SCOTT FORESMAN
READING STREET

COMMON CORE ©

Program Authors

Peter Afflerbach

Camille Blachowicz

Candy Dawson Boyd

Elena Izquierdo

Connie Juel

Edward Kame'enui

Donald Leu

Jeanne R. Paratore

P. David Pearson

Sam Sebesta

Deborah Simmons

Susan Watts Taffe

Alfred Tatum

Sharon Vaughn

Karen Kring Wixson

Glenview, Illinois

Boston, Massachusetts

Chandler, Arizona

Upper Saddle River, New Jersey

ALWAYS LEARNING   PEARSON

We dedicate Reading Street to
Peter Jovanovich.

His wisdom, courage,
and passion for education
are an inspiration to us all.

Accelerated Reader®

The Acknowledgments page appears in the back of the book immediately following the Oral Vocabulary section and constitutes an extension of this copyright page.

ISBN-13: 978-0-328-72531-1
ISBN-10:   0-328-72531-5
1 2 3 4 5 6 7 8 9 10 V003 16 15 14 13 12

Program Authors

Peter Afflerbach, Ph.D.
Professor; Department of Curriculum and Instruction,
University of Maryland; College Park, Maryland
Areas of Expertise: Common Core State Standards English Language Arts
Work Team, Assessment, and Comprehension

Camille L. Z. Blachowicz, Ph.D.
Professor; National College of Education, National-Louis University; Skokie, Illinois
Areas of Expertise: Vocabulary and Comprehension

Candy Dawson Boyd, Ph.D.
Professor, School of Education; Saint Mary's College; Moraga, California
Areas of Expertise: Children's Literature and Professional Development

Elena Izquierdo, Ph.D.
Associate Professor, University of Texas at El Paso
Area of Expertise: English Language Learners

Connie Juel, Ph.D.
Professor of Education; Stanford University; Stanford, California
Areas of Expertise: Phonics, Oral Vocabulary, and Intervention

Edward J. Kame'enui, Ph.D.
Dean-Knight Professor of Education and Director, Institute for the Development
of Educational Achievement, and the Center on Teaching and Learning;
College of Education; University of Oregon
Areas of Expertise: Assessment, Intervention, and Progress Monitoring

Donald J. Leu, Ph.D.
John and Maria Neag Endowed Chair in Literacy and Technology Board of Directors,
International Reading Association; University of Connecticut; Storrs, Connecticut
Areas of Expertise: Comprehension, Technology, and New Literacies

Jeanne R. Paratore, Ed.D.
Professor of Literacy, Language, and Cultural Studies, Boston University School
of Education; Boston, Massachusetts
Areas of Expertise: Intervention and Small Group Instruction

P. David Pearson, Ph.D.
Professor of Language, Literacy and Culture, and Human Development;
Graduate School of Education; University of California; Berkeley, California
Areas of Expertise: Common Core State Standards English Language Arts
Work Team, Comprehension

Sam L. Sebesta, Ph.D.
Professor Emeritus; Curriculum and Instruction College of Education,
University of Washington; Seattle, Washington
Areas of Expertise: Children's Literature, Reader Response, and Motivation

Deborah Simmons, Ph.D.
Professor in the Department of Educational Psychology, College of Education
and Human Development, Texas A&M University
Areas of Expertise: Literacy Development, Phonics, and Intervention

Susan Watts Taffe, Ph.D.
Associate Professor and Program Coordinator, Literacy and Second Language Studies,
School of Education; University of Cincinnati; Cincinnati, Ohio
Areas of Expertise: Vocabulary, Comprehension, and New Literacies

Alfred Tatum, Ph.D.
Associate Professor and Director, UIC Reading Clinic, University of Illinois at Chicago
Areas of Expertise: Adolescent Literacy, Reader Response, and Motivation

Sharon Vaughn, Ph.D.
H. E. Hartfelder/The Southland Corporation Regents Professor;
University of Texas; Austin, Texas
Areas of Expertise: Literacy Development, Intervention, Professional Development,
English Language Learners, Vocabulary, and Small Group Instruction

Karen Kring Wixson, Ph.D.
Dean of Education, University of North Carolina, Greensboro
Areas of Expertise: Common Core State Standards English Language Arts Work
Team, Assessment, Small Group Instruction

Consulting Authors

Jeff Anderson, M.Ed.
Author and National Literacy Staff Developer

Jim Cummins, Ph.D.
Professor; Department of Curriculum, Teaching and Learning; University of Toronto

Tahira A. DuPree Chase, Ed.D.
Director of Curriculum and Instruction, Mt. Vernon City School District, New York

Lily Wong Fillmore, Ph.D.
Professor Emerita; Graduate School of Education, University of California, Berkeley

Georgia Earnest Garcia, Ph.D.
Professor; Language and Literacy Division, Department of Curriculum and Instruction,
University of Illinois at Urbana-Champaign

George A. Gonzalez, Ph.D.
Professor (Retired); School of Education,
University of Texas-Pan American, Edinburg

Adria Klein, Ph.D.
Professor Emeritus; School of Education, California State University, San Bernadino

Lesley Maxwell, M.S., CCC-SLP
Director of Clinical Education, Clinical Associate Professor; Department of
Communication Sciences and Disorders, MGH Institute of Health Professions

Valerie Ooka Pang, Ph.D.
Professor; School of Teacher Education, San Diego State University

Sally M. Reis, Ph.D.
Board of Trustees Distinguished Professor; Department of Educational Psychology,
University of Connecticut

Jon Scieszka, M.F.A.
Children's Book Author and Founder of GUYS READ, First National Ambassador for
Young People's Literature 2008

Grant Wiggins, Ed.D.
President of Authentic Education, coauthor of *Understanding by Design*

iii

Nurture the love of reading.

Help students learn to read *and* love to read. *Reading Street Common Core* supports reading, writing, and language development. Amazing literature on amazing devices inspires students in a whole new way.

Literature students love

The best literary and informational text

On devices they crave!

Whiteboards, tablets, computers, mobile dev

Build a foundation for reading.

Reading Street Common Core helps students develop foundational skills for reading more complex text. Common Core experts helped design the plan. Classroom results prove it works.

Early Reading Success

Reading Street students outperformed their peers by 15 percentile points, even though they started below the comparison students.

Greater Reading Enjoyment Later

Fourth-grade *Reading Street* students had more positive attitudes toward reading.

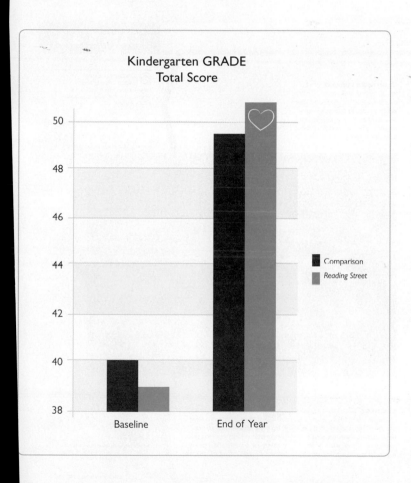

Kindergarten GRADE
Total Score

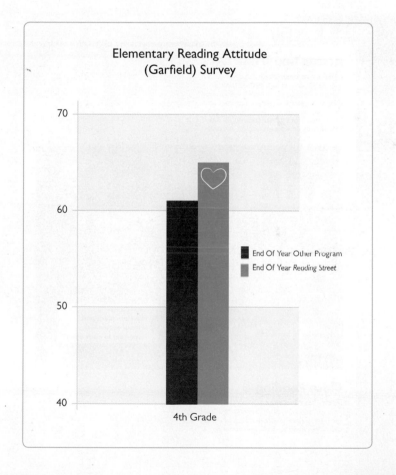

Elementary Reading Attitude
(Garfield) Survey

"The texts children read provide them with a foundation not just for what they're going to read, but also for what they're going to write and talk about."

Jeanne R. Paratore, Ed.D.
Program Author

Grow student capacity.

Reading Street Common Core builds students' capacity to read complex texts. Zoom in on elements critical to the Common Core State Standards.

Text-Based Comprehension

Modeling, analysis, and guided practice prepare students for more demanding text.

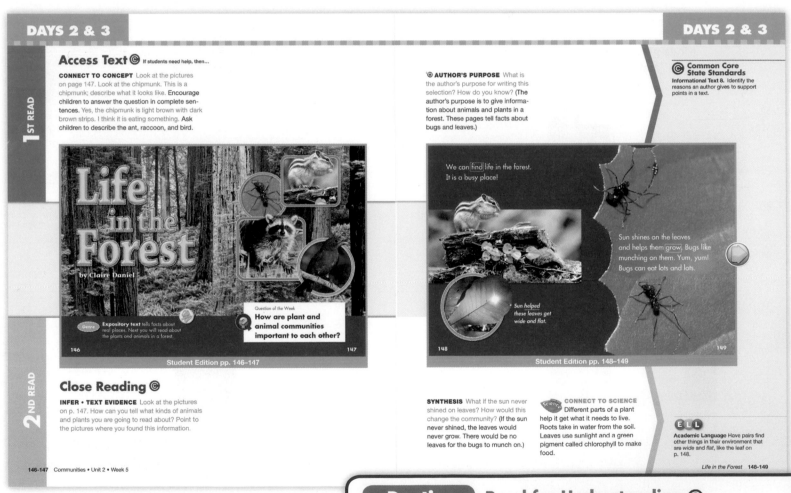

Read for Understanding Routine

Routines provide weekly opportunities to develop deep understanding and build higher-order thinking skills through Close Reading.

Routine | **Read for Understanding** ©

Deepen understanding by reading the selection multiple times.

1. **First Read**—use the **Access Text** notes to help children clarify understanding.

2. **Second Read**—use the **Close Reading** notes to help children draw knowledge from the text.

Content Knowledge

Weekly and unit instruction is built around science and social studies concepts. These concepts connect every piece of literature, vocabulary, and writing, allowing students to develop deep knowledge.

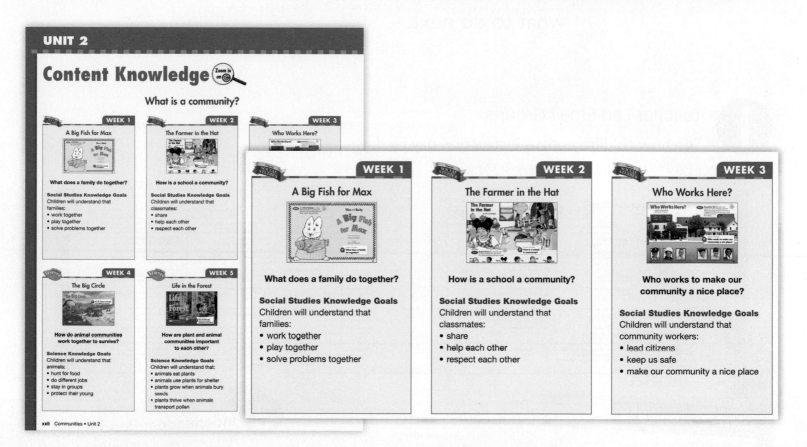

Writing

Varied writing tasks help students write to inform or explain.

DAILY

- 10-minute mini-lessons on writing traits and craft allow students to write in response to their reading
- Quick Write routine for writing on demand

WEEKLY

- Different writing product each week
- Writing mini-lessons and organizational models
- Mentor text to exemplify good traits

UNIT

- One- or two-week Writing Workshops
- Writing process lessons

Inspire confidence.

"What do I do in group time?" Follow the simple 3-step plan. *Reading Street Common Core* provides a road map to help you teach with confidence. You'll know exactly where to go and what to do next.

1 Teacher-Led Small Groups

See how to differentiate instruction day by day.

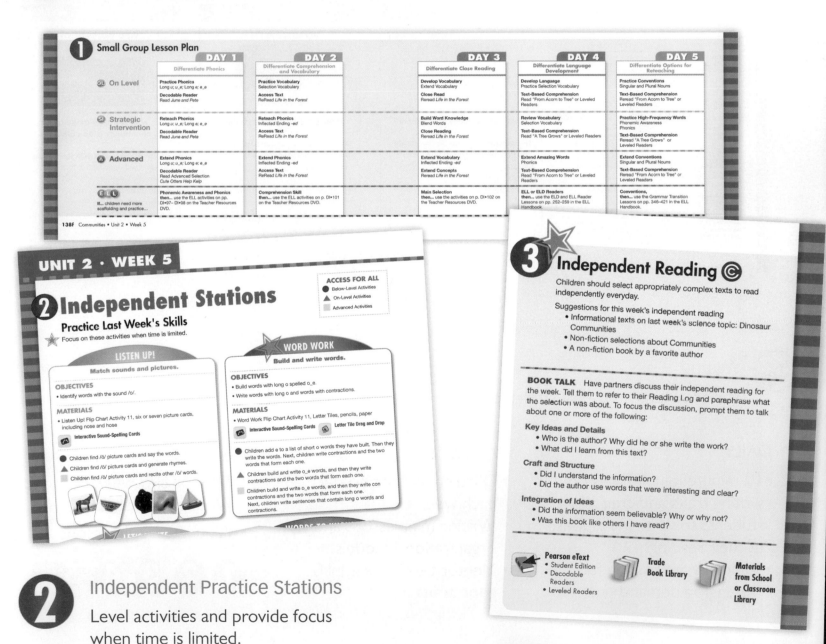

2 Independent Practice Stations

Level activities and provide focus when time is limited.

3 Independent Reading

Suggest concept-related reading and partner activities.

**Tier 2
Intervention**

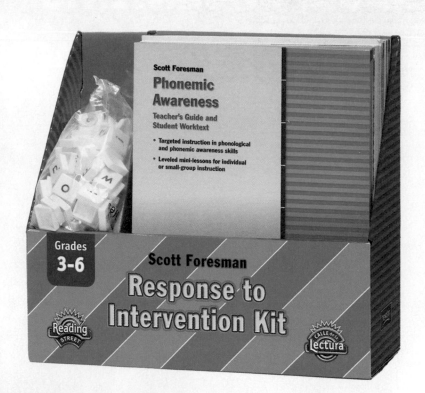

Response to Intervention Kit

Tier 2 RTI Kit provides a targeted focus and leveled mini-lessons for individuals and small groups.

**Intensive
Intervention**

My Sidewalks Intensive Intervention

Conceptually related to *Reading Street, My Sidewalks* provides 30 weeks of instruction for struggling readers.

"What we need to do is to increase the support strategies to help students cope with complex text."

P. David Pearson
Program Author

UNIT 5
Cultures

YOU ARE HERE

WEEK 1 ....190a
Suki's Kimono Realistic Fiction
Clothes: Bringing Cultures Together Expository Text
Small Group Time OL SI A E L L ....SG•1

WEEK 2 ....222a
I Love Saturdays y domingos Realistic Fiction
Communities Celebrate Cultures Textbook
Small Group Time OL SI A E L L ....SG•17

WEEK 3 ....254a
Good-Bye, 382 Shin Dang Dong Realistic Fiction
Sing a Song of People Poetry
Small Group Time OL SI A E L L ....SG•33

WEEK 4 ....288a
Jalapeño Bagels Realistic Fiction
Foods of Mexico: A Delicious Blend Expository Text
Small Group Time OL SI A E L L ....SG•49

WEEK 5 ....320a
Me and Uncle Romie Historical Fiction
Country to City Online Reference Sources
Small Group Time OL SI A E L L ....SG•65

WEEK 6 ....UR•1
Optional Review
Wrap Up Your Unit
Unit 5 Reading Poetry 360–361

UNIT 6
Freedom

WEEK 1 ....366a
The Story of the Statue of Liberty Narrative Nonfiction
A Nation of Immigrants Textbook
Small Group Time OL SI A E L L ....SG•1

WEEK 2 ....394a
Happy Birthday Mr. Kang Realistic Fiction
Once Upon a Constitution Expository Text
Small Group Time OL SI A E L L ....SG•17

WEEK 3 ....430a
Talking Walls: Art for the People Photo Essay
The History of Palindromes Palindromes
Small Group Time OL SI A E L L ....SG•33

WEEK 4 ....460a
Two Bad Ants Animal Fantasy
Hiking Safety Tips Evaluating Online Sources
Small Group Time OL SI A E L L ....SG•49

WEEK 5 ....494a
Atlantis Legend
The Monster in the Maze Drama
Small Group Time OL SI A E L L ....SG•65

WEEK 6 ....UR•1
Optional Review
Wrap Up Your Unit
Unit 6 Reading Poetry 532–533

TABLE OF CONTENTS

UNIT 1
Living and Learning

UNIT 2
Smart Solutions

UNIT 3
People and Nature

UNIT 4
One of a Kind

Cultures

What happens when two ways of life come together?

Suki's Kimono
REALISTIC FICTION

How does culture influence the clothes we wear?

Paired Selection
Clothes: Bringing Cultures Together
EXPOSITORY TEXT

I Love Saturdays y domingos
REALISTIC FICTION

How are cultures alike and different?

Paired Selection
Communities Celebrate Cultures
TEXTBOOK

Good-Bye, 382 Shin Dang Dong
REALISTIC FICTION

Why is it hard to adapt to a new culture?

Paired Selection
Sing a Song of People
POETRY

Jalapeño Bagels
REALISTIC FICTION

How can different cultures contribute to the foods we eat?

Paired Selection
Foods of Mexico: A Delicious Blend
EXPOSITORY TEXT

Me and Uncle Romie
HISTORICAL FICTION

How does city life compare to life in the country?

Paired Selection
Country to City
ONLINE REFERENCE SOURCES

UNIT 5

Skills Overview

 WEEK 1

 WEEK 2

 WEEK 3

Key
T Tested Skill
🎯 Target Skill

	WEEK 1 **Suki's Kimono** Realistic Fiction, pp. 198–211 **Clothes: Bringing Cultures Together** Expository Text, pp. 216–219	**WEEK 2** **I Love Saturdays y domingos** Realistic Fiction, pp. 230–245 **Communities Celebrate Cultures** Textbook, pp. 250–251	**WEEK 3** **Good-Bye, 382 Shin Dang Dong** Realistic Fiction, pp. 262–279 **Sing a Song of People** Poetry, pp. 284–285
Build Content Knowledge — Integrate Science and Social Studies	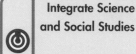 Cultures; Clothing; Festivals	Cultural Diversity	Cultures; Family Life; Location Skills
Weekly Question	*How does culture influence the clothes we wear?*	*How are cultures alike and different?*	*Why is it hard to adapt to a new culture?*
Knowledge Goals	Students will understand that people • wear special clothes for holidays • wear traditional clothing • react to clothing	Students will understand that cultures • have similarities and differences • usually value family • can be tied to countries	Students will understand that a new culture means • a new home and neighborhood • a new language • new traditions
Get Ready to Read — Phonics/Word Analysis	T 🎯 Syllable Pattern CV/VC	T 🎯 Homophones	T 🎯 Vowel Patterns for /ô/
Literary Terms	Word Choice	Point of View	Mood
Read and Comprehend — Comprehension	T 🎯 **Skill** Compare and Contrast 🎯 **Strategy** Visualize **Review Skill** Cause and Effect	T 🎯 **Skill** Main Idea and Details 🎯 **Strategy** Inferring **Review Skill** Compare and Contrast	T 🎯 **Skill** Sequence 🎯 **Strategy** Monitor and Clarify **Review Skill** Draw Conclusions
Vocabulary	T 🎯 Synonyms	T 🎯 Homophones	T 🎯 Compound Words
Fluency	Rate	Accuracy	Expression and Punctuation Cues
Language Arts — Writing	Letter to the Editor Trait: Organization	Personal Narrative Trait: Conventions	Poetry Trait: Word Choice
Conventions	T Adjectives and Articles	T Comparative and Superlative Adjectives	T Adverbs
Spelling	Syllable Pattern CV/VC	Homophones	Vowel Patterns *au, augh, ou, ough*
Listening and Speaking	Introduction	Drama	Song or Poem

WEEK 4

Jalapeño Bagels
Realistic Fiction, pp. 296–309
Foods of Mexico:
A Delicious Blend
Expository Text, pp. 314–317

 Food; Cultures

How can different cultures contribute to the foods we eat?

Students will understand that food
• comes from different cultures
• is shared
• can be a mix from different cultures

Vowel Patterns *ei, eigh*

Dialogue and Narration

T **Skill** Draw Conclusions
Strategy Summarize
Review Skill Sequence

T Unfamiliar Words

Accuracy

Invitation
Trait: Focus/Ideas

T Comparative and Superlative
Adverbs

Vowel Patterns *ei, eigh*

Radio Advertisement

WEEK 5

Me and Uncle Romie
Historical Fiction, pp. 328–349
Country to City
Online Reference Sources,
pp. 354–357

 Communities; Cultures: Housing; Cultures: Entertainment

How does city life compare to life in the country?

Students will understand that
• city life is busy
• cities have tall buildings
• the country has farms

Suffixes *-y, -ish, -hood, -ment*

Onomatopoeia

T **Skill** Author's Purpose
Strategy Background Knowledge
Review Skill Draw Conclusions

T Homonyms

Appropriate Phrasing

Book Review
Trait: Conventions

T Conjunctions

Suffixes *-y, -ish, -hood, -ment*

Retelling

WEEK 6

Optional Review

 Cultures

What happens when two ways of life come together?

Connect the Question of the Week to the Big Question

Review Unit 5 Target Comprehension Skills and Strategies

Review Unit 5 Target Vocabulary Skills

Review Unit 5 Fluency Skills

Quick Write for Fluency

Review Unit 5 Conventions

Review Unit 5 Spelling Patterns

Assessment

5 Steps to Success on Reading Street

RIGHT IN YOUR TEACHER'S EDITION

Step 1

Begin the Year

The Assessment Handbook provides ideas and support to begin the school year and beyond.

The Baseline Group Test helps identify where students are. Use the Baseline Test results to make initial grouping decisions and to differentiate instruction based on ability levels.

Online Assessment Save time by using digital assessments. All Reading Street assessments are available on ExamView and in SuccessTracker.

Step 2

Every Day

During the day, use these tools to monitor student progress.

• **Corrective Feedback** provides point of use support.

Corrective feedback | **If...** students are unable to answer the comprehension questions,
then... use the Reteach lesson in *First Stop.*

• **Monitor Progress** boxes each day check retelling, fluency, and oral vocabulary.

Don't Wait Until Friday **MONITOR PROGRESS** **Check Retelling**

If... students have difficulty retelling,
then... use the Retelling Cards/Story Sort to scaffold their retellings.

Step 3

Every Week

• **Weekly Assessments** on Day 5 check comprehension and fluency.

• **Weekly Tests** assess target skills for the week.

• **Fresh Reads** assesses fluency and comprehension as students read a new passage.

• **Reading Street Sleuth** assesses students' ability to find clues in text through close reading.

Step 4

Every Unit

- **Unit Benchmark Tests** assess mastery of unit skills: comprehension, vocabulary, phonics, conventions, and writing.

- **Unit Benchmark Tests** provide professional development and support with performance-based assessment.

- **Performance-Based Assessments** assess students' ability to demonstrate text-based comprehension and application of higher-order thinking skills.

Step 5

End the Year

- **End-of-Year Benchmark Test** measures student mastery of skills covered in all six units with options for performance-based assessment.

5 Steps to Success on Reading Street

1 Begin the Year

2 Every Day

3 Every Week

4 Every Unit

5 End the Year

. . . .

Digital Assessment

eInstruction®
EXAMVIEW®
ASSESSMENT SUITE

☆ SuccessTracker™

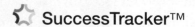
eSTREET INTERACTIVE
www.ReadingStreet.com

UNIT 5

Implementing eStreet Interactive
Power up your classroom and put time back on your side!

eSTREET INTERACTIVE
www.ReadingStreet.com

Additional Digital Support

AudioText CD
Background Building Audio CD
Teacher Resources DVD

Plan

Customize your daily plan
by clicking, dragging, and posting!

- Online Lesson Planner
- Online Teacher's Edition

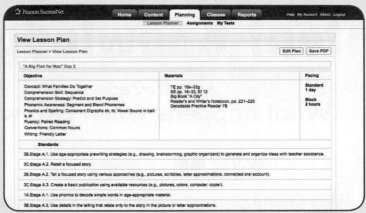

Online Lesson Planner

Teach

Engage through interactive media!

- Concept Talk Videos
- Letter Tile Drag and Drop
- Envision It! Animations
- Grammar Jammer

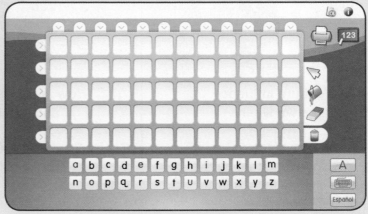

Letter Tile Drag and Drop

Practice

Motivate through personalized
practice activities!

- Story Sort
- Pearson eText
- Journal
- Vocabulary Activities
- Leveled Reader Database

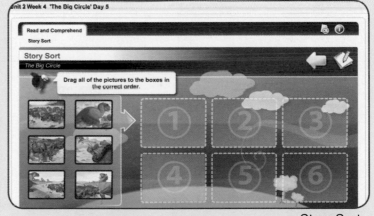

Story Sort

Manage and Assess

Respond to individual needs!

- Monitor student progress
- Assign
- Prescribe
- Remediate

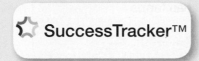

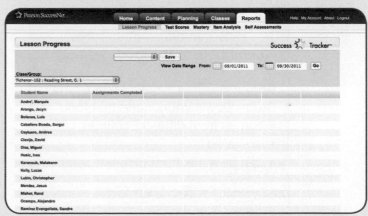

Class Management

UNIT 5

Content Knowledge

What happens when two ways of life come together?

WEEK 1

Suki's Kimono

How does culture influence the clothes we wear?

Social Studies Knowledge Goals
Students will understand that people
- wear special clothes for holidays
- wear traditional clothing
- react to clothing

WEEK 2

I Love Saturdays y domingos

How are cultures alike and different?

Social Studies Knowledge Goals
Students will understand that cultures
- have similarities and differences
- usually value family
- can be tied to countries

WEEK 3

Good-Bye, 382 Shin Dang Dong

Why is it hard to adapt to a new culture?

Social Studies Knowledge Goals
Students will understand that a new culture means
- a new home and neighborhood
- a new language
- new traditions

WEEK 4

Jalapeño Bagels

How can different cultures contribute to the foods we eat?

Social Studies Knowledge Goals
Students will understand that food
- comes from different cultures
- is shared
- can be a mix from different cultures

WEEK 5

Me and Uncle Romie

How does city life compare to life in the country?

Social Studies Knowledge Goals
Students will understand that
- city life is busy
- cities have tall buildings
- the country has farms

Indiana Common Core Edition

This Week's Target Skills and Strategies

Target Skills and Strategies	© Common Core State Standards for English Language Arts	Indiana Academic Standards for English Language Arts
Phonics and Spelling 🔊 Skill: Syllable Pattern CV/VC	CCSS Foundational Skills 3. Know and apply grade-level phonics and word analysis skills in decoding words. (Also CCSS Foundational Skills 3.c., CCSS Language 2.f.)	IN 3.1 Students understand the basic features of words. They select letter patterns and know how to translate them into spoken language using phonics, syllables, word parts, and context. They apply this knowledge to achieve fluent oral and silent reading.
Text-Based Comprehension 🔊 Skill: Compare and Contrast	CCSS Literature 1. Ask and answer questions to demonstrate understanding of a text, referring explicitly to the text as the basis for the answers. (Also CCSS Literature 2.)	IN 3.3 Students read and respond to a wide variety of significant works of children's literature.
🔊 Strategy: Visualize	CCSS Literature 1. Ask and answer questions to demonstrate understanding of a text, referring explicitly to the text as the basis for the answers. (Also CCSS Literature 10.)	IN 3.3 Students read and respond to a wide variety of significant works of children's literature.
Vocabulary 🔊 Skill: Synonyms **Strategy:** Context Clues	CCSS Language 5. Demonstrate understanding of word relationships and nuances in word meanings.	IN 3.1.4 Determine the meanings of words using knowledge of synonyms, antonyms, homophones, and homographs.
Fluency Skill: Rate	CCSS Foundational Skills 4.b. Read on-level prose and poetry orally with accuracy, appropriate rate, and expression on successive readings. (Also CCSS Foundational Skills 4.)	IN 3.1.3 Read aloud grade-level-appropriate literary and informational texts fluently and accurately and with appropriate timing, change in voice, and expression.
Listening and Speaking Introductions	CCSS Speaking/Listening 1.b. Follow agreed-upon rules for discussions (e.g., gaining the floor in respectful ways, listening to others with care, speaking one at a time about the topics and texts under discussion). (Also CCSS Speaking/Listening 4.)	The Indiana Academic Standards for Listening and Speaking are not currently assessed on ISTEP+ assessments. Educators and students should implement the Common Core Standards for Speaking and Listening as soon as possible.
Six-Trait Writing **Trait of the Week:** Organization	CCSS Writing 1.a. Introduce the topic or book they are writing about, state an opinion, and create an organizational structure that lists reasons. (Also CCSS Writing 4.)	IN 3.5.7 Write responses to literature.
Writing Letter to the Editor	CCSS Writing 1. Write opinion pieces on familiar topics or texts, supporting a point of view with reasons. (Also CCSS Writing 1.a., CCSS Writing 1.b.)	IN 3.5.7 Write responses to literature.
Conventions Skill: Adjectives and Articles	CCSS Language 1.a. Explain the function of nouns, pronouns, verbs, adjectives, and adverbs in general and their functions in particular sentences. (Also CCSS Language 5.c.)	IN 3.6.5 Identify and correctly use pronouns, adjectives, compound nouns, and articles in writing.

This Week's Cross-Curricular Standards and Resources

Cross-Curricular Indiana Academic Standards for Science and Social Studies

Science
IN 3.1.1 Generate sounds using different materials, objects and techniques. Record the sounds and then discuss and share the results.

Social Studies
IN 3.3.4 Explain that regions are areas that have similar physical and cultural characteristics. Identify Indiana and the local community as part of a specific region.
IN 3.3.9 Identify factors that make the region unique, including cultural diversity, industry, the arts and architecture.

Reading Street Sleuth

Celebrating Children and Tradition pp. 56–57

Follow the path to close reading using the Super Sleuth tips:

- Gather Evidence
- Ask Questions
- Make Your Case
- Prove it!

More Reading in Science and Social Studies

Concept Literacy

Below Level

On Level

Advanced

ELL

ELD

ISBN-13: 978-0-328-73391-0   ISBN-10: 0-328-73391-1

Your 90-Minute Reading Block

	Whole Group	Formative Assessment	Small Group — OL On Level SI Strategic Intervention A Advanced	Daily Independent Options
		How do I make my small groups flexible?	What are my other students reading and learning every day in Small Groups?	What do my other students do when I lead Small Groups?
DAY 1	**Content Knowledge** Build Oral Language/Vocabulary **Phonics/Word Analysis** **Read Decodable Reader** **Text-Based Comprehension** **Selection Vocabulary** **Research and Inquiry** Step 1–Identify and Focus Topic **Spelling Pretest** Connect to Phonics/Word Analysis	**Monitor Progress** Check Oral Vocabulary	*Differentiate Vocabulary* **Build Word Knowledge** OL Practice Amazing Words SI Reteach Amazing Words A Extend Amazing Words OL SI A **Text-Based Comprehension** **Read** *Reading Street Sleuth*, pp. 56–57 or Leveled Readers A Inquiry Project ELL Access Vocabulary	★ **Independent Reading** C Suggestions for this week's independent reading: • A folk tale that involves an animal • An animal fantasy • A nonfiction book about animal behavior **Book Talk** Foster critical reading and discussion skills through independent and close reading. Students should focus on discussing one or more of the following: • Key Ideas and Details • Craft and Structure • Integration of Ideas
DAY 2	**Content Knowledge** Build Oral Language/Vocabulary **Phonics/Word Analysis** **Vocabulary Skill** **Text-Based Comprehension** **Read** Main Selection, using Access Text Notes **Research and Inquiry** Step 2–Navigate/Search **Spelling** Connect to Phonics/Word Analysis	**Monitor Progress** Formative Assessment: Check Word Reading	*Differentiate Comprehension* **Build Word Knowledge** OL Practice Selection Vocabulary SI Reteach Selection Vocabulary A Extend Selection Vocabulary OL SI A **Access Text** **Read** *Suki's Kimono* A Inquiry Project ELL Access Comprehension Skill	
DAY 3	**Content Knowledge** Build Oral Language/Vocabulary **Phonics/Word Analysis** **Read Decodable Passage** **Text-Based Comprehension** **Read** Main Selection, using Close Reading Notes **Fluency** **Research and Inquiry** Step 3–Analyze Information **Spelling** Connect to Phonics/Word Analysis	**Monitor Progress** Check Retelling	*Differentiate Close Reading* OL SI **Reread to Develop Vocabulary** A **Reread to Extend Vocabulary** OL SI A **Close Reading** **Read** *Suki's Kimono* A Inquiry Project ELL Access Main Selection	**Pearson eText** • Student Edition • Decodable Readers • Leveled Readers **Trade Book Library** **Materials from School or Classroom Library**
DAY 4	**Content Knowledge** Build Oral Language/Vocabulary **Phonics/Word Analysis** **Read Decodable Passage** **Read Content Area Paired Selection with Genre Focus** **Let's Learn It!** Vocabulary/Fluency/Listening and Speaking **Research and Inquiry** Step 4–Synthesize **Spelling** Connect to Phonics/Word Analysis	**Monitor Progress** Check Fluency	*Differentiate Vocabulary* **Build Word Knowledge** OL Develop Language Using Amazing Words SI Review/Discuss Amazing Words A Extend Amazing Words and Selection Vocabulary OL SI A **Text-Based Comprehension** **Read** "Clothes: Bringing Culture Together" A Inquiry Project ELL Access Amazing Words	**Independent Stations** Practice Last Week's Skills ★ Focus on these activities when time is limited. ★ **Word Wise** **Word Work** ★ **Read for Meaning** **Let's Write!** **Words to Know** **Get Fluent**
DAY 5	**Content Knowledge** Build Oral Language/Vocabulary **Text-Based Comprehension** **Vocabulary Skill** **Phonics/Word Analysis** **Assessment** Fluency, Comprehension **Research and Inquiry** Step 5–Communicate **Spelling Test** Connect to Phonics/Word Analysis	**Monitor Progress** Formative Assessment: Check Oral Vocabulary **Monitor Progress** Fluency; Comprehension	*Differentiate Reteaching* OL **Practice Adjectives and Articles** SI **Review Adjectives and Articles** A **Extend Adjectives and Articles** OL SI A **Text-Based Comprehension** **Reread** *Reading Street Sleuth*, pp. 56–57 or Leveled Readers A Inquiry Project ELL Access Conventions and Writing	

Assessment Resources

Common Core Weekly Tests, pp. 121–126

Common Core Fresh Reads for Fluency and Comprehension, pp. 121–126

Common Core Unit 5 Benchmark Test

Common Core Success Tracker, ExamView, and Online Lesson Planner

Teaching the Common Core State Standards This Week

The Common Core State Standards for English Language Arts are divided into strands for **Reading** (including **Foundational Skills**), **Writing**, **Speaking and Listening**, and **Language**. The chart below shows some of the content you will teach this week, strand by strand. Turn to this week's 5-Day Planner on pages 190d–190e to see how this content is taught each day.

Reading Strand

- **Phonics/Word Analysis:** Syllable Pattern CV/VC
- **Text-Based Comprehension:** Compare and Contrast; Visualize
- **Fluency:** Rate

- **Literary Terms:** Word Choice
- **Genre:** Main Selection: Realistic Fiction; Paired Selection: Expository Text

Common Core State Standards for English Language Arts

Writing Strand

- **Writing Mini-Lesson:** Letter to the Editor
- **Trait:** Organization
- **Look Back and Write:** Text Evidence

Speaking and Listening Strand

- **Content Knowledge:** Build Oral Language
- **Listening and Speaking:** How-To Demonstrations – Introductions
- **Research and Inquiry**

Language Strand

- **Oral Vocabulary: Amazing Words** *traditional, fret, scarves, fabric, acceptable, inspire, robe, drape, elegant, stylish*
- **Vocabulary:** Synonyms; Context Clues
- **Selection Vocabulary:** *festival, snug, rhythm, paces, graceful, pale, cotton, handkerchief*

- **Academic Vocabulary:** *compare and contrast, adjective, articles, letter to the editor, fiction, Internet, realistic fiction, newsletter, synonyms*
- **Conventions:** Adjectives and Articles
- **Spelling:** Syllable Pattern CV/VC

Text-Based Comprehension

Text Complexity Measures

Use the rubric to familiarize yourself with the text complexity of **Suki's Kimono**.

Bridge to Complex Knowledge

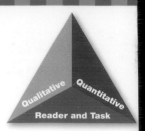

Quantitative Measures	Lexile	800L
	Average Sentence Length	11.51
	Word Frequency	3.60

Qualitative Measures	Levels of Meaning	understand the motivations of the characters
	Structure	simple graphics; conventional structure; flash-back
	Language Conventionality and Clarity	natural, conversational language; non-English words; close alignment between pictures and text
	Theme and Knowledge Demands	references to cultural experiences; uncommon perspective

Reader and Task Suggestions
FORMATIVE ASSESSMENT Based on assessment results, use the **Reader and Task Suggestions** in Access Main Selection to scaffold the selection or support independence for students as they read **Suki's Kimono**.

READER AND TASK SUGGESTIONS	
Preparing to Read the Text	**Leveled Tasks**
• Review the strategy of using synonyms as context clues. • Discuss how authors sometimes use flashbacks in realistic fiction. • Remind students they may need to read more slowly when they encounter foreign words in text.	• **Levels of Meaning • Analysis** If students have difficulty understanding Suki's motivation for wearing her kimono to school on the first day, have them read p. 201 and tell why Suki's kimono is special to her. • **Language Conventionality and Clarity** Students may have difficulty understanding complex sentences in the story. Remind them to break long sentences into smaller parts and identify the main action in each sentence.

Recommended Placement Both the qualitative and quantitative measures suggest this text should be placed in the Grade 4–5 text complexity band, which is where both the Common Core State Standards and *Scott Foresman Reading Street* have placed it.

Focus on Common Core State Standards ©

Main Selection, pp. 198–211

Paired Selection, pp. 216–219

Text-Based Comprehension

Compare and Contrast
CCSS Literature 1.,
CCSS Literature 2.

Visualize
CCSS Literature 1.,
CCSS Literature 10.

Fluency

Rate
CCSS Foundational Skills 4.,
CCSS Foundational Skills 4.b.

Writing and Conventions

Trait: Organization
CCSS Writing 1.a., CCSS Writing 4.

Writing Mini-Lesson: Letter to the Editor
CCSS Writing 1., CCSS Writing 1.a.,
CCSS Writing 1.b.

Conventions: Adjectives and Articles
CCSS Language 1.a.,
CCSS Language 5.c.

Oral Vocabulary

Amazing Words

traditional	inspire
fret	robe
scarves	drape
fabric	elegant
acceptable	stylish

CCSS Language 6.

Selection Vocabulary

Synonyms
CCSS Language 5.

Context Clues
CCSS Language 5.c.

cotton	handkerchief	rhythm
festival	paces	snug
graceful	pale	

Phonics and Spelling

Syllable Pattern CV/VC
CCSS Foundational Skills 2.f.,
CCSS Foundational Skills 3.,
CCSS Foundational Skills 3.c.

create	duo
medium	patio
piano	rodeo
idea	pioneer
radio	trio
video	stadium
studio	audio
violin	

Challenge Words

audience	Creole
radiate	recreation
cereal	

Listening and Speaking

Introduction
CCSS Speaking/Listening 1.b.,
CCSS Speaking/Listening 4.

Preview Your Week

How does culture influence the clothes we wear?

Main Selection, pp. 198–211

Genre: Realistic Fiction

Vocabulary: Synonyms

Text-Based Comprehension: Compare and Contrast

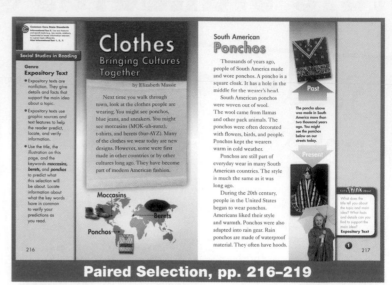

Paired Selection, pp. 216–219

Social Studies in Reading

Genre: Expository Text

Build Content Knowledge

Zoom in on ©

KNOWLEDGE GOALS

Students will understand that people

- wear special clothes for holidays
- wear traditional clothing
- react to clothing

THIS WEEK'S CONCEPT MAP

Develop a concept-related graphic organizer like the one below over the course of this week.

How culture influences the clothes we wear

Celebrations | Customs | Climate

BUILD ORAL VOCABULARY

This week, students will acquire the following academic vocabulary/domain-specific words.

Amazing Words

traditional	acceptable	drape
fret	inspire	elegant
scarves	robe	stylish
fabric		

OPTIONAL CONCEPT-BASED READING Use the Digital Path to access readers offering different levels of text complexity.

Concept Literacy

Below-Level

On-Level

Advanced

ELL

ELD

This Week's Digital Resources

eStreet Interactive
www.ReadingStreet.com

Get Ready to Read

 Big Question Video This video introduces students to the Big Question and facilitates discussion of the concept for the unit.

 Concept Talk Video Use this video on the Digital Path to pique interest and introduce the weekly concept of cultures.

 Pearson eText Read the eText of the Student Edition pages on Pearson SuccessNet for comprehension and fluency support.

 Envision It! Animations Use this vibrant animation on the Digital Path to explain the target comprehension skill, Compare and Contrast.

Read and Comprehend

 Journal Use the Word Bank on the Digital Path to have students write sentences using this week's selection vocabulary words.

 Background Building Audio CD This audio CD provides interesting background information about cultures to help students read and comprehend the weekly texts.

 Pearson eText Read the eText of the main selection, *Suki's Kimono,* and the paired selection, "Clothes: Bringing Cultures Together," with audio support on Pearson SuccessNet.

 Vocabulary Activities A variety of interactive vocabulary activities on the Digital Path help students practice selection vocabulary and concept-related words.

 Story Sort Use the Story Sort Activity on the Digital Path after reading *Suki's Kimono* to involve students in summarizing.

Language Arts

 Grammar Jammer Choose an appealing animation on the Digital Path to provide an engaging grammar lesson that will capture students' attention.

Pearson eText Find the Student Edition eText of the Let's Write It! and Let's Learn It! pages with audio support on Pearson SuccessNet.

Additional Resources

 Teacher Resources DVD-ROM Use the following resources on the TR DVD or on Pearson SuccessNet throughout the week:

- Amazing Word Cards
- Reader's and Writer's Notebook
- Writing Transparencies
- Daily Fix-It Transparencies
- Scoring Rubrics
- Grammar Transparencies
- ELL Support
- Let's Practice It!
- Graphic Organizers
- Vocabulary Cards

This Week's Skills

Phonics/Word Analysis
- Syllable Pattern CV/VC

Comprehension
- **Skill:** Compare and Contrast
- **Strategy:** Visualize

Language
- **Vocabulary:** Synonyms
- **Conventions:** Adjectives and Articles

Fluency
Rate

Writing
Letter to the Editor

5-Day Planner

DAY 1

Get Ready to Read

Content Knowledge 190j
Oral Vocabulary: *traditional, fret, scarves, fabric*

> **Monitor Progress**
> Check Oral Vocabulary

Phonics/Word Analysis 192a
- Syllable Pattern CV/VC
- **READ** Decodable Reader 21A
  Reread for Fluency

Read and Comprehend

Text-Based Comprehension 194a
- Compare and Contrast
- Visualize

Fluency 194–195
Rate

Selection Vocabulary 195a
cotton, festival, graceful, handkerchief, paces, pale, rhythm, snug

Language Arts

Research and Inquiry 195b
Identify and Focus Topic

Spelling 195c
Syllable Pattern CV/VC, Pretest

Conventions 195d
Adjectives and Articles

Handwriting 195d
Cursive Letters *A, C*

Writing 195e
Letter to the Editor

DAY 2

Get Ready to Read

Content Knowledge 196a
Oral Vocabulary: *acceptable, inspire*

Phonics/Word Analysis 196c
Syllable Pattern CV/VC

> **Monitor Progress**
> Check Word Reading

Literary Terms 196d
Word Choice

Read and Comprehend

Vocabulary Skill 196e
- Synonyms

Fluency 196–197
Rate

Text-Based Comprehension 198–199
- **READ** *Suki's Kimono*—1st Read

Language Arts

Research and Inquiry 205b
Navigate/Search

Conventions 205c
Adjectives and Articles

Spelling 205c
Syllable Pattern CV/VC

Writing 205d
Letter to the Editor

DAY 3

Get Ready to Read

Content Knowledge 206a
Oral Vocabulary: *robe, drape*

Word Analysis 206c
Syllable Pattern CV/VC
Fluent Word Reading
DECODE AND READ
Decodable Practice Passage 21B

Read and Comprehend

Text-Based Comprehension 206e
Check Understanding
READ *Suki's Kimono*—2nd Read
Monitor Progress Check Retelling

Fluency 213b
Rate

Language Arts

Research and Study Skills 213c
Newsletter

Research and Inquiry 213d
Analyze Information

Conventions 213e
Adjectives and Articles

Spelling 213e
Syllable Pattern CV/VC

Writing 214–215
Letter to the Editor

DAY 4

Get Ready to Read

Content Knowledge 216a
Oral Vocabulary: *elegant, stylish*

Phonics/Word Analysis 216c
Review Syllables VCCCV
Fluent Word Reading
DECODE AND READ
Decodable Practice Passage 21C

Read and Comprehend

Genre 216g
Expository Text
READ "Clothes: Bringing Cultures Together"—Paired Selection

Fluency 220–221
Rate
Monitor Progress Check Fluency

Vocabulary Skill 221a
Synonyms

Listening and Speaking 221a
Introductions

Language Arts

Research and Inquiry 221b
Synthesize

Conventions 221c
Adjectives and Articles

Spelling 221c
Syllable Pattern CV/VC

Writing 221d
Letter to the Editor

DAY 5

Get Ready to Read

Content Knowledge 221f
Review Oral Vocabulary
Monitor Progress
Check Oral Vocabulary

Read and Comprehend

Text-Based Comprehension 221h
Review Compare and Contrast

Vocabulary Skill 221h
Review Synonyms

Word Analysis 221i
Review Syllable Pattern CV/VC

Literary Terms 211i
Review Word Choice

Assessment 221j, 221l
Monitor Progress
Fluency; Compare and Contrast

Language Arts

Research and Inquiry 221n
Communicate

Spelling 221o
Syllable Pattern CV/VC, Test

Conventions 221o
Adjectives and Articles

Writing 221p
Letter to the Editor

Wrap Up Your Week! 221p

Access for All

What do I do in group time?
It's as easy as 1-2-3!

① TEACHER-LED SMALL GROUPS

② INDEPENDENT PRACTICE STATIONS

③ INDEPENDENT READING

Small Group Time

© Bridge to Common Core

SKILL DEVELOPMENT
- Syllable Pattern CV/VC
- Compare and Contrast
- Visualize
- Synonyms

DEEP UNDERSTANDING
This Week's Knowledge Goals
Students will understand that people
- wear special clothes for holidays
- wear traditional clothing
- react to clothing

① Small Group Lesson Plan

	DAY 1	DAY 2
	Differentiate Vocabulary	Differentiate Comprehension
OL On-Level pp. SG•2–SG•6	**Build Word Knowledge** Practice Amazing Words **Text-Based Comprehension** Read *Reading Street Sleuth*, pp. 56–57 or Leveled Readers	**Build Word Knowledge** Practice Selection Vocabulary **Access Text** Read *Suki's Kimono*
SI Strategic Intervention pp. SG•7–SG•11	**Build Word Knowledge** Reteach Amazing Words **Text-Based Comprehension** Read *Reading Street Sleuth*, pp. 56–57 or Leveled Readers	**Build Word Knowledge** Reteach Selection Vocabulary **Access Text** Read *Suki's Kimono*
A Advanced pp. SG•12–SG•16	**Build Word Knowledge** Extend Amazing Words **Text-Based Comprehension** Read *Reading Street Sleuth*, pp. 56–57 or Leveled Readers	**Build Word Knowledge** Extend Selection Vocabulary **Access Text** Read *Suki's Kimono*
Independent Inquiry Project	Identify Questions	Investigate
ELL If... students need more scaffolding and practice with...	**Vocabulary,** then... use the activities on pp. DI•17–DI•18 in the Teacher Resources section on SuccessNet.	**Comprehension Skill,** then... use the activities on p. DI•21 in the Teacher Resources section on SuccessNet.

Build Text-Based Comprehension

Suki's Kimono

Reading Street Sleuth

Provides access to grade-level text for all students
Focuses on finding clues in text through close reading
Builds capacity for complex text

Optional Leveled Readers

Concept Literacy   Below-Level   On-Level   Advanced   ELL   ELD

DAY 3	DAY 4	DAY 5
Differentiate Close Reading	**Differentiate Vocabulary**	**Differentiate Reteaching**
Reread to Develop Vocabulary **Close Reading** Read *Suki's Kimono*	**Build Word Knowledge** Develop Language Using Amazing Words **Text-Based Comprehension** Read "Clothes: Bringing Cultures Together"	**Practice Conventions** Adjectives and Articles **Text-Based Comprehension** Reread *Reading Street Sleuth*, pp. 56–57 or Leveled Readers
Reread to Develop Vocabulary **Close Reading** Read *Suki's Kimono*	**Build Word Knowledge** Review/Discuss Amazing Words **Text-Based Comprehension** Read "Clothes: Bringing Cultures Together"	**Review Conventions** Adjectives and Articles **Text-Based Comprehension** Reread *Reading Street Sleuth*, pp. 56–57 or Leveled Readers
Reread to Extend Vocabulary **Close Reading** Read *Suki's Kimono*	**Build Word Knowledge** Extend Amazing Words and Selection Vocabulary **Text-Based Comprehension** Read "Clothes: Bringing Cultures Together"	**Extend Conventions** Adjectives and Articles **Text-Based Comprehension** Reread *Reading Street Sleuth*, pp. 56–57 or Leveled Readers
Investigate	Organize	Communicate
Main Selection, **then...** use the activities on p. DI•22 in the Teacher Resources section on SuccessNet.	**Amazing Words,** **then...** use the Routine on pp. xxxvi–xxxvii in the *ELL Handbook.*	**Conventions and Writing,** **then...** use the Grammar Transition Lessons on pp. 312–386 in the *ELL Handbook.*

2 Independent Stations

Practice Last Week's Skills

Focus on these activities when time is limited.

ACCESS FOR ALL
- Below-Level Activities
- On-Level Activities
- Advanced Activities

WORD WISE

Spell and use words in sentences.

OBJECTIVES
- Spell words with VCCCV spelling pattern.

MATERIALS
- *Word Wise* Flip Chart Activity 21, teacher-made word cards, paper and pencils

 Letter Tile Drag and Drop

● Students choose and write five words, write sentences using the words, and write other words with the spelling pattern VCCCV.

▲ Students choose and write eight words, write sentences using the words, and write other words with the spelling pattern VCCCV.

■ Students choose and write ten words, write sentences using the words, and add other VCCCV words to their lists.

WORD WORK

Identify and pronounce words.

OBJECTIVES
- Identify and pronounce words with VCCCV spelling pattern.

MATERIALS
- *Word Work* Flip Chart Activity 21, teacher-made word cards, paper and pencils

 Letter Tile Drag and Drop

● Students say and list five words, write a rhyming word next to each, and then compose a four-line rhyming poem with some of the words.

▲ Students say and list eight words, write a rhyming word next to each, and write a four- or six-line rhyming poem with some of the words.

■ Students say and list ten words, write a rhyming word next to each, and write a six- or eight-line rhyming poem with some of the words.

LET'S WRITE!

Summarize.

OBJECTIVES
- Write a summary.

MATERIALS
- *Let's Write!* Flip Chart Activity 21, paper and pencils

 Grammar Jammer

● Students write a summary of a favorite book, using time-order words to tell the plot and main events.

▲ Students write a summary of a favorite book, using time-order words to tell the plot and then proofread their summaries, focusing on word choice.

■ Students summarize the plot of a favorite book, including details about plot elements, using time-order words, and retelling events in order.

WORDS TO KNOW

Determine word meanings.

OBJECTIVES
- Identify and define unknown words.

MATERIALS
- *Words to Know* Flip Chart Activity 21, magazines, paper and pencils

 Vocabulary Activities

● Students write three unfamiliar words from a magazine, define them using a dictionary, and write sentences using them.

▲ Students write five unfamiliar words from a magazine, define them using a dictionary, and write sentences using them.

■ Students write seven unfamiliar words from a magazine, define them using a dictionary, and write sentences using them.

READ FOR MEANING

Identify cause and effect.

OBJECTIVES

- Identify cause and effect in expository text.

MATERIALS

- *Read for Meaning* Flip Chart Activity 21, Leveled Readers, paper and pencils

 Pearson eText
- Leveled eReaders

Envision It! Animations

⬤ Students read a book, identify one event that causes another, and then write one sentence about the cause and one sentence about the effect.

▲ Students read a book and then write sentences explaining two causes and effects.

◼ Students read a book and then write a short paragraph about one effect and what caused it.

GET FLUENT

Practice fluent reading with partners.

OBJECTIVES

- Read aloud at an appropriate rate.

MATERIALS

- *Get Fluent* Flip Chart Activity 21, Leveled Readers

 Pearson eText
- Leveled eReaders

⬤ Partners take turns reading aloud at an appropriate rate from a Concept Literacy or Below-Level Reader and providing feedback.

▲ Partners take turns reading aloud at an appropriate rate from an On-Level Reader and providing feedback.

◼ Partners take turns reading aloud at an appropriate rate from an Advanced Reader and providing feedback.

Manage the Stations

Use these management tools to set up and organize your Practice Stations:

Practice Station Flip Charts

Classroom Management Handbook for Differentiated Instruction Practice Stations, p. 39

3 Independent Reading ©

Students should select appropriate complex texts to read and write about independently every day before, during, and after school.

Suggestions for this week's independent reading:
- A folk tale that involves an animal
- An animal fantasy
- A nonfiction book about animal behavior

BOOK TALK Have partners discuss their independent reading for the week. Tell them to refer to their Reading Logs and paraphrase what each selection was about. Then have students focus on discussing one or more of the following:

Key Ideas and Details
- What is the main idea or theme of the text? What details support it?
- What conclusions did you draw from reading the text?

Craft and Structure
- Identify one example of figurative or technical language. What does it mean?
- What was the author's purpose for writing this text?

Integration of Ideas
- How did the illustrations in the text help you understand the meaning?
- How does this text compare and contrast with other texts on the same topic that you have read?

 Pearson eText
- Student Edition
- Decodable Readers
- Leveled Readers

 Trade Book Library

 School or Classroom Library

Materials

- Student Edition
- Reader's and Writer's Notebook
- Decodable Reader

© Bridge to Common Core

INTEGRATION OF KNOWLEDGE/IDEAS
This week, students will read, write, and talk about culture and clothing.

Texts This Week
- "Surprise in the Attic"
- "The Boxed Lunch"
- "Pass It Down"
- *Suki's Kimono*
- "Clothes: Bringing Cultures Together"

Social Studies Knowledge Goals
Students will understand that people
- wear special clothes for holidays
- wear traditional clothing
- react to clothing

Street Rhymes!

Cultures have clothing that people buy and wear.
Some wear silk kimonos or scarves to cover hair.
Some wear elegant clothing and robes on occasion.
Some wear vibrant colors for a special celebration!

- To introduce this week's concept, read aloud the poem several times and ask students to join you.

Content Knowledge Zoom in on ©

Cultures and Clothing

CONCEPT TALK To explore the unit concept of Cultures, this week students will read, write, and talk about how culture influences the clothes people wear. Write the Question of the Week on the board *How does culture influence the clothes we wear?*

Build Oral Language

TALK ABOUT CULTURES AND CLOTHING Have students turn to pp. 190–191 in their Student Editions. Look at each of the photos. Then use the prompts to guide discussion and create a concept map.

- What kind of hat is the boy wearing? (It is called a *kufi*. It is a custom for people to wear these in Africa.) In some cultures, it is a custom for all males to wear a hat outside the home. Let's add *Customs* to our concept map.

- What are the two girls on the left wearing? (These traditional clothes are called *saris*. The fabric is light to help shield their skin from the hot sun.) Climate can influence what people wear. Let's add *Climate* to the concept map.

- Why might the people in these photos be dressed in such fancy outfits? (They might be part of a parade or celebration.) People often dress up for traditional celebrations. Let's add *Celebrations* to the concept map.

- After discussing the photos, ask: How does culture influence the clothes we wear?

Oral Vocabulary

Let's Talk About

Cultures and Clothing

- Ask relevant questions about how culture influences clothing.
- Work together to summarize ideas about wearing traditional clothing.
- Pose and answer questions about special clothes for holidays and traditions.

READING STREET ONLINE
CONCEPT TALK VIDEO
www.ReadingStreet.com

You've learned
1 9 7
Amazing Words
so far this year!

190

191

Student Edition, pp. 190–191

CONNECT TO READING Tell students that this week they will be reading about people from different cultures and why they wear what they do. Throughout the week, encourage students to add concept-related words to this week's concept map.

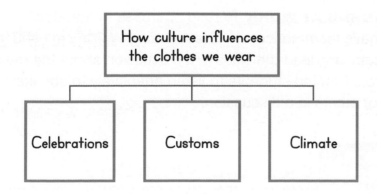

How culture influences the clothes we wear

| Celebrations | Customs | Climate |

eSTREET INTERACTIVE
www.ReadingStreet.com

Pearson eText
- Student Edition

Big Question Video

Concept Talk Video

ELL

Preteach Concepts Use the Day 1 instruction on ELL Poster 21 to build knowledge, develop concepts, and build oral vocabulary.

ELL Support Additional ELL support and modified instruction is provided in the *ELL Handbook* and in the ELL Support lessons found on the *Teacher Resources DVD-ROM*.

Suki's Kimono **190–191**

Amazing Words

You've learned **1 9 7** words so far.

You'll learn **0 1 0** words this week!

traditional	inspire
fret	robe
scarves	drape
fabric	elegant
acceptable	stylish

Content Knowledge Zoom in on

Build Oral Vocabulary

INTRODUCE AMAZING WORDS "Surprise in the Attic" on p. 191b is about a brother and sister who learn they have a rich cultural background. Tell students to listen for this week's Amazing Words—*traditional, fret, scarves,* and *fabric*—as you read the Teacher Read Aloud on p. 191b.

Amazing Words — Robust Vocabulary Routine

1. **Introduce** Write the word *traditional* on the board. Have students say the word aloud with you. In "Surprise in the Attic," we learn that students must wear *traditional* clothing to a Culture Fair. Does the author include any context clues that tell me the meaning of this word? Supply a student-friendly definition. *Traditional* means made or done according to tradition, or custom.

2. **Demonstrate** Have students answer questions to demonstrate understanding. What *traditional* clothing might students from Africa wear? What *traditional* clothing might students from Japan wear?

3. **Apply** Ask students to give an antonym for *traditional.*

4. **Display the Word** Write the word *traditional* on a card. Run your hand under the chunks *tra-di-tion-al* as you read the word.

See p. OV•1 to teach *fret, scarves,* and *fabric.*

Routines Flip Chart

AMAZING WORDS AT WORK Reread "Surprise in the Attic" aloud. As students listen, have them notice how the Amazing Words are used in context. To build oral vocabulary, lead the class in a discussion about the meanings of the Amazing Words. Remind students to listen attentively to speakers and to build on the ideas of others in a discussion.

 Don't Wait Until Friday **MONITOR PROGRESS** Check Oral Vocabulary

During discussion, listen for students' use of Amazing Words.

If... students are unable to use the Amazing Words in discussion,

then... use the Oral Vocabulary Routine in the Routines Flip Chart to demonstrate words in different contexts.

Teacher Read Aloud

MODEL FLUENCY As you read "Surprise in the Attic," model appropriate rate by reading at a speed that is appropriate to the text and will improve the reader's comprehension.

eSTREET INTERACTIVE
www.ReadingStreet.com

Teacher Resources
• Amazing Word Cards
• ELL Support

Surprise in the Attic

Ricky and Dana sat on the floor. They looked at the clothes they had dragged from the closet. They needed something to wear to the Culture Fair at school tomorrow. They had to find clothes that showed something about their family and the country they came from.

"The Culture Fair will help us learn about each other," their teacher had said. "Try to wear something that is special to your family. My family is from China, so I'll wear traditional Chinese clothes. Tomorrow, I bet we'll see clothes from countries all over the world."

"We come from Texas," Ricky said to his sister. "That's not another country!" Dana agreed that their family seemed dull compared to their friends' families. Her best friend Rosa came from Mexico. Ricky's best friend Ken came all the way from Japan.

Just then, the children's grandparents walked in the door. They lived down the street and had gone for a walk. "What's this?" their grandmother asked when she saw the pile of clothes on the floor. Ricky told her about the Culture Fair. Dana said they were worried. "We don't have a culture like our friends do," she said, "so Ricky and I have nothing to wear."

"That's not true," her grandfather said. "There's no need to fret. We have a rich culture you may not know anything about. Come to our house, and we'll

show you." The children followed their grandparents down the street to their house, and then up to their attic. In the attic, in a box, there were some very beautiful things.

"My family came from England a long time ago," the children's grandmother said. She pulled two lovely silk scarves out of the box. "My grandmother used to wear these scarves to English tea parties," she said. "I've had them since I was a child, but I think you should have them now." She handed the scarves to Dana, who smiled with delight.

The children's grandfather pulled out a folded piece of fabric. It was a red plaid skirt with fringe on the seam. "My great-great grandfather came from Scotland," he told Ricky. "He wore this kilt. Kilts are made of a fabric called tartan. A long time ago, the kind of tartan a man wore showed who he was and where he lived. Now it's your turn to wear it."

Ricky and Dana were very surprised. They were from cultures they never knew about! "I can't wait to go to the Culture Fair now," said Ricky. "I can't wait to wear my kilt!"

"And I can't wait to wear my scarves," said Dana. She wrapped both of them around her neck and pranced around the attic—just as if she were going to a fancy English tea party.

Support Listening Comprehension Before listening, have small groups of students discuss traditional clothing from their cultures and any experiences they have had with these traditional clothes. Share with the group. After listening, have students compare those experiences to what they heard in the Read Aloud.

ELL Support for Read Aloud Use the modified Read Aloud on p. DI•19 of the ELL Support lessons on the *Teacher Resources DVD-ROM* to prepare students to listen to "Surprise in the Attic."

Common Core State Standards

Foundational Skills 3. Know a and apply on-level phonics and word analysis skills in decoding words. **Foundational Skills 3.c.** Decode multisyllable words.

Skills Trace

Syllable Pattern CV/VC

Introduce U5W1D1

Practice U5W1D3; U5W1D4

Reteach/Review U5W1D5; U5W2D4

Assess/Test Weekly Test U5W1 Benchmark Test U5

KEY: U=Unit   W=Week   D=Day

Vocabulary Support

You may wish to explain the meanings of these words.

radiator a device that heats a room or keeps a car engine cool

annual happening once a year

Word Analysis

Teach/Model

⊙ Syllable Pattern CV/VC

CONNECT Connect today's lesson to previously learned vowel digraphs. Write *team* and *rain.* You already can read words like these. Each word has two vowels in a row. Today you'll learn to spell and read words with the syllabication pattern CV/VC: two vowels that appear together but are part of different syllables.

MODEL Write *lion. Lion* is a two-syllable word. When I see a word that has two vowels in a row, I usually say one vowel sound. But sometimes I can hear both vowels. That's because each vowel is in a different syllable. Draw a line between the *i* and *o* to divide *lion* into syllables. When I divide the word into syllables, I can tell that the word is not pronounced *line.* It is the two-syllable word *lion.*

GROUP PRACTICE Have students read *lion* with you. Write the words below. Have the group read the words with you. Then identify the syllables in each word.

gradu/ate	usu/al	the/ater	cre/ate	ne/on
di/ary	radi/ator	sci/ence	annu/al	cli/ent

REVIEW What do you know about reading words with two vowels that appear together but are part of different syllables? When vowels appear together in different syllables, divide the vowels, read each syllable first, and then read the whole word.

Guide Practice

MODEL Have students turn to p. 192 in their Student Editions. Each word on this page has the syllabication pattern CV/VC. The first word is *ideas.* I divide the vowels *e* and *a,* read each syllable, then read the whole word, *ideas.*

GROUP PRACTICE For each word in Words I Can Blend, ask students to divide the word into syllables. Make sure they are dividing the two vowels. Then have students read the words.

Corrective feedback	**If...** students have difficulty reading a word,
	then... model reading the parts and then the whole word, and then ask students to read it with you.

Phonics

Syllable Pattern CV/VC

Common Core State Standards
Foundational Skills 3. Know and apply grade-level phonics and word analysis skills in decoding words.

piano
CV/VC
READING STREET ONLINE
SOUND-SPELLING CARDS
www.ReadingStreet.com

Words I Can Blend

ideas
violets
piano
neon
create

Sentences I Can Read

1. Yesterday I had three great ideas.
2. Ginny placed a small vase of violets on the piano.
3. Some crafters use neon to create signs.

I Can Read!

Dear Diary,

This morning I was listening to the radio on our stereo as I ate my cereal. The announcer was reporting the news as usual, when suddenly there was a message about an annual geography contest in our area.

My friend Luis and I love to study geography. I think we might be able to cooperate to create an unusual project.

I phoned Luis immediately, and we got together to discuss a variety of ideas. I'll have more on this tomorrow, Diary.

You've learned
Syllable Pattern CV/VC

192

193

Student Edition, pp. 192–193

Apply

READ WORDS IN ISOLATION After students can successfully combine the word parts to read the words on p. 192, point to words in random order and ask students to read them naturally.

READ WORDS IN CONTEXT Have students read each of the sentences on p. 192. Have them identify words in the sentences that have the vowel pattern CV/VC.

 **Team Talk** Pair students and have them take turns reading each of the sentences aloud.

Chorally read the I Can Read! passage on p. 193 with students. Then have them read the passage aloud to themselves.

ON THEIR OWN For additional practice, use *Reader's and Writer's Notebook,* p. 316.

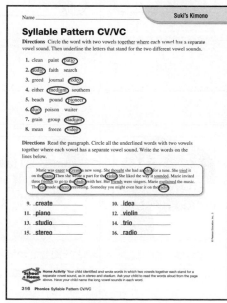

Suki's Kimono

Syllable Pattern CV/VC

Directions Circle the word with two vowels together where each vowel has a separate vowel sound. Then underline the letters that stand for the two different vowel sounds.

1. clean   paint   (patio)
2. (studio)   faith   search
3. greed   journal   (rodeo)
4. either   (medium)   southern
5. beach   pound   (pioneer)
6. (duo)   poison   waiter
7. grain   group   (stadium)
8. mean   freeze   (video)

Directions Read the paragraph. Circle all the underlined words with two vowels together where each vowel has a separate vowel sound. Write the words on the lines below.

Marie was eager to create a new song. She thought she had an idea for a tune. She tried it on the piano. Then she wrote a part for the violin. She liked the way it sounded. Marie invited three friends to go to the studio with her. Her friends were singers. Marie explained the music. They made a stereo recording. Someday you might even hear it on the radio.

9. create   10. idea
11. piano   12. violin
13. studio   14. trio
15. stereo   16. radio

Home Activity Your child identified and wrote words in which two vowels together each stand for a separate vowel sound, as in stereo and stadium. Ask your child to read the words aloud from the page above. Have your child name the long vowel sounds in each word.

316   Phonics Syllable Pattern CV/VC

Reader's and Writer's Notebook, p. 316

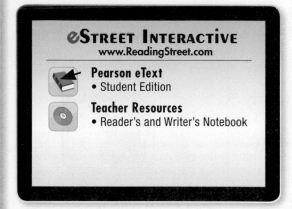

eSTREET INTERACTIVE
www.ReadingStreet.com

Pearson eText
• Student Edition

Teacher Resources
• Reader's and Writer's Notebook

ELL

Cognates Some English words with the V/V syllable pattern have cognates in Spanish: *create/crear, idea/idea, radio/radio, piano/piano.* Have Spanish speakers discuss the spellings and pronunciations of these word pairs in both languages.

Suki's Kimono   **192–193**

© Common Core State Standards

Foundational Skills 3. Know and apply on-level phonics and word analysis skills in decoding words. **Foundational Skills 3.c.** Decode multisyllable words. **Foundational Skills 3.d.** Read grade-appropriate irregularly spelled words. **Foundational Skills 4.** Read with sufficient accuracy and fluency to support comprehension.

Decodable Reader 21A

If students need help, then...

Read *Radio Days*

READ WORDS IN ISOLATION Have students turn to p. 61 of *Decodable Practice Readers* 3.2. Have students read each word.

Have students read the high-frequency words *you, watch, to, the, people, of, have, would, your, their, they, were, could, one, new, some,* and *laughed* on the first page.

PREVIEW Have students read the title and preview the story. Tell them that they will read words with the syllable pattern CV/VC.

READ WORDS IN CONTEXT Pair students for reading and listen as they read. One student begins. Students read the entire story, switching readers after each page. Partners reread the story. This time the other student begins. Make sure that students are monitoring their accuracy when they decode words.

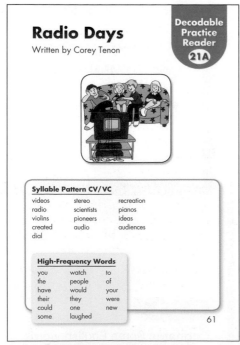

Decodable Practice Reader 21A

Corrective feedback	**If...** students have difficulty decoding a word, **then...** refer them to the *Sound-Spelling Cards* to identify the word parts. Have them read the word parts individually and then together to say the word. • What is the new word? • Is the new word a word you know? • Does it make sense in the story?

CHECK DECODING AND COMPREHENSION Have students retell the story to include characters, setting, and events. Then have students find words in the story that have the syllable pattern CV/VC. Students should supply *videos, recreation, scientists, pianos, violins, pioneers, ideas, created, audiences,* and *dial.*

Reread for Fluency

REREAD DECODABLE READER Have students reread *Decodable Practice Reader 21A* to develop automaticity decoding words with the syllable pattern CV/VC.

Routine   Oral Rereading

1. Read Have students read the entire book orally.

2. Reread To achieve optimal fluency, students should reread the text three or four times.

3. Corrective Feedback Listen as students read. Provide corrective feedback regarding their fluency and decoding.

Routines Flip Chart

Syllable Pattern CV/VC

Beginning Write several words with the syllable pattern CV/VC, such as *pioneers, dial, videos,* and *recreation,* from the *Decodable Practice Reader* on the board. Point to each word as you say it aloud. Then underline the two vowels that are together. Have students divide the vowels and then repeat the words with you.

Intermediate After reading, have students sort the following words into two columns, headed CVVC pattern and CV/VC pattern: *rain, radios, cream, create, dial, deep, pianos,* and *pains.*

Advanced After reading the story, have students write a short radio message or radio advertisement using 3 or 4 words with the CV/VC syllable pattern.

Zoom in on ©

© Common Core State Standards

Literature 1. Ask and answer questions to demonstrate understanding of a text, referring explicitly to the text as the basis for the answers. **Literature 2.** Recount stories, including fables, folktales, and myths from diverse cultures; determine the central message, lesson, or moral and explain how it is conveyed through key details in the text. **Foundational Skills 4.b.** Read on-level prose and poetry orally with accuracy, appropriate rate, and expression on successive readings. **Also Literature 10.**

Skills Trace

⊙ Compare and Contrast

Introduce U1W4D1; U2W2D1; U5W1D1

Practice U1W4D2; U1W4D3; U2W1D2; U2W1D3; U2W2D2; U2W2D3; U2W4D2; U2W4D3

Reteach/Review U1W4D5; U2W2D5; U5W1D5

Assess/Test Weekly Tests U1W4; U2W2; U5W1
Benchmark Tests U2; U5

KEY: U=Unit   W=Week   D=Day

Academic Vocabulary ©

compare and contrast a relationship between events, characters, or settings that expresses how they are alike and different

Comprehension Support

Students may also turn to pp. EI•5 and EI•27 to review the skill and strategy if necessary.

Text-Based Comprehension

⊙ Compare and Contrast
⊙ Visualize

READ Remind students of the weekly concept—Cultures and Clothing. Have students read "The Boxed Lunch" on p. 195.

MODEL A CLOSE READ

Think Aloud Have students follow along as you read the first paragraph of "The Boxed Lunch." The first paragraph describes Ky's lunch. Which words signal that things are the same? *(looked like)* What looks the same? (sausage and tiny octopus, hard-boiled eggs and baby chicks just hatching, rice ball covered with seaweed and a soccer ball) Which words signal that things are different? *(instead of)* What is different? (carrot sticks and hard-boiled eggs; tortilla chips and rice balls covered with seaweed)

As I read the end of the story, I formed a picture in my mind of how funny it would be to eat peanut butter and jelly sandwiches with chopsticks.

TEACH Have students read p. 194. Explain that the skill of compare and contrast and the strategy of visualizing are tools they can use to better understand the text. Review the bulleted items and explanations on p. 194. Then have students use a graphic organizer like the one on p. 194 to compare and contrast the food items in the passage.

GUIDE PRACTICE Have students reread "The Boxed Lunch" using the callouts as guides. Then ask volunteers to respond to the questions in the callouts, citing specific examples from the text to support their answers.

Skill Two different snack foods are being compared—tortilla chips and a rice ball covered in seaweed. They are different because the rice ball looks like a soccer ball and a tortilla chip does not.

Strategy I see a person who drops the sandwich and makes a mess.

APPLY Use *Reader's and Writer's Notebook* p. 317 for additional practice with comparing and contrasting.

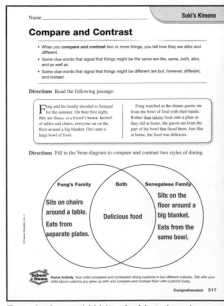
Reader's and Writer's Notebook, p. 317

Common Core State Standards
Literature 1. Ask and answer questions to demonstrate understanding of a text, referring explicitly to the text as the basis for the answers. **Also Literature 2., 10.**

Envision It! Skill Strategy

Skill

Compare and Contrast

Strategy

Visualize

READING STREET ONLINE
ENVISION IT! ANIMATIONS
www.ReadingStreet.com

Comprehension Skill

Compare and Contrast

• When you compare and contrast two or more things, you tell how they are alike and different.

• Clue words such as *like, both, also, but, however,* and *instead of* show comparisons and contrasts.

• Use what you learned about compare and contrast and the graphic organizer below as you read "The Boxed Lunch." Then write a short paragraph comparing the two lunches.

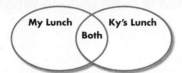

My Lunch — Both — Ky's Lunch

Comprehension Strategy

Visualize

While reading, look for words that help you form pictures in your mind. Forming pictures about what is happening in the story can help you enjoy and remember a story. Forming pictures in your mind can help you monitor and adjust or correct your comprehension as you read.

194

THE BOXED LUNCH

Ky was nervous about his first day in his new school. In Japan, Ky always brought his lunch in a bento box, which was carefully packed with eye-catching foods. Ky loved the sausage that looked like a tiny octopus. Instead of carrot sticks, he had hard-boiled eggs that looked like baby chicks just hatching. And instead of tortilla chips, he had a rice ball covered with pieces of dried seaweed so that it looked like a soccer ball.

At lunchtime, Ky's classmates began eating their lunches. Ky opened his box slowly, not sure of what his new friends would think. But they were very interested. He explained each item and showed them how to eat with chopsticks. Some boys asked to try the chopsticks. Ky promised to bring some for everyone the next day. One friend said, "I wonder how they'll work with peanut butter and jelly sandwiches."

Skill Note the clue words—*instead of.* What things are being compared? How are they the same or different?

Strategy Form a picture in your mind of a friend trying to eat a peanut butter and jelly sandwich with chopsticks. What do you see?

Your Turn!

Need a Review? See the *Envision It! Handbook* for help with comparing and contrasting and visualizing.

Let's Think About...

Ready to Try It? As you read *Suki's Kimono,* use what you've learned about comparing and contrasting and visualizing to understand the text.

195

Student Edition, pp. 194–195

Model Fluent Reading

RATE Have students listen as you read paragraph 2 of "The Boxed Lunch" at an appropriate rate. Explain that you will not read too fast or too slowly because you want your listeners to understand what you are saying.

Routine   Oral Rereading

1. **Select a Passage** Read paragraph 2 of "The Boxed Lunch."

2. **Model** Have students listen as you read at an appropriate rate.

3. **Guide Practice** Have students read along with you.

4. **On Their Own** For optimal fluency, students should reread three or four times at an appropriate rate.

Routines Flip Chart

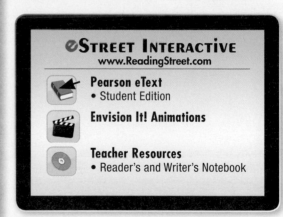

eSTREET INTERACTIVE
www.ReadingStreet.com

Pearson eText
• Student Edition

Envision It! Animations

Teacher Resources
• Reader's and Writer's Notebook

ELL

Compare and Contrast Provide oral practice by having students compare and contrast a house cat and a tiger. Help students speak in complete sentences and use clue words to signal sameness and difference. Then write their sentences on the board and have students take turns reading them aloud.

Common Core State Standards

Writing 7. Conduct short research projects that build knowledge about a topic. **Speaking/Listening 1.** Engage effectively in a range of collaborative discussions (one-on-one, in groups, and teacher-led) with diverse partners on grade 3 topics and texts, building on others' ideas and expressing their own clearly. **Language 4.** Determine or clarify the meaning of unknown and multiple-meaning words and phrases based on grade 3 reading and content, choosing flexibly from a range of strategies.

Selection Vocabulary

Use the following routine to introduce this week's tested selection vocabulary.

cotton cloth made from cotton fibers

festival a celebration or holiday

graceful showing beauty in movement

handkerchief a square piece of cloth used to wipe the face or nose

paces steps in walking

pale light in shade or color

rhythm a repeated beat, sound, or motion

snug fitting closely; tight

SEE IT/SAY IT Write *snug.* Scan across the word with your finger as you say it: *snug.*

HEAR IT Use the word in a sentence. My sweatshirt from last year is *snug* in the shoulders.

DEFINE IT Elicit definitions from students. How would you describe to another student what *snug* means? Clarify or give a definition when necessary. Yes, *snug* means "tight," or "fitting closely." Restate the word in student-friendly terms. So if something is *snug,* it's tight.

Team Talk Is it a good or bad thing to wear clothes that are *snug*? Does it depend on the type of clothing? Turn and talk to your partner about this. Be prepared to explain your answer. Allow students time to discuss. Ask for examples. Rephrase their examples for usage when necessary or to correct misunderstandings.

MAKE CONNECTIONS Have students discuss the word. Have you ever worn clothes that are *snug*? Turn and talk to your partner about this. Then be prepared to share. Have students share. Rephrase their ideas for usage when necessary or to correct misunderstandings.

RECORD Have students write the word and its meaning.

Continue this routine to introduce the remaining words in this manner.

> **Corrective feedback** | **If...** students are having difficulty understanding, **then...** review the definitions in small groups.

Research and Inquiry

Step 1 | Identify and Focus Topic

TEACH Discuss the Question of the Week: *How does culture influence the clothes we wear?* Tell students they will research how culture influences clothing in different parts of the world. They will write articles to present to the class on Day 5.

Think Aloud

MODEL I'll start by brainstorming specific inquiry questions about how culture influences the clothes people wear. I know that one thing that influences the clothes people wear is the customs of their culture. First I'll choose the custom of wearing a head covering. Some questions could be *Why do people wear head coverings? What style of head covering do people from different cultures wear?* and *What colors do people wear on their heads?*

GUIDE PRACTICE After students have brainstormed inquiry questions, explain that tomorrow they will conduct online research using their questions. Help students identify keywords that will guide their search.

ON THEIR OWN Have students work individually, in pairs, or in small groups to write an inquiry question.

21st Century Skills
Internet Guy *Don Leu*

Weekly Inquiry Project

STEP 1	Identify and Focus Topic
STEP 2	Navigate/Search
STEP 3	Analyze Information
STEP 4	Synthesize
STEP 5	Communicate

ELL

Multilingual Vocabulary Students can apply knowledge of their home languages to acquire new English vocabulary by using Multilingual Vocabulary Lists (*ELL Handbook*, pp. 433–444).

ELL

If... students need more scaffolding and practice with **Vocabulary, then...** use the activities on pp. DI•17–DI•18 in the Teacher Resources section on SuccessNet.

Day 1 | SMALL GROUP TIME • Differentiate Vocabulary, p. SG•1

OL On-Level	**SI** Strategic Intervention	**A** Advanced
• **Practice Vocabulary** Amazing Words	• **Reteach Vocabulary** Amazing Words	• **Extend Vocabulary** Amazing Words
• **Read** *Reading Street Sleuth*, pp. 56–57	• **Read** *Reading Street Sleuth*, pp. 56–57	• **Read** *Reading Street Sleuth*, pp. 56–57
		• **Introduce** Inquiry Project

Common Core State Standards

Language 1.a. Explain the function of nouns, pronouns, verbs, adjectives, and adverbs in general and their functions in particular sentences. **Language 2.f.** Use spelling patterns and generalizations (e.g., word families, position-based spellings, syllable patterns, ending rules, meaningful word parts) in writing words.

Spelling Pretest

Syllable Pattern CV/VC

INTRODUCE Some words contain the CV/VC syllable pattern.

PRETEST Say each word, read the sentence, and repeat the word.

1. **create** — I will **create** a poster of a cell for science.
2. **medium** — Alex is tall, and Damon is **medium** height.
3. **piano** — Sue played songs on the **piano.**
4. **idea** — I have an **idea** for my science project.
5. **radio** — We listened to songs on the **radio.**
6. **video** — They played a **video** of their wedding.
7. **studio** — The artist painted in his **studio.**
8. **violin** — Rebecca is practicing playing the **violin.**
9. **duo** — The two singers performed as a **duo.**
10. **patio** — We put a picnic table on the **patio.**
11. **rodeo** — They rode bulls at the **rodeo.**
12. **pioneer** — The **pioneer** arrived in a wagon.
13. **trio** — The three musicians formed a jazz **trio.**
14. **stadium** — We went to a baseball game at the **stadium.**
15. **audio** — We could not hear any **audio** on the broken television.

Challenge words
16. **audience** — The **audience** clapped loudly after the play.
17. **radiate** — Fireplaces **radiate** warmth.
18. **cereal** — Our family eats **cereal** together each morning.
19. **Creole** — Many **Creole** people live in southern Louisiana.
20. **recreation** — For **recreation,** we played kickball.

SELF-CORRECT Have students self-correct their pretests by rewriting misspelled words.

ON THEIR OWN Use *Let's Practice It!* p. 289 on the *Teacher Resources DVD-ROM.*

Let's Practice It! TR DVD•289

Conventions

Adjectives and Articles

MAKE CONNECTIONS To focus attention on adjectives and articles, ask volunteers to write descriptive sentences on the board. Have others point out the adjectives and articles.

TEACH Display Grammar Transparency 21, and read aloud the explanation and examples in the box. Point out each noun described by an adjective or article.

MODEL Model how to identify the adjective in items 1 and 2. Explain that in item 1, you found the adjective by asking, "What kind of cloth?" In item 2, you found the adjective by asking, "What kind of occasions?"

GUIDE PRACTICE Guide students to complete items 3 to 5. Record the correct responses on the transparency.

APPLY Have students read sentences 6–9 on the transparency and choose the article to correctly complete each sentence.

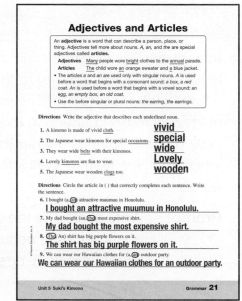

Adjectives and Articles

An **adjective** is a word that can describe a person, place, or thing. Adjectives tell more about nouns. *A, an,* and *the* are special adjectives called **articles.**

Adjectives Many people wore <u>bright</u> clothes to the <u>annual</u> parade.

Articles The child wore <u>an</u> orange sweater and <u>a</u> blue jacket.

• The articles *a* and *an* are used only with singular nouns. *A* is used before a word that begins with a consonant sound: *a box, a red coat. An* is used before a word that begins with a vowel sound: *an egg, an empty box, an old coat.*

• Use *the* before singular or plural nouns: *the earring, the earrings.*

Directions Write the adjective that describes each underlined noun.

1. A kimono is made of vivid <u>cloth</u>. **vivid**
2. The Japanese wear kimonos for special <u>occasions</u>. **special**
3. They wear wide <u>belts</u> with their kimonos. **wide**
4. Lovely <u>kimonos</u> are fun to wear. **Lovely**
5. The Japanese wear wooden <u>clogs</u> too. **wooden**

Directions Circle the article in ( ) that correctly completes each sentence. Write the sentence.

6. I bought (a, **an**) attractive muumuu in Honolulu.
   I bought an attractive muumuu in Honolulu.
7. My dad bought (an, **the**) most expensive shirt.
   My dad bought the most expensive shirt.
8. (**The**, An) shirt has big purple flowers on it.
   The shirt has big purple flowers on it.
9. We can wear our Hawaiian clothes for (a, **an**) outdoor party.
   We can wear our Hawaiian clothes for an outdoor party.

Unit 5 Suki's Kimono   Grammar **21**

Grammar Transparency 21, TR DVD

Academic Vocabulary ©

An **adjective** is a word that modifies a noun or pronoun. It usually comes before the word it describes. Most adjectives answer the questions *What kind?, How many?,* or *Which one? A, an,* and *the* are special adjectives called **articles.**

Daily Fix-It

1. The little girl wore a beautifull dress from japan. *(beautiful; Japan)*

2. She was prowd of the dress that her grandmother gived her. *(proud; gave)*

Handwriting

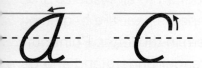

MODEL LETTER FORMATION, SIZE, AND SLANT Display the capital cursive letters *A* and *C.* Follow the stroke instruction pictured to model letter formation. Explain that writing legibly includes writing letters that are the correct size and slant. Model writing this sentence: *Archie and Cate ran a race.*

GUIDE PRACTICE Have students write these sentences: *Ceci saw cacti in Arizona. Alan ate chocolate ice cream.*

ELL

Language Production: Adjectives and Articles Have each student take an item out of his or her desk and identify it. Help students find adjectives to describe each item. Then add articles to the description of each item. Group several items together to illustrate how articles can change with plural nouns.

Vocabulary: Syllable Pattern CV/VC Clarify the pronunciation and meaning of each spelling word. Show the meaning of *create, violin, rodeo,* and *trio* with motions, objects, or pictures. Have students point out where the words are divided into syllables.

Common Core State Standards

Writing 1. Write opinion pieces on familiar topics or texts, supporting a point of view with reasons. **Writing 1.a.** Introduce the topic or text they are writing about, state an opinion, and create an organizational structure that lists reasons. **Also Writing 1.b., 10.**

Bridge to Common Core

TEXT TYPES AND PURPOSES

This week students write a letter to the editor bringing attention to an issue.

Opinion Writing

Through reading and discussion, students will gain a deeper understanding of cultures and clothing. They will use this knowledge from the texts to write and support letters to the editor.

Through the week, students will improve their range and content of writing through daily mini-lessons.

5-Day Plan

DAY 1	Read Like a Writer
DAY 2	Main Idea and Supporting Details
DAY 3	Keeping Your Letter Focused
DAY 4	Revise: Adding
DAY 5	Proofread for Adjectives and Articles

Writing

Letter to the Editor

Mini-Lesson   Read Like a Writer

■ **Introduce** This week you will write a letter to the editor. A letter to the editor is a formal letter written to a newspaper or magazine to bring attention to an issue. A newspaper publishes a letter to the editor when it thinks the letter will inform or help readers.

Prompt Write a letter to the editor about an issue occurring in your community or school.

Trait Organization

Mode Persuasive/Opinion

■ **Examine Model Text** Today, we will read an example of a letter to the editor that brings our attention to a problem at a school. Have students read the letter to the editor on p. 318 of their *Reader's and Writer's Notebook*.

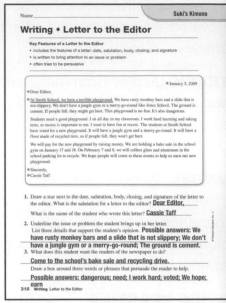

Reader's and Writer's Notebook, p. 318

■ **Key Features** A letter to the editor has the same features as other formal letters. It has a date, a salutation, a body, a closing, and a signature. Have students draw a star next to each of these features on the letter.

A letter to the editor is written to bring public attention to an issue or problem. Usually the problem is clearly stated and appears near the beginning of the letter. Ask students to underline the problem in the letter. Point out that the author uses specific details to help the reader understand and care about the problem.

A letter to the editor tries to persuade the reader to agree with the writer's opinion or position. It might ask the reader to take action. Help students identify what the author is trying to persuade the reader to think or do. Have students choose words and phrases from the text that persuade them that the author is right.

Review Key Features

Review the key features of a letter to the editor with students. Create a poster of the key features to display in your classroom.

Key Features of a Letter to the Editor

- includes the features of a letter: date, salutation, body, closing, and signature
- is written to bring attention to an issue or problem
- often tries to be persuasive

Routine **Quick Write for Fluency** **Team Talk**

1. **Talk** Have students discuss the features of letters to the editor with a partner, based on the prompts, "What is the purpose of a letter to the editor?" and "Who can write a letter to the editor?"

2. **Write** Have each student write a short answer to one of the prompts.

3. **Share** Have students read their answers aloud to a new partner.

Routines Flip Chart

eSTREET INTERACTIVE
www.ReadingStreet.com

Teacher Resources
- Reader's and Writer's Notebook
- Let's Practice It!

Academic Vocabulary ©

A **letter to the editor** is a formal letter written to a newspaper or magazine to bring attention to an issue.

ELL

Letter to the Editor Show students a newspaper containing several letters to the editor. Read one or two of the letters to them. Explain that a letter to the editor is written to bring public attention to an issue or problem. Then read the writing model aloud and clarify any unfamiliar words, phrases, or ideas for students. Ask students to identify problems that they think the public should know about.

Wrap Up Your Day!

✔ **Content Knowledge** Reread "Street Rhymes!" on p. 190j to students. Ask them what they learned this week about cultures and clothing.

✔ **Oral Vocabulary** Have students use the Amazing Words they learned in context sentences.

✔ **Homework** Send home this week's Family Times newsletter on *Let's Practice It!* pp. 290–291 on the *Teacher Resources DVD-ROM.*

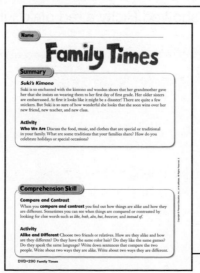

Let's Practice It!
TR DVD•290–291

Preview DAY 2

Tell students that tomorrow they will read about how and why a person's culture might be important to him or her.

Common Core State Standards

Speaking/Listening 1. Engage effectively in a range of collaborative discussions (one-on-one, in groups, and teacher-led) with diverse partners on grade 3 topics and texts, building on others' ideas and expressing their own clearly. **Language 6.** Acquire and use accurately grade-appropriate conversational, general academic, and domain-specific words and phrases, including those that signal spatial and temporal relationships (e.g., *After dinner that night we went looking for them*). **Also Speaking/Listening 1.b., 1.c.**

Content Knowledge

Cultures and Clothing

EXPAND THE CONCEPT Remind students of the weekly concept question, *How does culture influence the clothes we wear?* Tell students that today they will begin reading *Suki's Kimono.* As they read, encourage students to think about how cultures influence clothing.

Build Oral Language

TALK ABOUT SENTENCES AND WORDS Reread these sentences from the Read Aloud, "Surprise in the Attic."

The children's grandfather pulled out a folded piece of fabric. It was a red plaid skirt with fringe on the seam. "My great-great grandfather came from Scotland," he told Ricky. "He wore this kilt."

- What does *fabric* mean? (cloth)
- What context clues help you understand its meaning? (red plaid skirt; fringe on the seam)
- Why do you think the author included a description of the fabric? (so readers could visualize what it looked like)

Team Talk Have students turn to a partner and discuss the following question. Then ask them to share their responses.

- What is the shortest version of these sentences you can make without changing the basic meaning? (Possible response: Ricky's grandfather showed Ricky a red plaid kilt worn by his great-great grandfather.)

Build Oral Vocabulary

Amazing Words
Robust Vocabulary Routine

1. **Introduce** Write the Amazing Word *acceptable* on the board. Have students say it aloud with you. Relate *acceptable* to the photographs on pp. 190–191 and "Surprise in the Attic." Why do most people want to wear clothing that is *acceptable* to their culture? Have students determine the definition of the word. (Something is acceptable if it is seen to be proper or right.)

2. **Demonstrate** Have students answer questions to demonstrate understanding. What clothing might be *acceptable* in a hot climate but not in a cold climate? Would it be *acceptable* to wear a fancy beaded hat to play softball?

3. **Apply** Have students apply their understanding. What kinds of clothing are *acceptable* for school? (Possible response: clothes that are clean, tidy, and not sloppy)

4. **Display the Word** Write the word *acceptable* on a card. Run your hand under the syllables *ac-cept-a-ble* as you read the word.

See p. OV•1 to teach *inspire*.

Routines Flip Chart

Amazing Words

traditional	inspire
fret	robe
scarves	drape
fabric	elegant
acceptable	stylish

ADD TO THE CONCEPT MAP Use the photos on pp. 190–191 and the Read Aloud "Surprise in the Attic" to discuss how culture influences the clothes we wear and talk about the Amazing Words *traditional, fret, scarves,* and *fabric.* Add these and other concept-related words to the concept map to develop students' knowledge of the topic. Discuss the photos and vocabulary to generate questions about the topic. Encourage students to build on others' ideas when they answer. Add some of the words generated in discussion to the concept map.

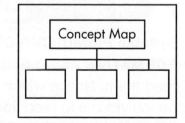
Concept Map

• What kinds of *fabric* do people use to make clothes?

Why do women wear *scarves*?

Why might people *fret* if they were not allowed to wear their *traditional* clothing?

Reinforce Vocabulary Use the Day 2 instruction on ELL Poster 21 to teach lesson vocabulary and discuss the lesson concept.

 **Common Core State Standards**

Foundational Skills 3. Know and apply grade-level phonics and word analysis skills in decoding words. **Foundational Skills 3.c.** Decode multisyllable words. **Language 3.a.** Choose words and phrases for effect.

Word Analysis

Syllable Pattern CV/VC

REVIEW Review the syllable pattern CV/VC, pointing out that the two vowels are split when in different syllables and are both pronounced.

READ WORDS IN ISOLATION Display these words. Have the class read the words. Then point to the words in random order and ask students to read them quickly.

poem	react	duet	stadium
medium	trial	cruel	pioneer

> **Corrective feedback** | Model reading the syllables and then have students read the whole word with you.

READ WORDS IN CONTEXT Display these sentences. Have the class read the sentences.

Josh **creates** songs to play on his **violin.**

The **poet** wrote about a wild **lion.**

Ken is **fluent** in Spanish.

 **Don't Wait Until Friday**

MONITOR PROGRESS Check Word Reading

Syllable Pattern CV/VC

FORMATIVE ASSESSMENT Write the following words and have the class read them. Notice which words students miss during the group reading. Call on individuals to read some of the words.

dial	trial	diet	truant	supplier	Spiral Review
always	screen	borrow	explain	approach ←	Row 2 reviews words with long vowel digraphs *ee, ea, ai, ay, oa, ow.*
obtain	denial	degree	realize	peanut ←	Row 3 reviews words with long vowel digraphs and words with syllable patterns CV/VC.

If... students cannot read words with the syllable pattern CV/VC at this point,

then... use the Day 1 Word Analysis lesson on p. 192a to reteach syllable pattern CV/VC. Use words from the *Decodable Practice Reader.* Continue to monitor students' progress using other instructional opportunities during the week. See the Skills Trace on p. 192a.

Literary Terms

Word Choice

TEACH Tell students that authors choose their words carefully. Their goal is to select words that make the selection more interesting and understandable. Word choice is important in fiction and nonfiction.

Think Aloud **MODEL** Let's look at "The Boxed Lunch" and "Pass It Down." Can you find words and phrases that help you experience the way things look, sound, smell, taste, or feel? (in "The Boxed Lunch," words that describe the appearance of each food item; in "Pass It Down," words that tell how nervous Emily Douglas felt)

GUIDE PRACTICE Find an example of interesting word choice on p. 204 of *Suki's Kimono.*

ON THEIR OWN Have students look for examples of descriptive word choice in other selections of their Student Edition.

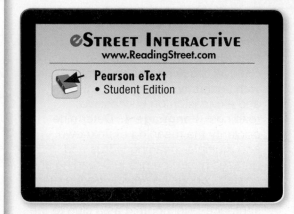

eSTREET INTERACTIVE
www.ReadingStreet.com

Pearson eText
• Student Edition

Academic Vocabulary

fiction a story that describes imaginary people and events

ⓒ Common Core State Standards

Foundational Skills 4.b. Read on-level prose and poetry orally with accuracy, appropriate rate, and expression on successive readings. **Language 4.** Determine or clarify the meaning of unknown and multiple-meaning words and phrases based on grade 3 reading and content, choosing flexibly from a range of strategies. **Language 4.a.** Use sentence-level context as a clue to the meaning of a word or phrase. **Also Language 5., 5.c.**

Selection Vocabulary

cotton cloth made from cotton fibers

festival a celebration or holiday

graceful showing beauty in movement

handkerchief a square piece of cloth used to wipe the face or nose

paces steps in walking

pale light in shade or color

rhythm a repeated beat, sound, or motion

snug fitting closely; tight

ⓒ Bridge to Common Core

VOCABULARY ACQUISITION AND USE
Looking for synonyms within a text helps students determine the meanings of unknown words and enables them to acquire a broad range of academic and domain-specific words. By using context clues to clarify the meaning of words, students demonstrate the ability to gather vocabulary knowledge on their own.

Vocabulary Support

Refer students to *Words!* on p. W•3 in the Student Edition for additional practice.

Vocabulary Skill

⟳ Synonyms

READ Have students read "Pass It Down" on p. 197. Use the vocabulary skill and strategy as tools to build comprehension.

TEACH CONTEXT CLUES Tell students that when they encounter an unfamiliar word, they should use context clues to find a synonym. Explain that context clues are found in nearby words and sentences and can sometimes be a synonym for the unfamiliar word.

Think Aloud **MODEL** Write on the board: *We clapped to the rhythm, or beat, of the music.* I don't know the meaning of the word *rhythm,* so I will read nearby words for clues. I notice that the words or *beat* immediately follow the word *rhythm.* These words are surrounded by commas. This tells me that the word *beat* means the same or almost the same as the word *rhythm. Beat* is a synonym for *rhythm.*

GUIDE PRACTICE Write these sentences on the board: *Our town holds a street festival every summer. Everyone enjoys this fun celebration.* Have students determine the meaning of the word *festival* using context clues that might include a synonym for the unfamiliar word. For additional support, use *Envision It! Pictured Vocabulary Cards* or *Tested Vocabulary Cards.*

ON THEIR OWN Have students reread "Pass It Down" on p. 197. Have them find examples of context clues that include synonyms for vocabulary words. For additional practice, use *Reader's and Writer's Notebook* p. 319.

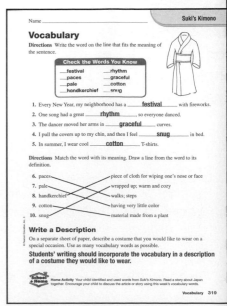

Reader's and Writer's Notebook, p. 319

Envision It! | Words to Know

festival

handkerchief

snug

cotton
graceful
paces
pale
rhythm

READING STREET ONLINE VOCABULARY ACTIVITIES
www.ReadingStreet.com

Vocabulary Strategy for

🔄 Synonyms

Context Clues Sometimes, you might read a word you don't know. The author may have used a synonym that gives you a clue to the meaning of the unknown word. A synonym is a word that has the same or almost the same meaning as another word. For example, *difficult* is a synonym for *hard*.

1. Look at the words and sentences near the unknown word. The author may have used a synonym.

2. Do you recognize a word that might be a synonym?

3. Use the synonym in place of the unknown word. Does it make sense?

Read "Pass It Down" on page 197. Use synonyms to help you understand the meanings of unknown words.

Words to Write Reread "Pass It Down." Recall a story about someone in your family. Write it down or make one up. Use words from the Words to Know list and synonyms in your story.

Pass It Down

Emily Douglas is named after her grandmother, Emily Kelly. Every summer Emily Kelly's village in Ireland held a dance festival and contest. Emily K. was eight the first time she entered the contest. She had practiced for weeks, but she was very nervous and started to worry. One shoe felt comfortably snug while the other felt too tight. When the fiddles began playing, her heart was thumping so loudly that she couldn't hear the rhythm. So she started a few paces, or steps, behind the beat. That's the way she did the entire dance!

When she finished, everyone applauded and cheered. The judges told her how graceful she was and how original her dance was! She won first prize—a pale blue cotton handkerchief embroidered with white flowers. When Emily K. came to the United States, the handkerchief was one of the few things she brought with her. Later she gave it to her granddaughter, Emily. Emily has kept the handkerchief. It makes her think about another girl named Emily.

Your Turn!

⏸ **Need a Review?** For additional help with synonyms, see *Words!*

▶ **Ready to Try It?** Read *Suki's Kimono* on pp. 198–211.

196   197

Reread for Fluency

RATE Read the first paragraph of "Pass It Down" aloud, keeping your rate comfortable. Tell students that you are reading the passage neither too slowly nor too quickly because you want them to understand what you are saying. Explain that you are pausing when you see a comma or period.

Routine | **Oral Rereading**

1. **Select a Passage** Read the first paragraph of "Pass It Down" aloud.

2. **Model** Have students listen as you read at an appropriate rate.

3. **Guide Practice** Have students read along with you.

4. **On Their Own** For optimal fluency, students should reread three or four times at an appropriate rate.

Routines Flip Chart

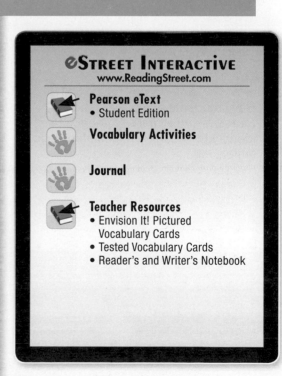

eSTREET INTERACTIVE
www.ReadingStreet.com

Pearson eText
• Student Edition

Vocabulary Activities

Journal

Teacher Resources
• Envision It! Pictured Vocabulary Cards
• Tested Vocabulary Cards
• Reader's and Writer's Notebook

Ⓒ **Common Core State Standards**

Literature 10. By the end of the year, read and comprehend literature, including stories, dramas, and poetry, at the high end of the grades 2–3 text complexity band independently and proficiently. **Also Literature 7.**

Ⓒ **Bridge to Common Core**

CRAFT AND STRUCTURE

Students analyze the structure of the selection and how its components relate to each other and the whole as they examine its genre. As they preview the selection and prepare to read, they come to see how genre shapes the content and style of the text.

Academic Vocabulary Ⓒ

realistic fiction a story with made-up characters and events that could happen in real life

Strategy Response Log

Have students use p. 27 in the *Reader's and Writer's Notebook* to identify the characteristics of realistic fiction.

Text-Based Comprehension

Introduce Main Selection

Student Edition, pp. 198–199

GENRE Explain that **realistic fiction** is a made-up story that contains characters that are believable and events that could happen in real life. Point out that the characters in the story could be like them or people they know. Explain that readers will be familiar with the events that occur because they take place in a familiar place, such as a home or school.

PREVIEW AND PREDICT Have students preview the title and illustrations for *Suki's Kimono.* Have them predict what will happen when Suki wears her kimono to school.

PURPOSE By analyzing *Suki's Kimono,* a realistic fiction selection, students will gain knowledge of how culture influences the clothes people wear.

Access Main Selection

READER AND TASK SUGGESTIONS

Preparing to Read the Text	Leveled Tasks
• Review the strategy of using synonyms as context clues. • Discuss how authors sometimes use flashbacks in realistic fiction. • Remind students they may need to read more slowly when they encounter foreign words in text.	• **Levels of Meaning • Analysis** If students have difficulty understanding Suki's motivation for wearing her kimono to school on the first day, have them read p. 201 and tell why Suki's kimono is special to her. • **Language Conventionality and Clarity** Students may have difficulty understanding complex sentences in the story. Remind them to break long sentences into smaller parts and identify the main action in each sentence.

See Text Complexity Measures for *Suki's Kimono* on the tab at the beginning of this week.

READ Tell students that today they will read *Suki's Kimono* for the first time. Use the Read for Understanding routine.

Routine Read for Understanding ©

Deepen understanding by reading the selection multiple times.

1. **First Read**—If students need support, then use the **Access Text** notes to help them clarify understanding.

2. **Second Read**—Use the **Close Reading** notes to help students draw knowledge from the text.

Day 2 SMALL GROUP TIME • Differentiate Comprehension, p. SG•1

OL On-Level	**SI** Strategic Intervention	**A** Advanced
• **Practice** Selection Vocabulary • **Read** *Suki's Kimono*	• **Reteach** Selection Vocabulary • **Read** *Suki's Kimono*	• **Extend** Selection Vocabulary • **Read** *Suki's Kimono* • **Investigate** Inquiry Project

eStreet Interactive
www.ReadingStreet.com

 Pearson eText
• Student Edition

 AudioText CD

 Teacher Resources
• Reader's and Writer's Notebook

 Background Building Audio CD

Access for All

A Advanced

Have students look through the story illustrations and discuss what each one might be saying about the characters.

ELL

Build Background To build background, review the selection summary in English in the *ELL Handbook*, p. 151. Use the Retelling Cards to provide visual support for the summary.

ELL

If... students need more scaffolding and practice with the **Comprehension Skill, then...** use the activities on p. DI•21 in the Teacher Resources section on SuccessNet.

Access Text © If students need help, then...

◎ COMPARE AND CONTRAST Ask students to compare and contrast Suki and her sisters as they get ready for the first day of school.

Think Aloud **MODEL** To compare and contrast, I look for clue words that show how things are alike and different. All the sisters are getting ready for the first day of school. That tells me what is alike. What words signal contrast? *(did not approve)* This shows me what is different: the sisters have different ideas about what to wear.

Close Reading ©

ANALYSIS • TEXT EVIDENCE Find a statement that shows Suki disagrees with her sisters. How are their beliefs different? (In the last paragraph on p. 200, it says *But Suki shook her head.* Suki's sisters believe she should wear something new and cool. Suki wants to wear her favorite thing, her kimono.)

O n the first day of school, Suki wanted to wear her kimono. Her sisters did not approve.

"You can't wear that," said Mari. "People will think you're weird."

"You can't wear that," said Yumi. "Everyone will laugh, and no one will play with you."

"You need something new, Suki."

"You need something cool."

But Suki shook her head. She didn't care for new. She didn't care for cool. She wanted to wear her favorite thing. And her favorite thing was her kimono.

Let's **Think** About...

How does the art help you form a picture in your mind of Suki in her kimono?

◎ Visualize

❶

200

Student Edition, p. 200

REREAD CHALLENGING TEXT Have students reread the first paragraph on p. 201 to practice fluent reading of the text and in particular the Japanese words *obāchan, kimono,* and *sōmen.* They may need to hear the correct pronunciations several times before saying the words fluently on their own.

ON THEIR OWN Have students reread pp. 200–201 to find more statements about things that are alike and different. For additional practice, see *Let's Practice It!* p. 292 on the *Teacher Resources DVD-ROM.*

Suki's obāchan had given her the kimono. The first time Suki wore it, her obāchan took her to a street festival where they slurped bowls of slippery, cold sōmen noodles and shared a cone of crunchy, shaved ice topped with a sweet red bean sauce.

Under strings of paper lanterns, Suki joined her obāchan in a circle dance. She followed her and copied her movements, trying to be as light and as graceful. She watched the other women and children who danced, especially those who were dressed in cotton kimonos like her.

Let's **Think** About...

The words in this description are meant to help you visualize. What can you do if you don't understand them?
◉ **Monitor and Clarify**

2

201

Student Edition, p. 201

Let's Think About...

…can imagine Suki running around in her kimono and flapping her arms …ke wings.

…can use context clues to clarify my understanding of the words.

© **Common Core State Standards**

Literature 1. Ask and answer questions to demonstrate understanding of a text, referring explicitly to the text as the basis for the answers. **Literature 3.** Describe characters in a story (e.g., their traits, motivations, or feelings) and explain how their actions contribute to the sequence of events.

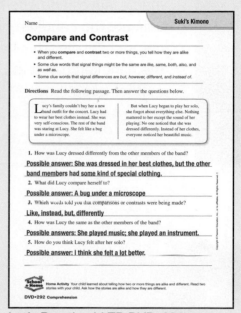

Let's Practice It! TR DVD•292

Connect to Social Studies

Japanese Festivals Several Japanese festivals honor children. One of these is Children's Day, which occurs on May 5. On this day children hang colorful kites shaped like carp, a kind of fish, outside their homes.

ELL

Activate Prior Knowledge Before reading, point out the clothing each sister is wearing in the illustrations. Have students discuss traditional and modern dress in their own cultures.

Access Text © If students need help, then...

VISUALIZE Have students read p. 202. Then ask them what words help them visualize what Suki's grandmother bought her.

Think Aloud **MODEL** When I read that the handkerchief is made of *pale pink linen,* I think of a light-colored, light-weight fabric. When I read that the handkerchief is *decorated with tiny maple leaves and cherry blossoms,* that tells me the handkerchief has dainty, colorful details. This helps me visualize the handkerchief that Suki's grand-mother bought her.

Let's **Think** About...

What words help you visualize the stage and the souvenir stand?

 Visualize

3

Later, Suki sat so close to the stage that when the taiko drummers performed, *bom-bom-bom-bom* she felt like she'd swallowed a ball of thunder, and her whole insides quaked and quivered.

Before they left the festival, Suki and her obāchan stopped at a souvenir stand. There were many things to choose from, but her obāchan found the prettiest thing of all—a handkerchief of pale pink linen, decorated with tiny maple leaves and cherry blossoms. When she gave it to Suki, she said, "This will help you remember our day."

Now, it was time for school. Mother checked Suki's obi one last time and took a picture of Mari, Yumi, and Suki together by the front steps.

202

Student Edition, p. 202

Close Reading ©

INFERENCE • TEXT EVIDENCE

What do the actions of Suki and her sisters on p. 203 tell you about them? Cite examples from the text to support your answers. (The sisters walk ahead of Suki and pretend they don't know her. This shows they want to be like everyone else and are embarrassed that Suki dresses differently. Suki, on the other hand, doesn't seem to mind being different; she feels very pleased to be dressed in her kimono.)

ON THEIR OWN Have students reread pp. 200–203 to find more words that help them visualize what is happening. Ask them to explain how these words help them see, feel, smell, touch, and taste what is happening in the story.

Then, as she watched, the three sisters made their way down the block to their school. Mari and Yumi stayed several paces ahead of Suki and pretended they didn't know her.

But Suki didn't mind.

She turned and waved to her mother before she clip-clopped along in her shiny red geta, feeling very pleased in her fan-patterned blue kimono.

Let's **Think** About...

What do you know about older brothers and sisters that helps you understand Mari and Yumi? **Background Knowledge**

203

Student Edition, p. 203

Let's Think About...

The words "swallowed a ball of thunder" help me imagine the sound of the taiko drummers. The words "many" and "prettiest" help me imagine all the things being sold.

Older brothers and sisters are often embarrassed by younger siblings.

Common Core State Standards

Literature 1. Ask and answer questions to demonstrate understanding of a text, referring explicitly to the text as the basis for the answers. **Literature 3.** Describe characters in a story (e.g., their traits, motivations, or feelings) and explain how their actions contribute to the sequence of events.

Access for All

SI Strategic Intervention

Invite students to work in pairs and write down the words and phrases that help them visualize something in the story.

ELL

Visualize Read aloud the first sentence on p. 202 and ask students if it is possible to swallow a ball of thunder. Explain that this expression is an exaggeration to help readers understand how the vibrations of the drum felt. Ask how our chests and stomachs feel when loud sounds occur. Help students determine the meaning of the words *quaked* and *quivered*. Then invite volunteers to use each word in a sentence.

Vocabulary Read aloud the last sentence on p. 203. Then ask students to use word and picture clues to determine the meaning of the Japanese word *geta*. Explain that the hyphenated word *clip-clopped* tells the sound Suki's geta made as she walked.

Access Text © If students need help, then...

Review CAUSE AND EFFECT Have students read the bottom half of p. 204. Ask what caused the children at Suki's school to stare and laugh at her.

Think Aloud **MODEL** A cause is why something happens, and an effect is what happens. When I read this, I remember how children often make fun of others who act or dress differently than they do. Suki's unusual clothing is the cause of the other children staring and laughing at her.

ON THEIR OWN Have students find other cause-and-effect relationships as they read the rest of the story. For additional practice, use *Let's Practice It!* p. 293 on the *Teacher Resources DVD-ROM*.

Close Reading ©

ANALYSIS • TEXT EVIDENCE What words does the author use to describe the sound of the swing? Why does she use those words? (On p. 205, the words "Swoosh, swoosh" describe the sound. The author wants us to imagine the sound of Suki and Penny swinging.)

Once in a while, Suki would lift her arms and let the butterfly sleeves flutter in the breeze. It made her feel like she'd grown her own set of wings.

Let's **Think** About...

How do you feel when others tease you? How might Suki feel? **Background Knowledge**

5

204

When they reached the school, Mari and Yumi hurried across the yard to a group of their friends. Suki stopped and looked around. Some of the children turned and stared at her, and others giggled and pointed at her kimono.

But Suki ignored them.

Student Edition, p. 204

HECK PREDICTIONS Have students look back at the predictions they ade earlier and discuss whether they were accurate. Then have stu- ents preview the rest of the selection and either adjust their predictions ccordingly or make new predictions.

She took a seat on a swing to wait for the bell. A girl dressed in overalls just like a pair Suki had at home sat on the swing beside her.

"Hi, Suki," said the girl.

"Hi, Penny," said Suki.

"How come you're dressed so funny?" Penny asked. "Where did you get those shoes?"

Suki lifted her feet off the sand and wiggled her toes. "I'm not dressed funny," she said. "My grandma gave me these shoes."

Suki started pumping her legs. After a moment, Penny did the same, and soon they were both swinging as fast and as high as they could. *Swoosh, swoosh,* up and up.

Let's **Think** About...

What do you think might happen next for Suki and Penny? **Predict**

6

If you want to teach this selection in two sessions, stop here.

If you want to continue reading this selection, turn to p. 206–207.

205

Student Edition, p. 205

Let's Think About...

hurts my feelings when I get teased. I think it upsets Suki a little, but ostly she is happy to be wearing her kimono.

hink Suki and Penny will become friends.

Common Core State Standards

Literature 1. Ask and answer questions to demonstrate understanding of a text, referring explicitly to the text as the basis for the answers. **Literature 3.** Describe characters in a story (e.g., their traits, motivations, or feelings) and explain how their actions contribute to the sequence of events.

Access for All

Ⓐ Advanced

Explain to students that characters' traits are revealed through their words and actions and how other characters treat them. Have students locate information in the story that reveals Suki's character traits.

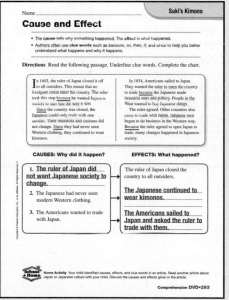

Let's Practice It! TR DVD•293

ELL

Text Features Read aloud the italicized words on p. 205, *Swoosh, swoosh,* and ask students why they think the author italicized them. Explain that writers often italicize sounds and words to draw attention to them.

Suki's Kimono **205a**

Common Core State Standards

Writing 7. Conduct short research projects that build knowledge about a topic. **Writing 8.** Recall information from experiences or gather information from print and digital sources; take brief notes on sources and sort evidence into provided categories. **Language 1.a.** Explain the function of nouns, pronouns, verbs, adjectives, and adverbs in general and their functions in particular sentences. **Language 2.f.** Use spelling patterns and generalizations (e.g., word families, position-based spellings, syllable patterns, ending rules, meaningful word parts) in writing words.

 Bridge to Common Core

RESEARCH TO BUILD AND PRESENT KNOWLEDGE

On Day 2 of the weeklong research project, students gather relevant information based on their focused questions from Day 1 through the use of a survey. They consult informational texts as well as digital sources, assessing the credibility of each one. This process enables students to demonstrate an understanding of the subject under investigation.

Research and Inquiry

Step 2 Navigate/Search

TEACH Have students generate a research plan for gathering information about their research topic. Be sure students include a survey in their plan. Explain how to conduct a survey in the classroom. Give examples of good questions to include on a survey, such as *What kind of clothes do you wear at home?* or *What kinds of clothes do people in other cultures wear?* Have students pass around sheets of paper with their survey questions to other members of a small group. They will use their classmates' suggestions to learn more on the Web.

 MODEL One of my classmates mentioned that some people in the desert wear coverings over their heads. When I looked for information about this, I found that desert people wear turbans to keep sand out of their faces. I will use keywords from this information, such as *turbans,* to lead me to more specific information. One fact I found using this keyword states, *In India men decorate their turbans with jewels to show their wealth and power.*

GUIDE PRACTICE Have students conduct an Internet search to learn more about the clothing their classmates listed. Students can read the descriptions to determine if a site contains valid information. Discuss with students the difference between paraphrasing information they want to use and plagiarizing. Also discuss the importance of using and citing valid reliable sources.

ON THEIR OWN Have students paraphrase any information they found that they will use in their article or identify the source of a direct quote.

Conventions

Adjectives and Articles

TEACH Write these phrases on the board: *a rectangular box, an unusual story,* and *the wooden clogs.* Identify the article in each phrase, and remind students that an article is a special kind of adjective. Then point out the descriptive adjective that modifies each noun.

GUIDE PRACTICE Write and read the articles and descriptive adjectives below. Help students add appropriate nouns that these adjectives might modify.

the colorful	the colorful butterflies
a delicious	a delicious meal

Have students look for and read aloud phrases that contain adjectives and articles in *Suki's Kimono.* (*a sweet red bean sauce,* p. 201; *the other dancers,* p. 209; *the three sisters, the pale pink handkerchief,* p. 211)

ON THEIR OWN For additional practice, use *Reader's and Writer's Notebook.* p. 320.

Spelling

Syllable Pattern CV/VC

TEACH Remind students that words with the syllable pattern CV/VC are divided between the vowels. Point out that segmenting words can help students decode and spell words. Say the word *medium.* Identify and write the three syllables of the word: *me-di-um.*

GUIDE PRACTICE Write the remaining spelling words on the board. Have students write them and underline the two vowels that appear side by side but are part of different syllables. Have them identify the letter sounds and word parts in each word.

ON THEIR OWN For additional practice, use *Reader's and Writer's Notebook,* p. 321.

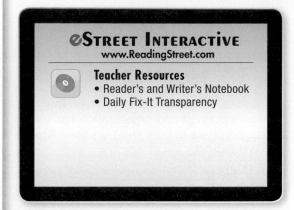

eStreet INTERACTIVE
www.ReadingStreet.com

Teacher Resources
• Reader's and Writer's Notebook
• Daily Fix-It Transparency

Daily Fix-It

3. The girls sisters told her not to wear a unusual costume. *(girl's; an)*
4. She didnt listen to her two sisters advice. *(didn't; sisters')*

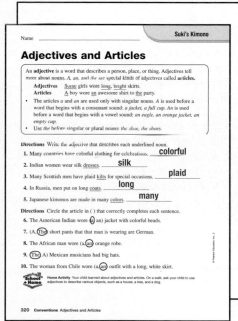

Reader's and Writer's Notebook, pp. 320–321

 ELL

Practice Articles Asian and Russian students may have difficulty with articles, as there are no articles in many of these languages. Guide students in writing descriptions of common classroom objects.

Common Core State Standards

Writing 1.b. Provide reasons that support the opinion. **Writing 4.** With guidance and support from adults, produce writing in which the development and organization are appropriate to task and purpose. **Also Writing 10.**

Writing

Letter to the Editor

Writing Trait: Organization

INTRODUCE THE PROMPT Remind students that a letter to the editor is a letter written to a newspaper or magazine that takes a position on an issue. Encourage students to keep the key features of a letter to the editor in mind as they plan their writing. Read aloud the writing prompt.

Writing Prompt

Write a letter to the editor about an issue occurring in your community or school.

SELECT A TOPIC

Think Aloud Let's brainstorm a list of issues in our school and community and write them in a chart. **Display a T-chart.** The letter to the editor we read yesterday discussed an issue or problem at school. I'm going to write *Issues at School* at the top of the first column in the chart. What topics can you think of that have become issues at our school? **Add relevant information to the first column of the chart (see examples below).** At the top of the other column, I'll write *Issues in the Community.* What issues can you think of that have become a problem on your street, in your neighborhood, or in the city? **Add relevant information to the second column of the chart.**

GATHER INFORMATION Remind students that they can do research to help them find out more about the issue they choose as a topic. Research might include interviews with other students, teachers, parents, or city officials. Research might also include finding articles on the topic in the local newspaper.

Issues at School	Issues in the Community
can't use the playground after school	litter on the streets
short recess	no buses on weekends
art class only once a week	the bike trail is closing

Corrective feedback Circulate around the room to check in with students who seem to be having trouble brainstorming or selecting a topic. Help struggling students identify issues that reflect their own interests as well as those of the school or community.

Mini-Lesson | Main Idea and Supporting Details

eStreet Interactive
www.ReadingStreet.com

Teacher Resources
• Reader's and Writer's Notebook
• Graphic Organizer

■ A graphic organizer can help organize information. I'm going to write about litter. **Draw a main idea chart.** My main idea is that I think litter is a problem. This will go at the beginning of my letter. In the top box, write *Litter is a problem in the neighborhood around our school.*

■ In the bottom boxes, I'll list details. In the left box, write *I see candy and food wrappers in the grass.* In the middle box, write *Litter is bad for plants, animals, and people.* In the right box, write *Littering is irresponsible.*

■ Below the chart, I'll write what I want readers to do about the problem. This will come at the end of my letter. Write *We need to clean up our neighborhood and keep it clean.* Have students fill in their own charts using the form on p. 322 of their *Reader's and Writer's Notebook.*

Routine | Quick Write for Fluency | Team Talk

. **Talk** Have pairs describe two topics they might write about.

. **Write** Have students write a short paragraph about each topic.

. **Share** Partners share their writing and choose a topic.

outines Flip Chart

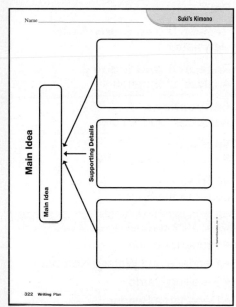

Reader's and Writer's Notebook, p. 322

Wrap Up Your Day!

✔ **Content Knowledge** What did you learn about how important people's cultures are to them?

✔ **Text-Based Comprehension** How did visualizing help you understand Suki's memories of the street festival?

Preview DAY 3

Tell students that tomorrow they will read more about a lesson that Suki teaches her classmates.

DAY 3
at a Glance

Materials

- Student Edition
- Reader's and Writer's Notebook
- Retelling Cards
- Decodable Reader

© Common Core State Standards

Speaking/Listening 1. Engage effectively in a range of collaborative discussions (one-on-one, in groups, and teacher-led) with diverse partners on grade 3 topics and texts, building on others' ideas and expressing their own clearly. **Language 6.** Acquire and use accurately grade-appropriate conversational, general academic, and domain-specific words and phrases, including those that signal spatial and temporal relationships (e.g., *After dinner that night we went looking for them*).

Content Knowledge

Cultures and Clothing

EXPAND THE CONCEPT Remind students of the weekly concept question, *How does culture influence the clothes we wear?* Discuss how the question relates to what Suki decides to wear to school. Encourage students to think about wearing traditional clothing and how Suki's choice is influenced by her culture.

Build Oral Language

TALK ABOUT SENTENCES AND WORDS Reread these sentences from Student Edition p. 201, *Suki's Kimono*.

Under strings of paper lanterns, Suki joined her obāchan. She followed her and copied her movements, trying to be as light and as graceful.

- What does *graceful* mean? (showing beauty in movement)
- What words from the passage describe *graceful* or how Suki was trying to dance? *(light; followed her and copied her movements)*
- What is another word for *graceful*? *(elegant; light-footed)*

Team Talk Have students work with a partner to replace key words in the sentence with synonyms. Use the following sentence frame.

She followed her and copied her movements, trying to be as _____ and _____.

Build Oral Vocabulary

Amazing Words

Robust Vocabulary Routine

1. Introduce Write the word *robe* on the board. Have students say it with you. Yesterday we learned that a kimono looks like a *robe.* Have students determine a definition of *robe.* (A *robe* is a long, loose garment.)

2. Demonstrate Have students answer questions to demonstrate understanding. Who might wear a *robe* on his or her job? (A judge might wear a robe.)

3. Apply Have students apply their understanding. When would a person wear a *robe*? (near bedtime)

4. Display the Word Students can segment the sounds in *robe* and then blend them.

See p. OV•1 to teach *drape.*

Routines Flip Chart

ADD TO THE CONCEPT MAP Discuss the Amazing Words *acceptable* and *inspire.* Add these and other concept-related words to the concept map. Use the following questions to develop students' understanding of the concept.

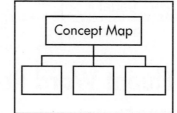

Clothing that is *acceptable* to one culture may not be *acceptable* to another. What determines whether or not an article of clothing is *acceptable*?

Suki loves learning about her Japanese culture. How might learning about your culture *inspire* you?

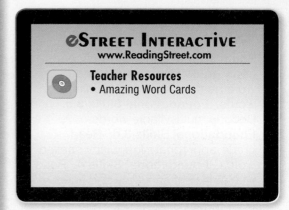

Amazing Words

traditional	inspire
fret	robe
scarves	drape
fabric	elegant
acceptable	stylish

ELL

Expand Vocabulary Use the Day 3 instruction on ELL Poster 21 to help students expand vocabulary.

© Common Core State Standards

Foundational Skills 3. Know and apply grade-level phonics and word analysis skills in decoding words. **Foundational Skills 3.c.** Decode multisyllable words. **Foundational Skills 3.d.** Read grade-appropriate irregularly spelled words. **Foundational Skills 4.** Read with sufficient accuracy and fluency to support comprehension. **Also Foundational Skills 4.b.**

Word Analysis

⊙ Syllable Pattern CV/VC

MODEL WORD SORTING Write *u/a, e/o, e/a, i/a,* and *i/e* as headings in a five-column chart. Now we are going to sort words. We'll put words that have the vowel *ua* divided between two syllables in the first column. Words with the vowels *eo* will go in the second column. Words with *ea* will go in the third column, words with *ia* will go in the fourth column, and words with *ie* will go in the last column. I will start. Write *graduate* and model how to read it, using the Word Analysis lesson on p. 192a. *Graduate* contains the vowels *u* and *a,* and both vowels stand for separate sounds. I will write *graduate* in the first column. Model reading *usual* and *theater* in the same way.

GUIDE PRACTICE Use practice words from the activity on p. 192a for the word sort. Point to a word. Have students read the word, identify its parts, and tell where it should be written on the chart.

> **Corrective feedback** | For corrective feedback, model reading each word as you read *graduate.*

u/a	e/o	e/a	i/a	i/e
graduate	neon	theater	diary	science
usual			radiator	client
annual				

Fluent Word Reading

MODEL Write *diet.* I know I will divide the two vowels and pronounce each vowel sound. I know the sounds for *d, i, e,* and *t.* I can blend them and read the word *diet.*

GUIDE PRACTICE Write the words below. Say the sounds in your head for each spelling you see. When I point to the word, we'll read it together. For the first reading, allow a previewing time of one second per word part.

| reuse | biology | denial | Canadian | appliance | preamble |

ON THEIR OWN Have students read the list above three or four times, until they can read one word part per second.

Decodable Passage 21B

students need help, then...

Read *Annual Music Fest*

READ WORDS IN ISOLATION Have students turn to p. 69 in *Decodable Practice Readers 3.2* and find the first list of words. Each word in this list has the syllable pattern CV/VC. Let's read these words. Be sure that students pronounce each vowel in the CV/VC pattern.

Next, have students read the high-frequency words.

PREVIEW Have students read the title and preview the story. Tell them that they will read words with the syllabication pattern CV/VC.

READ WORDS IN CONTEXT Chorally read the passage along with the students. Have students identify words in the passage that have the syllable pattern CV/VC. Make sure that students are monitoring their accuracy when they decode words.

Team Talk Pair students and have them take turns reading the passage aloud to each other. Monitor students as they read to check for proper pronunciation and appropriate pacing.

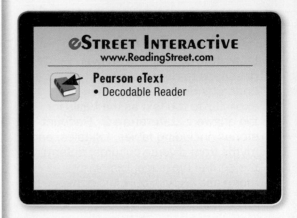

eSTREET INTERACTIVE
www.ReadingStreet.com

Pearson eText
• Decodable Reader

Access for All

A Advanced
Have students choose five words from the word sort activity and use each word in a sentence. Have students exchange their work with a partner and identify the words with the CV/VC pattern that appear in their sentences.

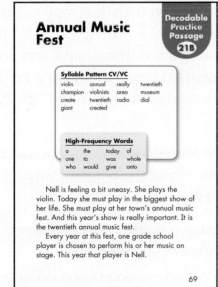

Annual Music Fest

Decodable Practice Passage **21B**

Syllable Pattern CV/VC

violin	annual	really	twentieth
champion	violinists	area	museum
create	twentieth	radio	dial
giant	created		

High-Frequency Words

a	the	today	of
one	to	was	whole
who	would	give	onto

Nell is feeling a bit uneasy. She plays the violin. Today she must play in the biggest show of her life. She must play at her town's annual music fest. And this year's show is really important. It is the twentieth annual music fest.

Every year at this fest, one grade school player is chosen to perform his or her music on stage. This year that player is Nell.

69

It was not easy to earn this spot. First at Nell's music school, she was named the champion violin player. And her school is filled with good violinists.

After that, Nell was named the champion violinist of the whole area! She beat many good players. That victory meant that she was the player who would perform in the annual fest.

The fest is held each year in back of the town's museum. It's a big deal for the whole town. The fest is even played over local radio.

Nell's music teacher had an idea. He asked Nell to create her own music for the fest. Nell liked to write music, so she agreed to create her own song.

At last, the town's twentieth annual music fest was underway. Nell was to go on soon. She was waiting backstage next to the radio. The radio dial was set on the show. Nell heard a voice on the radio say, "Next, please give a nice hand to Nell, our champion violinist!"

Nell grabbed her violin and ran onto the giant stage. She played the song she had created and then took a big bow. Nell had been tense, but she performed well. Nell now sat back and enjoyed the rest of her town's twentieth annual music fest.

70

Decodable Practice Passage 21B

Zoom in on ©

© **Common Core State Standards**

Literature 1. Ask and answer questions to demonstrate understanding of a text, referring explicitly to the text as the basis for the answers. **Literature 2.** Recount stories, including fables, folktales, and myths from diverse cultures; determine the central message, lesson, or moral and explain how it is conveyed through key details in the text.

Strategy Response Log

Have students revisit p. 27 in the *Reader's and Writer's Notebook* to identify the characteristics of realistic fiction.

Text-Based Comprehension

Check Understanding

Student Edition, pp. 198–199

If... you choose to read *Suki's Kimono* in two parts,
then... use the following questions to monitor students' understanding of pp. 198–205 of the selection. Encourage students to cite evidence from the text.

EVALUATION How do the passages describing the street festival help you understand the story better? Give an example of a descriptive detail that helped you visualize the scene. (They help me see, hear, taste, and smell what Suki is experiencing. The details "slurped bowls of slippery, cold sōmen noodles" (p. 201); and "her whole insides quaked and quivered" (p. 202) helped me visualize the scene.)

ANALYSIS How does the author use the technique of compare and contrast to introduce the lesson in this story? (She shows the different ways Suki and her two older sisters want to dress and why.)

RETELL Have students retell what they have read of *Suki's Kimono*. Encourage students to use the illustrations in their retellings.

> **Corrective feedback** | **If...** students leave out important details,
> **then...** have students look back through the illustrations in the selection.

READ Use the **Access Text** and **Close Reading** notes to finish reading *Suki's Kimono*.

If... you followed the Read for Understanding routine below,

then... ask students to retell the selection before you reread *Suki's Kimono*.

RETELL Have students retell what they have read of *Suki's Kimono*. Encourage students to use the illustrations in their retellings.

> **Corrective feedback**
>
> **If...** students leave out important details,
>
> **then...** have students look back through the illustrations in the selection.

READ Return to p. 200–201 and use the **2nd Read/Close Reading** notes to reread *Suki's Kimono*.

Read Main Selection

Routine   Read for Understanding ©

Deepen understanding by reading the selection multiple times.

1. **First Read**—If students need support, then use the **Access Text** notes to help them clarify understanding.

2. **Second Read**—Use the **Close Reading** notes to help students draw knowledge from the text.

 **Day 3** **SMALL GROUP TIME • Differentiate Close Reading, p. SG•1**

OL On-Level	**SI** Strategic Intervention	**A** Advanced
• **Reread** to Develop Vocabulary • **Read** *Suki's Kimono*	• **Reread** to Develop Vocabulary • **Read** *Suki's Kimono*	• **Reread** to Extend Vocabulary • **Read** *Suki's Kimono* • **Investigate** Inquiry Project

Check Retelling To support retelling, review the multilingual summary for *Suki's Kimono* with the appropriate Retelling Cards to scaffold understanding.

ELL

If... students need more scaffolding and practice with the **Main Selection,**

then... use the activities on p. DI•22 in the Teacher Resources section on SuccessNet.

Access Text © If students need help, then...

🔊 **SYNONYMS** Have students read p. 207. Ask them to find the word *snug* and any context clues that help them figure out the word's meaning.

(Think Aloud) **MODEL** When I don't know the meaning of a word, I look for nearby words that help me figure out the meaning. I read that Suki's obi is wrapped snug around her middle and that this helps her sit up straight and tall. How would something need to be wrapped to help me sit this way? **(tight)**

ON THEIR OWN Have students reread pp. 206–207 to find context clues for other unfamiliar words. Have them use these clues to understand the meanings for these words. For additional practice, use *Reader's and Writer's Notebook,* p. 323.

Close Reading ©

ANALYSIS • TEXT EVIDENCE What is the effect of one boy's comments about Suki's kimono? How do you know? (Suki is either angry or embarrassed. On p. 207, it says she felt her cheeks burn.)

Let's **Think** About...

Can you visualize why the boys say that Suki is a bat?

🔊 **Visualize**

7

206

When the bell rang, Suki and Penny jumped off their swings and ran to the gym for the first day assembly. Once they were finally taken to their new classroom, Suki chose a desk near the window. Penny chose a desk next to Suki.

As they waited for everyone to find a seat, two boys in front of Suki turned and snickered behind their hands. One of the boys reached over and snatched at Suki's sleeve. "Look at this," he said. "She's a bat!"

Student Edition, p. 206

DEVELOP LANGUAGE Have students reread the last paragraph on p. 206. *What does* snickered *mean? When have you* snickered, *and why?*

Suki felt her cheeks burn, but she did not respond. Instead, she concentrated on sitting up straight and tall, the way her obāchan always did. It was easy to do with an obi wrapped snug around her middle. Her obi was golden yellow, and in its folds Suki had tucked away her pale pink handkerchief.

"Welcome to the first grade," said the teacher. "My name is Mrs. Paggio." She smiled. "Let's introduce ourselves and tell everyone what we did this summer."

When it was her turn to speak, Suki stood up and told the teacher her name.

"Hello, Suki," said Mrs. Paggio. "What did you do this summer?"

"My grandma visited us," she said, straightening her sleeves. "She brought me my kimono and my geta." Suki raised her foot to show the teacher her wooden clog.

 Let's **Think** About...

As you visualize being Suki, are you sitting straight and tall? Do you feel the obi around you? What words help you by appealing to your senses?
Visualize

8

207

Student Edition, p. 207

Let's Think About...

...think the boys are making fun of Suki's sleeves. They are saying her sleeves look like bat wings.

...Yes. The words *wrapped snug* help me imagine how the kimono would feel and the words *golden yellow* help me picture how the obi would look.

 Common Core State Standards

Literature 1. Ask and answer questions to demonstrate understanding of a text, referring explicitly to the text as the basis for the answers. **Language 4.** Determine or clarify the meaning of unknown and multiple-meaning words and phrases based on grade 3 reading and content, choosing flexibly from a range of strategies.

Connect to Social Studies

American Cities Tell students that several American cities have large Asian populations. It's not unusual to see people dressed in traditional clothing such as kimonos and *cheongsam,* a Chinese-style dress.

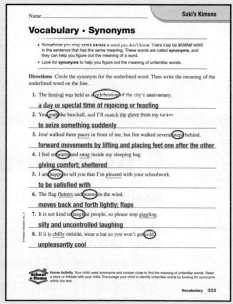

Reader's and Writer's Notebook, p. 323

Activate Prior Knowledge Ask children to recall and tell about a time when they might have seen someone dressed in a kimono such as the one Suki is wearing.

1ST READ

Access Text © If students need help, then...

◉ VISUALIZE Have students read the first sentence on p. 209. Ask students what words help them visualize that experience.

(Think Aloud) MODEL When I read that Suki danced barefoot in the open air on fresh-cut grass, I can smell the fresh air and the newly cut grass. What words help me feel the experience? *(fresh-cut grass that tickled her toes)* The first sentence helps me smell and feel the dancing experience Suki had.

Let's **Think** About...

Can you visualize Suki being so caught up in the dancing that she doesn't hear her classmates?
◉ Visualize

9

Somewhere in the classroom, someone laughed, but Suki took a deep breath and continued. "The best thing was that she took me to a festival. And there were dancing girls, dressed like me, and they danced like this." She took a few steps and swayed her arms sideways.

"Look, now she's *dancing*," someone said. But Suki didn't hear.

She hummed the music she remembered hearing at the festival.

2ND READ

Close Reading ©

SYNTHESIS Why didn't the students laugh at Suki after her dance? (They were fascinated by her performance. Suki had helped students *feel* the dance and what it meant to her.)

208

Student Edition, p. 208

ANALYSIS Help students generate text-based questions by providing the following question stem for them to complete: In the story, what did Suki do when _____?

ON THEIR OWN Have students reread p. 209 to find more words that help them visualize the circle dance. Ask them to explain how these words help them experience what happens in the story.

Common Core State Standards

Literature 1. Ask and answer questions to demonstrate understanding of a text, referring explicitly to the text as the basis for the answers. **Literature 3.** Describe characters in a story (e.g., their traits, motivations, or feelings) and explain how their actions contribute to the sequence of events.

She remembered how it felt to dance barefoot in the open air, on fresh-cut grass that tickled her toes.

She tried to picture the other dancers. How they moved forward in the circle with the rhythm of the music. How they stamped their feet, first right, then left, swung their arms, first up, then down. How they stepped back, and back, and back, then clapped.

When Suki couldn't remember the next step, she made it up, just to keep dancing. *One-two, one-two, one-two, stop.*

When she finished, the room seemed very quiet. Everyone was watching her.

Suki sat down, wondering if she was in trouble.

Let's Think About...

What words help you know how Suki dances? How did the other dancers look and act?
 Visualize

10

209

Student Edition, p. 209

Let's Think About...

Yes, I can visualize Suki having so much fun that she forgets she's in a classroom.

The words "stamped their feet," "swung their arms," and "clapped" helped me visualize how Suki and the other dancers look and act.

Access for All

A Advanced
Have students discuss which story character is the most realistic. Then have them present their arguments to the class.

ELL

Visualize Ask a group of volunteers to dramatize the dance movements Suki makes as you read aloud pp. 208–209. Encourage students to visualize, or experience with their senses, what they read.

Suki's Kimono **209a**

1ST READ

Access Text © If students need help, then...

⊙ **COMPARE AND CONTRAST** Write "as the three sisters walked home together, Mari and Yumi grumbled about their first day. But Suki just smiled." Have students compare the characters.

(Think Aloud) **MODEL** To find comparisons and contrasts, I look for clue words. *Sisters* and *together* show how the girls are alike. The word *but* signals contrast or difference. Mari and Yumi are grumbling, *but* Suki is smiling.

ON THEIR OWN Have students reread the story to find other examples of compare-and-contrast relationships.

CROSS-TEXT EVALUATION
Use a Strategy to Self-Check How did the Read Aloud, "Surprise in the Attic," help you understand this selection?

Let's **Think** About...
How do the sounds and sights help you visualize what happens after Suki dances?
⊙ **Visualize**

11

But Mrs. Paggio said, "That was wonderful, Suki." And she started to clap.
Then, so did Penny.
And after a moment, so did the entire class.

210

Student Edition, p. 210

2ND READ

Close Reading ©

SYNTHESIS Summarize how Suki stays true to herself in this story. (Even though she looks different, causing the other students to make fun of her, Suki delights in wearing her kimono. She shows pride in her Japanese heritage by dancing for her classmates.) What is the theme of this story? (Don't be afraid to be different.)

SYNTHESIS • TEXT EVIDENCE Using what you learned in this selection, tell how culture influences the clothes we wear. Have students cite examples from the text to support their responses.

CHECK PREDICTIONS Have students look back at the predictions they made earlier and confirm whether they were accurate.

After school, as the three sisters walked home together, Mari and Yumi grumbled about their first day.

"No one even noticed my new sweater," said Mari.

"No one even noticed my cool shoes," said Yumi.

But Suki just smiled.

As she clip-clopped along behind them, Suki pulled out the pale pink handkerchief from her obi and held it up over her head to catch the wind. And in her blue cotton kimono and in her shiny red geta, Suki danced all the way home.

Let's **Think** About...

What happens when Suki wears a kimono on the first day of school? Use evidence from the story to support your answer. **Summarize**

12

211

Student Edition, p. 211

Let's Think About...

The story says that everyone starts clapping. I can imagine that everyone is happy and impressed with Suki's dancing.

At first, some people make fun of her. After she performs a traditional dance, everyone in the class applauds.

Literature 1. Ask and answer questions to demonstrate understanding of a text, referring explicitly to the text as the basis for the answers. **Literature 2.** Recount stories, including fables, folktales, and myths from diverse cultures; determine the central message, lesson, or moral and explain how it is conveyed through key details in the text. **Literature 3.** Describe characters in a story (e.g., their traits, motivations, or feelings) and explain how their actions contribute to the sequence of events.

Access for All

Ⓐ Advanced

Have students discuss what the main characters learn in this story. Encourage them to consider why each sister wears what she does to school and what happens as a result.

ⒺⓁⓁ

Theme Explain to students that the theme of a story is its main idea or lesson. Reread p. 211 aloud. Have students retell what happens on this page and why. Then help students write a sentence explaining what the two sisters learn and another sentence explaining what Suki learns.

Common Core State Standards
Literature 1. Ask and answer questions to demonstrate understanding of a text, referring explicitly to the text as the basis for the answers. Also Literature 2., Writing 8.

Envision It! Retell

READING STREET ONLINE
STORY SORT
www.ReadingStreet.com

212

Think Critically

1. In "The Boxed Lunch," Ky is nervous about his first day at a new school. In what ways is Suki different from Ky? What evidence from *Suki's Kimono* tells you this? Text to Text

2. As you read the story, you get to know Suki. How does the author help you do that? Think Like an Author

3. At school, Suki meets her friend, Penny. How are Penny's clothes different from Suki's? Compare and Contrast

4. Imagine seeing Suki dancing in the classroom. How does she look? How do the other students look? How does the author's language help you clarify the image in your mind? What would you ask Suki if you were there? Visualize

5. **Look Back and Write** Look back at the question on page 199. Think about the day Suki wore her kimono to the street festival. Now write a response to the question. Provide evidence to support your answer.

Key Ideas and Details • Text Evidence

Meet the Author

Chieri Uegaki

Chieri Uegaki began writing at the age of 7 when she published a family newspaper called *The Pender Street Times*. At the time, she lived on Pender Street in Vancouver, British Columbia.

Ms. Uegaki says this about her writing: "It makes me very happy to think that something I've written could touch someone and perhaps even become someone's favorite." Ms. Uegaki based *Suki's Kimono* on her relationship with her Japanese grandmother.

Ms. Uegaki offers this advice to young writers: "Listen more than you speak. Read everything and take notes."

Read more books about children like Suki.

First Day, Hooray! by Nancy Poydar

It's Back to School We Go! First Day Stories from Around the World by Ellen Jackson

Use the *Reader's and Writer's Notebook* to record your independent reading.

213

Common Core State Standards

Literature 1. Ask and answer questions to demonstrate understanding of a text, referring explicitly to the text as the basis for the answers. **Also Literature 2., 3., Writing 8.**

Bridge to Common Core

RANGE OF READING AND LEVEL OF TEXT COMPLEXITY

To increase students' capacity for reading and comprehending complex texts independently and proficiently, have them read other literary texts by Chieri Uegaki or about the social studies topic, Cultures and Clothing. After students read closely for a sustained period of time, they should record their reading in their Reading Logs.

Think Critically

1. **TEXT TO TEXT** Unlike Ky, Suki is eager for the first day of school. She does not care about gaining her classmates' approval. She wants to please herself and wear her favorite thing—her Kimono. On p. 200, the last paragraph tells us how Suki feels.

2. **THINK LIKE AN AUTHOR** The author describes Suki's actions and her reactions to people and events.

3. **COMPARE AND CONTRAST** Penny is dressed casually in overalls. Suki is dressed formally in a long, flowing kimono.

4. **VISUALIZE** Suki's arms are sweeping up and down. She stamps her feet. Her classmates watch in silence. The language helps me imagine what Suki looked like. I would ask if she would teach me her dance.

5. **LOOK BACK AND WRITE • TEXT EVIDENCE** To build writing fluency, allow 10–15 minutes.

eStreet Interactive
www.ReadingStreet.com

Pearson eText
• Student Edition

Story Sort

Scoring Rubric Look Back and Write

TOP-SCORE RESPONSE A top-score response uses details to tell why Suki's kimono is so important to her.

A top-score response should include:

• Suki's kimono is a gift from her grandmother.
• Suki thinks the fan-patterned blue kimono is beautiful.
• Suki's kimono tells about her Japanese family.

Retell

Have students work in pairs to retell the selection, using the retelling strip in the Student Edition or the Story Sort as prompts. Monitor students' retellings.

Scoring Rubric Narrative Retelling

	4	3	2	1
Connections	Makes connections and generalizes beyond the text	Makes connections to other events, stories, or experiences	Makes a limited connection to another event, story, or experience	Makes no connection to another event, story, or experience
Author's Purpose	Elaborates on author's purpose	Tells author's purpose with some clarity	Makes some connection to author's purpose	Makes no connection to author's purpose
Characters	Describes the main character(s) and any character development	Identifies the main character(s) and gives some information about them	Inaccurately identifies some characters or gives little information about them	Inaccurately identifies the characters or gives no information about them
Setting	Describes the time and location	Identifies the time and location	Omits details of time or location	Is unable to identify time or location
Plot	Describes the problem, goal, events, and ending using rich detail	Tells the problem, goal, events, and ending with some errors that do not affect meaning	Tells parts of the problem, goal, events, and ending with gaps that affect meaning	Retelling has no sense of story

Don't Wait Until Friday

MONITOR PROGRESS Check Retelling

If… students have difficulty retelling,

Then… use the Retelling Cards/Story Sort to scaffold their retellings.

Plan to Assess Retelling

- ☑ **This week assess Strategic Intervention students.**
- ☐ **Week 2** Advanced
- ☐ **Week 3** Strategic Intervention
- ☐ **Week 4** On-Level
- ☐ **Week 5** Assess any students you have not yet checked during this unit.

Meet the Author

Have students read about author Chieri Uegaki on p. 213. Ask how Suki's relationship with her grandmother might be similar to the author's relationship with her own grandmother.

Read Independently

Have students enter their independent reading into their Reading Logs.

Retelling Use the Retelling Cards to discuss the selection with students. Place the cards in an incorrect order and have volunteers correct the mistake. Then have students explain where each card should go as they describe the sequence of the selection.

 **Common Core State Standards**

Informational Text 5. Use text features and search tools (e.g., key words, sidebars, hyperlinks) to locate information relevant to a given topic efficiently. **Foundational Skills 4.** Read with sufficient accuracy and fluency to support comprehension. **Foundational Skills 4.b.** Read on-level prose and poetry orally with accuracy, appropriate rate, and expression on successive readings.

Fluency

Rate

MODEL FLUENT READING Have students turn to p. 209 of *Suki's Kimono.* Have students follow along as you read this page. Tell them to notice the pace at which you read the author's description of Suki's dance. Adjust your pace according to punctuation and word choice.

GUIDE PRACTICE Have students follow along as you read the page again. Then have them reread the page as a group without you until they read at a comfortable rate and with no mistakes. Continue in the same way on pp. 210–211.

Corrective feedback	**If...** students are having difficulty reading at the correct rate, **then...** prompt:
	• Do you think you need to slow down or read more quickly?
	• Read the sentence more quickly. Now read it more slowly. Which helps you understand what you are reading?
	• Tell me the sentence. Read it at the rate that would help me understand it.

Reread for Fluency

Routine Oral Rereading

1. **Select a Passage** For *Suki's Kimono,* use p. 209.

2. **Model** Have students listen as you read at an appropriate rate.

3. **Guide Practice** Have students read along with you.

4. **On Their Own** For optimal fluency, students should reread three or four times at an appropriate rate.

Routines Flip Chart

Research and Study Skills

Newsletter

TEACH Ask students to explain a **newsletter** and why it is published. Students may know that a newsletter is a brief publication of a group that contains news of interest to group members. Show a newsletter from a local group and use it to review these terms:

A **table of contents** usually appears in a box on the front page of a newsletter. It tells what information the reader will find inside.

The **heading** is the name of the newsletter. It appears at the top of the first page in large, bold print.

The **date** of the newsletter appears just below the heading. It lists the period of time that the information in the newsletter covers—a specific week, month, or season.

A **header** is the title of an article in a newsletter. A header appears above an article in larger, bold print.

Explain that many newsletters are electronic newsletters. They feature the same information as a paper newsletter, but may be organized differently. Display an electronic newsletter to show how to navigate it.

GUIDE PRACTICE Discuss these questions:

How do you know how current the information in a newsletter is? (The date shows the period of time that the information covers.)

How can you determine whether the newsletter has the information you need? (The table of contents lists the topics covered.)

ON THEIR OWN Have students review and complete p. 324 of the *Reader's and Writer's Notebook.*

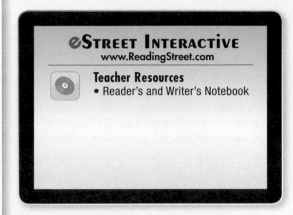

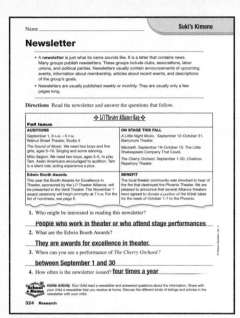

Reader's and Writer's Notebook, p. 324

Academic Vocabulary ©

newsletter A newsletter is a brief publication by a group or an organization that contains news of interest to the members of the group or organization.

Professional Development: What ELL Experts Say About Choral Reading "Repeated reading aloud of texts provides English language learners with multiple opportunities to match the text they read with the words they hear. When students participate in shared reading and echo the spoken text or read the words aloud chorally, anxiety about pronunciation or decoding errors is reduced." —Dr. Georgia Earnest García

 **Common Core State Standards**

Writing 5. With guidance and support from peers and adults, develop and strengthen writing as needed by planning, revising, and editing. **Language 1.a.** Explain the function of nouns, pronouns, verbs, adjectives, and adverbs in general and their functions in particular sentences. **Language 2.f.** Use spelling patterns and generalizations (e.g., word families, position-based spellings, syllable patterns, ending rules, meaningful word parts) in writing words.

Research and Inquiry

Step 3 Analyze Information

TEACH Tell students that today they will analyze their findings and may need to change the focus of their original inquiry question.

Think Aloud **MODEL** So far I have focused my research on the head coverings that people wear in different cultures. I am finding lots of information about this topic. I need to refocus my inquiry question so that I narrow my topic to a smaller population, such as men and women in the Middle East. Now my inquiry question is *How does culture influence the head coverings of men and women in the Middle East?*

GUIDE PRACTICE Have students analyze their findings. They may need to refocus their inquiry question to better fit the information they found. Remind students that if they have difficulty improving their focus, they can ask a reference librarian or a local expert for guidance.

Remind students that they will share their findings by writing a short informational article that might appear in a cultural newsletter.

ON THEIR OWN Have students discuss their findings with a small group and ask the group to evaluate their research.

Conventions

Adjectives and Articles

REVIEW Remind students that they learned this week that an adjective describes a person, place, or thing.

A, an, the, this, and *that* are special adjectives called *articles. A* and *an* are used with singular nouns. *The* is used with singular and plural nouns. Another kind of special adjective is a limiting adjective, such as *this* and *that,* as in *This desk is mine. That desk is Mia's.*

CONNECT TO ORAL LANGUAGE Have students identify the nouns in the sentences below. *(flag, cabin, shirt)* Then have them ask the questions "What kind?" or "Which one?" to find the adjectives. *(The American; cozy; this striped, that plain)*

> **The American flag waved in the breeze.**
>
> **They spent the weekend in a cozy cabin.**
>
> **Darius chose this striped shirt, not that plain shirt.**

ON THEIR OWN For additional support, use *Let's Practice It!* p. 294 on the *Teacher Resources DVD-ROM.*

Name _____ Suki's Kimono

Adjectives and Articles

Directions Complete each sentence by adding an adjective. Write the new sentence. **Possible answers:**
1. Everyone wore ___ clothes to the party.
   Everyone wore bright clothes to the party.
2. Amy had on her ___ blouse.
   Amy had on her red blouse.
3. The ___ shirt is Kevin's.
   The colorful shirt is Kevin's.
4. Julio and William came with ___ hats on their heads.
   Julio and William came with funny hats on their heads.
5. Kay's ___ pants made us laugh.
   Kay's baggy pants made us laugh.

Directions Write two sentences about your favorite outfit. Use at least two adjectives. Underline the adjectives. **Possible answer:**
I like my blue jeans and my green sweater. I wear comfortable jeans with a bright sweater.

DVD•294 Adjectives and Articles

Let's Practice It! TR DVD•294

Spelling

Syllable Pattern CV/VC

FREQUENTLY MISSPELLED WORDS The words *cousin* and *believe* are words that students often misspell. Think carefully before you write these words. Have students fill in each sentence with the correct word.

1. **She didn't _____ his story.** (believe)

2. **His aunt's son, Pete, was his _____.** (cousin)

ON THEIR OWN For additional support, use *Reader's and Writer's Notebook* p. 325.

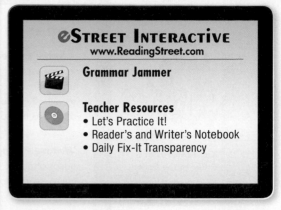

eSTREET INTERACTIVE
www.ReadingStreet.com

Grammar Jammer

Teacher Resources
• Let's Practice It!
• Reader's and Writer's Notebook
• Daily Fix-It Transparency

Access for All

SI Strategic Intervention

Have students in small groups compete to see which group can write more sentences using adjectives to describe a list of nouns, such as *children, firefighter, breakfast, school, island,* and *game.* Give extra points for using proper adjectives, such as *American* or *Texan.*

Daily Fix-It

5. The classes weared costumes and clothes from other countrys. *(wore; countries)*

6. James and him dressed like cowboys in a rodio. *(he; rodeo)*

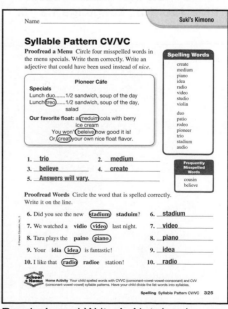

Name _____ Suki's Kimono

Syllable Pattern CV/VC

Proofread a Menu Circle four misspelled words in the menu specials. Write them correctly. Write an adjective that could have been used instead of *nice.*

Spelling Words
create
medium
piano
idea
radio
video
studio
violin

duo
patio
rodeo
pioneer
trio
stadium
audio

Pioneer Cáfe

Specials
Lunch duo.......1/2 sandwich, soup of the day
Lunch (treo).....1/2 sandwich, soup of the day, salad

Our favorite float: a (meduim) cola with berry ice cream
You won't (beleive) how good it is!
Or (creat) your own nice float flavor.

1. ___trio___   2. ___medium___
3. ___believe___ 4. ___create___
5. ___Answers will vary.___

Frequently Misspelled Words
cousin
believe

Proofread Words Circle the word that is spelled correctly. Write it on the line.
6. Did you see the new (stadium) staduim?   6. ___stadium___
7. We watched a vidio (video) last night.   7. ___video___
8. Tara plays the paino (piano).   8. ___piano___
9. Your idia (idea) is fantastic!   9. ___idea___
10. I like that (radio) radioe station!   10. ___radio___

Spelling Syllable Pattern CV/VC 325

Reader's and Writer's Notebook, p. 325

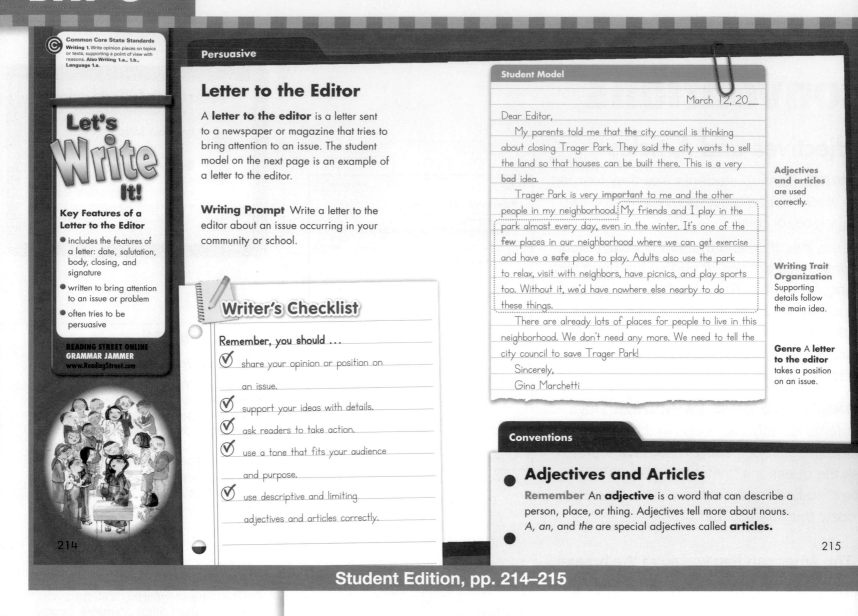

Common Core State Standards
Writing 1. Write opinion pieces on topics or texts, supporting a point of view with reasons. Also Writing 1.a., 1.b., Language 1.a.

Let's Write It!

Key Features of a Letter to the Editor

- includes the features of a letter: date, salutation, body, closing, and signature
- written to bring attention to an issue or problem
- often tries to be persuasive

READING STREET ONLINE
GRAMMAR JAMMER
www.ReadingStreet.com

214

Persuasive

Letter to the Editor

A **letter to the editor** is a letter sent to a newspaper or magazine that tries to bring attention to an issue. The student model on the next page is an example of a letter to the editor.

Writing Prompt Write a letter to the editor about an issue occurring in your community or school.

Writer's Checklist

Remember, you should . . .

☑ share your opinion or position on an issue.

☑ support your ideas with details.

☑ ask readers to take action.

☑ use a tone that fits your audience and purpose.

☑ use descriptive and limiting adjectives and articles correctly.

Student Model

March 12, 20___

Dear Editor,

My parents told me that the city council is thinking about closing Trager Park. They said the city wants to sell the land so that houses can be built there. This is a very bad idea.

Trager Park is very important to me and the other people in my neighborhood. My friends and I play in the park almost every day, even in the winter. It's one of the few places in our neighborhood where we can get exercise and have a safe place to play. Adults also use the park to relax, visit with neighbors, have picnics, and play sports too. Without it, we'd have nowhere else nearby to do these things.

There are already lots of places for people to live in this neighborhood. We don't need any more. We need to tell the city council to save Trager Park!

Sincerely,
Gina Marchetti

Adjectives and articles are used correctly.

Writing Trait Organization Supporting details follow the main idea.

Genre A **letter to the editor** takes a position on an issue.

Conventions

Adjectives and Articles

Remember An **adjective** is a word that can describe a person, place, or thing. Adjectives tell more about nouns. *A, an,* and *the* are special adjectives called **articles.**

215

Student Edition, pp. 214–215

Common Core State Standards

Writing 1. Write opinion pieces on familiar topics or texts, supporting a point of view with reasons. **Also Writing 1.a., 1.b., Language 1.a., 3.**

Let's Write It!

WRITE A LETTER TO THE EDITOR Use pp. 214–215 in the Student Edition. Direct students to read the key features of a letter to the editor, which appear on p. 214. Remind students that they can refer to the information in the Writer's Checklist as they write their own letters to the editor.

Read the student model on p. 215. Point out the date, salutation, body, closing, and signature in the model. Identify the issue or problem in the letter, and point out where the author tries to persuade the reader to take action.

CONNECT TO CONVENTIONS Remind students that an adjective is a word that describes a person, place, or thing. *A, an,* and *the* are special adjectives called *articles.* Point out the correct use of adjectives and articles in the model.

Writing

Letter to the Editor

Writing Trait: Focus/Ideas

DISPLAY RUBRIC Display Scoring Rubric 21 from the *Teacher Resources DVD-ROM* and go over the criteria for each trait under each score. Then, using the model in the Student Edition, choose students to explain why the model should score a 4 for one of the traits. If a student offers that the model should score below 4 for a particular trait, the student should offer support for that response. Remind students that this is the rubric that will be used to evaluate the letter to the editor they write.

Scoring Rubric Letter to the Editor

	4	3	2	1
Focus/Ideas	Clear, logical main idea; many supporting details; nonfiction	Clear main idea; some supporting details; nonfiction	Unclear, illogical main idea; few supporting details; seems like fiction	No main idea; no supporting details; fiction
Organization	Correct use of letter format	A few mistakes in letter format	Many mistakes in letter format	No attempt to use letter format
Voice	Clear, strong position; writer's personality clearly conveyed	Position conveyed; sense of writer's personality	Weak position; weak sense of writer's personality	No position; no sense of writer's personality
Word Choice	Strong use of persuasive language	Some use of persuasive language	Weak use of persuasive language	Informal, unpersuasive language
Sentences	Clear sentences of various lengths and types; strong variety of sentence beginnings	Sentences of a few lengths and types; variety of sentence beginnings	Sentences of similar length and type; weak variety of sentence beginnings	No attempt at sentences of various lengths and types; no variety of sentence beginnings
Conventions	Few, if any, errors; strong use of adjectives and articles; complete sentences	Several minor errors; use of adjectives and articles; mostly complete sentences	Many errors; weak use of adjectives and articles; few complete sentences	Numerous errors; no or incorrect use of adjectives and articles; no complete sentences

MAIN IDEA AND SUPPORTING DETAILS Have students refer to the main idea graphic organizer they worked on yesterday. If their charts are not complete, give them additional time and the necessary resources to complete them.

WRITE You will be using your main idea charts as you write the draft of your letter to the editor. Don't worry about mistakes as you write your draft. You will be able to revise it tomorrow.

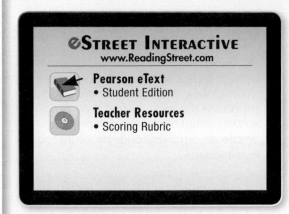

eSTREET INTERACTIVE
www.ReadingStreet.com

Pearson eText
• Student Edition

Teacher Resources
• Scoring Rubric

Access for All

 Advanced

Have each student choose a letter to the editor from a newspaper or magazine and score it using the rubric. Then invite students to trade letters with a partner and revise to see if they can improve the letter using the criteria in the rubric as a guide. Have a third student grade the revision, and then compare the two scores.

Letter to the Editor Illustrate how word choice can give writing or speech a formal or informal tone. Choose a problem—for example not having homework finished—and ask students to explain the problem (a) to a friend and (b) to their teacher.

Common Core State Standards

Writing 1. Write opinion pieces on familiar topics or texts, supporting a point of view with reasons. **Writing 1.a.** Introduce the topic or text they are writing about, state an opinion, and create an organizational structure that lists reasons.

Bridge to Common Core

RANGE OF WRITING

As students progress through the writing project, they routinely write for a range of tasks, purposes, and audiences. In this lesson, they learn to keep their letters to the editor focused on one main idea.

Writing

Letter to the Editor

Mini-Lesson | Keeping Your Letter Focused

■ **Introduce** Discuss the importance of focusing your letter to the editor on one main idea. The main idea of your letter should establish your position or opinion about the issue you have chosen as your topic. Use only details that logically and reasonably support this main idea. Display the Drafting Tips for students. Remind them that the purpose of drafting is to organize their thoughts. Then display Writing Transparency 21A.

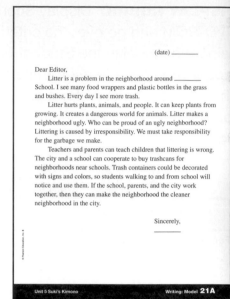

Writing Transparency 21A, TR DVD

Drafting Tips
✔ To get started, review your main idea chart.

✔ Make sure your main idea appears early in your letter.

✔ Use language that will persuade your audience to share your opinion and take action.

✔ Get your ideas down on paper without worrying about grammar or mechanics. You'll revise and proofread your letter later.

Think Aloud **MODEL** First, I'm going to write the date, the salutation, and the opening paragraph of my letter to the editor. My first sentence will be the main idea from my main idea chart. I'll also include my first supporting detail in the first paragraph, because it describes the problem in detail. The other supporting details describe the effects and cause of littering, so I'll put them together in the second paragraph. As I write my draft, I'll add adjectives and other details to help persuade the reader to agree with my opinion. I won't worry about revising or proofreading yet, since I'll have time for those tasks later.

Direct students to use the Drafting Tips to guide them in writing their drafts. Remind them that each detail should tell something about the problem or issue they are writing about.

eSTREET INTERACTIVE
www.ReadingStreet.com

Teacher Resources
• Writing Transparency

Routine | Quick Write for Fluency | Team Talk

. Talk Have pairs of students discuss how to identify good supporting details.

. Write Have students write one main idea, three good supporting details, and one poor supporting detail.

. Share Have students exchange their writing with their partners and pick out the poor supporting detail from the list.

Routines Flip Chart

Access for All

 Advanced

Have students interview two people with different views on the same issue. Invite students to share with the class what they've discovered about the two different positions on the issue, the details that support each position, and what solutions each side recommends for solving the problem. Have students choose a side with which they agree most strongly and tally the results.

Wrap Up Your Day!

✔ **Content Knowledge** What did you learn about how Suki felt about her culture?

✔ **Text-Based Comprehension** *Compare Penny's reaction to Suki's outfit with the reaction of the two boys in the classroom.* Encourage students to cite evidence from the text.

Preview DAY 4

Tell students that tomorrow they will read about how clothes from other cultures have become popular in our own.

Materials

- Student Edition
- Reader's and Writer's Notebook
- Decodable Reader

Common Core State Standards

Speaking/Listening 1. Engage effectively in a range of collaborative discussions (one-on-one, in groups, and teacher-led) with diverse partners on grade 3 topics and texts, building on others' ideas and expressing their own clearly. **Language 6.** Acquire and use accurately grade-appropriate conversational, general academic, and domain-specific words and phrases, including those that signal spatial and temporal relationships (e.g., *After dinner that night we went looking for them*).

Content Knowledge

Zoom in on ©

Cultures and Clothing

EXPAND THE CONCEPT Remind students of the weekly concept question, *How does culture influence the clothes we wear?* Have students discuss how clothes from different cultures have become popular in our own culture.

Build Oral Language

Team Talk **TALK ABOUT SENTENCES AND WORDS** Have students reread the following sentences from p. 209 of the Student Edition.

She remembered how it felt to dance barefoot in the open air, on fresh-cut grass that tickled her toes.

She tried to picture the other dancers. How they moved forward in the circle with the rhythm of the music.

- What does it mean to dance in the "open air"? (to dance outside)
- What does the word *picture* mean here? (form a picture in her mind, or remember) What are some synonyms for *picture,* as it is used here? *(visualize, see, remember, imagine)*
- What is Suki trying to *picture?* (She is trying to remember the way the dancers moved at the festival.)
- What does it mean to dance "with the rhythm of the music"? (to move your body to the same beat as the music)
- Have partners tell in their own words what is happening in these sentences from the story.

Build Oral Vocabulary

Amazing Words ⭐   Robust Vocabulary Routine

1. **Introduce** Write the concept word *elegant* on the board. Have students say it aloud with you. We learn that Suki danced in an *elegant* fan-patterned blue kimono with a yellow obi. How do the illustrations on page 208 explain the meaning of the word *elegant*? (The illustrations show how fine-looking and tasteful the kimono is.)

2. **Demonstrate** Have students answer questions to demonstrate understanding. What qualities of the kimono make it look *elegant*? (its long, loose appearance and its pretty fabric)

3. **Apply** Have students apply their understanding. When might a woman wear something *elegant*?

4. **Display the Word** Run your hand under the chunks in *el-e-gant* as you read the word. Have students say the word.

See p. OV•1 to teach *stylish*.

Routines Flip Chart

- -

ADD TO THE CONCEPT MAP Discuss the Amazing Words *robe* and *drape*. Add these and other concept-related words to the concept map. Use the following questions to develop students' understanding of the concept.

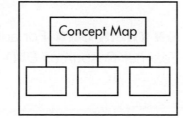

Suki's kimono looks like a *robe.* In what other cultures do people wear a garment that looks like a *robe?*

The sleeves of a kimono *drape* over a person's arms. What are some other clothes that *drape* over the arms and shoulders?

Amazing Words ⭐

traditional	inspire
fret	robe
scarves	drape
fabric	elegant
acceptable	stylish

Strategy Response Log

Have students review the characteristics of realistic fiction on p. 27 of the *Reader's and Writer's Notebook.* Then have them compare *Suki's Kimono* to another example of realistic fiction that they have read or know about.

Produce Oral Language Use the Day 4 instruction on ELL Poster 21 to extend and enrich the language.

Common Core State Standards

Foundational Skills 3. Know and apply grade-level phonics and word analysis skills in decoding words. **Foundational Skills 3.c.** Decode multisyllable words. **Foundational Skills 3.d.** Read grade-appropriate irregularly spelled words.

Name _____   **Suki's Kimono**

Syllable Patterns VCCCV

Directions Look at the words on the right. These words have the VCCCV syllable pattern. Divide each word into syllables. Write the syllables on the lines.

1. com + plete = complete
2. hun + dred = hundred
3. mer + chant = merchant
4. mon + ster = monster
5. pil + grim = pilgrim
6. sur + prise = surprise
7. twin + kle = twinkle
8. in + spect = inspect
9. com + plain = complain
10. ad + dress = address

Directions Underline the word that has the VCCCV syllable pattern in each sentence.

11. The pilot takes charge of the controls in the plane.
12. My brother José and I built a fortress in the snowbank.
13. I scraped my knuckles on the wood while sanding the porch railing.
14. My cat tried to distract me by climbing into my lap.
15. Strawberries ripen on the vine in springtime.
16. The store gave everyone a free sample.

Home Activity Your child wrote words with the VCCCV syllable pattern found in monster. Ask your child to write a sentence for each of the words in the first exercise. Have your child circle the word with the VCCCV syllable pattern.

Syllable Patterns VCCCV DVD•295

Let's Practice It! TR DVD•295

Word Analysis

Review Syllables VCCCV

REVIEW SOUND-SPELLINGS To review syllabication pattern VCCCV, write *children, exchange, thirsty, appliance,* and *compliance.* We learned to divide words that have three consonants in a row. Let's review by looking at these words. Have students identify the syllable pattern VCCCV in each word. What do you know about reading these words? (When a word has three consonants in the middle, divide it between the single consonant and the blend or digraph.) What is the digraph in *exchange*? *(ch)*

> **Corrective feedback** | If students are unable to answer questions about the VCCCV syllable pattern, refer them to *Sound-Spelling Card* 146.

GUIDE PRACTICE Display a T-chart with the headings VCCCV and CV/VC. Write these words on the board: *huddle, client, sample, science, inspect, address, diary,* and *medium.* Have students read and sort each word into the appropriate column. Then have students read the words together.

VCCCV	CV/VC
huddle	client
sample	science
inspect	diary
address	medium

ON THEIR OWN For additional practice, use *Let's Practice It!* p. 295 on the *Teacher Resources DVD-ROM.*

Fluent Word Reading

Spiral Review

READ WORDS IN ISOLATION Display these words. Tell students that they can already decode some words on this list. Explain that they should know other words because they appear often in reading.

Have students read the list three or four times until they can read at the rate of two to three seconds per word.

Word Reading

teacher	midweek	story	outdoors	a
the	was	chemist	to	more
preview	editor	overgrown	smart	from
turn	her	your	actress	bicycle

Corrective feedback	**If...** students have difficulty reading whole words, **then...** have them use sound-by-sound blending for decodable words or chunking for words that have word parts, or have them say and spell high-frequency words.
	If... students cannot read fluently at a rate of two to three seconds per word, **then...** have pairs practice the list until they can read it fluently.

eSTREET INTERACTIVE
www.ReadingStreet.com

 Teacher Resources
• Let's Practice It!
• Graphic Organizers

Interactive Sound-Spelling Cards

Access for All

SI Strategic Intervention

To assist students having difficulty with the syllable pattern VCCCV, have them write the letters VCCCV in small letters on a self-stick note. When decoding words in this lesson, allow students to use the self-stick note to track under the individual letters in the words and more readily identify the syllable pattern.

Spiral Review

These activities review:
• previously taught high-frequency words *the, was, your, to, a, from.*
• *r*-controlled vowels *er, ur, or, ar, ore;* prefixes *pre-, mid-, over-, out-, bi-;* suffixes *-er, -or, -ess, -ist.*

Fluent Word Reading Have students listen to a more fluent reader say the words. Then have them repeat the words.

Suki's Kimono **216d**

© Common Core State Standards

Foundational Skills 3. Know and apply grade-level phonics and word analysis skills in decoding words. **Foundational Skills 3.c.** Decode multisyllable words. **Foundational Skills 3.d.** Read grade-appropriate irregularly spelled words. **Foundational Skills 4.** Read with sufficient accuracy and fluency to support comprehension.

Fluent Word Reading

READ WORDS IN CONTEXT Display these sentences. Call on individuals to read a sentence. Then randomly point to review words and have students read them. To help you monitor word reading, high-frequency words are underlined and decodable words are italicized.

MONITOR PROGRESS Sentence Reading

The *teacher* asked the class to *preview* a *story* for next week.

The *actress* from the movie has *her* audition *midweek.*

The *smart chemist* works to control *overgrown* crops.

You should ride your *bicycle outdoors more* often.

The *editor* was able to *turn* his comments in on Monday.

If... students are unable to read an underlined high-frequency word,

then... read the word for them and spell it, having them echo you.

If... students have difficulty reading an italicized decodable word,

then... guide them in using sound-by-sound blending or chunking.

Reread for Fluency

Have students reread the sentences to develop automaticity decoding words.

Routine Oral Rereading

1. **Read** Have students read all the sentences orally.

2. **Reread** To achieve optimal fluency, students should reread the sentences three or four times.

3. **Corrective Feedback** Listen as students read. Provide corrective feedback regarding their fluency and decoding.

Routines Flip Chart

Decodable Passage 21C

...students need help, then...

Read *Leona's Poem*

READ WORDS IN ISOLATION Have students turn to p. 71 in *Decodable Practice Readers 3.2* and find the first list of words. Each word in this list has the syllabication pattern CV/VC. Let's read these words. Be sure that students pronounce each vowel in the CV/VC pattern.

Next, have students read the high-frequency words.

PREVIEW Have students read the title and preview the passage. Tell them that they will read words with the syllable pattern CV/VC.

READ WORDS IN CONTEXT Chorally read the passage along with the students. Have students identify words in the passage that have the syllable pattern CV/VC. Make sure that students are monitoring their accuracy when they decode words.

Team Talk Pair students and have them take turns reading the passage aloud to each other. Monitor students as they read to check for proper pronunciation and appropriate pacing.

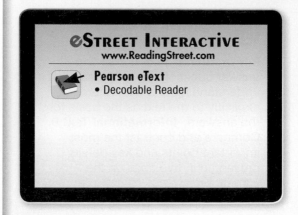

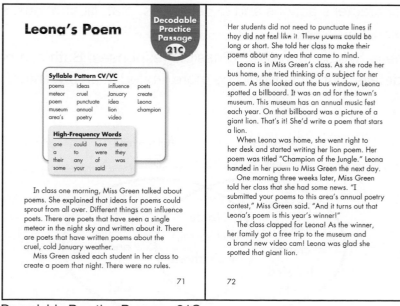

Decodable Practice Passage 21C

Access for All

A Advanced

Have students start a list of professions that use the suffixes *-er, -or, -ess,* and *-ist* from the sentences on p. 216e. Have them add as many additional words to the list as they can.

Common Core State Standards

Informational Text 1. Ask and answer questions to demonstrate understanding of a text, referring explicitly to the text as the basis for the answers. **Informational Text 9.** Compare and contrast the most important points and key details presented in two texts on the same topic.

 Bridge to Common Core

KEY IDEAS AND DETAILS
Comparing the central ideas and purposes of expository text and adventure stories will lead students to better understand each genre and how they are alike and different. By studying each genre, students will know the benefits of reading each genre and the features they include.

 # Social Studies in Reading

Expository Text

INTRODUCE Explain to students that what we read is structured differently depending on the author's reasons for writing and the kind of information he or she wishes to convey. Different types of texts are called genres. Tell students that an expository text is one type of genre.

DISCUSS THE GENRE Discuss with students how an expository text might provide information about a topic that interests them. For example, ask: Where might you look to learn about snowboarding? (Possible responses: a sports magazine, a reference book, the Internet) Explain that students could also learn about snowboarding by reading an adventure story in which someone snowboards. Which kind of text might provide you with more facts and details about snowboarding? (an expository text) Let's compare and contrast an expository text and an adventure story.

GROUP PRACTICE Display a Venn diagram like the one below. Label the sides *Expository Text* and *Adventure Story.* Ask the following questions:

- What features might an expository text use to share information? (Possible responses: facts and details, photos, illustrations, captions, diagrams, charts, maps, bulleted lists)

- How might an adventure story share information? (Possible responses: through a character's actions and experiences, plot, illustrations, some facts and details)

- How are these two genres alike? (Possible responses: Both can provide facts and details, but facts would be more limited in an adventure story.)

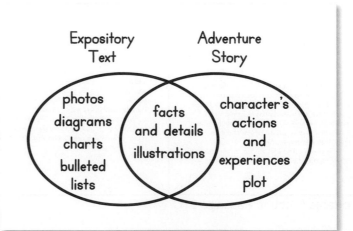

Team Talk Then, have students work in pairs to list the benefits of reading an expository text to learn about a topic. Have them list the text features the text might use and examples of the kinds of information each feature might provide. Ask students to share their lists with the class.

READ Tell students that they will now read about clothes from other cultures that have become fashionable in the United States.

ELL

Expository Article Have small groups of students examine an expository article. Point out each feature of the article and briefly explain its function. Then have students name each feature and its function.

ELL

If... students need more scaffolding and practice with the **Amazing Words,**
then... use the Routine on pp. xxxvi–xxxvii in the *ELL Handbook.*

Day 4 **SMALL GROUP TIME • Differentiate Vocabulary, p. SG•1**

OL On-Level	**SI** Strategic Intervention	**A** Advanced
Develop Language Using Amazing Words	• **Review/Discuss** Amazing Words	• **Extend** Amazing Words and Selection Vocabulary
Read "Clothes: Bringing Cultures Together"	• **Read** "Clothes: Bringing Cultures Together"	• **Read** "Clothes: Bringing Cultures Together"
		• **Organize** Inquiry Project

DAY 4

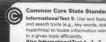

Common Core State Standards
Informational Text 5. Use text features
and search tools (e.g., key words, sidebars,
hyperlinks) to locate information relevant
to a given topic efficiently.
Also Informational Text 1., 2., 7.

Social Studies in Reading

Genre
Expository Text

- Expository texts are nonfiction. They give details and facts that support the main idea about a topic.
- Expository texts use graphic sources and text features to help the reader predict, locate, and verify information.
- Use the title, the illustration on this page, and the keywords *moccasins, berets,* and *ponchos* to predict what this selection will be about. Locate information about what the key words have in common to verify your predictions as you read.

216

Clothes
Bringing Cultures Together

by Elizabeth Massie

Next time you walk through town, look at the clothes people are wearing. You might see ponchos, blue jeans, and sneakers. You might see moccasins (MOK-uh-sunz), t-shirts, and berets (bur-AYZ). Many of the clothes we wear today are new designs. However, some were first made in other countries or by other cultures long ago. They have become part of modern American fashion.

Moccasins

Berets

Ponchos →

South American
Ponchos

Thousands of years ago, people of South America made and wore ponchos. A poncho is a square cloak. It has a hole in the middle for the wearer's head.

South American ponchos were woven out of wool. The wool came from llamas and other pack animals. The ponchos were often decorated with flowers, birds, and people. Ponchos kept the wearers warm in cold weather.

Ponchos are still part of everyday wear in many South American countries. The style is much the same as it was long ago.

During the 20th century, people in the United States began to wear ponchos. Americans liked their style and warmth. Ponchos were also adapted into rain gear. Rain ponchos are made of waterproof material. They often have hoods.

Past

The poncho above was made in South America more than two thousand years ago. You might see the ponchos below on our streets today.

Present

Let's **Think** About...

What does the title tell you about the topic and main idea? What facts and details can you find to support the main idea?
Expository Text

①

217

Student Edition, pp. 216–217

Common Core State Standards

Informational Text 1. Ask and answer questions to demonstrate understanding of a text, referring explicitly to the text as the basis for the answers. **Informational Text 5.** Use text features and search tools (e.g., key words, sidebars, hyperlinks) to locate information relevant to a given topic efficiently. **Informational Text 7.** Use information gained from illustrations (e.g., maps, photographs) and the words in a text to demonstrate understanding of the text (e.g., where, when, why, and how key events occur). **Also Informational Text 2., 10.**

Access Text ©

TEACH Expository Text Have students preview "Clothes: Bringing Cultures Together" on pp. 216–217. Have them look at the map on p. 216 and discuss what information it shares. Then ask: What does the map tell you about each article of clothing?

Corrective feedback	**If...** students are unable to identify what the map tells about the articles of clothing, **then...** use the model to guide students in identifying this information.

216–217 Cultures • Unit 5 • Week 1

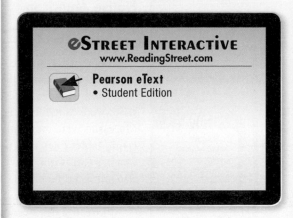

Think Aloud

MODEL I see the names and pictures of three articles of clothing on the world map. Each arrow points to some part of the world. I think the map shows that each article of clothing comes from the culture in that part of the world.

ON THEIR OWN Have students work in pairs to design a different way of presenting the information in the map. Encourage them to use other kinds of text features, such as charts, diagrams, and bulleted lists, and so on, to provide the same information.

Close Reading ©

ANALYSIS • TEXT EVIDENCE Reread p. 217. How do ponchos worn in the United States today compare with those worn thousands of years ago in South America? (Ponchos worn today often have hoods and are sometimes made of a waterproof material. Years ago, ponchos had no hoods and were decorated with birds, flowers, and people. They were made from the wool of pack animals.)

EVALUATION How has the poncho become part of modern American fashion? (Americans have adapted the original poncho design to wear in many situations and under many circumstances.)

Genre

LET'S THINK ABOUT... As you read "Clothes: Bringing Cultures Together," use Let's Think About in the Student Edition to help students focus on the features of expository text.

It tells me that this section will be about ponchos worn in South America. Ponchos are woven out of wool. They are often decorated with flowers, birds, and people.

eSTREET INTERACTIVE
www.ReadingStreet.com

 Pearson eText
• Student Edition

Access for All

 Strategic Intervention

Work with a small group of students to identify how the original poncho and today's American design are alike and different. Have each student create a T-chart and label the two columns *North American* and *South American*. Have students list the qualities of each poncho in its column. Then discuss the similarities and differences.

A **Advanced**

Have students write a brief paragraph that summarizes what they have learned about ponchos.

Vocabulary Point out the pronunciation of the words *moccasins* and *berets* on p. 216. Have students practice saying these words aloud.

Suki's Kimono **217a**

Native American
Moccasins

Long ago, native people of North America made shoes out of animal hides. These shoes were called moccasins. Moccasins were tough and comfortable. They kept the wearer's feet warm. They also protected feet from cold, rough ground.

Moccasin styles were different from tribe to tribe. You could tell what tribe people belonged to by looking at their shoes. For example, the Blackfeet tribe was called that because they dyed their moccasins black.

Native Americans taught European settlers how to make moccasins. Trappers and explorers wore these shoes in the wilderness. Even Lewis and Clark made and wore moccasins on their trip west.

Today, Americans of many backgrounds wear moccasins. They like the soft comfort of the shoe.

Past

Members of the Blackfeet tribe (top) wore moccasins that were dyed black. These colorful moccasins (above) were made years ago by Native Americans. The moccasins below are similar to those worn today.

Present

218

Let's Think About...

How do the illustrations and captions verify the information from the text? **Expository Text**

②

Let's Think About...

How did moccasins connect Native American cultures? How do moccasins bring together Native American cultures and ours today? **Expository Text**

③

Basque
Berets

A beret is a soft, round hat. Hundreds of years ago, the Basque (BASK) people made these hats out of wool. Basque shepherds tended their flocks in the cold mountains between France and Spain. These hats kept their heads warm.

In the 1920s, British tank soldiers started wearing black berets. The hats were comfortable. They didn't show grease stains. During World War II, some British soldiers gave American soldiers berets to wear. The hats were seen as special. Today, some units of the United States military wear berets.

Berets became popular with American women in the 1930s. Berets are still worn by men, women, and children as part of everyday outfits.

Past

Present

British General Bernard Law Montgomery, above, popularized the use of berets during World War II. Even today, traditional clothes for Basque men, below, often include berets.

219

Let's Think About...

What text feature separates the topic of this page from the topic on the previous page? What are the different topics? **Expository Text**

④

Let's Think About...

Reading Across Texts Elizabeth Massie describes ponchos, moccasins, and berets in "Clothes: Bringing Cultures Together." How might she describe Suki's kimono?

Writing Across Texts Write what you think the author's description of Suki's kimono would be.

Student Edition, pp. 218–219

Common Core State Standards

Informational Text 1. Ask and answer questions to demonstrate understanding of a text, referring explicitly to the text as the basis for the answers. **Informational Text 3.** Describe the relationship between a series of historical events, scientific ideas or concepts, or steps in technical procedures in a text, using language that pertains to time, sequence, and cause/effect. **Informational Text 10.** By the end of the year, read and comprehend informational texts, including history/social studies, science, and technical texts, at the high end of the grades 2–3 text complexity band independently and proficiently. **Also Informational Text 8., Writing 10.**

Access Text ©

TEACH Expository Text Explain that the author of an expository text must choose the best way to present information. Then ask: How does the author order the information on pages 218–219?

Corrective feedback | **If...** students are unable to determine the order of information, **then...** use the model to guide them in understanding the order.

MODEL I notice that the author begins each section by telling how each article of clothing came into use years ago. She continues by explaining how the item has changed over time. She ends each section by telling how the article of clothing is used today. She uses time order to present information.

ON THEIR OWN Have students examine other expository texts to determine how information is presented.

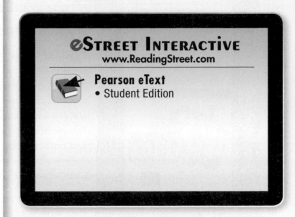
Close Reading

EVALUATION Why does it make sense to use time order to explain how culture influences clothing? (Clothing styles evolve, or develop, over time.)

ANALYSIS • TEXT EVIDENCE Reread the first paragraph of p. 219. Why were berets created? (Basque shepherds created berets from wool because they wanted to keep their heads warm while they tended their sheep.)

Genre

LET'S THINK ABOUT... features of expository text.

They show how moccasins have changed over the years.

Each tribe had a different style of moccasin. The Native Americans taught European settlers how to make them.

A head separates the information; moccasins and berets are the topics.

Reading and Writing Across Texts

Have students reread *Suki's Kimono* and take notes on the different ways the author and illustrator portray the girl's kimono. Next, have students use their notes to write an informational paragraph describing Suki's kimono. Instruct them to begin by writing a central idea in a topic sentence and then using facts and details to describe the kimono's color, design, fabric, and movement.

 Have partners locate books by the same author. After reading, have them compare and contrast characters, setting, and plot to see how the books are alike and how they are different. Suggest the partners use a Venn diagram to make their comparisons.

Access for All

SI Strategic Intervention
Help pairs of students sequence the information about berets. Have them use approximate dates (1942 for WWII) to list and explain how the beret has been used over time. Then ask students to use their lists to explain what they have learned.

A Advanced
Have students research the origin of another popular article of clothing and share their findings with the class. Possible clothing: clogs, vests, ties, shawls, capes

 Connect to Social Studies

Basque People The Basques live in a region of the Pyrenees Mountains that lies in both France and Spain. Most of the people in this region live in Spain. The Basque language, known as Euskara, is believed to be one of the oldest living languages in Europe.

ELL

Text Features Point out the Past/Present feature on each page and explain the information each feature provides. Then have students take turns explaining how the feature helps them understand the differences between past and present dress.

Let's **Learn** It!

READING STREET ONLINE
ONLINE STUDENT EDITION
www.ReadingStreet.com

Vocabulary

Synonyms

Context Clues An analogy is a way to show relationships between words. Read the analogy: *take* is to *snatch* as *sway* is to *move*. *Take* and *snatch* are synonyms just like *sway* and *move* are synonyms. The relationship between words before and after *as* is the same in an analogy.

Practice It! Finish the analogy by writing a synonym from *Suki's Kimono*. Then write your own analogies. *Look* is to *stare* as *laugh* is to _____. *Shoes* is to *geta* as *outfit* is to _____. *Laugh* is to *giggle* as *copy* is to _____.

Fluency

Rate

When reading, sometimes you come to a part of a story that has more difficult words. Your rate of reading might slow down. Reviewing the difficult words and practicing reading them will help you read at an appropriate rate.

Practice It! With your partner, practice reading *Suki's Kimono*, page 201. Before you begin, practice the difficult words, such as *Suki's, obāchan, kimono,* and *sōmen noodles.* Then practice reading the entire paragraph until you can read it at an appropriate rate.

220

Listening and Speaking

Get Ready For Middle School

Follow the etiquette, or rules, for conversation, including making eye contact.

Introduction

Introductions are conversations that follow rules for polite ways of meeting people in a culture.

Practice It! Think about how we make introductions in our culture. Follow oral directions for making introductions in groups. Role play other people, such as a teacher or coach, as you practice introductions.

Tips

Listening ...
• Execute multi-step directions.

Speaking ...
• Speak clearly and distinctly.
• Use adjectives and articles correctly.

Teamwork ...
• Restate the directions to the group to make sure you understand them.
• Give clear directions to your group before role playing other people.

221

Student Edition, pp. 220–221

Fluency

Rate

GUIDE PRACTICE Use the Fluency activity as an assessment tool. Make sure the passage is at least 200 words long. As students read, make sure their rate is appropriate and sounds natural.

 Don't Wait Until Friday **MONITOR PROGRESS** Check Fluency

FORMATIVE ASSESSMENT As students reread, monitor progress toward their individual fluency goals.

Current Goal: 102–112 words correct per minute
End-of-Year Goal: 120 words correct per minute

If... students cannot read fluently at a rate of 102–112 words correct per minute,

then... have students practice with text at their independent levels.

Vocabulary Skill

◎ Synonyms

TEACH SYNONYMS • CONTEXT CLUES Write this analogy on the board.
***Shook** is to **quaked** as **grabbed** is to **snatched**.*

Explain that *shook* and *quaked* are synonyms and that *grabbed* and *snatched* are synonyms. Point out that the words *quaked* and *snatched* appear in the story.

GUIDE PRACTICE Have students complete the following analogy on their own. Tell them to use context clues to find a synonym for *celebration* on the page of *Suki's Kimono* where the author describes a celebration.
***Focused** is to **concentrated** as **celebration** is to _____.*

ON THEIR OWN Walk around the room as students work with partners to complete the analogies on p. 220. Check to make sure the synonyms they write are words from the story.

Listening and Speaking

Introductions

TEACH Explain to students that our culture has certain standards for making introductions. Remind students to be polite and speak slowly and distinctly as they make an introduction. Explain that people being introduced should maintain attention at all times. People introducing and those being introduced should always face the other person and make eye contact with him or her. They should shake hands with the other person if that person extends his or her hand.

GUIDE PRACTICE Be sure students are speaking slowly and clearly as they make their introductions. Remind those being introduced to listen attentively and make eye contact with each other.

ON THEIR OWN Have students restate the oral instructions to the group. Have them follow the instructions by making introductions in groups of three. Be sure students give clear directions to their group before role playing other people.

eStreet Interactive
www.ReadingStreet.com

Pearson eText
• Student Edition

Introductions
Point out to students that they need to be aware of when a person needs an introduction. If they are unsure whether or not people know each other, they should simply ask.

 Bridge to Common Core

COMPREHENSION AND COLLABORATION
When students make introductions, they should be polite and speak slowly and distinctly. To participate effectively in the introduction, they should maintain attention, make eye contact with the person they are being introduced to, and shake hands with him or her to show they understand the standards for making introductions.

ELL
Synonyms Help students find the page of the story where a synonym for each word might appear. For example, suggest that they ask themselves: *On what page are people laughing?* and *On what page is someone copying?* Help students read these pages carefully to look for a synonym to complete each analogy.

Practice Pronunciation Assist pairs of students by modeling the correct pronunciation of the words used in the analogies and then having them repeat after you. Pair students with mixed language proficiencies together to practice pronunciation and employ self-corrective techniques.

Common Core State Standards

Writing 2. Write informative/explanatory texts to examine a topic and convey ideas and information clearly. **Language 1.a.** Explain the function of nouns, pronouns, verbs, adjectives, and adverbs in general and their functions in particular sentences. **Language 2.f.** Use spelling patterns and generalizations (e.g., word families, position-based spellings, syllable patterns, ending rules, meaningful word parts) in writing words.

Research and Inquiry

Step 4 Synthesize

TEACH Have students synthesize their research findings and results. Tell students they will be writing an informational article on the research they conducted. Explain that they will present their articles on Day 5. Remind students that when they organize information, they pull it together and arrange it in an orderly, functional way. Review how to choose relevant information from a number of sources and organize it logically. Suggest that students use available software, such as graphing or charting programs, to synthesize their information.

GUIDE PRACTICE Have students use a word-processing program to write drafts of their articles for the cultural newsletter. Suggest to students that they organize their ideas into paragraphs that each begin with a topic sentence. If necessary, review how to write a topic sentence. Have students use a dictionary and the computer to find and check correct spellings.

ON THEIR OWN Have students write a brief explanation of their research findings. Then have them organize and combine information for their presentation.

Conventions

Adjectives and Articles

TEST PRACTICE Remind students that grammar skills, such as identifying and using adjectives and articles, are often addressed on important tests. Remind students that:

- An adjective describes a person, place, or thing.

- *A, an,* and *the* are special adjectives called *articles.*

- *This* and *that* are special adjectives called *limiting adjectives.*

ON THEIR OWN For additional practice, use *Reader's and Writer's Notebook,* p. 326.

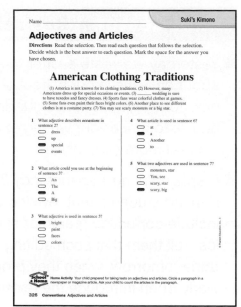

Reader's and Writer's Notebook, p. 326

Spelling

Syllable Pattern CV/VC

PRACTICE SPELLING STRATEGY Supply pairs of students with index cards on which the spelling words have been written. Have one student read a word while the other writes it. Then have students switch roles. Have them use the cards to check their spelling and correct any misspelled words.

ON THEIR OWN For additional practice, use *Let's Practice It!* p. 296 on the *Teacher Resources DVD-ROM.*

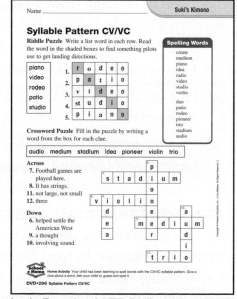

Let's Practice It! TR DVD•296

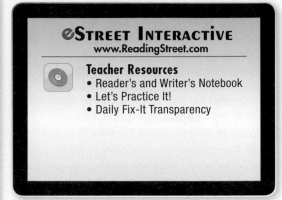

Daily Fix-It

7. Now Cara and Linda has a idea for a party. *(have; an)*

8. Childrens will bring food from diffrent countries. *(Children; different)*

Bridge to Common Core

CONVENTIONS OF STANDARD ENGLISH

As students identify and use adjectives and articles correctly, they are demonstrating command of the conventions of standard English. Your guidance will help them use correct grammar, usage, and spelling to convey meaning when they speak and write.

Common Core State Standards

Writing 5. With guidance and support from peers and adults, develop and strengthen writing as needed by planning, revising, and editing. **Language 3.a.** Choose words and phrases for effect.

Write Guy *by Jeff Anderson*

Conferencing Is Listening

Conferring about student's writing is more about teachers *listening* than teachers speaking. What is the student trying to say? What help does he need? We can ask questions to keep kids speaking: "What do you want your reader to know? Wow, how did you think of this vivid phrase?"

Writing

Letter to the Editor

Mini-Lesson Revise: Adding

■ Yesterday we wrote a letter to the editor about an issue in our school or community. Today we will revise our drafts. The goal is to make your writing more interesting and more persuasive.

■ Display Writing Transparency 21B. Remind students that revising does not include correcting grammar and mechanics. Tell them that such editing will be done tomorrow, when they proofread their work. Then introduce the revising strategy of adding.

■ When you revise a letter to the editor, you ask yourself, "What words will persuade the reader to feel and think the way I do?" Add details that will persuade the reader to agree with your opinion and support your position. **Illustrate how to do this.**

Writing Transparency 21B, TR DVD

Remind students to look for other ways to improve their writing by adding adjectives or articles, or by changing details.

Revising Tips

✔ Use negative words to define your problem.

✔ Use positive words to persuade people to agree with your opinion or to take action.

✔ Use more facts or evidence than feelings to support your position. Be logical, and use sound reasoning.

PEER CONFERENCING • PEER REVISION Have students exchange letters with a partner for peer revision. Give each student four sticky notes. Direct each student to read his or her partner's letter and write the main idea on one sticky note. On the remaining sticky notes, students should write three words, phrases, or ideas that persuade the reader to agree with the writer's position and want to take action. If the letter does not contain three strong instances of such language, instruct students to suggest some.

DAY 4

Have students revise their letters to the editor using the feedback from their Peer Revision partners as well as the key features of a letter to the editor to guide them.

Corrective feedback | Circulate around the room to answer questions and confer with students as they revise. When you see students correcting errors, remind them that they will have time to edit tomorrow.

Routine **Quick Write for Fluency** **Team Talk**

1. **Talk** Have pairs of students brainstorm a list of words and phrases that help persuade an audience to share a writer's opinion.

2. **Write** Direct students to write a pair of sentences: one, a good example of persuasive writing, and the other, a bad example of persuasive writing.

3. **Share** Invite students to exchange sentences with their partners and identify the effective and ineffective persuasive writing.

Routines Flip Chart

Choral Reading Collect the main idea sentences from several proficient English users' letters to the editor. Have students chorally read these sentences to emphasize the similarity in tone, concept, and sentence structure.

Wrap Up Your Day!

✔ **Content Knowledge** Have students discuss the reasons clothes from other cultures have become popular in our own.

✔ **Oral Vocabulary** Monitor students' use of oral vocabulary as they respond: *Why might clothing from other cultures be considered elegant and stylish in our culture?*

✔ **Text Features** Discuss how reading heads and captions helps you understand text.

Preview DAY 5

Remind students to think about how culture affects our clothing choices.

Suki's Kimono **221e**

Materials

- Student Edition
- Weekly Test
- Reader's and Writer's Notebook

Bridge to Common Core

INTEGRATION OF KNOWLEDGE AND IDEAS

This week, students have integrated content presented in diverse media and analyzed how different texts address similar topics. They have developed knowledge about cultures and clothing to expand the unit topic of Cultures.

Social Studies Knowledge Goals

Students have learned that people
- wear special clothes for holidays
- wear traditional clothing
- react to clothing

Content Knowledge Zoom in on

Cultures and Clothing

REVIEW THE CONCEPT Have students look back at the reading selections to find examples that best demonstrate how culture influences the clothes we wear.

Build Oral Language

REVIEW AMAZING WORDS Display and review this week's concept map. Remind students that this week they have learned ten Amazing Words related to clothing. Have students use the Amazing Words and the concept map to answer the Question of the Week, *How does culture influence the clothes we wear?*

Build Oral Vocabulary

Team Talk **CONNECT TO AMAZING IDEAS** Have pairs of students discuss how the Question of the Week connects to the question for this unit of study: *What happens when two ways of life come together?* Tell students to use the concept map and what they have learned from this week's discussions and reading selections to form an Amazing Idea—a realization or "big idea" about Cultures. Remind partners to pose and answer questions with appropriate detail and to give suggestions that build on each other's ideas. Then ask pairs to share their Amazing Ideas with the class.

Amazing Ideas might include these key concepts:

• A culture's climate influences the fabric, style, and color of its clothing.

• People express who they are through the clothes they wear.

• The materials available to make clothing affect what people wear.

WRITE ABOUT IT Have students write a few sentences about their Amazing Idea, beginning with "This week I learned . . ."

eSTREET INTERACTIVE
www.ReadingStreet.com

Concept Talk Video

Teacher Resources
• Amazing Word Cards

Story Sort

Amazing Words

traditional	inspire
fret	robe
scarves	drape
fabric	elegant
acceptable	stylish

Don't Wait Until Friday

MONITOR PROGRESS **Check Oral Vocabulary**

FORMATIVE ASSESSMENT Have individuals use this week's Amazing Words to describe clothes from different cultures. Monitor students' abilities to use the Amazing Words and note which words you need to reteach.

If... students have difficulty using the Amazing Words,

then... reteach using the Oral Vocabulary Routine on pp. 191a, 196b, 206b, 216b, OV•1.

ELL

Concept Map Work with students to add new words to the concept map.

Check Concepts and Language Use the Day 5 instruction on ELL Poster 21 to monitor students' understanding of the lesson concept.

Zoom in on ©

Common Core State Standards

Literature 1. Ask and answer questions to demonstrate understanding of a text, referring explicitly to the text as the basis for the answers. **Foundational Skills 3.** Know and apply grade-level phonics and word analysis skills in decoding words. **Language 3.a.** Choose words and phrases for effect. **Language 4.** Determine or clarify the meaning of unknown and multiple-meaning words and phrases based on grade 3 reading and content, choosing flexibly from a range of strategies.

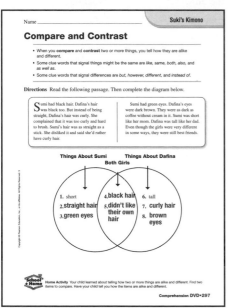

Let's Practice It! TR DVD•297

Selection Vocabulary

cotton cloth made from cotton fibers

festival a celebration or holiday

graceful showing beauty in movement

handkerchief a square piece of cloth used to wipe the face or nose

paces steps in walking

pale light in shade or color

rhythm a repeated beat, sound, or motion

snug fitting closely; tight

Text-Based Comprehension

Review © Compare and Contrast

TEACH Review the definition of compare and contrast on p. 194. Remind students that when they compare and contrast two things or ideas, they tell how they are alike and different. Remind students of the clue words that signal comparison and contrast. For additional support, have students review p. EI•5 on comparing and contrasting.

GUIDE PRACTICE Have student pairs find an example of a compare-and-contrast relationship in *Suki's Kimono.* Then have pairs tell how things are alike and different and what clue words signal this.

ON THEIR OWN For additional practice with comparing and contrasting, use *Let's Practice It!* p. 297 on the *Teacher Resources DVD-ROM.*

Vocabulary Skill

Review © Synonyms

TEACH Remind students to use context clues to find synonyms for unfamiliar words.

GUIDE PRACTICE Write the following sentence on the board and review how to use context clues to find a synonym for *snug. One shoe felt snug, but not so tight that it caused me pain.*

ON THEIR OWN Have students work with partners to write sentences using synonyms for this week's lesson vocabulary words. Partners can trade sentences and identify the context clues that help them find the synonym for each unfamiliar word.

Word Analysis

Review 💿 Syllable Pattern CV/VC

TEACH Write the following sentences on the board. Have students read each one, first quietly to themselves and then aloud as you track the print.

1. The garden had a <u>variety</u> of <u>violet</u> flowers.
2. He wore <u>casual</u> clothes to the <u>recreation</u> center.
3. We had to <u>rearrange</u> all the <u>appliances</u> in the house.
4. The <u>audience</u> listened <u>quietly</u>.
5. The cast did not <u>reenter</u> the <u>theater</u>.

Team Talk Have students identify with a partner which words in the sentences have the CV/VC syllable pattern. Then point to the underlined words at random and have the group read them together.

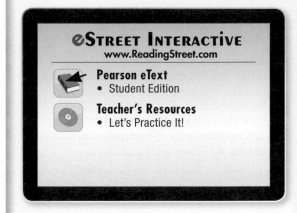

eStreet Interactive
www.ReadingStreet.com

Pearson eText
• Student Edition

Teacher's Resources
• Let's Practice It!

Literary Terms

Review Word Choice

TEACH Have students reread pp. 200–201 of *Suki's Kimono.* Remind students that authors choose words that make their selection more interesting and understandable.

GUIDE PRACTICE Find an example of an interesting word choice on these pages. Discuss with students why the author chose the words she did. Have students point out other examples of interesting words on these pages and discuss.

ON THEIR OWN Have students make a T-chart with the headings *word choice* and *adds to the story.* Ask them to list examples of interesting words from the selection and tell how each one adds to the story.

Compare and Contrast If students have trouble locating signal words that suggest comparing and contrasting, model how to find them. Have students read the sentence aloud and explain what is being compared or contrasted. Have students find another example.

Syllable Pattern CV/VC Supply students with a list of words that have the CV/VC syllable pattern. Have students write each word and circle the CV/VC pattern.

Suki's Kimono **221i**

Common Core State Standards

Literature 10. By the end of the year, read and comprehend literature, including stories, dramas, and poetry, at the high end of the grades 2–3 text complexity band independently and proficiently. **Foundational Skills 4.** Read with sufficient accuracy and fluency to support comprehension. **Also Foundational Skills 4.a., 4.b.**

Plan to Assess Fluency

☑ **This week assess On-Level students.**

☐ **Week 2** Strategic Intervention

☐ **Week 3** On-Level

☐ **Week 4** Strategic Intervention

☐ **Week 5** Assess any students you have not yet checked during this unit.

Set individual goals for students to enable them to reach the year-end goal.

• Current Goal: 102–112 WCPM

• Year-End Goal: 120 WCPM

Assessment

Monitor Progress

FLUENCY Make two copies of the fluency passage on p. 221k. As the student reads the text aloud, mark mistakes on your copy. Also mark where the student is at the end of one minute. To check the student's comprehension of the passage, have him or her retell what was read. To figure words correct per minute (WCPM), subtract the number of mistakes from the total number of words read in one minute.

RATE

Corrective feedback	**If...** students cannot read fluently at a rate of 102–112 WCPM, **then...** make sure they practice with text at their independent reading level. Provide additional fluency practice by pairing nonfluent readers with fluent readers.
	If... students already read at 120 WCPM, **then...** have them read a book of their choice independently.

ELL

If... students need more scaffolding and practice with **Conventions and Writing,** **then...** use the Grammar Transition Lessons on pp. 312–386 in the *ELL Handbook.*

Day 5 SMALL GROUP TIME • Differentiate Reteaching, p. SG•1

OL On-Level	**SI** Strategic Intervention	**A** Advanced
• **Practice** Adjectives and Articles	• **Review** Adjectives and Articles	• **Extend** Adjectives and Articles
• **Reread** *Reading Street Sleuth,* pp. 56–57	• **Reread** *Reading Street Sleuth,* pp. 56–57	• **Reread** *Reading Street Sleuth,* pp. 56–57
		• **Communicate** Inquiry Project

Name _____

Cinco de Mayo

"What if I forget the dance, Mama?" Carmen said. She looked 11

at her red cotton dress in the mirror and twirled. Her skirt spun in a 26

graceful circle around her feet. Carmen loved to dance; she didn't love 38

an audience. 40

"You'll remember. You and Manuel are a beautiful dancing duo," 50

Mama said. 52

"Besides," Manuel said, "no one at the festival knows the steps 63

we practiced at the studio. If you make a mistake, smile and keep 76

dancing." 77

Carmen tried to smile. She tried to eat her breakfast cereal, but 89

she was still nervous. They drove to the Cinco de Mayo Festival at the 103

county rodeo grounds. There was a stage across from the stadium. 114

Carmen and Manuel helped their parents unpack the guitar, violin, 124

and audio equipment. Their cousin Maria came to play piano in the 136

family trio. 138

"Carmen, you're as pale as a handkerchief," Maria said. "Are you 149

nervous?" 150

Carmen nodded. 152

"Just think about the rhythm of the music and keeping pace with 164

your brother," Maria said. "The audience won't see a frightened girl. 175

They'll see a graceful *dama*—a young lady—who is proud of her 188

heritage." 189

That afternoon at the performance, Carmen didn't think about the 199

audience or the video cameras. She thought, *This is my family's music.* 211

I am proud to dance with them. 218

MONITOR PROGRESS • Check Fluency

Common Core State Standards

Informational Text 1. Ask and answer questions to demonstrate understanding of a text, referring explicitly to the text as the basis for the answers. **Informational Text 3.** Describe the relationship between a series of historical events, scientific ideas or concepts, or steps in technical procedures in a text, using language that pertains to time, sequence, and cause/effect.

Assessment

Monitor Progress

For a written assessment of Syllable Pattern CV/VC, Compare and Contrast, and Selection Vocabulary, use Weekly Test 21, pp. 121–126.

○ COMPARE AND CONTRAST Use "Cowboy Clothes" on p. 221m to check students' understanding of compare and contrast.

1. Why did cowboys in the Old West wear the clothes they did? (Their clothes were practical and helped them on their jobs.)

2. Compare and contrast the reason cowboys wore boots years ago with the reason people wear them today. (Years ago, cowboys wore boots to keep their feet in the stirrups and slip them out fast, but today people wear cowboy boots because they look great and are comfortable.)

3. Compare and contrast the reasons cowboys wore bandannas years ago with the reasons people wear them today. (Years ago, cowboys wore bandannas to protect their necks and faces from dust on the trails. Today some people wear bandannas for the same reason, but also because they like the look.)

> **Corrective feedback** | **If...** students are unable to answer the comprehension questions,
> **then...** use the Reteach lesson in *First Stop.*

Name _____

Cowboy Clothes

Today, folks wear cowboy clothing because they like the style. In the Old West, a cowboy wasn't worried much about fashion. His clothes were practical and aided him in his job. When a cowboy rode a horse and herded cattle, he was outside all day in all kinds of weather. It was incredibly tough work.

These days, you see big-brimmed cowboy hats on a lot of people. An Old West cowboy wore a big-brimmed hat as protection from sun, rain, and snow. The hat also had a bigger top to help keep his head cool. In addition, his hat could be a tool of sorts. It could be a water scooper, a flag, or even a fan.

Cowboy's boots are popular today. They look great and are comfortable. However, a real cowboy wore them because he sat on a saddle on his horse. A saddle has stirrups, which are big rings for a cowboy's feet. The heels of cowboy boots were designed to help a cowboy keep his feet in the stirrups. The design also let him slip his feet out fast if he were to fall off his horse. That way the horse wouldn't drag the cowboy!

People today wear bandannas around their necks. Some people do this because they like the look. But others wear them for the same reasons that a cowboy did. A bandanna keeps dust and dirt from going down a shirt. A cowboy also used a bandanna to cover his face on dusty trails. We don't see dusty trails much in today's cities!

MONITOR PROGRESS   • **Compare and Contrast**

Common Core State Standards

Speaking/Listening 4. Report on a topic or text, tell a story, or recount an experience with appropriate facts and relevant, descriptive details, speaking clearly at an understandable pace. **Language 1.a.** Explain the function of nouns, pronouns, verbs, adjectives, and adverbs in general and their functions in particular sentences. **Language 2.f.** Use spelling patterns and generalizations (e.g., word families, position-based spellings, syllable patterns, ending rules, meaningful word parts) in writing words.

Research and Inquiry

Step 5 Communicate

PRESENT IDEAS Have students share their inquiry results by giving a brief talk on their research and then reading aloud the informational article they wrote for a cultural newsletter.

SPEAKING Remind students how to be good speakers and how to communicate effectively with their audience.

• Respond to relevant questions with appropriate details.

• Speak clearly and loudly.

• Keep eye contact with audience members.

LISTENING Review with students these tips for being a good listener.

• Wait until the speaker has finished before raising your hand to ask a relevant question or make a comment.

• Be polite, even if you disagree.

LISTEN TO IDEAS Have students listen attentively to the various presentations. Have them make pertinent comments, closely related to the topic.

Spelling Test

Syllable Pattern CV/VC

To administer the spelling test, refer to the directions, words, and sentences on p. 195c.

Conventions

Adjectives and Articles

MORE PRACTICE Remind students that an adjective describes a person, place, or thing. *A, and,* and *the* are special adjectives called *articles*. *A* and *an* are used with singular nouns. *A* is used with nouns that begin with a consonant sound, while *an* is used with nouns that begin with a vowel sound. *The* is used with both singular and plural nouns.

GUIDE PRACTICE Have students in groups of four take turns describing unusual clothing they have worn or seen. Have students in each group choose the most unusual clothing to share with the class.

> I saw <u>article</u> <u>noun</u> wearing <u>article</u> <u>adjective</u> <u>noun</u>.
>
> (e.g., I saw <u>a dog</u> wearing <u>a pink tutu</u>.)

ON THEIR OWN Write the sentences below. Have students look back in *Suki's Kimono* to find the correct adjectives and articles to fill in the blanks. Sentence number 5 does not need articles. Students should complete *Let's Practice It!* p. 298 on the *Teacher Resources DVD-ROM.*

1. At _____ _____ festival, Suki ate _____, _____ sōmen noodles. (the street; cold; slippery)

2. Under strings of _____ lanterns, Suki joined her obāchan in _____ _____ dance. (paper; a circle)

3. Suki's kimono had _____ _____ _____obi, or belt. (a golden yellow)

4. _____ _____ class clapped after Suki's dance. (The whole)

5. No one noticed Mari's _____ sweater or Yumi's _____ shoes. (new; cool)

Daily Fix-It

9. Polly will creat a salad from spain. *(create; Spain)*

10. The students will enjoy they're meal from around the world. *(their; world)*

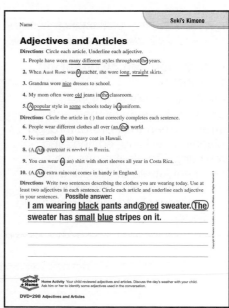

Let's Practice It! TR DVD•298

Writing 5. With guidance and support from peers and adults, develop and strengthen writing as needed by planning, revising, and editing. **Language 1.** Demonstrate command of the conventions of standard English grammar and usage when writing or speaking. **Language 2.** Demonstrate command of the conventions of standard English capitalization, punctuation, and spelling when writing.

Teacher Note

Writing Self-Evaluation Make copies of the Writing Self-Evaluation Guide on p. 39 of the *Reader's and Writer's Notebook* and hand out to students.

Ⓒ Bridge to Common Core

PRODUCTION AND DISTRIBUTION OF WRITING

Over the course of the week, students have developed and strengthened their drafts through planning, revising, editing, and rewriting. The final drafts are coherent letters to the editor in which the organization and style are appropriate to the purpose and audience.

Writing 🔍 Zoom in on Ⓒ

Letter to the Editor

REVIEW REVISING Remind students that yesterday they revised their letters, with special attention to the language we use when we want to persuade the reader to agree with us. Tell students that today they will proofread their letters.

Mini-Lesson Proofread

Proofread for Adjectives and Articles

■ **Teach** Proofreading is the final stage of writing. When we proofread, we look for errors in format, grammar, and spelling, punctuation, and capitalization. Today we will also check to see if we are using adjectives and articles correctly.

■ **Model** First, we will proofread a paragraph from the letter we read yesterday. Display Writing Transparency 21C. Explain that you will edit for grammar and mechanics first. Make corrections on the transparency. Then identify adjectives and articles in the letter. Change *a school* to *the school* and *cleaner* to *cleanest.* Then add the adjectives *large, bold,* and *bright.* Explain that these adjectives will help the reader imagine the solution. Encourage students to read their letters several times for errors and to add adjectives.

Proofreading Marks			
Take Out	⤶	Uppercase letter	≡
Add	∧	Lowercase letter	/
Period	⊙	New paragraph	¶
Check spelling	◯	Insert quotes	⌄
Insert space	#	Insert apostrophe	⌄

Teachers and parents can teach children that littering is wrong. The city and a school can cooperate to buy trashcans for neighborhoods near schools. Trash containers could be decorated with signs and colors, so students walking to and from school will notice and use them. If the school, parents, and the city work together, then they can make the neighborhood the cleaner neighborhood in the city.

Unit 5 Suki's Kimono   Writing: Proofread **21C**

Writing Transparency 21C, TR DVD

PROOFREAD Display the Proofreading Tips. Ask students to proofread their compositions, using the Proofreading Tips and paying particular attention to adjectives and articles. Circulate around the room answering students' questions. When students have finished editing their own work, have pairs proofread one another's letters to the editor.

Proofreading Tips

✔ Be sure that the letter contains a date, salutation, body, closing, and signature.

✔ Check sentences for an initial capital letter and end punctuation.

✔ Add adjectives to bring the writing to life.

PRESENT Have students incorporate revisions and proofreading edits into their letters to the editor to create a final draft.

Students may either send their letters to the local newspaper, or they may post their letters on your school or class Web site. When students have finished, have them complete the Writing Self-Evaluation Guide.

Routine **Quick Write for Fluency** Team Talk

. **Talk** Pairs discuss reasons a citizen might write a letter to the editor.

.. **Write** Have students write short paragraphs describing what they learned about letters to the editor.

. **Share** Have students exchange, read, and discuss their paragraphs.

Routines Flip Chart

Wrap Up Your Week!

Cultures and Clothing

How does culture influence the clothes we wear?

Think Aloud In *Suki's Kimono* and "Clothes: Bringing Cultures Together," we learned about the clothing in other cultures.

Team Talk Have students recall their Amazing Ideas about cultures and use these ideas to help them demonstrate their understanding of the Question of the Week.

Next Week's Concept
Comparing Cultures

How are cultures alike and different?

Poster Preview Prepare students for next week by using Week 2, ELL Poster 22. Read the Talk-Through to introduce the concept and vocabulary. Ask students to identify and describe actions in the art.

Selection Summary Send home the summary of next week's selection, *I Love Saturdays y domingos,* in English and in students' home languages, if available in the *ELL Handbook.* They can read the summary with family members.

How are cultures alike and different? Tell students that next week they will read about a little girl who spends time with her grandparents.

Preview Next Week

Assessment Checkpoints for the Week

Weekly Assessment

Use pp. 121–126 of *Weekly Tests* to check:

✔ ◉ **Phonics/Word Analysis** Syllable Pattern CV/VC

✔ ◉ **Comprehension** Compare and Contrast

✔ Review **Comprehension** Cause and Effect

✔ **Selection Vocabulary**

cotton	handkerchief	rhythm
festival	paces	snug
graceful	pale	

Weekly Tests

Differentiated Assessment

Advanced

On-Level

Use pp. 121–126 of *Fresh Reads for Fluency and Comprehension* to check:

✔ ◉ **Comprehension** Compare and Contrast

✔ Review **Comprehension** Cause and Effect

✔ **Fluency** Words Correct Per Minute

Strategic Intervention

Fresh Reads for Fluency and Comprehension

Managing Assessment

Use *Assessment Handbook* for:

✔ **Weekly Assessment Blackline Masters for Monitoring Progress**

✔ **Observation Checklists**

✔ **Record-Keeping Forms**

✔ **Portfolio Assessment**

Assessment Handbook

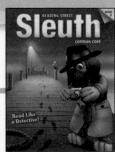

DAY 1 Differentiate Vocabulary

- **Word Knowledge** Amazing Words
- **Read** "Celebrating Children and Tradition"
- **Inquiry** Identify Questions

"Celebrating Children and Tradition,"
pp. 56–57

DAY 2 Differentiate Comprehension

- **Word Knowledge** Selection Vocabulary
- **Access Text** Read *Suki's Kimono*
- **Inquiry** Investigate

DAY 3 Differentiate Close Reading

- **Word Knowledge** Develop Vocabulary
- **Close Reading** Read *Suki's Kimono*
- **Inquiry** Investigate

DAY 4 Differentiate Vocabulary

- **Word Knowledge** Amazing Words
- **Read** "Clothes: Bringing Cultures Together"
- **Inquiry** Organize

DAY 5 Differentiate Reteaching

- **Conventions** Adjectives and
  Articles
- **Reread** "Celebrating Children and
  Tradition" or Leveled Readers
- **Inquiry** Communicate

Teacher Guides and Student pages can be found in the
Leveled Reader Database.

 Place English Language Learners in the groups that correspond to their reading abilities.
If... students need scaffolding and practice,
then... use the ELL Notes on the instructional pages.

ndependent Practice

**Independent
Practice Stations**

See pp. 190h and 190i for
Independent Stations.

**Pearson Trade Book
Library**

See the Leveled Reader
Database for lesson plans
and student pages.

**Reading Street
Digital Path**

Independent Practice
Activities are available in
the Digital Path.

**Independent
Reading**

See p. 190i for
independent reading
suggestions.

© Common Core State Standards

Literature 1. Ask and answer questions to demonstrate understanding of a text, referring explicitly to the text as the basis for the answers. **Foundational Skills 4.** Read with sufficient accuracy and fluency to support comprehension. **Speaking/ Listening 1.** Engage effectively in a range of collaborative discussions (one-on-one, in groups, and teacher-led) with diverse partners on grade 3 topics and texts, building on others' ideas and expressing their own clearly. **Language 4.a.** Use sentence-level context as a clue to the meaning of a word or phrase. **Language 5.** Demonstrate understanding of word relationships and nuances in word meanings.

Independent Reading Options

Trade Book Library

eSTREET INTERACTIVE
www.ReadingStreet.com

Teacher Guides are available on the Leveled Reader Database.

ELL

If... students need more scaffolding and practice with **Vocabulary, then...** use the activities on pp. DI•17–DI•18 in the Teacher Resources section on SuccessNet.

 On-Level

1 Build Word Knowledge
Practice Amazing Words

DEFINE IT Elicit the definition for the word *traditional* from students. Ask: How would you describe something *traditional* to another student? (Possible response: Something *traditional* is part of a country's or group's custom.) Clarify or give a definition when necessary. Continue with the words *fabric* and *scarves*.

Team Talk **TALK ABOUT IT** Have partners internalize meanings. Ask: How can you group the Amazing Words together in a sentence? (Possible response: My beautiful *scarves* are made from the same *traditional fabric*.) Allow time for students to play with the words. Review the concept map with students. Discuss other words they can add to the concept map.

2 Text-Based Comprehension
Read

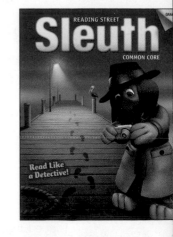

READ ALOUD "Celebrating Children and Tradition" Have partners read "Celebrating Children and Tradition" from *Reading Street Sleuth* on pp. 56–57.

ACCESS TEXT Discuss the Sleuth Work section with students before they work on it. Remind students that they can use these steps with other texts they read.

Gather Evidence Talk together about the importance of kimonos to the Japanese culture. Have partners work together to make a list of evidence from the text that supports this discussion. Invite students to share whether the evidence they found is factual or not.

Ask Questions Talk together about questions that are based on facts and questions that are based on opinions. Discuss the questions students wrote. Have students identify their questions as factual or opinion based.

Make Your Case Have students share the holiday they would like to see celebrated. Remind students that in order to convince others to join in such a celebration, they need to support their idea with convincing reasons.

On-Level

① Build Word Knowledge

Practice Selection Vocabulary

cotton	festival	graceful	handkerchief
paces	pale	rhythm	snug

DEFINE IT Discuss the definition for the word *handkerchief* with students. Ask: How would you describe a *handkerchief* to another student? (Possible response: A *handkerchief* is a square piece of cloth you can use instead of a tissue.) Continue with the remaining words.

Team Talk **TALK ABOUT IT** Have pairs use the selection vocabulary in sentences to internalize meaning. Ask: How can you group the selection vocabulary words together in a sentence? (Possible response: The *handkerchief* was made from a *pale* piece of *cotton*.) Allow time for students to play with the words and then share their sentences.

② Read

Suki's Kimono

If you read *Suki's Kimono* during whole group time, then use the following instruction.

ACCESS TEXT Reread the paragraphs on the bottom of p. 201 and the first two paragraphs on p. 202. Ask questions to check understanding. What does Suki do when she dances? (She tries to copy her grandmother's movements and be as light and graceful as her grandmother and the other women.) How does Suki feel when she hears the drums? (like she'd swallowed thunder; her whole insides quaked and quivered) What does her grandmother find for Suki? Why does she give it to her? (She finds her a handkerchief and tells her it will help her remember their day together.)

Have students identify sections from today's reading that they did not completely understand. Reread them aloud and clarify misunderstandings.

If you are reading *Suki's Kimono* during small group time, then return to pp. 200–205a to guide the reading.

eSTREET INTERACTIVE
www.ReadingStreet.com

Pearson eText
• Student Edition
• Leveled Reader Database
• *Reading Street Sleuth*

More Reading for Group Time

ON-LEVEL

Reviews
• Compare and Contrast
• Visualize
• Selection Vocabulary

Use this suggested Leveled Reader or other text at students' instructional level.

eSTREET INTERACTIVE
www.ReadingStreet.com

Use the Leveled Reader Database for lesson plans and student pages for *Cowboy Slim's Dude Ranch.*

SMALL GROUP TIME

Suki's Kimono **SG•3**

© Common Core State Standards

Informational Text 1. Ask and answer questions to demonstrate understanding of a text, referring explicitly to the text as the basis for the answers. **Language 1.a.** Explain the function of nouns, pronouns, verbs, adjectives, and adverbs in general and their functions in particular sentences. **Language 4.a.** Use sentence-level context as a clue to the meaning of a word or phrase. **Language 5.** Demonstrate understanding of word relationships and nuances in word meanings. **Also Writing 10., Language 5.c.**

On-Level

1 Build Word Knowledge
Develop Vocabulary

REREAD FOR VOCABULARY Reread the first paragraph on p. 207. Introduce: Let's read this paragraph to figure out what *concentrated* means. To help students understand the word *concentrated,* ask questions related to the context, such as: What does Suki do instead of responding to the boys' teasing? Why does Suki focus on sitting up straight? Have students use online sources to find out more information about the word *concentrated.*

2 Read
Suki's Kimono

If you read *Suki's Kimono* during whole group time, then use the following instruction.

CLOSE READING Read pp. 208–209. Have students search through the text for action words. As a class, make a list of Suki's actions in the order they appear. *(took, swayed, hummed, remembered, tried, couldn't remember, made, finished, sat, and wondering)*

Ask: What do these words tell you about Suki? (Suki likes to sing and dance. Also, she is brave and imaginative because she makes up steps when she can't remember them.) How do her classmates act before and after the dance? (At first, they laugh at her. Afterwards, they are silent and watch her carefully.)

If you are reading *Suki's Kimono* during small group time, then return to pp. 206–211a to guide the reading.

ELL

If... students need more scaffolding and practice with the **Main Selection, then...** use the activities on p. DI•22 in the Teacher Resources section on SuccessNet.

OL On-Level

① Build Word Knowledge
Practice Amazing Words

traditional	fret	scarves	fabric	acceptable
inspire	robe	drape	elegant	stylish

Team Talk **LANGUAGE DEVELOPMENT** Have partners practice building more complex sentences. Display a sentence starter and have students add ral phrases or clauses using the Amazing Words. For example: The _____ be _____. (The *elegant* robe was *traditional* / and made / of such *stylish* bric / that it *inspired* people.) Guide students to add at least three phrases or auses per sentence.

② Read
"Clothes: Bringing Cultures Together"

EFORE READING Read aloud e genre information on p. 216 bout expository text. Explain at students will encounter xpository text when they do esearch. Have students preview nd set a purpose for reading. Ask:

What are some other examples of expository text? (encyclopedia articles, most newspaper and magazine articles, many Web sites, and reference books)

How do the arrows on the pictures reflect the idea of the article? (They indicate the early and the modern forms of the item of clothing and also their origin.)

Why are the words in the text in parentheses? (They tell how to pronounce unfamiliar words.)

DURING READING Have students read with you while tracking along with e print. Ask: How does the article explain the name of the Blackfeet tribe? People called them that because they wore moccasins that were dyed black.)

AFTER READING Have students share their reaction to "Clothes: Bringing ultures Together." Ask them to research an item of clothing, such as kimo- os, blue jeans, or neckties, and then write a brief description of its origins.

eStreet Interactive
www.ReadingStreet.com

Pearson eText
• Student Edition

SMALL GROUP TIME

Independent Reading Options

Trade Book Library

eStreet Interactive
www.ReadingStreet.com

Teacher Guides are available on the Leveled Reader Database.

OL On-Level

© Common Core State Standards

Literature 1. Ask and answer questions to demonstrate understanding of a text, referring explicitly to the text as the basis for the answers. **Foundational Skills 4.** Read with sufficient accuracy and fluency to support comprehension. **Writing 7.** Conduct short research projects that build knowledge about a topic. **Speaking/ Listening 1.** Engage effectively in a range of collaborative discussions (one-on-one, in groups, and teacher-led) with diverse partners on grade 3 topics and texts, building on others' ideas and expressing their own clearly. **Language 4.a.** Use sentence-level context as a clue to the meaning of a word or phrase. **Language 5.** Demonstrate understanding of word relationships and nuances in word meanings.

More Reading for Group Time

ON-LEVEL

Reviews
• Compare and Contrast
• Visualize
• Selection Vocabulary

Use this suggested Leveled Reader or other text at students' instructional level.

eSTREET INTERACTIVE
www.ReadingStreet.com

Use the Leveled Reader Database for lesson plans and student pages for *Cowboy Slim's Dude Ranch.*

1 Build Word Knowledge
Practice Adjectives and Articles

IDENTIFY Read aloud the instruction on the bottom of p. 215 to help students understand how to use adjectives and articles, explaining that articles are a special kind of adjective. Have partners reread the model letter to the editor to find examples of how the writer used adjectives and articles. Allow time for students to discuss their examples and correct any misunderstandings.

2 Text-Based Comprehension
Read

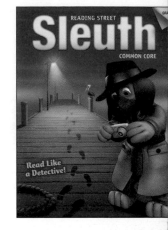

REREAD "Celebrating Children and Tradition" Have partners reread "Celebrating Children and Tradition."

EXTEND UNDERSTANDING Talk together about symbols and traditions of the Japanese culture, such as Children's Day, carp banners, and the kimono. Have students make connections to traditions and symbols that are important to their own families.

PERFORMANCE TASK • Prove It! Have students design a poster that celebrates children around the world. Help students research clothing worn in other nations. The poster should include their wishes for children around the world. Invite students to include a paragraph that tells about the traditional clothing of that nation.

COMMUNICATE Have small groups share their posters with each other. Encourage students to discuss how children may differ or be alike in many nations.

SI Strategic Intervention

① Build Word Knowledge

Reteach Amazing Words

Repeat the definition of the word. We learned that *traditional* means part of a country's or group's custom. Then use the word in a sentence. My mother made a *traditional* Mexican meal for the party.

Team Talk **TALK ABOUT IT** Have partners take turns using the word *traditional* in a sentence. Continue this routine to practice the Amazing Words *fabric* and *scarves*. Review the concept map with students. Discuss other words they can add to the concept map.

> **Corrective feedback** | **If...** students need more practice with the Amazing Words, **then...** use visuals from the Student Edition or online sources to clarify meaning.

② Text-Based Comprehension

Read

REREAD "Celebrating Children and Tradition" Have students track the print as you read "Celebrating Children and Tradition" from *Reading Street Sleuth* on pp. 56–57.

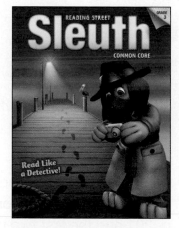

ACCESS TEXT Discuss the Sleuth Work section with students and provide support as needed as they work on it. Remind students that they can use these steps with other texts they read.

Gather Evidence Discuss the importance of kimonos to the Japanese culture. Together, make a list of evidence from the text that supports this discussion. Invite students to talk about whether the evidence is based on facts or opinions.

Ask Questions Have students work with a partner to write several questions. As students share their questions, have them identify their questions as factual or opinion based.

Make Your Case Talk together about holiday ideas that might be celebrated in your community. Have students work with a partner to write about a holiday they would like to see celebrated. Remind students that in order to convince others to join in such a celebration, they need to support their idea with convincing reasons.

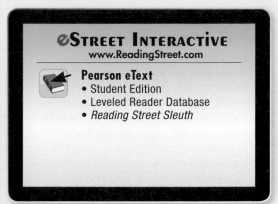

eSTREET INTERACTIVE
www.ReadingStreet.com

Pearson eText
• Student Edition
• Leveled Reader Database
• *Reading Street Sleuth*

SMALL GROUP TIME

More Reading for Group Time

CONCEPT LITERACY
Practice
Concept Words

BELOW-LEVEL
Reviews
• Compare and Contrast
• Visualize
• Selection Vocabulary

Use these suggested Leveled Readers or other text at students' instructional level.

eSTREET INTERACTIVE
www.ReadingStreet.com

Use the Leveled Reader Database for lesson plans and student pages for *Kiko's Kimono* and *A Tea Party with Obâchan*.

SI Strategic Intervention

Common Core State Standards

Literature 1. Ask and answer questions to demonstrate understanding of a text, referring explicitly to the text as the basis for the answers. **Literature 7.** Explain how specific aspects of a text's illustrations contribute to what is conveyed by the words in a story (e.g., create mood, emphasize aspects of a character or setting). **Language 4.a.** Use sentence-level context as a clue to the meaning of a word or phrase. **Language 5.** Demonstrate understanding of word relationships and nuances in word meanings. **Also Language 5.c.**

1 Build Word Knowledge
Reteach Selection Vocabulary

DEFINE IT Describe a *festival* to a friend. Give a definition when necessary. Restate the word in student-friendly terms and clarify meaning with a visual. A *festival* is a celebration, often of cultural events. Page 201 shows a street festival that celebrates traditional Japanese culture.

cotton	festival	graceful
handkerchief	paces	pale
rhythm	snug	

Team Talk **TALK ABOUT IT** Have you ever been to a festival? Turn and tal to your partner about this. Allow time for students to discuss. Ask for examples. Rephrase students' examples for usage when necessary or to correct misunderstandings. Continue with the remaining words.

Corrective feedback | **If...** students need more practice with selection vocabulary, **then...** use the *Envision It! Pictured Vocabulary Cards.*

2 Read
Suki's Kimono

If you read *Suki's Kimono* during whole group time, then use the instruction below.

ACCESS TEXT Reread the paragraphs on the bottom of p. 201 and the first two paragraphs on p. 202. Ask questions to check understanding. Who is Suki's obāchan? (her grandmother) What does she give Suki? Where does she take Suki? (a kimono; to a Japanese festival) What does Suki try to do when she dances? (be graceful like her grandmother and the other women) Why does Suki's grandmother give her a handkerchief? (She wants Suki to remember thei day together.)

Have students identify sections they did not understand. Reread them aloud. Clarify the meaning of each section to build understanding.

If you are reading *Suki's Kimono* during small group time, then return to pp. 200–205a to guide the reading.

Independent Reading Options

Trade Book Library

eSTREET INTERACTIVE
www.ReadingStreet.com

Teacher Guides are available on the Leveled Reader Database.

SI Strategic Intervention

1 Build Word Knowledge

Develop Vocabulary

REREAD FOR VOCABULARY Reread the first paragraph on p. 207. Let's read this paragraph to figure out what *concentrated* means. To help students understand the word *concentrated,* ask questions related to the context, such as: What is Suki doing at her desk? How does she feel? What is she focusing on?

| Corrective feedback | **If...** students have difficulty understanding the word *concentrated,* **then...** lead students in additional class discussion of the word. |

2 Read

Suki's Kimono

If you read *Suki's Kimono* during whole group time, then use the instruction below.

CLOSE READING Read pp. 208–209. Have students search through the text for action words. As a class, make a list of Suki's actions in the order they appear. *(took, swayed, hummed, remembered, tried, couldn't remember, made, finished, sat, wondering)*

Use the action words to retell what happened in this part of the story. (Suki took a few dance steps and then swayed as she hummed the music she remembered from the festival. She tried to remember the steps. When she couldn't remember, she made up new steps. When she finished her dance, she sat down, wondering why the room was so quiet and if she was in trouble.)

If you are reading *Suki's Kimono* during small group time, then return to pp. 206–211a to guide the reading.

eSTREET INTERACTIVE
www.ReadingStreet.com

Pearson eText
• Student Edition

ELL

If... students need more scaffolding and practice with the **Main Selection, then...** use the activities on p. DI•22 in the Teacher Resources section on SuccessNet.

Common Core State Standards

Informational Text 1. Ask and answer questions to demonstrate understanding of a text, referring explicitly to the text as the basis for the answers. **Foundational Skills 4.** Read with sufficient accuracy and fluency to support comprehension. **Writing 7.** Conduct short research projects that build knowledge about a topic. **Language 4.a.** Use sentence-level context as a clue to the meaning of a word or phrase. **Language 5.** Demonstrate understanding of word relationships and nuances in word meanings. **Also Writing 10., Language 5.c.**

SI Strategic Intervention

① Build Word Knowledge
Review Amazing Words

traditional	fret	scarves	fabric	acceptable
inspire	robe	drape	elegant	stylish

Team Talk **LANGUAGE DEVELOPMENT** Have partners practice building more complex sentences. Display a sentence starter and have students add oral phrases or clauses using the Amazing Words.

Corrective feedback | **If...** students have difficulty using the Amazing Words orally, **then...** review the meaning of each of the words.

② Read
"Clothes: Bringing Cultures Together"

BEFORE READING Read aloud the genre information on p. 216 about expository text. Expository text gives you facts and details about a real-life topic. You will find examples of expository text in news magazines and reference books. Have students scan the pages, noting the map and photographs. How can these photographs help you as you read? (They help the reader picture what the article describes.) How does the caption help you understand the picture? (It tells what the picture shows and may add some important details.)

DURING READING Read the article aloud while students track the print. Pause to discuss the captions and how they explain the past and present clothing shown in the pictures.

AFTER READING Have students share their reactions to the selection. Then guide them through the Reading Across Texts and Writing Across Texts activities. Look closely at the first picture of Suki wearing her kimono. How is her kimono special?

 ELL

If... students need more scaffolding and practice with Amazing Words, **then...** use the Routine on pp. xxxvi–xxxvii in the *ELL Handbook*.

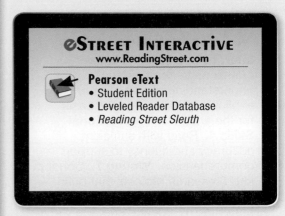

eStreet Interactive
www.ReadingStreet.com

Pearson eText
• Student Edition
• Leveled Reader Database
• *Reading Street Sleuth*

SI **Strategic Intervention**

① Build Word Knowledge
Review Adjectives and Articles

IDENTIFY Read aloud the instruction on the bottom of p. 215 to help students review how to use adjectives and articles. Have partners reread the model letter to the editor on p. 215 to find examples of how the writer used adjectives and articles. Allow time for students to discuss their examples and correct any misunderstandings.

② Text-Based Comprehension
Read

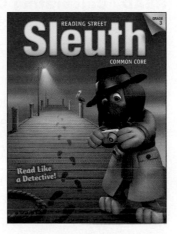

REREAD "Celebrating Children and Tradition" Have partners reread "Celebrating Children and Tradition," with partners alternating paragraphs.

EXTEND UNDERSTANDING Talk together about the Japanese holiday Children's Day. Have students relate how they would feel if the United States celebrated this type of holiday.

PERFORMANCE TASK • Prove It! Have students design a poster that celebrates children around the world. Help students research clothing worn in other nations. The poster should include their wishes for children around the world. Invite students to work with a partner to create their posters.

COMMUNICATE Have pairs share their posters with other pairs. Encourage students to restate the wishes on each poster and make connections to the wishes Japanese parents have for their children.

More Reading for Group Time

CONCEPT LITERACY
Practice
Concept Words

BELOW-LEVEL
Reviews
• Compare and Contrast
• Visualize
• Selection Vocabulary

Use these suggested Leveled Readers or other text at students' instructional level.

eStreet Interactive
www.ReadingStreet.com

Use the Leveled Reader Database for lesson plans and student pages for *Kiko's Kimono* and *A Tea Party with Obâchan.*

SMALL GROUP TIME

Advanced

1 Build Word Knowledge

Extend Amazing Words

Team Talk Have partners define *traditional*. Discuss synonyms and uses for *traditional*. Continue with *fabric* and *scarves*. Have students use all three words in a sentence.

2 Text-Based Comprehension

Read

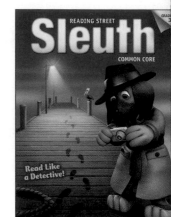

READ "Celebrating Children and Tradition" Have students read "Celebrating Children and Tradition" from *Reading Street Sleuth* on pp. 56–57.

ACCESS TEXT Discuss the Sleuth Work section with students before they work on it. Remind students that they can use these steps with other texts they read.

Gather Evidence Have students revisit the text and make a list of evidence that supports the importance of wearing kimonos. Invite students to share whether the evidence they found is factual or not.

Ask Questions Have students share the questions they wrote, identifying them as based on facts or opinions. Invite discussion about why students asked the questions they asked.

Make Your Case Have students write a paragraph or two that describes the holiday and the clothing. Remind them to include convincing reasons in their paragraphs so as to encourage others to support their holiday idea.

3 Inquiry: Extend Concepts

IDENTIFY QUESTIONS Have students think of questions they have about certain cultures' traditional clothing. Have them use their questions to research the clothing and create a poster or digital presentation of the clothing that includes callouts explaining what each item represents, when it is worn, and what it is made of. Throughout the week, they will gather information. On Day 5, they will present what they have learned.

A Advanced

Build Word Knowledge

Extend Selection Vocabulary

Team Talk Have partners use the selection vocabulary in sentences to internalize their meanings. Have students use as many of the words as they can while making sure the sentence is grammatically correct. (Possible response: After standing in the sun at the *festival,* she used her *cotton handkerchief* to wipe her *pale* brow.) Continue with additional selection vocabulary words.

cotton	festival	graceful
handkerchief	paces	pale
rhythm	snug	

Read

Suki's Kimono

If you read *Suki's Kimono* during whole group time, then use the instruction below.

ACCESS TEXT Reread the paragraphs on the bottom of p. 201 and the first two paragraphs on p. 202. Discuss comparisons in the paragraphs. (Comparison: Suki tried to make her dancing as light and graceful as her grandmother's; Suki saw other women and children dressed in kimonos like her; her insides felt like she had swallowed a ball of thunder.) Ask: How do these comparisons help you understand the story? (These comparisons helped me understand how Suki feels and what she sees at the festival. It also helps me understand what she is like.)

If you are reading *Suki's Kimono* during small group time, then return to p. 198–205a to guide the reading.

Inquiry: Extend Concepts

INVESTIGATE Encourage students to use materials at their independent reading levels or student-friendly search engines to identify relevant and credible sites to gather information about traditional clothing. Have students consider how they will present their information.

eStreet Interactive
www.ReadingStreet.com

Pearson eText
• Student Edition
• Leveled Reader Database
• *Reading Street Sleuth*

More Reading for Group Time

ADVANCED

Reviews
• Compare and Contrast
• Visualize

Use this suggested Leveled Reader or other text at students' instructional level.

eStreet Interactive
www.ReadingStreet.com

Use the Leveled Reader Database for lesson plans and student pages for *His Favorite Sweatshirt.*

SMALL GROUP TIME

Common Core State Standards

Literature 1. Ask and answer questions to demonstrate understanding of a text, referring explicitly to the text as the basis for the answers. **Writing 7.** Conduct short research projects that build knowledge about a topic. **Language 4.a.** Use sentence-level context as a clue to the meaning of a word or phrase. **Language 5.** Demonstrate understanding of word relationships and nuances in word meanings. **Also Informational Text 1.**

Independent Reading Options

Trade Book Library

eSTREET INTERACTIVE
www.ReadingStreet.com

Teacher Guides are available on the Leveled Reader Database.

ELL

If... students need more scaffolding and practice with the **Main Selection, then...** use the activities on p. DI•22 in the Teacher Resources section on SuccessNet.

A Advanced

1 Build Word Knowledge
Develop Vocabulary

REREAD FOR VOCABULARY Reread the last paragraph on p. 207. Let's read this paragraph to figure out what *geta* means. Discuss meaning and context—as well as the illustration—with students.

2 Read
Suki's Kimono

If you read *Suki's Kimono* during whole group time, then use the instruction below.

CLOSE READING Read pp. 208–209. Have students create a T-chart with the heads **Action Words** and **Sensory Words.** Have students search through the text to identify references to actions and write them in the order they occur. Then students should find words that appeal to the senses.

Action Words	Sensory Words
took	swayed
swayed	fresh-cut grass
hummed	tickled
remembered	stamped
tried	clapped
made	quiet
finished	
wondered	

Ask: What do you notice about the author's language? (The words are vivid and interesting.) How does the author's use of vivid or strong language help you as you read the story? (The language helps me visualize the story and imagine Suki's actions and memories.)

If you are reading *Suki's Kimono* during small group time, then return to pp. 206–211a to guide the reading.

3 Inquiry: Extend Concepts

INVESTIGATE Provide time for students to investigate their topics in books or online. If necessary, help them locate information that is focused on their topics.

Advanced

eSTREET INTERACTIVE
www.ReadingStreet.com

Pearson eText
• Student Edition

1 Build Word Knowledge

Extend Amazing Words and Selection Vocabulary

traditional	fret	scarves	cotton	festival	graceful
fabric	acceptable	inspire	handkerchief	paces	pale
robe	drape	elegant	rhythm	snug	
stylish					

Team Talk Have partners practice building more complex sentences. Display sentence starter and have students add oral phrases or clauses using the Amazing Words and the selection vocabulary.

2 Read

"Clothes: Bringing Cultures Together"

BEFORE READING Read aloud the panel information on expository text on pp. 216–219. Have students use the text features to set a purpose for reading. Then have students read "Clothes: Bringing Cultures Together" on their own.

DURING READING Have students read the selection. Encourage them to think critically and creatively. What generalization could you make about why ponchos, moccasins, and berets became part of modern American fashion? (Americans liked the way they looked and thought they were comfortable or useful.)

AFTER READING Have students discuss Reading Across Texts. Then have them do Writing Across Texts independently.

3 Inquiry: Extend Concepts

ORGANIZE INFORMATION Provide time for students to organize their information into a format that will effectively communicate their findings to their audience. Provide any necessary materials, such as posterboard, markers and other supplies, or computer time.

SMALL GROUP TIME

Independent Reading Options

Trade Book Library

eSTREET INTERACTIVE
www.ReadingStreet.com

Teacher Guides are available on the Leveled Reader Database.

A Advanced

Common Core State Standards

Literature 1. Ask and answer questions to demonstrate understanding of a text, referring explicitly to the text as the basis for the answers. **Foundational Skills 4.** Read with sufficient accuracy and fluency to support comprehension. **Writing 7.** Conduct short research projects that build knowledge about a topic. **Speaking/Listening 4.** Report on a topic or text, tell a story, or recount an experience with appropriate facts and relevant, descriptive details, speaking clearly at an understandable pace. **Language 4.a.** Use sentence-level context as a clue to the meaning of a word or phrase. **Language 5.** Demonstrate understanding of word relationships and nuances in word meanings.

More Reading for Group Time

ADVANCED

Reviews
• Compare and Contrast
• Visualize

Use this suggested Leveled Reader or other text at students' instructional level.

eStreet Interactive
www.ReadingStreet.com

Use the Leveled Reader Database for lesson plans and student pages for *His Favorite Sweatshirt*.

❶ Build Word Knowledge
Extend Adjectives and Articles

IDENTIFY AND EXTEND Read aloud the instruction on the bottom of p. 215 and have students discuss how to use adjectives and articles. Encourage partners to reread the model letter to the editor to find examples of how the writer used adjectives and articles. Then have students write single-paragraph letters to the editor using rich adjectives. Allow time for students to discuss their work and correct any misunderstandings.

❷ Text-Based Comprehension
Read

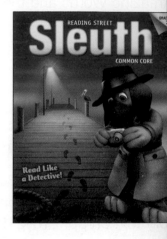

REREAD "Celebrating Children and Tradition" Have partners reread the selection. Then have partners discuss how they might have felt to be the narrator attending an event that included unfamiliar traditions.

EXTEND UNDERSTANDING Talk together about traditional celebrations students have participated in. These celebrations might have been through school assemblies, family gatherings, or community events. Invite students to share their thoughts on the importance of these traditional celebrations.

PERFORMANCE TASK • Prove It! Have students design a poster that celebrates children around the world. Help students research clothing worn in other nations. The poster should include their wishes for children around the world. Encourage students to include a map of the nation they have researched so others can pinpoint its location.

COMMUNICATE Have students share their posters in small groups. Invite discussion about what students learned from each others' posters.

❸ Inquiry: Extend Concepts

COMMUNICATE Have students share their inquiry projects on traditional clothing with the rest of the class. Provide the following tips for presenting.

• Point to your visuals as you describe the clothing.

• Ask questions to make sure your audience understands the information.

• Speak slowly and pause briefly after key points.

This Week's Target Skills and Strategies

Target Skills and Strategies	© Common Core State Standards for English Language Arts	Indiana Academic Standards for English Language Arts
Phonics and Spelling Skill: Homophones	**CCSS Foundational Skills 4.c.** Use context to confirm or self-correct word recognition and understanding, rereading as necessary. **(Also CCSS Language 2.e.)**	**IN 3.1** Students understand the basic features of words. They select letter patterns and know how to translate them into spoken language using phonics, syllables, word parts, and context. They apply this knowledge to achieve fluent oral and silent reading.
Text-Based Comprehension Skill: Main Idea and Details	**CCSS Informational Text 2.** Determine the main idea of a text; recount the key details and explain how they support the main idea.	**IN 3.2.5** Distinguish the main idea and supporting details in expository (informational) text.
Strategy: Inferring	**CCSS Informational Text 1.** Ask and answer questions to demonstrate understanding of a text, referring explicitly to the text as the basis for the answers.	**IN 3.2.2** Ask questions and support answers by connecting prior knowledge with literal information from the text. **(Also IN 3.2.3)**
Vocabulary Skill: Homophones Strategy: Context Clues	**CCSS Language 4.** Determine or clarify the meaning of unknown and multiple-meaning words and phrases based on *grade 3* reading and content, choosing flexibly from a range of strategies. **(Also CCSS Language 4.a.)**	**IN 3.1.6** Use sentence and word context to find the meaning of unknown words.
Fluency Skill: Accuracy	**CCSS Foundational Skills 4.b.** Read on-level prose and poetry orally with accuracy, appropriate rate, and expression on successive readings.	**IN 3.1.3** Read aloud grade-level-appropriate literary and informational texts fluently and accurately and with appropriate timing, change in voice, and expression.
Listening and Speaking Drama	**CCSS Speaking/Listening 4.** Report on a topic or text, tell a story, or recount an experience with appropriate facts and relevant, descriptive details, speaking clearly at an understandable pace.	The Indiana Academic Standards for Listening and Speaking are not currently assessed on ISTEP+ assessments. Educators and students should implement the Common Core Standards for Speaking and Listening as soon as possible.
Six-Trait Writing Trait of the Week: Conventions	**CCSS Writing 3.** Write narratives to develop real or imagined experiences or events using effective technique, descriptive details, and clear event sequences. **(Also CCSS Language 1., CCSS Language 1.e.)**	**IN 3.5.1** Write narratives.
Writing Personal Narrative	**CCSS Writing 3.** Write narratives to develop real or imagined experiences or events using effective technique, descriptive details, and clear event sequences. **(Also CCSS Writing 3.a.)**	**IN 3.5.1** Write narratives.
Conventions Skill: Comparative and Superlative Adjectives	**CCSS Language 1.g.** Form and use comparative and superlative adjectives and adverbs, and choose between them depending on what is to be modified.	**IN 3.6.5** Identify and correctly use pronouns, adjectives, compound nouns, and articles in writing.

This Week's Cross-Curricular Standards and Resources

Cross-Curricular Indiana Academic Standards for Social Studies

Social Studies
IN 3.3.9 Identify factors that make the region unique, including cultural diversity, industry, the arts and architecture.

Reading Street Sleuth

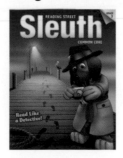

A Visit to Vietnam
pp. 58–59

Follow the path to close reading
using the Super Sleuth tips:

- Gather Evidence
- Ask Questions
- Make Your Case
- Prove it!

More Reading in Science and Social Studies

Concept Literacy

Below Level

On Level

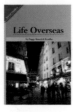
Advanced

ELL

ELD

ISBN-13: 978-0-328-73391-0   ISBN-10: 0-328-73391-1

Your 90-Minute Reading Block

	Whole Group	Formative Assessment	Small Group OL On Level SI Strategic Intervention A Advanced	Daily Independent Options
		How do I make my small groups flexible?	What are my other students reading and learning every day in Small Groups?	What do my other students do when I lead Small Groups?
DAY 1	**Content Knowledge** Build Oral Language/Vocabulary **Phonics/Word Analysis** **Read Decodable Reader** **Text-Based Comprehension** **Selection Vocabulary** **Research and Inquiry** Step 1–Identify and Focus Topic **Spelling Pretest** Connect to Phonics/Word Analysis	**Monitor Progress** Check Oral Vocabulary	**Differentiate Vocabulary** **Build Word Knowledge** OL Practice Amazing Words SI Reteach Amazing Words A Extend Amazing Words OL SI A Text-Based Comprehension **Read** *Reading Street Sleuth*, pp. 58–59 or Leveled Readers A Inquiry Project ELL Access Vocabulary	⭐ **Independent Reading** © Suggestions for this week's independent reading: • Informational texts on last week's social studies topic: How culture influences the clothes we wear. • A high-quality magazine article about clothing in several cultures. • An information-rich Web site about clothing in different cultures.
DAY 2	**Content Knowledge** Build Oral Language/Vocabulary **Phonics/Word Analysis** **Vocabulary Skill** **Text-Based Comprehension** **Read** Main Selection, using Access Text Notes **Research and Inquiry** Step 2–Navigate/Search **Spelling** Connect to Phonics/Word Analysis	**Monitor Progress** Formative Assessment: Check Word Reading	**Differentiate Comprehension** **Build Word Knowledge** OL Practice Selection Vocabulary SI Reteach Selection Vocabulary A Extend Selection Vocabulary OL SI A Access Text **Read** *I Love Saturdays y domingos* A Inquiry Project ELL Access Comprehension Skill	**Book Talk** Foster critical reading and discussion skills through independent and close reading. Students should focus on discussing one or more of the following: • Key Ideas and Details • Craft and Structure • Integration of Ideas
DAY 3	**Content Knowledge** Build Oral Language/Vocabulary **Phonics/Word Analysis** **Read Decodable Passage** **Text-Based Comprehension** **Read** Main Selection, using Close Reading Notes **Fluency** **Research and Inquiry** Step 3–Analyze Information **Spelling** Connect to Phonics/Word Analysis	**Monitor Progress** Check Retelling	**Differentiate Close Reading** OL SI **Reread to Develop Vocabulary** A **Reread to Extend Vocabulary** OL SI A **Close Reading** **Read** *I Love Saturdays y domingos* A Inquiry Project ELL Access Main Selection	**Pearson eText** • Student Edition • Decodable Readers • Leveled Readers
DAY 4	**Content Knowledge** Build Oral Language/Vocabulary **Phonics/Word Analysis** **Read Decodable Passage** **Read Content Area Paired Selection with Genre Focus** **Let's Learn It!** Vocabulary/Fluency/Listening and Speaking **Research and Inquiry** Step 4–Synthesize **Spelling** Connect to Phonics/Word Analysis	**Monitor Progress** Check Fluency	**Differentiate Vocabulary** **Build Word Knowledge** OL Develop Language Using Amazing Words SI Review/Discuss Amazing Words A Extend Amazing Words and Selection Vocabulary OL SI A Text-Based Comprehension **Read** "Communities Celebrate Cultures" A Inquiry Project ELL Access Amazing Words	**Trade Book Library** **Materials from School or Classroom Library** **Independent Stations** Practice Last Week's Skills ⭐ Focus on these activities when time is limited. **Word Wise** ⭐ **Word Work** ⭐ **Read for Meaning** ⭐ **Let's Write!** **Words to Know** **Get Fluent**
DAY 5	**Content Knowledge** Build Oral Language/Vocabulary **Text-Based Comprehension** **Vocabulary Skill** **Phonics/Word Analysis** **Assessment** Fluency, Comprehension **Research and Inquiry** Step 5–Communicate **Spelling Test** Connect to Phonics/Word Analysis	**Monitor Progress** Formative Assessment: Check Oral Vocabulary **Monitor Progress** Fluency; Comprehension	**Differentiate Reteaching** OL **Practice Comparative and Superlative Adjectives** SI **Review Comparative and Superlative Adjectives** A **Extend Comparative and Superlative Adjectives** OL SI A **Text-Based Comprehension** **Reread** *Reading Street Sleuth*, pp. 58–59 or Leveled Readers A Inquiry Project ELL Access Conventions and Writing	

Assessment Resources

Common Core Weekly Tests, pp. 127–132

Common Core Fresh Reads for Fluency and Comprehension, pp. 127–132

Common Core Unit 5 Benchmark Test

Common Core Success Tracker, ExamView, and Online Lesson Planner

Teaching the Common Core State Standards This Week

 The Common Core State Standards for English Language Arts are divided into strands for **Reading** (including **Foundational Skills**), **Writing**, **Speaking and Listening**, and **Language**. The chart below shows some of the content you will teach this week, strand by strand. Turn to this week's 5-Day Planner on pages 222d–222e to see how this content is taught each day.

Reading Strand

- **Phonics/Word Analysis:** Homophones
- **Text-Based Comprehension:** Main Idea and Details; Inferring
- **Fluency:** Accuracy

- **Literary Terms:** Point of View
- **Genre:** Main Selection: Realistic Fiction; Paired Selection: Textbook

Writing Strand

- **Writing Mini-Lesson:** Personal Narrative
- **Trait:** Conventions
- **Look Back and Write:** Text Evidence

Common Core State Standards for English Language Arts

Speaking and Listening Strand

- **Content Knowledge:** Build Oral Language
- **Listening and Speaking:** Drama
- **Research and Inquiry**

Language Strand

- **Oral Vocabulary: Amazing Words** *clan, dwelling, shield, headdress, concentrate, barbeque, belief, chant, procession, settler*
- **Vocabulary:** Homophones; Context Clues
- **Selection Vocabulary:** *circus, nibbling, bouquet, difficult, pier, swallow, soars*

- **Academic Vocabulary:** *comparative adjective, superlative adjective, personal narrative, first person, third person, realistic fiction*
- **Conventions:** Comparative and Superlative Adjectives
- **Spelling:** Homophones

Text-Based Comprehension

Text Complexity Measures

Use the rubric to familiarize yourself with the text complexity of *I Love Saturdays y Domingos*.

Bridge to Complex Knowledge

Quantitative Measures	Lexile	510L
	Average Sentence Length	8.01
	Word Frequency	3.50

Qualitative Measures	Levels of Meaning	identify realistic situations; non-English words and sentences are presented
	Structure	flash-back; use of non-English words and punctuation
	Language Conventionality and Clarity	non-English words; close alignment of images and text
	Theme and Knowledge Demands	non-English words; references to cultural experiences; basic understanding of identifying similarities and patterns in non-English words

Reader and Task Suggestions	**FORMATIVE ASSESSMENT** Based on assessment results, use the **Reader and Task Suggestions** in Access Main Selection to scaffold the selection or support independence for students as they read *I Love Saturdays y Domingos*.

READER AND TASK SUGGESTIONS

Preparing to Read the Text	Leveled Tasks
• Review listening for context clues to determine the meanings of homophones. • Discuss how authors use italic type to focus attention on foreign words. • Remind students that they may need to read more slowly as they encounter unfamiliar words.	• **Language Conventionality and Clarity** If students have difficulty understanding the foreign words and foreign punctuation in the story, remind them to search for context and picture clues as they read. • **Structure** Students may have difficulty understanding what is happening when the main character in the story speaks in Spanish. Have students note similarities and differences between the pictures and words on the top of the page and those on the bottom of the page.

Recommended Placement Generally the qualitative and quantitative measures suggest this text should be placed in the Grade 2–3 text complexity band, which is where both the Common Core State Standards and *Scott Foresman Reading Street* have placed it. Scaffolded support that stresses the use of context clues for the non-English words in the selection will help some students access the content of the story.

Focus on Common Core State Standards ©

Main Selection, pp. 230–245

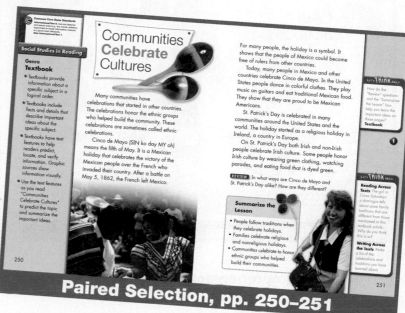

Paired Selection, pp. 250–251

Text-Based Comprehension

Main Idea and Details
CCSS Informational Text 2.

Inferring
CCSS Informational Text 1.

Fluency

Accuracy
CCSS Foundational Skills 4.b.

Writing and Conventions

Trait: Conventions
CCSS Writing 3.,
CCSS Language 1.,
CCSS Language 1.e.

Writing Mini-Lesson: Personal Narrative
CCSS Writing 3., CCSS Writing 3.a.

Conventions: Comparative and Superlative Adjectives
CCSS Language 1.g.

Oral Vocabulary

Amazing Words

clan	barbecue
dwelling	belief
shield	chant
headdress	procession
concentrate	settler

CCSS Language 6.

Selection Vocabulary

Homophones
CCSS Language 4.

Context Clues
CCSS Language 4.,
CCSS Language 4.a

bouquet	nibbling	soars
circus	pier	swallow
difficult		

Phonics and Spelling

Homophones
CCSS Foundational Skills 4.c.,
CCSS Language 2.e.

to	stare
too	bear
two	bare
week	write
weak	right
road	new
rode	knew
stair	

Challenge Words

their	weather
there	whether
they're	

Listening and Speaking

Drama
CCSS Speaking/Listening 4.

Preview Your Week

How are cultures alike and different?

Main Selection, pp. 230–245

Genre: Realistic Fiction

⊙ **Text-Based Comprehension:** Main Idea and Details

⊙ **Vocabulary:** Homophones

Paired Selection, pp. 250–251

Social Studies in Reading
Genre: Textbook

Build Content Knowledge

 Zoom in on ©

Time for SOCIAL STUDIES

KNOWLEDGE GOALS
Students will understand that cultures

- have similarities and differences
- usually value family
- can be tied to countries

THIS WEEK'S CONCEPT MAP
Develop a concept-related graphic organizer like the one below over the course of this week.

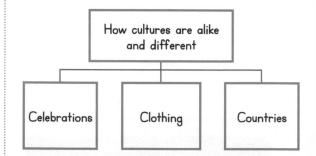

How cultures are alike and different

| Celebrations | Clothing | Countries |

BUILD ORAL VOCABULARY
This week, students will acquire the following academic vocabulary/domain-specific words.

Amazing Words

clan	concentrate	chant
dwelling	barbecue	processio
shield	belief	settler
headdress		

OPTIONAL CONCEPT-BASED READING Use the Digital Path to access readers offering different levels of text complexity.

Concept Literacy

Below-Level

On-Level

Advanced

ELL

ELD

This Week's Digital Resources

eStreet Interactive
www.ReadingStreet.com

Get Ready to Read

 Concept Talk Video   Use this video on the Digital Path to engage interest and introduce the weekly concept of comparing cultures.

 Pearson eText   Read the eText of the Student Edition pages on Pearson SuccessNet for comprehension and fluency support.

 Envision It! Animations   Use this stimulating animation on the Digital Path to explain the target comprehension skill, Main Idea and Details.

Read and Comprehend

 Journal   Use the Word Bank on the Digital Path to have students write sentences using this week's selection vocabulary words.

 Background Building Audio CD   This audio CD provides essential background information about cultures to help students read and comprehend the weekly texts.

 Pearson eText   Read the eText of the main selection, *I Love Saturdays y domingos*, and the paired selection, "Communities Celebrate Cultures," with audio support on Pearson SuccessNet.

 Vocabulary Activities   A variety of interactive vocabulary activities on the Digital Path help students practice selection vocabulary and concept-related words.

 Story Sort   Use the Story Sort Activity on the Digital Path after reading *I Love Saturdays y domingos* to involve students in summarizing.

Language Arts

 Grammar Jammer   Select a lighthearted animation on the Digital Path to provide an engaging grammar lesson that will hold students' attention.

Pearson eText   Find the Student Edition eText of the Let's Write It! and Let's Learn It! pages with audio support on Pearson SuccessNet.

Additional Resources

 Teacher Resources DVD-ROM Use the following resources on the TR DVD or on Pearson SuccessNet throughout the week:

- Amazing Word Cards
- Reader's and Writer's Notebook
- Writing Transparencies
- Daily Fix-It Transparencies
- Scoring Rubrics
- Grammar Transparencies
- ELL Support
- Let's Practice It!
- Graphic Organizers
- Vocabulary Cards

This Week's Skills

Phonics/Word Analysis
⊙ Homophones

Comprehension
⊙ **Skill:** Main Idea and Details
⊙ **Strategy:** Inferring

Language
⊙ **Vocabulary:** Homophones
Conventions: Comparative and Superlative Adjectives

Fluency
Accuracy

Writing
Personal Narrative

5-Day Planner

DAY 1

Get Ready to Read

Content Knowledge 222j
Oral Vocabulary: *clan, dwelling, shield, headdress*

Monitor Progress
Check Oral Vocabulary

Phonics/Word Analysis 224a
⊙ Homophones
READ Decodable Reader 22A
Reread for Fluency

Read and Comprehend

Text-Based Comprehension 226a
⊙ Main Idea and Details
⊙ Inferring

Fluency 226–227
Accuracy

Selection Vocabulary 227a
bouquet, circus, difficult, nibbling, pier, soars, swallow

Language Arts

Research and Inquiry 227b
Identify and Focus Topic

Spelling 227c
Homophones, Pretest

Conventions 227d
Comparative and Superlative Adjectives

Handwriting 227d
Cursive Letters *E* and *O*

Writing 227e
Personal Narrative

DAY 2

Get Ready to Read

Content Knowledge 228a
Oral Vocabulary: *concentrate, barbecue*

Phonics/Word Analysis 228c
⊙ Homophones
Monitor Progress
Check Word Reading

Literary Terms 228d
Point of View

Read and Comprehend

Vocabulary Skill 228e
⊙ Homophones

Fluency 228–229
Accuracy

Text-Based Comprehension 230–231
READ *I Love Saturdays y domingos*
—1st Read

Language Arts

Research and Inquiry 237b
Navigate/Search

Conventions 237c
Comparative and Superlative Adjectives

Spelling 237c
Homophones

Writing 237d
Personal Narrative

DAY 3

Get Ready to Read

Content Knowledge 238a
Oral Vocabulary: *belief, chant*

Word Analysis 238c
⦿ Homophones
Fluent Word Reading
DECODE AND READ
Decodable Practice Passage 22B

Read and Comprehend

Text-Based Comprehension 238e
Check Understanding
READ *I Love Saturdays y domingos*
—2nd Read

> **Monitor Progress**
> Check Retelling

Fluency 247b
Accuracy

Language Arts

Research and Study Skills 247c
Maps

Research and Inquiry 247d
Analyze Information

Conventions 247e
Comparative and Superlative
Adjectives

Spelling 247e
Homophones

Writing 248–249
Personal Narrative

DAY 4

Get Ready to Read

Content Knowledge 250a
Oral Vocabulary: *procession, settler*

Phonics/Word Analysis 250c
Review Syllable Pattern CV/VC
Fluent Word Reading
DECODE AND READ
Decodable Practice Passage 22C

Read and Comprehend

Genre 250g
Textbook
READ "Communities Celebrate
Cultures"—Paired Selection

Fluency 252–253
Accuracy

> **Monitor Progress** Check Fluency

Vocabulary Skill 253a
⦿ Homophones

Listening and Speaking 253a
Drama

Language Arts

Research and Inquiry 253b
Synthesize

Conventions 253c
Comparative and Superlative
Adjectives

Spelling 253c
Homophones

Writing 253d
Personal Narrative

DAY 5

Get Ready to Read

Content Knowledge 253f
Review Oral Vocabulary

> **Monitor Progress**
> Check Oral Vocabulary

Read and Comprehend

Text-Based Comprehension 253h
Review ⦿ Main Idea and Details

Vocabulary Skill 253h
Review ⦿ Homophones

Word Analysis 253i
Review ⦿ Homophones

Literary Terms 253i
Review Point of View

Assessment 253j, 253l

> **Monitor Progress**
> Fluency; Main Idea and Details

Language Arts

Research and Inquiry 253n
Communicate

Spelling 253o
Homophones, Test

Conventions 253o
Comparative and Superlative
Adjectives

Writing 253p
Personal Narrative

Wrap Up Your Week! 253q

Access for All

What do I do in group time?
It's as easy as 1-2-3!

1 TEACHER-LED SMALL GROUPS → **2** INDEPENDENT PRACTICE STATIONS → **3** INDEPENDENT READING

Small Group Time

© Bridge to Common Core

SKILL DEVELOPMENT
- Main Idea and Details
- Inferring
- Homophones

DEEP UNDERSTANDING
This Week's Knowledge Goals
Students will understand that cultures
- have similarities and differences
- usually value family
- can be tied to countries

1 Small Group Lesson Plan

		DAY 1	DAY 2
		Differentiate Vocabulary	Differentiate Comprehension
OL	**On-Level** pp. SG•18–SG•22	**Build Word Knowledge** Practice Amazing Words **Text-Based Comprehension** Read *Reading Street Sleuth*, pp. 58–59 or Leveled Readers	**Build Word Knowledge** Practice Selection Vocabulary **Access Text** Read *I Love Saturdays y domingos*
SI	**Strategic Intervention** pp. SG•23–SG•27	**Build Word Knowledge** Reteach Amazing Words **Text-Based Comprehension** Read *Reading Street Sleuth*, pp. 58–59 or Leveled Readers	**Build Word Knowledge** Reteach Selection Vocabulary **Access Text** Read *I Love Saturdays y domingos*
A	**Advanced** pp. SG•28–SG•32	**Build Word Knowledge** Extend Amazing Words **Text-Based Comprehension** Read *Reading Street Sleuth*, pp. 58–59 or Leveled Readers	**Build Word Knowledge** Extend Selection Vocabulary **Access Text** Read *I Love Saturdays y domingos*
	Independent Inquiry Project	Identify Questions	Investigate
ELL	If... students need more scaffolding and practice with...	**Vocabulary,** then... use the activities on pp. DI•42–DI•43 in the Teacher Resources section on SuccessNet.	**Comprehension Skill,** then... use the activities on p. DI•46 in the Teacher Resources section on SuccessNet.

Build Text-Based Comprehension

I Love Saturdays y domingos

Optional Leveled Readers

   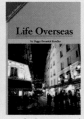  

| Concept Literacy | Below-Level | On-Level | Advanced | ELL | ELD |

Reading Street Sleuth

Provides access to grade-level text for all students

Focuses on finding clues in text through close reading

Builds capacity for complex text

DAY 3	**DAY 4**	**DAY 5**
Differentiate Close Reading	**Differentiate Vocabulary**	**Differentiate Reteaching**
Reread to Develop Vocabulary **Close Reading** Read *I Love Saturdays y domingos*	**Build Word Knowledge** Develop Language Using Amazing Words **Text-Based Comprehension** Read "Communities Celebrate Cultures"	**Practice Comparative and Superlative Adjectives** **Text-Based Comprehension** Reread *Reading Street Sleuth,* pp. 58–59 or Leveled Readers
Reread to Develop Vocabulary **Close Reading** Read *I Love Saturdays y domingos*	**Build Word Knowledge** Review/Discuss Amazing Words **Text-Based Comprehension** Read "Communities Celebrate Cultures"	**Review Comparative and Superlative Adjectives** **Text-Based Comprehension** Reread *Reading Street Sleuth,* pp. 58–59 or Leveled Readers
Reread to Extend Vocabulary **Close Reading** Read *I Love Saturdays y domingos*	**Build Word Knowledge** Extend Amazing Words and Selection Vocabulary **Text-Based Comprehension** Read "Communities Celebrate Cultures"	**Extend Comparative and Superlative Adjectives** **Text-Based Comprehension** Reread *Reading Street Sleuth,* pp. 58–59 or Leveled Readers
Investigate	Organize	Communicate
Main Selection, **then...** use the activities on p. DI•47 in the Teacher Resources section on SuccessNet.	**Amazing Words,** **then...** use the Routine on pp. xxxvi–xxxvii in the *ELL Handbook.*	**Conventions and Writing,** **then...** use the activities on pp. DI•49–DI•50 in the Teacher Resources section on SuccessNet.

2 Independent Stations
Practice Last Week's Skills

 Focus on these activities when time is limited.

WORD WISE

Spell and use words in sentences.

OBJECTIVES

- Spell words with syllable pattern CV/VC.

MATERIALS

- *Word Wise* Flip Chart Activity 22, word cards, paper and pencils

 Letter Tile Drag and Drop

● Students write five words, draw slashes to break them into syllables, and write sentences using the words.

▲ Students write seven words, draw slashes to break them into syllables, and write sentences using the words.

■ Students write ten words, draw slashes to break them into syllables, identify each word's part of speech, and write sentences using the words.

WORD WORK

Identify and pronounce words.

OBJECTIVES

- Identify and pronounce words with syllable pattern CV/VC.

MATERIALS

- *Word Work* Flip Chart Activity 22, teacher-made word cards, paper and pencils

 Letter Tile Drag and Drop

● Students write six words, say each word, and write a one-paragraph fictional story using the words.

▲ Students write eight words, say each word, and write a two-paragraph fictional story using the words.

■ Students write ten words, say each word, and write a fictional story using the words.

LET'S WRITE!

Write to persuade.

OBJECTIVES

- Write a letter to the editor.

MATERIALS

- *Let's Write!* Flip Chart Activity 22, paper and pencils

Grammar Jammer

● Students write a letter to the editor explaining a school or community problem and suggesting a solution.

▲ Students write a letter to the editor explaining in detail a school or community problem and suggesting a solution.

■ Students write a letter to the editor explaining a school or community problem in detail, suggesting possible solutions, and supporting one.

WORDS TO KNOW

Determine word meanings.

OBJECTIVES

- Identify the meanings of synonyms.

MATERIALS

- *Words to Know* Flip Chart Activity 22, teacher-made word cards, thesaurus, paper and pencils

 Vocabulary Activities

● Students write three words, write a synonym for each, and write sentences for the synonym pairs to show how the meanings are similar.

▲ Students write five words, write a synonym for each, and write sentences for the synonym pairs to show how the meanings are similar.

■ Students write seven words, write a synonym for each, and write sentences for the synonym pairs to show how the meanings are similar.

Manage the Stations

Use these management tools to set up and organize your Practice Stations:

Practice Station Flip Charts

Classroom Management Handbook for Differentiated Instruction Practice Stations, p. 40

 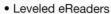

READ FOR MEANING

Read to compare and contrast.

OBJECTIVES

• Identify comparison and contrast.

MATERIALS

• *Read for Meaning* Flip Chart Activity 22, Leveled Readers, paper and pencils

Pearson eText
• Leveled eReaders

Envision It! Animations

⬤ Students read a book and write one sentence comparing characters and one sentence contrasting them.

▲ Students read a book and write two sentences comparing characters and two sentences contrasting them.

■ Students read a book and write a short paragraph comparing characters and a short paragraph contrasting them.

GET FLUENT

Practice fluent reading with partners.

OBJECTIVES

• Read aloud at an appropriate rate.

MATERIALS

• *Get Fluent* Flip Chart Activity 22, Leveled Readers

Pearson eText
• Leveled eReaders

⬤ Partners take turns reading aloud from a Concept Literacy or Below-Level Reader at an appropriate rate and providing feedback.

▲ Partners take turns reading aloud from an On-Level Reader at an appropriate rate and providing feedback.

■ Partners take turns reading aloud from an Advanced Reader at an appropriate rate and providing feedback.

3 Independent Reading ©

Students should select appropriate complex texts to read and write about independently every day before, during, and after school.

Suggestions for this week's independent reading:
• Informational texts on last week's social studies topic: How culture influences the clothes we wear.
• A high-quality magazine article about clothing in several cultures.
• An information-rich Web site about clothing in different cultures.

BOOK TALK Have partners discuss their independent reading for the week. Tell them to refer to their Reading Logs and paraphrase what each selection was about. Then have students focus on discussing one or more of the following:

Key Ideas and Details
• Write the main idea of the text in your own words. What text details support it?

Craft and Structure
• How did the body paragraphs of the text relate to the introduction?

Integration of Ideas
• How did the illustrations help explain the text?
• How is the information in other texts you have read similar or different?

 Pearson eText
• Student Edition
• Decodable Readers
• Leveled Readers

 Trade Book Library

 School or Classroom Library

Materials

- Student Edition
- Reader's and Writer's Notebook
- Decodable Reader

© Bridge to Common Core

INTEGRATION OF KNOWLEDGE/IDEAS
This week, students will read, write, and talk about comparing cultures.

Texts This Week
- "The First Texans"
- "The Best Game"
- "Island Vacation"
- *I Love Saturdays y domingos*
- "Communities Celebrate Cultures"

Social Studies Knowledge Goals
Students will understand that cultures
- have similarities and differences
- usually value family
- can be tied to countries

Street Rhymes!

Some cultures live in dwellings made of mud and bricks.
Others live in houseboats or houses made of sticks.
Some cultures cook pasta, rice, or barbecue.
Others cook seafood. Tell me what you do!

- To introduce this week's concept, read aloud the poem several times and ask students to join you.

Content Knowledge

Comparing Cultures

CONCEPT TALK To further explore the unit concept of Cultures, this week students will read, write, and talk about how cultures are alike and different. Write the Question of the Week on the board, *How are cultures alike and different?*

Build Oral Language

TALK ABOUT COMPARING CULTURES Have students turn to pp. 222–223 in their Student Editions. Look at each of the photos. Then use the prompts to guide discussion and create a concept map.

- What are the people in all the photos doing? **(They are celebrating.)** Many cultures have celebrations. That is one way that cultures are alike. Let's add *Celebrations* to our concept map.
- What is the girl on p. 223 wearing? **(some sort of costume)** Many cultures have costumes or specific clothing that they wear. Let's add *Clothing* to the concept map.
- What are the children holding? **(flags)** There are cultural ties to different countries. Countries have special flags to represent them. Let's add *Countries* to our concept map.
- After discussing the photos, ask: How are cultures alike and different?

Oral Vocabulary

Let's Talk About

Comparing Cultures

- Ask questions about how cultures are alike and different.
- Express and listen to comments about cultural values.
- Pose and answer questions about cultural ties to different countries.

READING STREET ONLINE
CONCEPT TALK VIDEO
www.ReadingStreet.com

You've learned
207
Amazing Words ☆
so far this year!

Student Edition, pp. 222–223

CONNECT TO READING Tell students that this week they will be reading about people from different cultures. Encourage students to add concept-related words to this week's concept map.

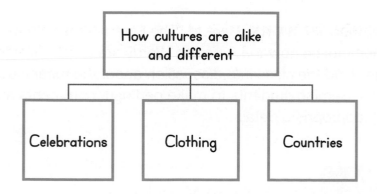

How cultures are alike and different

- Celebrations
- Clothing
- Countries

eSTREET INTERACTIVE
www.ReadingStreet.com

Pearson eText
- Student Edition

Concept Talk Video

ELL

Preteach Concepts Use the Day 1 instruction on ELL Poster 22 to assess and build background knowledge, develop concepts, and build oral vocabulary.

ELL Support Additional ELL support and modified instruction are provided in the *ELL Handbook* and in the ELL Support lessons found on the *Teacher Resources DVD-ROM*.

I Love Saturdays y domingos **222–223**

Ⓒ **Common Core State Standards**

Language 4. Determine or clarify the meaning of unknown and multiple-meaning words and phrases based on grade 3 reading and content, choosing flexibly from a range of strategies. **Language 4.a.** Use sentence-level context as a clue to the meaning of a word or phrase. **Language 6.** Acquire and use accurately grade-appropriate conversational, general academic, and domain-specific words and phrases, including those that signal spatial and temporal relationships (e.g., *After dinner that night we went looking for them*).

Amazing Words

You've learned **2 0 7** words so far.

You'll learn **0 1 0** words this week!

clan	barbecue
dwelling	belief
shield	chant
headdress	procession
concentrate	settler

Content Knowledge

Build Oral Vocabulary

INTRODUCE AMAZING WORDS "The First Texans" on p. 223b is about two Native American tribes. Tell students to listen for this week's Amazing Words—*clan, dwelling, shield,* and *headdress*—as you read the Teacher Read Aloud on p. 223b.

Amazing Words   Robust Vocabulary Routine

1. **Introduce** Write the word *clan* on the board. Have students say the word aloud with you. What context clues does the author give to help us figure out the meaning of *clans*? (the words *or groups*) Supply a student-friendly definition. A *clan* is a group of people who are related by blood or by a common trait.

2. **Demonstrate** Have students answer questions with appropriate detail to demonstrate understanding. Is the word *clan* used correctly in this sentence? We had the *clan* over to watch the football game. Explain.

3. **Apply** Have students apply their understanding by using *clan* in a sentence.

4. **Display the Word** Students can decode the word *clan*. Have them name other words that begin with *cl*.

See p. OV•2 to teach *dwelling, shield,* and *headdress.*

Routines Flip Chart

AMAZING WORDS AT WORK Reread "The First Texans" aloud. As students listen, have them notice how the Amazing Words are used in context. To build oral vocabulary, lead the class in a discussion about the meanings of the Amazing Words. Remind students to make pertinent comments and answer questions with appropriate detail.

 Don't Wait Until Friday **MONITOR PROGRESS** **Check Oral Vocabulary**

During discussion, listen for students' use of Amazing Words.

If... students are unable to use the Amazing Words in discussion,

then... use the Oral Vocabulary Routine in the Routines Flip Chart to demonstrate words in different contexts.

Teacher Read Aloud

MODEL FLUENCY As you read "The First Texans," model accuracy with smooth, fluent reading.

The First Texans

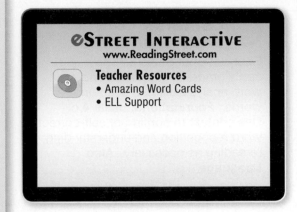

eSTREET INTERACTIVE
www.ReadingStreet.com

Teacher Resources
• Amazing Word Cards
• ELL Support

Many groups of people once lived in the area we now call the state of Texas. Two of these groups were the Caddo Native Americans and the Comanche Native Americans. They lived in different parts of the state and lived in very different ways.

The Caddo people lived in the eastern part of Texas, close to what is now the state of Louisiana. They lived in clans, or groups, near rivers and by the Gulf of Mexico. Each clan had 10 members. They made canoes out of logs so they could travel in the water.

The Comanche people lived further west in the state. They lived far from the coast and therefore could not travel by water. Instead, they used dog sleds to travel over the land. The Comanche people followed the buffalo. They hunted for food, so as the buffalo moved, they moved as well.

The land where the Caddo lived had good rich soil for planting crops. Although they did do some hunting, the Caddo planted crops of corn, beans, sunflowers, and pumpkins. Because the Comanche followed the buffalo herds, they did not plant. They did, however, gather fruits, berries, and nuts. They also ate potatoes that grew wild.

A Comanche dwelling and a Caddo dwelling were different, too, because of the way they lived. The Comanche built their homes out of buffalo skins and wood. Their homes could be easily taken down and moved when the group moved. The Caddo built their homes from the rich soil, and thatched their roofs with grass.

The Comanche hunter and the Caddo hunter both used a bow and arrow for hunting. The Comanche hunter made a shield out of buffalo hides as well. A Comanche man wore a feather headdress when he fought and when he hunted. A Caddo man wore what is called a roach headdress. This type of headdress was made from dyed stiff animal hair that was attached to a bone or to leather in a way that made the hair stand straight up.

The Caddo were well known for their pottery craftsmanship. The Comanche people were well known for their beautiful jewelry and intricate beadwork. They continue these artful traditions today as a way of keeping their customs alive.

Both the Comanche and Caddo Native Americans have passed down stories of their lives in early Texas. Many of the Comanche's stories include buffaloes in them. Many Caddo stories are told through dance. The Caddo used dance for many reasons in their early history, and today many of those same dances are still performed by members of Caddo clans.

Support Listening Comprehension
To increase understanding of the vocabulary heard in the Read Aloud, use visuals to support understanding of words students may not know such as *headdress, dog sleds, intricate beadwork, canoes, buffalo,* and *Native Americans.*

ELL Support for Read Aloud Use the modified Read Aloud on p. DI•44 of the ELL Support lessons on the *Teacher Resources DVD-ROM* to prepare students to listen to "The First Texans."

Common Core State Standards

Foundational Skills 3. Know and apply grade-level phonics and word analysis skills in decoding words. **Foundational Skills 4.c.** Use context to confirm or self-correct word recognition and understanding, rereading as necessary. **Also Language 4.a.**

Skills Trace

Homophones

Introduce U5W2D1

Practice U5W2D3; U5W2D4

Reteach/Review U5W2D5; U5W3D4

Assess/Test Weekly Test U5W2 Benchmark Test U5

KEY: U=Unit W=Week D=Day

Vocabulary Support

You may wish to explain the meanings of these words.

dear loved or especially valued

peace freedom from war

Word Analysis

Teach/Model

Homophones

CONNECT Connect to previously learned digraphs: /ē/ spelled *ee, ea*. Write *screeching* and *easel.* You already can read words like these. Each has the long e sound, but it is spelled differently. Today you'll learn how to read and spell *homophones*—words that sound the same, but have different spellings and meanings.

MODEL Write *meat* and *meet*. How do you pronounce the first word? (/m//ē//t/) How do you pronounce the second word? (/m//ē//t/) Which word makes sense in this sentence? *I'll _____ you in the gym. (meet)* Which word makes sense in this sentence? *We ate _____ for dinner. (meat)* Homophones sound alike, but have different spellings and meanings. When a word that's a homophone doesn't make sense in a sentence, I need to make sure I'm using the correct spelling and meaning for the homophone.

GROUP PRACTICE Continue the process. This time have students read the words with you. Identify the spelling differences in each pair and the different meanings of each word.

piece	through	way	dear
peace	threw	weigh	deer

REVIEW What do you know about reading homophones? When the meaning of a word that's a homophone doesn't make sense in a sentence, make sure you are using the correct spelling and meaning for the homophone.

Guide Practice

MODEL Have students turn to p. 224 in their Student Editions. Each pair of words on this page is a homophone. The first pair of words is *stare/stair*. These words sound the same, but I know they are spelled differently and have different meanings.

GROUP PRACTICE For each word in Words I Can Blend, ask students to read each word part and then read them together.

> **Corrective feedback** **If...** students have difficulty reading a word,
> **then...** model reading the parts and then the whole word, and then ask students to read it with you.

Phonics

Homophones

Common Core State Standards
Foundational Skills 4.c. Use context to
confirm or self-correct word recognition and
understanding, rereading as necessary.

Envision It! Sounds to Know

sun

son

READING STREET ONLINE
SOUND-SPELLING CARDS
www.ReadingStreet.com

Words I Can Blend

stare	stair
rays	raise
chili	chilly

Sentences I Can Read

1. Did you see him stare at me from under the stair?
2. The golden rays of the sun helped raise my spirits.
3. Chili is my favorite food on a chilly day.

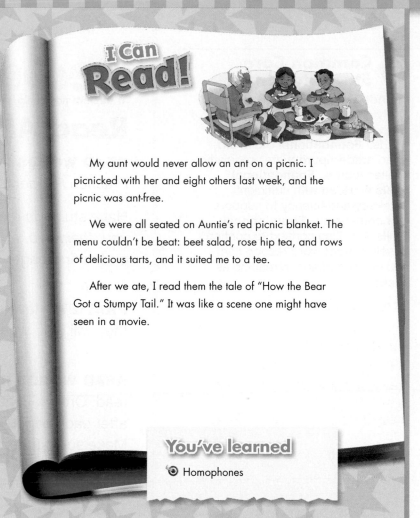

I Can Read!

My aunt would never allow an ant on a picnic. I picnicked with her and eight others last week, and the picnic was ant-free.

We were all seated on Auntie's red picnic blanket. The menu couldn't be beat: beet salad, rose hip tea, and rows of delicious tarts, and it suited me to a tee.

After we ate, I read them the tale of "How the Bear Got a Stumpy Tail." It was like a scene one might have seen in a movie.

You've learned

Homophones

224   225

Student Edition, pp. 224–225

Apply

READ WORDS IN ISOLATION After students can successfully combine the word parts to read the words on p. 224 in their Student Editions, point to words in random order and ask students to read them naturally.

READ WORDS IN CONTEXT Have students read each of the sentences on p. 224. Have them identify words in the sentences that are homophones.

Team Talk Pair students and have them take turns reading each of the sentences aloud.

ON THEIR OWN For additional practice, use *Reader's and Writer's Notebook* p. 327.

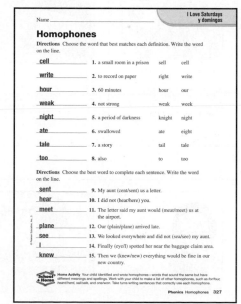

Reader's and Writer's Notebook, p. 327

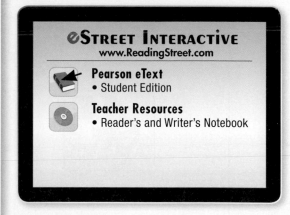

eSTREET INTERACTIVE
www.ReadingStreet.com

Pearson eText
• Student Edition

Teacher Resources
• Reader's and Writer's Notebook

ELL

Homophones Homophones exist in many languages. If possible, use home-language resources to locate and present examples of homophones in students' home languages. In Latin-American Spanish, examples of homophones include *casa (house)/caza (hunt)*, *ciento (one hundred)/siento (I feel)*, and *hola (hello)/ola (wave)*.

I Love Saturdays y domingos **224–225**

Common Core State Standards

Foundational Skills 3. Know and apply grade-level phonics and word analysis skills in decoding words. **Foundational Skills 3.d.** Read grade-appropriate irregularly spelled words. **Foundational Skills 4.** Read with sufficient accuracy and fluency to support comprehension. **Foundational Skills 4.c.** Use context to confirm or self-correct word recognition and understanding, rereading as necessary.

Decodable Reader 22A

If students need help, then...

Read *All Week Long*

READ WORDS IN ISOLATION Have students turn to p. 73 of *Decodable Practice Readers 3.2.* Have students read each word.

Have students read the high-frequency words *said, to, what, do, was, the, of, you, their, two, a, there, were, many, one, would, they, watched, full,* and *sure* on the first page.

PREVIEW Have students read the title and preview the story. Tell them that they will read words that are homophones.

READ WORDS IN CONTEXT Pair students for reading and listen as they read. One student begins. Students read the entire story, switching readers after each page. Partners reread the story. This time the other student begins. Make sure students are monitoring their accuracy when they decode words.

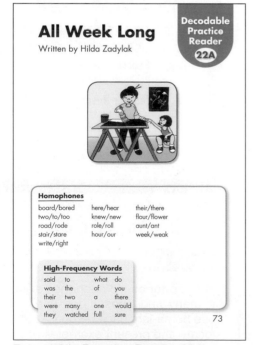

Decodable Practice Reader 22A

eSTREET INTERACTIVE
www.ReadingStreet.com

Pearson eText
• Decodable Reader

Interactive Sound-Spelling Cards

Corrective feedback	**If...** students have difficulty decoding a word, **then...** refer them to the *Sound-Spelling Cards* to identify the word parts. Have them read the word parts individually and then together to say the word.

- What is the new word?
- Is the new word a word you know?
- Does it make sense in the story?

CHECK DECODING AND COMPREHENSION Have students retell the story to include characters, setting, and events. Then have students find words in the story that are homophones. Students should supply *board/bored, here/hear, their/there, two/to/too, knew/new, flour/flower, road/rode, role/roll, aunt/ant, stair/stare, hour/our, week/weak,* and *write/right.*

Reread for Fluency

REREAD DECODABLE READER Have students reread *Decodable Practice Reader 22A* to develop automaticity decoding words with homophones.

Routine   Oral Rereading

1. **Read** Have students read the entire book orally.

2. **Reread** To achieve optimal fluency, students should reread the text three or four times.

3. **Corrective Feedback** Listen as students read. Provide corrective feedback regarding their fluency and decoding.

Routines Flip Chart

Homophones

Beginning Have students write seven pairs of homophones from the *Decodable Practice Reader* on 14 separate index cards. Have students shuffle the cards and match the words that are homophones. Repeat with the remaining six pairs of homophones.

Intermediate After reading, have students identify homophones in the *Decodable Practice Reader* and use the homophones in a single sentence. For example, *Come* here *because I can't* hear *you.*

Advanced After reading the story, have students write a diary entry about one week in their life. What special things do they observe? Challenge students to use 4 pairs of homophones in their writing.

Zoom in on

Common Core State Standards

Informational Text 1. Ask and answer questions to demonstrate understanding of a text, referring explicitly to the text as the basis for the answers. **Informational Text 2.** Determine the main idea of a text; recount the key details and explain how they support the main idea. **Foundational Skills 4.b.** Read on-level prose and poetry orally with accuracy, appropriate rate, and expression on successive readings.

Skills Trace

Main Idea and Details

Introduce U2W1D1; U2W5D1; U5W2D1

Practice U2W1D2; U2W1D3; U2W3D2; U2W3D3; U2W5D2; U2W5D3; U4W2D2; U5W2D2; U5W2D3

Reteach/Review U2W1D5; U2W5D5; U5W2D5

Assess/Test Weekly Tests U2W1; U2W5; U5W2
Benchmark Tests U2; U5
KEY: U=Unit W=Week D=Day

Comprehension Support

Students may also turn to pp. EI•9 and EI•20 to review the skill and strategy if necessary.

Text-Based Comprehension

Main Idea and Details
Inferring

TEACH Remind students of the weekly concept—Comparing Cultures. Have students read "The Best Game" on p. 227.

MODEL A CLOSE READ

Think Aloud Today we're going to read about games the narrator likes to play. Have students follow along as you read the first paragraph of "The Best Game." I know that the topic is games but I'm not sure what the most important idea is yet. I'll have to keep reading. The boy and his sister disagree on which game is best. I can infer what the main idea is: Which game is best? I can infer information after reading facts that the author presents. The author tells how the narrator likes board games and the narrator's sister likes charades. I can infer that the sister would rather play games that involve a lot of moving around and creativity.

TEACH Have students read p. 226. Explain that the skill of identifying the main idea and details and the strategy of inferring are tools they can use to demonstrate an understanding of the text. Review the bulleted items and explanations on p. 226. Then have students use a graphic organizer like the one on p. 226 and identify the topic, main idea, and details from the passage.

GUIDE PRACTICE Have students reread "The Best Game" using the callouts as guides. Then ask volunteers to respond to the questions in the callouts, citing specific examples from the text to support their answers.

Strategy The author is trying to convince me that board games are the best family activity.
Skill Thousands of board games are sold every year; everything you need to play the game is in the box; the rules for playing a game are printed out.
Strategy the sister; it's the game she likes best

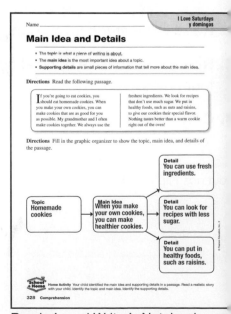

Reader's and Writer's Notebook, p. 328

APPLY Use *Reader's and Writer's Notebook*, p. 328 for additional practice with main idea and details.

Common Core State Standards
Informational Text 1. Ask and answer
questions to demonstrate understanding of
a text, referring explicitly to the text as the
basis for the answers.
Also Informational Text 2.

Envision It! Skill Strategy

Skill

Main Idea and Details

Strategy

Inferring

READING STREET ONLINE
ENVISION IT! ANIMATIONS
www.ReadingStreet.com

Comprehension Skill

Main Idea and Details

- The topic is what a piece of writing is about. The main idea is the most important idea about the topic.

- Details are pieces of information that tell more about the main idea.

- Use what you learned about main idea and details and a graphic organizer like the one below as you read "The Best Game." Then use the organizer to help you write a summary of the text.

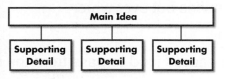

Main Idea

Supporting Detail	Supporting Detail	Supporting Detail

Comprehension Strategy

Inferring

When you infer, you combine your background knowledge with evidence in the text to come up with your own ideas or conclusions about what the author is saying. Active readers infer the ideas, morals, lessons, and themes of a written work.

The Best Game

I think board games are the best family activity. Playing a board game with family or friends is my favorite thing to do on a rainy day. However, my sister doesn't agree. She likes playing charades with a group. To her, board games are boring.

Strategy What do you think the author is trying to persuade you to think or do?

Board games include everything you need right in the box. There is nothing to think up or to make. The rules are printed out. That's the best part! There shouldn't be any arguments among players. Thousands of board games are sold every year. The people who buy them can't all be wrong.

Skill What details does this paragraph include about board games?

On the other hand, my sister says charades is a creative game. Players must think of books, movies, or songs that will stump the other team. Players have a great time using their imagination and acting.

Strategy Who do you think is better at charades—the narrator or the sister? Why do you think so?

Here you have two kinds of games, two people, and two ideas. Which game is best? You decide.

Your Turn!

⏸ **Need a Review?** See the *Envision It! Handbook* for information about main ideas and details and inferring.

▶ **Ready to Try It?** As you read *I Love Saturdays y domingos*, use what you've learned about main ideas and details and inferring to understand the text.

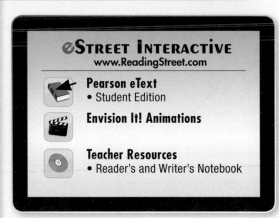

226 / 227

Student Edition, pp. 226–227

Model Fluent Reading

ACCURACY Have students listen as you read paragraph one of "The Best Game" with accuracy. Explain that you will read all the words correctly without leaving out or substituting any words.

Routine | Oral Rereading

1. **Read** Have students read paragraph two of "The Best Game" orally.

2. **Reread** To achieve optimal fluency, students should reread the text three to four times with accuracy.

3. **Corrective Feedback** Have students read aloud without you. Provide feedback about their accuracy and encourage them to read each word correctly.

Routines Flip Chart

eSTREET INTERACTIVE
www.ReadingStreet.com

Pearson eText
- Student Edition

Envision It! Animations

Teacher Resources
- Reader's and Writer's Notebook

ELL

Main Idea and Details Provide oral practice by having students say detail sentences to support this main idea sentence: *You can learn so much at school.* Then write their sentences on the board and read them aloud. Have students evaluate and discuss whether each sentence is a detail that supports the main idea sentence.

I Love Saturdays y domingos **226–227**

Common Core State Standards

Writing 7. Conduct short research projects that build knowledge about a topic. **Writing 8.** Recall information from experiences or gather information from print and digital sources; take brief notes on sources and sort evidence into provided categories. **Speaking/Listening 1.** Engage effectively in a range of collaborative discussions (one-on-one, in groups, and teacher-led) with diverse partners on grade 3 topics and texts, building on others' ideas and expressing their own clearly. **Speaking/ Listening 1.d.** Explain their own ideas and understanding in light of the discussion. **Language 4.** Determine or clarify the meaning of unknown and multiple-meaning words and phrases based on grade 3 reading and content, choosing flexibly from a range of strategies. **Language 6.** Acquire and use accurately grade-appropriate conversational, general academic, and domain-specific words and phrases, including those that signal spatial and temporal relationships (e.g., *After dinner that night we went looking for them*). **Also Writing 10.**

Selection Vocabulary

Use the following routine to introduce this week's tested selection vocabulary.

bouquet a bunch of flowers

circus a show that includes acrobats, clowns, and trained animals

difficult hard to do; not easy to understand

nibbling eating or biting in a quick, gentle way

pier a walkway that stretches out over water

soars rises high in the air

swallow the action that causes food to pass from the mouth to the stomach

SEE IT/SAY IT Write *bouquet.* Scan across the word with your finger as you say it: *bou-quet.*

HEAR IT Use the word in a sentence. My teacher received a *bouquet* of flowers for her birthday.

DEFINE IT Elicit definitions from students. What would you tell your friend the word *bouquet* means? Clarify or give a definition when necessary. Yes, it means "an arrangement of flowers." Restate the word in student-friendly terms. A *bouquet* of flowers is a bunch of flowers.

Team Talk Do people receive *bouquets* of flowers only for holidays or birthdays? On what other occasions do people receive a *bouquet* of flowers? Turn and talk to your partner about this. Be prepared to explain your answer. Allow students time to discuss. Ask for examples. Rephrase their examples for usage when necessary or to correct misunderstandings.

MAKES CONNECTIONS Have students discuss the word. Have you ever seen a *bouquet* of flowers or given someone a *bouquet* of flowers? Turn and talk to your partner about this. Then be prepared to share. Have students share. Rephrase their ideas for usage when necessary or to correct misunderstandings.

RECORD Have students write the word and its meaning.

Continue this routine to introduce the remaining words in this manner.

Corrective feedback | **If...** students are having difficulty understanding, **then...** review the definitions in small groups.

Research and Inquiry

Step 1 | Identify and Focus Topic

TEACH Discuss the Question of the Week: *How are cultures alike and different?* Tell students that they will research a cultural celebration. Tell students to generate their research topics from personal interests. Explain that they will use the information they learn to create a flyer for a cultural celebration. They will present the flyer to the class on Day 5.

Think Aloud

MODEL I'll start by brainstorming a list of questions about cultural festivals and celebrations. First, I'll choose a culture. My grandmother comes from Japan. I don't know that much about her background. Some possible questions could be *What are some Japanese celebrations or festivals? Are there special foods they eat? Are there special clothes they wear?*

GUIDE PRACTICE After students have formulated open-ended inquiry questions, explain that tomorrow they will research their questions using written and online information. Help students identify the key words they will use to guide their search and the types of books and other reference materials they will use as resources.

ON THEIR OWN Have students work individually, in pairs, or in small groups to write an inquiry question. Then have them generate a research plan for gathering relevant information about their question. This can include interviewing people as well as researching written material.

---

eStreet Interactive
www.ReadingStreet.com

Teacher Resources
- Envision It! Pictured Vocabulary Cards
- Tested Vocabulary Cards

21st Century Skills
Internet Guy *Don Leu*

Weekly Inquiry Project

STEP 1	Identify and Focus Topic
STEP 2	Navigate/Search
STEP 3	Analyze Information
STEP 4	Synthesize
STEP 5	Communicate

Access for All

A Advanced
Have students brainstorm a list of people they know who might be able to help them in their research.

ELL

Multilingual Vocabulary Students can apply knowledge of their home languages to acquire new English vocabulary by using Multilingual Vocabulary Lists (*ELL Handbook* pp. 433–444).

ELL

If... students need more scaffolding and practice with **Vocabulary,**

then... use the activities on pp. DI•42–DI•43 in the Teacher Resources section on SuccessNet.

Day 1 | SMALL GROUP TIME • Differentiate Vocabulary, p. SG•17

OL On-Level	**SI Strategic Intervention**	**A Advanced**
• **Practice Vocabulary** Amazing Words	• **Reteach Vocabulary** Amazing Words	• **Extend Vocabulary** Amazing Words
• **Read** *Reading Street Sleuth,* pp. 58–59	• **Read** *Reading Street Sleuth,* pp. 58–59	• **Read** *Reading Street Sleuth,* pp. 58–59
		• **Introduce** Inquiry Project

Common Core State Standards

Language 1.g. Form and use comparative and superlative adjectives and adverbs, and choose between them depending on what is to be modified. **Language 2.f.** Use spelling patterns and generalizations (e.g., word families, position-based spellings, syllable patterns, ending rules, meaningful word parts) in writing words. **Also Language 1.a., 2.e.**

Spelling Pretest

Homophones

INTRODUCE Explain to students that homophones are words that sound alike but are spelled differently and have different meanings.

PRETEST Say each word, read the sentence, and repeat the word.

1. to	I am going **to** the store.	5
2. too	Jess enjoys pizza **too.**	3
3. two	He has **two** sisters.	1
4. week	My birthday is next **week.**	2
5. weak	I was **weak** after running all day.	6
6. road	Don't play in the middle of the **road.**	4
7. rode	I **rode** my bike to school today.	7
8. stair	I slipped on the second **stair.**	8
9. stare	Cats can **stare** out the window.	10
10. bear	The baby sleeps with her teddy **bear.**	9
11. bare	After the leaves fell the trees were **bare.**	13
12. write	I will **write** a story for class.	12
13. right	She told us the **right** answer.	14
14. new	I have a **new** bicycle.	11
15. knew	I **knew** the way home.	15

Challenge words

16. their	We will go to **their** home for dinner.	16
17. there	**There** are many colors in the rainbow.	18
18. they're	After school, **they're** going to soccer practice.	20
19. weather	We will cancel the picnic because of the **weather.**	17
20. whether	Decide **whether** or not you will play.	19

SELF-CORRECT Have students self-correct their pretests by rewriting misspelled words.

ON THEIR OWN Use *Let's Practice It!* p. 299 on the *Teacher Resources DVD-ROM.*

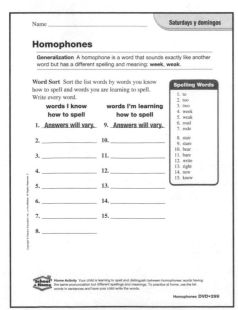

Let's Practice It! TR DVD•299

Conventions

Comparative and Superlative Adjectives

MAKE CONNECTIONS Write the following sentences on the board. Call on a student to underline the adjective in each sentence. Then have them tell whether the adjective compares two things or three or more.

> **My friend's hair is longer than mine.** (longer; two things)
>
> **His truck was the oldest in the lot.** (oldest; three or more things)

TEACH Remind students that adjectives are words that describe nouns. Then display Grammar Transparency 22, and read aloud the explanation and examples in the box.

MODEL Model choosing the correct adjective for items 1 and 2. Explain how you chose the correct adjectives using the rules for comparatives and superlatives.

GUIDE PRACTICE Guide students to complete items 3 and 4. Remind them to read the sentence both ways before choosing the correct adjective.

APPLY Have students read sentences 5–7 on the transparency, using the correct adjective to correctly combine each pair of sentences.

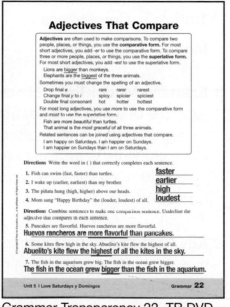

Adjectives That Compare

Adjectives are often used to make comparisons. To compare two people, places, or things, you use the **comparative form**. For most short adjectives, you add -er to use the comparative form. To compare three or more people, places, or things, you use the **superlative form**. For most short adjectives, you add -est to use the superlative form.

Lions are bigger than monkeys.
Elephants are the biggest of the three animals.

Sometimes you must change the spelling of an adjective.

Drop final e	rare	rarer	rarest
Change final y to i	spicy	spicier	spiciest
Double final consonant	hot	hotter	hottest

For most long adjectives, you use more to use the comparative form and most to use the superlative form.

Fish are more beautiful than turtles.
That animal is the most graceful of all three animals.

Related sentences can be joined using adjectives that compare.

I am happy on Saturdays. I am happier on Sundays.
I am happier on Sundays than I am on Saturdays.

Directions Write the word in ( ) that correctly completes each sentence.

1. Fish can swim (fast, faster) than turtles. — **faster**
2. I wake up (earlier, earliest) than my brother. — **earlier**
3. The piñata hung (high, higher) above our heads. — **high**
4. Mom sang "Happy Birthday" the (louder, loudest) of all. — **loudest**

Directions Combine sentences to make one comparison sentence. Underline the adjective that compares in each sentence.

5. Pancakes are flavorful. Huevos rancheros are more flavorful.
Huevos rancheros are more flavorful than pancakes.

6. Some kites fly high in the sky. Abuelito's kite flew the highest of all.
Abuelito's kite flew the highest of all the kites in the sky.

7. The fish in the aquarium grew big. The fish in the ocean grew bigger.
The fish in the ocean grew bigger than the fish in the aquarium.

Unit 5 I Love Saturdays y Domingos — Grammar **22**

Grammar Transparency 22, TR DVD

Handwriting

MODEL LETTER FORMATION AND SPACING Display the uppercase letters *E* and *O*. Follow the stroke instruction pictured to model letter formation. Explain that it is important to pay attention to the spaces between letters and words in addition to the form of the letters themselves. Letters in a word should have even spacing. Spaces between words should be slightly larger. Model writing this sentence with correct spacing: *Even Olivia and Evan like oatmeal.*

GUIDE PRACTICE Have students write this sentence: *Every day I feed my dog Ollie.* Circulate around the room, guiding students.

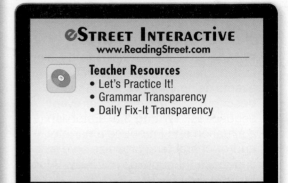

eSTREET INTERACTIVE
www.ReadingStreet.com

Teacher Resources
• Let's Practice It!
• Grammar Transparency
• Daily Fix-It Transparency

Daily Fix-It

1. Carlas family came from Puerto Rico to weeks ago. *(Carla's; two)*
2. Which is the biggest city, San Juan or New york? *(bigger; York)*

Academic Vocabulary ©

A **comparative adjective** is an adjective that compares two things.

A **superlative adjective** is an adjective that compares three or more things.

ELL

Homophones Clarify the pronunciation and meaning of each spelling word. Demonstrate the meaning of *stair, stare, week,* and *weak* with motions and facial expressions. Provide additional examples.

Language Production: Comparative and Superlative Adjectives Write the adjectives *small, big,* and *heavy.* Have students generate the comparative and superlative forms of each. Gather classroom objects and have students use the adjectives to compare the objects.

Writing 3. Write narratives to develop real or imagined experiences or events using effective technique, descriptive details, and clear event sequences. **Writing 3.a.** Establish a situation and introduce a narrator and/or characters; organize an event sequence that unfolds naturally. **Also Writing 3.c., 8., 10.**

© **Bridge to Common Core**

TEXT TYPES AND PURPOSES

This week students write a personal narrative about a real event that has happened to them.

Narrative Writing

Through reading and discussion, students will gain a deeper understanding of cultures. They will use this knowledge from the texts to write and support personal narratives.

Through the week, students will improve their range and content of writing through daily mini-lessons.

5-Day Plan

DAY 1	Read Like a Writer
DAY 2	Describing Events
DAY 3	Evaluation
DAY 4	Put Events in Order
DAY 5	Revise

Write Guy *by Jeff Anderson*

Let's Use Books

If a student wants to write dialogue, she can look at how the author of a recently read story wrote dialogue. Have the student ask herself, "What do I like about how these characters speak?" *Young writers can use models.*

Writing
Personal Narrative

| **Mini-Lesson** | Writing for Tests: Read Like a Writer |

- **Introduce** This week you will write a personal narrative. A personal narrative is a story of real events that happened to you. It is written from your own point of view.

  Genre   Personal Narrative

  Trait   Conventions

  Mode   Narrative

- **Examine Model Text** Let's read an example of a personal narrative written in response to a writing prompt on a test. Have students read "Costume Party" on p. 329 of their *Reader's and Writer's Notebook.*

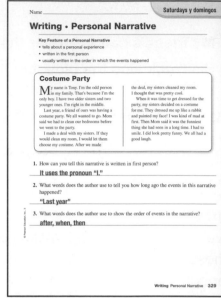

Reader's and Writer's Notebook, p. 329

- **Key Features** A personal narrative tells about a personal experience and may tell the writer's opinion of the experience. Have students summarize the experience this narrative tells about. (a boy's sisters dress him up like a bunny for a costume party)

  A personal narrative is written in the first person, from the writer's point of view. This means the writer uses the pronoun *I*. Have students circle the word *I* each time it is used.

  Personal narratives usually are written in the order in which the events happened. Have students name the events in the story in order. (Tony's mom tells them to clean their rooms before the party. Tony makes a deal with his sisters. Then they clean his room. Then they dress him as a bunny for a costume party. Then his mother thinks it is funny.)

Review Key Features

Review the key features of personal narratives with students. You may want to post the key features in the classroom for students to refer to as they work on their compositions.

Key Features of a Personal Narrative

- tells about a personal experience
- written in first person
- usually written in the order in which the events happened

Routine | **Quick Write for Fluency** | **Team Talk**

1. **Talk** Have pairs take a few minutes to discuss the features of a personal narrative.

2. **Write** Each student writes a definition of personal narrative.

3. **Share** Partners share their definitions with one another.

Routines Flip Chart

eStreet Interactive
www.ReadingStreet.com

Teacher Resources
- Reader's and Writer's Notebook
- Let's Practice It!

Academic Vocabulary ©

A **personal narrative** is a retelling of a true personal experience.

ELL

Model Text Read aloud the writing model "Costume Party" and help students understand it. Discuss with students that the events in a personal narrative are real events. Have students restate the events in the narrative. List them on the board.

Wrap Up Your Day!

✔ **Content Knowledge** Reread "Street Rhymes!" on p. 222j to students. Ask them what they learned this week about comparing cultures.

✔ **Oral Vocabulary** Have students use the Amazing Words they learned in context sentences.

✔ **Homework** Send home this week's Family Times newsletter on *Let's Practice It!* pp. 300–301 on the *Teacher Resources DVD-ROM.*

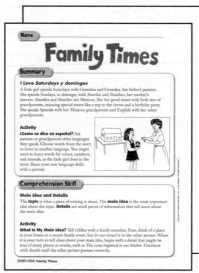

Let's Practice It!
TR DVD•300–301

Preview DAY 2

Tell students that tomorrow they will read about a girl and her grandparents.

Materials

- Student Edition
- Reader's and Writer's Notebook

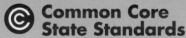

Common Core State Standards

Speaking/Listening 1. Engage effectively in a range of collaborative discussions (one-on-one, in groups, and teacher-led) with diverse partners on grade 3 topics and texts, building on others' ideas and expressing their own clearly. **Language 6.** Acquire and use accurately grade-appropriate conversational, general academic, and domain-specific words and phrases, including those that signal spatial and temporal relationships (e.g., *After dinner that night we went looking for them*). **Also Informational Text 7.**

Content Knowledge

Comparing Cultures

EXPAND THE CONCEPT Remind students of the weekly concept question, *How are cultures alike and different?* Tell students that today they will begin reading *I Love Saturdays y domingos*. As they read, encourage students to think about how the two cultures of the little girl are alike and how they are different.

Build Oral Language

TALK ABOUT SENTENCES AND WORDS Reread these sentences from the Read Aloud, "The First Texans."

The Comanche hunter and the Caddo hunter both used a bow and arrow for hunting. The Comanche hunter made a shield out of buffalo hides as well.

- What is a *shield?* (protective gear held by straps or a handle)
- Why would a hunter need a shield? (to protect himself from other animals or arrows)
- For what reason does the author tell readers about the hunters and what they used when hunting? (to better understand how they hunted and to visualize what they looked like)

Team Talk Have students turn to a partner and discuss the following question. Then ask them to share their responses.

- What is the shortest version of these sentences that can be made without changing the basic meaning? (Possible response: The Caddo hunter used a bow and arrow. The Comanche used these and a shield.)

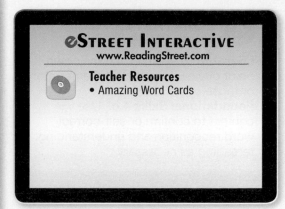

Build Oral Vocabulary

Amazing Words — Robust Vocabulary Routine

1. **Introduce** Write the Amazing Word *concentrate* on the board. Have students say it aloud with you. Relate *concentrate* to the photographs on pp. 222–223 and "The First Texans." The girls need to *concentrate* on their dancing so they don't make a mistake. Do you think the hunters needed to *concentrate* while hunting? Explain. Have students determine the definition of the word *concentrate*. (*Concentrate* means "to focus on or give attention to.")

2. **Demonstrate** Have students answer questions to demonstrate understanding. Why do athletes have to *concentrate* during a game? Why would a student need to *concentrate* when taking a test?

3. **Apply** Have students apply their understanding. Give an example of a time when it was important for you to *concentrate* on what you were doing.

4. **Display the Word** Run your hand under the word parts in *con-cen-trate*. Clap the syllables with students.

See p. OV•2 to teach *barbecue*.

Routines Flip Chart

Amazing Words

clan	barbecue
dwelling	belief
shield	chant
headdress	procession
concentrate	settler

ADD TO THE CONCEPT MAP Use the photos on pp. 222–223 and the Read Aloud, "The First Texans," to talk about the Amazing Words *clan, dwelling, shield,* and *headdress*. Add these and other concept-related words to the concept map to develop students' knowledge of the topic. Discuss the following questions. Encourage students to build upon the ideas of others when they answer.

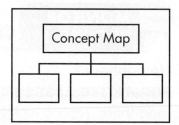
Concept Map

Describe your *dwelling*.

Do you have a large *clan*? Do you all get together for holidays?

On what occasions might you see a *headdress* worn?

If you were to make a *shield* to protect yourself, what would you make it out of? Why?

Reinforce Vocabulary Use the Day 2 instruction on ELL Poster 22 to teach lesson vocabulary and the lesson concept.

Common Core State Standards

Literature 6. Distinguish their own point of view from that of the narrator or those of the characters.
Foundational Skills 4.c. Use context to confirm or self-correct word recognition and understanding, rereading as necessary.

Word Analysis

Homophones

REVIEW Review that homophones are words that sound alike but have different spellings and meanings.

READ WORDS IN ISOLATION Have the class read these words. Then point to the words in random order and ask students to read them quickly.

meddle	Sunday	marry	pale
medal	sundae	merry	pail

Corrective feedback | Model reading the word parts and then have students read the whole word with you.

READ WORDS IN CONTEXT Have the class read the sentences below.

Team Talk Have pairs take turns reading the sentences naturally.

Jeff felt **weak** after being sick for a **week.**

The **two** sisters are flying **to** France.

Our family is going to leave for the party in an **hour.**

MONITOR PROGRESS **Check Word Reading**

Homophones

FORMATIVE ASSESSMENT Write the following words and have the class read them. Notice which words students miss during the group reading. Call on individuals to read some of the words.

role	roll	acts	ax	**Spiral Review**
peer	pier	wring	right	Row 2 reviews homophones.
bass	row	wind	tear	Row 3 contrasts homographs, words that have the same spelling but different pronunciations and different meanings, with homophones.

If... students cannot read words that are homophones at this point,

then... use the Day 1 Word Analysis lesson on p. 224a to reteach homophones. Use words from the *Decodable Practice Passages* (or Reader). Continue to monitor students' progress using other instructional opportunities during the week. See the Skills Trace on p. 224a.

Literary Terms

Point of View

TEACH Tell students that point of view is the perspective from which an author presents the actions and characters in a story. There are two main points of view: first person and third person. The first person is when the narrator is a character in the story who uses *I* or *we* when telling the story. The third person is when the story is told by a narrator who is not a character in the story and who uses pronouns such as *he, she, it,* and *they.*

Think Aloud

MODEL Let's look at "The Best Game" on p. 227. The first sentence says *I think board games are the best family activity.* Which word tells the reader that this passage is written in the first-person point of view? (*I*) Since the narrator is telling the story about him or herself, the point of view is first person.

GUIDE PRACTICE Look at the first two sentences of *I Love Saturdays y domingos* on p. 232. Ask students to find pronouns that signal which point of view the story is told in *(my, I).* Then ask them to identify the point of view. (first person)

ON THEIR OWN Have students determine the point of view in other selections in their Student Editions.

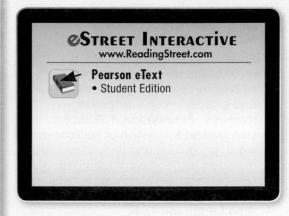

eStreet Interactive
www.ReadingStreet.com

Pearson eText
• Student Edition

Academic Vocabulary ©

first person the one speaking (I, we)

third person the one spoken of (he, she, it, they)

© **Common Core State Standards**

Foundational Skills 4.b. Read on-level prose and poetry orally with accuracy, appropriate rate, and expression on successive readings. **Foundational Skills 4.c.** Use context to confirm or self-correct word recognition and understanding, rereading as necessary. **Language 4.a.** Use sentence-level context as a clue to the meaning of a word or phrase. **Also Language 4., 5.**

Selection Vocabulary

bouquet a bunch of flowers

circus a show that includes acrobats, clowns, and trained animals

difficult hard to do; not easy to understand

nibbling eating or biting in a quick, gentle way

pier a walkway that stretches out over water

soars rises high in the air

swallow the action that causes food to pass from the mouth to the stomach

© **Bridge to Common Core**

VOCABULARY ACQUISITION AND USE

When students interact with this week's selection vocabulary words, they are learning about word relationships they will need to succeed in school and beyond. Teaching the strategy of context clues to determine and clarify the meanings of homophones will help students gain independence when they encounter them in other contexts.

Vocabulary Support

Refer students to *Words!* on p. W•12 in the Student Edition for additional practice.

Vocabulary Skill

⟳ Homophones

READ Have students read "Island Vacation" on p. 229. Use the vocabulary skill and strategy as tools to build comprehension.

TEACH CONTEXT CLUES Tell students that words that sound the same but have different meanings and spellings are called homophones. *Sea* and *see* are examples of homophones. Explain that using the strategy of context clues can help students determine the meaning of the word.

Think Aloud

MODEL Listen to this sentence: *My brother's team won their basketball game.* The word *won* in this sentence sounds like the word for the number one. But that would not make sense here. The team played a game. Usually in a game one team wins and the other loses. So in this case, the word *won* must mean that they were victorious.

GUIDE PRACTICE Write this sentence on the board: *We ate breakfast at eight o'clock in the morning.* Have students identify the homophones and determine their meanings using context clues. For additional support, use *Envision It! Pictured Vocabulary Cards* or *Tested Vocabulary Cards.*

ON THEIR OWN Have students reread "Island Vacation" on p. 229. Have students identify the words in the story that have homophones and write the other words that sound the same. Then have them use each homophone in a sentence. For additional practice use *Reader's and Writer's Notebook* p. 330.

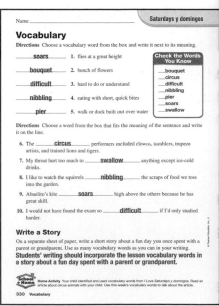

Reader's and Writer's Notebook, p. 330

Common Core State Standards
Language 4.a. Use sentence-level context as a clue to the meaning of a word or phrase. Also Foundational Skills 4.c., Language 4., 5.

Envision It! | Words to Know

bouquet

circus

pier

difficult
nibbling
soars
swallow

READING STREET ONLINE
VOCABULARY ACTIVITIES
www.ReadingStreet.com

Vocabulary Strategy for

🔊 Homophones

Context Clues You may read or hear a word you know, but the meaning doesn't make sense in the sentence. The word might be a homophone. Homophones are words that are pronounced the same but have different meanings and spellings. For example, the words *bear* and *bare* are homophones. A *bear* is "a large mammal" and *bare* means "not covered."

1. If the word you know doesn't make sense in the sentence, it might be a homophone.
2. Look at the words around it. Can you figure out another meaning?
3. Try the new meaning in the sentence. Does it make sense?

Read "Island Vacation" on page 229. Use context clues to determine the meanings of homophones.

Words to Write Reread "Island Vacation." What kind of places are you interested in traveling to? Write about your interest. Use homophones and words from the Words to Know list.

Island Vacation

Every summer my family goes to Cherry Island for a vacation. It is my favorite place in the whole world. Cherry Island is a small island with just a few cabins and houses. You can't drive to Cherry Island because there is no bridge. You have to take a boat.

My sisters and I play all over the island. We like to pick wildflowers and make a bouquet for our mother. We also like to pack a picnic lunch and eat it down by the water. We sit on the pier, nibbling on sandwiches. Sometimes a gull soars over us while we eat. Once my sister, Jane, threw some pieces of bread in the water. A huge crowd of gulls came and tried to eat the bread. It was like a circus, so crowded and noisy! Now I am always careful not to leave my sandwich on the pier because I know a gull might grab it and swallow it in one big bite.

At the end of our vacation, it is always difficult to say good-bye to Cherry Island. As the boat pulls away, I start counting the days until I can come back again.

Your Turn!

⏸ **Need a Review?** For additional help with homophones, see *Words!*

▶ **Ready to Try It?** Read *I Love Saturdays y domingos* on pp. 230–245.

228

229

Student Edition, pp. 228–229

Reread for Fluency

ACCURACY Read paragraph 1 of "Island Vacation" aloud, reading each word accurately. Tell students that you are reading the passage with accuracy, pronouncing each word correctly without replacing or skipping any words.

Routine Oral Rereading

1. **Read** Have students read paragraph 1 of "Island Vacation" orally.

2. **Reread** To achieve optimal fluency, students should reread the text three or four times.

3. **Corrective Feedback** Have students read aloud without you. Provide feedback about their accuracy. Encourage them to read each word without skipping or replacing any words.

Routines Flip Chart

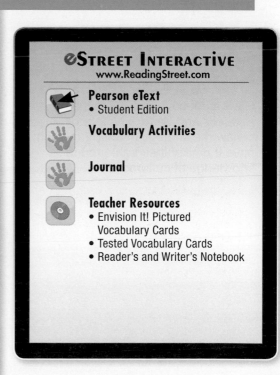

eSTREET INTERACTIVE
www.ReadingStreet.com

📖 **Pearson eText**
• Student Edition

✋ **Vocabulary Activities**

✋ **Journal**

💿 **Teacher Resources**
• Envision It! Pictured Vocabulary Cards
• Tested Vocabulary Cards
• Reader's and Writer's Notebook

© **Common Core State Standards**

Literature 10. By the end of the year, read and comprehend literature, including stories, dramas, and poetry, at the high end of the grades 2–3 text complexity band independently and proficiently. **Also Literature 7., Foundational Skills 4.a.**

© **Bridge to Common Core**

CRAFT AND STRUCTURE

Students analyze the structure of the selection and how its illustrations and words in bold relate to each other and the whole. As they preview the selection and prepare to read, they come to see how purpose and genre shape the content and style of the text.

Academic Vocabulary ©

realistic fiction a made-up story that could happen in real life

Strategy Response Log

Have students use p. 28 in the *Reader's and Writer's Notebook* to review the strategy of inferring. Then have them list their background knowledge of cultures.

Text-Based Comprehension

Introduce Main Selection

Student Edition, pp. 230–231

GENRE Explain that **realistic fiction** is a made-up story with characters, a setting, and events that seem real. In realistic fiction, there are no fantastic solutions to problems. Story endings are reasonable and believable.

PREVIEW AND PREDICT Have students preview the illustrations in *I Love Saturdays y domingos.* Have them notice the introductory text box and the many words in bold italics. Have them predict what they will find out as they read.

PURPOSE By analyzing *I Love Saturdays y domingos,* a realistic fiction selection, students will gain knowledge of how different cultures compare.

Access Main Selection

READER AND TASK SUGGESTIONS

Preparing to Read the Text	Leveled Tasks
• Review listening for context clues to determine the meanings of homophones. • Discuss how authors use italic type to focus attention on foreign words. • Remind students that they may need to read more slowly as they encounter unfamiliar words.	• **Language Conventionality and Clarity** If students have difficulty understanding the foreign words and foreign punctuation in the story, remind them to search for context and picture clues as they read. • **Structure** Students may have difficulty understanding what is happening when the main character in the story speaks in Spanish. Have students note similarities and differences between the pictures and words on the top of the page and those on the bottom of the page.

See Text Complexity Measures for *I Love Saturdays y domingos* on the tab at the beginning of this week.

READ Tell students that today they will read *I Love Saturdays y domingos* for the first time. Use the Read for Understanding routine.

Routine   Read for Understanding

Deepen understanding by reading the selection multiple times.

1. First Read—If students need support, then use the **Access Text** notes to help them clarify understanding.

2. Second Read—Use the **Close Reading** notes to help students draw knowledge from the text.

Day 2   SMALL GROUP TIME • Differentiate Comprehension, p. SG•17

OL On-Level	**SI** Strategic Intervention	**A** Advanced
• **Practice** Selection Vocabulary • **Read** *I Love Saturdays y domingos*	• **Reteach** Selection Vocabulary • **Read** *I Love Saturdays y domingos*	• **Extend** Selection Vocabulary • **Read** *I Love Saturdays y domingos* • **Investigate** Inquiry Project

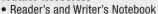

eStreet Interactive
www.ReadingStreet.com

Pearson eText
• Student Edition

AudioText CD

Teacher Resources
• Reader's and Writer's Notebook

Background Building Audio CD

Access for All

A **Advanced**

Have students make a Venn diagram comparing and contrasting two different cultures.

Build Background Review the selection summary in English (*ELL Handbook* p. 157). Use the Retelling Cards to provide visual support for the summary.

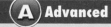

If... students need more scaffolding and practice with the **Comprehension Skill, then...** use the activities on p. DI•46 in the Teacher Resources section on SuccessNet.

Access Text © If students need help, then...

⟲ MAIN IDEA AND DETAILS

Write the following paragraph on the board: *My grandparents are the best! They are so nice. They spend lots of time with me.* Ask students to identify the main idea and the details that support it.

Think Aloud **MODEL** The topic of the paragraph is grandparents. So I think the main idea is *My grandparents are the best!* The sentences that support the main idea would be the ones that tell why the grandparents are the best. The details are *They are so nice* and *They spend lots of time with me.*

Saturdays and Sundays are my special days. I call Sundays *domingos,* and you'll soon see why.

On Saturdays, I go visit Grandpa and Grandma. Grandpa and Grandma are my father's parents. They are always happy to see me. I say, "Hi, Grandpa! Hi, Grandma!" as I walk in. And they say, "Hello, sweetheart! How are you? Hello, darling!"

232

Student Edition, p. 232

Close Reading ©

ANALYSIS • TEXT EVIDENCE Why is the detail that the girl calls Sundays *domingos* important? Use evidence from the selection to support your answer. (On p. 233, it says she visits her Spanish-speaking grandparents on Sundays. One way the visits with her grandparents are different is that she speaks Spanish on Sundays.)

ON THEIR OWN Have students reread pp. 232–233 to identify the main idea of the story so far. For additional practice, use *Let's Practice It!* p. 302 on the *Teacher Resources DVD-ROM.*

Common Core State Standards

Literature 1. Ask and answer questions to demonstrate understanding of a text, referring explicitly to the text as the basis for the answers. **Literature 2.** Recount stories, including fables, folktales, and myths from diverse cultures; determine the central message, lesson, or moral and explain how it is conveyed through key details in the text.

I spend *los domingos* with *Abuelito y Abuelita.*
Abuelito y Abuelita are my mother's parents.
They are always happy to see me.
I say: —¡*Hola, Abuelito!* ¡*Hola, Abuelita!*— as I get out of the car.
And they say: —¡*Hola, hijita! ¿Cómo estás?*
¡*Hola, mi corazón!*

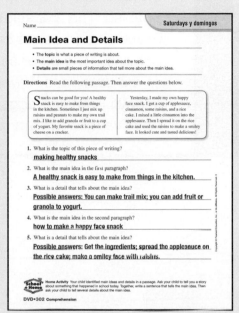

Let's Practice It! TR DVD•302

233

Student Edition, p. 233

Access for All

SI Strategic Intervention

Make a T-chart. Label the columns *Spanish* and *English.* Write the words or phrases that are in italics (Spanish words or phrases) from pp. 232–233 in the left column under *Spanish.* Then write the English equivalent in the right column.

EVALUATION Why are some words in boldface and italics? (Those are in a different language—Spanish. The author chose the different treatment to make those words stand out so the reader notices them.

ELL

Extend Language Have Spanish speakers read the Spanish words and then read them again in English. Have them explain why, "Hi, Grandpa" and "Hi, Grandma" are the same as *"Hola, Abuelito"* and *"Hola, Abuelita."*

I Love Saturdays y domingos **233a**

Access Text © If students need help, then...

◉ INFERRING Have students read the first sentence of the first paragraph and the first sentence of the fifth paragraph on p. 234. Ask students to make inferences to determine the meaning of the word *Abuelita.*

Think Aloud **MODEL** The author often says what the girl did on Saturdays in English and then says something very similar that she did on Sundays in Spanish. The first sentence says that Grandma serves her breakfast on Saturday. The other sentence says that on *los domingos Abuelita* serves her papaya juice and eggs. I can infer that *Abuelita* means "Grandma."

Close Reading ©

ANALYSIS • TEXT EVIDENCE

Compare and contrast the girl's visits to her grandparents' houses. Cite evidence from the selection. (**Same:** On p. 234, both grandmothers make breakfast for her. On p. 235, it says they both have pets. **Different:** On p. 234, her grandmother serves her pancakes, scrambled eggs, and milk. Her *abuelita* serves *huevos rancheros* and papaya juice.)

On Saturdays, Grandma serves me breakfast: milk, scrambled eggs, and pancakes.
The pancakes are spongy. I like to put a lot of honey on my pancakes.
Grandma asks me, "Do you like them sweetheart?"
And I answer, "Oh, yes, Grandma, I love them!"

Los domingos,
Abuelita serves me a large glass of papaya juice and a plate of eggs called *huevos rancheros.*
The *huevos rancheros* are wonderful.
No one makes them better than *Abuelita.*
    Abuelita asks me if I like them: —¿*Te gustan, hijita?*
    First I need to swallow, and then I answer: —*Sí, Abuelita, ¡me encantan!*

234

Student Edition, p. 234

SYNTHESIS Based on what you have read so far, how does the girl feel about her grandparents? (She loves them and loves spending time with them.)

ON THEIR OWN Have students look at p. 235 to infer the meaning of what the girl tells the dog in the last sentence.

Common Core State Standards

Literature 1. Ask and answer questions to demonstrate understanding of a text, referring explicitly to the text as the basis for the answers. **Literature 3.** Describe characters in a story (e.g., their traits, motivations, or feelings) and explain how their actions contribute to the sequence of events. **Language 4.** Determine or clarify the meaning of unknown and multiple-meaning words and phrases based on grade 3 reading and content, choosing flexibly from a range of strategies.

Grandma has a tabby cat. Her name is Taffy. I roll on the carpet and call, "Come, Taffy, let´s play."

Abuelita has a dog. His name is *Canelo*. When I go out to the garden, *Canelo* follows me. I call out to him: —*Ven, Canelo. ¡Vamos a jugar!*

235

Student Edition, p. 235

Access for All

SI Strategic Intervention

Show students illustrations or photos of different people or scenes. Ask them to infer the meaning of what is happening in the visuals.

A Advanced

Tell students to make a list of inferences based on the following sentence and their prior knowledge: *Our teacher is so happy today.*

EVALUATION How does using the same phrases in English and Spanish help the author make clear her reason for writing the story? (The author wants to show how the cultures of the grandparents are alike even though there are differences.)

Inferring Read aloud the last line on p. 232. Ask students how they think the grandparents feel about the girl based on what they said. (They call her sweetheart and darling, so they love her.)

I Love Saturdays y domingos **235a**

Access Text © If students need help, then...

🌀 HOMOPHONES Write the following sentence on the board: *We heard the herd of cows moo very loudly.* Ask students to identify the homophones.

Think Aloud MODEL When I read the sentence, the words *heard* and *herd* sound the same. *Heard* is the past tense for the verb *to hear* and *herd* means a group. The first homophone is something people do so that must be the past tense of *hear.* The second is about cows so that must refer to a group.

ON THEIR OWN Have students reread p. 236 to identify any words that are homophones. Then ask them to use the homophone correctly in a sentence. For additional practice, see *Reader's and Writer's Notebook,* p. 334.

Grandma collects owls. Every time that she and Grandpa go on a trip she brings back an owl for her collection.

Each one is different. I count them: One, two, three, four, five, six, seven, eight, nine, ten, eleven, twelve…to see how her collection is growing.

Abuelita loves animals. When she was little she lived on a farm. She is glad that now they have a large backyard so she can keep chickens.

One of her hens has been sitting on her eggs for many days. Now the chicks have hatched. I count them: — *Uno, dos, tres, cuatro, cinco, seis, siete, ocho, nueve, diez, once, doce…*

236

Student Edition, p. 236

Close Reading ©

ANALYSIS • TEXT EVIDENCE Find the word *eight* on p. 236. How can you tell if it is the number *eight* or the past tense of the word *eat?* (I can look at the context. The girl is counting owls. It must be the number.)

EVALUATION • TEXT EVIDENCE How does *Abuelita* feel about animals? How do you know? (She loves them. The text on p. 236 says she grew up on a farm and that she is glad to have a large enough backyard to have chickens.)

CHECK PREDICTIONS Have students look back at the predictions they made earlier and discuss whether they were accurate. Then have students preview the rest of the selection and either adjust their predictions accordingly or make new predictions.

One Saturday, Grandpa and Grandma play a movie about the circus for me on their VCR.

"I like the circus, especially the lions and tigers," says Grandpa.

"And the giraffes," says Grandma.

When Grandma and Grandpa ask me what part I like best, I answer:

"I like the mother elephant and her little elephant best."

Un domingo, Abuelito y Abuelita take me to a real circus.

—*Me encanta el circo, Abuelito*—I say.

—*Mira los leones y los tigres*—says *Abuelita*.

—*¡Y las jirafas!*—*Abuelito* adds.

When they ask me what I like best, I say:

—*La mamá elefanta y su elefantito.*

237

Student Edition, p. 237

REREAD CHALLENGING TEXT Ask a Spanish speaker to reread the Spanish/English text at the bottom of p. 237 aloud to provide an example of proper pronunciation. Then have partners take turns rereading the text until they can do so fluently.

Common Core State Standards

Literature 1. Ask and answer questions to demonstrate understanding of a text, referring explicitly to the text as the basis for the answers. **Literature 3.** Describe characters in a story (e.g., their traits, motivations, or feelings) and explain how their actions contribute to the sequence of events. **Foundational Skills 4.c.** Use context to confirm or self-correct word recognition and understanding, rereading as necessary. **Also Literature 4., Language 4.a.**

Access for All

SI Strategic Intervention

Make a T-chart and list words on the left side that have a homophone. Ask students to help you to list the homophones for each word on the right side of the chart.

If you want to teach this selection in two sessions, stop here.

If you want to continue reading this selection, turn to page 238–239.

Name _____ Saturdays y domingos

Vocabulary • Homophones

- A **cygnet** is a baby swan and a **signet** is a heavy gold ring. The two words sound exactly alike, but they look different and they mean different things. Words that sound alike but look different and have different meanings are called **homophones**.
- You can use **context clues** to figure out the correct homophone to use in a sentence.

Directions Next to each word below, write its homophone.

1. brake **break** _____ 2. waist **waste** _____
3. pane **pain** _____ 4. pause **paws** _____
5. soar **sore** _____ 6. rap **wrap** _____
7. suite **sweet** _____ 8. reed **read** _____

Directions Each sentence below has a pair of homophones in ( ). Use context clues to choose the correct homophone and underline it.

9. The bald eagle and the stars and stripes are (cymbals, <u>symbols</u>) of the U.S.A.
10. The driver slammed his foot on the (<u>brake</u>, break) when he saw the deer.
11. Someday I hope to (right, <u>write</u>) a play as famous as Macbeth.
12. The squirrel (<u>hoards</u>, hordes) acorns all fall so she can eat during the winter.
13. The crowds cheered for the speaker until they were (<u>hoarse</u>, horse).
14. Don't forget to (ring, <u>wring</u>) out the dishcloth after you clean the sink.
15. The streets of San Francisco are often hidden in the morning (missed, <u>mist</u>).
16. The long, hot August afternoon had left me feeling (board, <u>bored</u>) and restless.
17. A (bare, <u>bear</u>) got into our kitchen and ate all our food while we were on vacation.
18. It would take two weeks for the catcher's injured shoulder to (<u>heal</u>, heel).

School + Home **Home Activity** Your child identified and compared homophones. Read a short story with your child. Point to words that have homophones, such as stare. Take turns with your child defining the word in the story, then spelling and defining the homophone (i.e., stair).

334 Vocabulary

Reader's and Writer's Notebook, p. 334

Cognates Point out the Spanish cognates: *giraffe/jirafa, tiger/tigre,* and *elephant/elefante.*

I Love Saturdays y domingos **237a**

Common Core State Standards

Writing 2.b. Develop the topic with facts, definitions, and details. **Writing 7.** Conduct short research projects that build knowledge about a topic. **Writing 8.** Recall information from experiences or gather information from print and digital sources; take brief notes on sources and sort evidence into provided categories. **Language 1.g.** Form and use comparative and superlative adjectives and adverbs, and choose between them depending on what is to be modified. **Also Language 2.e., 2.f.**

Bridge to Common Core

RESEARCH TO BUILD AND PRESENT KNOWLEDGE

On Day 2 of the weeklong research project, students generate a plan for gathering information about their topics. They consult multiple print and digital sources, skimming and scanning to identify data. This process enables students to develop an understanding of the subject under investigation.

Research and Inquiry

Step 2 Navigate/Search

TEACH Have students generate a research plan for gathering information about their topics. Suggest that students search multiple written sources in the library and online using their inquiry questions and keywords. Tell them to use skimming and scanning techniques to identify data by looking for words in italics. Point out that words in italics are often in other languages and may help students find important information. Encourage students to look for graphs and other visual sources that show the kinds of celebrations that are popular within different cultures. Remind students to take notes as they gather information.

Think Aloud **MODEL** When looking for information on cultural celebrations, I looked up Japan in encyclopedias and book indexes. Once I found information about Japan, I skimmed and scanned the pages, focusing on heads and words in italics for specific information about Japanese celebrations. I found that in Japan there are celebrations all the time. New Year's is a big day. So are Children's Day and the Emperor's Birthday.

GUIDE PRACTICE Have students continue their review of the books and Web sites they identified. Remind them to collect information from multiple sources.

ON THEIR OWN Have students keep track of all their reference sources—books, encyclopedias, magazines, and Web sites. Remind them to look for graphs and other visual sources of information.

Conventions

Comparative and Superlative Adjectives

TEACH Draw two circles on the board to illustrate the descriptive adjectives *small* and *smaller*. Tell students that one circle is smaller than the other. When two things are compared, the ending *-er* is added to an adjective to make the comparative form. Draw a smaller circle. Tell students that the superlative form *smallest* illustrates the comparison of all three circles.

GUIDE PRACTICE Write the following words: *bigger, red, fastest, golden, smarter, large*. Have students identify if the adjective is used to compare.

ON THEIR OWN For more practice, use *Reader's and Writer's Notebook* p. 331.

Spelling

Homophones

TEACH Remind students that their spelling words for this week are homophones. Tell students that the way these words are spelled depends on their meanings. Yet, students can use knowledge of letter sounds, word parts, and syllables to help them spell the homophones.

GUIDE PRACTICE Write the spelling words on the board. Have a student volunteer use one in a sentence. Then have another volunteer choose the correct spelling. Ask students to explain their choices.

ON THEIR OWN For more practice, use *Reader's and Writer's Notebook* p. 332.

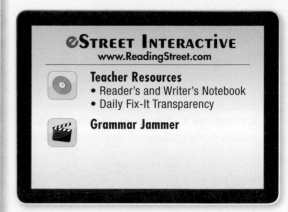

eStreet Interactive
www.ReadingStreet.com

Teacher Resources
• Reader's and Writer's Notebook
• Daily Fix-It Transparency

Grammar Jammer

Daily Fix-It

3. The family gone to the circus and enjoyed seeing the animalls. *(went; animals)*

4. It was the most greatest days they had ever spend. *(the greatest day; spent)*

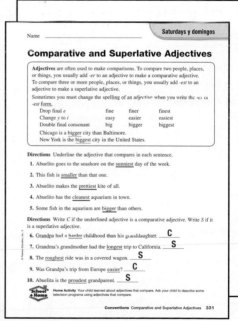

Reader's and Writer's Notebook, pp. 331–332

Conventions To give students more practice using comparative and superlative adjectives, use the modified grammar lessons in the *ELL Handbook* and Grammar Jammer online at:
www.ReadingStreet.com

I Love Saturdays y domingos **237c**

Common Core State Standards

Writing 3. Write narratives to develop real or imagined experiences or events using effective technique, descriptive details, and clear event sequences. **Language 1.** Demonstrate command of the conventions of standard English grammar and usage when writing or speaking. **Also Writing 3.a., 3.b., Language 3.a.**

Writing

Personal Narrative

INTRODUCE THE PROMPT Remind students that yesterday they learned about the key features of a personal narrative. Tell them today they will practice writing for tests by creating a personal narrative that addresses the prompt. Read aloud the writing prompt.

Writing Prompt

Think about an important happy memory you have. Now write a personal narrative about it.

Mini-Lesson | Writing for Tests: Describing Events

■ Before you start writing, decide on a topic. Choose a happy memory that you can remember well.

■ Explain to students that thinking about the order in which each event in the memory happened can help them choose which details are most important. Have them think about which details are necessary to understand the story, and which are most interesting.

■ Explain to students that sensory details will make their writing more vivid and interesting. Good descriptions rely on verbs and descriptive adjectives to clearly tell about an event or opinion. As an example, have students visualize "Jon *went* to the store" and "Jon *rushed* to the grocery store." Point out that the second sentence includes a more interesting verb and an adjective.

■ Have students close their eyes and visualize the memory they chose to write about. Have them think about what they see, hear, smell, touch, and taste in the memory.

DISCUSS RUBRIC Discuss the Scoring Rubric found on p. 333 in the *Reader's and Writer's Notebook.* Go over the criteria for each trait under each score. Remind students that this is the rubric that will be used to evaluate the personal narratives they write.

SAMPLE TEST Direct students to get paper and pencil ready to take a writing test. Display the writing prompt for students and give them appropriate time to write to the prompt. Remind students to allow themselves a couple of minutes after writing to reread what they've written and make changes or additions.

Routine   Quick Write for Fluency   Team Talk

1. **Talk** Have pairs discuss the events in their narratives.

2. **Write** Have students write two sentences summarizing what happens in their narratives.

3. **Share** Have students share what they wrote with the class.

Routines Flip Chart

eStreet Interactive
www.ReadingStreet.com

Teacher Resources
• Reader's and Writer's Notebook

Name _____   Saturdays y domingos

Scoring Rubric: Writing for Tests: Personal Narrative

	4	3	2	1
Focus/Ideas	Focuses on specific, real memory; told from writer's point of view	Includes events from writer's memory; told from writer's point of view	Includes some events from writer's memory; mostly told from writer's point of view	Narrative does not focus on real events from writer's memory
Organization	Clear order of events	Can follow order of events	Unclear order of events	No order of events
Voice	Writer shows personal emotions, thoughts, and opinions	Writer shows some personal emotions, thoughts, and opinions	Writer shows few personal emotions, thoughts, and opinions	Writer shows no personal emotions, thoughts, and opinions
Word Choice	Strong use of verbs and adjectives to bring the story to life	Good try at using verbs and adjectives	Poor use of verbs and adjectives; story lacks description	No effort made to use verbs and adjectives
Sentences	Clear sentences of different lengths and types	Sentences of a few lengths and types	Sentences of similar length and type	No variety of sentence length and type
Conventions	Few, if any, errors; correct use of verbs and adjectives	Several small errors; use of verbs and adjectives	Many errors; weak use of verbs and adjectives	Many serious errors; incorrect or no use of verbs and adjectives

Writing Writing for Tests 333

Reader's and Writer's Notebook, p. 333

Wrap Up Your Day!

✓ **Content Knowledge** What did you learn about how the cultures of the grandparents are alike and different?

✓ **Text-Based Comprehension** How did finding the main idea and details make the story easier to understand?

Preview DAY 3

Tell students that tomorrow they will read more about the girl and her grandparents.

DAY 3
at a Glance

Content Knowledge
Oral Vocabulary

Phonics/Word Analysis
Homophones

Text-Based Comprehension
Main Idea and Details
Inferring

Fluency
Accuracy

Research and Study Skills
Maps

Research and Inquiry
Analyze Information

Conventions
Comparative and Superlative Adjectives

Spelling
Homophones

Writing
Writing for Tests: Personal Narrative

Materials
- Student Edition
- Reader's and Writer's Notebook
- Retelling Cards
- Decodable Reader

Common Core State Standards

Speaking/Listening 1. Engage effectively in a range of collaborative discussions (one-on-one, in groups, and teacher-led) with diverse partners on grade 3 topics and texts, building on others' ideas and expressing their own clearly. **Language 6.** Acquire and use accurately grade-appropriate conversational, general academic, and domain-specific words and phrases, including those that signal spatial and temporal relationships (e.g., *After dinner that night we went looking for them*). **Also Language 4.a., 5.b.**

Content Knowledge

Comparing Cultures

EXPAND THE CONCEPT Remind students of the weekly concept question, *How are cultures alike and different?* Discuss how the question relates to *I Love Saturdays y domingos.* Encourage students to think about how the grandparents' cultures are alike and different.

Build Oral Language

TALK ABOUT SENTENCES AND WORDS Reread sentences from Student Edition p. 237, *I Love Saturdays y domingos*

One Saturday, Grandpa and Grandma play a movie about the circus for me on their VCR. "I like the circus, especially the lions and tigers," says Grandpa.

- What is a *circus?* (a traveling group of acrobats, clowns, and animals)
- What context clues could you use to help you understand what you might see at a *circus?* (It says Grandpa likes the lions and tigers at the circus. I know I might see them there.)
- If you wanted to learn more about the *circus,* where could you look? (in a dictionary, online, or in a book about the circus)

Team Talk Have students work with a partner to replace key words in the sentences with synonyms. Use the following sentence frame.

One Saturday, Grandpa and Grandma play a movie about the _____ for me on their VCR. "I like the _____, especially the _____ and _____," says Grandpa.

Build Oral Vocabulary

Amazing Words

Robust Vocabulary Routine

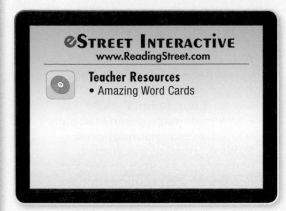
. Introduce Write the word *belief* on the board. Have students say it with you. Yesterday we read about a girl who probably has *beliefs* based on what she learned from her grandparents. Have students determine a definition of *belief*. (A *belief* is something someone thinks is true or is his or her point of view.)

2. Demonstrate Have students answer questions with appropriate detail to demonstrate understanding. What is a *belief* that the girl might have from her mother's parents? (Possible response: It's great to have your own chickens and watch the chicks hatch.)

3. Apply Have students apply their understanding. What is a *belief* that is connected to your culture?

. Display the Word Students can decode the sounds in *belief* and blend them.

ee p. OV•2 to teach *chant*.

Routines Flip Chart

Amazing Words

clan	barbecue
dwelling	belief
shield	chant
headdress	procession
concentrate	settler

ADD TO THE CONCEPT MAP Discuss the Amazing Words *concentrate* and *barbecue*. Add these and other concept-related words to the concept map. Use the following questions to develop students' understanding of the concept.

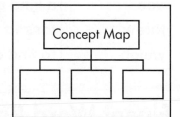

Concept Map

When I want to learn about my culture I *concentrate* on what my grandparents are telling me. What do you *concentrate* on when you are reading?

We had a *barbecue* and cooked hamburgers and hot dogs. What do you like to eat when you have a *barbecue*? Explain.

Expand Vocabulary Use the Day 3 instruction on ELL Poster 22 to help students expand vocabulary.

Common Core State Standards

Foundational Skills 3. Know and apply grade-level phonics and word analysis skills in decoding words. **Foundational Skills 3.d.** Read grade-appropriate irregularly spelled words. **Foundational Skills 4.** Read with sufficient accuracy and fluency to support comprehension. **Foundational Skills 4.b.** Read on-level prose and poetry orally with accuracy, appropriate rate, and expression on successive readings. **Foundational Skills 4.c.** Use context to confirm or self-correct word recognition and understanding, rereading as necessary.

Word Analysis

🔊 Homophones

MODEL WORD SORTING Display a T-chart and write these definitions in the right column: the absence of war; between the parts of; how something can be done; precious; a part of something; a kind of animal; tossed; to find out how heavy something is. Now we are going to match words to their definitions. I will start. Write *peace* and *piece,* and model how to read them and find their definitions. I know long e can be spelled *ea* and *ie,* so both of these words are pronounced the same. I know *peace* means "no fighting," so I'll put it next to the definition "the absence of war." Model finding the definition for *piece.*

GUIDE PRACTICE Use the practice words from the activity on p. 224a for the word sort. Point to a set of homophones. Have students read the homophones identify their different spellings, and match them to the correct definitions.

> **Corrective feedback** | For corrective feedback, model reading each word and using that word in a sentence.

peace	the absence of war
through	between the parts of
way	how something can be done
dear	precious
piece	a part of something
deer	a kind of animal
threw	tossed
weigh	to find out how heavy something is

Fluent Word Reading

MODEL Write *tea* and *tee.* I know *ea* and *ee* both stand for the long e sound so these words are pronounced the same. They are homophones, which means they sound the same but have different spellings and meanings.

GUIDE PRACTICE Write the words below. Say the sounds in your head for each spelling you see. When I point to the word, we'll read it together. Allow one second per word part previewing time for the first reading.

principle   principal   mustered   mustard   bolder   boulder

ON THEIR OWN Have students read the list above three or four times, until they can read one word per second.

Decodable Passage 22B

If students need help, then...

Read *Brett's Day at the Inn*

READ WORDS IN ISOLATION Have students turn to p. 81 in *Decodable Practice Readers 3.2* and find the first list of words. Each word in this list is a homophone. Let's read these words. Be sure that students pronounce pairs of homophones the same.

Next, have students read the high-frequency words.

PREVIEW Have students read the title and preview the passage. Tell them that they will read words that are homophones.

READ WORDS IN CONTEXT Chorally read the passage along with the students. Have students identify words in the passage that are homophones. Make sure that students are monitoring their accuracy when they decode words.

Team Talk Pair students and have them take turns reading the passage aloud to each other. Monitor students as they read to check for proper pronunciation and appropriate pacing.

eStreet Interactive
www.ReadingStreet.com

Pearson eText
• Decodable Reader

Teacher Resources
• Graphic Organizer

Access for All

A Advanced

Have students add more homophones and their definitions to the T-chart. Students may use a dictionary to check spellings and meanings.

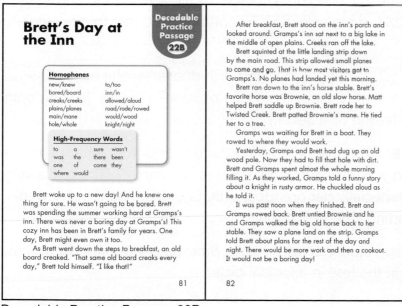

Decodable Practice Passage 22B

© **Common Core State Standards**

Literature 2. Recount stories, including fables, folktales, and myths from diverse cultures; determine the central message, lesson, or moral and explain how it is conveyed through key details in the text. **Literature 3.** Describe characters in a story (e.g., their traits, motivations, or feelings) and explain how their actions contribute to the sequence of events. **Also Literature 7., Speaking/ Listening 4.**

Strategy Response Log

Have students use their background knowledge and clues from the text to make inferences about cultures. Use p. 28 in the *Reader's and Writer's Notebook* to list clues students found in the text.

Text-Based Comprehension
Check Understanding

Student Edition, pp. 230–231

If... you choose to read *I Love Saturdays y domingos* in two parts, **then...** use the following questions to monitor students' understanding of pp. 230–237 of the selection. Encourage students to cite evidence from the text.

ANALYSIS When the girl visits her grandparents, she says "They are always happy to see me." Is this a fact or an opinion? Explain. (It is an opinion. An opinion is a feeling or a belief.)

INFERENCE By looking at the illustrations and from what you have read so far, what can you infer about the girl and her family? (The girl is very close to her family, especially her grandparents. She sees them every weekend and enjoys spending time with them.)

RETELL Have students retell *I Love Saturdays y domingos,* summarizing information in the text in a logical order.

Corrective feedback | **If...** students leave out important details, **then...** have students look back through the illustrations in the selection.

READ Use the **Access Text** and **Close Reading** notes to finish reading *I Love Saturdays y domingos.*

eSTREET INTERACTIVE
www.ReadingStreet.com

Pearson eText
• Student Edition

AudioText CD

Teacher Resources
• Reader's and Writer's Notebook

If... you followed the Read for Understanding routine below,

then... ask students to retell the selection before you reread *I Love Saturdays y domingos.*

RETELL Have students retell *I Love Saturdays y domingos,* summarizing information in the text in a logical order.

| **Corrective feedback** | **If...** students leave out important details, **then...** have students look back through the illustrations in the selection. |

READ Return to p. 232–233 and use the **2nd Read/Close Reading** notes to reread *I Love Saturdays y domingos.*

Read Main Selection

Routine | **Read for Understanding** ©

1. **First Read**—If students need support, then use the **Access Text** notes to help them clarify understanding.

2. **Second Read**—Use the **Close Reading** notes to help students draw knowledge from the text.

ELL

Check Retelling To support retelling, review the multilingual summary for *I Love Saturdays y domingos* with the appropriate Retellings Cards to scaffold understanding.

Day 3 SMALL GROUP TIME • Differentiate Close Reading, p. SG•17

OL On-Level	**SI Strategic Intervention**	**A Advanced**
• **Reread** to Develop Vocabulary	• **Reread** to Develop Vocabulary	• **Reread** to Extend Vocabulary
• **Read** *I Love Saturdays y domingos*	• **Read** *I Love Saturdays y domingos*	• **Read** *I Love Saturdays y domingos*
		• **Investigate** Inquiry Project

ELL

If... students need more scaffolding and practice with the **Main Selection**, **then...** use the activities on p. DI•47 in the Teacher Resources section on SuccessNet.

1ST READ

Access Text © If students need help, then...

Review COMPARE AND CONTRAST
Have students compare and contrast the ways that the grandfathers like to watch fish.

Think Aloud MODEL What does it mean to compare and contrast? (to look at ways things are alike and different) First, let's see what is alike about the way the grandfathers like to watch fish. They both pointed out the big fish so they are the same in that way. We can read more to see how the way they watch fish is different.

ON THEIR OWN Have students reread p. 238 to find something different about the way the two grandfathers like to watch fish. For additional practice, see *Let's Practice It!* p. 303 on the *Teacher Resources DVD-ROM.*

Grandpa has a beautiful aquarium. He keeps it very clean.

"Look at that big fish!" Grandpa says, and points to a big yellow fish.

"I like the little ones," I answer.

It's fun to watch the big and little fish. I watch, my nose pressed against the glass, for a long time.

2ND READ

Close Reading ©

ANALYSIS • TEXT EVIDENCE
Compare and contrast the grandfathers. Use evidence from the selection. (**Same:** They both bring the girl colorful presents. **Different:** Grandpa brings her balloons and *Abuelito* brings her a kite.)

Abuelito takes me to the seashore. He loves to walk by the ocean. We sit on the pier and look down at the water.

—*Mira el pez grande*— *Abuelito* says. He points to a big fish.

—*Me gustan los chiquitos*— I answer, and show him some little silver fish that are nibbling by a rock.

We stay at the pier *un buen rato,* for a long time.

238

Student Edition, p. 238

INFERENCE Do you think the girl has any brothers or sisters? Explain. (No, because if she did, they would probably be with her on her visits with her grandparents.)

DEVELOP LANGUAGE Have students reread the first paragraph on p. 238. What does *aquarium* mean? What is something else you might see in an *aquarium* besides fish?

Grandpa knows I love surprises.

One Saturday, when I arrive, he has blown up a bunch of balloons for me. The balloons look like a big bouquet of flowers: yellow, red, orange, blue, and green.

"What fun, Grandpa" I say, and run with my balloons up and down the yard.

Un domingo, Abuelito also has a special surprise for me. He has made me a kite. The kite is made of colored paper and looks like a giant butterfly: *amarillo, rojo, anaranjado, azul, y verde.*

—*¡Qué divertido, Abuelito!*— I say. And I hold on to the string of my kite as it soars high in the air.

239

Student Edition, p. 239

SYNTHESIS What does the girl say the balloons look like? (a bouquet of flowers) Why do you think she says they look like a bouquet? (Flowers are colorful, and a bouquet of flowers is a bunch of flowers tied together. The balloons are also colorful and are tied together.)

Common Core State Standards

Literature 1. Ask and answer questions to demonstrate understanding of a text, referring explicitly to the text as the basis for the answers. **Literature 3.** Describe characters in a story (e.g., their traits, motivations, or feelings) and explain how their actions contribute to the sequence of events. **Literature 4.** Determine the meaning of words and phrases as they are used in a text, distinguishing literal from nonliteral language.

Access for All

SI Strategic Intervention

Have students work with a partner to compare and contrast two of the family members.

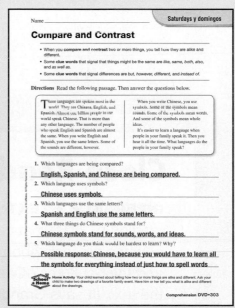

Let's Practice It! TR DVD•303

ELL

Learn New Words Explain to students that an *aquarium* is a container or tank where fish are kept. Have students who have seen an aquarium describe it. Point out that buildings in which fish are kept also are called aquariums. Show photos of each if possible.

Access Text © If students need help, then...

◉ INFERRING Have students read p. 240. Ask what they learned about the grandfathers when they were young. What can you infer about the grandfathers when they were young?

Think Aloud **MODEL** Grandpa delivered papers early in the morning when he was a young boy. *Abuelito* was in charge of his siblings and he helped in the fields when he was only twelve. I can infer that both were very responsible and hard workers.

Grandpa likes to tell stories. He tells me about how his mother, his father, and his older brother came to America in a big ship from Europe.

He also tells me about growing up in New York City. When he was a young boy, he delivered papers early in the morning, before school, to help his family.

Close Reading ©

INFERENCE • TEXT EVIDENCE After reading p. 241, what can you infer about how the girl feels about her ancestors and their cultures? Cite evidence from the text. (It says Grandma was proud of her grandmother and her *abuelita* was proud of her Indian blood and her *mamá*, so I think the girl is proud too.)

Abuelito also likes to tell stories. He tells me about the times when he was growing up on a *rancho* in Mexico. He worked in the fields when he was very young.

He also tells me how his father went to Texas, looking for work, and *Abuelito* was left in charge of his family. And he was only twelve!

240

Student Edition, p. 240

EVALUATION What makes this story realistic fiction? (The story is realistic because it tells about events that could really happen. Many children are close with their grandparents. Many grandparents speak different languages.)

ON THEIR OWN Have students reread p. 241 and make inferences about either of the grandmothers from what they have read and what they already know.

Grandma loves to tell me about her grandmother whose parents came to California in a covered wagon. It was a long and difficult trip.

Grandma's grandmother was born on the trail. Later she became a teacher.

Grandma is very proud of her grandmother. I feel proud too.

Abuelita loves to tell me about her *abuelita* and her *mamá.* Her *abuelita*'s family are Native Americans.

Abuelita is very proud of her Indian blood because the Indians really know how to love the land.

Abuelita feels *orgullo,* and I feel *orgullo,* too.

241

ANALYSIS Why do you think the author chose to tell the story from the point of view of the little girl? (The reader gets a strong feeling about how happy the girl is visiting both sets of grandparents.)

Common Core State Standards

Literature 1. Ask and answer questions to demonstrate understanding of a text, referring explicitly to the text as the basis for the answers. **Literature 3.** Describe characters in a story (e.g., their traits, motivations, or feelings) and explain how their actions contribute to the sequence of events.

Access for All

A Advanced

Have students write a short story that is realistic fiction. Remind them that realistic fiction is a made-up story that could actually happen in real life.

Connect to Social Studies

Native Tribes The original inhabitants of the area that is now called Texas included the Apache tribe, Caddo tribe, and Comanche tribe.

Inferring Show students a photo of a person. Ask students what the person is doing and how the person feels. Then have students make inferences about the person in the photo based on what they see and prior knowledge.

Access Text ⓒ If students need help, then...

◉ **HOMOPHONES** Write the following sentence on the board: *It took us an hour to get to our house.* Ask students to identify the homophones and their meanings.

(Think Aloud) **MODEL** I know the homophones mean a "measure of time" and "belonging to us." The words "it took us" tell me that the first word refers to an amount of time, so it must be *hour*. The other word describes the house, so it must be *our*.

It's my birthday. This time, Grandpa and Grandma come to our house. They have brought me a new doll. Grandma has made her a dress in my favorite color.

"What a beautiful doll, Grandpa!" I tell him, and I give him a big kiss.

"What a pretty blue dress! Thank you, Grandma, I love you very much!" I say.

242

Student Edition, p. 242

Close Reading ⓒ

SYNTHESIS • TEXT EVIDENCE
Why did the girl conclude that *Abuelita* and Grandma had planned the surprise together? Use evidence from the selection. (Grandma makes a doll and a dress in the girl's favorite color. *Abuelita* made a dollhouse and a dress just like the doll's dress. Because the presents go together, she knows *Abuelita* and Grandma planned it.)

ANALYSIS Help students generate text-based questions by providing the following question stem: In the selection, what did the girl say to her grandparents when _____?

ON THEIR OWN Have students look at p. 242 to identify two words that [h]ave homophones. Have them spell both sets of homophones. Then have [t]hem use each homophone in a sentence.

Abuelito y Abuelita also come.
Abuelito has made me a dollhouse.
Abuelita has made me a dress for my birthday
party. The dress is exactly like my doll's dress.
Abuelita and Grandma must have planned
this surprise together!
—*¡Qué linda casa de muñecas, Abuelito!*
¡Gracias!— I say, and give Abuelito a big hug.
¡Y qué bonito vestido azul, Abuelita! El
azul es mi color favorito— I tell her. —*Gracias,*
Abuelita. Te quiero mucho.

243

Student Edition, p. 243

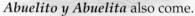

[IN]**FERENCE** What do you think will happen next? Why? (The girl says [it']s her birthday and both sets of grandparents are at her house, so I think [t]here will be a birthday party.)

Common Core State Standards

Literature 1. Ask and answer questions to demonstrate understanding of a text, referring explicitly to the text as the basis for the answers. **Foundational Skills 4.c.** Use context to confirm or self-correct word recognition and understanding, rereading as necessary. **Also Foundational Skills 3.**

ELL

Build Vocabulary Have Spanish speakers read the Spanish words on p. 243. Then call on volunteers to translate the text into English.

Homophones Homophones can be particularly confusing for English learners. Have students make a four-column chart that lists homophones and their meanings side by side to refer to as they read and write. They can use a dictionary or glossary to find the correct meanings.

I Love Saturdays y domingos **243a**

Access Text © If students need help, then...

⊙ MAIN IDEA AND DETAILS Have students read pp. 244–245. Ask them what the main idea is.

(Think Aloud) MODEL These pages are about the girl having a birthday party. I know she is having a good time because she says, "For me, it's a wonderful day." I think the main idea of these pages is that the girl is happy to be celebrating her birthday with her entire family and her friends.

ON THEIR OWN Have students reread pp. 244–245. Ask them to look for details that support the main idea.

Close Reading ©

EVALUATION What is the main idea of the entire story? Give some details to support that main idea. (A girl is proud of her cultures and loves her grandparents. She likes to visit and go places with both sets of grandparents.)

CROSS-TEXT EVALUATION
Use a Strategy to Self-Check How did the Read Aloud, "The First Texans," help you understand this selection?

All my cousins and friends come to the party. We gather together to break the *piñata* that my Mom has filled with gifts.

Abuelito is holding the rope to make the *piñata* go up and down.

We all line up. The younger kids in front.

Abuelita covers our eyes with a folded scarf so that we can't see the *piñata*.

244

Student Edition, p. 244

SYNTHESIS • TEXT EVIDENCE Using what you learned in this selection, tell what we can learn by comparing cultures. Have students cite examples from the text to support their responses.

CHECK PREDICTIONS Have students return to the predictions they made earlier and confirm whether they were accurate.

Some say, "Happy birthday!" and some say —*¡Feliz cumpleaños!*
For me it's a wonderful day, *un día maravilloso.*

245

Student Edition, p. 245

ANALYSIS • TEXT EVIDENCE Use details from the selections to compare and contrast what the grandparents do at the party. (On p. 244, it says that *Abuelito* is holding the rope of the piñata. *Abuelita* covers the children's eyes. From the illustrations on p. 244, I can see Grandpa and Grandma are just watching.)

Common Core State Standards

Literature 1. Ask and answer questions to demonstrate understanding of a text, referring explicitly to the text as the basis for the answers. **Literature 2.** Recount stories, including fables, folktales, and myths from diverse cultures; determine the central message, lesson, or moral and explain how it is conveyed through key details in the text. **Also Literature 3.**

Access for All

SI **Strategic Intervention**

Have students work with a partner to review the story and find the main idea on each spread. Have them use that information to figure out the main idea of the story.

A **Advanced**

The girl celebrated her birthday with a *piñata.* Have students write about how they celebrate their birthdays.

Celebrations Have students discuss the ways in which they celebrate birthdays or other special days with their families. List any words related to the celebrations. Have students explain their meanings to the group. They can show or draw pictures if appropriate.

I Love Saturdays y domingos **245a**

DAY 3

Common Core State Standards
Literature 1. Ask and answer questions to demonstrate understanding of a text, referring explicitly to the text as the basis for the answers. Also Literature 2., Writing 8.

Envision It! Retell

246

Think Critically

1. In the story, the author writes about a girl visiting her grandparents on the weekends. Do you ever visit with your grandparents or other relatives? What you do during your visits? What would you like to do if you had a chance?
Text to Self

2. The author of *I Love Saturdays y domingos* has a purpose. What do you think the author's purpose is for writing this story? What would you ask the author if you had a chance?
Think Like an Author

3. Look back at the story. What do you think is the main idea? Find details that support your choice. Main Idea and Details

4. What do you think the author feels about different cultures and families? Explain your answer using details from the story.
Inferring

5. Look Back and Write Look back at the question on page 231. How are the girl's two sets of grandparents alike? How are they different? Use information from the selection to write about how they each celebrate their culture. Provide evidence to support your answer.
Key Ideas and Details • Text Evidence

Meet the Author

Alma Flor Ada

Alma Flor Ada was born in Cuba and has lived in Spain and Peru. She currently lives in California and teaches at the University of San Francisco. Ms. Ada writes most of her books, such as *Jordi's Star* and *Gathering the Sun*, in both English and Spanish and her daughter does a lot of her translations!

Use the *Reader's and Writer's Notebook* to record your independent reading.

247

Student Edition, pp. 246–247

Common Core State Standards

Literature 1. Ask and answer questions to demonstrate understanding of a text, referring explicitly to the text as the basis for the answers. **Also Literature 2., Writing 8., Speaking/Listening 4., Language 3.**

Bridge to Common Core

RANGE OF READING AND LEVEL OF TEXT COMPLEXITY

To increase students' capacity for reading and comprehending complex texts independently and proficiently, have them read other literary texts by Alma Flor Ada or about the topic of comparing cultures. After students read closely for a sustained period of time, they should record their reading in their Reading Logs.

Think Critically

1. TEXT TO SELF Students should tell about what they do with their grandparents or relatives and what they would like to do if they had a chance.

2. THINK LIKE AN AUTHOR The author wants to compare the two cultures and entertain the reader. I would ask her how she came up with the idea.

3. MAIN IDEA AND DETAILS The main idea is that although the girl's grandparents do things a bit differently, she loves them equally. I know this because she is happy when she visits them.

4. INFERRING I think the author enjoys experiencing different cultures because the main character in the story loves eating foods from different cultures and learning about her family. She must have a close family because the characters love each other and enjoy being together.

5. LOOK BACK AND WRITE • TEXT EVIDENCE To build writing fluency, assign a 10–15 minute time limit.

Scoring Rubric | Look Back and Write

TOP-SCORE RESPONSE A top-score response uses details to tell how the grandparents are alike and different.

A top-score response should include:

• One set of grandparents speaks English while the other speaks Spanish.

• Both sets of grandparents love their granddaughter and see her every weekend.

• They all love to tell the girl stories about their childhood but their stories are all different.

Retell

Have students work in pairs to retell the selection, using the retelling strip in the Student Edition or the Story Sort as prompts. Monitor students' retellings.

Scoring Rubric | Narrative Retelling

	4	3	2	1
Connections	Makes connections and generalizes beyond the text	Makes connections to other events, stories, or experiences	Makes a limited connection to another event, story, or experience	Makes no connection to another event, story, or experience
Author's Purpose	Elaborates on author's purpose	Tells author's purpose with some clarity	Makes some connection to author's purpose	Makes no connection to author's purpose
Characters	Describes the main character(s) and any character development	Identifies the main character(s) and gives some information about them	Inaccurately identifies some characters or gives little information about them	Inaccurately identifies the characters or gives no information about them
Setting	Describes the time and location	Identifies the time and location	Omits details of time or location	Is unable to identify time or location
Plot	Describes the problem, goal, events, and ending using rich detail	Tells the problem, goal, events, and ending with some errors that do not affect meaning	Tells parts of the problem, goal, events, and ending with gaps that affect meaning	Retelling has no sense of story

MONITOR PROGRESS | Check Retelling

If... students have difficulty retelling,

then... use the Retelling Cards/Story Sort to scaffold their retellings.

Plan to Assess Retelling

☐ **Week 1** Strategic Intervention

☑ **This week assess Advanced students.**

☐ **Week 3** Strategic Intervention

☐ **Week 4** On-Level

☐ **Week 5** Assess any students you have not yet checked during this unit.

Meet the Author

Have students read about author Alma Flor Ada on p. 247. Ask them how she tells about her culture in *I Love Saturdays y domingos*.

Read Independently

Have students enter their independent reading into their Reading Logs.

Retelling Use the Retelling Cards to discuss the selection with students. Place the cards in an incorrect order and have volunteers correct the order. Then have students explain where each card should go as they describe the sequence of the selection.

 **Common Core State Standards**

Informational Text 7. Use information gained from illustrations (e.g., maps, photographs) and the words in a text to demonstrate understanding of the text (e.g., where, when, why, and how key events occur). **Foundational Skills 4.b.** Read on-level prose and poetry orally with accuracy, appropriate rate, and expression on successive readings. **Also Foundational Skills 4.**

Fluency

Accuracy

MODEL FLUENT READING Have students turn to p. 238 of *I Love Saturdays y domingos.* Have students follow along as you read the top half of the page. Tell them to listen to how you read each word without skipping or replacing any words.

GUIDE PRACTICE Have students follow along as you read the paragraphs again. Then have them reread the page as a group without you until they read each word correctly and do not skip any words. Ask questions to be sure they comprehend the text. Continue in this way with the rest of the page.

Corrective feedback	**If...** students are having difficulty reading with accuracy, **then...** prompt them as follows:

- Did you read every word? Where do you see difficult words?
- How can you read with better accuracy?
- Read the sentence again. Make sure you read carefully and do not miss any words.

Reread for Fluency

Routine Oral Rereading

1. **Read** Have students read the first three paragraphs on p. 239 of *I Love Saturdays y domingos* orally.

2. **Reread** To achieve optimal fluency, students should reread the text three or four times.

3. **Corrective Feedback** Have the class read aloud without you. Provide feedback about their accuracy and encourage them to read each word correctly without skipping or replacing any.

Routines Flip Chart

Research and Study Skills

Maps

TEACH Ask students what kinds of texts use **maps.** Students may mention textbooks, newspapers, nonfiction books, or magazines. Show a map from a content area text and use it to review these terms:

- A map is a **drawing of a place** and shows where something is or where something happened.

- Maps have a **legend** that contains a compass rose, a scale, and symbols to show landmarks, such as airports, schools, and churches.

- A **compass rose** shows the directions north, south, east, and west.

- A **scale** shows distance. Usually an inch equals a certain distance in miles or kilometers.

Provide groups with examples of different kinds of maps. Have each group show its map to the class, telling what it shows and pointing out the features of the map.

GUIDE PRACTICE Discuss these questions:

What is the purpose of a map? (to locate places, to determine how to get somewhere, to find out how far apart locations are)

How can a map help you when you read? (Possible response: You can look to see where places you read about are. You can see what places you know about are close to them. It can give you a better idea of what the place is like.)

ON THEIR OWN Have students review and complete p. 335 of the *Reader's and Writer's Notebook.*

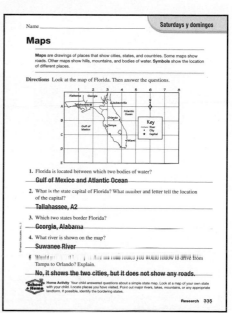

Reader's and Writer's Notebook,
p. 335

Access for All

A Advanced

Have students create a map of a make-believe town including symbols to represent various landmarks in the town. Remind students to include a legend to describe the symbols and to include a compass rose and a scale.

 **Common Core State Standards**

Writing 5. With guidance and support from peers and adults, develop and strengthen writing as needed by planning, revising, and editing. **Language 1.g.** Form and use comparative and superlative adjectives and adverbs, and choose between them depending on what is to be modified. **Also Writing 7., Language 4., 4.a.**

Research and Inquiry

Step 3 Analyze Information

TEACH Tell students they will analyze their findings and may need to change the focus of their original inquiry question.

Think Aloud **MODEL** Originally, I thought looking up Japanese celebrations in an encyclopedia would give me all the information I needed but the article didn't go into a lot of details. Then I found some books and articles that talked about all kinds of celebrations around the world. These let me find detailed information about Japanese New Year's celebrations and see how they compare to those in other places. I will refocus my inquiry question to be specifically about Japanese New Year's celebrations: *What makes Japanese New Year's celebrations unique?*

GUIDE PRACTICE Have students analyze their findings. They may need to refocus their inquiry question to better fit the information they found. Remind students that if they have difficulty improving their focus they can ask local members of the community they are researching for guidance.

Remind students that their flyers should present information in an easy-to-read format with an eye-catching design.

ON THEIR OWN Have students survey one another about cultural celebrations that their families observe or ones they have heard of. Students should then compare their research results to the survey they conducted in class.

Conventions

Comparative and Superlative Adjectives

REVIEW Write the word *lighter* on the board. Ask students how many things they can compare with this word. Remind students that comparative adjectives compare two people, places, or things. Recall that comparative adjectives are formed by adding -*er* to the end of an adjective.

Write the word *lightest* on the board. Ask students how many things they can compare with this word. Remind students that superlative adjectives compare three or more people, places, or things. Recall that superlative adjectives are formed by adding -*est* to the end of an adjective.

CONNECT TO ORAL LANGUAGE Have the class complete these sentence frames orally.

> Running is _____ than walking.
>
> But biking is the _____.

ON THEIR OWN For additional support, use *Let's Practice It!* p. 304 on the *Teacher Resources DVD-ROM*.

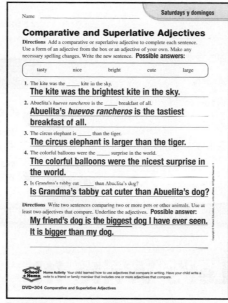

Let's Practice It! TR DVD•304

Spelling

Homophones

FREQUENTLY MISSPELLED WORDS The words *for/four, maid/made,* and *ear/here* are common words that students often misspell. These words are difficult because they are homophones—they sound the same but are spelled differently. You have to know from the context which word and spelling to use. Have students practice by writing sentences using each word.

ON THEIR OWN For more support, use *Reader's and Writer's Notebook,* p. 336.

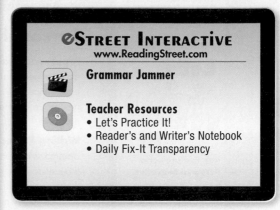

eStreet Interactive
www.ReadingStreet.com

Grammar Jammer

Teacher Resources
• Let's Practice It!
• Reader's and Writer's Notebook
• Daily Fix-It Transparency

Daily Fix-It

5. Mom will right a letter to her nefew in Mexico. *(write; nephew)*

6. Isnt he a great sircus performer? *(Isn't; circus)*

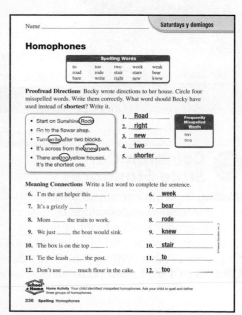

Reader's and Writer's Notebook, p. 336

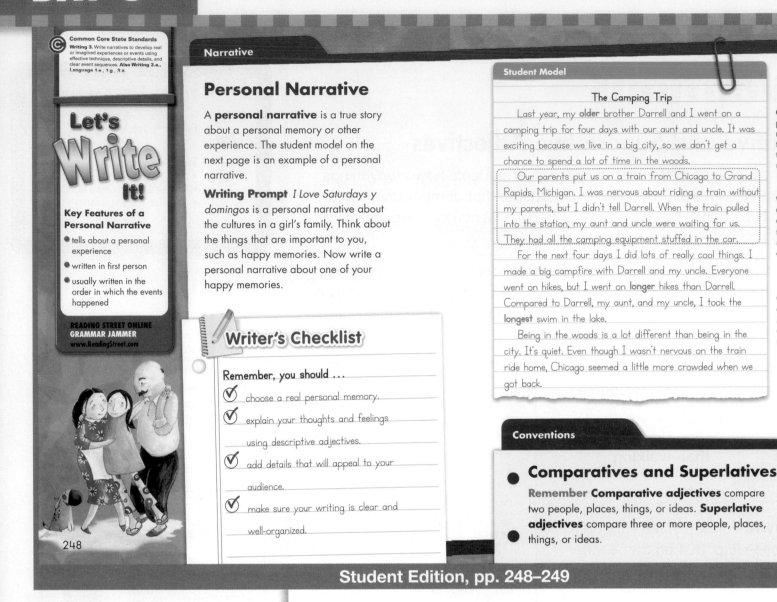

Narrative

Personal Narrative

A **personal narrative** is a true story about a personal memory or other experience. The student model on the next page is an example of a personal narrative.

Writing Prompt *I Love Saturdays y domingos* is a personal narrative about the cultures in a girl's family. Think about the things that are important to you, such as happy memories. Now write a personal narrative about one of your happy memories.

Writer's Checklist

Remember, you should ...

☑ choose a real personal memory.

☑ explain your thoughts and feelings using descriptive adjectives.

☑ add details that will appeal to your audience.

☑ make sure your writing is clear and well-organized.

248

Student Model

The Camping Trip

Last year, my older brother Darrell and I went on a camping trip for four days with our aunt and uncle. It was exciting because we live in a big city, so we don't get a chance to spend a lot of time in the woods.

Our parents put us on a train from Chicago to Grand Rapids, Michigan. I was nervous about riding a train without my parents, but I didn't tell Darrell. When the train pulled into the station, my aunt and uncle were waiting for us. They had all the camping equipment stuffed in the car.

For the next four days I did lots of really cool things. I made a big campfire with Darrell and my uncle. Everyone went on hikes, but I went on longer hikes than Darrell. Compared to Darrell, my aunt, and my uncle, I took the longest swim in the lake.

Being in the woods is a lot different than being in the city. It's quiet. Even though I wasn't nervous on the train ride home, Chicago seemed a little more crowded when we got back.

Genre A personal narrative tells about a true personal memory.

Writing Trait Conventions Consistent verb tense helps make meaning clear.

Comparative and superlative adjectives are used correctly.

Conventions

Comparatives and Superlatives

Remember Comparative adjectives compare two people, places, things, or ideas. **Superlative adjectives** compare three or more people, places, things, or ideas.

249

Student Edition, pp. 248–249

Key Features of a Personal Narrative

- tells about a personal experience
- written in first person
- usually written in the order in which the events happened

READING STREET ONLINE
GRAMMAR JAMMER
www.ReadingStreet.com

Common Core State Standards

Writing 3. Write narratives to develop real or imagined experiences or events using effective technique, descriptive details, and clear event sequences. **Also Writing 3.a., 3.b., 10., Language 1.e., 1.g., 3., 3.a.**

Let's Write It!

WRITE A PERSONAL NARRATIVE Use pp. 248–249 in the Student Edition. Direct students to read the key features of a personal narrative, which appears on p. 248. Remind students to review the information in the Writer's Checklist as they write their own personal narratives.

Read the student model on p. 249. Point out the key features of personal narratives in the model.

CONNECT TO CONVENTIONS Remind students that comparative adjectives compare two things, while superlative adjectives are used to compare three or more things. Point out the correct use of comparative and superlative adjectives in the model.

Writing  Zoom in on ©

Personal Narrative

Writing for Tests: Evaluation

DISPLAY RUBRIC Have students return to the scoring rubric from p. 333 of the *Reader's and Writer's Notebook* that you reviewed on Day 2. Then explain to students that they will use this rubric to evaluate the personal narratives they wrote yesterday.

Scoring Rubric Personal Narrative			
4	**3**	**2**	**1**
Focus/Ideas Focuses on specific, real memory; told from writer's point of view	Includes events from writer's memory; told from writer's point of view	Includes some events from writer's memory; mostly told from writer's point of view	Narrative does not focus on real events from writer's memory
Organization Clear order of events	Can follow order of events	Unclear order of events	No order of events
Voice Writer shows personal emotions, thoughts, and opinions	Writer shows some personal emotions, thoughts, and opinions	Writer shows few personal emotions, thoughts, and opinions	Writer makes no effort to show personal emotions, thoughts, and opinions
Word Choice Strong use of verbs and adjectives to bring the story to life	Good try at using verbs and adjectives	Poor use of verbs and adjectives; story lacks description	No effort made to use verbs and adjectives
Sentences Clear sentences of different lengths and types	Sentences of a few lengths and types	Sentences of similar length and type	No variety of sentence length and type
Conventions Few, if any, errors; correct use of verbs and adjectives	Several small errors; use of verbs and adjectives	Many errors; weak use of verbs and adjectives	Many serious errors; incorrect or no use of verbs and adjectives

Key Features Have students take turns asking each other questions about their personal narratives: *What is your personal narrative about? What happens first in your narrative? What happens next in your narrative? Is your narrative a true personal memory? Did you write in the first person?*

DAY 3

Common Core State Standards

Writing 3. Write narratives to develop real or imagined experiences or events using effective technique, descriptive details, and clear event sequences. **Language 1.** Demonstrate command of the conventions of standard English grammar and usage when writing or speaking. **Language 1.a.** Explain the function of nouns, pronouns, verbs, adjectives, and adverbs in general and their functions in particular sentences. **Also Language 3.a.**

Bridge to Common Core

RANGE OF WRITING

Throughout the week, students produce writing in which the organization and style are appropriate to the task of writing for tests as they complete personal narratives. They also develop and strengthen their revising and editing skills through self-evaluation.

Writing

Personal Narrative

Mini-Lesson | **Writing for Tests: Evaluation**

- ■ **Introduce** Explain that when you evaluate writing with a rubric, you are evaluating different traits in the writing. Have students read aloud a few of the six traits in the rubric.

- ■ **Evaluate a Trait** Tell students that they will evaluate their sample writing test based on 1 of the 6 traits in the rubric. We will focus on trait 4, word choice. Remind students that good word choice creates an interesting narrative that helps the reader visualize the writer's experience. According to the rubric, we want to make sure that we evaluate our use of verbs and adjectives. These descriptive words bring a narrative to life. Verbs describe the action in the sentence, so we want interesting, exciting verbs rather than boring ones. Adjectives describe the people, places, and things in our narrative (wooden; decrepit; rectangular; soothing).

  Have students review their personal narratives and circle all the verbs and adjectives. Then, using the rubric as a guide, have them assess their use of descriptive verbs and adjectives on a scale from 4 to 1.

- ■ **Apply Scoring** Direct students to continue evaluating their personal narratives based on the other 5 traits on the rubric. Remind students that they may receive different number scores for each of the different traits, but that is all right. Lower or higher scores for different traits can help them see where their strengths lie, and where they might need to focus more attention and effort.

Writing Trait: Conventions

Inconsistent use of verb tenses in writing can confuse the reader and make it more difficult to follow a story line. As students review their writing, remind them that consistent verb tense helps make meaning clear. Write several sentences on the board with inconsistent past and present verb tenses. Have partners look for the inconsistencies and tell how they would fix them to make sense.

Routine Quick Write for Fluency Team Talk

1. **Talk** Pairs talk about how using descriptive language can bring a narrative to life.

2. **Write** Students write one sentence using a boring verb, and then revise it using an exciting verb.

3. **Share** Students read their sentences to a partner. Partners suggest adjectives that would help improve the sentence.

Routines Flip Chart

Access for All

SI Strategic Intervention

To help students who struggle with identifying verbs and adjectives, write several of each on index cards. Make one pile of adjectives and one of verbs. Have students take turns drawing one card from each pile. Then have students make a sentence that uses both words.

Wrap Up Your Day!

✔ **Content Knowledge** Have students discuss how the cultures of the grandparents were alike and how they were different.

✔ **Text-Based Comprehension** How can inferring help you understand the text?

Preview DAY 4

Tell students that tomorrow they will read about cultural celebrations.

Materials

- Student Edition
- Reader's and Writer's Notebook
- Decodable Reader

© Common Core State Standards

Speaking/Listening 1. Engage effectively in a range of collaborative discussions (one-on-one, in groups, and teacher-led) with diverse partners on grade 3 topics and texts, building on others' ideas and expressing their own clearly. **Language 6.** Acquire and use accurately grade-appropriate conversational, general academic, and domain-specific words and phrases, including those that signal spatial and temporal relationships (e.g., *After dinner that night we went looking for them*). **Also Speaking/Listening 1.d.**

Content Knowledge

Comparing Cultures

EXPAND THE CONCEPT Remind students of the weekly concept question, *How are cultures alike and different?* Have students discuss how cultures are alike and different.

Build Oral Language

Team Talk **TALK ABOUT SENTENCES AND WORDS** Ask students to reread the first paragraph on Student Edition p. 244.

All my cousins and friends come to the party. We gather together to break the piñata *that my Mom has filled with gifts.*

- What is another word for *gather? (group, get together, join)*
- What word is a homophone? *(break)* What is the homophone for *break* and what is its definition? *(brake;* "a device that presses against the wheels to slow or stop the motion of a vehicle" or "the action of slowing or stopping by using a brake")
- If you didn't know what a *piñata* was, what could you infer from the surrounding text? (It's something you break, it's filled with gifts, and you find it at a party. It must be some kind of game.)
- How could we combine these sentences without changing their basic meaning? Have students turn to a partner and share. (Possible response: All my cousins and friends gather to break the *piñata* that my Mom has filled with gifts.)

Build Oral Vocabulary

Amazing Words
Robust Vocabulary Routine

1. **Introduce** Write the Amazing Word *procession* on the board. Have students say it aloud with you. Some people celebrate certain holidays by having a parade or *procession.* Have students determine a definition of *procession.* (A *procession* is a type of organized movement forward done by people or vehicles that move slowly together, usually as part of a celebration.)

2. **Demonstrate** Have students answer questions to demonstrate understanding. Have you ever seen a *procession?* Where were you? What did you see? (Possible response: Yes, it was a Martin Luther King Jr. Day parade. I saw bands marching and playing music.)

3. **Apply** Have students apply their understanding. Where else or when might there be a *procession?* (Possible response: at a wedding ceremony)

4. **Display the Word** Point out the different vowel sound-spellings in the word *procession* as you read it.

See p. OV•2 to teach *settler.*

Routines Flip Chart

ADD TO THE CONCEPT MAP Discuss the Amazing Words *belief* and *chant.* Add these and other concept-related words to the concept map. Use the following questions to develop students' understanding of the concept.

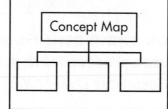

Think about a *belief* that the girl's grandparents might have. What are some *beliefs* that your parents have?

Sometimes when people have a *piñata,* they sing a *chant.* Do you have any *chants* that you sing when you play certain games? Explain.

eStreet Interactive
www.ReadingStreet.com
Teacher Resources
• Amazing Word Cards
• Reader's and Writer's Notebook

Amazing Words

clan	barbecue
dwelling	belief
shield	chant
headdress	procession
concentrate	settler

Strategy Response Log

Have students interpret or make new inferences about *I Love Saturdays y domingos.* Then have them complete p. 28 in *Reader's and Writer's Notebook.*

Produce Oral Language Use the Day 4 instruction on ELL Poster 22 to extend and enrich language.

@ **Common Core State Standards**

Foundational Skills 3. Know and apply grade-level phonics and word analysis skills in decoding words. **Foundational Skills 3.c.** Decode multisyllable words. **Also Foundational Skills 3.d.**

Word Analysis

Review Syllable Pattern CV/VC

REVIEW SOUND-SPELLINGS To review syllable pattern CV/VC, write this sentence: *The gentle giant is not cruel.* You studied the syllable pattern CV/VC. Let's review this syllable pattern by looking at the sentence. Read the sentence to yourself. Raise your hand when you see words that have two vowels in a row. *(giant, cruel)* Have students identify where to divide the words into syllables. How many vowel sounds do you hear in each word? **(two)** How many syllables do you hear in each word? **(two)** Where should we divide the words? *(giant: between the i and the a; cruel: between the u and the e)*

> **Corrective feedback** | If students are unable to answer the questions about the CV/VC syllable pattern, refer them to *Sound-Spelling Card* 116.

GUIDE PRACTICE Display a four-column chart with the headings *u/i, i/o, u/a,* and *i/a.* We'll put words that have the vowel *ui* divided between two syllables in the first column. Words with the vowels *io* will go in the second column, words with *ua* in the third column, and words with *ia* in the fourth column. **Have students write these words in the appropriate column:** *casual, fluid, patios, denial, period, violet, truant,* and *radiator.* Then have students read the words and ask volunteers to draw a slash mark between the two vowels that get divided.

u/i	i/o	u/a	i/a
fluid	patios	casual	denial
	period	truant	radiator
	violet		

ON THEIR OWN For additional practice, use *Let's Practice It!* p. 305 on the *Teacher Resources DVD-ROM.*

Name _____   Saturdays y domingos

Syllable Pattern CV/VC

Directions Draw a / mark to correctly divide each word into syllables. Write the syllables on the lines. (Example: *di/ary*).

1. create _____ cre/ate _____
2. giant _____ gi/ant _____
3. piano _____ pi/a/no _____
4. realize _____ re/al/ize _____
5. pioneer _____ pi/o/neer _____
6. violin _____ vi/o/lin _____
7. riot _____ ri/ot _____
8. Indian _____ In/di/an _____

Directions Each sentence contains an underlined word. Divide the word into syllables correctly. Write the syllables on the line, with a / mark between them.

9. The block castle lay in ruins on the playroom floor.
_____ ru/ins _____

10. Cats must have meat in their diet in order to survive.
_____ di/et _____

11. Mr. Mills reminded the students to study for the science test.
_____ sci/ence _____

12. The team played baseball in a small minor league stadium.
_____ sta/di/um _____

Home Activity Your child divided CV/VC words correctly into syllables. Read an article about Mexican culture with your child. Point to words that have two vowels together that have different sounds. Have your child pronounce them correctly.

Syllable Pattern CV/VC DVD•305

Let's Practice It! TR DVD•305

Fluent Word Reading

Spiral Review

READ WORDS IN ISOLATION Display these words. Tell students that they can already decode some words on this list. Explain that they should know other words because they appear often in reading.

Have students read the list three or four times until they can read at the rate of two to three seconds per word.

Word Reading

people	hungry	inventor	outside	have
complain	what	instant	hostess	complete
presoak	midnight	should	surprise	two
writer	artist	overtime	you	bifocals

Corrective feedback

If... students have difficulty reading whole words,

then... have them use sound-by-sound blending for decodable words or chunking for words that have word parts, or have them say and spell high-frequency words.

If... students cannot read fluently at a rate of two to three seconds per word,

then... have pairs practice the list until they can read it fluently.

eSTREET INTERACTIVE
www.ReadingStreet.com

Teacher Resources
• Let's Practice It!

Interactive Sound-Spelling Cards

Access for All

SI Strategic Intervention

Have students copy the words from the four-column chart onto a piece of paper. When students copy the words, have them use a different color ink for the two vowels that appear together. This will help students visually see that each vowel sound should be pronounced.

Spiral Review

These activities review:
• previously taught high-frequency words *people, what, should, you, have, two.*
• syllables VCCCV; prefixes *(pre-, mid-, over-, out-, bi-)*; suffixes *(-er, -or, -ess, -ist).*

Fluent Word Reading Have students listen to a more fluent reader say the words. Then have them repeat the words.

Common Core State Standards

Foundational Skills 3. Know and apply grade-level phonics and word analysis skills in decoding words. **Foundational Skills 3.d.** Read grade-appropriate irregularly spelled words. **Foundational Skills 4.** Read with sufficient accuracy and fluency to support comprehension. **Foundational Skills 4.b.** Read on-level prose and poetry orally with accuracy, appropriate rate, and expression on successive readings. **Foundational Skills 4.c.** Use context to confirm or self-correct word recognition and understanding, rereading as necessary.

Fluent Word Reading

READ WORDS IN CONTEXT Display these sentences. Call on individuals to read a sentence. Then randomly point to review words and have students read them. To help you monitor word reading, high-frequency words are underlined and decodable words are italicized.

MONITOR PROGRESS | **Sentence Reading**

What will the *hostess* serve the *hungry* people *outside*?

Should the *artist* paint a famous *inventor* or *writer*?

Was it a *complete surprise* that you needed *bifocals*?

Don't *complain* that the game went into *overtime* until *midnight*.

In an *instant* you can *presoak* the two dirty shirts you have.

If... students are unable to read an underlined high-frequency word,

then... read the word for them and spell it, having them echo you.

If... students have difficulty reading an italicized decodable word,

then... guide them in using sound-by-sound blending or chunking.

Reread for Fluency

Have students reread the sentences to develop automaticity decoding words.

Routine | **Oral Rereading**

1. **Read** Have students read all the sentences orally.

2. **Reread** To achieve optimal fluency, students should reread the sentences three or four times.

3. **Corrective Feedback** Listen as students read. Provide corrective feedback regarding their fluency and decoding.

Routines Flip Chart

Decodable Passage 22C

f students need help, then...

Read *Jobs*

READ WORDS IN ISOLATION Have students turn to p. 83 in *Decodable Practice Readers 3.2* and find the first list of words. Each word in this list is a homophone. Let's read these words. Be sure that students pronounce pairs of homophones the same.

Next, have students read the high-frequency words.

PREVIEW Have students read the title and preview the passage. Tell them that they will read words that are homophones.

READ WORDS IN CONTEXT Chorally read the passage along with the students. Have students identify words in the passage that are homophones. Make sure that students are monitoring their accuracy when they decode words.

Team Talk Pair students and have them take turns reading the passage aloud to each other. Monitor students as they read to check for proper pronunciation and appropriate pacing.

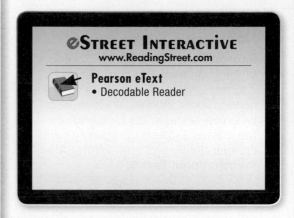

eStreet Interactive
www.ReadingStreet.com

Pearson eText
• Decodable Reader

Access for All

A **Advanced**

Have students make a list of the words with prefixes in the sentences on p. 250e (*outside, bifocals, overtime, midnight, presoak*). Ask students to sort the words by the prefix they contain and add as many other words as they can to each list.

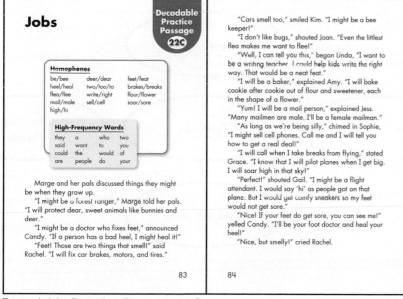

Jobs

Decodable Practice Passage 22C

Homophones

be/bee	deer/dear	feet/feat
heel/heal	two/too/to	brakes/breaks
flea/flee	write/right	flour/flower
mail/male	sell/cell	soar/sore
high/hi		

High-Frequency Words

they	a	who	two
said	want	to	you
could	the	would	of
are	people	do	your

Marge and her pals discussed things they might be when they grow up.

"I might be a forest ranger," Marge told her pals. "I will protect dear, sweet animals like bunnies and deer."

"I might be a doctor who fixes feet," announced Candy. "If a person has a bad heel, I might heal it!"

"Feet! Those are two things that smell!" said Rachel. "I will fix car brakes, motors, and tires."

"Cars smell too," smiled Kim. "I might be a bee keeper!"

"I don't like bugs," shouted Joan. "Even the littlest flea makes me want to flee!"

"Well, I can tell you this," began Linda, "I want to be a writing teacher. I could help kids write the right way. That would be a neat feat."

"I will be a baker," explained Amy. "I will bake cookie after cookie out of flour and sweetener, each in the shape of a flower."

"Yum! I will be a mail person," explained Jess. "Many mailmen are male. I'll be a female mailman."

"As long as we're being silly," chimed in Sophie, "I might sell cell phones. Call me and I will tell you how to get a real deal!"

"I will call when I take breaks from flying," stated Grace. "I know that I will pilot planes when I get big. I will soar high in that sky!"

"Perfect!" shouted Gail. "I might be a flight attendant. I would say 'hi' as people got on that plane. But I would get comfy sneakers so my feet would not get sore."

"Nice! If your feet do get sore, you can see me!" yelled Candy. "I'll be your foot doctor and heal your heel!"

"Nice, but smelly!" cried Rachel.

83   84

Decodable Practice Passage 22C

Common Core State Standards

Informational Text 10. By the end of the year, read and comprehend informational texts, including history/social studies, science, and technical texts, at the high end of the grades 2–3 text complexity band independently and proficiently. **Also Informational Text 5.**

Bridge to Common Core

KEY IDEAS AND DETAILS

Analyzing the structure and purpose of textbooks will lead students to identify the elements of a textbook. By thinking about textbooks, students will be able to approach their reading with an understanding of the genre.

Social Studies in Reading

Textbook

INTRODUCE Explain to students that what we read is structured differently depending on the author's reason for writing and what kind of information he or she wishes to convey. Different types of texts are called genres. Tell students that a textbook is one type of genre.

DISCUSS THE GENRE Ask students what they already know about textbooks. We use textbooks in school. Usually textbooks have many pages and contain a lot of information. We usually use the same textbook for the entire school year.

GROUP PRACTICE Display a concept web. Label the middle circle *Textbooks.* Ask the following questions:

- When do we usually read textbooks? (at school)

- What kind of information is found in textbooks? (It varies. There are textbooks for all subject areas. There is information in them and sometimes activities to complete.)

- How are textbooks arranged? (Sometimes in chapters or by themes or stories; sometimes by skills.)

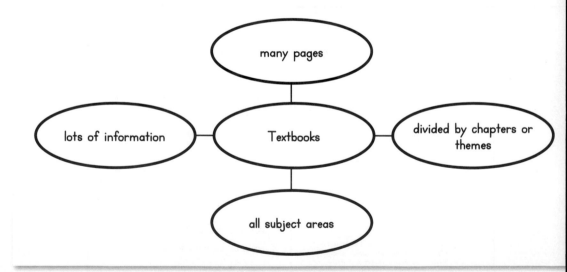

Team Talk Have have students work with a partner to discuss and identify he elements of a textbook.

READ Tell students that they will now read a passage from a textbook about communities celebrating culture. Have the class think about times when reading a textbook might be interesting or informative.

Day 4 SMALL GROUP TIME • Differentiate Vocabulary, p. SG•17

OL On-Level	**SI** Strategic Intervention	**A** Advanced
• **Develop** Language Using Amazing Words	• **Review/Discuss** Amazing Words	• **Extend** Amazing Words and Selection Vocabulary
• **Read** "Communities Celebrate Cultures"	• **Read** "Communities Celebrate Cultures"	• **Read** "Communities Celebrate Cultures"
		• **Organize** Inquiry Project

If... students need more scaffolding and practice with the **Amazing Words,**
then... use the Routine on pp. xxxvi–xxxvii in the *ELL Handbook*.

Common Core State Standards
Informational Text 5. Use text features and search tools (e.g., key words, sidebars, hyperlinks) to locate information relevant to a given topic efficiently.
Also Informational Text 1.

Social Studies in Reading

Genre
Textbook

- Textbooks provide information about a specific subject in a logical order.
- Textbooks include facts and details that describe important ideas about the specific subject.
- Textbooks have text features to help readers predict, locate, and verify information. Graphic sources show information visually.
- Use the text features as you read "Communities Celebrate Cultures" to predict the topic and summarize the important ideas.

Communities Celebrate Cultures

Many communities have celebrations that started in other countries. The celebrations honor the ethnic groups who helped build the community. These celebrations are sometimes called ethnic celebrations.

Cinco de Mayo (SIN ko day MY oh) means the fifth of May. It is a Mexican holiday that celebrates the victory of the Mexican people over the French who invaded their country. After a battle on May 5, 1862, the French left Mexico.

For many people, the holiday is a symbol. It shows that the people of Mexico could become free of rulers from other countries.

Today, many people in Mexico and other countries celebrate Cinco de Mayo. In the United States people dance in colorful clothes. They play music on guitars and eat traditional Mexican food. They show that they are proud to be Mexican Americans.

St. Patrick's Day is celebrated in many communities around the United States and the world. The holiday started as a religious holiday in Ireland, a country in Europe.

On St. Patrick's Day both Irish and non-Irish people celebrate Irish culture. Some people honor Irish culture by wearing green clothing, watching parades, and eating food that is dyed green.

REVIEW In what ways are Cinco de Mayo and St. Patrick's Day alike? How are they different?

Summarize the Lesson

- People follow traditions when they celebrate holidays.
- Families celebrate religious and nonreligious holidays.
- Communities celebrate to honor ethnic groups who helped build their communities.

Let's Think About...

How do the "Review" questions and the "Summarize the Lesson" box help you learn the important ideas on these pages?
Textbook

Let's Think About...

Reading Across Texts The girl in *I Love Saturdays y domingos* tells about some family traditions that are different from those mentioned in this textbook article. Why do you think this is so?

Writing Across the Texts Make a list of the celebrations and traditions you have learned about.

250

251

Student Edition, pp. 250–251

Common Core State Standards

Informational Text 1. Ask and answer questions to demonstrate understanding of a text, referring explicitly to the text as the basis for the answers. **Informational Text 2.** Determine the main idea of a text; recount the key details and explain how they support the main idea. **Informational Text 5.** Use text features and search tools (e.g., key words, sidebars, hyperlinks) to locate information relevant to a given topic quickly and efficiently. **Also Informational Text 9., 10.**

Access Text ©

TEACH Genre: Textbook Have students preview "Communities Celebrate Cultures" on pp. 250–251. Have them look at the photographs and preview the text. Then ask: What is the subject of this passage? What point of view is this passage written in? (The subject is community celebrations. It is written in the third person.)

Corrective feedback	If... students are unable to identify the subject,
	then... use the model to guide students in identifying the subject of the textbook passage.

Think Aloud

MODEL Textbooks provide information in a logical order about a specific subject. I can read the title and look at the illustrations to determine what the subject is. The photos of the maracas and dancers tell me that it will be about a Mexican celebration. The photo of the woman and the clover tell me that it will also be about an Irish celebration. I think the Mexican celebration will be presented first, and then the Irish celebration. I can infer this by looking at the placement of the photos. The point of view is third person. I know because textbooks are always written in the third person.

ON THEIR OWN Have students work with partners to discuss any cultural celebrations that they or their families observe.

Close Reading ©

EVALUATION • TEXT EVIDENCE What is the main idea of the passage? What are the details to support the main idea? (The main idea is that communities have celebrations that honor ethnic groups. The details are Cinco de Mayo is a Mexican holiday that is celebrated by people in Mexico and other countries. St. Patrick's Day is an Irish holiday celebrated in many communities in the United States and the world.)

ANALYSIS How are the two celebrations alike? How are they different? (People wear special clothing and eat certain foods during their celebrations but they are different in that they eat Mexican food for Cinco de Mayo and food that is dyed green on St. Patrick's Day.)

Genre

LET'S THINK ABOUT... As you read "Communities Celebrate Cultures," use Let's Think About in the Student Edition to help students focus on the features of a textbook.

They summarize what is in the text and tell me the important facts or main ideas of the passage.

Reading and Writing Across Texts

There are many kinds of traditions. Have students create a concept web listing the traditions in I Love Saturdays y domingos and the main features of those traditions. Have them complete a similar concept web for "Communities Celebrate Cultures." Then have students create a T-chart. On the left side, have them list the celebrations and traditions they learned about. On the right side, have them write the corresponding culture or ethnic group.

Connect to Social Studies

Cinco de Mayo Cinco de Mayo means the fifth of May. Some mistake this to be Mexican Independence Day, but it is actually a national holiday in Mexico that celebrates the anniversary of the Battle of Puebla. The Mexican victory at Puebla has come to symbolize a struggle for freedom and independence.

Activate Prior Knowledge Create a 2-column chart to record students' prior knowledge of Cinco de Mayo and St. Patrick's Day. Ask them what they already know about the celebrations. Record students' answers in the chart, adding to it as students read the selection.

Common Core State Standards
Language 4.a. Use sentence-level context as a clue to the meaning of a word or phrase. Also Foundational Skills 4.b., Speaking/Listening 4., Language 4.

Let's Learn It!

READING STREET ONLINE
ONLINE STUDENT EDITION
www.ReadingStreet.com

Vocabulary

Homophones

Context Clues Homophones are words that sound the same, but have different meanings and spellings, such as *pause* and *paws*. Context clues can help you determine the meanings of homophones.

Practice It! As you read *I Love Saturdays y domingos*, make a list of three or four words that have homophones. Write both the word and its homophone. Then write down the definition of each homophone.

Fluency

Accuracy

It is important to read with accuracy so you can understand the text. Reading each word as it is written on the page makes this possible. Listen to yourself as you read to make sure what you are reading makes sense.

Practice It! With a partner, practice reading aloud *I Love Saturdays y domingos*, page 238. Help each other pronounce difficult words correctly. How many words did you misread? Reread the section. Did your accuracy improve?

252

Listening and Speaking

Work productively and acknowledge others' contributions.

Drama

In a dramatization, people act out scenes from a story or play. Actors can use clues in the dialogue to show the emotions of the characters.

Practice It! Work in groups to write a dramatization of *I Love Saturdays y domingos*. Choose one event in the story to create a script for a scene in the dramatization. Determine the character assignments, including a narrator. Perform your scene in front of the class.

Tips

Listening ...

• Determine their purpose for listening, such as for enjoyment.
• Listen to identify emotional clues.

Speaking ...

• Speak at an appropriate pace.
• Use expression and emotion.

Teamwork ...

• Make suggestions to help improve the performance.
• Give, follow, and restate directions for staging the dramatization.

253

Student Edition, pp. 252–253

Common Core State Standards

Speaking/Listening 4. Report on a topic or text, tell a story, or recount an experience with appropriate facts and relevant, descriptive details, speaking clearly at an understandable pace. **Language 3.b.** Recognize and observe differences between the conventions of spoken and written standard English. **Language 4.a.** Use sentence-level context as a clue to the meaning of a word or phrase. **Also Foundational Skills 4., 4.b., Language 3., 4.**

Fluency

Accuracy

GUIDE PRACTICE Use the Student Edition activity as an assessment tool. Make sure the reading passage is at least 200 words in length. Make sure the accuracy is appropriate to enhance the meaning of what they are reading.

Don't Wait Until Friday

MONITOR PROGRESS Check Fluency

FORMATIVE ASSESSMENT As students reread, monitor progress toward their individual fluency goals.
Current Goal: 102–112 words correct per minute.
End-of-Year Goal: 120 words correct per minute.

If... students cannot read fluently at a rate of 102–112 words correct per minute,

then... have students practice with text at their independent levels.

Vocabulary Skill

⊙ Homophones

TEACH HOMOPHONES • CONTEXT CLUES Write these sentences on the board: *Mom used flour, sugar, and other ingredients to make a cake. Then she used frosting to decorate the cake with pink flowers.*

Point out the homophones *flour* and *flower.* Tell students to read the words around the homophones to determine the meaning of each homophone.

GUIDE PRACTICE Have students determine which context clues tell them the meaning of *flour* (sugar, make a cake) and *flower* (pink, decorated). Then ask them to determine the meaning of *flour* (finely ground cereal grains) and *flower* (colored part of a plant).

ON THEIR OWN Walk around the room as students work with partners to make sure the words and homophones they have written are correct. Check to make sure partners know the meanings of the words and their homophones.

Listening and Speaking

Drama

TEACH Tell students that in order for a dramatization to be successful, everyone must work together and acknowledge others' contributions. Remind students that there should be a narrator, and the rest of the group members are the characters. The characters perform all the lines of dialogue and the narrator reads the rest.

GUIDE PRACTICE Be sure students speak coherently when presenting the story. Point out that spoken communication of the characters may be less formal than written communication. Remind students to listen attentively to one another so they know when it is their turn to speak.

ON THEIR OWN Have students take turns performing the dramatization. Have the viewers (listeners) evaluate the performance, using the story in the Student Edition to support their opinions.

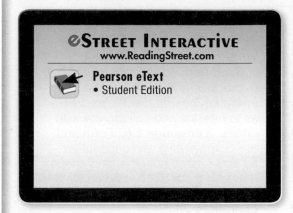

eStreet Interactive
www.ReadingStreet.com

Pearson eText
• Student Edition

Drama

Remind students that they should speak their lines as their character would, paying special attention to any punctuation cues that could be clues to expression. Encourage students to use any props that might aid their performance.

 Bridge to Common Core

COMPREHENSION AND COLLABORATION

Students work together to create and present their dramatizations. They should speak coherently when presenting and listen attentively to one another so they know when it is their turn to speak. Students should recognize that for the dramatization to be successful, everyone in the group must contribute.

ELL

Practice Pronunciation Assist pairs of students by modeling the correct pronunciation of the words and their homophones. Have students repeat the words after you. Remind students that even though the spellings are different the words are pronounced the same.

Common Core State Standards

Writing 6. With guidance and support from adults, use technology to produce and publish writing (using keyboarding skills) as well as to interact and collaborate with others. **Language 1.g.** Form and use comparative and superlative adjectives and adverbs, and choose between them depending on what is to be modified. **Also Writing 2., 10., Language 2.f.**

Research and Inquiry

Step 4 Synthesize

TEACH Have students synthesize their research findings and results. Remind them that when they synthesize, they integrate important and relevant ideas from various sources to create an answer to their inquiry questions. Students may choose to include a graph on their flyers to show comparisons among different cultural celebrations. Review how to choose relevant information from a number of sources and organize it logically.

GUIDE PRACTICE Guide students to use a word-processing program to prepare the flyer they will make for their presentation on Day 5. Tell students their flyers should contain information about the cultural celebration so readers will know what kind of celebration it will be and when it will be held. Be sure to have them explain any unfamiliar words they use.

ON THEIR OWN Have students write a brief explanation of their research findings to present with their flyers. Then have them review the flyer to be sure that it includes all necessary information and is easy to read.

Conventions

Comparative and Superlative Adjectives

TEST PRACTICE Explain that many tests assess the use of comparative and superlative adjectives. Review the forms: How many people, places, or things does a comparative adjective compare? (two) How many people, places, or things does a superlative adjective compare? (three or more) Then ask students to identify whether the sentences below use a comparative or superlative.

The cheetah is the fastest animal on Earth. (superlative)

My new pillow is softer than my old pillow. (comparative)

ON THEIR OWN For additional practice, use *Reader's and Writer's Notebook* p. 337.

Reader's and Writer's Notebook, p. 337

Spelling

Homophones

PRACTICE SPELLING STRATEGY

Remind students to segment words by letter sounds, syllables, and word parts to spell words correctly. Supply pairs of students with index cards on which the spelling words have been written. Have one student read a word and then say a sentence containing that word, while the other writes it. Then have students switch roles. Have them use the cards to check their spelling and correct any misspelled words.

ON THEIR OWN For additional practice, use *Let's Practice It!* p. 306 on the *Teacher Resources DVD-ROM*.

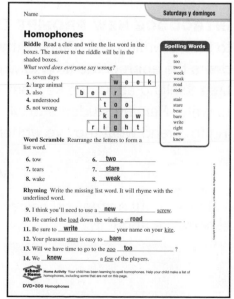

Let's Practice It! TR DVD•306

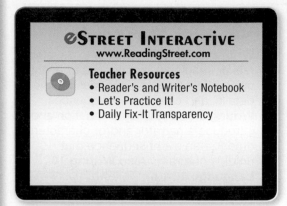

eSTREET INTERACTIVE
www.ReadingStreet.com

Teacher Resources
• Reader's and Writer's Notebook
• Let's Practice It!
• Daily Fix-It Transparency

Daily Fix-It

7. Papa new english before he moved to America. *(knew; English)*

8. Dan and her helped their parents with new werds. *(she; words)*

Bridge to Common Core

CONVENTIONS OF STANDARD ENGLISH

As students identify and use comparative and superlative adjectives, they are demonstrating command of the conventions of standard English. Your guidance will help them use correct grammar, usage, and spelling to convey meaning when they speak and write.

Common Core State Standards

Writing 3. Write narratives to develop real or imagined experiences or events using effective technique, descriptive details, and clear event sequences. **Writing 3.a.** Establish a situation and introduce a narrator and/or characters; organize an event sequence that unfolds naturally. **Also Writing 10., Language 1., 1.e.**

Write Guy *by Jeff Anderson*

Powerful Words, Powerful Verbs

Students can have fun making a complete statement by adding together subjects *(David)* and powerful verbs *(laughed, talked, punched): David laughed.*

Writing

Personal Narrative

REVIEW Review the key features of a personal narrative. Stress the importance of using better word choices, particularly verbs and descriptive adjectives, to make a narrative more interesting.

Mini-Lesson | Writing for Tests: Put Events in Order

■ Yesterday we evaluated our test writing sample based on a writing rubric. Today we will prepare to write to another writing prompt.

■ Remind students that one of the key features of a personal narrative is that the events occur in the order that they really happened. Explain to students that using a consistent verb tense can help readers understand the correct order of events.

■ We use the past tense of a verb *(said)* to talk about something that has already happened. We use the present tense *(says; is saying)* to describe something that is happening now. We use the future tense *(will say)* to talk about something that will happen in the future.

■ Tell students that as they put the events of their narrative in order, they should write in either the present tense (as in *I Love Saturdays y domingos*) or the past tense. It is important to use the same verb tense throughout the narrative.

INTRODUCE NEW PROMPT Direct students to get paper and pencil ready to take a writing test. Display the prompt by writing it on the board. Allow students the appropriate time to write to the prompt. Tell students to spend some time thinking about the key features of a personal narrative before beginning to write. Remind students to allow themselves a couple of minutes after writing to reread what they've written and make changes or additions.

Writing Prompt

Think about a time you helped another person. Now write a personal narrative about it.

Routine   Quick Write for Fluency   Team Talk

. Talk Pairs discuss how verb tenses affect personal narratives.

. Write Students write two sentences about something that happened—one sentence in the present tense and one sentence in the past tense.

. Share Students share what they wrote with their partners.

outines Flip Chart

ELL

Verb Tense Have students practice using both the present tense and the past tense to tell the same story. Use the following sentence frames to practice.

I _____ to the park to play with my friends. (went)

Each day I _____ to the park to play with friends. (go)

Wrap Up Your Day!

✔ **Content Knowledge** Have students discuss the similarities and differences among cultural celebrations.

✔ **Oral Vocabulary** Monitor students' use of oral vocabulary as they respond to this question: *Why might someone hold a shield in a celebratory procession?*

✔ **Text Features** Discuss how the illustrations helped students understand text.

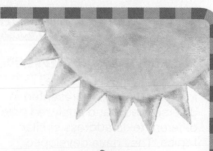

Preview DAY 5

Remind students to think about how cultures are alike and different.

Materials

- Student Edition
- Weekly Test
- Reader's and Writer's Notebook

© Bridge to Common Core

INTEGRATION OF KNOWLEDGE/IDEAS

This week, students have integrated content presented in diverse media and analyzed how different texts address similar topics. They have developed knowledge about comparing cultures to expand the unit topic of Cultures.

Social Studies Knowledge Goals

Students have learned that cultures

- have similarities and differences
- usually value family
- can be tied to countries

Content Knowledge Zoom in on ©

Comparing Cultures

REVIEW THE CONCEPT Have students look back at the reading selections to find examples that best demonstrate how cultures are alike and different.

Build Oral Language

REVIEW AMAZING WORDS Display and review this week's concept map. Remind students that this week they have learned ten Amazing Words related to how cultures are alike and different. Have students use the Amazing Words and the concept map to answer the Question of the Week, *How are cultures alike and different?*

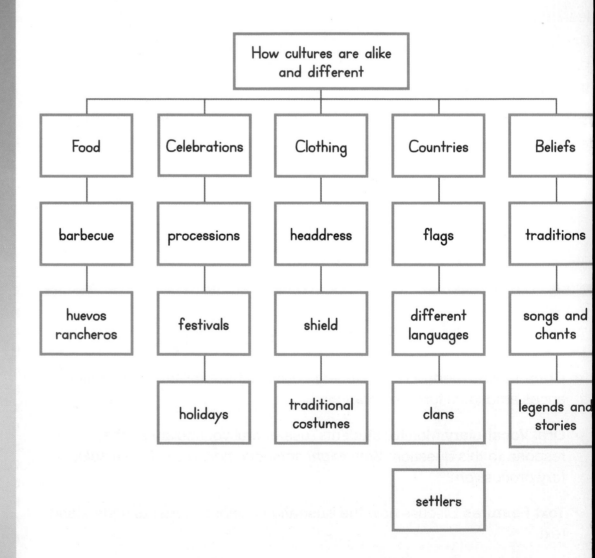

Build Oral Vocabulary

Team Talk **CONNECT TO AMAZING IDEAS** Have pairs of students discuss how the Question of the Week connects to the question for this unit of study: *What happens when two ways of life come together?* Tell students to use the concept map and what they have learned from this week's discussions and reading selections to form an Amazing Idea—a realization or "big idea" about Cultures. Remind partners to pose and answer questions with appropriate detail and to give suggestions that build on each other's ideas. Then ask pairs to share their Amazing Ideas with the class.

Amazing Ideas might include these key concepts:

People from different cultures can share the things that are the same and learn from their differences.

People are all basically the same even if they seem very different.

People should be proud of their cultures and let others know what makes them unique.

WRITE ABOUT IT Have students write a few sentences about their Amazing Idea, beginning with "This week I learned . . ."

eStreet Interactive
www.ReadingStreet.com

Concept Talk Video

Teacher Resources
• Amazing Word Cards

Story Sort

Amazing Words

clan	barbecue
dwelling	belief
shield	chant
headdress	procession
concentrate	settler

MONITOR PROGRESS **Check Oral Vocabulary**

FORMATIVE ASSESSMENT Have individuals use this week's Amazing Words to describe cultures. Monitor students' abilities to use the Amazing Words and note which words you need to reteach.

If... students have difficulty using the Amazing Words,

then... reteach using the Oral Vocabulary Routine, pp. 223a, 228b, 238b, 250b, OV•2.

 ELL

Check Concepts and Language Use the Day 5 instruction on ELL Poster 22 to monitor students' understanding of the lesson concept.

Concept Map Work with students to add new words to the concept map.

Common Core State Standards

Literature 2. Recount stories, including fables, folktales, and myths from diverse cultures; determine the central message, lesson, or moral and explain how it is conveyed through key details in the text. **Foundational Skills 4.c.** Use context to confirm or self-correct word recognition and understanding, rereading as necessary. **Also Literature 6.**

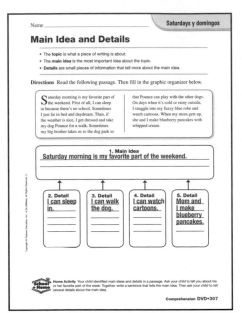

Let's Practice It! TR DVD•307

Selection Vocabulary

bouquet a bunch of flowers

circus a show that includes acrobats, clowns, and trained animals

difficult hard to do; not easy to understand

nibbling eating or biting in a quick, gentle way

pier a walkway that stretches out over water

soars rises high in the air

swallow the action that causes food to pass from the mouth to the stomach

Text-Based Comprehension

Review 🎯 Main Idea and Details

TEACH Review the definition of main idea and details on p. 226. For additional support have students review p. EI•9 on main idea and details.

GUIDE PRACTICE Have student pairs determine the main idea in *I Love Saturdays y domingos*. Then have pairs find an example of a detail that supports the main idea.

ON THEIR OWN For additional practice, use *Let's Practice It!* p. 307 on the *Teacher Resources DVD-ROM*.

Vocabulary Skill

Review 🎯 Homophones

TEACH Remind students that homophones are words that sound the same but have different meanings and spellings. Looking at words and sentences around a homophone may give you a clue to its meaning.

GUIDE PRACTICE Read the first paragraph of "Island Vacation" on p. 229, and ask students if they see words that have homophones. *(to, too, two; in, inn; you, ewe; there, their, they're; whole, hole; no, know).*

ON THEIR OWN Have students work with partners to write sentences using this week's selection words and some homophones.

Word Analysis

Review Homophones

TEACH Write the following sentences on the board. Have students read each one, first quietly to themselves and then aloud as you track the print.

GUIDE PRACTICE

1. My great-grandpa mined copper during the reign of Queen Victoria.
2. Do you two mind the rain?
3. We passed a herd of cattle as we drove on the road past the farm.
4. The knight rode on a beautiful horse.
5. We went to the camp at night.

Team Talk Have students discuss with a partner which words are homophones. Call on individuals to underline the homophones in each sentence. Then point to underlined words at random and have students read them together.

Literary Terms

Review Point of View

TEACH Have students reread "The Best Game" on p. 227. Remind students that point of view is the perspective from which an author presents the actions and characters in a story.

GUIDE PRACTICE Identify the point of view in "The Best Game." Have students point out the words or pronouns that helped them determine the point of view.

ON THEIR OWN Have students make a T-chart with the headings *First Person* and *Third Person*. Ask them to review other selections they have recently read and determine the point of view for each. Have them list the titles in the corresponding columns of the T-chart.

eStreet Interactive
www.ReadingStreet.com

Pearson eText
• Student Edition

Teacher's Resources
• Let's Practice It!

ELL

Homophones Supply students with various homophones written on separate cards. Have students arrange the cards to match up the words that are homophones. Tell them to say the words aloud as they match them.

© Common Core State Standards

Literature 10. By the end of the year, read and comprehend literature, including stories, dramas, and poetry, at the high end of the grades 2–3 text complexity band independently and proficiently. **Foundational Skills 4.b.** Read on-level prose and poetry orally with accuracy, appropriate rate, and expression on successive readings.

Plan to Assess Fluency

☐ **Week 1** Advanced

☑ **This week assess Strategic Intervention students.**

☐ **Week 3** On-Level

☐ **Week 4** Strategic Intervention

☐ **Week 5** Assess any students you have not yet checked during this unit.

Set individual goals for students to enable them to reach the year-end goal.

• Current Goal: 102–112 WCPM

• Year-End Goal: 120 WCPM

Assessment

Monitor Progress

FLUENCY Make two copies of the fluency passage on p. 253k. As the student reads the text aloud, mark mistakes on your copy. Also mark where the student is at the end of one minute. To check the student's comprehension of the passage, have him or her retell what was read. To figure words correct per minute (WCPM), subtract the number of mistakes from the total number of words read in one minute.

RATE

| Corrective feedback | **If...** students cannot read fluently at a rate of 102–112 WCPM, **then...** make sure they practice with text at their independent reading level. Provide additional fluency practice by pairing nonfluent readers with fluent readers. **If...** students already read at 120 WCPM, **then...** have them read a book of their choice independently. |

ELL

If... students need more scaffolding and practice with **Conventions and Writing,** **then...** use the activities on pp. DI•49–DI•50 in the Teacher Resources section on SuccessNet.

Day 5 SMALL GROUP TIME • Differentiate Reteaching, p. SG•17

OL On-Level	**SI** Strategic Intervention	**A** Advanced
• **Practice** Comparative and Superlative Adjectives	• **Review** Comparative and Superlative Adjectives	• **Extend** Comparative and Superlative Adjectives
• **Reread** *Reading Street Sleuth,* pp. 58–59	• **Reread** *Reading Street Sleuth,* pp. 58–59	• **Reread** *Reading Street Sleuth,* pp. 58–59
		• **Communicate** Inquiry Project

Name _____

A Day at the Circus

Once upon a time there were eight dwarfs, the usual seven plus   12
Sweepy. Sweepy came to clean the dwarfs' cottage after Snow White   23
left. One Saturday, after a long week of working in the mines, the   36
dwarfs were weak and tired too. They decided to take a long nap and   50
then go to the circus.   55

The dwarfs paid the bus fare to get to the fairgrounds where the   68
circus was performing. When they got there, they bought peanuts to   79
nibble and pears for a snack. They ate the snack on the grass outside   93
the circus tent. They were sure to spill plenty of treats on the ground for   108
mice and swallows to eat. Then the dwarfs found their seats, and the   121
circus began.   123

They watched a pair of trapeze artists soar through the air. They   135
watched two high-wire walkers do a difficult dance overhead. The   145
dwarfs clapped until their hands were sore. Everyone had a favorite   156
act. Some liked the lions, jugglers, and horses best. Others liked the   168
acrobats, dogs, and clowns.   172

At the end of the show, the elephants made a parade around the   185
ring, and all the circus performers took a bow. On the way home,   198
Sweepy picked a bouquet of wildflowers for the cottage. It would   209
remind them all of their happy day at the circus.   219

MONITOR PROGRESS   • Check Fluency

Common Core State Standards

Literature 2. Recount stories, including fables, folktales, and myths from diverse cultures; determine the central message, lesson, or moral and explain how it is conveyed through key details in the text. **Literature 10.** By the end of the year, read and comprehend literature, including stories, dramas, and poetry, at the high end of the grades 2–3 text complexity band independently and proficiently.

Assessment

Monitor Progress

For a written assessment of Homophones, Main Idea and Details, and Selection Vocabulary, use Weekly Test 22, pp. 127–132.

⦿ MAIN IDEAS AND DETAILS Use "New Words!" on p. 253m to check student's understanding of main idea and details.

1. What are the new words that John learned? (*lift, boot,* and *petrol*)

2. What is the main idea of the passage? (English people speak English, but they use some words differently than we do in the United States.)

3. What are the details to support the main idea? (*lift* means "elevator," *boot* means "car trunk," and *petrol* means "gas")

> **Corrective feedback**
>
> **If...** students are unable to answer the comprehension questions,
> **then...** use the Reteach lesson in *First Stop*.

Name _____

New Words!

John lived on the sixth floor of a huge Dallas skyscraper. From his balcony, he could see the street below. Today, he watched carefully. His aunt, uncle, and cousins were arriving soon for a visit. They lived in England and seldom traveled to the United States. John had never met them.

"Mom, are you sure they really speak English?" John questioned. "They live in a foreign country."

"Yes, they're citizens of England," Mom answered with a chuckle. "English people speak the English language! But they do use some words differently than we do."

"They do?" asked John.

"Yes, for example, English people call an elevator a *lift*," said Mom.

"That makes sense because an elevator lifts people," said John.

"And they call a car's trunk a *boot*," explained Mom.

That didn't make sense! But before John could say that, he spotted a taxicab down below. "They're here, Mom!" he said.

Mom and John took the elevator down to the ground floor. Then they stood by the building's front door and watched as their English guests got out of the taxicab. John's uncle said to the driver, "I'll get the suitcases out of the boot."

Boot! John looked at Mom.

One of John's cousins said, "I'll carry them to the lift." Lift! John looked again at Mom.

Then John's aunt said to the driver, "We used a bit of petrol getting here from the airport."

"*Petrol* means gasoline," Mom whispered to John.

John smiled. This visit was going to be fun!

MONITOR PROGRESS

• **Main Idea and Details**

Common Core State Standards

Speaking/Listening 1.b. Follow agreed-upon rules for discussions (e.g., gaining the floor in respectful ways, listening to others with care, speaking one at a time about the topics and texts under discussion). **Speaking/Listening 4.** Report on a topic or text, tell a story, or recount an experience with appropriate facts and relevant, descriptive details, speaking clearly at an understandable pace. **Language 1.g.** Form and use comparative and superlative adjectives and adverbs, and choose between them depending on what is to be modified. **Also Speaking/ Listening 1.c., 3., Language 2.f.**

Research and Inquiry

Step 5 Communicate

PRESENT IDEAS Have students share their inquiry results by displaying their flyers and giving a brief talk on their research. Students will answer questions after their presentations.

SPEAKING Remind students how to be good speakers and how to communicate effectively with their audience.

• Respond to relevant questions with appropriate details.

• Speak clearly and loudly.

• Keep eye contact with audience members.

LISTENING Review with students these tips for being a good listener.

• Listen attentively to speakers.

• Wait until the speaker has finished before raising your hand to ask a relevant question or make a pertinent comment.

• Be polite, even if you disagree.

LISTEN TO IDEAS Have students listen attentively to the various presentations of their flyers and talks about their research. Have them make pertinent comments, closely related to the topic.

Spelling Test

Homophones

To administer the spelling test, refer to the directions, words, and sentences on p. 227c.

eStreet Interactive
www.ReadingStreet.com

Teacher Resources
• Let's Practice It!
• Daily Fix-It Transparency

Conventions

Comparative and Superlative Adjectives

MORE PRACTICE Explain to students that not all comparatives and superlatives follow the pattern *small/smaller/smallest.* Write the word *fun* on the board. Then show students that this word forms the comparative by adding "more" before it: *more fun*. It forms the superlative by adding "most": *most fun.*

GUIDE PRACTICE Guide students in choosing the correct comparative and superlative adjectives for the following sentences.

> John Is _____ at soccer than Marcus. (better)
>
> Stuart is the _____ player on the team. (best)
>
> The trip to the museum was fun, but the park was _____. (more fun)

ON THEIR OWN Have students find the correct comparative and superlative adjectives in *I Love Saturdays y domingos* to complete the sentences below. Students should complete *Let's Practice It!* p. 308 on the *Teacher Resources DVD-ROM.*

> 1. No one makes them _____ than *Abuelita.* (better)
> 2. I like the mother elephant and her little elephant _____. (best)
> 3. Grandpa tells me about how his mother, his father, and his _____ brother came to America. (older)

Daily Fix-It

9. Of all the familys, the Gomezes had the easier time finding a home. *(families; easiest)*

10. They was helpfull to others who came from Mexico. *(were; helpful)*

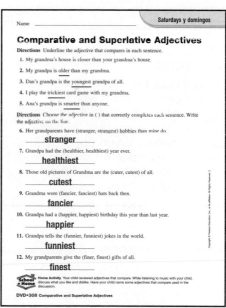

Name _____   Saturdays y domingos

Comparative and Superlative Adjectives

Directions Underline the adjective that compares in each sentence.
1. My grandma's house is closer than your grandma's house.
2. My grandpa is older than my grandma.
3. Dan's grandpa is the youngest grandpa of all.
4. I play the trickiest card game with my grandma.
5. Ana's grandpa is smarter than anyone.

Directions Choose the adjective in ( ) that correctly completes each sentence. Write the adjective on the line.
6. Her grandparents have (stranger, strangest) hobbies than mine do.
   _____ stranger _____
7. Grandpa had the (healthier, healthiest) year ever.
   _____ healthiest _____
8. Those old pictures of Grandma are the (cuter, cutest) of all.
   _____ cutest _____
9. Grandma wore (fancier, fanciest) hats back then.
   _____ fancier _____
10. Grandpa had a (happier, happiest) birthday this year than last year.
    _____ happier _____
11. Grandpa tells the (funnier, funniest) jokes in the world.
    _____ funniest _____
12. My grandparents give the (finer, finest) gifts of all.
    _____ finest _____

Home Activity Your child reviewed adjectives that compare. While listening to music with your child, discuss what you like and dislike. Have your child name some adjectives that compare used in the discussion.

DVD•308 Comparative and Superlative Adjectives

Let's Practice It! TR DVD•308

Common Core State Standards

Writing 5. With guidance and support from peers and adults, develop and strengthen writing as needed by planning, revising, and editing. **Writing 10.** Write routinely over extended time frames (time for research, reflection, and revision) and shorter time frames (a single sitting or a day or two) for a range of discipline-specific tasks, purposes, and audiences. **Also Writing 3., Language 1.a., 1.g.**

Teacher Note

Writing Self-Evaluation Make copies of the Writing Self-Evaluation Guide on p. 39 of the *Reader's and Writer's Notebook* and hand out to students.

Bridge to Common Core

PRODUCTION AND DISTRIBUTION OF WRITING

Throughout the week, students developed writing in which organization and style were appropriate to the task, purpose, and audience. Given opportunities to practice writing for shorter time frames, students expand their range and ability of writing.

Writing

Personal Narrative

REVIEW Remind students that yesterday they learned more about how to make the order of events in a narrative clear to the reader. Then they wrote to another prompt. Today they will evaluate their second writing sample.

Mini-Lesson | Writing for Tests: Revise

■ Yesterday we wrote personal narratives about a time we helped another person. Part of effectively writing for tests is using some of the test-taking time to revise and edit what we have written. The goal is to make the writing as clear, interesting, and correct as possible. Today we will focus on making sure we used comparative and superlative adjectives correctly.

■ Remind students that comparative adjectives compare two things, while superlatives compare three or more things. Tell students that comparatives often end in *-er*, while superlatives often end in *-est*. Students should make sure these adjectives, as well as other adjectives, are spelled and used correctly.

■ Look for places where you can use comparative or superlative adjectives to make your personal narrative more interesting.

DISPLAY Display the following Revising Tips for students.

Revising Tips
✔ Review writing to make sure the writing is clear and interesting.
✔ Make sure to use a variety of adjectives, including descriptive, comparative, and superlative.

VALUATE Have students spend a few minutes editing and revising the writ-
ng they wrote on Day 4. When students have finished editing, have them use
he Scoring Rubric that they used on Day 3 to evaluate this writing.

Routine   Quick Write for Fluency   Team Talk

1. Talk Pairs discuss how a personal narrative is similar to realistic fiction.

2. Write Students write a sentence comparing the two types of writing.

3. Share Students read their sentence to their partners.

Routines Flip Chart

Wrap Up Your Week!

Comparing Cultures

How are cultures alike and different?

 Think Aloud In *I Love Saturdays y domingos* and "Communities Celebrate Cultures," we learned about different cultures and how they are alike and different.

Team Talk Have students recall their Amazing Ideas about cultures and use these ideas to help them demonstrate their understanding of the Question of the Week.

Next Week's Concept
Adapting to a New Culture

Why is it hard to adapt to a new culture?

Poster Preview Prepare students for next week by using Week 3 ELL Poster 23. Read the Talk-Through to introduce the concept and vocabulary. Ask students to identify and describe actions in the art.

Selection Summary Send home the summary of next week's selection, *Good-Bye, 382 Shin Dang Dong,* in English and in students' home languages, if available in the *ELL Handbook.* They can read the summary with family members.

Why is it hard to adapt to a new culture? Tell students that next week they will read about adapting to new cultures.

Preview Next Week ➡

Assessment Checkpoints for the Week

Weekly Assessment

Use pp. 127–132 of *Weekly Tests* to check:

✔ 🔵 **Phonics/Word Analysis** Homophones

✔ 🔵 **Comprehension** Main Idea and Details

✔ **Review** **Comprehension** Compare and Contrast

✔ **Selection Vocabulary**

bouquet	pier
circus	soars
difficult	swallow
nibbling	

Weekly Tests

Differentiated Assessment

 A Advanced

 OL On-Level

SI Strategic Intervention

Use pp. 127–132 of *Fresh Reads for Fluency and Comprehension* to check:

✔ 🔵 **Comprehension** Main Idea and Details

✔ **Review** **Comprehension** Compare and Contrast

✔ **Fluency** Words Correct Per Minute

Fresh Reads for Fluency and Comprehension

Managing Assessment

Use *Assessment Handbook* for:

✔ **Weekly Assessment Blackline Masters for Monitoring Progress**

✔ **Observation Checklists**

✔ **Record-Keeping Forms**

✔ **Portfolio Assessment**

Assessment Handbook

TEACHER NOTES

DAY 1 Differentiate Vocabulary

- **Word Knowledge** Amazing Words
- **Read** "A Visit to Vietnam"
- **Inquiry** Identify Questions

"A Visit to Vietnam,"
pp. 58–59

DAY 2 Differentiate Comprehension

- **Word Knowledge** Selection Vocabulary
- **Access Text** Read *I Love Saturdays y domingos*
- **Inquiry** Investigate

DAY 3 Differentiate Close Reading

- **Word Knowledge** Develop Vocabulary
- **Close Reading** Read *I Love Saturdays y domingos*
- **Inquiry** Investigate

DAY 4 Differentiate Vocabulary

- **Word Knowledge** Amazing Words
- **Read** "Communities Celebrate Cultures"
- **Inquiry** Organize

DAY 5 Differentiate Reteaching

- **Conventions** Comparative and
  Superlative Adjectives
- **Reread** "A Visit to Vietnam" or
  Leveled Readers
- **Inquiry** Communicate

Teacher Guides and Student pages can be found in the
Leveled Reader Database.

 Place English Language Learners in the groups that correspond to their reading abilities.
If... students need scaffolding and practice,
then... use the ELL Notes on the instructional pages.

Independent Practice

**Independent
Practice Stations**

See pp. 222h and 222i for
Independent Stations.

**Pearson Trade Book
Library**

See the Leveled Reader
Database for lesson plans
and student pages.

**Reading Street
Digital Path**

Independent Practice
Activities are available in
the Digital Path.

**Independent
Reading**

See p. 222i for
independent reading
suggestions.

OL On-Level

Common Core State Standards

Literature 3. Describe characters in a story (e.g., their traits, motivations, or feelings) and explain how their actions contribute to the sequence of events. **Foundational Skills 4.** Read with sufficient accuracy and fluency to support comprehension. **Speaking/Listening 4.** Report on a topic or text, tell a story, or recount an experience with appropriate facts and relevant, descriptive details, speaking clearly at an understandable pace. **Language 4.** Determine or clarify the meaning of unknown and multiple-meaning words and phrases based on grade 3 reading and content, choosing flexibly from a range of strategies. **Language 4.a.** Use sentence-level context as a clue to the meaning of a word or phrase.

Independent Reading Options

Trade Book Library

eSTREET INTERACTIVE
www.ReadingStreet.com

Teacher Guides are available on the Leveled Reader Database.

 ELL

If... students need more scaffolding and practice with **Vocabulary, then...** use the activities on pp. DI•42–DI•43 in the Teacher Resources section on SuccessNet.

1 Build Word Knowledge
Practice Amazing Words

DEFINE IT Elicit the definition for the word *clan* from students. Ask: How would you describe a clan to another student? (Possible response: A clan is a group of people who are related.) Clarify or give a definition when necessary. Continue with the words *headdress* and *shield*.

Team Talk **TALK ABOUT IT** Have partners internalize meanings. Ask: How can you group the Amazing Words together in a sentence? (Possible response: Each warrior of the *clan* wore a special *headdress* and carried a *shield* during the ceremony.) Allow time for students to play with the words. Review the concept map with students. Discuss other words they can add to the concept map.

2 Text-Based Comprehension
Read

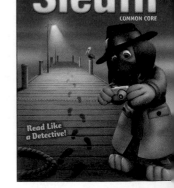

READ ALOUD "A Visit to Vietnam" Have partners read "A Visit to Vietnam" from *Reading Street Sleuth* on pp. 58–59.

ACCESS TEXT Discuss the Sleuth Work section with students before they work on it. Remind students that they can use these steps with other texts they read.

Gather Evidence Revisit the text together, skimming for words and phrases that help readers understand Benjamin's point of view. With students, make a list of these words and phrases.

Ask Questions Have students share their questions with a partner. Together, discuss the kinds of questions students asked and where they might look for the answers. If time permits, have students research the answer to one of their factual questions.

Make Your Case Have students select a position on this issue. Encourage students who took the same side of the issue to work together and make a list of convincing reasons for supporting that side. Invite students to share their most convincing reasons with the group.

 **On-Level**

① Build Word Knowledge
Practice Selection Vocabulary

bouquet	circus	difficult	nibbling
pier	soars	swallow	

DEFINE IT Discuss the definition for the word *circus* with students. Ask: How would you describe a *circus* to another student? (Possible response: A *circus* is a group of clowns and performers who travel with animals and perform in a big tent.) Continue with the remaining words.

Team Talk **TALK ABOUT IT** Have pairs use the selection vocabulary in sentences to internalize meaning. Ask: How can you group the selection vocabulary together in a sentence? (Possible response: *Circus* performers can do many *difficult* tricks, such as *swallowing* fire.) Allow time for students to play with the words and then share their sentences.

② Read
I Love Saturdays y domingos

If you read *I Love Saturdays y domingos* during whole group time, then use the following instruction.

ACCESS TEXT Reread the paragraphs on pp. 232–233. Ask questions to check understanding. Who are *Abuelito* and *Abuelita*? (They are the girl's mother's parents, or her grandparents.) How are they similar to and different from Grandpa and Grandma? (Like Grandpa and Grandma, they are happy to see the girl and ask how she is. But unlike Grandpa and Grandma, they see the girl on Sundays, not Saturdays. They speak Spanish, not English, with her.)

Have students identify sections from today's reading that they did not completely understand. Reread them aloud and clarify misunderstandings.

If you are reading *I Love Saturdays y domingos* during small group time, then return to pp. 232–237a to guide the reading.

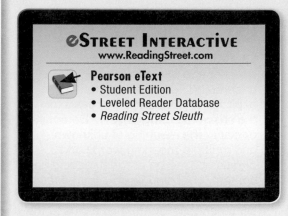
More Reading for Group Time

ON-LEVEL

Reviews
• Main Idea and Details
• Inferring
• Selection Vocabulary

Use this suggested Leveled Reader or other text at students' instructional level.

eSTREET INTERACTIVE
www.ReadingStreet.com

Use the Leveled Reader Database for lesson plans and student pages for *Celebrate Around the World*.

I Love Saturdays y domingos **SG•19**

SMALL GROUP TIME

On-Level

ⓒ Common Core State Standards

Literature 1. Ask and answer questions to demonstrate understanding of a text, referring explicitly to the text as the basis for the answers. **Language 4.** Determine or clarify the meaning of unknown and multiple-meaning words and phrases based on grade 3 reading and content, choosing flexibly from a range of strategies. **Language 4.a.** Use sentence-level context as a clue to the meaning of a word or phrase.

❶ Build Word Knowledge

Develop Vocabulary

REREAD FOR VOCABULARY Reread the first four paragraphs on p. 238. Introduce: Let's read this paragraph to find out what *aquarium* means. To help students understand the word *aquarium*, ask questions related to context, such as: What does Grandpa have that the girl likes to watch? Which fish does she like? Where does she press her nose? Have students use online sources to find out more information about an aquarium.

❷ Read

I Love Saturdays y domingos

If you read *I Love Saturdays y domingos* during whole group time, then use the following instruction.

CLOSE READING Read pp. 240–241. Have students search the text to find different references to the places where each grandparent came from and grew up. As a class, make a list of the different places. (Europe, New York City, Mexico, California) Ask: What do you learn about the girl's grandparents? (They or their families all came from different places and different cultures.)

If you are reading *I Love Saturdays y domingos* during small group time, then return to pp. 238–245a to guide the reading.

If... students need more scaffolding and practice with the **Main Selection, then...** use the activities on p. DI•47 in the Teacher Resources section on SuccessNet.

On-Level

1 Build Word Knowledge

Practice Amazing Words

clan	dwelling	shield	headdress	concentrate
barbecue	belief	chant	procession	settler

Team Talk **LANGUAGE DEVELOPMENT** Have partners practice building more complex sentences. Display a sentence starter and have students add oral phrases or clauses using the Amazing Words. For example: Clan members _____. (*Clan* members went / to the simple *dwelling* / to *chant* and share their *beliefs*.) Guide students to add at least three phrases or clauses per sentence.

2 Read

"Communities Celebrate Cultures"

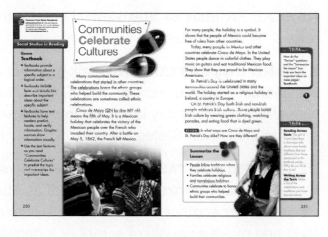

BEFORE READING Read aloud the genre information about textbooks on p. 250. Explain that textbooks are used in classes to help students learn about a subject. Have students preview "Communities Celebrate Cultures" and set a purpose for reading. Ask: The photographs on these pages do not have captions. How do you know what they are pictures of? (The photographs go with the information in the main text.) Based on the title and photographs, what do you think the main idea of the selection will be? (how different communities celebrate cultures with costumes and dancing)

DURING READING Have students read with you. Ask: What kind of information do you expect to find in a textbook? (factual information and explanations about the subject) What is the meaning of "SIN ko day MY oh" in the second paragraph on the first page? (It tells the reader how to pronounce a Spanish term, *Cinco de Mayo*.)

AFTER READING Have students share their reactions. Then have them research another holiday with roots in a foreign country and write a description of it.

SMALL GROUP TIME

Independent Reading Options

Trade Book Library

eSTREET INTERACTIVE
www.ReadingStreet.com

Teacher Guides are available on the Leveled Reader Database.

Common Core State Standards

Literature 3. Describe characters in a story (e.g., their traits, motivations, or feelings) and explain how their actions contribute to the sequence of events. **Informational Text 1.** Ask and answer questions to demonstrate understanding of a text, referring explicitly to the text as the basis for the answers. **Foundational Skills 4.** Read with sufficient accuracy and fluency to support comprehension. **Writing 8.** Recall information from experiences or gather information from print and digital sources; take brief notes on sources and sort evidence into provided categories. **Speaking/ Listening 4.** Report on a topic or text, tell a story, or recount an experience with appropriate facts and relevant, descriptive details, speaking clearly at an understandable pace. **Language 4.** Determine or clarify the meaning of unknown and multiple-meaning words and phrases based on grade 3 reading and content, choosing flexibly from a range of strategies. **Also Language 1.g, 4.a.**

More Reading for Group Time

ON-LEVEL

Reviews
• Main Idea and Details
• Inferring
• Selection Vocabulary

Use this suggested Leveled Reader or other text at students' instructional level.

eStreet Interactive
www.ReadingStreet.com

Use the Leveled Reader Database for lesson plans and student pages for *Celebrate Around the World.*

 **On-Level**

1 Build Word Knowledge
Practice Comparative and Superlative Adjectives

IDENTIFY Read aloud the instruction on the bottom of p. 249 and explain comparative and superlative adjective forms, discussing the suffixes *-er* and *-est,* as well as the words *more* and *most.* Have students work in groups to reread the model personal narrative and look for examples of comparative and superlative adjectives. Allow time for students to discuss their examples and correct any misunderstandings.

2 Text-Based Comprehension
Read

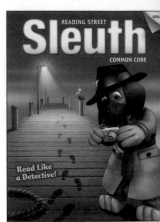

REREAD "A Visit to Vietnam" Have partners reread "A Visit to Vietnam."

EXTEND UNDERSTANDING Talk together about the characteristics of Ho Chi Minh City. Invite discussion about how this city is similar to or different from cities in the United States.

PERFORMANCE TASK • Prove It! Have students work together to make a scrapbook of a virtual visit to Vietnam or another foreign country. Have one group of students research food and make a couple of scrapbook pages related to the food. Have other groups research the language, dress, music, landscape, and weather of the chosen country. Each group should add scrapbook pages related to their topic. Remind students to include factual information on their scrapbook pages.

COMMUNICATE Have groups share their scrapbook pages with the others. Invite discussion about the kinds of things students learned about this country from the exercise.

SI Strategic Intervention

1 Build Word Knowledge

Reteach Amazing Words

Repeat the definition of the word. We learned that a *clan* is a group of people who are related. Then use the word in a sentence. The *clan* celebrated the traditional holiday together.

Team Talk **TALK ABOUT IT** Have partners take turns using the word *shield* in a sentence. Continue this routine to practice the Amazing Words *headdress* and *shield*. Review the concept map with students. Discuss other words they can add to the concept map.

> **Corrective feedback** | **If...** students need more practice with the Amazing Words, **then...** use visuals from the Student Edition or online sources to clarify meaning.

2 Text-Based Comprehension

Read

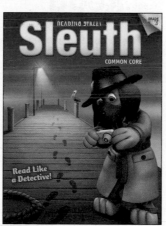

READ "A Visit to Vietnam" Have students track the print as you read "A Visit to Vietnam" from *Reading Street Sleuth* on pp. 58–59.

ACCESS TEXT Discuss the Sleuth Work section with students and provide support as needed.

Gather Evidence Talk together about how Benjamin felt about his Vietnam trip. With students, revisit the text and list words and phrases that support his feelings. Invite discussion about the author's use of opinions to express Benjamin's point of view.

Ask Questions Have students work with a partner to write questions about Vietnam. Encourage students to write at least one question that requires a factual answer. Talk together about how students might research the answers to their questions. If time permits, have partners work together to find an answer to one of their questions.

Make Your Case Talk together about travel experiences students have had. Take a poll asking students whether they would like to travel to a place they know well or to a new place. Invite students from both sides of the issue to back up their opinions with convincing reasons.

SMALL GROUP TIME

More Reading for Group Time

CONCEPT LITERACY
Practice
Concept Words

BELOW-LEVEL
Reviews
• Main Idea and Details
• Inferring
• Selection Vocabulary

Use these suggested Leveled Readers or other text at students' instructional level.

Use the Leveled Reader Database for lesson plans and student pages for *Happy New Year!* and *Celebrate Independence Day/Celebrar El Día de la Independencia.*

Common Core State Standards

Literature 3. Describe characters in a story (e.g., their traits, motivations, or feelings) and explain how their actions contribute to the sequence of events. **Language 4.** Determine or clarify the meaning of unknown and multiple-meaning words and phrases based on grade 3 reading and content, choosing flexibly from a range of strategies. **Language 4.a.** Use sentence-level context as a clue to the meaning of a word or phrase.

① Build Word Knowledge
Reteach Selection Vocabulary

DEFINE IT Describe a *circus* to a friend. Give a definition when necessary. Restate the word in student-friendly terms and clarify meaning with a visual. A *circus* is a traveling show with animals and clowns. Page 237 shows circus animals.

bouquet	circus	difficult
nibbling	pier	soars
swallow		

Team Talk **TALK ABOUT IT** Have you ever seen a circus? Turn and talk to your partner about this. Rephrase students' examples for usage when necessary or to correct misunderstandings. Continue with the remaining words.

Corrective feedback | **If...** students need more practice with selection vocabulary, **then...** use the *Envision It! Pictured Vocabulary Cards.*

② Read
I Love Saturdays y domingos

If you read *I Love Saturdays y domingos* during whole group time, then use the instruction below.

ACCESS TEXT Reread the paragraphs on pp. 232–233. Ask questions to check understanding. Who are *Abuelito* and *Abuelita*? (They are the girl's mother's parents, or her grandparents.) Why are some words on p. 233 bold and italicized? (They are Spanish words). How can you understand these words? (The English words are on p. 232.) How are *Abuelito* and *Abuelita* similar to and different from Grandpa and Grandma? (Like Grandpa and Grandma, they are happy to see the girl, and they ask how she is. Unlike Grandpa and Grandma, they see the girl on Sundays, not Saturdays. They speak Spanish, not English, with her.)

Have students identify sections they did not understand. Reread them aloud. Clarify the meaning of each section to build understanding.

If you are reading *I Love Saturdays y domingos* during small group time, then return to pp. 232–237a to guide the reading.

Independent Reading Options

Trade Book Library

eSTREET INTERACTIVE
www.ReadingStreet.com

Teacher Guides are available on the Leveled Reader Database.

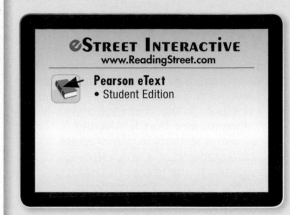

SI Strategic Intervention

① Build Word Knowledge

Develop Vocabulary

REREAD FOR VOCABULARY Reread the first three paragraphs on p. 238. Let's read this paragraph to find out what *aquarium* means. To help students understand the word *aquarium,* ask questions related to context, such as: What are the girl and her grandfather looking at? What does she do when looking at the fish? How do the words *glass* and *fish* help you understand the word *aquarium?*

Corrective feedback | **If...** students have difficulty understanding the word *aquarium,* **then...** guide students to use the illustration on p. 238 to guess its meaning.

② Read

I Love Saturdays y domingos

you read *I Love Saturdays y domingos* during whole group time, then use the instruction below.

CLOSE READING Read pp. 240–241. Have students search through the text for references to each grandparent's heritage or culture. As a class, make a list of the different places and cultures that each character talks about in the order they occur. (Grandpa: Europe, New York City. *Abuelito*: Mexico, rancho, Texas. Grandma: California; her grandmother was born on the trail. *Abuelita*: Native American, Indian)

Now use what you learned to summarize or retell each grandparent's family history. (Grandpa's family came to New York City from Europe. *Abuelito's* family grew up on a ranch in Mexico; his dad went to Texas looking for work. Grandma's family went to California in a covered wagon. Her grandmother was born on the trail. *Abuelita's* family are Native Americans.)

you are reading *I Love Saturdays y domingos* during small group time, then return to pp. 238–245a to guide the reading.

SMALL GROUP TIME

 ELL

If... students need more scaffolding and practice with the **Main Selection, then...** use the activities on p. DI•47 in the Teacher Resources section on SuccessNet.

Strategic Intervention

Common Core State Standards

Literature 3. Describe characters in a story (e.g., their traits, motivations, or feelings) and explain how their actions contribute to the sequence of events. **Informational Text 1.** Ask and answer questions to demonstrate understanding of a text, referring explicitly to the text as the basis for the answers. **Foundational Skills 4.** Read with sufficient accuracy and fluency to support comprehension. **Writing 8.** Recall information from experiences or gather information from print and digital sources; take brief notes on sources and sort evidence into provided categories. **Language 1.g.** Form and use comparative and superlative adjectives and adverbs, and choose between them depending on what is to be modified. **Language 4.a.** Use sentence-level context as a clue to the meaning of a word or phrase. **Also Writing 10., Language 4.**

1 Build Word Knowledge
Review Amazing Words

| clan | dwelling | shield | headdress | concentrate |
| barbecue | belief | chant | procession | settler |

Team Talk **LANGUAGE DEVELOPMENT** Have partners practice building more complex sentences. Display a sentence starter and have students add oral phrases or clauses using the Amazing Words.

Corrective feedback | **If...** students have difficulty using the Amazing Words orally, **then...** review the meaning of each of the words.

2 Read

"Communities Celebrate Cultures"

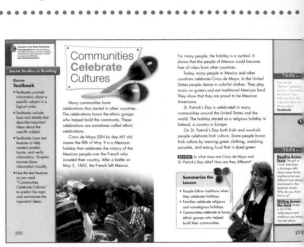

BEFORE READING Read aloud the genre information about text-books on p. 250. Textbooks help students learn about a topic. They often include diagrams, charts, lists, photographs, illustrations, and text separated into sections with subtitles.

DURING READING Have students read with you while tracking along with the text. Stop to discuss difficult vocabulary, such as *ethnic, invaded,* and *symbol*.

AFTER READING Have students share their reactions to the paired selection. Then guide them through the Reading Across Texts and Writing Across Texts activities.

- Do you think the main character in *I Love Saturdays y domingos* celebrates Cinco de Mayo? Why? (Yes; one of her grandfathers is from Mexico.)
- Why do you think this textbook discusses another cultural holiday? (so that St. Patrick's Day could be compared to Cinco de Mayo)
- What celebrations and traditions did you learn about? (Cinco de Mayo and St. Patrick's Day)

ELL

If... students need more scaffolding and practice with Amazing Words, **then...** use the Routine on pp. xxxvi–xxxvii in the *ELL Handbook*.

SI Strategic Intervention

eSTREET INTERACTIVE
www.ReadingStreet.com

Pearson eText
• Student Edition
• Leveled Reader Database
• *Reading Street Sleuth*

1 Build Word Knowledge

Review Comparative and Superlative Adjectives

IDENTIFY Read aloud the instruction on the bottom of p. 249 to review comparative and superlative adjective forms. Have students work in groups to reread the model personal narrative on p. 249 and look for examples of comparative and superlative adjectives. Allow time for students to discuss their examples and correct any misunderstandings.

2 Text-Based Comprehension

Read

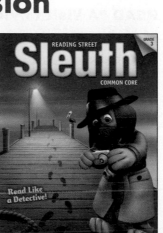

REREAD "A Visit to Vietnam" Have partners reread "A Visit to Vietnam," with partners alternating paragraphs.

EXTEND UNDERSTANDING Talk together about the Americanization of Ho Chi Minh City. Have students find evidence in the text that supports this idea.

PERFORMANCE TASK • Prove It! Have students work together to make a "scrapbook" of a virtual visit to Vietnam or another foreign country. Have the group of students research food and make a couple of scrapbook pages related to the food. Have other groups research the language, dress, music, landscape, and weather of the chosen country. Each group should add scrapbook pages related to their topic. Encourage students to find photos that capture their topic and add captions to those photos to share facts they have learned.

COMMUNICATE Have groups share the scrapbook pages they made. Invite others to ask questions about the information presented on the pages.

More Reading for Group Time

CONCEPT LITERACY	BELOW-LEVEL
Practice Concept Words	**Reviews** • Main Idea and Details • Inferring • Selection Vocabulary

Use these suggested Leveled Readers or other text at students' instructional level.

eSTREET INTERACTIVE
www.ReadingStreet.com

Use the Leveled Reader Database for lesson plans and student pages for *Happy New Year!* and *Celebrate Independence Day/Celebrar El Día de la Independencia.*

SMALL GROUP TIME

A Advanced

Common Core State Standards

Literature 3. Describe characters in a story (e.g., their traits, motivations, or feelings) and explain how their actions contribute to the sequence of events. **Foundational Skills 4.** Read with sufficient accuracy and fluency to support comprehension. **Speaking/Listening 4.** Report on a topic or text, tell a story, or recount an experience with appropriate facts and relevant, descriptive details, speaking clearly at an understandable pace. **Language 4.** Determine or clarify the meaning of unknown and multiple-meaning words and phrases based on grade 3 reading and content, choosing flexibly from a range of strategies. **Language 4.a.** Use sentence-level context as a clue to the meaning of a word or phrase. **Also Writing 7.**

1 Build Word Knowledge

Extend Amazing Words

Team Talk Have pairs of students define *clan*. Discuss other names for a *clan*. Continue with *headdress* and *shield*.

2 Text-Based Comprehension

Read

READ "A Visit to Vietnam" Have partners read "A Visit to Vietnam" from *Reading Street Sleuth* on pp. 58–59.

ACCESS TEXT Discuss the Sleuth Work section with students before they work on it. Remind students that they can use these steps with other texts they read.

Gather Evidence Have students revisit the text to find words and phrases that tell Benjamin's opinion about visiting Vietnam. Encourage students to make a list with this evidence, sharing their list then with a partner. Discuss whether the evidence is fact, opinion, or both.

Ask Questions Have students share their questions with the group. Discuss how answers might be researched. If time permits, have students research their most interesting question.

Make Your Case Have students select a position on this issue. Encourage students to make a list of convincing reasons that support their side of the issue. Invite students to share their most convincing reasons with the group.

3 Inquiry: Extend Concepts

IDENTIFY QUESTIONS Have students think about questions they have about their family histories and use these questions to learn about a place from which a family member emigrated, or moved, to the United States. Students should retell some of the history of that place and create a poster about traditions and symbols associated with it. Throughout the week, they will gather information. On Day 5, they will present what they have learned.

ELL

If... students need more scaffolding and practice with **Vocabulary, then...** use the activities on pp. DI•42–DI•43 in the Teacher Resources section on SuccessNet.

A Advanced

① Build Word Knowledge

Extend Selection Vocabulary

Team Talk Have partners use the selection vocabulary in sentences to internalize their meanings. Have students use as many of the words as they can while making sure the sentence is grammatically correct. Continue with additional selection vocabulary.

bouquet	circus	difficult
nibbling	pier	soars
swallow		

② Read

I Love Saturdays y domingos

If you read *I Love Saturdays y domingos* during whole group time, then use the instruction below.

ACCESS TEXT Reread the paragraphs on pp. 232–233. Discuss the bold and italicized words and their meanings. Then have students use a Venn diagram to compare and contrast the sets of grandparents. (Similar: Both are happy to see the girl and ask how she is. Grandma and Grandpa: See the girl on Saturday; speak English. *Abuelito* and *Abuelita*: See her on Sunday; speak Spanish.)

Ask: Why do you think the author shows two sets of grandparents who are similar and different? (She wants to show that even though people come from different cultures, they have similarities. The grandparents speak different languages, but they both love her and have fun with her.)

If you are reading *I Love Saturdays y domingos* during small group time, then turn to pp. 232–237a to guide the reading.

③ Inquiry: Extend Concepts

INVESTIGATE Encourage students to use materials at their independent reading levels or student-friendly search engines to identify relevant and credible sites to gather information about a place associated with their family's history. Have students consider how they will present their information.

eStreet Interactive
www.ReadingStreet.com

Pearson eText
• Student Edition
• Leveled Reader Database
• *Reading Street Sleuth*

More Reading for Group Time

ADVANCED

Reviews
• Main Idea and Details
• Inferring

Use this suggested Leveled Reader or other text at students' instructional level.

eStreet Interactive
www.ReadingStreet.com

Use the Leveled Reader Database for lesson plans and student pages for *Life Overseas*.

Common Core State Standards

Literature 3. Describe characters in a story (e.g., their traits, motivations, or feelings) and explain how their actions contribute to the sequence of events. **Language 4.** Determine or clarify the meaning of unknown and multiple-meaning words and phrases based on grade 3 reading and content, choosing flexibly from a range of strategies. **Language 4.a.** Use sentence-level context as a clue to the meaning of a word or phrase. **Also Writing 7.**

Independent Reading Options

Trade Book Library

eStreet Interactive
www.ReadingStreet.com

Teacher Guides are available on the Leveled Reader Database.

ELL

If... students need more scaffolding and practice with the **Main Selection, then...** use the activities on p. DI•47 in the Teacher Resources section on SuccessNet.

A   Advanced

1 Build Word Knowledge
Develop Vocabulary

REREAD FOR VOCABULARY Reread the first paragraph on p. 238. Let's read this paragraph to find out what *aquarium* means. Discuss meaning and context with students.

2 Read
I Love Saturdays y domingos

If you read *I Love Saturdays y domingos* during whole group time, then use the instruction below.

CLOSE READING Reread pp. 240–241. Have students create a four-column chart in which they list the different backgrounds of each grandparent. Have students search through the text for references to different cultures, people, or places and write them in the chart.

Grandpa	Grandma	*Abuelito*	*Abuelita*
Europe, New York City	California, on the trail	Mexico, ranch, Texas	Native American, Indian

Ask: What idea is the author developing by making each grandparent so different? (that different cultures or backgrounds make our families interesting) What do you think that the author is trying to say about America or American families? (America is a place where people of many backgrounds come together in families.)

If you are reading *I Love Saturdays y domingos* during small group time, then return to pp. 238–245a to guide the reading.

3 Inquiry: Extend Concepts

INVESTIGATE Provide time for students to investigate their topics in books or online. If necessary, help them locate information that is focused on their topics.

A Advanced

Build Word Knowledge

Extend Amazing Words and Selection Vocabulary

eSTREET INTERACTIVE
www.ReadingStreet.com

Pearson eText
• Student Edition

clan	dwelling	shield	bouquet	circus	difficult
headdress	concentrate	barbecue	nibbling	pier	soars
belief	chant	procession	swallow		
settler					

Team Talk Have partners practice building more complex sentences. Display a sentence starter and have students add oral phrases or clauses using the Amazing Words and the selection vocabulary. For example: *The settler lived _____.* (The *settler* lived / in a simple *dwelling* / away from his *clan* / so that he could *concentrate* / on the *difficult* task / of creating *headdresses* and *shields*.) Guide students to add at least three phrases or clauses per sentence.

Read

"Communities Celebrate Cultures"

BEFORE READING Read the panel information on textbooks on p. 250. Then have students use the text features to set a purpose for reading.

DURING READING Have students read the selection. Encourage students to think critically. For example, ask: Why do you think non-Irish people celebrate Irish culture on St. Patrick's Day? (They enjoy participating in the activities associated with the holiday; they may have Irish friends they want to honor.)

AFTER READING Have students discuss Reading Across Texts. Then have them complete the Writing Across Texts activity independently.

Inquiry: Extend Concepts

ORGANIZE INFORMATION Provide time for students to organize their information into a format that will effectively communicate their findings to their audience. Provide any necessary materials or computer time.

Independent Reading Options

Trade Book Library

eSTREET INTERACTIVE
www.ReadingStreet.com

Teacher Guides are available on the Leveled Reader Database.

SMALL GROUP TIME

Common Core State Standards

Informational Text 1. Ask and answer questions to demonstrate understanding of a text, referring explicitly to the text as the basis for the answers. **Foundational Skills 4.** Read with sufficient accuracy and fluency to support comprehension. **Speaking/Listening 4.** Report on a topic or text, tell a story, or recount an experience with appropriate facts and relevant, descriptive details, speaking clearly at an understandable pace. **Writing 8.** Recall information from experiences or gather information from print and digital sources; take brief notes on sources and sort evidence into provided categories. **Language 1.g.** Form and use comparative and superlative adjectives and adverbs, and choose between them depending on what is to be modified. **Language 4.a.** Use sentence-level context as a clue to the meaning of a word or phrase. Also **Speaking/Listening 1.b., Language 4.**

More Reading for Group Time

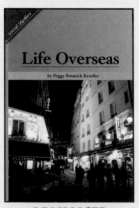

ADVANCED

Reviews
• Main Idea and Details
• Inferring

Use this suggested Leveled Reader or other text at students' instructional level.

eSTREET INTERACTIVE
www.ReadingStreet.com

Use the Leveled Reader Database for lesson plans and student pages for *Life Overseas.*

A Advanced

1 Build Word Knowledge
Extend Comparative and Superlative Adjectives

IDENTIFY AND EXTEND Read aloud the instruction on the bottom of p. 249 and encourage students to explain comparative and superlative adjective forms. Have students work in groups to reread the model personal narrative and look for examples of comparative and superlative adjectives. Then ask students to write their own personal narratives using comparative and superlative adjectives. Allow time for students to discuss their work and correct any misunderstandings.

2 Text-Based Comprehension
Read

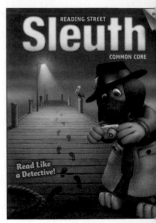

REREAD "A Visit to Vietnam" Have partners reread the selection. Have partners discuss why Benjamin feels the way he does about the trip.

EXTEND UNDERSTANDING Talk together about connections students can make to Benjamin's excitement over visiting a place he's been to before. Have students share their own similar experiences.

PERFORMANCE TASK • Prove It! Have students work together to make a "scrapbook" of a virtual visit to Vietnam or another foreign country. Have one group of students research food and make a couple of scrapbook pages related to the food. Have other groups research the language, dress, music, landscape, and weather of the chosen country. Each group should add scrapbook pages related to their topic. Encourage students to include information on their scrapbook pages that would be most interesting for children of their age.

COMMUNICATE Have groups share their scrapbook pages. Invite discussio about how this country compares and contrasts to the United States.

3 Inquiry: Extend Concepts

COMMUNICATE Have students share their inquiry projects on holidays with the rest of the class. Provide the following tips for presenting.
• Speak loudly and clearly.
• Make eye contact when answering questions.
• Speak slowly and pause briefly after key points.

Indiana Common Core Edition

This Week's Target Skills and Strategies

Target Skills and Strategies	Common Core State Standards for English Language Arts	Indiana Academic Standards for English Language Arts
Phonics and Spelling Skill: Vowel Patterns *au, augh, ou, ough*	**CCSS Foundational Skills 3.** Know and apply grade-level phonics and word analysis skills in decoding words. **(Also CCSS Language 2.f.)**	**IN 3.1** Students understand the basic features of words. They select letter patterns and know how to translate them into spoken language using phonics, syllables, word parts, and context. They apply this knowledge to achieve fluent oral and silent reading.
Text-Based Comprehension Skill: Sequence	**CCSS Literature 3.** Describe characters in a story (e.g., their traits, motivations, or feelings) and explain how their actions contribute to the sequence of events.	**IN 3.3.3** Determine what characters are like by what they say or do and by how the author or illustrator portrays them.
Strategy: Monitor and Clarify	**CCSS Literature 1.** Ask and answer questions to demonstrate understanding of a text, referring explicitly to the text as the basis for the answers.	**IN 3.3** Students read and respond to a wide variety of significant works of children's literature.
Vocabulary Skill: Compound Words Strategy: Word Structure	**CCSS Foundational Skills 3.** Know and apply grade-level phonics and word analysis skills in decoding words. **(Also CCSS Language 4.)**	**IN 3.1.2** Read words with several syllables.
Fluency Skill: Expression and Punctuation Cues	**CCSS Foundational Skills 4.b.** Read on-level prose and poetry orally with accuracy, appropriate rate, and expression on successive readings.	**IN 3.1.3** Read aloud grade-level-appropriate literary and informational texts fluently and accurately and with appropriate timing, change in voice, and expression.
Listening and Speaking Song or Poem	**CCSS Speaking/Listening 1.b.** Follow agreed-upon rules for discussions (e.g., gaining the floor in respectful ways, listening to others with care, speaking one at a time about the topics and texts under discussion). **(Also CCSS Speaking/Listening 4.)**	The Indiana Academic Standards for Listening and Speaking are not currently assessed on ISTEP+ assessments. Educators and students should implement the Common Core Standards for Speaking and Listening as soon as possible.
Six-Trait Writing Trait of the Week: Word Choice	**CCSS Language 3.a.** Choose words and phrases for effect.	**IN 3.5.4** Use varied word choices to make writing interesting.
Writing Poetry: Free Verse	**CCSS Writing 3.** Write narratives to develop real or imagined experiences or events using effective technique, descriptive details, and clear event sequences. **(Also CCSS Writing 3.a., CCSS Language 3.a.)**	**IN 3.5.1** Write narratives.
Conventions Skill: Adverbs	**CCSS Language 1.a.** Explain the function of nouns, pronouns, verbs, adjectives, and adverbs in general and their functions in particular sentences.	**IN 3.6** Students write using Standard English conventions appropriate to this grade level.

This Week's Cross-Curricular Standards and Resources

Cross-Curricular Indiana Academic Standards for Science and Social Studies

Science
IN 3.3.1 Identify the common structures of a plant including its roots, stems, leaves, flowers, fruits and seeds. Describe their functions.

Social Studies
IN 3.3.6 Explain the basic Earth/sun relationship, including how it influences climate, and identify major climate regions of the United States.
IN 3.3.9 Identify factors that make the region unique, including cultural diversity, industry, the arts and architecture.

Reading Street Sleuth

A Day at School in Japan
pp. 60–61

Follow the path to close reading using the Super Sleuth tips:

• Gather Evidence

• Ask Questions

• Make Your Case

• Prove it!

More Reading in Science and Social Studies

Concept Literacy

Below Level

On Level

Advanced

ELL

ELD

ISBN-13: 978-0-328-73391-0   ISBN-10: 0-328-73391-1

Your 90-Minute Reading Block

	Whole Group	Formative Assessment	Small Group OL On Level SI Strategic Intervention A Advanced	Daily Independent Options
		How do I make my small groups flexible?	What are my other students reading and learning every day in Small Groups?	What do my other students do when I lead Small Groups?
DAY 1	**Content Knowledge** Build Oral Language/Vocabulary **Phonics/Word Analysis** **Read Decodable Reader** **Text-Based Comprehension** **Selection Vocabulary** **Research and Inquiry** Step 1–Identify and Focus Topic **Spelling Pretest** Connect to Phonics/Word Analysis	**Monitor Progress** Check Oral Vocabulary	Differentiate Vocabulary **Build Word Knowledge** OL Practice Amazing Words SI Reteach Amazing Words A Extend Amazing Words OL SI A Text-Based Comprehension **Read** *Reading Street Sleuth*, pp. 60–61 or Leveled Readers A Inquiry Project ELL Access Vocabulary	★ **Independent Reading** © Suggestions for this week's independent reading: • Nonfiction selections about different cultures • A high-quality magazine article about different cultures • An information-rich Web site about how cultures are alike and different
DAY 2	**Content Knowledge** Build Oral Language/Vocabulary **Phonics/Word Analysis** **Vocabulary Skill** **Text-Based Comprehension** **Read** Main Selection, using Access Text Notes **Research and Inquiry** Step 2–Navigate/Search **Spelling** Connect to Phonics/Word Analysis	**Monitor Progress** Formative Assessment: Check Word Reading	Differentiate Comprehension **Build Word Knowledge** OL Practice Selection Vocabulary SI Reteach Selection Vocabulary A Extend Selection Vocabulary OL SI A Access Text **Read** *Good-Bye, 382 Shin Dang Dong* A Inquiry Project ELL Access Comprehension Skill	**Book Talk** Foster critical reading and discussion skills through independent and close reading. Students should focus on discussing one or more of the following: • Key Ideas and Details • Craft and Structure • Integration of Ideas
DAY 3	**Content Knowledge** Build Oral Language/Vocabulary **Phonics/Word Analysis** **Read Decodable Passage** **Text-Based Comprehension** **Read** Main Selection, using Close Reading Notes **Fluency** **Research and Inquiry** Step 3–Analyze Information **Spelling** Connect to Phonics/Word Analysis	**Monitor Progress** Check Retelling	Differentiate Close Reading OL SI **Reread to Develop Vocabulary** A **Reread to Extend Vocabulary** OL SI A **Close Reading** **Read** *Good-Bye, 382 Shin Dang Dong* A Inquiry Project ELL Access Main Selection	**Pearson eText** • Student Edition • Decodable Readers • Leveled Readers **Trade Book Library**
DAY 4	**Content Knowledge** Build Oral Language/Vocabulary **Phonics/Word Analysis** **Read Decodable Passage** **Read Content Area Paired Selection with Genre Focus** **Let's Learn It!** Vocabulary/Fluency/Listening and Speaking **Research and Inquiry** Step 4–Synthesize **Spelling** Connect to Phonics/Word Analysis	**Monitor Progress** Check Fluency	Differentiate Vocabulary **Build Word Knowledge** OL Develop Language Using Amazing Words SI Review/Discuss Amazing Words A Extend Amazing Words and Selection Vocabulary OL SI A Text-Based Comprehension **Read** "Sing a Song of People" A Inquiry Project ELL Access Amazing Words	**Materials from School or Classroom Library** **Independent Stations** Practice Last Week's Skills ★ Focus on these activities when time is limited. **Word Wise** **Word Work** ★ **Read for Meaning** **Let's Write!** ★ **Words to Know** **Get Fluent**
DAY 5	**Content Knowledge** Build Oral Language/Vocabulary **Text-Based Comprehension** **Vocabulary Skill** **Phonics/Word Analysis** **Assessment** Fluency, Comprehension **Research and Inquiry** Step 5–Communicate **Spelling Test** Connect to Phonics/Word Analysis	**Monitor Progress** Formative Assessment: Check Oral Vocabulary **Monitor Progress** Fluency; Comprehension	Differentiate Reteaching OL **Practice Adverbs** SI **Review Adverbs** A **Extend Adverbs** OL SI A **Text-Based Comprehension** **Reread** *Reading Street Sleuth*, pp. 60–61 or Leveled Readers A Inquiry Project ELL Access Conventions and Writing	

Assessment Resources

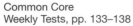

Common Core
Weekly Tests, pp. 133–138

Common Core Fresh Reads for Fluency and Comprehension, pp. 133–138

Common Core
Unit 5 Benchmark Test

Common Core Success Tracker, ExamView, and Online Lesson Planner

Teaching the Common Core State Standards This Week

 The Common Core State Standards for English Language Arts are divided into strands for **Reading** (including **Foundational Skills**), **Writing**, **Speaking and Listening**, and **Language**. The chart below shows some of the content you will teach this week, strand by strand. Turn to this week's 5-Day Planner on pages 254d–254e to see how this content is taught each day.

Reading Strand

- **Phonics/Word Analysis:** Vowel Patterns *a*, *au*, *aw*, *al*, *augh*, *ough*
- **Text-Based Comprehension:** Sequence; Monitor and Clarify
- **Fluency:** Expression and Punctuation Cues
- **Literary Terms:** Mood
- **Genre:** Main Selection: Realistic Fiction; Paired Selection: Poetry

Writing Strand

- **Writing Mini-Lesson:** Poetry – Free Verse
- **Trait:** Word Choice
- **Look Back and Write:** Text Evidence

Common Core State Standards for English Language Arts

Speaking and Listening Strand

- **Content Knowledge:** Build Oral Language
- **Listening and Speaking:** Song or Poem
- **Research and Inquiry**

Language Strand

- **Oral Vocabulary: Amazing Words** *native, homeland, aspect, advantage, sponsor, habit, impolite, manner, conscious, insult*
- **Vocabulary:** Compound Words; Word Structure
- **Selection Vocabulary:** *homesick, airport, raindrops, memories, farewell, curious, described, delicious, cellar*
- **Academic Vocabulary:** *adverb, free verse, mood, rising action, atlas*
- **Conventions:** Adverbs
- **Spelling:** Vowel Patterns *a*, *au*, *aw*, *al*, *augh*, *ough*

Text-Based Comprehension

Text Complexity Measures

Use the rubric to familiarize yourself with the text complexity of *Goodbye, 382 Shin Dang Dong*.

Qualitative Quantitative
Reader and Task

Bridge to Complex Knowledge

Quantitative Measures	Lexile	610L
	Average Sentence Length	8.84
	Word Frequency	3.46

Qualitative Measures	Levels of Meaning	identify realistic situations in the story
	Structure	flash-back
	Language Conventionality and Clarity	non-English words; close alignment of images and text; conversational language
	Theme and Knowledge Demands	singular perspective; references to other cultural experiences; text assumes some knowledge of Korea's location and culture

Reader and Task Suggestions	**FORMATIVE ASSESSMENT** Based on assessment results, use the **Reader and Task Suggestions** in Access Main Selection to scaffold the selection or support independence for students as they read *Goodbye, 382 Shin Dang Dong*.

READER AND TASK SUGGESTIONS	
Preparing to Read the Text	**Leveled Tasks**
• Review strategies for understanding compound words. • Discuss the features of realistic fiction. • Remind students there are foreign words in this selection. They may need to read more slowly and use context clues to understand the text.	• **Levels of Meaning • Evaluation** If students have difficulty identifying the story as realistic fiction, have them look for connections between their lives and the situations in the story. • **Theme and Knowledge Demands** Students may not understand where Korea is or how far Jangmi moved when she came to America. Have them take notes about places to locate on a map.

Recommended Placement Generally the qualitative and quantitative measures suggest this text should be placed in the Grade 2–3 text complexity band, which is where both the Common Core State Standards and *Scott Foresman Reading Street* have placed it. Scaffolded support for unfamiliar words will help students stretch to reach the content of the selection.

Focus on Common Core State Standards ©

Main Selection, pp. 262–279

Paired Selection, pp. 284–285

Text-Based Comprehension

Sequence
CCSS Literature 3.

Monitor and Clarify
CCSS Literature 1.

Fluency

Expression and Punctuation Cues
CCSS Foundational Skills 4.b.

Writing and Conventions

Trait: Word Choice
CCSS Writing 3.b., CCSS Language 3.a.

Writing Mini-Lesson: Poetry:
Free Verse
CCSS Writing 3., CCSS Writing 3.a.,
CCSS Language 3.a.

Conventions: Adverbs
CCSS Language 1.a.

Oral Vocabulary

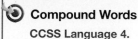

Amazing Words

native	habit
homeland	impolite
aspect	manner
advantage	conscious
sponsor	insult

CCSS Language 6.

Selection Vocabulary

Compound Words
CCSS Language 4.

Word Structure
CCSS Foundational Skills 3.,
CCSS Language 4.

airport	delicious	homesick
cellar	described	memories
curious	farewell	raindrops

Phonics and Spelling

Vowel Patterns *au, augh, ou, ough*
CCSS Foundational Skills 3.,
CCSS Language 2.f.

bccause	enough
though	sausage
taught	fought
bought	should
touch	faucet
would	daughter
author	brought
could	

Challenge Words

laundry	auditorium
distraught	overwrought
afterthought	

Listening and Speaking

Song or Poem
CCSS Speaking/Listening 1.b.,
CCSS Speaking/Listening 4.

Preview Your Week

Why is it hard to adapt to a new culture?

Main Selection, pp. 262–279

Genre: Realistic Fiction

🔊 **Vocabulary:** Compound Words

🔊 **Text-Based Comprehension:** Sequence

Paired Selection, pp. 284–285

Social Studies in Reading

Genre: Poetry

Build Content Knowledge

Zoom in on ©

Time for SOCIAL STUDIES

KNOWLEDGE GOALS
Students will understand that a new culture means

• a new home and neighborhood
• a new language
• new traditions

THIS WEEK'S CONCEPT MAP
Develop a concept-related graphic organizer like the one below over the course of this week.

BUILD ORAL VOCABULARY
This week, students will acquire the following academic vocabulary/domain-specific words.

Amazing Words

native	sponsor	manner
homeland	habit	conscious
aspect	impolite	insult
advantage		

Concept Literacy

Below-Level

On-Level

Advanced

ELL

ELD

OPTIONAL CONCEPT-BASED READING Use the Digital Path to access readers offering different levels of text complexity.

This Week's Digital Resources

eStreet Interactive
www.ReadingStreet.com

Get Ready to Read

 Concept Talk Video Use this video on the Digital Path to capture interest and introduce the weekly concept of adapting to new cultures.

 Pearson eText Read the eText of the Student Edition pages on Pearson SuccessNet for comprehension and fluency support.

 Envision It! Animations Use this vivid animation on the Digital Path to explain the target comprehension skill, Sequence.

Read and Comprehend

 Journal Use the Word Bank on the Digital Path to have students write sentences using this week's selection vocabulary words.

 Background Building Audio CD This audio CD provides key background information about cultures to help students read and comprehend the weekly texts.

 Pearson eText Read the eText of the main selection, *Good-Bye, 382 Shin Dang Dong,* and the paired selection, "Sing a Song of People," with audio support on Pearson SuccessNet.

 Vocabulary Activities A variety of interactive vocabulary activities on the Digital Path help students practice selection vocabulary and concept-related words.

 Story Sort Use the Story Sort Activity on the Digital Path after reading *Good-Bye, 382 Shin Dang Dong* to involve students in summarizing.

Language Arts

 Grammar Jammer Opt for a whimsical animation on the Digital Path to provide an engaging grammar lesson that will grab students' attention.

 Pearson eText Find the Student Edition eText of the Let's Write It! and Let's Learn It! pages with audio support on Pearson SuccessNet.

Additional Resources

Teacher Resources DVD-ROM Use the following resources on the TR DVD or on Pearson SuccessNet throughout the week:

- Amazing Word Cards
- Reader's and Writer's Notebook
- Writing Transparencies
- Daily Fix-It Transparencies
- Scoring Rubrics
- Grammar Transparencies
- ELL Support
- Let's Practice It!
- Graphic Organizers
- Vocabulary Cards

This Week's Skills

Phonics/Word Analysis
- Vowel Patterns for /ȯ/

Comprehension
- **Skill:** Sequence
- **Strategy:** Monitor and Clarify

Language
- **Vocabulary:** Compound Words
- **Conventions:** Adverbs

Fluency
Expression and Punctuation Cues

Writing
Poetry: Free Verse

5-Day Planner

DAY 1

Get Ready to Read

Content Knowledge 254j
Oral Vocabulary: *native, homeland, aspect, advantage*

Monitor Progress
Check Oral Vocabulary

Phonics/Word Analysis 256a
- Vowel Patterns for /ȯ/
READ Decodable Reader 23A
Reread for Fluency

Read and Comprehend

Text-Based Comprehension 258a
- Sequence
- Monitor and Clarify

Fluency 258–259
Expression and Punctuation Cues

Selection Vocabulary 259a
airport, cellar, curious, delicious, described, farewell, homesick, memories, raindrops

Language Arts

Research and Inquiry 259b
Identify and Focus Topic

Spelling 259c
Vowel Patterns *au, augh, ou, ough,* Pretest

Conventions 259d
Adverbs

Handwriting 259d
Cursive Letters *H* and *K*

Writing 259e
Poetry: Free Verse

DAY 2

Get Ready to Read

Content Knowledge 260a
Oral Vocabulary: *sponsor, habit*

Phonics/Word Analysis 260c
Vowel Patterns for /ȯ/

Monitor Progress
Check Word Reading

Literary Terms 260d
Mood

Read and Comprehend

Vocabulary Skill 260e
- Compound Words

Fluency 260–261
Expression and Punctuation Cues

Text-Based Comprehension 262–263
READ *Good-Bye, 382 Shin Dang Dong*—1st Read

Language Arts

Research and Inquiry 271b
Navigate/Search

Conventions 271c
Adverbs

Spelling 271c
Vowel Patterns *au, augh, ou, ough*

Writing 271d
Poetry: Free Verse

DAY 3

Get Ready to Read

Content Knowledge 272a
Oral Vocabulary: *impolite, manner*

Phonics/Word Analysis 272c
◉ Vowel Patterns for /ô/
Fluent Word Reading
DECODE AND READ
Decodable Practice Passage 23B

Read and Comprehend

Text-Based Comprehension 272e
Check Understanding
READ *Good-Bye, 382 Shin Dang Dong*—2nd Read

> **Monitor Progress**
> Check Retelling

Fluency 281b
Expression and Punctuation Cues

Language Arts

Research and Study Skills 281c
Atlas

Research and Inquiry 281d
Analyze Information

Conventions 281e
Adverbs

Spelling 281e
Vowel Patterns *au, augh, ou, ough*

Writing 282–283
Poetry: Free Verse

DAY 4

Get Ready to Read

Content Knowledge 284a
Oral Vocabulary: *conscious, insult*

Phonics/Word Analysis 284c
Review Homophones
Fluent Word Reading
DECODE AND READ
Decodable Practice Passage 23C

Read and Comprehend

Genre 284g
Poetry
READ "Sing a Song of People"
—Paired Selection

Fluency 286–287
Expression and Punctuation Cues
> **Monitor Progress** Check Fluency

Vocabulary Skill 287a
◉ Compound Words

Listening and Speaking 287a
Song or Poem

Language Arts

Research and Inquiry 287b
Synthesize

Conventions 287c
Adverbs

Spelling 287c
Vowel Patterns *au, augh, ou, ough*

Writing 287d
Poetry: Free Verse

DAY 5

Get Ready to Read

Content Knowledge 287f
Review Oral Vocabulary

> **Monitor Progress**
> Check Oral Vocabulary

Read and Comprehend

Text-Based Comprehension 287h
Review ◉ Sequence

Vocabulary Skill 287h
Review ◉ Compound Words

Word Analysis 287i
Review ◉ Vowel Patterns for /ô/

Literary Terms 287i
Review Mood

Assessment 287j, 287l
> **Monitor Progress**
> Fluency; Sequence

Language Arts

Research and Inquiry 287n
Communicate

Spelling 287o
Vowel Patterns *au, augh, ou, ough*,
Test

Conventions 287o
Adverbs

Writing 287p
Poetry: Free Verse

Wrap Up Your Week! 287q

Access for All

What do I do in group time?
It's as easy as 1-2-3!

① TEACHER-LED SMALL GROUPS ➔ **②** INDEPENDENT PRACTICE STATIONS ➔ **③** INDEPENDENT READING

Small Group Time

© Bridge to Common Core

SKILL DEVELOPMENT
- ➲ Sequence
- ➲ Monitor and Clarify
- ➲ Compound Words

DEEP UNDERSTANDING

This Week's Knowledge Goals
Students will understand that a new culture means
- a new home and neighborhood
- a new language
- new traditions

① Small Group Lesson Plan

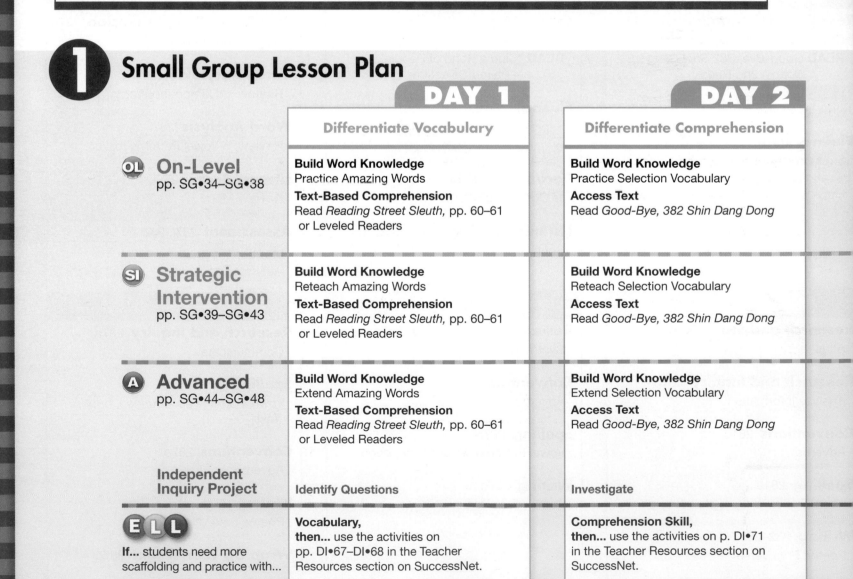

		DAY 1 Differentiate Vocabulary	**DAY 2** Differentiate Comprehension
OL	**On-Level** pp. SG•34–SG•38	**Build Word Knowledge** Practice Amazing Words **Text-Based Comprehension** Read *Reading Street Sleuth*, pp. 60–61 or Leveled Readers	**Build Word Knowledge** Practice Selection Vocabulary **Access Text** Read *Good-Bye, 382 Shin Dang Dong*
SI	**Strategic Intervention** pp. SG•39–SG•43	**Build Word Knowledge** Reteach Amazing Words **Text-Based Comprehension** Read *Reading Street Sleuth*, pp. 60–61 or Leveled Readers	**Build Word Knowledge** Reteach Selection Vocabulary **Access Text** Read *Good-Bye, 382 Shin Dang Dong*
A	**Advanced** pp. SG•44–SG•48	**Build Word Knowledge** Extend Amazing Words **Text-Based Comprehension** Read *Reading Street Sleuth*, pp. 60–61 or Leveled Readers	**Build Word Knowledge** Extend Selection Vocabulary **Access Text** Read *Good-Bye, 382 Shin Dang Dong*
	Independent Inquiry Project	Identify Questions	Investigate
ELL	**If...** students need more scaffolding and practice with...	**Vocabulary,** **then...** use the activities on pp. DI•67–DI•68 in the Teacher Resources section on SuccessNet.	**Comprehension Skill,** **then...** use the activities on p. DI•71 in the Teacher Resources section on SuccessNet.

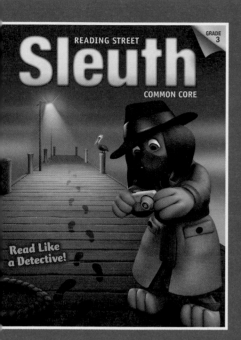

Build Text-Based Comprehension

Good-Bye, 382 Shin Dang Dong

Optional Leveled Readers

| Concept Literacy | Below-Level | On-Level | Advanced | ELL | ELD |

Reading Street Sleuth

Provides access to grade-level text for all students

Focuses on finding clues in text through close reading

Builds capacity for complex text

DAY 3

Differentiate Close Reading

Reread to Develop Vocabulary
Close Reading
Read *Good-Bye, 382 Shin Dang Dong*

Reread to Develop Vocabulary
Close Reading
Read *Good-Bye, 382 Shin Dang Dong*

Reread to Extend Vocabulary
Close Reading
Read *Good-Bye, 382 Shin Dang Dong*

Investigate

Main Selection,
then... use the activities on p. DI•72 in the Teacher Resources section on SuccessNet.

DAY 4

Differentiate Vocabulary

Build Word Knowledge
Develop Language Using Amazing Words
Text-Based Comprehension
Read "Sing a Song of People"

Build Word Knowledge
Review/Discuss Amazing Words
Text-Based Comprehension
Read "Sing a Song of People"

Build Word Knowledge
Extend Amazing Words and Selection Vocabulary
Text-Based Comprehension
Read "Sing a Song of People"

Organize

Amazing Words,
then... use the Routine on pp. xxxvi–xxxvii in the *ELL Handbook.*

DAY 5

Differentiate Reteaching

Practice Adverbs
Text-Based Comprehension
Reread *Reading Street Sleuth,* pp. 60–61 or Leveled Readers

Review Adverbs
Text-Based Comprehension
Reread *Reading Street Sleuth,* pp. 60–61 or Leveled Readers

Extend Adverbs
Text-Based Comprehension
Reread *Reading Street Sleuth,* pp. 60–61 or Leveled Readers

Communicate

Conventions and Writing,
then... use the Grammar Transition Lessons on pp. DI•312–DI•386 in the *ELL Handbook.*

2 # Independent Stations
Practice Last Week's Skills

Focus on these activities when time is limited.

WORD WISE

Spell and use words in sentences.

OBJECTIVES

- Spell homophones.

MATERIALS

- *Word Wise* Flip Chart Activity 23, teacher-made word cards, paper and pencils

 Letter Tile Drag and Drop

● Students write three pairs of homophones side by side and write a definition for each.

▲ Students write four pairs of homophones side by side and write a definition in their own words for each.

■ Students write five words that do not sound alike, write a homophone for each, and write sentences for each pair.

WORD WORK

Identify and pronounce words.

OBJECTIVES

- Identify and pronounce homophones.

MATERIALS

- *Word Work* Flip Chart Activity 23, teacher-made word cards, paper and pencils

 Letter Tile Drag and Drop

● Students write and say four pairs of homophones and then add other homophones to the list.

▲ Students write and say five pairs of homophones and then add other homophones to the list.

■ Students write and say six pairs of homophones and then add other homophones to the list.

LET'S WRITE!

Write to narrate.

OBJECTIVES

- Write a personal narrative.

MATERIALS

- *Let's Write!* Flip Chart Activity 23, paper and pencils

 Grammar Jammer

● Students write a personal narrative about an important event in their lives, include details about feelings, and use the pronoun *I*.

▲ Students write a personal narrative about an important event in their lives, include details about feelings, and use consistent verb tense.

■ Students write a personal narrative about an important event in their lives, include details about feelings and the event, and use consistent verb tense.

WORDS TO KNOW

Determine word meanings.

OBJECTIVES

- Identify the meanings of homophones.

MATERIALS

- *Words to Know* Flip Chart Activity 23, teacher-made word cards, paper and pencils

 Vocabulary Activities

● Students write three pairs of homophones and sentences for each pair that show their different meanings.

▲ Students write four pairs of homophones and sentences for each pair that show their different meanings.

■ Students write five pairs of homophones and sentences for each pair with context clues to show their different meanings.

Manage the Stations

Use these management tools to set up and organize your Practice Stations:

Practice Station Flip Charts

Classroom Management Handbook for Differentiated Instruction Practice Stations, p. 41

READ FOR MEANING

Use comprehension skills.

OBJECTIVES

• Identify comparison and contrast.

MATERIALS

• *Read for Meaning* Flip Chart Activity 23, Leveled Readers, paper and pencils

Pearson eText
• Leveled eReaders

Envision It! Animations

● Students read a book and write a sentence telling the main idea and a sentence about a supporting detail.

▲ Students read a book and write a sentence telling the main idea and two sentences about supporting details.

■ Students read a book and write a paragraph stating the main idea and explaining supporting details.

3 Independent Reading ©

Students should select appropriate complex texts to read and write about independently every day before, during, and after school.

Suggestions for this week's independent reading:
• Nonfiction selections about different cultures
• A high-quality magazine article about different cultures
• An information-rich Web site about how cultures are alike and different

BOOK TALK   Have partners discuss their independent reading for the week. Tell them to refer to their Reading Logs and paraphrase what each selection was about. Then have students focus on discussing one or more of the following:

Key Ideas and Details
• State the main idea of the text in your own words.
• Summarize the key ideas in the text.

Craft and Structure
• How is the information in the text organized?
• How do you know that the text is nonfiction? What text features did you notice?

Integration of Ideas
• What claims does the author make?
• How well does the author support his or her claims?

GET FLUENT

Practice reading fluently with partners.

OBJECTIVES

• Read aloud using correct expression.

MATERIALS

• *Get Fluent* Flip Chart Activity 23, Leveled Readers

Pearson eText
• Leveled eReaders

● Partners take turns reading aloud with correct expression from a Concept Literacy or Below-Level Reader and providing feedback.

▲ Partners take turns reading aloud with correct expression from an On-Level Reader and providing feedback.

■ Partners take turns reading aloud with correct expression from an Advanced Reader and providing feedback.

 Pearson eText
• Student Edition
• Decodable Readers
• Leveled Readers

 Trade Book Library

School or Classroom Library

Materials

- Student Edition
- Reader's and Writer's Notebook
- Decodable Reader

Ⓒ **Bridge to Common Core**

INTEGRATION OF KNOWLEDGE/IDEAS
This week, students will read, write, and talk about adapting to a new culture.

Texts This Week
- "Welcome to America!"
- "Moving Day"
- "How to Do a Move"
- *Good-Bye, 382 Shin Dang Dong*
- "Sing a Song of People"

Social Studies Knowledge Goals
Students will understand that a new culture means
- a new home and neighborhood
- a new language
- new traditions

Street Rhymes!

Hugo left Peru and moved to Idaho.
He knew a bit of English, but some words
   he didn't know.
He felt a little homesick for his homeland far away.
Then he met some friends and felt better every day!

- To introduce this week's concept, read aloud the poem several times and ask students to join you.

Content Knowledge

Adapting to a New Culture

CONCEPT TALK To further explore the unit concept of Cultures, this week students will read, write, and talk about how people adjust when they move to a new place with a different culture. Write the Question of the Week on the board *Why is it hard to adapt to a new culture?*

Build Oral Language

TALK ABOUT ADAPTING TO A NEW CULTURE Have students turn to pp. 254–255 in their Student Editions. Look at each of the photos. Then use the prompts to guide discussion and create the concept map.

- If someone is new to America, what difficulties might the person have with a subway map? **(He or she might not know how to read it.)** When you go to a new country, you might not be able to speak the language or communicate with other people. Let's add *Communication* to the concept map.

- What forms of transportation are the children using? **(subway, bicycles, bus)** Depending on where you live, there are different customs, or ways of doing things. Let's add *Customs* to our concept map.

- What kinds of places do you see in the photos? **(There is a dry, dusty place. There are places with trees and roads.)** Different countries have different climates. Some people might leave a rural area and have to learn how to live in a city. Let's add *Climate* to our concept map.

- After discussing the photos, ask: What makes it hard to live in a new culture?

Oral Vocabulary

Let's Talk About

Adapting to a New Culture

- Make and listen to comments about adapting to a new home or neighborhood.

- Ask about and describe new traditions.

- Pose and answer questions about what it might be like to adapt to a new culture.

READING STREET ONLINE
CONCEPT TALK VIDEO
www.ReadingStreet.com

You've learned

2 1 7

Amazing Words ⭐
so far this year!

254

255

Student Edition, pp. 254–255

CONNECT TO READING Tell students that this week they will be reading about people who must learn how to live in a new culture. Throughout the week, encourage students to add concept-related words to this week's concept map.

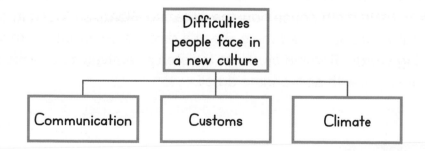

```
        Difficulties
        people face in
        a new culture
        /      |      \
Communication   Customs   Climate
```

eSTREET INTERACTIVE
www.ReadingStreet.com

Pearson eText
• Student Edition

Concept Talk Video

ELL

Preteach Concepts Use the Day 1 instruction on ELL Poster 23 to assess and build background knowledge, develop concepts, and build oral vocabulary.

ELL Support Additional ELL support and modified instruction is provided in the *ELL Handbook* and in the ELL Support lessons on the *Teacher Resources DVD-ROM*.

Ⓒ Common Core State Standards

Speaking/Listening 1.c. Ask questions to check understanding of information presented, stay on topic, and link their comments to the remarks of others. **Language 4.** Determine or clarify the meaning of unknown and multiple-meaning words and phrases based on grade 3 reading and content, choosing flexibly from a range of strategies. **Language 6.** Acquire and use accurately grade-appropriate conversational, general academic, and domain-specific words and phrases, including those that signal spatial and temporal relationships (e.g., *After dinner that night we went looking for them*). **Also Speaking/ Listening 1., 3., Language 4.a.**

Amazing Words

You've learned | 2 | 1 | 7 | words so far.

You'll learn | 0 | 1 | 0 | words this week!

native	habit
homeland	impolite
aspect	manner
advantage	conscious
sponsor	insult

Content Knowledge

Build Oral Vocabulary

INTRODUCE AMAZING WORDS "Welcome to America!" on p. 255b is about a boy who moves to America from Germany. Tell students to listen for this week's Amazing Words—*native, homeland, aspect, advantage*—as you read the Teacher Read Aloud on p. 255b.

Amazing Words Robust Vocabulary Routine

1. **Introduce** Write the word *advantage* on the board. Have students say the word aloud with you. In "Welcome to America!" we learn that it is an *advantage* to have relatives in the country you are going to immigrate to. Supply a student-friendly definition. An *advantage* is anything that is in your favor, or is a benefit to you.

2. **Demonstrate** Have students answer questions to demonstrate understanding. Would it be an *advantage* to know the answers to a test? Why? Name an *advantage* that a grown-up has over a child.

3. **Apply** Ask students to give a personal example of *advantage*.

4. **Display the Word** Run your hand under the chunks in *ad-van-tage* as you read it. Have students say the word again.

See p. OV•3 to teach *native, homeland,* and *aspect*.

Routines Flip Chart

AMAZING WORDS AT WORK Reread "Welcome to America!" aloud. As students listen, have them notice how the Amazing Words are used in context. To build oral vocabulary, lead the class in a discussion about the meanings of the Amazing Words. Remind students to listen attentively to speakers and to answer questions with appropriate detail.

 **MONITOR PROGRESS** Check Oral Vocabulary

During discussion, listen for students' use of Amazing Words.

If... students are unable to use the Amazing Words in discussion,

then... use the Oral Vocabulary Routine in the Routines Flip Chart to demonstrate words in different contexts.

Teacher Read Aloud

MODEL FLUENCY As you read "Welcome to America!," model appropriate expression by adjusting your voice to demonstrate lively, fluent reading.

Welcome to America!

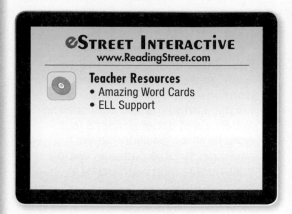

Oscar grabbed his father's hand tightly as they stood on deck of their steamship, the KAISER WILHELM II. And there it was—barely visible on the horizon—their new home in Boston. Oscar wondered what America would be like. Would there be streets of gold? Wild cowboys? Oscar laughed to himself. He knew Boston was not like that. Oscar's uncle and his family had gone to America four years ago, and they had told them that Massachusetts was a lot like Germany. Its climate was similar, and even the landscape would look familiar.

Still, Oscar felt that it could never replace the forests and woodlands of his native homeland. No new friends would ever take the place of his friends back home. No strudel would taste as good in this new land as the ones made in his mother's oven back home.

Despite his doubts, Oscar was anxious to get there. They had been on the ship for two weeks, and the trip had been hard. Oscar's family was not wealthy, and they, along with 900 other passengers, had been crammed into the ship for the passage to America. There had been little to do, so Oscar's mother had taught him English the entire trip. As for the food, it had been awful—an insult to the taste buds! Oscar longed for the scrumptious sausages and potatoes that his mother made at home. But his mother had a completely different attitude—if this is what people in America were used to eating, her bakery

in Boston would surely be a huge success! His mother's specialties were sweet breads and flaky pastries.

"Being able to make money is only one aspect of our new life," his mother said to Oscar. "You will get a better education and go to college. Don't forget that your father and I have an advantage over most immigrants. Your father is a skilled carpenter and I am a master baker. Soon we will have a new life, filled with success and happiness."

His mother was filled with confidence and enthusiasm, but to Oscar, America was the big unknown. Would he truly be happy there?

Leaving the ship was a long, tough process, and the strange sound of English words swirled in and out of his ears. Even though he had studied the language for months, most of it still didn't make sense. Then finally his aunt and uncle found them in the crowd. Their German words of greeting settled over Oscar like a warm blanket of welcome.

Oscar's two cousins stood shyly next to their parents. The boy, Paul, smiled at Oscar and handed him a hand-carved wooden toy. He said in English, "I made it for you. Welcome to America." For the briefest moment, Oscar felt happy. Maybe his parents were right, and America would provide a good life for them. Even Oscar knew that there was only one way to find out!

Support Listening Comprehension
English learners will benefit from additional visual support to understand the key terms in the concept map. Use the pictures on pp. 254–255 to scaffold understanding.

ELL Support for Read Aloud Use the modified Read Aloud on p. DI•69 of the *ELL Support* lessons to prepare students to listen to "Welcome to America!"

Common Core State Standards

Foundational Skills 3. Know and apply grade-level phonics and word analysis skills in decoding words. **Language 2.f.** Use spelling patterns and generalizations (e.g., word families, position-based spellings, syllable patterns, ending rules, meaningful word parts) in writing words.

Skills Trace

⦿ **Vowel Patterns for** /ȯ/

Introduce U5W3D1

Practice U5W3D3; U5W3D4

Reteach/Review U5W3D5; U5W4D4

Assess/Test Weekly Test U5W3
Benchmark Test U5

KEY: U=Unit   W=Week   D=Day

Vocabulary Support

You may wish to explain the meanings of these words.

scald to burn with hot liquid or steam

stalk stem of a plant; to follow quietly

awkward clumsy

Phonics

Teach/Model

⦿ **Vowel Patterns for** /ȯ/

CONNECT Write the words *word* and *bird*. Ask students what they know about the vowel sounds. (Both words have the vowel sound /ėr/, but the spelling patterns are different.) Today you will learn how to decode words with the sound /ȯ/ spelled *a, au, aw, al, augh,* and *ough*.

USE SOUND-SPELLING CARDS Display Card 56. Point to *au*. The sound /ȯ/ can be spelled *au*. Have students say /ȯ/ several times as you point to *au*. Follow the same procedure with Card 105, /ȯ/ spelled *a*; Card 58, /ȯ/ spelled *aw*; Card 106, /ȯ/ spelled *al*; Card 57, /ȯ/ spelled *augh*; and Card 97, /ȯ/ spelled *ough*.

MODEL Write *law*. In this word, the letters *aw* stand for the sound /ȯ/. Point to each spelling as you say its sound. Then blend the word: /l/ /ȯ/, *law*. Follow this procedure to model *chalk* and *launch*.

GROUP PRACTICE Continue the process. This time have students blend with you. Remind students that *a* followed by *l, u,* or *w* usually stands for the sound /ȯ/.

awe	scald	caught	raw	pause	thought
daughter	stalk	fault	haunt	recall	awkward

REVIEW What do you know about reading these words? When you see *a, au, aw, al, augh,* or *ough* in a word, try the sound /ȯ/.

Guide Practice

MODEL Have students turn to p. 256 in their Student Editions. Each word on this page has the vowel sound /ȯ/. The first word is *ought*. I hear /ȯ/ in this word. In *ought,* /ȯ/ is spelled *ough*. When I say *daughter,* I hear /ȯ/ in the first syllable. In *daughter,* /ȯ/ is spelled *augh*.

GROUP PRACTICE For each word in Words I Can Blend, ask for the sound of each letter or group of letters. Make sure that students identify the correct sounds for the spelling patterns *a, au, aw, al, augh,* and *ough*.

Corrective feedback	**If...** students have difficulty blending a word, **then...** model blending the word, and then ask students to blend it with you.

Envision It! Sounds to Know

thought

ough

daughter

audience

augh

au

ball

chalk

a

hawk

al

aw

READING STREET ONLINE SOUND-SPELLING CARDS
www.ReadingStreet.com

256

Phonics

Vowel Patterns *a, au, aw, al, augh, ough*

Words I Can Blend

o u g h t
d a u gh t e r
b a l l
f a u l t
y a w n e d
w a l k i n g

Sentences I Can Read

1. The woman ought to buy her daughter a new dress.
2. He missed the ball, but it wasn't his fault.
3. Tracy yawned while walking home.

I Can Read!

One fall day at school I saw Paula draw a picture on the sidewalk with chalk. I talked to her about what she had drawn, and she said she did it because it brought her joy.

Paula calmly taught me how to crawl around on the pavement and launch my own art. I thought I ought to try it. My first drawing was awful, but I sought to improve.

Now I wouldn't call all my drawings works of art, but I have improved in small ways.

You've learned

Vowel Patterns
a, au, aw, al, augh, ough

257

Apply

READ WORDS IN ISOLATION After students can successfully segment and blend the words on p. 256 in their Student Editions, point to words in random order and ask students to read them naturally.

READ WORDS IN CONTEXT Have students read each of the sentences on p. 256. Have them identify words in the sentences that have the vowel sound /ȯ/.

Team Talk Pair students and have them take turns reading each of the sentences aloud.

ON THEIR OWN For additional practice, use *Reader's and Writer's Notebook*, p. 338.

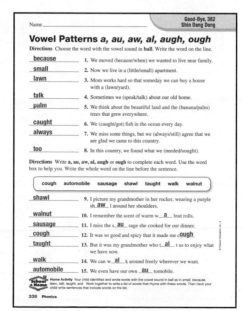

Name _____

Good-Bye, 382 Shin Dang Dong

Vowel Patterns *a, au, aw, al, augh, ough*

Directions Choose the word with the vowel sound in **ball**. Write the word on the line.

because — 1. We moved (because/when) we wanted to live near family.
small — 2. Now we live in a (little/small) apartment.
lawn — 3. Mom works hard so that someday we can buy a house with a (lawn/yard).
talk — 4. Sometimes we (speak/talk) about our old home.
palm — 5. We think about the beautiful land and the (banana/palm) trees that grew everywhere.
caught — 6. We (caught/got) fish in the ocean every day.
always — 7. We miss some things, but we (always/still) agree that we are glad we came to this country.
too — 8. In this country, we found what we (needed/sought).

Directions Write **a, au, aw, al, augh** or **ough** to complete each word. Use the word box to help you. Write the whole word on the line before the sentence.

| cough | automobile | sausage | shawl | taught | walk | walnut |

shawl — 9. I picture my grandmother in her rocker, wearing a purple sh_aw_l around her shoulders.
walnut — 10. I remember the scent of warm w_a_lnut rolls.
sausage — 11. I miss the s_au_sage she cooked for our dinner.
cough — 12. It was so good and spicy that it made me c_ough_.
taught — 13. But it was my grandmother who t_au_t us to enjoy what we have now.
walk — 14. We can w_al_k around freely wherever we want.
automobile — 15. We even have our own _au_tomobile.

School + Home Home Activity Your child identified and wrote words with the vowel sound in ball as in small, because, lawn, talk, taught, and Work together to write a list of words that rhyme with these words. Then have your child write sentences that include words on the list.

338 Phonics

Reader's and Writer's Notebook, p. 338

eSTREET INTERACTIVE
www.ReadingStreet.com

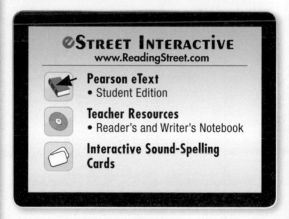

Pearson eText
• Student Edition

Teacher Resources
• Reader's and Writer's Notebook

Interactive Sound-Spelling Cards

ELL

Articulation Tip English language learners may need help with *augh* and *ough* words, such as *caught* and *bought*, in which the digraph *gh* is silent. Have students practice these words along with *au* words such as *auto* and *sauce*.

Good-Bye, 382 Shin Dang Dong **256–257**

Common Core State Standards

Foundational Skills 3. Know and apply grade-level phonics and word analysis skills in decoding words. **Foundational Skills 3.c.** Decode multisyllable words. **Foundational Skills 3.d.** Read grade-appropriate irregularly spelled words. **Foundational Skills 4.** Read with sufficient accuracy and fluency to support comprehension. **Also Foundational Skills 4.a.**

Decodable Reader 23A

If students need help, then...

Read *All That Moms Do*

READ WORDS IN ISOLATION Have students turn to p. 85 of *Decodable Practice Readers 3.2*. Have students read each word.

Have students read the high-frequency words *the, of, was, a, there, to, one, want, your, said, you, here, of, something, mother, again, off, what's,* and *what* on the first page.

PREVIEW Have students read the title and preview the story. Tell them that they will read words with the vowel sound /ô/ spelled *a, au, aw, al, augh,* and *ough*.

READ WORDS IN CONTEXT Pair students for reading and listen as they read. One student begins. Students read the entire story, switching readers after each page. Partners reread the story. This time the other student begins. Make sure students are monitoring their accuracy when they decode words.

Decodable Practice Reader 23A

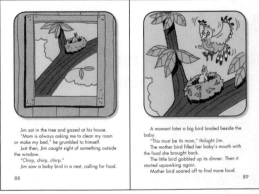

Corrective feedback	**If...** students have difficulty decoding a word, **then...** refer them to the *Sound-Spelling Cards* to identify the sounds in the word. Then prompt them to blend the word.

- What is the new word?
- Is the new word a word you know?
- Does it make sense in the story?

CHECK DECODING AND COMPREHENSION Have students retell the story to include characters, setting, and events. Then have students find words in the story that have the vowel sound /ȯ/. Students should supply *lawn, tall, walnut, thought, because, ought, always, caught, saw, calling, brought, squawking, sought, all, small, bought, walked, hall, taught.*

Reread for Fluency

REREAD DECODABLE READER Have students reread *Decodable Practice Reader 23A* to develop automaticity decoding words with /ȯ/ spelled *a, au, aw, al, augh,* and *ough.*

Routine   Oral Reading

1. **Read** Have students read the entire book orally.

2. **Reread** To achieve optimal fluency, students should reread the text three or four times.

3. **Corrective Feedback** Listen as students read. Provide corrective feedback regarding their fluency and decoding.

Routines Flip Chart

Vowel Patterns for /ȯ/

Beginning Write several words with the vowel sound /ȯ/ from the *Decodable Practice Reader* on the board, such as *lawn, tall, ought,* and *walnut.* Point to each word as you say it aloud. Then underline the letters that represent the spelling pattern for /ȯ/ in each word. Have students repeat the words with you.

Intermediate After reading, have students find pairs of rhyming words with the vowel sound /ȯ/. Some examples are *small* and *hall, bought* and *caught.*

Advanced After reading the story, have students choose four or five words with the vowel sound /ȯ/ and write a sentence for each word.

Good-Bye, 382 Shin Dang Dong **257b**

Common Core State Standards

Literature 1. Ask and answer questions to demonstrate understanding of a text, referring explicitly to the text as the basis for the answers. **Literature 3.** Describe characters in a story (e.g., their traits, motivations, or feelings) and explain how their actions contribute to the sequence of events. **Foundational Skills 4.** Read with sufficient accuracy and fluency to support comprehension. **Foundational Skills 4.b.** Read on-level prose and poetry orally with accuracy, appropriate rate, and expression on successive readings.

Skills Trace

◉ Sequence

Introduce U1W2D1; U1W3D1; U5W3D1

Practice U1W2D2; U1W2D3; U1W3D3; U1W5D3; U5W3D2; U5W4D3

Reteach/Review U1W2D5; U1W3D5; U5W3D5

Assess/Test Weekly Tests U1W2; U1W3; U5W3
Benchmark Tests U1

KEY: U=Unit   W=Week   D=Day

Comprehension Support

Students may also turn to pp. EI•14 and EI•21 to review the skill and strategy if necessary.

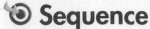

Text-Based Comprehension

◉ Sequence
◉ Monitor and Clarify

READ Remind students of the weekly concept—Adapting to a New Culture. Have students read "Moving Day" on p. 259.

MODEL A CLOSE READ

Think Aloud Today we're going to read about a boy whose family is moving. **Have students follow along as you read the first two paragraphs.** The second paragraph describes how Tom helped his parents pack. The author uses some clue words and phrases to help us follow the sequence of events. *First* tells me what they did first. *After that* tells what they did next. *When they were done* tells me that they finished packing.

As I read, I can use the strategy of monitor and clarify to make adjustments or corrections to my understanding. For example, at the end of the first paragraph, it says the family has lots to do before they move. I know that when people move, they pack up all their belongings. I can read on to find out if this is what Tom's family is doing.

TEACH Have students read p. 258. Explain that the skill of sequence and the strategy of monitor and clarify are tools they can use to ask and answer questions to demonstrate understanding of a text. Review the bulleted items and explanations on p. 258. Then have students use a graphic organizer like the one on p. 258 and identify the sequence of events in the passage.

GUIDE PRACTICE Have students reread "Moving Day" using the callouts as guides. Then ask volunteers to respond to the questions in the callouts, citing specific examples from the text to support their answers.

Skill First, Tom helps his dad pack tools in the garage. Then Tom helps his mom wrap treasures in the attic.
Strategy I can reread any section that I don't understand.

APPLY Use *Reader's and Writer's Notebook,* p. 339 for additional practice with sequence.

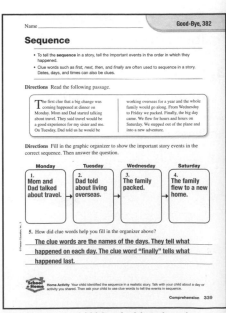

Reader's and Writer's Notebook, p. 339

Common Core State Standards

Literature 3. Describe characters in a story (e.g., their traits, motivations, or feelings) and explain how their actions contribute to the sequence of events. Also Literature 1.

Envision It! Skill | Strategy

Skill

Strategy

READING STREET ONLINE
ENVISION IT! ANIMATIONS
www.ReadingStreet.com

Comprehension Skill

Sequence

* To sequence the events in a story, tell the order in which events happen.
* Transition words such as *first, next, then,* and *finally* are often used to sequence events in a story.
* Use what you learned about sequence and a graphic organizer like the one below as you read "Moving Day." Then write a paragraph to summarize the story in order, maintaining the meaning of the story.

first → next → then → finally

Comprehension Strategy

Monitor and Clarify

When reading, stop after a paragraph or two and ask, "What did I learn?" "What doesn't make sense?" and "How does this connect to what I already know?" Reread aloud to clarify or read on to look for answers. Monitoring and clarifying will help you understand what you read.

258

MOVING DAY

Tom's family was getting ready to move to Chicago. Tom's mom was starting a new job in two weeks. There was a lot to do to get ready for moving day!

Mom and Dad decided to pack things that they didn't need every day. Tom would help. First, he helped his dad pack tools in the garage. After that, Tom helped his mom carefully wrap special treasures from the attic. When they were done, the house seemed strange and there were boxes everywhere.

The day before moving day Tom got up early to pack his own clothes. After lunch, Tom packed all of his toys and other belongings. When Tom went to bed that night, his room was almost empty.

Moving day finally arrived. While the movers loaded all of their belongings into the truck, Tom helped his parents make sure nothing was forgotten. It had been a tremendous amount of work to get ready for moving day!

Skill Here are some clue words. In what sequence have events happened so far?

Strategy If you lost track of the events, what can you do to adjust or correct your comprehension?

Your Turn!

⏸ **Need a Review?** See the *Envision It! Handbook* for help with sequence and monitoring and clarifying.

▶ **Ready to Try It?** As you read *Good-Bye, 382 Shin Dang Dong,* use what you've learned about sequence and monitoring and clarifying.

259

Student Edition, pp. 258–259

Model Fluent Reading

EXPRESSION AND PUNCTUATION CUES Have students listen as you read paragraphs 2 and 3 of "Moving Day" with appropriate expression. Explain that you will adjust your voice level to show excitement and use punctuation cues to decide how to read and where to pause and stop.

Routine Paired Reading

1. **Select a Passage** Use the first two paragraphs of "Moving Day."

2. **Reader 1** Students read the paragraphs, switching readers at the end of the first paragraph.

3. **Reader 2** Partners reread the paragraphs. This time the other student begins.

4. **Reread** For optimal fluency, have partners continue to read three or four times.

5. **Corrective Feedback** Listen as students read. Provide feedback about their expression. Encourage them to adjust their voice level to stress important words and phrases.

Routines Flip Chart

Sequence Perform a simple three-step activity. Ask: What did I do first? What did I do next? What did I do last? Guide students to use sequence words in their responses.

Good-Bye, 382 Shin Dang Dong **258–259**

Common Core State Standards

Writing 7. Conduct short research projects that build knowledge about a topic. **Speaking/Listening 1.** Engage effectively in a range of collaborative discussions (one-on-one, in groups, and teacher-led) with diverse partners on grade 3 topics and texts, building on others' ideas and expressing their own clearly. **Language 4.a.** Use sentence-level context as a clue to the meaning of a word or phrase. **Language 6.** Acquire and use accurately grade-appropriate conversational, general academic, and domain-specific words and phrases, including those that signal spatial and temporal relationships (e.g., *After dinner that night we went looking for them*). **Also Language 4.**

Selection Vocabulary

Use the following routine to introduce this week's tested selection vocabulary.

airport a place where airplanes are able to take off and land

cellar an underground room or rooms, usually under a building

curious eager to find out or learn about new things

delicious tastes very good

described told about in words or writing

farewell good-bye

homesick wanting to go home

memories everything a person remembers

raindrops drops of rain

SEE IT/SAY IT Write *farewell*. Scan across the word with your finger as you say it: *fare-well*.

HEAR IT Use the word in a sentence. I said *farewell* to my neighbor before he moved to another state.

DEFINE IT Elicit definitions from students. How would you explain the meaning of *farewell* to a friend? Clarify or give a definition when necessary. Yes, *farewell* means "good-bye." Restate the word in student-friendly terms. When you say *farewell,* you are saying good-bye.

Team Talk When do people say *farewell* to each other? Is it a happy or sad time when you say *farewell*? Turn and talk to your partner about this. Be prepared to explain your answer. Allow students time to discuss. Ask for examples. Rephrase their examples for usage when necessary or to correct misunderstandings.

MAKE CONNECTIONS Have students discuss the word. Have you ever said *farewell* or heard someone else say *farewell*? Turn and talk to your partner about this. Then be prepared to share. Have students share. Rephrase their ideas for usage when necessary or to correct misunderstandings.

RECORD Have students write the word and its meaning.

Continue this routine to introduce the remaining words in this manner.

Corrective feedback | **If...** students are having difficulty understanding, **then...** review the definitions in small groups.

Research and Inquiry

Step 1 Identify and Focus Topic

TEACH Discuss the Question of the Week: *Why is it hard to adapt to a new culture?* Tell students they will research how people overcome difficulties when they move to a new country. They will write articles to present to the class on Day 5.

Think Aloud

MODEL I'll start by brainstorming a list of questions about the difficulties immigrants face in America. I know that people come here from many different countries and they may have different customs. Some possible questions could be *What do immigrants leave behind in their homeland? What challenges do they face in America?* and *Who can help them adapt?*

GUIDE PRACTICE After students have brainstormed inquiry questions, explain that tomorrow they will conduct research using their questions. Help students identify keywords that will guide their search.

ON THEIR OWN Have students work individually, in pairs, or small groups to write an inquiry question. Encourage them to generate their research topics from personal interests.

eSTREET INTERACTIVE
www.ReadingStreet.com

Teacher Resources
- Envision It! Pictured Vocabulary Cards
- Tested Vocabulary Cards

21st Century Skills
Internet Guy *Don Leu*

Weekly Inquiry Project

STEP 1	Identify and Focus Topic
STEP 2	Navigate/Search
STEP 3	Analyze Information
STEP 4	Synthesize
STEP 5	Communicate

ELL

Multilingual Vocabulary Students can apply knowledge of their home languages to acquire new English vocabulary by using the Multilingual Vocabulary Lists (*ELL Handbook*, pp. 433–444).

ELL

If... students need more scaffolding and practice with **Vocabulary, then...** use the activities on pp. DI•67–DI•68 in the Teacher Resources section on SuccessNet.

Day 1 SMALL GROUP TIME • Differentiate Vocabulary, p. SG•33

OL On-Level	**SI** Strategic Intervention	**A** Advanced
• **Practice Vocabulary** Amazing Words	• **Reteach Vocabulary** Amazing Words	• **Extend Vocabulary** Amazing Words
• **Read** *Reading Street Sleuth*, pp. 60–61	• **Read** *Reading Street Sleuth*, pp. 60–61.	• **Read** *Reading Street Sleuth*, pp. 60–61
		• **Introduce** Inquiry Project

Common Core State Standards

Language 1.a. Explain the function of nouns, pronouns, verbs, adjectives, and adverbs in general and their functions in particular sentences. **Language 2.f.** Use spelling patterns and generalizations (e.g., word families, position-based spellings, syllable patterns, ending rules, meaningful word parts) in writing words. **Also Language 2.**

Spelling Pretest

Vowel Patterns *au, augh, ou, ough*

INTRODUCE This week we will spell words with the vowel patterns *au, augh, ou,* and *ough.*

PRETEST Say each word, read the sentence, and repeat the word.

1. **because**	I stayed home **because** I am sick.
2. **though**	It is sunny now, **though** later it will rain.
3. **taught**	He **taught** me how to tie my shoes.
4. **bought**	Max **bought** a new skateboard today.
5. **touch**	She reached out to **touch** the goat's soft nose.
6. **would**	**Would** you like a piece of cake?
7. **author**	The **author** read from her book.
8. **could**	If Hannah **could,** she would stay up all night.
9. **enough**	Did you get **enough** to eat?
10. **sausage**	I ate **sausage** for breakfast.
11. **fought**	The policeman **fought** the robber and won.
12. **should**	The mail **should** be here any minute.
13. **faucet**	Please turn off the **faucet** when you are done.
14. **daughter**	Jackie's baby **daughter** is very sweet.
15. **brought**	We **brought** games to play tonight.

Challenge words

16. **laundry**	We always do the **laundry** on Saturdays.
17. **distraught**	Julie is **distraught** over the bad news.
18. **afterthought**	He went back for his umbrella as an **afterthought.**
19. **auditorium**	People gathered in the **auditorium** before the play.
20. **overwrought**	Kiera was **overwrought** from the busy day.

SELF-CORRECT Have students self-correct their pretests by rewriting misspelled words.

ON THEIR OWN Use *Let's Practice It!* p. 309 on the *Teacher Resources DVD-ROM.*

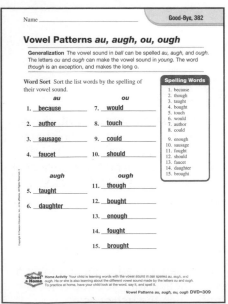

Let's Practice It! TR DVD•309

Conventions

Adverbs

MAKE CONNECTIONS Write the following sentences on the board. Underline the adverb in each sentence. Have students tell whether each underlined word tells *how, when,* or *where* something happens.

I wrote the letter <u>neatly</u>. (how)

He is coming <u>tomorrow</u>. (when)

We had to come <u>inside</u>. (where)

TEACH Display Grammar Transparency 23, and read aloud the explanation and examples in the box. Point out the adverbs *yesterday* and *inside*. Adverbs tell when, where, or how something happens. Some adverbs come before the verb, such as *yesterday*. Some adverbs come after the verb, such as *inside*. Adverbs such as *first, then, finally,* and *last* tell when something happens and are called time-order transition words.

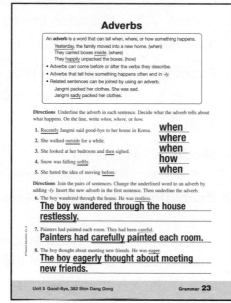

Grammar Transparency 23, TR DVD

MODEL Model completing item 1. The word *Recently* is an adverb. It tells when Jangmi said good-bye. I will underline the word *Recently*.

GUIDE PRACTICE Guide students to complete items 2–5. Remind them that adverbs tell when, where, or how something happens.

APPLY Have students read sentences 6–8 on the transparency and connect the sentences by rewriting the underlined word as an adverb with an *-ly* ending.

Handwriting

MODEL LETTER FORMATION AND PROPER WORD SPACING Display the cursive uppercase letters *H* and *K*. Follow the stroke instruction pictured to model letter formation. Explain to students that when they write in cursive, they need to make sure there is enough space between each word in a sentence. Model proper word spacing by writing the sentences *Honolulu is in Hawaii* and *Kansas is a state in the Midwest*.

GUIDE PRACTICE Have students write this sentence: *Helen and Keith are brother and sister*.

eSTREET INTERACTIVE
www.ReadingStreet.com

Teacher Resources
• Let's Practice It!
• Grammar Transparency
• Daily Fix-It Transparency

Daily Fix-It

1. Jangmi moved happy to her knew home. *(happily; new)*

2. Her familys' house has a big laun. *(family's; lawn)*

Academic Vocabulary ©

An **adverb** is a word that can tell how, when, or where something happens.

Adverbs Reinforce the meanings of various adverbs by having students act out the adverbs. For example, you might say "Can you walk slowly?" Then you can substitute different adverbs for students to act out. *(quickly, angrily, lazily)*

Handwriting To provide extra practice in handwriting cursive uppercase letters *H* and *K* and to extend language opportunities, have students write a list of names that begin with *H* and *K*. *(Harry, Henry; Ken, Karen)*

Common Core State Standards

Literature 5. Refer to parts of stories, dramas, and poems when writing or speaking about a text, using terms such as chapter, scene, and stanza; describe how each successive part builds on earlier sections. **Writing 3.** Write narratives to develop real or imagined experiences or events using effective technique, descriptive details, and clear event sequences. **Writing 4.** With guidance and support from adults, produce writing in which the development and organization are appropriate to task and purpose. **Also Language 3.a.**

TEXT TYPES AND PURPOSES

This week students write a free verse poem about a time when they were new to something or someplace.

Narrative Writing

Through reading and discussion, students will gain a deeper understanding of what it's like to adapt to a new culture. They will use this knowledge from the texts to write free verse poetry.

Through the week, students will improve their range and content of writing through daily mini-lessons.

5-Day Plan

DAY 1	Read Like a Writer
DAY 2	Writing Trait: Organization
DAY 3	Writer's Craft: Figurative Language
DAY 4	Revise: Adding
DAY 5	Proofread for Adverbs

Write Guy by Jeff Anderson

Experiment and Use What You Know!

Encourage students to experiment—or stretch themselves to try new things—with spelling, punctuation, and grammar. They can make an attempt to use all that they know and stretch.

Writing

Poetry: Free Verse

Mini-Lesson | **Read Like a Writer**

■ **Introduce** Free verse poetry is poetry that does not rhyme or follow a fixed rhythmic structure; instead, the writer creates his or her own pattern and rhythm. A poem written in free verse may sound like a conversation, or even a person thinking aloud.

Prompt Think about a time you were new to something or someplace. Write a free verse poem about the experience.

Trait Word Choice

Mode Narrative

■ **Examine Model Text** Let's read an example of a free verse poem about a new experience. Have students read "music class" on p. 340 of their *Reader's and Writer's Notebook*.

■ **Key Features** Free verse poetry may contain a few rhyming words, but it usually has no fixed rhyme scheme or rhyming pattern. **Have students circle the last word of each line in the first stanza and say whether or not the words rhyme.**

The words are arranged in lines of various lengths, which draw readers' attention to specific words. Also, the lines in free verse poetry may or may not be arranged in stanzas. **Have students identify varying line lengths in the second stanza.**

Writers of free verse choose words carefully to create a picture, convey meaning, and make readers feel a certain way. **Point out and have students underline the words *tinkling, fingers, running,* and *stretching* in the third stanza. Explain that the words are intended to give a mental picture of someone playing a piano.**

Punctuation is also important in free verse because it draws attention to specific words. **Point out that the model contains no punctuation except for the end mark on the final line. Have students circle the end mark.**

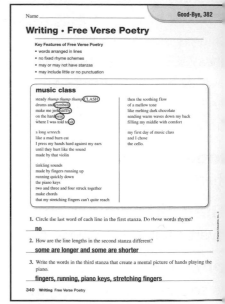

Reader's and Writer's Notebook, p. 340

Review Key Features

Review the key features of free verse poetry with students. You may want to post the features in the classroom for students to refer to as they work on their poems.

Key Features of Free Verse Poetry

- words are arranged in lines of various lengths
- no fixed rhyme schemes or rhyming patterns
- lines may or may not be arranged in stanzas
- may include little or no punctuation

Routine   Quick Write for Fluency   Team Talk

Talk Have pairs talk about the features of free verse poetry.

Write Students should write a sentence about a feature that they would like to use in their own poems.

Share Partners should share their sentences and ideas.

Routines Flip Chart

---

eSTREET INTERACTIVE
www.ReadingStreet.com

Teacher Resources
- Reader's and Writer's Notebook
- Let's Practice It!

Academic Vocabulary

Free verse is a form of poetry without a fixed structure or regular rhyme scheme.

ELL

Read Like a Writer Read the writing model aloud and help students understand that free verse poetry uses specific words to help create pictures in readers' minds. Explain that the model tells about a student's first day in music class, in which the student listens to different instruments before choosing one to learn. Ask students to think about how this experience is shared through the images created by the writer.

Wrap Up Your Day!

✔ **Content Knowledge** Reread "Street Rhymes!" on p. 254j to students. Ask them what they learned this week about adapting to a new culture.

✔ **Oral Vocabulary** Have students use the Amazing Words they learned in context sentences.

✔ **Homework** Send home this week's Family Times newsletter on *Let's Practice It!* pp. 310–311 on the *Teacher Resources* DVD-ROM.

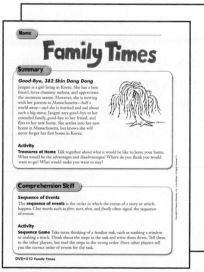

Let's Practice It!
TR DVD•310–311

Preview DAY 2

Tell students that tomorrow they will read about a young girl who has to adapt to life in the United States.

Content Knowledge
Oral Vocabulary

Phonics/Word Analysis
© Vowel Patterns for /ȯ/

Literary Terms
Mood

Vocabulary Skill
© Compound Words

Fluency
Expression and Punctuation Cues

Research and Inquiry
Navigate/Search

Conventions
Adverbs

Spelling
Vowel Patterns *au, augh, ou, ough*

Writing
Poetry: Free Verse

Materials
- Student Edition
- Reader's and Writer's Notebook

© Common Core State Standards

Speaking/Listening 1. Engage effectively in a range of collaborative discussions (one-on-one, in groups, and teacher-led) with diverse partners on grade 3 topics and texts, building on others' ideas and expressing their own clearly. **Language 6.** Acquire and use accurately grade-appropriate conversational, general academic, and domain-specific words and phrases, including those that signal spatial and temporal relationships (e.g., *After dinner that night we went looking for them*). **Also Speaking/ Listening 1.c., 1.d., Language 5.b.**

Content Knowledge

Adapting to a New Culture

EXPAND THE CONCEPT Remind students of the weekly concept question, *Why is it hard to adapt to a new culture?* Tell students that today they will begin reading *Good-Bye, 382 Shin Dang Dong.* As they read, encourage students to think about the difficulties people face when they move to a new place with a different culture.

Build Oral Language

TALK ABOUT SENTENCES AND WORDS Reread sentences from the Rea Aloud, "Welcome to America!"

Still, Oscar felt that it could never replace the forests and woodlands of his native homeland. No new friends would ever take the place of his friends back home.

- What does *native* mean? (where a person is born)
- What does *homeland* mean? (the state or country where a person is born; hometown)
- What does the author mean when he or she says that Oscar felt that it coul never replace his native homeland? (Oscar knows he will miss his hometow and that nothing in the new town will replace his memories and the forests and woodlands.)

Team Talk Have students turn to a partner and discuss the following question. Then ask them to share their responses.

- What is the shortest version of these sentences you can make without changing the basic meaning? (Possible response: Oscar felt that nothing could replace the forests and woodlands of his homeland or his friends back home.)

Build Oral Vocabulary

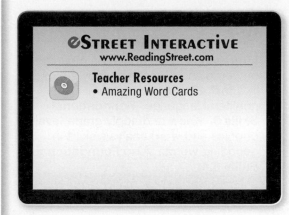

eSTREET INTERACTIVE
www.ReadingStreet.com
Teacher Resources
• Amazing Word Cards

Amazing Words   Robust Vocabulary Routine

Introduce Write the Amazing Word *sponsor* on the board. Have students say it aloud with you. Relate *sponsor* to the photos on pp. 254–255 and "Welcome to America!" Which family member is Oscar's *sponsor*? How will his uncle be able to help Oscar's family adapt to life in America? Have students determine the definition of the word. (A *sponsor* is a person responsible in some way for another person or thing.)

Demonstrate Have students answer questions to demonstrate understanding. What makes Oscar's uncle and cousins good *sponsors*? (They can teach Oscar's family English and show them how things are done in America.)

Apply Have students apply their understanding. What qualities would a good *sponsor* have?

Display the Word Run your finger under the syllables *spon-sor* as you say the word.

ee p. OV•3 to teach *habit*.

utines Flip Chart

Amazing Words

native	habit
homeland	impolite
aspect	manner
advantage	conscious
sponsor	insult

DD TO THE CONCEPT MAP Use the photos
n pp. 254–255 and the Read Aloud "Welcome to
merica!" to talk about the Amazing Words *native*,
meland, aspect,* and *advantage.* Add the words to
e concept map to develop students' knowledge of
e topic. Discuss the following questions. Encourage
udents to build on others' ideas when they answer.

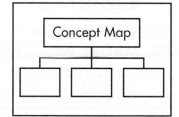

Concept Map

What things might people have to leave behind in their *homeland* when they
move?

What *aspect* of moving to a new country would be most difficult for you?

What *advantage* do *native* people have over immigrants?

Reinforce Vocabulary Use the Day 2 instruction on ELL Poster 23 to teach lesson vocabulary and discuss the lesson concept.

Good-Bye, 382 Shin Dang Dong **260b**

Common Core State Standards

Literature 4. Determine the meaning of words and phrases as they are used in a text, distinguishing literal from nonliteral language. **Foundational Skills 3.** Know and apply grade-level phonics and word analysis skills in decoding words. **Also Foundational Skills 3.c.**

Phonics

Vowel Patterns for /ȯ/

REVIEW Review the /ȯ/ spelling patterns *a, au, aw, al, augh,* and *ough* using Sound-Spelling Cards 56, 57, 58, 97, 105, and 106.

READ WORDS IN ISOLATION Have the class read the words. Then point to the words in random order and ask students to read them quickly.

draw	because	taught
always	almost	talking
brought	false	

....

Corrective feedback | Model blending decodable words. Ask students to blend them with you.

....

READ WORDS IN CONTEXT Display the sentences. Have the class read them.

Team Talk Have pairs take turns reading the sentences naturally.

I feel **awful** about the way I treated you.

The recipe **calls** for one **stalk** of celery.

My **daughter thought** our new **walkway** looked nice.

Don't Wait Until Friday

MONITOR PROGRESS Check Word Reading

Vowel Patterns for /ȯ/

FORMATIVE ASSESSMENT Write the following words and have the class read them. Notice which words students miss during the group reading. Call on individuals to read some of the words.

stall	paw	saucer	haul
disturb	worm	third	earl
auburn	curl	swirl	astronaut

Spiral Review
Row 2 reviews words with /ėr/ spelled *ir, ear, or, ur.*

Row 3 contrasts words with /ȯ/ spelled *a, au, aw, al, augh, ough,* and words with /ėr/ spelled *ir, ear, or, ur.*

If... students cannot read words with /ȯ/ spelling patterns at this point,

then... use the Day 1 Phonics lesson on p. 256a to reteach vowel patterns for /ȯ/. Use words from the *Decodable Practice Passages* (or Reader). Continue to monitor students' progress using other instructional opportunitie during the week. See the Skills Trace on p. 256a.

Literary Terms

Mood

TEACH Tell students that the mood of a story is the atmosphere or feeling it has. The author creates the mood through the setting, the characters, and the details that describe them. Explain that a scary story might have a creepy or eerie mood, while a humorous story would have a fun, playful mood.

Think Aloud **MODEL** Let's look at "Moving Day." In this story, I get a sense of excitement as the family prepares to move. The mood of the story is happy as the family works together. How might the author change this story to make the mood sad? (The author could include details about what Tom will miss about his old home.)

GUIDE PRACTICE Read p. 264 of *Good-Bye, 382 Shin Dang Dong* and point out how the authors create a sad mood through the setting (rainy day) and descriptive details (Jangmi's empty room, all her possessions in a box).

ON THEIR OWN Have students choose a scene from another story they have read, describe its mood, and tell how the setting, characters, and details help create that mood.

Academic Vocabulary

mood the atmosphere or feeling a story has

rising action the events in a story that show how a character reacts to a problem

Common Core State Standards

Foundational Skills 4.a. Read on-level text with purpose and understanding. **Foundational Skills 4.b.** Read on-level prose and poetry orally with accuracy, appropriate rate, and expression on successive readings. **Language 4.** Determine or clarify the meaning of unknown and multiple-meaning words and phrases based on grade 3 reading and content, choosing flexibly from a range of strategies.

Selection Vocabulary

airport a place where airplanes are able to take off and land

cellar an underground room or rooms, usually under a building

curious eager to find out or learn about new things

delicious tastes very good

described told about in words or writing

farewell good-bye

homesick wanting to go home

memories everything a person remembers

raindrops drops of rain

Bridge to Common Core

VOCABULARY ACQUISITION AND USE

When students interact with this week's selection vocabulary words, they are learning words they will need to succeed in school and beyond. Teaching the strategy of looking at a word's structure to determine and clarify the meanings of compound words will help students gain independence when they encounter compound words in other contexts.

Vocabulary Support

Refer students to *Words!* on p. W•9 in the Student Edition for additional practice.

Vocabulary Skill

Compound Words

READ Have students read "How to Do a Move" on p. 261. Use the vocabulary skill and strategy as tools to build comprehension.

TEACH WORD STRUCTURE Tell students that a compound word is made of two smaller words. Explain that using the strategy of looking at a compound word's structure can help them determine the word's meaning.

Think Aloud **MODEL** When I see an unfamiliar word, I can look for smaller words that I do know. The word *airport* is made up of two smaller words, *air* and *port*. I know the meanings of these two smaller words. *Air* can mean the space above us. A *port* is a place where boats load and unload goods. This helps me figure out what *airport* means. An *airport* is a place where airplanes land and take off.

GUIDE PRACTICE Write this sentence on the board: *I hear raindrops hitting the roof*. Have students identify the compound word and the two smaller words in it. Guide them to use the meanings of the two smaller words to determine the meaning of *raindrops*. For additional support, use *Envision It! Pictured Vocabulary Cards* or *Tested Vocabulary Cards*.

ON THEIR OWN Have students reread "How to Do a Move" on p. 261. Have them identify all four compound words in the Words to Know on p. 260. Then ask students to look at the word structure of *homesick* and *farewell* and determine their meanings. For additional practice use *Reader's and Writer's Notebook*, p. 341.

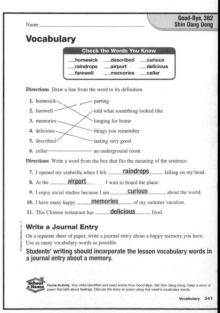

Reader's and Writer's Notebook, p. 341

Envision It! | Words to Know

airport

delicious

raindrops

cellar
curious
described
farewell
homesick
memories

**READING STREET ONLINE
VOCABULARY ACTIVITIES**
www.ReadingStreet.com

Vocabulary Strategy for

🎯 Compound Words

Word Structure You may come across a long word when you are reading. Look closely at it. Do you see two small words in it? Then it is a compound word. Use the two small words to figure out the meaning of the compound word. For example, a *classroom* is a room where a class is held.

1. Divide the compound word into its two small words.

2. Think of the meaning of each small word and then put the two meanings together. Does this help you understand the meaning of the compound word?

3. Try the new meaning in the context of the sentence. Does it make sense?

Read "How to Do a Move" on page 261. Use the two small words in each compound word to help you figure out its meaning.

Words to Write Reread "How to Do a Move." Write about what you think it would be like to move to a new place. Use words from the Words to Know list.

How to Do a Move

So you're moving. When you heard the news, did your stomach drop to the cellar? Did you become homesick before you had even left? Don't wait until you get to the airport to get ready for a move. Start planning now.

• Recognize that, just as raindrops are wet, you are going to be upset and unhappy. But that's OK. Just set a time limit. When the time is up, do something to make yourself feel better.

• Keep the memories. Take pictures of your old home, neighborhood, and friends. Make a scrapbook.

• Have a farewell party. Exchange addresses and telephone numbers with your friends.

• Be curious about your new town. Research the area at the library and on the Internet. It might be described in guidebooks. It might be known for a famous person or a delicious food. The more you know about the place, the more familiar it will feel when you get there.

Your Turn!

⏸ **Need a Review?** For additional help with compound words, see *Words!*

▶ **Ready to Try It?** Read *Good-Bye, 382 Shin Dang Dong* on pp. 262–279.

260

261

Student Edition, pp. 260–261

Reread for Fluency

EXPRESSION AND PUNCTUATION CUES Read the first paragraph of "How to Do a Move" aloud, keeping your expression slow and steady and using changes of voice level for emphasis. Tell students that you are reading the passage with expression, paying special attention to the end punctuation.

Routine | Paired Reading

Select a Passage Use paragraphs 1 and 2 of "How to Do a Move."

Reader 1 Students read the paragraphs, switching readers at the end of the first paragraph.

Reader 2 Partners reread the paragraphs. This time the other student begins.

Reread For optimal fluency, have partners continue to read three times.

Corrective Feedback Listen as students read. Provide corrective feedback regarding their oral reading, paying special attention to their expression.

Routines Flip Chart

eSTREET INTERACTIVE
www.ReadingStreet.com

Pearson eText
• Student Edition

Vocabulary Activities

Journal

Teacher Resources
• Envision It! Pictured Vocabulary Cards
• Tested Vocabulary Cards
• Reader's and Writer's Notebook

DAY 2

© Common Core State Standards

Literature 10. By the end of the year, read and comprehend literature, including stories, dramas, and poetry, at the high end of the grades 2–3 text complexity band independently and proficiently. **Also Literature 7.**

© Bridge to Common Core

CRAFT AND STRUCTURE

When students preview the selection, they analyze how portions of the text relate to the selection as a whole. As they prepare to read, they come to see how its genre impacts the content and style of the text.

Academic Vocabulary ©

realistic fiction a made-up story that could happen in real life

Strategy Response Log

Have students use p. 29 in the *Reader's and Writer's Notebook* to review and use the monitor and clarify strategy. Have them apply the strategy as they read *Good-Bye, 382 Shin Dang Dong.*

Text-Based Comprehension

Introduce Main Selection

Student Edition, pp. 262–263

GENRE Explain that **realistic fiction** is a made-up story with characters, a setting, and events that seem real. The characters in realistic fiction do and say things that real people do. The settings and problems are ones that readers will recognize from real life.

PREVIEW AND PREDICT Have students preview the title and illustrations for *Good-Bye, 382 Shin Dang Dong.* Have them predict what they will find ou as they read.

PURPOSE By analyzing *Good-Bye, 382 Shin Dang Dong,* a realistic fiction selection, students will gain knowledge of the difficulties of adapting to a new culture.

Access Main Selection

READER AND TASK SUGGESTIONS	
Preparing to Read the Text	**Leveled Tasks**
Review strategies for under-standing compound words.	• **Levels of Meaning • Evaluation** If students have difficulty identifying the story as realistic fiction, have them look for connections between their lives and the situations in the story.
Discuss the features of realistic fiction.	
Remind students that there are foreign words in this selection. They may need to read more slowly and use context clues to understand the text.	• **Theme and Knowledge Demands** Students may not understand where Korea is or how far Jangmi moved when she came to America. Have them take notes about places to locate on a map.

ee Text Complexity Measures for *Good-Bye, 382 Shin Dang Dong* on the tab the beginning of this week.

EAD Tell students that today they will read *Good-Bye, 382 Shin Dang Dong* r the first time. Use the Read for Understanding routine.

Routine — Read for Understanding ©

eepen understanding by reading the selection multiple times.

First Read—If students need support, then use the **Access Text** notes to help them clarify understanding.

Second Read—Use the **Close Reading** notes to help students draw knowledge from the text.

Day 2 — SMALL GROUP TIME • Differentiate Comprehension, p. SG•33

OL On-Level	**SI** Strategic Intervention	**A** Advanced
Practice Selection Vocabulary	• **Reteach** Selection Vocabulary	• **Extend** Selection Vocabulary
Read *Good-Bye, 382 Shin Dang Dong*	• **Read** *Good-Bye, 382 Shin Dang Dong*	• **Read** *Good-Bye, 382 Shin Dang Dong*
		• **Investigate** Inquiry Project

eSTREET INTERACTIVE
www.ReadingStreet.com

Pearson eText
• Student Edition

AudioText CD

Teacher Resources
• Reader's and Writer's Notebook

Background Building Audio CD

Access for All

A Advanced

Have students use resources to learn about Korean culture, including homes, foods, and clothing.

Build Background To build background, review the selection summary in English (*ELL Handbook*, p. 163). Use the Retelling Cards to provide visual support for the summary.

If... students need more scaffolding and practice with the **Comprehension Skill, then...** use the activities on p. DI•71 in the Teacher Resources section on SuccessNet.

Access Text © If students need help, then...

Review **DRAW CONCLUSIONS** Ask students to read the first page and find information that helps them draw a conclusion about how the narrator feels. (She mentions *one very sad memory*. She feels unhappy.)

(Think Aloud) **MODEL** In the first paragraph, the narrator mentions *one very sad memory*. This tells me she is thinking about a time in her past when she felt unhappy. What other information in the story shows that the narrator is unhappy or upset? **(She says her** *heart sank*.)

Close Reading ©

ANALYSIS • TEXT EVIDENCE In the last paragraph on p. 264, what information helps you draw a conclusion about how the narrator feels about moving to the United States? **(The text says she "frowns" and says she is going to a "strange, foreign place." She is scared and unhappy about moving.)**

My heart beats in two places: Here, where I live, and also in a place where I once lived. You see, I was born in Korea. One day my parents told me we were moving to America. I was eight years old, old enough to keep many lovely memories of my birthplace alive in my heart forever. But one very sad memory stays with me too. The day I cried, "Good-bye, 382 Shin Dang Dong!"

On that summer day I woke up to the sound of light rain tapping on my window. The monsoon season was coming. I didn't even need to open my eyes to know that. It was that time of year. It was also time to move.

In a few hours, I would be on an airplane.

When I opened my eyes, my heart sank. My bedroom was so bare! No hand-painted scrolls or colorful fans on my walls. No silk cushions or straw mats on my floor. All my possessions were packed away in a big brown box marked "Lovely Things."

I frowned and listened to the raindrops. One, two, three. . . . Soon the thick of the monsoon would arrive, and a thousand raindrops would hit our clay-tiled roof all at once. But I wouldn't be here to listen to them. I would be halfway around the world in a strange, foreign place called 112 Foster Terrace, Brighton, Massachusetts, U.S.A.

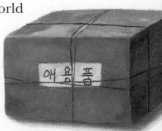

264

N THEIR OWN Have students list other details that show how the arrator feels. For additional practice, use *Let's Practice It!* p. 313 on e *Teacher Resources DVD-ROM*.

265

Student Edition, p. 265

YNTHESIS • TEXT EVIDENCE Use clues in the story and in the stration on p. 265 to tell the meaning of *monsoon*. Use a dictionary check the meaning. (The text mentions that *monsoon* is a season. also mentions rain tapping on the window and that a thousand rain- ops would soon hit the roof at once. The illustration shows rain outside ngmi's window. A *monsoon* must be a rainy season. The dictionary ys it is a season of strong winds and heavy rains.)

© **Common Core State Standards**

Literature 1. Ask and answer questions to demonstrate understanding of a text, referring explicitly to the text as the basis for the answers. **Literature 7.** Explain how specific aspects of a text's illustrations contribute to what is conveyed by the words in a story (e.g., create mood, emphasize aspects of a character or setting). **Also Literature 4., 10., Language 4.d.**

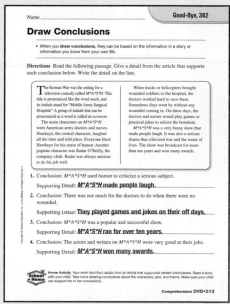

Let's Practice It! TR DVD•313

Access for All

SI Strategic Intervention

Display images of Korean scrolls, fans, cushions, and straw mats. Have students describe the objects. Explain how each one is used. Then have students compare and contrast them to what is in their own bedrooms.

ELL

Activate Prior Knowledge Explain that many people keep important or special items in their bedroom. Have students tell about things they keep in their room and explain why these are important or special.

Vocabulary: Idioms Point out the expression *my heart sank* on p. 264. Explain that we normally talk about a boat or another object that sank in the water. Here, Jangmi says her heart sank because she was reminded that she was moving to a faraway place, and she didn't want to go.

Good-Bye, 382 Shin Dang Dong **265a**

Access Text © <small>If students need help, then...</small>

⊙ MONITOR AND CLARIFY Point out that on page 266, Kisuni and Jangmi go to an open market. How can you figure out what this means?

MODEL When I see a word or term I don't know, I can look at the picture. I see that the girls are outside in an area where people are selling food. I can also think about words I know. I know that a supermarket is a store that sells food. I think an open market is a place outside where people sell food.

Close Reading ©

EVALUATION • TEXT EVIDENCE
What clues in the text tell you that Jangmi and her parents have very different feelings about moving to America? (The first sentence on p. 266 says her parents were "very excited." Jangmi shows she is upset about moving because she mentions "no friends" in America and says she doesn't "want to leave her best friend.")

My parents were very excited.

"Jangmi, you will like America," Dad tried to assure me.

"Are the seasons the same?" I wondered.

"Oh, yes."

"With monsoon rains?"

"No, Jangmi, no monsoon rains."

"No friends either," I moaned.

"You will make many new friends in America," Mom promised me, "in your new home."

But I loved my home right here! I didn't want to go to America and make new friends. I didn't want to leave my best friend, Kisuni.

After breakfast, Kisuni and I ran out into the rain and to the open market. Monsoon season was also the season for sweet, yellow melons called *chummy*. Kisuni and I would often peel and eat chummy under the willow tree that stood outside my bedroom window. But today, the chummy were for guests who were coming over for a farewell lunch.

At the market we peered into endless baskets and took our time choosing the ripest, plumpest chummy we could find.

"Do they have chummy in America?" Kisuni wondered.

"No," I replied. "But my mom says they have melons called *honeydew*."

"Honeydew," Kisuni giggled. "What a funny name!"

266

N THEIR OWN Have students identify another word they had trouble
ith and use pictures, prior knowledge, and context clues to determine
e word's meaning.

1ALYSIS How does the author show ways that life in Korea and
1erica will be different for Jangmi? **(The weather will be different.
th places will have melons, but America will have honeydew instead
the Korean *chummy*.)**

 Common Core State Standards

Literature 1. Ask and answer questions to demonstrate understanding of a text, referring explicitly to the text as the basis for the answers. **Literature 3.** Describe characters in a story (e.g., their traits, motivations, or feelings) and explain how their actions contribute to the sequence of events. **Literature 7.** Explain how specific aspects of a text's illustrations contribute to what is conveyed by the words in a story (e.g., create mood, emphasize aspects of a character or setting). **Also Language 4.**

Access for All

A Advanced

Have students brainstorm several more ways that life will be different in Korea and America for Jangmi. Challenge them also to think of ways her life will be the same. Then use their responses to create a Venn diagram on the board.

 Connect to Social Studies

Monsoons and Rice Rice is one of the main crops in Korea, and rice is a staple of the Korean diet. The monsoon rains provide the necessary water for irrigation of the country's rice fields.

ELL

Monitor and Clarify Read aloud the second sentence of the tenth paragraph on p. 266. Model how to reread, read ahead, and use pictures to clarify. *I wonder what chummy is. I can reread the text. It says that chummy are melons. I think this means chummy are a type of fruit. I can read on to get more information.* Read aloud the next sentence. Have students identify the additional information they learn about *chummy*. Then have them look for details in the picture that would help them clarify their understanding.

Good-Bye, 382 Shin Dang Dong **267a**

Access Text © If students need help, then...

1ST READ

Review DRAW CONCLUSIONS
After students read p. 269, ask them what Jangmi will miss most after moving to America. (her best friend, Kisuni)

Think Aloud **MODEL** When I read about the going-away party, I notice that Jangmi leaves her friends and family and goes outside to be with Kisuni. I think she will miss her friend more than the food, or her home, or anyone else.

ON THEIR OWN Have students reread p. 269 and draw a conclusion about how the family's relatives feel about their move to the United States.

268

Student Edition, p. 268

Close Reading ©

2ND READ

ANALYSIS • TEXT EVIDENCE Which words help you understand the mood of the going-away party on p. 269? (In the second paragraph, the words *sad, love, laughter,* and *tears* tell me that this is a sad party, but people are making the most of their time together. They are trying to have a good time.)

REREAD CHALLENGING TEXT Have students reread paragraphs 4–9 on p. 269 to practice reading dialogue fluently. Some students may need help with appropriate intonation and expression.

EVELOP LANGUAGE Have students reread the last four paragraphs
n page 269. What does *moan* mean? In what situations might a person
oan?

Soon after we returned, family and friends began
to arrive, carrying pots and plates of food. One by
one they took off their shoes, then entered the house.
Grandmother was dressed in her most special occasion
hanbok. She set up the long *bap sang* and before I could
even blink, on it were a big pot of dumpling soup and
the prettiest pastel rice cakes I had ever seen.
Kisuni and I peeled and sliced our chummy
and carefully arranged the pieces on a plate.

Then everybody ate and sang traditional
Korean songs and celebrated in a sad way. Love
and laughter and tears rippled through our house. How
I wanted to pack these moments into a big brown box and
bring them with me to America.

Kisuni and I sneaked outside and sat beneath the
willow tree. We watched the rain with glum faces.

"Kisuni, I wish we never had to move from this spot,"
I said.

"Me, too," she sighed. "Jangmi, how far away is America?"

"My mom says that it's halfway around the world. And my
dad told me that when the moon is shining here, the sun is
shining there. That's how far apart we'll be," I moaned.

"That's really far," Kisuni moaned back.

We watched the rain and grew more glum than ever.
Then Kisuni perked up.

"So when you're awake, I'll be asleep. And when I'm
awake, you'll be asleep," she declared. "At least we'll always
know what the other one is doing."

269

Student Edition, p. 269

YNTHESIS • TEXT EVIDENCE Use context clues on p. 269 to tell the
eaning of the word *glum.* (The girls are talking about how far apart they
ill be. This makes them feel sad. *Glum* means "sad" or "miserable.")

ⓒ **Common Core State Standards**

Literature 1. Ask and answer questions to demonstrate understanding of a text, referring explicitly to the text as the basis for the answers. **Literature 3.** Describe characters in a story (e.g., their traits, motivations, or feelings) and explain how their actions contribute to the sequence of events. **Language 4.** Determine or clarify the meaning of unknown and multiple-meaning word and phrases based on grade 3 reading and content, choosing flexibly from a range of strategies. **Also Literature 10., Language 4.a., 5.b.**

Connect to Social Studies

Korean Houses Explain to students that in Korea, the traditional house has walls that are built with wood, clay, or pounded earth. Because it is such a diverse country with people from all over the world, it has many different styles of houses. Some are modeled after the traditional houses of Korea as well as those of many other cultures.

ELL

Monitor Comprehension Read aloud the first paragraph on p. 269. Model using the reading strategy of monitoring comprehension by saying: I wonder what a *hanbok* is. I can reread the sentence to look for clues. The text says that Jangmi's grandmother was dressed in a *hanbok.* That tells me that a *hanbok* is a piece of clothing. Guide students to use context clues to figure out what a *bap sang* is. (a Korean table where food is served)

Good-Bye, 382 Shin Dang Dong **269a**

DAY 2

Access Text © If students need help, then...

SEQUENCE List on the board several events from the story. Have students put the events in sequence. Jangmi's family celebrates at a farewell dinner. Jangmi and Kisuni buy *chummy* at the market. Jangmi's parents tell her they are moving.

MODEL One way I can check the sequence of the events is to go back through the story. On p. 264, Jangmi's parents tell her they are moving. On p. 266, I see that the second event is when the girls go to the market. What is the third event? (farewell dinner)

ON THEIR OWN Have students choose another event from the story and tell where it would go in the sequence of events. For additional practice use *Let's Practice It!* p. 312 on the *Teacher Resources DVD-ROM*.

That moment our faces brightened. But a moment later we had to say good-bye.

Kisuni held back her tears. "Promise you'll write to me, Jangmi."

"I promise, Kisuni."

It was time to go to the airport.

"Kimpo Airport," Dad instructed the taxi driver.

The taxi slowly pulled away. I looked at our beautiful home one last time. Like rain on the window, tears streaked down my face.

"Good-bye, 382 Shin Dang Dong!" I cried.

270

Student Edition, p. 270

Close Reading ©

EVALUATION Which event on pp. 270–271 do you think was the hardest for Jangmi? Why? (I think the hardest event for Jangmi was saying good-bye to Kisuni because Jangmi has no friends in America.)

INFERENCE • TEXT EVIDENCE What does Jangmi say when the taxi pulls away from their house? Why do you think she says that? (She says, "Good-bye, 382 Shin Dang Dong." That must be the address, so she is saying good-bye to her house.)

HECK PREDICTIONS Have students look back at the predictions they made earlier and discuss whether they were accurate. Then have students preview the rest of the selection and either adjust their predictions accordingly or make new predictions.

On the long ride to the airport, Dad asked me, "Do you want to know what your new home looks like?"

"Okay," I shrugged.

"Let's see," Dad began, "it's a row house."

"A house that's attached to other houses," Mom explained.

"And inside the house are wooden floors," Dad added.

"No *ondal* floors?" I asked him. "How will we keep warm in the winter without ondal floors?"

"There are radiators in every room!" Mom said with an enthusiastic clap. "And a fireplace in the living room! Imagine!"

No, I could not imagine that. In our home we had a fire in the cellar called the *ondal*. It stayed lit all the time. The heat from the ondal traveled through underground pipes and kept our wax-covered floors warm and cozy. A fireplace in the living room sounded peculiar to me.

"And the rooms are separated by wooden doors," Mom added.

"No rice-paper doors?" I wondered.

My parents shook their heads. "No, Jangmi."

My eyes closed with disappointment. I had a hard time picturing this house. Would it ever feel like home?

271

If you want to teach this selection in two sessions, stop here.

If you want to continue reading this selection, turn to p. 272–273.

Student Edition, p. 271

ANALYSIS • TEXT EVIDENCE How does Jangmi feel about the new house? Use evidence from the text to support your answer. (She already knows that she is going to feel uncomfortable there because it will be so different from her house in Korea. The floors, doors, and the way of heating the house will all be totally different from what she is used to.)

 Common Core State Standards

Literature 1. Ask and answer questions to demonstrate understanding of a text, referring explicitly to the text as the basis for the answers. **Literature 3.** Describe characters in a story (e.g., their traits, motivations, or feelings) and explain how their actions contribute to the sequence of events. **Also Literature 10.**

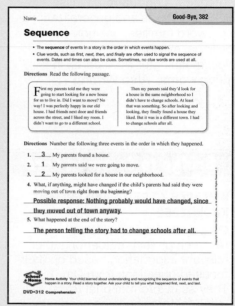

Let's Practice It! TR DVD•312

Sequence Have students draw a picture to represent each event and then number their pictures to show the order of events.

Good-Bye, 382 Shin Dang Dong **271a**

Common Core State Standards

Informational Text 5. Use text features and search tools (e.g., key words, sidebars, hyperlinks) to locate information relevant to a given topic efficiently. **Writing 8.** Recall information from experiences or gather information from print and digital sources; take brief notes on sources and sort evidence into provided categories. **Language 1.a.** Explain the function of nouns, pronouns, verbs, adjectives, and adverbs in general and their functions in particular sentences. **Language 2.f.** Use spelling patterns and generalizations (e.g., word families, position-based spellings, syllable patterns, ending rules, meaningful word parts) in writing words. **Also Writing 7.**

Bridge to Common Core

RESEARCH TO BUILD AND PRESENT KNOWLEDGE

On Day 2 of the weeklong research project, students gather relevant information based on their focused questions from Day 1. They scan informational texts using features such as headings, illustrations, captions, and highlighting as they look for answers to their inquiry questions. This process enables students to demonstrate an understanding of the subject matter under investigation.

Research and Inquiry

Step 2 Navigate/Search

TEACH Have students generate a research plan for gathering information about their topic. Be sure students search reference texts using their inquiry questions and keywords. Tell them to skim and scan each book for information that helps answer their inquiry question or leads them to specific information that will be useful. Have students look for features such as headings, illustrations, captions, or highlighting. Remind students to take notes as they gather information.

Think Aloud

MODEL When looking for information on what it is like to move to a new country, I found: *The first Korean immigrants arrived in Hawaii on January 13, 1903*. I will use keywords from this information, such as *Korean immigrants* and *Hawaii,* to lead me to more specific information. One fact I found using these keywords states, *Most of the first immigrants were young men who left their homeland to make a better life for themselves*.

GUIDE PRACTICE Have students continue their review of sources they identified. Tell students to make sure to skim and scan for further keywords that might lead to more information.

ON THEIR OWN Have students write down book titles, authors, and the book publishers and publication dates and create a Works Cited page.

Conventions

Adverbs

TEACH On the board, write the sentence *Yesterday, the movers gently packed our lamps.* Ask students *when* the movers packed and *how* the movers packed. *(yesterday; gently)* Remind students that adverbs tell when, where, or how something happens. Some adverbs, such as *yesterday* and *gently,* come before the word they describe. Other adverbs come after the words they describe.

GUIDE PRACTICE Write these words on the board: *soon, weakly, daily, around, quickly, near.* Guide students in identifying whether the adverbs tell *when, where,* or *how.*

ON THEIR OWN For more practice, use the *Reader's and Writer's Notebook,* p. 342.

Spelling

Vowel Patterns *au, augh, ou, ough*

TEACH Remind students that their spelling words have the vowel patterns *au, augh, ou,* and *ough.* Ask students to spell aloud the words *taught, bought, could,* and *faucet.* As each word is spelled, write it on the board and underline the vowel pattern.

GUIDE PRACTICE Have students write the remaining spelling words and underline the vowel patterns.

ON THEIR OWN For more practice, use the *Reader's and Writer's Notebook,* p. 343.

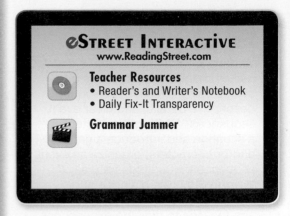

eStreet Interactive
www.ReadingStreet.com

Teacher Resources
• Reader's and Writer's Notebook
• Daily Fix-It Transparency

Grammar Jammer

Daily Fix-It

3. The family landed safe in they're new country. *(safely; their)*
4. Her parents and her were afraid she would disslike the new place. *(she; dislike)*

Reader's and Writer's Notebook, pp. 342–343

Conventions To provide students with practice on adverbs, use the modified grammar lessons in the *ELL Handbook* and Grammar Jammer online at: www.ReadingStreet.com

Common Core State Standards

Writing 3. Write narratives to develop real or imagined experiences or events using effective technique, descriptive details, and clear event sequences. **Writing 3.a.** Establish a situation and introduce a narrator and/or characters; organize an event sequence that unfolds naturally. **Writing 3.b.** Use dialogue and descriptions of actions, thoughts, and feelings to develop experiences and events or show the response of characters to situations. **Also Writing 4., 10.**

Writing

Poetry: Free Verse

Writing Trait: Organization

INTRODUCE THE PROMPT Review the key features of free verse poetry with students. Remind them to keep these features in mind as they plan their writing. Then explain that today they will begin the writing process for a free verse poem. Read aloud the writing prompt.

Writing Prompt

Think about a time when you were new to something or someplace. Write a free verse poem about the experience.

SELECT A TOPIC

Think Aloud Display a T-chart on the board. To help choose a topic, let's think about this week's readings. The main character, Jangmi, moves from Korea to the United States. This is a new experience, so I'll write it in the chart. The narrator in "music class" experienced the first day of music class. I'll write this in the chart as well.

GATHER INFORMATION Now let's think about new things that we've experienced in our own lives. Ask students to name important events from their own lives, and fill in the chart as they give examples.

Experiences in the lives of characters	Experiences in our own lives
Jangmi moves to a new country	Moving to a new house
A student goes to music class for the first time	Trying out for a sports team
	Learning a new skill
	Meeting a new friend

Corrective feedback Circulate around the room as students choose an experience to write about. Have brief discussions with students who are having problems making a choice. Guide them by asking questions, such as *What is something you did or tried for the first time?*

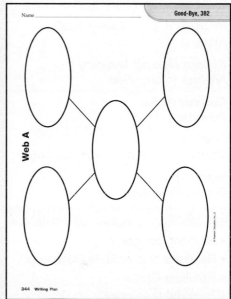

eSTREET INTERACTIVE
www.ReadingStreet.com

Teacher Resources
• Reader's and Writer's Notebook
• Graphic Organizer

Mini-Lesson | Writing Trait: Organization

You can prepare to write your free verse poem by creating an organizational web. I have decided to write about a young girl's experience of moving to a new house. Write the words *moving to a new house* in the middle of the web.

Think about how you felt before, during, and after your experience. Write these emotions in the surrounding circles. The narrator of my poem is excited about moving because she thinks it is an adventure. Write *feels excited* in an outlying circle of the web.

Did another person share in your experience? If so, write his or her name in another circle. My narrator shares her experience of moving with her dog, Ritz. Write *Ritz* in another circle. Have students begin their own organizational web using the form on p. 344 of their *Reader's and Writer's Notebook*. Explain that they will fill in their web with information about the new experience they have chosen to write about.

Routine | Quick Write for Fluency | Team Talk

. **Talk** Have pairs discuss how the web helped them plan their writing.

. **Write** Each student writes a sentence about how the web helped him or her.

. **Share** Partners exchange sentences.

outines Flip Chart

Reader's and Writer's Notebook, p. 344

Wrap Up Your Day!

✔ **Content Knowledge** What did you learn about Jangmi's life in Korea?

✔ **Text-Based Comprehension** How were you able to use the sequence of events to understand the story?

Preview DAY 3

Tell students that tomorrow they will read more about how Jangmi adjusts to life in the United States.

Ⓒ Common Core State Standards

Speaking/Listening 1. Engage effectively in a range of collaborative discussions (one-on-one, in groups, and teacher-led) with diverse partners on grade 3 topics and texts, building on others' ideas and expressing their own clearly. **Language 6.** Acquire and use accurately grade-appropriate conversational, general academic, and domain-specific words and phrases, including those that signal spatial and temporal relationships (e.g., *After dinner that night we went looking for them*). **Also Language 5.b.**

Content Knowledge

Adapting to a New Culture

EXPAND THE CONCEPT Remind students of the weekly concept question, *Why is it hard to adapt to a new culture?* Discuss how the question relates to moving to a new country. Encourage students to think about what makes it hard for Jangmi to feel comfortable in her new home.

Build Oral Language

TALK ABOUT SENTENCES AND WORDS Reread sentences from Student Edition p. 264, *Good-Bye, 382 Shin Dang Dong.*

I was eight years old, old enough to keep many lovely memories of my birthplace alive in my heart forever. But one very sad memory stays with me too. The day I cried, "Good-bye, 382 Shin Dang Dong!"

- What are *memories?* (things a person remembers)
- What context clues help you understand the meaning of *memories?* (the words *lovely, alive in my heart forever, one very sad, stays with me too*)
- What does Jangmi mean when she says that she will keep many lovely memories of her birthplace "alive in my heart forever"? (She means she will never forget what she remembers of her birthplace.)

Team Talk Have students work with a partner to replace words in the sentence with synonyms. Use the following sentence frames.

I was eight years old, old enough to keep many lovely _____ of my _____ alive in my heart forever. But one very sad _____ stays with me too. The day I cried, "Good-bye, 382 Shin Dang Dong!

Build Oral Vocabulary

Amazing Words
Robust Vocabulary Routine

- **Introduce** Write the word *impolite* on the board. Have students say it with you. Yesterday we learned that when Korean people enter someone's home, they remove their shoes so they do not track dirt inside. It would be considered *impolite* behavior to keep your shoes on. Have students determine a definition of *impolite*. (Acting *impolite* is behaving in a rude way.)

- **Demonstrate** Have students answer questions to demonstrate understanding. What behavior would be considered *impolite* at the dinner table? (Possible response: eating before everyone is seated; eating with your mouth open)

- **Apply** Have students apply their understanding. When have you shown *impolite* behavior? How did the people around you react?

- **Display the Word** Point out the base word *polite* in *impolite.* Identify the prefix *im-*. Students can decode the word.

See p. OV•3 to teach *manner*.

Routines Flip Chart

ADD TO THE CONCEPT MAP Discuss the Amazing Words *sponsor* and *habit*. Add these words to the concept map. Use the following questions to develop students' understanding of the concept. Add words generated in the discussion to the concept map.

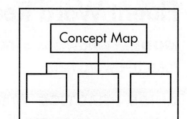

If a family does not have a *sponsor* in their new country, why might they have a hard time adapting to their new home?

Think about your own *habits* and what you are used to doing. What is one *habit* you would have to change if you moved to a new place? How would this make you feel?

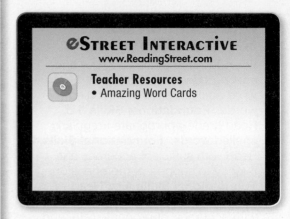

eStreet Interactive
www.ReadingStreet.com
Teacher Resources
• Amazing Word Cards

Amazing Words

native	habit
homeland	impolite
aspect	manner
advantage	conscious
sponsor	insult

Expand Vocabulary Use the Day 3 instruction on ELL Poster 23 to help students expand vocabulary.

© **Common Core State Standards**

Foundational Skills 3. Know and apply grade-level phonics and word analysis skills in decoding words. **Foundational Skills 3.d.** Read grade-appropriate irregularly spelled words. **Foundational Skills 4.** Read with sufficient accuracy and fluency to support comprehension. **Foundational Skills 4.b.** Read on-level prose and poetry orally with accuracy, appropriate rate, and expression on successive readings. **Also Foundational Skills 4.a.**

Phonics

🔊 Vowel Patterns for /ȯ/

MODEL WORD SORTING Write *a, au, aw, al, augh,* and *ough* as heads in a six-column chart. Now we are going to sort words. We'll put words with the /ȯ/ spelling pattern *a* in the first column. Words with the /ȯ/ spelling pattern *au* will go in the second column. Words with the /ȯ/ spelling pattern *aw* will go in the third column. Continue until all the columns have been identified. I will start. Write *pause* and model how to read it. I hear the vowel sound /ȯ/ in *pause*. The letters *au* spell the /ȯ/ sound, so I will write *pause* in the second column. Model reading *awe* and *recall* in the same way.

GUIDE PRACTICE Use the practice words from the activity on p. 256a for the word sort. Point to a word. Have students read the word, identify the spelling pattern of /ȯ/, and tell where it should be written on the chart.

> **Corrective feedback** | For corrective feedback, model blending the word to read it.

a	au	aw	al	augh	ough
stalk	pause	awe	recall	caught	thought
	fault	raw	scald	daughter	
	haunt	awkward			

Fluent Word Reading

MODEL Write *haul*. I know the sounds for *h, au,* and *l*. I can blend them and read the word *haul*.

GUIDE PRACTICE Write the words below. Say the sounds in your head for each spelling you see. When I point to the word, we'll read it together. Allow one second per sound previewing time for the first reading.

| sausage | taught | straw | bought | applause | almost |

ON THEIR OWN Have students read the list above three or four times, until they can read one word per second.

Decodable Passage 23B

If students need help, then...

Read *Paul Shops for Mom*

READ WORDS IN ISOLATION Have students turn to p. 93 in *Decodable Practice Readers 3.2* and find the first list of words. Each word in this list includes the vowel sound /ȯ/ spelled *a, au, aw, al, augh,* or *ough.* Let's blend and read these words. Be sure that students correctly pronounce the vowel sound in each word.

Next, have students read the high-frequency words.

PREVIEW Have students read the title and preview the story. Tell them that they will read words that include the /ȯ/ spelling patterns *a, au, aw, al, augh,* and *ough.*

READ WORDS IN CONTEXT Chorally read the story along with students. Have students identify words in the story that include /ȯ/ spelled *a, au, aw, al, ugh,* and *ough.* Make sure that students are monitoring their accuracy when they decode words.

Team Talk Pair students and have them take turns reading the story aloud to each other. Monitor students as they read to check for proper pronunciation and appropriate pacing.

Access for All

SI Strategic Intervention

Write words with two or three different spellings of the vowel sound /ȯ/ on cards. Have students practice sorting the words by vowel pattern. Use words such as *jaw, cough, jaunt, autumn, thought,* and *shawl.*

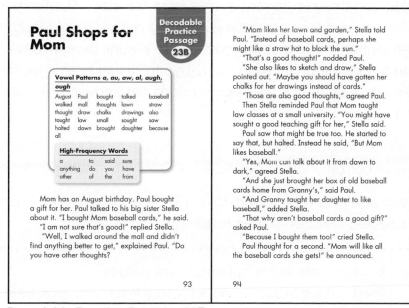

Decodable Practice Passage 23B

© **Common Core State Standards**

Literature 1. Ask and answer questions to demonstrate understanding of a text, referring explicitly to the text as the basis for the answers. **Literature 2.** Recount stories, including fables, folktales, and myths from diverse cultures; determine the central message, lesson, or moral and explain how it is conveyed through key details in the text. **Literature 3.** Describe characters in a story (e.g., their traits, motivations, or feelings) and explain how their actions contribute to the sequence of events.

Strategy Response Log

Have students revisit the text and identify places they had difficulty with comprehension. Have them use p. 29 in the *Reader's and Writer's Notebook* to identify a fix-up strategy to use to clarify their understanding.

Text-Based Comprehension
Check Understanding

Student Edition, pp. 262–263

If... you chose to read *Good-Bye, 382 Shin Dang Dong* in two parts,

then... use the following questions to monitor students' understanding of pp. 262–271 of the selection. Encourage students to cite evidence from the text

EVALUATION List three important events from the story. Put them in sequence. Choose one event and explain why it is important. (Jangmi's family has a farewell dinner; Jangmi says good-bye to Kisuni; Jangmi says good-bye to her Korean home. Jangmi saying good-bye to Kisuni is an important event because they are best friends and Jangmi does not know if she will ever see Kisuni again.)

ANALYSIS Why is Jangmi's room empty when the story begins? (She has packed up all of her belongings because her family is moving to America.)

RETELL Have students retell *Good-Bye, 382 Shin Dang Dong.* Encourage students to use text features in their retellings.

Corrective feedback | **If...** students leave out important details, **then...** have students do a Picture Walk and look back through the illustrations in the selection.

READ Use the **Access Text** and **Close Reading** notes to finish reading *Good-Bye, 382 Shin Dang Dong.*

f... you followed the Read for Understanding routine below,

hen... ask students to retell the selection before you reread *Good-Bye, 82 Shin Dang Dong.*

RETELL Have students retell *Good-Bye, 382 Shin Dang Dong,* referring o details in the text. Encourage students to use the text features in their etellings.

Corrective feedback	**If...** students leave out important details, **then...** have students do a Picture Walk and look back through the illustrations in the selection.

READ Return to p. 264–265 and use the **2nd Read/Close Reading** notes to eread *Good-Bye, 382 Shin Dang Dong.*

Read Main Selection

Routine   **Read for Understanding** ©

Deepen understanding by reading the selection multiple times.

. **First Read**—If students need support, then use the **Access Text** notes to help them clarify understanding.

. **Second Read**—Use the **Close Reading** notes to help students draw knowledge from the text.

ELL

Check Retelling To support retelling, review the multilingual summary for *Good-Bye, 382 Shin Dang Dong* with the appropriate Retelling Cards to scaffold understanding.

Day 3	**SMALL GROUP TIME • Differentiate Close Reading, p. SG•33**

OL On-Level	**SI** Strategic Intervention	**A** Advanced
• **Reread** to Develop Vocabulary	• **Reread** to Develop Vocabulary	• **Reread** to Extend Vocabulary
• **Read** *Good-Bye, 382 Shin Dang Dong*	• **Read** *Good-Bye, 382 Shin Dang Dong*	• **Read** *Good-Bye, 382 Shin Dang Dong*
		• **Investigate** Inquiry Project

ELL

If... students need more scaffolding and practice with the **Main Selection,** then... use the activities on p. DI•72 in the Teacher Resources section on SuccessNet.

Access Text © If students need help, then...

COMPOUND WORDS Remind students that compound words are made up of two smaller words. Ask students to identify the two smaller words in *newspaper* and how knowing those two words helps them tell the meaning of *newspaper*.

Think Aloud MODEL I see the word *newspaper*. I know this word is made up of the words *news* and *paper*. This means it is a compound word. I can use these words to help me figure out the meaning of *newspaper*. I think *newspaper* describes paper that has news printed on it.

Close Reading ©

ANALYSIS Find the compound word in paragraph 1 on p. 272. Use the smaller words and context clues to figure out its meaning. (The compound word is *homesick*. Feeling *homesick* means feeling sick or sad because you are away from home.)

On the airplane, I sat by the window. We flew over rice fields and clay-tiled roofs. Already I felt homesick.

The next thing I knew, we were flying over the ocean. At first I could see fishing boats rocking in the waters. As we climbed higher into the clouds, the boats grew smaller and smaller. Suddenly, the world looked very big to me.

"Good-bye, 382 Shin Dang Dong," I cried again.

Dad sat back in his seat and began to read an American newspaper. The words were all foreign.

"Dad," I asked, "how will I ever learn to understand English?"

"It's not so hard," he said. "Would you like to learn an English word?"

"Okay," I sighed.

After a pause, Dad came up with—

"Rose."

"Rose?" I repeated. "What does that mean?"

"That's the English translation of your Korean name," Mom said.

"Rose means Jangmi?" I asked.

"Yes," my parents nodded.

"Rose," I said over and over.

"Would you like to adopt Rose as your American name?" Mom asked me.

"No, I like *my* name," I insisted.

272

Student Edition, p. 272

INFERENCE • TEXT EVIDENCE Why do you think Jangmi does not want to change her name to Rose? Use evidence from the story to support your reasoning. (I don't think she is ready to change anything else in her life. When asked if she wanted to change it she says, "No, I like *my* name.")

ON THEIR OWN Have students scan the first half of the story and find other compound words (p. 264: *bedroom*; p. 266: *outside, bedroom*; p. 270–271: *airport, fireplace, underground*). For additional practice use *Reader's and Writer's Notebook,* p. 345.

Student Edition, p. 273

ANALYSIS How can you tell Jangmi is concerned about adapting to a new culture? (She asks her father how she will learn English. She practices saying her English name over and over.)

Common Core State Standards

Literature 1. Ask and answer questions to demonstrate understanding of a text, referring explicitly to the text as the basis for the answers. **Literature 3.** Describe characters in a story (e.g., their traits, motivations, or feelings) and explain how their actions contribute to the sequence of events. **Language 4.** Determine or clarify the meaning of unknown and multiple-meaning words and phrases based on grade 3 reading and content, choosing flexibly from a range of strategies. **Also Writing 10., Language 4.a.**

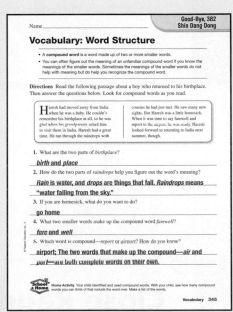

Reader's and Writer's Notebook, p. 345

Vocabulary: Compound Words
Have students work in pairs to find a compound word from the first half of the story. Have students use context clues to read the sentence for understanding of meaning and then restate its meaning to the class. Prompt discussion with questions such as these: Where does Jangmi keep her special things? Where does Jangmi like to sit with her friend? Why are Jangmi and her family riding in a taxi?

Good-Bye, 382 Shin Dang Dong **273a**

Access Text  If students need help, then...

MONITOR AND CLARIFY Have students reread the second paragraph on p. 275. Have them explain what the last sentence means to Jangmi. (Everything looks unfamiliar and strange to her. The people she sees don't look like Koreans.)

Think Aloud **MODEL** To find the meaning of the sentence, I think about the things Jangmi describes. I notice that she is contrasting things in America with things in Korea. The roads, homes, stores, people's faces, even the weather are all very different. Nothing looks the way it did at home.

Close Reading ©

ANALYSIS • TEXT EVIDENCE How do Jangmi's parents try to make her feel comfortable in their new home? Use details from the text to support your answer. (Her father says the tree outside is "just like the one at home." Jangmi's mother says "the movers are here!")

274

Student Edition, p. 274

EVALUATION Why do you think the authors include references to the address of Jangmi's new and old home? (Her new address stands for her new life in America. Her old address reminds her of Korea.)

IN THEIR OWN Have students read on to find other examples of things that are foreign or strange to Jangmi.

 Common Core State Standards

Literature 1. Ask and answer questions to demonstrate understanding of a text, referring explicitly to the text as the basis for the answers. **Also Literature 3., 10.**

Access for All

 Strategic Intervention

Identify descriptive details about Jangmi's new home in the text and have students find matching details in the illustration on p. 274.

On a foggy morning four days later, we arrived in Massachusetts. After we gathered our luggage, we climbed into an airport taxi.

Even through the fog, I could see that things were very different in America. There were big, wide roads called *highways*. The rooftops were shingled instead of clay-tiled. People shopped in glass-enclosed stores instead of open markets. No rice fields, no monsoon rains. So many foreign faces.

Slowly, the taxi pulled up to a row house on a quiet street. Red brick steps led up to a wooden door.

"Here we are, Jangmi," Dad said, "112 Foster Terrace, Brighton, Massachusetts, U.S.A."

The house was just as my parents had described. I took off my shoes and walked on wooden floors. They felt very cold. I opened wooden doors. They felt very heavy. Outside, the fog had lifted. But inside, everything felt dark and strange.

"Look," Dad pointed out the window, "there's a tree just like the one at home."

"No, it's not, Dad. It's not a willow tree," I said.

"No," he agreed. "It's a maple tree. But isn't it beautiful?"

382 Shin Dang Dong, 382 Shin Dang Dong. I wanted to go home to 382 Shin Dang Dong right now. Only a knock at the door saved me from tears.

Mom announced, "The movers are here!"

275

Student Edition, p. 275

ANALYSIS Help students generate text-based questions by providing the following question stem: In the selection, how did Jangmi respond when _____?

Figurative Language Point out the third paragraph on p. 275 and explain to students that "pulled up" means "to arrive or stop at a location." Ask students, Would you pull up to a desk? Would you pull up to the school?

Access Text © If students need help, then...

◉ **MONITOR AND CLARIFY** Have students reread p. 276. Ask them if Jangmi likes the new girl.

Think Aloud **MODEL** If I can't find the answer on the page I'm reading, I can read ahead. When I read ahead, I can find out new information to help me clarify important details in the story. I can see that Jangmi says that she made a new friend and is excited about spending time with her.

Close Reading ©

ANALYSIS • TEXT EVIDENCE What can you tell about the new girl's personality? Cite details from the story. (The new girl seems friendly and eager to help Jangmi. On p. 276, she shares a bowl of fruit with Jangmi and tells her the English names of the fruit. The girl also tries to learn more about Jangmi by asking her what fruit she ate in Korea.)

The house quickly filled up with furniture and big brown boxes. The box marked "Lovely Things" was the last to arrive.

I unpacked all my possessions. I hung my hand-painted scrolls and colorful fans on the walls. I placed my silk cushions and straw mats on the floor.

Then came another knock. To our surprise a parade of neighbors waltzed in carrying plates of curious food. There were pink-and-white iced cakes and warm pans containing something called *casseroles*.

A girl my age wandered up to me with a small glass bowl. Inside the bowl were colorful balls. They smelled fruity.

She pointed to a red ball and said, "Watermelon!" She pointed to an orange ball and said, "Cantaloupe!" Lastly she pointed to a green ball and said, "Honeydew!"

I took a green ball and tasted it. Mmm . . . it was as sweet and delicious as chummy.

The girl asked me a question. But I couldn't understand her.

"She wants to know what kind of fruit you eat in Korea," Dad stepped in.

"Chummy," I replied.

"Chummy," the girl repeated, then giggled—just like Kisuni!

276

N THEIR OWN Have students share a question they have about the
·ory and then reread or read ahead to look for information that helps
em answer their question.

277

Student Edition, p. 277

NALYSIS Compare and contrast Jangmi's first meal in America with the
·rewell meal she had in Korea. (Korea: family ate traditional foods and
·elebrated the family's move; America: neighbors brought American food
· welcome them. The foods and fruits all seemed strange to Jangmi.)

 **Common Core
State Standards**

Literature 1. Ask and answer
questions to demonstrate
understanding of a text, referring
explicitly to the text as the basis for
the answers. **Literature 3.** Describe
characters in a story (e.g., their
traits, motivations, or feelings) and
explain how their actions contribute
to the sequence of events. **Also
Literature 10.**

 **Connect to
Social Studies**

American Potlucks A potluck is
a gathering where neighbors bring
a variety of prepared foods to one
family's home or to a community
gathering place for a large meal. In
America, people sometimes welcome
new neighbors with a potluck.

Cognates Point out the Spanish
cognates from this week's selection
vocabulary: *curious/curioso* and
delicious/delicioso.

Good-Bye, 382 Shin Dang Dong **277a**

Access Text © If students need help, then...

Review DRAW CONCLUSIONS Ask students how they think Jangmi feels after her first day in America.

(Think Aloud) MODEL The text says that Jangmi smiles and says she made a new friend. This tells me she is happy to meet someone. But she still thinks of her friend back in Korea. She is trying to adapt to the new place, but it will take time.

ON THEIR OWN Have students use information in the story to draw a conclusion about the likelihood of a friendship between Jangmi and Mary.

Close Reading ©

INFERENCE • TEXT EVIDENCE Why do you think Jangmi sits under the maple tree? Use details to support your reasoning. (The tree reminds her of the one outside her home in Korea. On p. 278 she says, "maybe I would come to love it as much as our willow tree back home in Korea." Doing something that feels familiar makes her feel more comfortable in her new home.)

CROSS-TEXT EVALUATION

Use a Strategy to Self-Check How did the Read Aloud "Welcome to America!" help you understand this selection?

She asked me another question.

"She wants to know your name," Dad said.

Maybe someday I would adopt Rose as my American name. But not today.

"Jangmi," I replied.

"Jangmi," the girl smiled. "My name is Mary."

"Mary," I smiled back.

I had made a new friend.

Later, when all the guests had gone, I went outside and sat under the maple tree. Dad was right, it *was* beautiful. Maybe someday Mary and I would sit beneath this tree and watch the rain fall. And maybe I would come to love it as much as our willow tree back home in Korea. But not today.

I began to write.

Dear Kisuni. . . .

My best friend was so far away from me. So very, very far. But at least I knew where Kisuni was and what she was doing. She was halfway around the world, sleeping to the sound of a thousand raindrops hitting her clay-tiled roof all at once.

278

Student Edition, p. 278

SYNTHESIS • TEXT EVIDENCE Using what you learned in this selection, tell how hard it can be adapting to a new culture. Have students cite examples from the text to support their responses.

HECK PREDICTIONS Have students return to the predictions they
ade earlier and confirm whether they were accurate.

279

Student Edition, p. 279

VALUATION Why do you think the authors chose to end the story with
ngmi sitting under a tree? (In Korea she sat under a tree and talked to
r best friend. Jangmi hopes she can soon do the same thing in her new
me with her new friend.)

 **Common Core
State Standards**

Literature 1. Ask and answer
questions to demonstrate
understanding of a text, referring
explicitly to the text as the basis for
the answers. **Literature 3.** Describe
characters in a story (e.g., their traits,
motivations, or feelings) and explain
how their actions contribute to the
sequence of events.

Access for All

 Advanced

Have students list all the main events
from the story and then use them to
create a time line.

Draw Conclusions Remind
students that they can use their
own background knowledge and
experiences to help them draw
conclusions about the text. Ask
students to describe how they felt
on their first day in a new school
or a new place. Help them make
connections between their feelings
and Jangmi's feelings.

Good-Bye, 382 Shin Dang Dong **279a**

Common Core State Standards
Literature 1. Ask and answer questions to demonstrate understanding of a text, referring explicitly to the text as the basis for the answers. Also Literature 2., Writing 8.

Envision It! Retell

READING STREET ONLINE
STORY SORT
www.ReadingStreet.com

280

Think Critically

1. Think about moving. Tell how you or someone you know feels about moving. Explain why. Text to Self

2. Why do you think the authors wrote this story? Look at the Meet the Authors on page 281 for ideas. Think Like an Author

3. Make a time line showing the sequence of events during Jangmi's first day in her new home. Sequence

4. Was anything in this story confusing at first? How did you figure out the parts that were unclear? Did reading on, creating sensory images, using background knowledge, or asking questions help you? Monitor and Clarify

5. Look Back and Write Look back at the question on page 263. Think about Jangmi's life at 382 Shin Dang Dong. Now write a paragraph telling why she might have a hard time adapting to a new culture. Provide evidence to support your answer.

Key Ideas and Details • Text Evidence

Meet the Authors

Frances and Ginger Park

Frances and Ginger Park are sisters. They often work as a team to create a book.

Ginger Park, the younger sister, loves to tell stories. Frances Park is more of a poet. She says, "I've always been in love with the beauty of language. For me, it's music—my way of playing an instrument." Together, they have written books for both children and adults.

Although their parents came from Korea, Frances and Ginger Park were born near Washington, D.C. The sisters own a chocolate shop in Washington, D.C., called Chocolate Chocolate. People often stop by to talk about their books. "We pack up their truffles, and then talk books," says Frances.

Read two more books by Frances Park and Ginger Park.

My Freedom Trip

Where on Earth Is My Bagel?

Use the *Reader's and Writer's Notebook* to record your independent reading.

281

Student Edition, pp. 280–281

Common Core State Standards

Literature 1. Ask and answer questions to demonstrate understanding of a text, referring explicitly to the text as the basis for the answers. **Also Literature 2., 3., 10., Speaking/Listening 4.**

Bridge to Common Core

RANGE OF READING AND LEVEL OF TEXT COMPLEXITY

To increase students' capacity for reading and comprehending complex texts independently and proficiently, have them read other literary texts by Frances and Ginger Park or about the social studies topic, Adapting to a New Culture. After students read closely for a sustained period of time, they should record their reading in their Reading Logs.

Think Critically

1. TEXT TO SELF I moved from a small town in Mexico to Dallas. It was scary to move to a place that was so crowded.

2. THINK LIKE AN AUTHOR I think they wrote this to show that even though it is difficult to move to a new place, it can also be exciting.

3. SEQUENCE First, Jangmi walks through her new home. Then, neighbors bring food. Next, Jangmi meets Mary. Finally, Jangmi sits under the tree and writes to Kisuni.

4. MONITOR AND CLARIFY I didn't understand some of the Korean words. I reread to look for clues and read on to find more information.

5. LOOK BACK AND WRITE • TEXT EVIDENCE To build writing fluency, assign a 10–15 minute time limit.

eSTREET INTERACTIVE
www.ReadingStreet.com

Pearson eText
• Student Edition

Story Sort

Scoring Rubric   Look Back and Write

TOP-SCORE RESPONSE A top-score response uses details to support the writer's conclusions about adapting to new culture.

A top-score response should include:
• Jangmi has many good memories of her old home.
• She will be away from old friends.
• Things in America look different, and Jangmi doesn't understand the language.

Retell

Have students work in pairs to retell the selection, using the retelling strip in the Student Edition or the Story Sort as prompts. Monitor students' retellings.

Scoring Rubric   Narrative Retelling

	4	3	2	1
Connections	Makes connections and generalizes beyond the text	Makes connections to other events, stories, or experiences	Makes a limited connection to another event, story, or experience	Makes no connection to another event, story, or experience
Author's Purpose	Elaborates on author's purpose	Tells author's purpose with some clarity	Makes some connection to author's purpose	Makes no connection to author's purpose
Characters	Describes the main character(s) and any character development	Identifies the main character(s) and gives some information about them	Inaccurately identifies some characters or gives little information about them	Inaccurately identifies the characters or gives no information about them
Setting	Describes the time and location	Identifies the time and location	Omits details of time or location	Is unable to identify time or location
Plot	Describes the problem, goal, events, and ending using rich detail	Tells the problem, goal, events, and ending with some errors that do not affect meaning	Tells parts of the problem, goal, events, and ending with gaps that affect meaning	Retelling has no sense of story

MONITOR PROGRESS   Check Retelling

If... students have difficulty retelling,

then... use the Retelling Cards/Story Sort to scaffold their retellings.

Plan to Assess Retelling

☐ **Week 1** Strategic Intervention
☐ **Week 2** Advanced
☑ **This week assess Advanced students.**
☐ **Week 4** On-Level
☐ **Week 5** Assess any students you have not yet checked during this unit.

Meet the Authors

Have students read about Frances and Ginger Park on p. 281. Ask them how the authors made Jangmi and her family seem like real people in *Good-Bye, 382 Shin Dang Dong*.

Read Independently

Have students enter their independent reading information into their Reading Logs.

Ⓒ Common Core State Standards

Informational Text 7. Use information gained from illustrations (e.g., maps, photographs) and the words in a text to demonstrate understanding of the text (e.g., where, when, why, and how key events occur). **Foundational Skills 4.** Read with sufficient accuracy and fluency to support comprehension. **Foundational Skills 4.b.** Read on-level prose and poetry orally with accuracy, appropriate rate, and expression on successive readings.

Fluency

Expression and Punctuation Cues

MODEL FLUENT READING Have students turn to p. 271 of *Good-Bye, 382 Shin Dang Dong*. Have students follow along as you read the page. Tell them to listen to the changes in the expression of your voice as you show the excitement of Jangmi's parents and Jangmi's sadness. Explain that you will use punctuation cues to decide how to read.

GUIDE PRACTICE Have students follow along as you read the page again. Then have them reread the page as a group without you until they read with the right expression and with no mistakes in punctuation cues. Ask questions to be sure students comprehend the text. Continue in the same way on p. 272.

Corrective feedback	**If...** students are having difficulty reading with the right expression, **then...** prompt them as follows: • Which word is the problem? Let's read it together. • Read the sentence again to be sure you understand it. • Tell me the sentence. Now read it as if you are speaking to me.

Reread for Fluency

Routine **Paired Reading**

1. **Select a Passage** Use p. 269 of *Good-Bye, 382 Shin Dang Dong*.

2. **Reading 1** Students read p. 269, switching readers before the first full paragraph.

3. **Reading 2** Partners reread the page. This time the other student begins.

4. **Reread** For optimal fluency, have partners continue to read three or four times.

5. **Corrective Feedback** Listen as students read. Provide corrective feedback regarding their oral reading, paying special attention to their expression.

Routines Flip Chart

Research and Study Skills

Atlas

TEACH Ask students what kind of resource they would use to find a map of a specific country. If available, display various atlases. Remind students that an atlas is a book of maps. Atlases contain information on specific regions such as road maps of cities, landmarks, and features. There are many types of atlases. Explain that students can use text features on a map to locate information. Show a map and use it to review these features:

Every map includes a legend. The legend features a compass rose that shows directions. Most maps show north at the top. The legend also includes a scale. A scale shows distance on the map.

A map includes various symbols, colors, and shapes to help you differentiate between various things. Dots and stars are often used to indicate cities. Blue is used to indicate bodies of water, such as oceans, lakes, and rivers.

The size and styles of print used for names is important. Usually, the larger type size is used for bigger cities.

GUIDE PRACTICE Discuss these questions:

Which part of a map tells you what the symbols stand for? (the legend)

What can you use to determine the distance between two places on a map? (the scale)

Which symbol indicates a city? (a black dot or star)

Have students locate specific places on the map, such as cities and rivers.

ON THEIR OWN Have students review and complete p. 346 of the *Reader's and Writer's Notebook.*

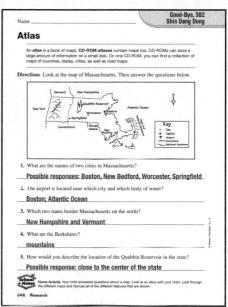

Reader's and Writer's Notebook, p. 346

Academic Vocabulary

atlas a book of maps

ELL

Atlas Show students a map that includes your city or state. Have them identify places they know. Ask them to describe maps they have seen or used. Have them tell why maps are useful.

Good-Bye, 382 Shin Dang Dong **281c**

Common Core State Standards

Writing 5. With guidance and support from peers and adults, develop and strengthen writing as needed by planning, revising, and editing. **Language 1.a.** Explain the function of nouns, pronouns, verbs, adjectives, and adverbs in general and their functions in particular sentences. **Language 2.f.** Use spelling patterns and generalizations (e.g., word families, position-based spellings, syllable patterns, ending rules, meaningful word parts) in writing words. **Also Informational Text 5., Writing 7.**

Research and Inquiry

Step 3 Analyze Information

TEACH Tell students that today they will analyze their findings and may need to change the focus of their original inquiry question.

Think Aloud **MODEL** Originally, I thought I would focus on what immigrants lost o their native culture when they moved to America. Part of my research was to ask my neighbor, who is from Korea, about her experiences. She told me that many Koreans keep a strong sense of Korean culture even when they live in America. I will refocus my question on what challenges Korean immigrants must overcome in America.

GUIDE PRACTICE Have students analyze their findings. They may need to refocus their inquiry question to better fit the information they found. Remind students that if they have difficulty improving their focus they can ask a reference librarian or a local expert for guidance. Remind students that they can use an atlas to locate countries and cities that come up in their research.

ON THEIR OWN Have students survey one another about what they think is the most difficult part of moving to a new country. Students should then com pare their research results to the survey they conducted in class.

Conventions

Adverbs

REVIEW Remind students that this week they learned about adverbs. Adverbs tell when, where, and how something happens.

Adverbs such as *first, then, finally,* and *last* tell when something happens and are also called time-order transition words.

Adverbs such as *beautifully* and *carefully* describe the manner in which something is done.

CONNECT TO ORAL LANGUAGE Have the class complete these sentences orally, using different adverbs before and after the verb.

I _____ clean my room.
I clean my room _____.
_____, I made my bed.
I made my bed _____.

ON THEIR OWN For additional support, use *Let's Practice It!* p. 314 on the *Teacher Resources DVD-ROM.*

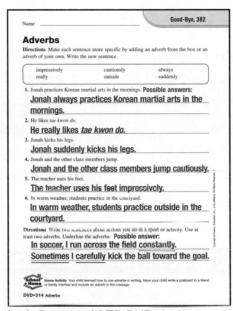

Name _____   Good-Bye, 382

Adverbs

Directions Make each sentence more specific by adding an adverb from the box or an adverb of your own. Write the new sentence.

impressively	cautiously	always
really	outside	suddenly

1. Jonah practices Korean martial arts in the mornings. **Possible answers:**
   Jonah always practices Korean martial arts in the mornings.
2. He likes *tae kwon do.*
   He really likes *tae kwon do.*
3. Jonah kicks his legs.
   Jonah suddenly kicks his legs.
4. Jonah and the other class members jump.
   Jonah and the other class members jump cautiously.
5. The teacher uses his feet.
   The teacher uses his feet impressively.
6. In warm weather, students practice in the courtyard.
   In warm weather, students practice outside in the courtyard.

Directions Write two sentences about actions you do in a sport or activity. Use at least two adverbs. Underline the adverbs. **Possible answer:**
In soccer, I run across the field constantly.
Sometimes I carefully kick the ball toward the goal.

Home Activity Your child learned how to use adverbs in writing. Have your child write a postcard to a friend or family member and include an adverb in the message.

DVD•314 Adverbs

Let's Practice It! TR DVD•314

Spelling

Vowel Patterns *au, augh, ou, ough*

FREQUENTLY MISSPELLED WORDS The words *because, caught,* and *ought* are words that students frequently misspell. These words are difficult because uncommon spellings are used for the vowel sounds. Have students choose the correct word to complete the sentence and then write it correctly.

1. The teacher _____ them whispering in the hall. (caught)
2. Mia stood on tiptoe _____ she couldn't reach it. (because)
3. Nick _____ about going to the park. (thought)

ON THEIR OWN For additional practice, use *Reader's and Writer's Notebook,* p. 347.

Access for All

SI Strategic Intervention
Extend students' understanding of various adverbs by asking questions such as "When would you _____? How would you _____? Where would you _____?" Have students brainstorm various responses to the question stems.

Daily Fix-It

5. Jangmi and she has almoast finished unpacking the pretty things for her room. *(have; almost)*
6. She has did it very cheerful. *(She did or has done; cheerfully)*

Name _____   Good-Bye, 382

Vowel Patterns *au, augh, ou, ough*

Spelling Words

because	though	taught	bought	touch
would	author	enough	sausage	brought
fought	should	faucet	daughter	though

Proofread a List Ella wrote about her day in class. Circle the four spelling mistakes. Write the words correctly. Write the word Ella should have used in the last sentence instead of better.

Class was very interesting becauze we had a guest speaker. She was an author. She brougt her book with her. The book was about goals. She said we shoold always have goals. She tawt us to aim high and be the better we can be.

1. because
2. brought
3. should
4. taught
5. best

Frequently Misspelled Words
because
caught
thought

Proofread Words Fill in a circle to show which word is spelled correctly. Write the word.

6. ○ fout   ○ fawt   ● fought   fought
7. ● faucet   ○ fawcet   ○ foucet   faucet
8. ○ tuch   ● touch   ○ toucgh   touch
9. ○ enuff   ○ enouh   ● enough   enough
10. ○ woud   ● would   ○ woughd   would
11. ● could   ○ cood   ○ coud   could
12. ○ thogh   ○ thow   ● though   though

Home Activity Your child wrote words with au, augh, ou, and ough that make different vowel sounds. Ask your child to circle the four hardest words for him or her to spell and then write them.

Spelling Vowel Patterns au, augh, ou, ough 347

Reader's and Writer's Notebook, p. 347

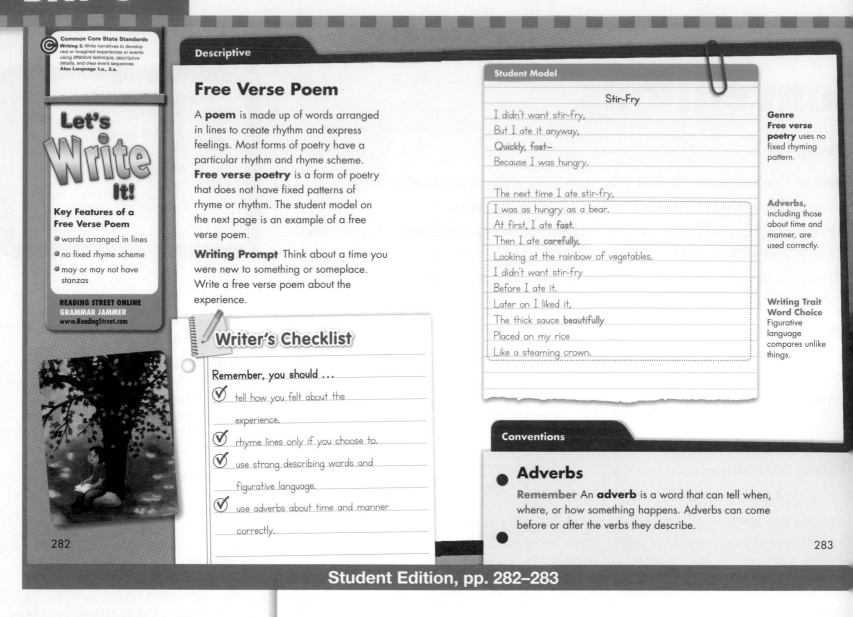

Common Core State Standards
Writing 3. Write narratives to develop real or imagined experiences or events using effective technique, descriptive details, and clear event sequences. Also Language 1.a., 3.a.

Let's Write It!

Key Features of a Free Verse Poem

- words arranged in lines
- no fixed rhyme scheme
- may or may not have stanzas

**READING STREET ONLINE
GRAMMAR JAMMER
www.ReadingStreet.com**

Descriptive

Free Verse Poem

A **poem** is made up of words arranged in lines to create rhythm and express feelings. Most forms of poetry have a particular rhythm and rhyme scheme. **Free verse poetry** is a form of poetry that does not have fixed patterns of rhyme or rhythm. The student model on the next page is an example of a free verse poem.

Writing Prompt Think about a time you were new to something or someplace. Write a free verse poem about the experience.

Writer's Checklist

Remember, you should ...

- ☑ tell how you felt about the experience.
- ☑ rhyme lines only if you choose to.
- ☑ use strong describing words and figurative language.
- ☑ use adverbs about time and manner correctly.

Student Model

Stir-Fry

I didn't want stir-fry,
But I ate it anyway,
Quickly, fast—
Because I was hungry.

The next time I ate stir-fry,
I was as hungry as a bear.
At first, I ate fast.
Then I ate carefully,
Looking at the rainbow of vegetables.
I didn't want stir-fry
Before I ate it.
Later on I liked it,
The thick sauce beautifully
Placed on my rice
Like a steaming crown.

Genre
Free verse poetry uses no fixed rhyming pattern.

Adverbs, including those about time and manner, are used correctly.

**Writing Trait
Word Choice** Figurative language compares unlike things.

Conventions

● **Adverbs**

Remember An **adverb** is a word that can tell when, where, or how something happens. Adverbs can come before or after the verbs they describe.

282

283

Student Edition, pp. 282–283

Common Core State Standards

Writing 3. Write narratives to develop real or imagined experiences or events using effective technique, descriptive details, and clear event sequences. **Writing 4.** With guidance and support from adults, produce writing in which the development and organization are appropriate to task and purpose. **Language 3.a.** Choose words and phrases for effect. **Also Writing 5., Language 1.a., 3.**

Let's Write It! ©

WRITE A FREE VERSE POEM Use pp. 282–283 in the Student Edition. Direct students to read the key features of a free verse poem that appear on p. 282. Remind students that they can refer to the information in the Writer's Checklist as they write their own free verse poem.

Read the student model on p. 283. Point out the words arranged in lines, the line breaks, and the stanzas in the model. Make sure that students recognize the lack of a set structure and rhyme scheme.

CONNECT TO CONVENTIONS Remind students that adverbs can tell about time or manner, showing *how, when,* or *where* something happens. Adverbs can come before or after the verb they describe. Point out the correct use of adverbs in the model.

Writing

oetry: Free Verse

Writer's Craft: Figurative Language

ISPLAY RUBRIC Display Scoring Rubric 23 from the *Teacher Resources* VD-ROM and go over the criteria for each trait under each score. Then, sing the model in the Student Edition, choose students to explain why the odel should score a 4 for one of the traits. If a student offers that the model ould score below 4 for a particular trait, the student should offer support r that response. Remind students that this is the rubric that will be used to aluate the free verse poem they write.

Scoring Rubric Poetry: Free Verse

	4	3	2	1
ocus/Ideas	Vivid, well-developed narrative	Good narrative with adequate development	Narrative lacking focus	Narrative with no focus
rganization	Correct use of free verse format (no set structure or rhyme scheme)	Some use of free verse format	Incorrect use of free verse format	No attempt at using free verse format
oice	Clear, distinct, engaging voice	Somewhat clear, distinct, engaging voice	Unclear, indistinct, unengaging voice	No attempt to create a clear, distinct, engaging voice
ord Choice	Strong use of exact nouns, vivid verbs, and figurative language, including similes, metaphors, and sensory details	Some use of exact nouns, vivid verbs, and figurative language, including similes, metaphors, and sensory details	Weak use of exact nouns, vivid verbs, and figurative language, including similes, metaphors, and sensory details	Little or no use of exact nouns, vivid verbs, or figurative language, including similes, metaphors, and sensory details
entences	Clear sentences of various lengths and types	Sentences of a few lengths and types	Sentences of similar length and type	No attempt at sentences of various lengths and types
onventions	Few, if any, errors; strong use of adverbs	Several minor errors; use of adverbs	Many errors; weak use of adverbs	Numerous errors, no use of adverbs

RGANIZATIONAL WEB Have students refer to the organizational web they orked on yesterday. If their webs are not complete, allow extra time for them finish in preparation for writing.

RITE You will be using your organizational web as you write your first draft a free verse poem. When you are drafting, don't worry if your poem does t sound exactly as you want it. You will have a chance to revise your poem morrow.

Access for All

Ⓐ Advanced

Discuss with students the narrator's view of the subject in "Stir-Fry." Students should understand that at first the narrator did not care much for the food but later on grew to appreciate it.

Figurative Language Students may have difficulty grasping the figurative meaning of certain phrases. Point out the phrase *rainbow of vegetables* in the Let's Write It! student model. Explain that this is not a literal vegetable rainbow, but that the narrator is using figurative language to say that the vegetables on the plate are very colorful, like a rainbow.

Writing 3. Write narratives to develop real or imagined experiences or events using effective technique, descriptive details, and clear event sequences. **Writing 3.b.** Use dialogue and descriptions of actions, thoughts, and feelings to develop experiences and events or show the response of characters to situations. **Language 3.a.** Choose words and phrases for effect. **Language 5.** Demonstrate understanding of word relationships and nuances in word meanings. **Language 5.a.** Distinguish the literal and nonliteral meanings of words and phrases in context (e.g., take steps). **Also Writing 10.**

Bridge to Common Core

RANGE OF WRITING

As students progress through the writing project, they routinely write for a range of tasks, purposes, and audiences. In this lesson, they learn the importance of using figurative language in free verse poetry to help readers visualize the experience.

Writing

Poetry: Free Verse

Mini-Lesson | **Writer's Craft: Figurative Language**

■ **Introduce** Explain to students that figurative language refers to words or phrases used to compare unlike things, which help readers form pictures in their minds. Tell students that a common form of figurative language is a *simile.* A simile compares two things using *like* or *as* (e.g., *She dances like a butterfly*). Remind students to use figurative language in their free verse poems to help readers visualize the experience.

Sunshine filled my eyes today—
the day I discovered my new home.

Getting out of the car, my legs shook
with excitement!
Ritz barked and got out after me
and at first we stood breathlessly
but just for a minute
then we ran to the door, impatient
to know what lay on the other side.

The air smelled thickly of new paint
but I didn't mind—
My footsteps echoed loudly
in the empty rooms, but I knew the house was happy
and so it sounded like clapping.

I found my room next
and I careful pushed open the white door—
and I knew it had been waiting for me.
The tall windows filled my room with light
I could see the corners of the room waited impatient
for me to fill them with my favorite things.
I rested easily against the cool wall, and thought for a minute after
exploring more—

thinking that my room suited me beautifully
because it held the sunshine in my eyes.

Unit 5 Good-Bye, 382 Shin Dang Dong   Writing: Model **23A**

Writing Transparency 23A, TR DVD

Drafting Tips

✔ Include carefully chosen words and figurative language arranged in lines.

✔ Include exact nouns and vivid adjectives and verbs.

✔ Make sure to get down the main idea you want to communicate.

Think Aloud **MODEL** Display Writing Transparency 23A and explain the process of drafting using the Writing Transparency. This is the first draft of my poem about a girl who moves to a new house. When I draft, I develop my ideas and try out new words and new ways of saying things. I use vivid words and figurative language that describe how the character feels and what she sees. I won't worry about spelling and grammar right now. I will revise my writing later. My goal in the first draft is to get my ideas on paper.

Direct students to use the Drafting Tips as a guide in writing the first drafts of their poems. Remind students to use figurative language to describe the ideas and events in their poems.

Writing Trait: Word Choice

Review the importance of choosing the best possible words when writing. Good writers use specific nouns, vivid adjectives, and strong verbs. They replace vague, weak words, such as *thing, nice,* and *go,* with precise, vivid words. They want their readers to be able to imagine exactly what is happening. Help students improve their word choices by writing sentences with vague, weak words and having them replace the words with more vivid, precise words.

Routine   Quick Write for Fluency   Team Talk

Talk Have pairs talk about examples of figurative language that they used in their drafts.

Write Have students write one example of figurative language used.

Share Partners should read each others' examples and check that figurative language is used correctly.

Routines Flip Chart

eStreet Interactive
www.ReadingStreet.com

Teacher Resources
• Writing Transparency

Access for All

 Advanced

As students draft their poems, have them create a mental picture of the experience they are writing about. Prompt them to recall the location, season, time of day, how they felt, and how things looked to them. Challenge them to describe the picture in their minds in their poems, using similes.

Wrap Up Your Day!

✔ **Content Knowledge** What did you learn about adapting to a new culture?

✔ **Text-Based Comprehension** How does the sequence of events explain the different emotions Jangmi feels in this selection?

Preview DAY 4

Tell students that tomorrow they will read a poem about people.

Materials

- Student Edition
- Reader's and Writer's Notebook
- Decodable Reader

Common Core State Standards

Speaking/Listening 1. Engage effectively in a range of collaborative discussions (one-on-one, in groups, and teacher-led) with diverse partners on grade 3 topics and texts, building on others' ideas and expressing their own clearly. **Language 6.** Acquire and use accurately grade-appropriate conversational, general academic, and domain-specific words and phrases, including those that signal spatial and temporal relationships (e.g., *After dinner that night we went looking for them*).

Content Knowledge

Adapting to a New Culture

EXPAND THE CONCEPT Remind students of the weekly concept question *Why is it hard to adapt to a new culture?* Have students discuss the difficultie people face when they move to a new place that has a different culture.

Build Oral Language

Team Talk **TALK ABOUT SENTENCES AND WORDS** Ask students to reread the last two sentences in the third paragraph on Student Edition p. 27

To our surprise a parade of neighbors waltzed in carrying plates of curi-ous food. There were pink-and-white iced cakes and warm pans containing something called casseroles.

- What other words could we use in place of *curious*? Have students share synonyms for *curious*. Ask students to also provide antonyms for *curious*.
- How would you describe what it would look like if a person "waltzed into a room"? Have students share descriptions with a partner and then demon-strate for the class.
- Have students reread the sentences and identify words with the vowel pat-tern /ȯ/. *(waltzed, called)* Then have them write a new sentence using each word.

Build Oral Vocabulary

Amazing Words

Robust Vocabulary Routine

eSTREET INTERACTIVE
www.ReadingStreet.com

Teacher Resources
• Amazing Word Cards
• Reader's and Writer's Notebook

1. **Introduce** Write the word *conscious* on the board. Have students say it with you. We read how Jangmi was *conscious* of how different things in America are compared to Korea. She notices things about the buildings and people that show how strange America is to her. This makes her *conscious* of how out of place she feels. Have students determine a definition of *conscious*. (*Conscious* means to be aware or know.)

2. **Demonstrate** Have students answer questions to demonstrate their understanding. What was Jangmi *conscious* of as she walked through her new home? (how different the home is from her home in Korea)

3. **Apply** Have students apply their understanding. What words are synonyms for the word *conscious?* *(aware, know)*

4. **Display the Word** Run your finger under the syllables *con-scious* as you read the word. Clap the syllables with students.

See p. OV•3 to teach *insult*.

Routines Flip Chart

Amazing Words

native	habit
homeland	impolite
aspect	manner
advantage	conscious
sponsor	insult

Strategy Response Log

Have students continue to monitor and clarify their comprehension. If students were successful in comprehending the text, have them write a brief summary of the selection.

ADD TO THE CONCEPT MAP Discuss the Amazing Words *impolite* and *manner*. Add these and other concept-related words to the concept map. Use the following questions to develop students' understanding of the concept.

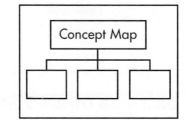

In some cultures it is considered *impolite* to shake hands. Why is it important to learn what behavior is considered *impolite* in a new country?

What does it mean for a person to have a kind *manner?*

ELL

Produce Oral Language Use the Day 4 instruction on ELL Poster 23 to extend and enrich language.

Common Core State Standards

Foundational Skills 3. Know and apply grade-level phonics and word analysis skills in decoding words. **Foundational Skills 3.c.** Decode multisyllable words. **Foundational Skills 4.b.** Read on-level prose and poetry orally with accuracy, appropriate rate, and expression on successive readings. **Also Language 2.e.**

Homophones

Name _____ Good-Bye, 382

Directions Circle the homophone that matches the definition.

1. a number between seven and nine — ate — (eight)
2. belonging to us — hour — (our)
3. two of a kind — (pair) — pear
4. to be aware of sounds — (hear) — here
5. just and right — (fair) — fare
6. big strong animal covered in fur — bare — (bear)
7. precious and beloved — (dear) — deer

Directions Each sentence contains two words in ( ). Underline the word that belongs in the sentence.

8. A bicycle has (too, two) wheels and a tricycle has three.
9. Vegetable gardens need a lot of (rain, reign) to grow.
10. My mother likes to add a pinch of (thyme, time) to her stew recipe.
11. Ti Su and Jacques invited us to (there, their) party.
12. The first flower to bloom in my garden was a pink (rose, rows).

Directions Choose three words from the above list and write a sentence for each word.
13. Sentences will vary.
14. _____
15. _____

Home Activity Your child used context clues to choose the correct homophone. Read a folk tale aloud to your child. When you come to a homophone, have your child spell and define it.

Homophones DVD•315

Let's Practice It! TR DVD•315

Word Analysis

Review Homophones

REVIEW SOUND-SPELLINGS To review last week's word analysis skill, write *hour* and *our*. You studied words like these last week. What do you know about homophones? (The words are pronounced the same but have different spellings and different meanings.) Write the following sentence on the board: *Our class worked on the art project for over an hour.* Have students identify the homophones in the sentence. (*our, hour*) What does the homophone *o-u-r* mean? (belongs to us) What does *h-o-u-r* mean? (sixty minutes) Continue in the same way for homophone pairs *not* and *knot, wood* and *would,* and *made* and *maid.*

Corrective feedback | If students are unable to answer the questions about homophones, refer them to *Sound-Spelling Card* 137.

GUIDE PRACTICE Display a 2-column chart with the headings shown below. Listen as I say a word and write it in the first column. Think about what the word means. Write *allowed*. Model reading the word. Then have students read *allowed* and explain its meaning. How is the homophone *aloud* spelled? Write *aloud* in the second column. Have students read the word and explain its meaning. Model reading and defining the other homophone pairs in the same way.

Homophone 1	Homophone 2
allowed	aloud
patients	patience
mussel	muscle
presents	presence

ON THEIR OWN For additional practice, use *Let's Practice It!* p. 315 on the *Teacher Resources DVD-ROM.*

Fluent Word Reading

Spiral Review

READ WORDS IN ISOLATION Display these words. Tell students that they can already decode some words on this list. Explain that they should know other words because they appear often in reading.

Have students read the list three or four times until they can read at the rate of two to three seconds per word.

Word Reading

swimmer	ostrich	video	laughed	idea
friends	artist	creative	inspect	some
surprised	people	impress	violets	hungry
dial	want	radio	into	actor

Corrective feedback	**If...** students have difficulty reading whole words, **then...** have them use sound-by-sound blending for decodable words or chunking for words that have word parts, or have them say and spell high-frequency words.
	If... students cannot read fluently at a rate of two to three seconds per word, **then...** have pairs practice the list until they can read it fluently.

Access for All

 Strategic Intervention

To assist students having difficulty decoding multisyllabic words, use the Multisyllabic Word Strategy Routine on the Routines Flip Chart to practice segmenting and reading words.

Spiral Review

These activities review

• previously taught high-frequency words *friends, into, laughed, people, some, want.*

• syllable patterns CV/VC, VCCCV; suffixes -*er*, -*or*, -*ist.*

Fluent Word Reading Have students listen to a more fluent reader say the words. Then have them repeat the words.

Good-Bye, 382 Shin Dang Dong **284d**

ⓒ Common Core State Standards

Foundational Skills 3. Know and apply grade-level phonics and word analysis skills in decoding words. **Foundational Skills 3.c.** Decode multisyllable words. **Foundational Skills 3.d.** Read grade-appropriate irregularly spelled words. **Foundational Skills 4.** Read with sufficient accuracy and fluency to support comprehension. **Foundational Skills 4.b.** Read on-level prose and poetry orally with accuracy, appropriate rate, and expression on successive readings.

Fluent Word Reading

READ WORDS IN CONTEXT Display these sentences. Call on individuals to read a sentence. Then randomly point to review words and have students read them. To help you monitor word reading, high-frequency words are underlined and decodable words are italicized.

MONITOR PROGRESS Sentence Reading

Lisa's *creative idea surprised* <u>some</u> of her <u>friends</u>.

In the *video,* a *swimmer* jumps <u>into</u> the pool.

We <u>laughed</u> when a *hungry ostrich* chased the *actor.*

Does Dad <u>want</u> to *inspect* the *dial* on the *radio*?

The *artist's* painting of *violets* will *impress* <u>people</u>.

If... students are unable to read an underlined high-frequency word,

then... read the word for them and spell it, having them echo you.

If... students have difficulty reading an italicized decodable word,

then... guide them in using sound-by-sound blending or chunking.

Reread for Fluency

Have students reread the sentences to develop automaticity decoding words

Routine Oral Rereading

1. **Read** Have students read all the sentences orally.

2. **Reread** To achieve optimal fluency, students should reread the sentences three or four times.

3. **Corrective Feedback** Listen as students read. Provide corrective feedback regarding their fluency and decoding.

Routines Flip Chart

Decodable Passage 23C

students need help, then...

Read *Dawn and Baseball*

READ WORDS IN ISOLATION Have students turn to p. 95 in *Decodable Practice Readers 3.2* and find the first list of words. Each word in this list as the vowel sound /ȯ/ spelled *a, au, aw, al, augh,* or *ough.* Let's blend and ead these words. Be sure that students identify the correct vowel sound in ach word.

ext, have students read the high-frequency words.

PREVIEW Have students read the title and preview the story. Tell them that ey will read words with the vowel sound /ȯ/.

READ WORDS IN CONTEXT Chorally read the story along with students. ave students identify words in the story that have the vowel sound /ȯ/. ake sure that students are monitoring their accuracy when they decode ords.

Team Talk Pair students and have them take turns reading the story aloud to ach other. Monitor students as they read to check for proper pronunciation nd appropriate pacing.

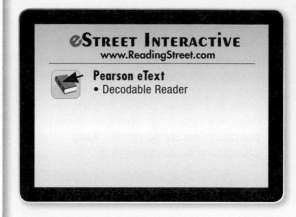

eStreet Interactive
www.ReadingStreet.com

Pearson eText
• Decodable Reader

Access for All

A **Advanced**

Have students write their own sentences using some of the decodable words found in the sentences on p. 284e.

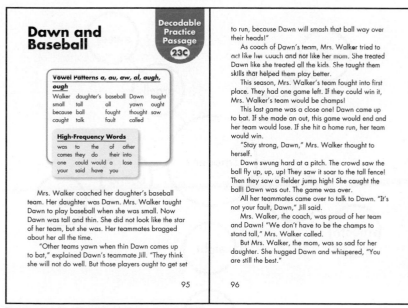

Decodable Practice Passage 23C

Common Core State Standards

Literature 5. Refer to parts of stories, dramas, and poems when writing or speaking about a text, using terms such as *chapter, scene,* and *stanza;* describe how each successive part builds on earlier sections. **Also Literature 4., Language 5.**

Bridge to Common Core

KEY IDEAS AND DETAILS

Discussing characteristics of poetry and the things described in poetry helps students understand more about this genre. In this lesson, they determine possible techniques to use to appeal to the five senses so that readers can visualize what is being described.

 # Social Studies in Reading

Poetry

INTRODUCE Explain to students that what we read is structured differently depending on the author's reasons for writing and what kind of information he or she wishes to convey. Different types of texts are called genres. Tell them that poetry is one type of genre.

DISCUSS THE GENRE Ask students to name or tell about poems they know or have heard. Discuss characteristics that the poems share. Ask: What kinds of things do poets describe? (Possible response: people, places, things Explain that poets often use imagery, or words that appeal to the five senses, to help readers visualize what is being described.

GROUP PRACTICE Use students' responses to create a concept map like the one below. Label the main circle *Imagery*. Ask the following questions:

- What are the five senses? (sight, sound, smell, taste, and touch.)
- What descriptive words could a poet use to appeal to these senses? (Possible response: sight—*blue;* sound—*loud;* smell—*sweet;* taste—*salty;* touch—*smooth*.)

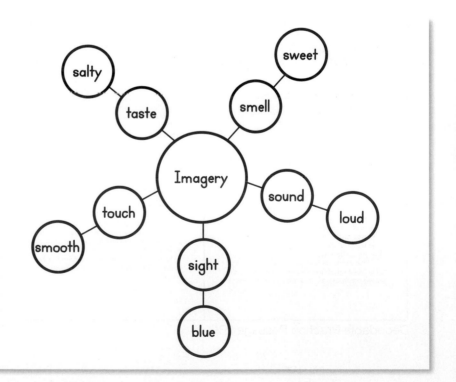

Team Talk Have students work in pairs to copy the concept map and add other sensory words to it. Have pairs share their words with the class.

READ Tell students that they will now read a poem about many different people on a crowded city street. Have them think about poems they have heard or read that describe a person or a place.

ELL

Cognates The Spanish word *poema* may be familiar to Spanish speakers as the cognate for *poem*.

Day 4 **SMALL GROUP TIME • Differentiate Vocabulary, p. SG•33**

OL On-Level	**SI** Strategic Intervention	**A** Advanced
Develop Language Using Amazing Words	• **Review/Discuss** Amazing Words	• **Extend** Amazing Words and Selection Vocabulary
Read "Sing a Song of People"	• **Read** "Sing a Song of People"	• **Read** "Sing a Song of People"
		• **Organize** Inquiry Project

ELL

If... students need more scaffolding and practice with **Amazing Words, then...** use the Routine on pp. xxxvi–xxxvii in the *ELL Handbook*.

Genre
Poetry

- Poetry is a creative expression of language, usually written to entertain or express feelings.
- Many poems have rhythm and rhyme, much like music.
- Poems use imagery, or sensory language that helps the reader picture the way something looks, sounds, feels, tastes, and smells.
- As you read "Sing a Song of People," try to picture what the poet is describing.

Sing a Song of People
by Lois Lenski

Sing a song of people
Walking fast or slow;
People in the city,
Up and down they go.

People on the sidewalk,
People on the bus;
People passing, passing,
In back and front of us.
People on the subway
Underneath the ground;
People riding taxis
Round and round and round.

People with their hats on,
Going in the doors;
People with umbrellas
When it rains and pours.
People in tall buildings
And in stores below;
Riding elevators
Up and down they go.

People walking singly,
People in a crowd;
People saying nothing,
People talking loud.
People laughing, smiling,
Grumpy people too;
People who just hurry
And never look at you!

Let's **Think** About...

How can I tell that "Sing a Song of People" is a poem and not a story?

1

Let's **Think** About...

How does the poet create an image of a crowded city street using words?

2

Let's **Think** About...

Reading Across Texts Which of Jangmi's homes is more like the place described in this poem, her old home in Korea or her new one in the United States?

Writing Across Texts Create a Venn diagram that compares Jangmi's home to the place described in "Sing a Song of People."

Common Core State Standards

Literature 5. Refer to parts of stories, dramas, and poems when writing or speaking about a text, using terms such as *chapter, scene,* and *stanza;* describe how each successive part builds on earlier sections. **Literature 10.** By the end of the year, read and comprehend literature, including stories, dramas, and poetry, at the high end of the grades 2–3 text complexity band independently and proficiently. **Also Writing 10., Language 3., 4., 5.**

Access Text ©

TEACH Genre: Poetry Have students preview "Sing a Song of People" on pp. 284–285. Then ask: How can you tell this selection is a poem? (The words are grouped in stanzas, and some of the end words rhyme.)

Corrective feedback | **If...** students are unable to identify the characteristics of a poem,
then... use the model to discuss the features of poetry.

Think Aloud

MODEL I see that this selection is made up of short lines of text rather than paragraphs. The lines are grouped together in stanzas with a space in between each stanza. I also notice that some of the words t the end of the lines, such as *slow* and *go* in the first stanza, rhyme. The use f rhyming words and the organization of the text into stanzas tells me this election is a poem.

N THEIR OWN Have students work in pairs to identify the beginning and nd of each stanza and identify all the rhyming words in the poem.

Close Reading ©

NALYSIS Which words would you use to describe this place? Why? (I would se the words *busy, noisy,* and *crowded* to describe this place because there re a lot of people and vehicles. Everything and everyone is moving and doing omething or going somewhere.)

NALYSIS Identify the compound word in the second stanza. Use your under- anding of word structure to determine what it means. (The compound word is *dewalk*. A sidewalk is a walkway that goes along the side of the street.)

Genre

T'S THINK ABOUT... As you read "Sing a Song of People," use Let's Think bout in the Student Edition to help students focus on the features of a poem.

he text is made up of short lines rather than paragraphs. Some of the words the end of the lines rhyme.

he poet mentions things on the street, such as a bus, the subway, and taxis. he also repeats the word *people* over and over to give the impression of rge crowds. She describes what the people are doing and where they are oing.

Reading and Writing Across Texts

ave students create a three-column chart that lists descriptive details about angmi's Korean home, her American home, and the place described in the oem. Then have students create a Venn diagram that compares Jangmi's ome to the place described in the poem. Ask them to use their diagrams write a paragraph about the similarities and differences between the two aces.

Access for All

SI Strategic Intervention

Use the illustrations and other visual aids to help students understand the meaning of words such as *bus, subway, taxis,* and *elevators.* Then have students use these words in sentences.

A Advanced

Have students write two to four lines to add to the poem. Have them share their work with the class.

Graphic Organizers Provide support to students when creating the three- column chart and the Venn diagram. Help them label their organizers, and then work together to add details to each one.

Good-Bye, 382 Shin Dang Dong **285a**

Let's Learn It!

READING STREET ONLINE
ONLINE STUDENT EDITION
www.ReadingStreet.com

Common Core State Standards
Language 4. Determine or clarify the meaning of unknown and multiple-meaning words and phrases based on grade 3 reading and content, choosing flexibly from a range of strategies. Also Foundational Skills 4.b., Speaking/Listening 1.b., 4.

Vocabulary

Compound Words

Word Structure Remember that a compound word is one word made up of two smaller words, such as *airplane* or *halfway*. The two smaller words can help you figure out the meaning of the compound word.

Practice It! Read each riddle. Have a partner choose the compound word from *Good-Bye, 382 Shin Dang Dong* that answers the riddle. Then write your own riddles. Riddles: "room with a bed," "place for a fire," "place of your birth," "drops of rain," "sick for home," "papers full of news," and "watery melon."

Fluency

Expression

Show expression in your voice when reading aloud to make your reading lively. Note words in quotation marks and whether a sentence ends with a period or a question mark, and show these in your voice.

Practice It! Read aloud the first half of page 266 with a partner. Read the words of the characters as you think they might say them. Let your voice fall at the end of statements and rise at the end of questions.

286

Listening and Speaking

Make eye contact with your audience during a performance.

Song or Poem

The words, images, rhythm, and rhyme in a song or poem come alive when it is performed.

Practice It! Choose a song or poem you like and perform it from memory for the class. Your performance should last less than three minutes. Consider using props for your performance.

Tips

Listening ...
• Listen attentively.
• Ask relevant questions and make pertinent comments about the song or poem.

Speaking ...
• Create a mood using volume, rate, and expression.
• Use adverbs and time-order transition words correctly.

Teamwork ...
• Ask and answer questions about how you connect to the poem.

287

Student Edition, pp. 286–287

Common Core State Standards

Foundational Skills 4.b. Read on-level prose and poetry orally with accuracy, appropriate rate, and expression on successive readings. **Speaking/Listening 1.b.** Follow agreed-upon rules for discussions (e.g., gaining the floor in respectful ways, listening to others with care, speaking one at a time about the topics and texts under discussion). **Speaking/Listening 4.** Report on a topic or text, tell a story, or recount an experience with appropriate facts and relevant, descriptive details, speaking clearly at an understandable pace. **Language 4.** Determine or clarify the meaning of unknown and multiple-meaning words and phrases based on grade 3 reading and content, choosing flexibly from a range of strategies.

Fluency

Expression and Punctuation Cues

GUIDE PRACTICE Use the Student Edition activity as an assessment tool. Make sure the passage is at least 200 words in length. As students read, make sure their expression changes to enhance the meaning of what they are reading.

Don't Wait Until Friday

MONITOR PROGRESS Check Fluency

FORMATIVE ASSESSMENT As students reread, monitor progress toward their individual fluency goals.

Current Goal: 102–112 words correct per minute

End-of-Year Goal: 120 words correct per minute

If... students cannot read fluently at a rate of 102–112 words correct per minute

then... have students practice with text at their independent levels.

Vocabulary Skill

◉ Compound Words

TEACH COMPOUND WORDS • WORD STRUCTURE Write *classroom* and *backpack* on the board. Point out that these are compound words and their meanings comes from the two smaller words. Ask students to tell the meaning of each word.

GUIDE PRACTICE Tell students that they will use these words to solve riddles. Ask: What is a pack you wear on your back? (backpack) What is a room for a class? (classroom) Point out that each riddle contains clues to the answer.

ON THEIR OWN As students work with partners, walk around the room to make sure they are identifying the correct answers. Provide a list of compound words from the story if necessary.

Listening and Speaking

Song or Poem

TEACH Have students work in pairs. Tell them that when they work with a partner, it is important that each person contributes to the assignment or activity. Remind students to take turns as they share their own ideas and then listen to their partner's ideas. Students should listen attentively to their partner and then ask relevant questions and make appropriate comments or suggestions. Both partners should offer ideas for songs and poems and then agree on which one to perform. Remind students to listen to their partner's performance and then offer constructive feedback on things such as expression, rate, and volume. Have students think about props that would enhance their performance.

GUIDE PRACTICE Be sure both students are making contributions and acknowledging their partner's ideas. Remind students to stand up straight and make eye contact with the audience during their performance.

ON THEIR OWN Have students perform their song or poem for the class.

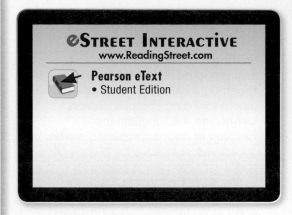

eStreet Interactive
www.ReadingStreet.com

Pearson eText
• Student Edition

Teamwork

Remind students that it is important to listen to and acknowledge others' ideas when you work as a team. Tell students that listening to their partner's comments and suggestions can help them improve their performance.

Ⓒ **Bridge to Common Core**

COMPREHENSION AND COLLABORATION

As students work together to prepare to present their songs or poems, they should take turns as they share their ideas, make comments, and offer suggestions and constructive feedback.

Echo Reading Pair less-fluent speakers with more-fluent students. Have the less-fluent students echo read the song or poem with their partner several times. Allow students to write out the words to their song or poem so they may refer to the written copy during their performance.

Common Core State Standards

Writing 2.a. Introduce a topic and group related information together; include illustrations when useful to aiding comprehension. **Language 1.a.** Explain the function of nouns, pronouns, verbs, adjectives, and adverbs in general and their functions in particular sentences. **Language 2.f.** Use spelling patterns and generalizations (e.g., word families, position-based spellings, syllable patterns, ending rules, meaningful word parts) in writing words. **Also Writing 2., 2.b., 4., 6., 7., 8., 10.**

Research and Inquiry

Step 4 Synthesize

TEACH Have students synthesize their research findings and results. Students may choose to include a map from an atlas to illustrate the location of a specific country or part of the world. Review how to choose relevant details from a number of oral and written sources and organize them logically.

GUIDE PRACTICE Have students use a word-processing program to prepare an outline of their article for Day 5. If students are including maps, check to see that they are clearly labeling names of key locations, such as countries, cities, and oceans.

ON THEIR OWN Have students organize and combine their research findings and then use this information to write an article about their inquiry topic. Remind students to create a Works Cited page from their notes. The page should include the author, title, publisher, and publication year for each source.

Conventions

Adverbs

TEST PRACTICE Remind students that grammar skills, such as adverbs, are often assessed on important tests. Remind students that adverbs are words that describe other words by telling **how** *(carefully, beautifully)*, **when** *(before, next)*, or **where** *(westward, here)* something happens.

ON THEIR OWN For additional practice, use *Reader's and Writer's Notebook,* p. 348.

Reader's and Writer's Notebook,
p. 348

Spelling

Vowel Patterns *au, augh, ou, ough*

PRACTICE SPELLING STRATEGY Supply pairs of students with index cards on which the spelling words have been written. Have one student read a word while the other writes it. Then have students switch roles. Have them use the cards to check their spelling and correct any misspelled words.

ON THEIR OWN For additional practice, use *Let's Practice It!* p. 316 on the *Teacher Resources DVD-ROM.*

Let's Practice It! TR DVD•316

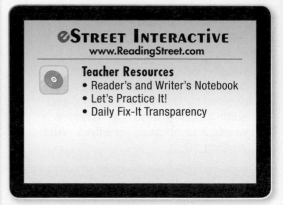

Daily Fix-It

7. The Korean girls' had an American dish with sawsages. *(girls; sausages)*

8. American foods is cooked different than Korean foods. *(are; differently)*

© Bridge to Common Core

CONVENTIONS OF STANDARD ENGLISH

As students identify and use adverbs, they are demonstrating command of the conventions of standard English. Your guidance will help them use correct grammar, usage, and spelling to convey meaning when they speak and write.

Common Core State Standards

Writing 5. With guidance and support from peers and adults, develop and strengthen writing as needed by planning, revising, and editing. **Language 3.a.** Choose words and phrases for effect. **Also Writing 10.**

Write Guy *by Jeff Anderson*

Let Me Check My List

Encourage students to keep lists of words they come across that are exciting or interesting to them. They can use their lists to increase their vocabulary and incorporate them in their own writing. This is a great way to improve vocabulary and word choice.

Writing

Poetry: Free Verse

Mini-Lesson   Revise: Adding

■ Yesterday we wrote free verse poetry about new experiences. Today we will revise our drafts. The goal is to make your writing clearer and more interesting.

■ Display Writing Transparency 23B. Remind students that revising does not include corrections of grammar and mechanics. Tell them that this will be done during the lesson as they proofread their work. Then introduce the revising strategy of adding.

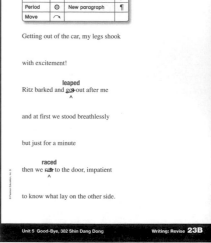

Writing Transparency 23B, TR DVD

■ Today we will look for places to add vivid verbs to make our drafts more descriptive. I see that the second stanza needs a few more vivid verbs, so I will change *got* to *leaped* and *ran* to *raced*. These verbs will help readers better visualize the action in their minds.

Tell students that as they revise, they should ask themselves questions about their writing, such as *What can I add to make the writing better?* and *How can I help readers create a picture in their minds?*

Revising Tips
✔ Make sure that the writing focuses on a central idea.

✔ Review writing to make sure that it makes sense and is engaging.

✔ Add details or change dull verbs to vivid verbs to make the writing more interesting and descriptive.

PEER CONFERENCING • PEER REVISION Have students exchange draft for peer revision. Students should read the drafts carefully, looking for places where information could be added or where dull words could be replaced with more vivid words to make the writing more clear and interesting. Have students write their suggestions for additions and comments directly on their partner's draft.

𝑒STREET INTERACTIVE
www.ReadingStreet.com

Teacher Resources
• Writing Transparency

Have students revise their free verse poems. They should use the suggestions and feedback that their partner wrote during Peer Revision as well as the key features of free verse poetry. Be sure that students are using the revising strategy of adding.

Corrective feedback Circulate around the room to monitor and confer with students as they revise. Remind students correcting errors that they will have time to edit tomorrow. They should be working on content and word choice today.

Routine | Quick Write for Fluency | Team Talk

- **Talk** Have pairs locate and discuss examples of figurative language in the main selection.

- **Write** Instruct students to write about one example of figurative language that helped them create a picture in their minds.

- **Share** Partners should exchange sentences and then check each other's writing for the use of vivid language.

Routines Flip Chart

Modify the Prompt Allow beginning English speakers to work with a partner, dictating their poems as their partner records them as a list. In the revising step, have students add words to make their poems more detailed and descriptive.

Wrap Up Your Day!

✔ **Content Knowledge** Have students discuss what city life is like in this poem.

✔ **Oral Vocabulary** Monitor students' use of oral vocabulary as they respond to this question: *What aspects of the city described in this poem might confuse someone from a different culture?*

✔ **Text Features** Discuss how the illustrations help students understand the text.

Preview DAY 5

Remind students to think about why it is hard to adapt to a new culture.

Materials

- Student Edition
- Weekly Test
- Reader's and Writer's Notebook

Bridge to Common Core

INTEGRATION OF KNOWLEDGE/IDEAS

This week, students have integrated content presented in diverse media and analyzed how different texts address similar topics. They have developed knowledge about adapting to a new culture to expand the unit topic of Cultures.

Social Studies Knowledge Goals

Students have learned that a new culture means

- a new home and neighborhood
- a new language
- new traditions

Content Knowledge

Adapting to a New Culture

REVIEW THE CONCEPT Have students look back at the reading selections to find examples that best demonstrate why it is hard to adapt to a new culture.

Build Oral Language

REVIEW AMAZING WORDS Display and review this week's concept map. Remind students that this week they have learned ten Amazing Words related to adapting to a new culture. Have students use the Amazing Words and the concept map to answer the Question of the Week, *Why is it hard to adapt to a new culture?* Be sure their answers include appropriate detail.

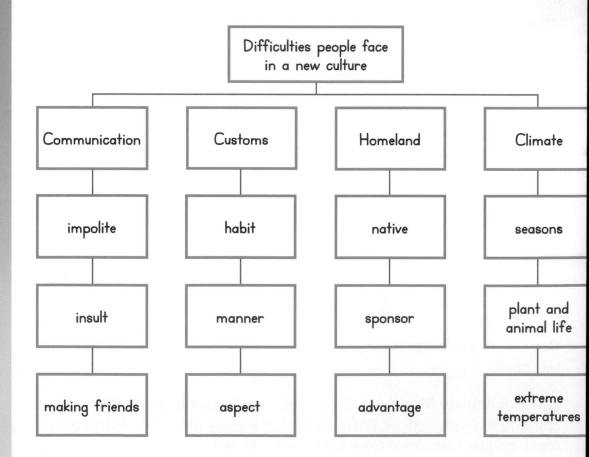

Build Oral Vocabulary

Team Talk **CONNECT TO AMAZING IDEAS** Have pairs of students discuss how the Question of the Week connects to the question for this unit of study: *What happens when two ways of life come together?* Tell students to use the concept map and what they have learned from this week's discussions and reading selections to form an Amazing Idea—a realization or "big idea" about Cultures. Remind partners to pose and answer questions with appropriate detail and to give suggestions that build on each other's ideas. Then ask pairs to share their Amazing Ideas with the class.

Amazing Ideas might include these key concepts:

- It's difficult to feel comfortable in a new culture when you don't know the language or customs—everything seems strange and foreign.
- Sponsors can help newcomers learn about the new culture and help them overcome their fears.
- Two specific cultures can be very different, but all cultures share common elements, such as food, clothing, and homes. It can be scary to leave one's homeland, but it can be exciting to learn about a new one.

WRITE ABOUT IT Have students write a few sentences about their Amazing Idea, beginning with "This week I learned . . ."

MONITOR PROGRESS **Check Oral Vocabulary**

FORMATIVE ASSESSMENT Have individuals use this week's Amazing Words to describe changes people make when they have to adapt to a new culture. Monitor students' abilities to use the Amazing Words and note which words you need to reteach.

If... students have difficulty using the Amazing Words,

then... reteach using the Oral Vocabulary Routine, pp. 255a, 260b, 272b, 284b, OV•3.

eStreet Interactive
www.ReadingStreet.com
Concept Talk Video
Teacher Resources • Amazing Word Cards
Story Sort

Amazing Words

native	habit
homeland	manner
aspect	impolite
advantage	conscious
sponsor	insult

 ELL

Check Concepts and Language Use the Day 5 instruction on ELL Poster 23 to monitor students' understanding of the lesson concept.
Concept Map Work with students to add new words to the concept map.

Good-Bye, 382 Shin Dang Dong **287g**

Zoom in on ©

© Common Core State Standards

Literature 3. Describe characters in a story (e.g., their traits, motivations, or feelings) and explain how their actions contribute to the sequence of events. **Foundational Skills 3.** Know and apply grade-level phonics and word analysis skills in decoding words. **Language 4.** Determine or clarify the meaning of unknown and multiple-meaning words and phrases based on grade 3 reading and content, choosing flexibly from a range of strategies. **Also Literature 1., Language 5.**

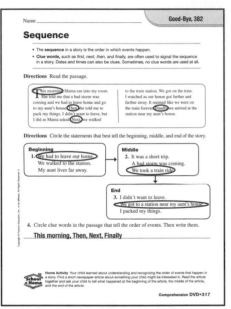
Let's Practice It! TR DVD•317

Selection Vocabulary

airport a place where airplanes are able to take off and land

cellar an underground room or rooms, usually under a building

curious eager to find out or learn about new things

delicious tastes very good

described told about in words or writing

farewell good-bye

homesick wanting to go home

memories everything a person remembers

raindrops drops of rain

Text-Based Comprehension

Review ☉ Sequence

TEACH Review the definition of sequence on p. 258. Remind students that the sequence is the order in which things happen in a story. For additional support have students review p. EI•14 on sequence.

GUIDE PRACTICE Have student pairs identify three important events in *Good-Bye, 382 Shin Dang Dong.* Then have pairs write the events in sequence.

ON THEIR OWN For additional practice with sequence, use *Let's Practice It!* p. 317 on the *Teacher Resources DVD-ROM.*

Vocabulary Skill

Review ☉ Compound Words

TEACH Remind students that a compound word is made up of two smaller words. Explain that students can look at a word's structure to help them figure out its meaning.

GUIDE PRACTICE Write the word *homesick* on the board and ask students to identify the two smaller words. Underline *home* and *sick*. Remind students that they can use the two smaller words to help them figure out the meaning of the compound word.

ON THEIR OWN Have students identify the two smaller words in *raindrops* and tell what the compound word means.

Phonics

Review Vowel Patterns for /ȯ/

TEACH Write the following sentences on the board. Have students read each one, first quietly to themselves and then aloud as you track the print.

1. I thought the August sunrises were awesome.
2. The kitten used its paws and claws to climb.
3. We ought to draw pictures of the lovely autumn trees.
4. He hauled away a bag of laundry.
5. His soccer ball crushed the stalks of the flowers.

Team Talk Have students discuss with a partner which words have the vowel sound /ȯ/, and ask them to identify the letters that spell each sound. Then call on individuals to share with the class.

Literary Terms

Review Mood

TEACH Have students reread p. 269 of *Good-Bye, 382 Shin Dang Dong.* Remind them that the mood of a story is the atmosphere or feeling it has.

GUIDE PRACTICE Ask students to describe the mood the authors create on p. 269. Guide them to identify details about the setting and character that create the mood.

ON THEIR OWN Have students choose another section from the selection and describe the mood. Ask them to list specific examples from the text that create the mood.

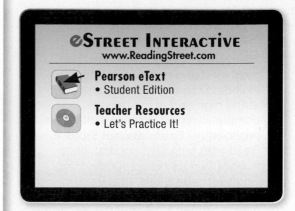

eSTREET INTERACTIVE
www.ReadingStreet.com

Pearson eText
• Student Edition

Teacher Resources
• Let's Practice It!

ELL

Articulation Tip If students have trouble pronouncing words with the vowel sound /ȯ/, demonstrate how to pronounce them by slowly repeating words. Have students practice saying them until they develop confidence.

Mood Create different moods in the classroom to demonstrate how authors create specific feelings. Smile and play upbeat music to create a happy mood. Turn out the lights and speak in a creepy voice to create a scary mood. Invite students to suggest other ways to create a specific mood.

Good-Bye, 382 Shin Dang Dong **287i**

Ⓒ Common Core State Standards

Literature 10. By the end of the year, read and comprehend literature, including stories, dramas, and poetry, at the high end of the grades 2–3 text complexity band independently and proficiently. **Foundational Skills 4.** Read with sufficient accuracy and fluency to support comprehension. **Foundational Skills 4.b.** Read on-level prose and poetry orally with accuracy, appropriate rate, and expression on successive readings.

Plan to Assess Fluency

☐ **Week 1** Advanced

☐ **Week 2** Strategic Intervention

☑ **This week assess On-Level students.**

☐ **Week 4** Strategic Intervention

☐ **Week 5** Assess any students you have not yet checked during this unit.

Set individual goals for students to enable them to reach the year-end goal.

• Current Goal: 102–112 WCPM
• Year-End Goal: 120 WCPM

Assessment

Monitor Progress

FLUENCY Make two copies of the fluency passage on p. 287k. As the student reads the text aloud, mark mistakes on your copy. Also mark where the student is at the end of one minute. To check the student's comprehension of the passage, have him or her retell what was read. To figure words correct per minute (WCPM), subtract the number of mistakes from the total number of words read in one minute.

RATE

Corrective feedback	**If...** students cannot read fluently at a rate of 102–112 WCPM, **then...** make sure they practice with text at their independent reading level. Provide additional fluency practice by pairing nonfluent readers with fluent readers. **If...** students already read at 120 WCPM, **then...** have them read a book of their choice independently.

ELL

If... students need more scaffolding and practice with **Conventions and Writing,** **then...** use the Grammar Transition Lessons on pp. 312–386 in the *ELL Handbook.*

Day 5 SMALL GROUP TIME • Differentiate Reteaching, p. SG•33

OL On-Level	SI Strategic Intervention	A Advanced
• **Practice** Adverbs	• **Review** Adverbs	• **Extend** Adverbs
• **Reread** *Reading Street Sleuth,* pp. 60–61	• **Reread** *Reading Street Sleuth,* pp. 60–61	• **Reread** *Reading Street Sleuth,* pp. 60–61
		• **Communicate** Inquiry Project

Name _____

Stuck at the Airport

June 13, 10:43 a.m.   4

Dear Diary,   6

It's the first day of summer vacation. Am I at the beach with my   20

friends? No, because I am stuck at the airport, waiting for a plane   33

to Grandma's house in Kansas. What normal person goes to Kansas   44

for the summer? All morning Dad has been describing Grandma's   54

delicious cooking. She makes her own sausage. She also makes   64

homemade applesauce. Dad's the one who's homesick for Grandma's   73

house. I think he should go!   79

June 13, 11:19 a.m.   83

Dear Diary,   85

Now it's Mom's turn to talk my ear off. "Call if you get homesick.   99

Wear sunscreen. If there's a tornado warning, go straight for the   110

cellar," she says. "You will be safe there." I promise that I'll run and   124

hide the minute I feel a raindrop.   131

June 13, 11:52 a.m.   135

Dear Diary,   137

Grandma called and said she was glad she caught me. She told   149

me that her neighbor gave her a straw-colored cocker spaniel puppy.   161

She said he's very active and curious, and he's going to need a lot of   176

attention. Grandma asked if I would please teach him not to dig up the   190

lawn.   191

This is going to be the best summer ever!   200

MONITOR PROGRESS   • **Check Fluency**

 **Common Core State Standards**

Literature 1. Ask and answer questions to demonstrate understanding of a text, referring explicitly to the text as the basis for the answers. **Literature 3.** Describe characters in a story (e.g., their traits, motivations, or feelings) and explain how their actions contribute to the sequence of events. **Foundational Skills 4.** Read with sufficient accuracy and fluency to support comprehension. **Foundational Skills 4.a.** Read on-level text with purpose and understanding. **Also Literature 10.**

Assessment

Monitor Progress

For a written assessment of Vowel Patterns for /ò/, Sequence, and Selection Vocabulary, use Weekly Test 23, pp. 133–138.

SEQUENCE Use "Berta Is Lonely" on p. 287m to check students' understanding of sequence.

1. Why is Berta lonely? (She can't find any other kids to play with her.)

2. What does Berta do first to meet other kids? (She walks up and down the street.)

3. What does Berta do next? (She walks down the street with a baseball mitt and ball.) What does she do last? (She bounces a soccer ball as she walks

Corrective feedback	**If...** students are unable to answer the comprehension questions, **then...** use the Reteach lesson in *First Stop*.

Berta Is Lonely

Berta sat on Grandpa's front stoop and gazed around, but she didn't see any kids. In fact, she hadn't seen any kids since she arrived at Grandpa's yesterday.

Berta had been looking forward to this visit to Mexico for a long time. She was really thrilled about seeing her dad's old neighborhood. Some of his childhood friends still lived nearby. She knew she would meet them later. Right now, however, Berta was a little bit bored. She wished there were kids around.

Suddenly, Berta had a brilliant idea. She asked Grandpa if she could stroll up and down the street. Maybe she would meet some kids that way.

Berta took her walk, but it didn't work. She didn't see any kids, and if kids saw her, they didn't come out to say hello. Berta had to try something else.

Then Berta grabbed her dad's old baseball mitt and a ball. She walked down the street again. As she did, Berta tossed the ball up in the air and caught it, over and over. She thought some boy or girl might see her and come out to play catch. That didn't work either.

Next, Berta saw her dad's old soccer ball. She walked down the street again and bounced the ball. She hoped the bouncing sound would get some attention. It did. As she passed a house, a door opened. Three kids came running out. In Spanish, they asked if they could play soccer with her.

Yes! Berta was happy.

MONITOR PROGRESS • Sequence

Common Core State Standards

Speaking/Listening 4. Report on a topic or text, tell a story, or recount an experience with appropriate facts and relevant, descriptive details, speaking clearly at an understandable pace. **Language 1.a.** Explain the function of nouns, pronouns, verbs, adjectives, and adverbs in general and their functions in particular sentences. **Language 2.f.** Use spelling patterns and generalizations (e.g., word families, position-based spellings, syllable patterns, ending rules, meaningful word parts) in writing words. **Also Speaking/Listening 1.a, 1.b., 3.**

Research and Inquiry

Step 5 Communicate

PRESENT IDEAS Have students share their inquiry results by reading aloud their articles and giving a brief talk on their research. Have students display any maps they copied or created on Day 3.

SPEAKING Remind students how to be good speakers and how to communicate effectively with their audience.

• Respond to relevant questions with appropriate details.

• Speak clearly and loudly.

• Keep eye contact with audience members.

LISTENING Review with students these tips for being a good listener.

• Wait until the speaker has finished before raising your hand to ask a relevant question.

• Be polite, even if you disagree.

LISTEN TO IDEAS Have students listen attentively as students read their articles and give brief talks. Have them make pertinent comments, closely related to the topic.

Spelling Test

Vowel Patterns *au, augh, ou, ough*

To administer the spelling test, refer to the directions, words, and sentences on p. 259c.

Conventions

Adverbs

MORE PRACTICE Remind students that adverbs tell how, when, or where something happens.

GUIDE PRACTICE Remind students that adding adverbs to their writing can make actions more specific and interesting. On the board, write *The cat meowed.* Model how to expand the sentence by adding adverbs. Write on the board *Yesterday the cat meowed sadly outside.* To tell when the cat meowed, I added a time-order transition adverb, *yesterday*. To tell how the cat meowed, I added the adverb *sadly*. To tell where the cat meowed, I added a third adverb, *outside*.

ON THEIR OWN Write these sentences on the board. Have students fill in the blanks by choosing an appropriate adverb from the following list: *before, next, carefully, beautifully, fastest, first, last, finally, then, after, sometimes, happily, noisily, soon, kindly.* Students should complete *Let's Practice It!* p. 318 on the *Teacher Resources DVD-ROM.*

1. **Kamil _____ lifted the puppy.** (carefully)

2. **_____ dinner, Dad _____ takes a nap.** (After; sometimes)

3. **The dogs barked _____ to go outside.** (noisily)

4. **The gentleman _____ opened the door for me.** (kindly)

5. **I hope to go home _____.** (soon)

6. **_____, I finished the test.** (Finally)

7. **This is the _____ step in the process.** (next)

8. **She plays piano _____.** (beautifully)

9. **He is the _____ runner on the team.** (fastest)

10. **Nathan's turn is _____ mine.** (before)

eStreet Interactive
www.ReadingStreet.com

Teacher Resources
• Let's Practice It!
• Daily Fix-It Transparency

Daily Fix-It

9. Was the voiage from Asia hard for Mom and she? *(voyage; her)*

10. It wasnt the easyest trip for them. *(wasn't; easiest)*

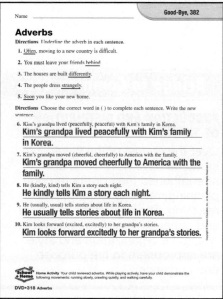

Let's Practice It! TR DVD•318

Ⓒ Common Core State Standards

Writing 5. With guidance and support from peers and adults, develop and strengthen writing as needed by planning, revising, and editing. **Language 1.** Demonstrate command of the conventions of standard English grammar and usage when writing or speaking. **Language 1.a.** Explain the function of nouns, pronouns, verbs, adjectives, and adverbs in general and their functions in particular sentences. **Language 2.** Demonstrate command of the conventions of standard English capitalization, punctuation, and spelling when writing.

Teacher Note

Writing Self-Evaluation Make copies of the Writing Self-Evaluation Guide on p. 39 of the *Reader's and Writer's Notebook* and hand out to students.

Ⓒ Bridge to Common Core

PRODUCTION AND DISTRIBUTION OF WRITING

Over the course of the week, students have developed and strengthened their drafts through planning, revising, editing, and rewriting. The final drafts are clear and coherent free verse poems in which the organization and style are appropriate to the purpose and audience.

Writing Zoom in on Ⓒ

Poetry: Free Verse

REVIEW REVISING Remind students that yesterday they revised their free verse poems, paying particular attention to adding vivid verbs to make the writing detailed and interesting. Today students will proofread their poems and edit for correct use of adverbs.

Mini-Lesson   Proofread

Proofread for Adverbs

■ **Teach** When we proofread, we look closely at our work, searching for errors in mechanics such as spelling, capitalization, punctuation, and grammar. Today we will focus on making sure that adverbs are used correctly.

■ **Model** Let's look at another paragraph from the poem we revised yesterday. Display Writing Transparency 23C. Explain that you will look for errors in the use of adverbs. There is an error in the second line—the adjective *careful* should be changed to the adverb *carefully* because it describes the verb *pushed*. The adjective *impatient* should also be changed to an adverb, so I will change it to *impatiently*. In the last line, the adverb *after* is incorrect because the narrator hasn't thoroughly explored the new house yet. I will change this adverb to *before*. Explain to students that they should reread their free verse poems several times, each time looking for different types of errors: spelling, punctuation, capitalization, and grammar.

Writing Transparency 23C, TR DVD

PROOFREAD Display the Proofreading Tips. Ask students to proofread their free verse poems, using the Proofreading Tips and paying particular attention to the correct use of adverbs. Circulate around the room answering students' questions. When students have finished editing their own work, have pairs proofread each other's free verse poems.

Proofreading Tips

✔ Be sure that all adverbs are used correctly.

✔ Check for correct spelling, punctuation, capitalization, and grammar.

PRESENT Have students incorporate revisions and proofreading edits to create a final draft. Give students two options for presenting: an oral presentation to the class, or an illustrated copy. When students have finished, have each student complete the Writing Self-Evaluation Guide. Then collect the poems, along with any illustrations, and bind them into a class book.

Routine Quick Write for Fluency Team Talk

• **Talk** Have pairs discuss what they learned about writing free verse poetry.

• **Write** Have students write two sentences about two things that they learned.

• **Share** Partners should read their writing to each other.

Routines Flip Chart

Wrap Up Your Week!

Adapting to a New Culture

Why is it hard to adapt to a new culture?

Think Aloud In *Good-Bye, 382 Shin Dang Dong* and "Sing a Song of People," we learned about how hard it can be to adapt to a new culture and the similarities and differences between people.

Team Talk Have students recall their Amazing Ideas about cultures and use these ideas to help them demonstrate their understanding of the Question of the Week.

Next Week's Concept
Foods from Different Cultures

How can different cultures contribute to the foods we eat?

ELL

Poster Preview Prepare students for next week by using Week 4 ELL Poster 24. Read the Talk-Through to introduce the concept and vocabulary. Ask students to identify and describe actions in the art.

Selection Summary Send home the summary of the next week's selection, *Jalapeño Bagels,* in English and in students' home languages, if available in the *ELL Handbook.* They can read the summary with family members.

How can different cultures contribute to the food we eat? Tell students that next week they will read about food and what part our culture plays in what we like to eat.

Preview Next Week

Assessment Checkpoints for the Week

Weekly Assessment

Use pp. 133–138 of *Weekly Tests* to check:

✔ 🔵 **Phonics** Vowel Patterns for /ó/

✔ 🔵 **Comprehension** Sequence

✔ **Review** **Comprehension** Draw Conclusions

✔ **Selection Vocabulary**

airport	described	raindrops
cellar	farewell	
curious	homesick	
delicious	memories	

Weekly Tests

Differentiated Assessment

Advanced

Use pp. 133–138 of *Fresh Reads for Fluency and Comprehension* to check:

✔ 🔵 **Comprehension** Sequence

On-Level

✔ **Review** **Comprehension** Draw Conclusions

✔ **Fluency** Words Correct Per Minute

SI

Strategic Intervention

Fresh Reads for Fluency and Comprehension

Managing Assessment

Use *Assessment Handbook* for:

✔ **Weekly Assessment Blackline Masters for Monitoring Progress**

✔ **Observation Checklists**

✔ **Record-Keeping Forms**

✔ **Portfolio Assessment**

Assessment Handbook

TEACHER NOTES

DAY 1 Differentiate Vocabulary

- **Word Knowledge** Amazing Words
- **Read** "A Day at School in Japan"
- **Inquiry** Identify Questions

"A Day at School in Japan,"
pp. 60–61

DAY 2 Differentiate Comprehension

- **Word Knowledge** Selection Vocabulary
- **Access Text** Read *Good-Bye, 382 Shin Dang Dong*
- **Inquiry** Investigate

DAY 3 Differentiate Close Reading

- **Word Knowledge** Develop Vocabulary
- **Close Reading** Read *Good-Bye, 382 Shin Dang Dong*
- **Inquiry** Investigate

DAY 4 Differentiate Vocabulary

- **Word Knowledge** Amazing Words
- **Read** "Sing a Song of People"
- **Inquiry** Organize

DAY 5 Differentiate Reteaching

- **Conventions** Adverbs
- **Reread** "A Day at School in Japan" or Leveled Readers
- **Inquiry** Communicate

Teacher Guides and Student pages can be found in the Leveled Reader Database.

 Place English Language Learners in the groups that correspond to their reading abilities.
If... students need scaffolding and practice,
then... use the ELL Notes on the instructional pages.

ndependent Practice

Independent Practice Stations

See pp. 254h and 254i for Independent Stations.

Pearson Trade Book Library

See the Leveled Reader Database for lesson plans and student pages.

Reading Street Digital Path

Independent Practice Activities are available in the Digital Path.

Independent Reading

See p. 254i for independent reading suggestions.

© Common Core State Standards

Literature 1. Ask and answer questions to demonstrate understanding of a text, referring explicitly to the text as the basis for the answers. **Literature 3.** Describe characters in a story (e.g., their traits, motivations, or feelings) and explain how their actions contribute to the sequence of events. **Informational Text 6.** Distinguish their own point of view from that of the author of a text. **Language 4.** Determine or clarify the meaning of unknown and multiple-meaning words and phrases based on grade 3 reading and content, choosing flexibly from a range of strategies. **Also Informational Text 10.**

Independent Reading Options

Trade Book Library

❡STREET INTERACTIVE
www.ReadingStreet.com

Teacher Guides are available on the Leveled Reader Database.

ELL

If... students need more scaffolding and practice with **Vocabulary, then...** use the activities on pp. DI•67–DI•68 in the Teacher Resources section on SuccessNet.

OL On-Level

① Build Word Knowledge
Practice Amazing Words

DEFINE IT Elicit the definition for the word *advantage* from students. Ask: How would you describe an *advantage* to another student? (Possible response: An *advantage* is a benefit.) Clarify or give a definition when necessary. Continue with the words *native* and *homeland*.

Team Talk **TALK ABOUT IT** Have partners internalize meanings. Ask: How can you pair the Amazing Words together in a sentence? (Possible response: One *advantage* of my *native homeland* is that everyone speaks two languages.) Allow time for students to play with the words. Review the concept map with students. Discuss other words they can add to the concept map.

② Text-Based Comprehension
Read

READ ALOUD "A Day at School in Japan"
Have partners read "A Day at School in Japan" from *Reading Street Sleuth* on pp. 60–61.

ACCESS TEXT Discuss the Sleuth Work section with students before they work on it. Remind students that they can use these steps with other texts they read.

Gather Evidence Have partners take notes of text evidence. Invite students to share the evidence they found in the article. If time permits, have students highlight the evidence that supports the position that the school experiences in Japan and the United States are similar.

Ask Questions Talk together about the questions students would like to ask. Invite students to identify these questions as requiring factual or opinion based answers. If time permits, have students research pen pals from Japan so that they may ask their questions.

Make Your Case Encourage students to choose a side and work with a partner to cite reasons for their opinions. Have students share their paragraphs with the group, pointing out the most convincing reasons for their opinions.

 **On-Level**

① Build Word Knowledge

Practice Selection Vocabulary

eStreet Interactive
www.ReadingStreet.com

Pearson eText
• Student Edition
• Leveled Reader Database
• *Reading Street Sleuth*

airport	cellar	curious	delicious	described
farewell	homesick	memories	raindrops	

DEFINE IT Discuss the definition for the word *airport* with students. Ask: How would you describe an *airport* to another student? (Possible response: An *airport* is a place where airplanes take off and land.) Continue with the remaining words.

Team Talk **TALK ABOUT IT** Have pairs use the selection vocabulary in sentences to internalize meaning. Ask: How can you pair the selection vocabulary together in a sentence? (Possible response: After we said *farewell* at the airport, I felt *homesick*.) Allow time for students to play with the words and then share their sentences.

② Read

Good-Bye, 382 Shin Dang Dong

If you read *Good-Bye, 382 Shin Dang Dong* during whole group time, then use the following instruction.

ACCESS TEXT Reread pp. 270–271. Ask students questions to check understanding. Why is Jangmi crying? (She is sad because she is moving away from her home in Korea.) Why does she say good-bye to her home? (She loves her home and country and will miss them.) Why is Jangmi having a hard time picturing what her new home will look like? (It is so different from the home she has lived in her whole life.)

Have students identify sections from today's reading that they did not completely understand. Reread them aloud and clarify misunderstandings.

If you are reading *Good-Bye, 382 Shin Dang Dong* during small group time, then return to pp. 264–271a to guide the reading.

SMALL GROUP TIME

More Reading for Group Time

ON-LEVEL

Reviews
• Sequence
• Monitor and Clarify
• Selection Vocabulary

Use this suggested Leveled Reader or other text at students' instructional level.

eStreet Interactive
www.ReadingStreet.com

Use the Leveled Reader Database for lesson plans and student pages for *Joanie's House Becomes a Home*.

On-Level

Common Core State Standards

Literature 1. Ask and answer questions to demonstrate understanding of a text, referring explicitly to the text as the basis for the answers. **Literature 3.** Describe characters in a story (e.g., their traits, motivations, or feelings) and explain how their actions contribute to the sequence of events. **Language 4.** Determine or clarify the meaning of unknown and multiple-meaning words and phrases based on grade 3 reading and content, choosing flexibly from a range of strategies. **Also Language 4.a., 5.b., 6.**

① Build Word Knowledge

Develop Vocabulary

REREAD FOR VOCABULARY Reread the second paragraph on p. 275. Introduce: Let's read this paragraph to find out what *shingled* means. To help students understand the word *shingled,* ask questions related to context, such as: What part of the house are they describing? How are the rooftops of American houses different from the rooftops of Korean houses? Have students use online sources to find out more information about the word *shingled*.

② Read

Good-Bye, 382 Shin Dang Dong

If you read *Good-Bye, 382 Shin Dang Dong* during whole group time, then use the following instruction.

CLOSE READING Read pp. 272 and 275. Have students work with a partner and search through the text to find references to the changes that make Jangmi feel sad. (In Korea, her plane travels over rice fields, clay-tiled roofs, and the ocean; the newspaper has foreign words; in America, there are no rice fields or monsoon rains; there are wide roads; the new house has shingles and wooden floors and doors; the tree outside is maple instead of willow.)

Ask: How does Jangmi feel about the changes she experiences? (She is not happy. She feels sad and wants to cry.) How do you know? (She thinks about her house and wants to go home.)

If you are reading *Good-Bye, 382 Shin Dang Dong* during small group time, then return to pp. 272–279a to guide the reading.

If... students need more scaffolding and practice with the **Main Selection, then...** use the activities on p. DI•72 in the Teacher Resources section on SuccessNet.

OL On-Level

① Build Word Knowledge

Practice Amazing Words

native	homeland	aspect	advantage	sponsor
habit	impolite	manner	conscious	insult

Team Talk **LANGUAGE DEVELOPMENT** Have partners practice building more complex sentences. Display a sentence starter and have students add ral phrases or clauses using the Amazing Words. For example: In my _____ omeland _____. (In my *native homeland* / it is considered *impolite* / if you o not make a *habit* / of greeting your neighbors.) Guide students to add at east three phrases or clauses per sentence.

② Read

"Sing a Song of People"

BEFORE READING Read aloud he genre information about oetry on p. 284. Discuss the dea that poets use language in reative ways to express ideas nd that many poems describe eople and places in a way that helps readers visualize them. Have students review "Sing a Song of People" and set a purpose for reading. Ask:

What looks different about this poem compared to the story in *Good-Bye, 382 Shin Dang Dong?* (The lines are shorter, and many more words repeat.)

Based on the illustrations, what do you think this poem will be about? (a city filled with busy people)

DURING READING Have students read with you. Then ask:

Why does the poet use the word *people* so often? (because the poem is about lots of different people)

What are some of the different things the people do? (travel, talk loudly, say nothing)

AFTER READING Have students share their reactions to "Sing a Song of eople." Then have partners write a short verse to add to the poem. Tell students to model their writing on one of the verses in the poem.

Independent Reading Options

Trade Book Library

Teacher Guides are available on the Leveled Reader Database.

SMALL GROUP TIME

On-Level

Common Core State Standards

Informational Text 1. Ask and answer questions to demonstrate understanding of a text, referring explicitly to the text as the basis for the answers. **Informational Text 6.** Distinguish their own point of view from that of the author of a text. **Writing 5.** With guidance and support from peers and adults, develop and strengthen writing as needed by planning, revising, and editing. **Writing 8.** Recall information from experiences or gather information from print and digital sources; take brief notes on sources and sort evidence into provided categories. **Language 4.** Determine or clarify the meaning of unknown and multiple-meaning words and phrases based on grade 3 reading and content, choosing flexibly from a range of strategies. **Also Informational Text 10., Writing 10., Speaking/ Listening 1., Language 1., 1.a., 6.**

More Reading for Group Time

ON-LEVEL

Reviews
- Sequence
- Monitor and Clarify
- Selection Vocabulary

Use this suggested Leveled Reader or other text at students' instructional level.

eStreet Interactive
www.ReadingStreet.com

Use the Leveled Reader Database for lesson plans and student pages for *Joanie's House Becomes a Home.*

1 Build Word Knowledge
Practice Adverbs

IDENTIFY Choral read the bottom of p. 283 with students and discuss the form and function of adverbs, explaining that adverbs tell where, when, why, and under what conditions something happens. Then have students work independently to reread the free verse poem to find examples of adverbs. Allow time for students to discuss their examples and correct any misunderstandings.

2 Text-Based Comprehension
Read

REREAD "A Day at School in Japan" Have partners reread "A Day at School in Japan."

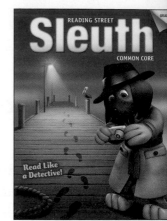

EXTEND UNDERSTANDING Talk together about the kind of handwriting Japanese people use. Ask students if they feel this would be a hard language to learn. Encourage them to support their opinions with convincing reasons.

PERFORMANCE TASK • Prove It! Have students write a letter to a Japanese student that describes a typical school day in the United States. Remind students to use descriptive details so that Japanese students can get a true understanding of a typical day.

COMMUNICATE Have partners share their letters with each other. Encourage students to prompt the letter writer with ways to improve the letter by adding or removing details.

SI Strategic Intervention

1 Build Word Knowledge

Reteach Amazing Words

Repeat the definition of the word. We learned that *advantage* means a benefit. Then use the word in a sentence. One *advantage* of having grandparents from another country is learning two languages.

Team Talk **TALK ABOUT IT** Have partners take turns using the word *advantage* in a sentence. Continue this routine to practice the Amazing Words *native* and *homeland*. Review the concept map with students. Discuss other words they can add to the concept map.

> **Corrective feedback** **If...** students need more practice with the Amazing Words, **then...** use visuals from the Student Edition or online sources to clarify meaning.

2 Text-Based Comprehension

Read

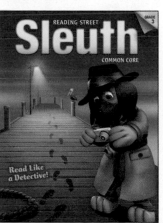

READ "A Day at School in Japan" Have students track the print as you read "A Day at School in Japan" from *Reading Street Sleuth* on pp. 60–61.

ACCESS TEXT Discuss the Sleuth Work section with students and provide support as needed as they work on it.

Gather Evidence Create a Venn diagram with students. Talk together about the evidence found in the article that shows how a school day in Japan compares to a school day in the United States. While completing the Venn diagram, have students make statements that compare the two school days.

Ask Questions Talk together about the questions students would like to ask. Invite students to think about how they might answer these same questions if asked by a Japanese student. Would they answer with a factual answer or an answer that shares an opinion?

Make Your Case Review together the differences between a school day in Japan and one in the United States. Then encourage students to choose a side and work with a partner to cite reasons for their opinions. Have students share their paragraphs with the group, pointing out the most convincing reasons for their opinions.

eSTREET INTERACTIVE
www.ReadingStreet.com

Pearson eText
• Student Edition
• Leveled Reader Database
• *Reading Street Sleuth*

More Reading for Group Time

CONCEPT LITERACY
Practice
Concept Words

BELOW-LEVEL
Reviews
• Sequence
• Monitor and Clarify
• Selection Vocabulary

Use these suggested Leveled Readers or other text at students' instructional level.

eSTREET INTERACTIVE
www.ReadingStreet.com

Use the Leveled Reader Database for lesson plans and student pages for *Our New Home* and *A Child's Life in Korea*.

SMALL GROUP TIME

Common Core State Standards

Literature 1. Ask and answer questions to demonstrate understanding of a text, referring explicitly to the text as the basis for the answers. **Literature 3.** Describe characters in a story (e.g., their traits, motivations, or feelings) and explain how their actions contribute to the sequence of events. **Language 4.** Determine or clarify the meaning of unknown and multiple-meaning words and phrases based on grade 3 reading and content, choosing flexibly from a range of strategies. **Also Speaking/Listening 4., Language 4.a., 6.**

Independent Reading Options

Trade Book Library

eSTREET INTERACTIVE
www.ReadingStreet.com

Teacher Guides are available on the Leveled Reader Database.

SI Strategic Intervention

① Build Word Knowledge
Reteach Selection Vocabulary

DEFINE IT Describe *raindrops* to a friend. Give a definition when necessary. Restate the word in student-friendly terms and clarify meaning with a visual. *Raindrops* means water that falls from the sky in the shape of droplets. Pages 265, 267, and 270 show raindrops.

airport	cellar	curious
delicious	described	farewell
homesick	memories	raindrops

Team Talk **TALK ABOUT IT** Have you ever seen raindrops? Turn and talk to your partner about this. Rephrase students' examples for usage when necessary or to correct misunderstandings. Continue with the remaining words.

Corrective feedback | **If...** students need more practice with selection vocabulary, **then...** use the *Envision It! Pictured Vocabulary Cards*.

② Read

Good-Bye, 382 Shin Dang Dong

If you read *Good-Bye, 382 Shin Dang Dong* during whole group time, then use the instruction below.

ACCESS TEXT Reread the paragraphs on pp. 270–271. Ask students questions to check understanding. Why is Jangmi crying? (She is sad because she is moving away.) What is 382 Shin Dang Dong? (the address of her home in Korea) Why is it hard for Jangmi to picture her new home? (It is so different from her home.) What makes it so different? (It has a fireplace, wooden floors, and wooden doors.)

Have students identify sections they did not understand. Reread them aloud. Clarify the meaning of each section to build understanding.

If you are reading *Good-Bye, 382 Shin Dang Dong* during small group time, then return to pp. 264–271a to guide the reading.

Strategic Intervention

Build Word Knowledge
Develop Vocabulary

REREAD FOR VOCABULARY Reread the second paragraph on p. 275. Let's read this paragraph to find out what *shingled* means. To help students understand the word *shingled,* ask questions related to context, such as: What part of the house is Jangmi describing? How are the rooftops in America different? How does *clay-tiled* help you understand what *shingled* means.

Corrective feedback	**If...** students have difficulty understanding the word *shingled,* **then...** provide them with an illustration of a shingled roof.

2 Read
Good-Bye, 382 Shin Dang Dong

If you read *Good-Bye, 382 Shin Dang Dong* during whole group time, then use the instruction below.

CLOSE READING Read p. 272 and 275. Have students search through the text for descriptive words. As a class, make a list of these words in the order they occur in the story. (*higher, smaller, big, foreign, hard, wide, shingled, clay-tiled, quiet, wooden, cold, heavy, dark, strange, beautiful*)

Now use the descriptive words you listed to tell about the changes Jangmi experiences in this part of the story. (On the plane, Jangmi notices how things appear *smaller,* and the world feels *big.* She notices *foreign* words and faces. She observes that American rooftops are *shingled* instead of *clay-tiled.* She notices that her new house is on a *quiet* street, and inside it has *cold wooden* floors, *heavy wooden* doors, and is *dark* and *strange.*)

If you are reading *Good-Bye, 382 Shin Dang Dong* during small group time, then return to pp. 272–279a to guide the reading.

eSTREET INTERACTIVE
www.ReadingStreet.com

Pearson eText
• Student Edition

SMALL GROUP TIME

If... students need more scaffolding and practice with the **Main Selection, then...** use the activities on p. DI•72 in the Teacher Resources section on SuccessNet.

Strategic Intervention

Common Core State Standards

Literature 1. Ask and answer questions to demonstrate understanding of a text, referring explicitly to the text as the basis for the answers. **Literature 3.** Describe characters in a story (e.g., their traits, motivations, or feelings) and explain how their actions contribute to the sequence of events. **Language 1.a.** Explain the function of nouns, pronouns, verbs, adjectives, and adverbs in general and their functions in particular sentences. **Language 4.** Determine or clarify the meaning of unknown and multiple-meaning words and phrases based on grade 3 reading and content, choosing flexibly from a range of strategies.

① Build Word Knowledge
Review Amazing Words

native	homeland	aspect	advantage	sponsor
habit	impolite	manner	conscious	insult

Team Talk **LANGUAGE DEVELOPMENT** Have partners practice building more complex sentences. Display a sentence starter and have students add oral phrases or clauses using the Amazing Words. Guide students to add at least two phrases or clauses per sentence.

Corrective feedback | **If...** students have difficulty using the Amazing Words orally, **then...** review the meaning of each of the words.

② Read
"Sing a Song of People"

BEFORE READING Read aloud the genre information about poetry on p. 284. Ask students to sing a song that they like and then write the first few lines on the board. Point out how the song's lines are like a poem because of the rhythmic language. Then have students preview the poem, noticing how some words rhyme. Remind them that although some poems rhyme, not all do.

DURING READING Have students perform a choral reading of the poem. If necessary, model reading the first few lines so that students understand the rhythm of the words. What are some of the rhyming words in the poem? (slow and go, bus and us, ground and round)

AFTER READING Have students share their reactions to the poem. Then guide them through the Reading Across Texts and Writing Across Texts activities, prompting if necessary. What country do you think the poet means to describe? What makes you think so? (The poem is set in the United States because the poem is written in English, and the verses describe such common American items as buses, subways, and elevators.)

If... students need more scaffolding and practice with Amazing Words, **then...** use the Routine on pp. xxxvi–xxxvii in the *ELL Handbook*.

SI Strategic Intervention

① Build Word Knowledge

Review Adverbs

IDENTIFY Choral read the bottom of p. 283 with students to review adverbs. Then have students work independently to reread the free verse poem on p. 283 to find examples of adverbs. Allow time for students to discuss their examples and correct any misunderstandings.

② Text-Based Comprehension

Read

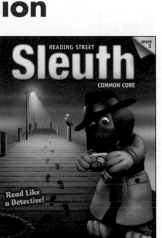

REREAD "A Day at School in Japan" Have partners reread "A Day at School in Japan," with partners alternating paragraphs.

EXTEND UNDERSTANDING Talk together about students' opinions on the advantages and disadvantages of being in school in Japan.

PERFORMANCE TASK • Prove It! Have students write a letter to a Japanese student that describes a typical school day in the United States. Invite students to work with a partner to write their letter.

COMMUNICATE Have partners share their letters with other pairs of students. Encourage students to help the letter writer communicate his or her thoughts with accuracy.

SMALL GROUP TIME

More Reading for Group Time

CONCEPT LITERACY	BELOW-LEVEL
Practice Concept Words	**Reviews** • Sequence • Monitor and Clarify • Selection Vocabulary

Use these suggested Leveled Readers or other text at students' instructional level.

eSTREET INTERACTIVE
www.ReadingStreet.com

Use the Leveled Reader Database for lesson plans and student pages for *Our New Home* and *A Child's Life in Korea.*

A Advanced

Common Core State Standards

Literature 1. Ask and answer questions to demonstrate understanding of a text, referring explicitly to the text as the basis for the answers. **Literature 4.** Determine the meaning of words and phrases as they are used in a text, distinguishing literal from nonliteral language. **Informational Text 6.** Distinguish their own point of view from that of the author of a text. **Writing 7.** Conduct short research projects that build knowledge about a topic. **Language 4.** Determine or clarify the meaning of unknown and multiple-meaning words and phrases based on grade 3 reading and content, choosing flexibly from a range of strategies.

1 Build Word Knowledge
Extend Amazing Words

Team Talk Have partners define *advantage*. Discuss other names for *advantage*. Continue with *native* and *homeland*. Have them find synonyms and antonyms for each word.

2 Text-Based Comprehension
Read

READ "A Day at School in Japan" Have students read "A Day at School in Japan" from *Reading Street Sleuth* on pp. 60–61.

ACCESS TEXT Discuss the Sleuth Work section with students before they work on it. Remind students that they can use these steps with other texts they read.

Gather Evidence Have partners take notes of text evidence. Invite students to share the evidence they found in the article. If time permits, have students write a short paragraph that states two similaritie and two differences.

Ask Questions Have students share the questions they would like to ask a Japanese student. Encourage discussion about how students might find a way to get their questions answered.

Make Your Case Have students share their paragraphs with the group, pointing out the most convincing reasons for their opinions.

3 Inquiry: Extend Concepts

IDENTIFY QUESTIONS Have students look at a map or a globe and randomly choose a country far from their homes. Have students think of a list of ten questions they would ask about this place if they were going to move there. Then have them research to find the answers to their questions and create a poster or online presentation about it, complete with illustrations and maps. Throughout the week, they will gather information. On Day 5, they will present what they have learned.

If... students need more scaffolding and practice with **Vocabulary, then...** use the activities on pp. DI•67–DI•68 in the Teacher Resources section on SuccessNet.

Advanced

① Build Word Knowledge

Extend Selection Vocabulary

Team Talk Have partners use the selection vocabulary in sentences to internalize their meanings. Have students use as many of the words as they can while making sure the sentence is grammatically correct. (Possible response: The *memories* of saying *farewell* to my family at the *airport* made me *homesick*.) Continue with additional selection vocabulary words.

airport	cellar	curious
delicious	described	farewell
homesick	memories	raindrops

② Read

Good-Bye, 382 Shin Dang Dong

If you read *Good-Bye, 382 Shin Dang Dong* during whole group time, then use the instruction below.

ACCESS TEXT Reread the paragraphs on pp. 270–271. Discuss action words and phrases that describe or reveal emotions. (*held back her tears, tears streaked, I shrugged, enthusiastic clap, closed with disappointment*)

Ask: How do these words and phrases help you understand the story? (It shows me how Jangmi feels and helps me visualize her as she leaves Korea. I understand her sadness and disappointment at having to leave her home.)

If you are reading *Good-Bye, 382 Shin Dang Dong* during small group time, then return to pp. 264–271a to guide the reading.

③ Inquiry: Extend Concepts

INVESTIGATE Encourage students to use materials at their independent reading levels or student-friendly search engines to identify relevant and credible sites to gather information about moving to a different country. Have students consider how they will present their information.

SMALL GROUP TIME

More Reading for Group Time

ADVANCED

Reviews
• Sequence
• Monitor and Clarify

Use this suggested Leveled Reader or other text at students' instructional level.

Use the Leveled Reader Database for lesson plans and student pages for *It's a World of Time Zones.*

Advanced

Ⓒ Common Core State Standards

Literature 1. Ask and answer questions to demonstrate understanding of a text, referring explicitly to the text as the basis for the answers. **Literature 3.** Describe characters in a story (e.g., their traits, motivations, or feelings) and explain how their actions contribute to the sequence of events. **Writing 7.** Conduct short research projects that build knowledge about a topic. **Language 4.** Determine or clarify the meaning of unknown and multiple-meaning words and phrases based on grade 3 reading and content, choosing flexibly from a range of strategies. **Also Writing 8., Language 4.a.**

Independent Reading Options

Trade Book Library

eStreet Interactive
www.ReadingStreet.com

Teacher Guides are available on the Leveled Reader Database.

If... students need more scaffolding and practice with the **Main Selection, then...** use the activities on p. DI•72 in the Teacher Resources section on SuccessNet.

① Build Word Knowledge

Develop Vocabulary

REREAD FOR VOCABULARY Reread the second paragraph on p. 275. Let's read this paragraph to find out what *shingled* means. Discuss meaning and context with students.

② Read

Good-Bye, 382 Shin Dang Dong

If you read *Good-Bye, 382 Shin Dang Dong* during whole group time, then use the instruction below.

CLOSE READING Read pp. 272 and 275. Have students create a T-chart with the heads **Action Words** and **Adjectives.** Have students search the text to find action words that reveal feelings and to write them in the chart in the order they occur. Then find adjectives that describe or suggest feelings.

Action Words	Adjectives
felt	homesick
cried	cold
sighed	heavy
insisted	dark
	strange
	beautiful

Ask: What does the author's choice of words tell you about how Jangmi feels as she travels to her new American home? **(She is sad and homesick and does not like her new home.)** Why does the author use words such as *cold, heavy, dark,* and *strange* to describe Jangmi's new home? **(The author is trying to show how strongly Jangmi feels about her new home.)**

If you are reading *Good-Bye, 382 Shin Dang Dong* during small group time, then return to pp. 272–279a to guide the reading.

③ Inquiry: Extend Concepts

INVESTIGATE Provide time for students to investigate their topics in books or online. If necessary, help them locate information that is focused on their topics.

Advanced

① Build Word Knowledge

Extend Amazing Words and Selection Vocabulary

native	homeland	aspect	insult
advantage	sponsor	habit	
impolite	manner	conscious	

airport	cellar	curious
delicious	described	farewell
homesick	memories	raindrops

Team Talk Have students practice building more complex sentences. Display a sentence starter and have students add oral phrases or clauses using the Amazing Words and the selection vocabulary.

② Read

"Sing a Song of People"

BEFORE READING Read aloud the panel information on poetry on p. 284. Then have students use the text features to set a purpose for reading. Finally, have students read "Sing a Song of People" on their own.

DURING READING Point out that the poet sometimes uses unconventional grammar to express her ideas. Where in the poem can you find a line that does not follow strict grammar rules? Why do you think the poet wrote it that way? ("People talking loud" is not standard; *loudly* would be more correct. But *loudly* would not fit the rhythm and would not rhyme with *crowd*.)

AFTER READING Have students discuss Reading Across Texts. Then have them complete the Writing Across Texts activity independently.

③ Inquiry: Extend Concepts

ORGANIZE INFORMATION Provide time for students to organize their information into a format that will effectively communicate their findings to their audience. Provide any necessary materials or computer time.

eSTREET INTERACTIVE
www.ReadingStreet.com

Pearson eText
• Student Edition

SMALL GROUP TIME

Independent Reading Options

Trade Book Library

eSTREET INTERACTIVE
www.ReadingStreet.com

Teacher Guides are available on the Leveled Reader Database.

Common Core State Standards

Writing 5. With guidance and support from peers and adults, develop and strengthen writing as needed by planning, revising, and editing. **Speaking/Listening 1.b.** Follow agreed-upon rules for discussions (e.g., gaining the floor in respectful ways, listening to others with care, speaking one at a time about the topics and texts under discussion). **Speaking/Listening 4.** Report on a topic or text, tell a story, or recount an experience with appropriate facts and relevant, descriptive details, speaking clearly at an understandable pace. **Also Writing 10., Language 1., 1.a.**

More Reading for Group Time

ADVANCED

Reviews
• Sequence
• Monitor and Clarify

Use this suggested Leveled Reader or other text at students' instructional level.

eSTREET INTERACTIVE
www.ReadingStreet.com

Use the Leveled Reader Database for lesson plans and student pages for *It's a World of Time Zones.*

SG•48 Cultures • Unit 5 • Week 3

A Advanced

① Build Word Knowledge
Extend Adverbs

IDENTIFY AND EXTEND Choral read the bottom of p. 283 with students and have them explain the form and function of adverbs, encouraging them to offer examples that go beyond *-ly* words, such as *very* and *quite*. Have students work independently to reread the free verse poem to find examples of adverbs. Then encourage students to write their own free verse poems using a mix of adverbs. Allow time for students to discuss their work and correct any misunderstandings.

② Text-Based Comprehension
Read

REREAD "A Day at School in Japan" Have partners reread the selection. Have partners discuss the length of the school year in Japan. Invite discussion about how a longer school year might be helpful to students in the United States.

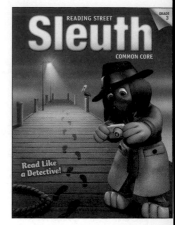

EXTEND UNDERSTANDING Talk together about the kind of chores Japanese students are asked to do in school. How do these compare to some of the ways students help out in their own classrooms in the United States?

PERFORMANCE TASK • Prove It! Have students write a letter to a Japanese student that describes a typical school day in the United States. Encourage students to share details of a typical school day as well as special events that take place at school, such as assemblies and field trips.

COMMUNICATE Have students share their letters with a small group. Encourage discussion about the details students included. Were they accurate details? What details seemed to be missing?

③ Inquiry: Extend Concepts

COMMUNICATE Have students share their inquiry projects on a faraway country with the rest of the class. Provide the following tips for presenting.
• Match your tone of voice and your pitch to your content.
• Speak at an appropriate rate.
• Make eye contact when answering questions and pointing to your visuals.

Indiana Common Core Edition

This Week's Target Skills and Strategies

Target Skills and Strategies	Common Core State Standards for English Language Arts	Indiana Academic Standards for English Language Arts
Phonics and Spelling 🔊 Skill: Vowel Patterns *ei, eigh*	**CCSS Foundational Skills 3.** Know and apply grade-level phonics and word analysis skills in decoding words. **(Also CCSS Language 2.f.)**	**IN 3.1** Students understand the basic features of words. They select letter patterns and know how to translate them into spoken language using phonics, syllables, word parts, and context. They apply this knowledge to achieve fluent oral and silent reading.
Text-Based Comprehension 🔊 Skill: Draw Conclusions	**CCSS Informational Text 1.** Ask and answer questions to demonstrate understanding of a text, referring explicitly to the text as the basis for the answers.	**IN 3.2.2** Ask questions and support answers by connecting prior knowledge with literal information from the text. **(Also IN 3.2.3)**
🔊 Strategy: Summarize	**CCSS Informational Text 2.** Determine the main idea of a text; recount the key details and explain how they support the main idea.	**IN 3.2.5** Distinguish the main idea and supporting details in expository (informational) text.
Vocabulary 🔊 Skill: Unfamiliar Words Strategy: Context Clues	**CCSS Language 4.** Determine or clarify the meaning of unknown and multiple-meaning words and phrases based on *grade 3 reading and content,* choosing flexibly from a range of strategies. **(Also CCSS Language 4.a., CCSS Language 5.)**	**IN 3.1.6** Use sentence and word context to find the meaning of unknown words.
Fluency Skill: Accuracy	**CCSS Foundational Skills 4.** Read with sufficient accuracy and fluency to support comprehension. **(Also CCSS Foundational Skills 4.b.)**	**IN 3.1.3** Read aloud grade-level-appropriate literary and informational texts fluently and accurately and with appropriate timing, change in voice, and expression.
Listening and Speaking Radio Advertisement	**CCSS Speaking/Listening 4.** Report on a topic or text, tell a story, or recount an experience with appropriate facts and relevant, descriptive details, speaking clearly at an understandable pace.	The Indiana Academic Standards for Listening and Speaking are not currently assessed on ISTEP+ assessments. Educators and students should implement the Common Core Standards for Speaking and Listening as soon as possible.
Six-Trait Writing Trait of the Week: Focus/Ideas	**CCSS Writing 2.a.** Introduce a topic and group related information together; include illustrations when useful to aiding comprehension. **(Also CCSS Writing 2.b.)**	**IN 3.5.2** Write descriptive pieces about people, places, things, or experiences. **(Also IN 3.5.7)**
Writing Invitation	**CCSS Writing 2.** Write informative/explanatory texts to examine a topic and convey ideas and information clearly. **(Also CCSS Writing 2.a., CCSS Writing 2.b.)**	**IN 3.5.2** Write descriptive pieces about people, places, things, or experiences. **(Also IN 3.5.7)**
Conventions Skill: Comparative and Superlative Adverbs	**CCSS Language 1.g.** Form and use comparative and superlative adjectives and adverbs, and choose between them depending on what is to be modified.	**IN 3.6** Students write using Standard English conventions appropriate to this grade level.

This Week's Cross-Curricular Standards and Resources

Cross-Curricular Indiana Academic Standards for Social Studies

Social Studies
IN 3.3.9 Identify factors that make the region unique, including cultural diversity, industry, the arts and architecture.
IN 3.4.2 Give examples of goods and services provided by local business and industry.

Reading Street Sleuth

Pizza, Pizza Everywhere
pp. 62–63

Follow the path to close reading using the Super Sleuth tips:

• Gather Evidence

• Ask Questions

• Make Your Case

• Prove it!

More Reading in Science and Social Studies

Concept Literacy

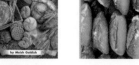
Below Level

On Level

Advanced

ELL

ELD

ISBN-13: 978-0-328-73391-0   ISBN-10: 0-328-73391-1

Your 90-Minute Reading Block

	Whole Group	**Formative Assessment** How do I make my small groups flexible?	**Small Group** (OL) On Level (SI) Strategic Intervention (A) Advanced What are my other students reading and learning every day in Small Groups?	**Daily Independent Options** What do my other students do when I lead Small Groups?
DAY 1	**Content Knowledge** Build Oral Language/Vocabulary **Phonics/Word Analysis** **Read Decodable Reader** **Text-Based Comprehension** **Selection Vocabulary** **Research and Inquiry** Step 1–Identify and Focus Topic **Spelling Pretest** Connect to Phonics/Word Analysis	**Monitor Progress** Check Oral Vocabulary	Differentiate Vocabulary **Build Word Knowledge** (OL) Practice Amazing Words (SI) Reteach Amazing Words (A) Extend Amazing Words (OL)(SI)(A) **Text-Based Comprehension** **Read** *Reading Street Sleuth,* pp. 62–63 or Leveled Readers (A) Inquiry Project (ELL) Access Vocabulary	★ **Independent Reading** © Suggestions for this week's independent reading: • Informational text on last week's topic: the difficulty of adapting to a new culture • Nonfiction selections about living in a new culture • An information-rich Web site about moving to a new culture
DAY 2	**Content Knowledge** Build Oral Language/Vocabulary **Phonics/Word Analysis** **Vocabulary Skill** **Text-Based Comprehension** Read Main Selection, using Access Text Notes **Research and Inquiry** Step 2–Navigate/Search **Spelling** Connect to Phonics/Word Analysis	**Monitor Progress** Formative Assessment: Check Word Reading	Differentiate Comprehension **Build Word Knowledge** (OL) Practice Selection Vocabulary (SI) Reteach Selection Vocabulary (A) Extend Selection Vocabulary (OL)(SI)(A) **Access Text** Read *Jalapeño Bagels* (A) Inquiry Project (ELL) Access Comprehension Skill	**Book Talk** Foster critical reading and discussion skills through independent and close reading. Students should focus on discussing one or more of the following: • Key Ideas and Details • Craft and Structure • Integration of Ideas
DAY 3	**Content Knowledge** Build Oral Language/Vocabulary **Phonics/Word Analysis** **Read Decodable Passage** **Text-Based Comprehension** Read Main Selection, using Close Reading Notes **Fluency** **Research and Inquiry** Step 3–Analyze Information **Spelling** Connect to Phonics/Word Analysis	**Monitor Progress** Check Retelling	**Differentiate Close Reading** (OL)(SI) **Reread to Develop Vocabulary** (A) **Reread to Extend Vocabulary** (OL)(SI)(A) **Close Reading** Read *Jalapeño Bagels* (A) Inquiry Project (ELL) Access Main Selection	**Pearson eText** • Student Edition • Decodable Readers • Leveled Readers **Trade Book Library** **Materials from School or Classroom Library**
DAY 4	**Content Knowledge** Build Oral Language/Vocabulary **Phonics/Word Analysis** **Read Decodable Passage** **Read Content Area Paired Selection with Genre Focus** **Let's Learn It!** Vocabulary/Fluency/Media Literacy **Research and Inquiry** Step 4–Synthesize **Spelling** Connect to Phonics/Word Analysis	**Monitor Progress** Check Fluency	Differentiate Vocabulary **Build Word Knowledge** (OL) Develop Language Using Amazing Words (SI) Review/Discuss Amazing Words (A) Extend Amazing Words and Selection Vocabulary (OL)(SI)(A) **Text-Based Comprehension** Read "Foods of Mexico: A Delicious Blend" (A) Inquiry Project (ELL) Access Amazing Words	**Independent Stations** Practice Last Week's Skills ★ Focus on these activities when time is limited. **Word Wise** ★ **Word Work** **Read for Meaning** ★ **Let's Write!** **Words to Know** **Get Fluent**
DAY 5	**Content Knowledge** Build Oral Language/Vocabulary **Text-Based Comprehension** **Vocabulary Skill** **Phonics/Word Analysis** **Assessment** Fluency, Comprehension **Research and Inquiry** Step 5–Communicate **Spelling Test** Connect to Phonics/Word Analysis	**Monitor Progress** Formative Assessment: Check Oral Vocabulary **Monitor Progress** Fluency; Comprehension	Differentiate Reteaching (OL) **Practice Comparative and Superlative Adverbs** (SI) **Review Comparative and Superlative Adverbs** (A) **Extend Comparative and Superlative Adverbs** (OL)(SI)(A) **Text-Based Comprehension** **Reread** *Reading Street Sleuth,* pp. 62–63 or Leveled Readers (A) Inquiry Project (ELL) Access Conventions and Writing	

Assessment Resources

Common Core
Weekly Tests, pp. 139–144

Common Core Fresh Reads for Fluency
and Comprehension, pp. 139–144

Common Core
Unit 5 Benchmark Test

Common Core Success Tracker,
ExamView, and Online Lesson Planner

Teaching the Common Core State Standards This Week

The Common Core State Standards for English Language Arts are divided into strands for **Reading** (including **Foundational Skills**), **Writing**, **Speaking and Listening**, and **Language**. The chart below shows some of the content you will teach this week, strand by strand. Turn to this week's 5-Day Planner on pages 288d–288e to see how this content is taught each day.

Reading Strand

- **Phonics/Word Analysis:** Vowel Patterns *ei*, *eigh*
- **Text-Based Comprehension:** Draw Conclusions; Summarize
- **Fluency:** Accuracy

- **Literary Terms:** Dialogue and Narration
- **Genre:** Main Selection: Realistic Fiction; Paired Selection: Expository Text

Writing Strand

- **Writing Mini-Lesson:** Invitation
- **Trait:** Focus/Ideas
- **Look Back and Write:** Text Evidence

Common Core State Standards for English Language Arts

Speaking and Listening Strand

- **Content Knowledge:** Build Oral Language
- **Media Literacy:** Radio Advertisement
- **Research and Inquiry**

Language Strand

- **Oral Vocabulary: Amazing Words** *nutrition, calorie, flavor, spice, nutmeg, grumble, allergic, wholesome, grate, agent*
- **Vocabulary:** Unfamiliar Words; Context Clues
- **Selection Vocabulary:** *bakery, ingredients, batch, mixture, dough, braided, boils*

- **Academic Vocabulary:** *comparative adverbs, superlative adverbs, invitation, narration, realistic fiction, advertisement*
- **Conventions:** Comparative and Superlative Adverbs
- **Spelling:** Vowel Patterns *ei, eigh*

Text-Based Comprehension

Text Complexity Measures

Use the rubric to familiarize yourself with the text complexity of *Jalapeño Bagels*.

Qualitative   Quantitative

Reader and Task

Bridge to Complex Knowledge

Quantitative Measures	Lexile	600L
	Average Sentence Length	9.69
	Word Frequency	3.44

Qualitative Measures	**Levels of Meaning**	understand how setting contributes to the story and how the jalapeño bagels are used as symbols
	Structure	events happen chronologically; recipe format
	Language Conventionality and Clarity	natural, conversational language
	Theme and Knowledge Demands	references to other cultural experiences

Reader and Task Suggestions	**FORMATIVE ASSESSMENT** Based on assessment results, use the **Reader and Task Suggestions** in Access Main Selection to scaffold the selection or support independence for students as they read *Jalapeño Bagels*.

READER AND TASK SUGGESTIONS	
Preparing to Read the Text	**Leveled Tasks**
• Review using context clues to understand unfamiliar words. • Discuss how setting contributes to a story. • Remind students that when they encounter unfamiliar words, they should adjust their reading rate.	• **Structure** If students have difficulty following the chronology of the selection, have them identify the bakery items one-by-one, as Pablo's parents create them. • **Levels of Meaning • Analysis** If students don't understand why Pablo decides to bring jalapeño bagels to school for International Day, have them identify the cultural backgrounds of Pablo's parents. Then have them point out which cultural traditions use jalapeño peppers in their cooking and which prepare bagels.

Recommended Placement Generally the qualitative and quantitative measures suggest this text should be placed in the Grade 2–3 text complexity band, which is where both the Common Core State Standards and *Scott Foresman Reading Street* have placed it. Students should be encouraged to use context clues to access any unfamiliar words in the selection. Provide scaffolded support as needed.

Focus on Common Core State Standards ©

Main Selection, pp. 296–309

Paired Selection, pp. 314–317

Text-Based Comprehension

Draw Conclusions
CCSS Informational Text 1.

Summarize
CCSS Informational Text 2.

Fluency

Accuracy
CCSS Foundational Skills 4.,
CCSS Foundational Skills 4.b.

Writing and Conventions

Trait: Focus/Ideas
CCSS Writing 2.a., CCSS Writing 2.b.

Writing Mini-Lesson: Invitation
CCSS Writing 2., CCSS Writing 2.a.,
CCSS Writing 2.b.

Conventions: Comparative and
Superlative Adverbs
CCSS Language 1.g.

Oral Vocabulary

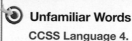

Amazing Words

nutrition	grumble
calorie	allergic
flavor	wholesome
spice	grate
nutmeg	agent

CCSS Language 6.

Selection Vocabulary

Unfamiliar Words
CCSS Language 4.

Context Clues
CCSS Language 4.a.,
CCSS Language 5.

bakery	braided	ingredients
batch	dough	mixture
boils		

Phonics and Spelling

Vowel Patterns *ei, eigh*
CCSS Foundational Skills 3.,
CCSS Language 2.f.

ceiling	protein
neighbor	freight
either	receive
eighteen	weigh
height	deceive
neither	sleigh
weight	conceited
leisure	

Challenge Words

receipt	deceitful
eightieth	featherweight
neighborly	

Media Literacy

Radio Advertisement
CCSS Speaking/Listening 4.

Jalapeño Bagels **288a**

Preview Your Week

How can different cultures contribute to the foods we eat?

Main Selection, pp. 296–309

Genre: Realistic Fiction

 **Vocabulary:** Unfamiliar Words

Text-Based Comprehension: Draw Conclusions

Paired Selection, pp. 314–317

Social Studies in Reading

Genre: Expository Text

Build Content Knowledge Zoom in on

Time for SOCIAL STUDIES

KNOWLEDGE GOALS

Students will understand that food

- comes from different cultures
- is shared
- can be a mix from different cultures

THIS WEEK'S CONCEPT MAP

Develop a concept-related graphic organizer like the one below over the course of this week.

```
How different
cultures contribute
to the foods we eat
```
```
Flavors    Nutrition    Traditions
```

BUILD ORAL VOCABULARY

This week, students will acquire the following academic vocabulary/domain-specific words.

Amazing Words

nutrition	nutmeg	wholesome
calorie	grumble	grate
flavor	allergic	agent
spice		

OPTIONAL CONCEPT-BASED READING Use the Digital Path to access readers offering different levels of text complexity.

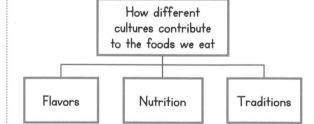      

| Concept Literacy | Below-Level | On-Level | Advanced | ELL | ELD |

This Week's Digital Resources

eStreet Interactive
www.ReadingStreet.com

Get Ready to Read

 Concept Talk Video Use this video on the Digital Path to build momentum and introduce the weekly concept of cultures.

 Pearson eText Read the eText of the Student Edition pages on Pearson SuccessNet for comprehension and fluency support.

 Envision It! Animations Use this colorful animation on the Digital Path to explain the target comprehension skill, Draw Conclusions.

Read and Comprehend

 Journal Use the Word Bank on the Digital Path to have students write sentences using this week's selection vocabulary words.

 Background Building Audio CD This audio CD provides essential background information about cultures to help students read and comprehend the weekly texts.

 Pearson eText Read the eText of the main selection, *Jalapeño Bagels,* and the paired selection, "Foods of Mexico: A Delicious Blend," with audio support on Pearson SuccessNet.

 Vocabulary Activities A variety of interactive vocabulary activities on the Digital Path help students practice selection vocabulary and concept-related words.

 Story Sort Use the Story Sort Activity on the Digital Path after reading *Jalapeño Bagels* to involve students in summarizing.

Language Arts

 Grammar Jammer Select a fun-filled animation on the Digital Path to provide an engaging grammar lesson that will capture students' attention.

 Pearson eText Find the Student Edition eText of the Let's Write It! and Let's Learn It! pages with audio support on Pearson SuccessNet.

Additional Resources

 Teacher Resources DVD-ROM Use the following resources on the TR DVD or on Pearson SuccessNet throughout the week:

- Amazing Word Cards
- Reader's and Writer's Notebook
- Writing Transparencies
- Daily Fix-It Transparencies
- Scoring Rubrics
- Grammar Transparencies
- ELL Support
- Let's Practice It!
- Graphic Organizers
- Vocabulary Cards

This Week's Skills

Phonics/Word Analysis
⦿ Vowel Patterns *ei, eigh*

Comprehension
⦿ **Skill:** Draw Conclusions
⦿ **Strategy:** Summarize

Language
⦿ **Vocabulary:** Unfamiliar Words
Conventions: Comparative and Superlative Adverbs

Fluency
Accuracy

Writing
Invitation

5-Day Planner

DAY 1

Get Ready to Read

Content Knowledge 288j
Oral Vocabulary: *nutrition, calorie, flavor*

> **Monitor Progress**
> Check Oral Vocabulary

Phonics/Word Analysis 290a
⦿ Vowel Patterns *ei, eigh*
READ Decodable Reader 24A
Reread for Fluency

Read and Comprehend

Text-Based Comprehension 292a
⦿ Draw Conclusions
⦿ Summarize

Fluency 292–293
Accuracy

Selection Vocabulary 293a
bakery, batch, boils, braided, dough, ingredients, mixture

Language Arts

Research and Inquiry 293b
Identify and Focus Topic

Spelling 293c
Vowel Patterns *ei, eigh*, Pretest

Conventions 293d
Comparative and Superlative Adverbs

Handwriting 293d
Cursive Letters *N, M, U*

Writing 293e–293f
Invitation

DAY 2

Get Ready to Read

Content Knowledge 294a
Oral Vocabulary: *spice, nutmeg*

Phonics/Word Analysis 294c
Vowel Patterns *ei, eigh*

> **Monitor Progress**
> Check Word Reading

Literary Terms 294d
Dialogue and Narration

Read and Comprehend

Vocabulary Skill 294e
⦿ Unfamiliar Words

Fluency 294–295
Accuracy

Text-Based Comprehension 296–297
READ *Jalapeño Bagels*—1st Read

Language Arts

Research and Inquiry 303b
Navigate/Search

Conventions 303c
Comparative and Superlative Adverbs

Spelling 303c
Vowel Patterns *ei, eigh*

Writing 303d
Invitation

DAY 3

Get Ready to Read

Content Knowledge 304a
Oral Vocabulary: *grumble, allergic*

Word Analysis 304c
Vowel Patterns *ei, eigh*
Fluent Word Reading
DECODE AND READ
Decodable Practice Passage 24B

Read and Comprehend

Text-Based Comprehension 304e
Check Understanding
READ *Jalapeño Bagels*—2nd Read
Monitor Progress
Check Retelling

Fluency 311b
Accuracy

Language Arts

Research and Study Skills 311c
Outlining

Research and Inquiry 311d
Analyze Information

Conventions 311e
Comparative and Superlative Adverbs

Spelling 311e
Vowel Patterns *ei, eigh*

Writing 312–313
Invitation

DAY 4

Get Ready to Read

Content Knowledge 314a
Oral Vocabulary: *wholesome, grate, agent*

Phonics/Word Analysis 314c
Review Vowel Patterns for /ō/
Fluent Word Reading
DECODE AND READ
Decodable Practice Passage 24C

Read and Comprehend

Genre 314g
Expository Text
READ "Foods of Mexico: A Delicious Blend"—Paired Selection

Fluency 318–319
Accuracy
Monitor Progress Check Fluency

Vocabulary Skill 319a
Unfamiliar Words

Media Literacy 319a
Radio Advertisement

Language Arts

Research and Inquiry 319b
Synthesize

Conventions 319c
Comparative and Superlative Adverbs

Spelling 319c
Vowel Patterns *ei, eigh*

Writing 319d
Invitation

DAY 5

Get Ready to Read

Content Knowledge 319f
Review Oral Vocabulary
Monitor Progress
Check Oral Vocabulary

Read and Comprehend

Text-Based Comprehension 319h
Review Draw Conclusions

Vocabulary Skill 319h
Review Unfamiliar Words

Phonics/Word Analysis 319i
Review Vowel Patterns *ei, eigh*

Literary Terms 319i
Review Dialogue and Narration

Assessment 319j, 319l
Monitor Progress
Fluency; Draw Conclusions

Language Arts

Research and Inquiry 319n
Communicate

Spelling 319o
Vowel Patterns *ei, eigh*, Test

Conventions 319o
Comparative and Superlative Adverbs

Writing 319p–319q
Invitation

Wrap Up Your Week! 319q

Access for All

What do I do in group time?
It's as easy as 1-2-3!

① TEACHER-LED SMALL GROUPS ➡ **②** INDEPENDENT PRACTICE STATIONS ➡ **③** INDEPENDENT READING

Small Group Time

Bridge to Common Core

SKILL DEVELOPMENT
- Draw Conclusions
- Summarize
- Unfamiliar Words

DEEP UNDERSTANDING
This Week's Knowledge Goals
Students will understand that food
- comes from different cultures
- is shared
- can be a mix from different cultures

① Small Group Lesson Plan

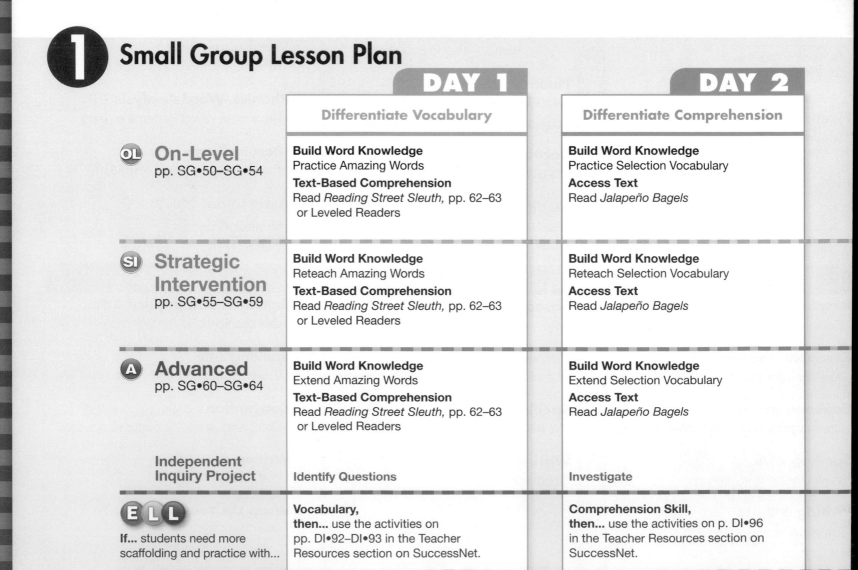

	DAY 1 Differentiate Vocabulary	DAY 2 Differentiate Comprehension
OL On-Level pp. SG•50–SG•54	**Build Word Knowledge** Practice Amazing Words **Text-Based Comprehension** Read *Reading Street Sleuth*, pp. 62–63 or Leveled Readers	**Build Word Knowledge** Practice Selection Vocabulary **Access Text** Read *Jalapeño Bagels*
SI Strategic Intervention pp. SG•55–SG•59	**Build Word Knowledge** Reteach Amazing Words **Text-Based Comprehension** Read *Reading Street Sleuth*, pp. 62–63 or Leveled Readers	**Build Word Knowledge** Reteach Selection Vocabulary **Access Text** Read *Jalapeño Bagels*
A Advanced pp. SG•60–SG•64	**Build Word Knowledge** Extend Amazing Words **Text-Based Comprehension** Read *Reading Street Sleuth*, pp. 62–63 or Leveled Readers	**Build Word Knowledge** Extend Selection Vocabulary **Access Text** Read *Jalapeño Bagels*
Independent Inquiry Project	Identify Questions	Investigate
ELL If... students need more scaffolding and practice with...	**Vocabulary,** then... use the activities on pp. DI•92–DI•93 in the Teacher Resources section on SuccessNet.	**Comprehension Skill,** then... use the activities on p. DI•96 in the Teacher Resources section on SuccessNet.

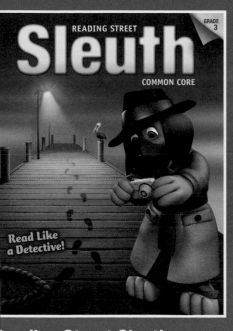

Reading Street Sleuth

- Provides access to grade-level text for all students
- Focuses on finding clues in text through close reading
- Builds capacity for complex text

Build Text-Based Comprehension

Jalapeño Bagels

Optional Leveled Readers

Concept Literacy	Below-Level	On-Level	Advanced	ELL	ELD

DAY 3	**DAY 4**	**DAY 5**
Differentiate Close Reading	**Differentiate Vocabulary**	**Differentiate Reteaching**
Reread to Develop Vocabulary **Close Reading** Read *Jalapeño Bagels*	**Build Word Knowledge** Develop Language Using Amazing Words **Text-Based Comprehension** Read "Foods of Mexico: A Delicious Blend"	**Practice Comparative and Superlative Adverbs** **Text-Based Comprehension** Reread *Reading Street Sleuth*, pp. 62–63 or Leveled Readers
Reread to Develop Vocabulary **Close Reading** Read *Jalapeño Bagels*	**Build Word Knowledge** Review/Discuss Amazing Words **Text-Based Comprehension** Read "Foods of Mexico: A Delicious Blend"	**Review Comparative and Superlative Adverbs** **Text-Based Comprehension** Reread *Reading Street Sleuth*, pp. 62–63 or Leveled Readers
Reread to Extend Vocabulary **Close Reading** Read *Jalapeño Bagels*	**Build Word Knowledge** Extend Amazing Words and Selection Vocabulary **Text-Based Comprehension** Read "Foods of Mexico: A Delicious Blend"	**Extend Comparative and Superlative Adverbs** **Text-Based Comprehension** Reread *Reading Street Sleuth*, pp. 62–63 or Leveled Readers
Investigate	**Organize**	**Communicate**
Main Selection, **then...** use the activities on p. DI•97 in the Teacher Resources section on SuccessNet.	**Amazing Words,** **then...** use the Routine on pp. xxxvi–xxxvii in the *ELL Handbook.*	**Conventions and Writing,** **then...** use the activities on pp. DI•99–DI•100 in the Teacher Resources section on SuccessNet.

2 Independent Stations
Practice Last Week's Skills

 Focus on these activities when time is limited.

WORD WISE

Spell and use words in sentences.

OBJECTIVES

• Spell words with vowel patterns *a, au, aw, al, augh, ough.*

MATERIALS

• *Word Wise* Flip Chart Activity 24, teacher-made word cards, paper and pencils

 Letter Tile Drag and Drop

● Students choose and write five words, underline the vowel pattern, and add other words with the vowel patterns to their lists.

▲ Students choose and write seven words, write sentences using the words, and add other words with the vowel patterns to their lists.

■ Students choose and write nine words, use them in sentences, and add other words with the vowel patterns to their lists.

WORD WORK

Identify and pronounce words.

OBJECTIVES

• Identify and pronounce words with vowel patterns *a, au, aw, al, augh, ough.*

MATERIALS

• *Word Work* Flip Chart Activity 24, teacher-made word cards, paper and pencils

 Letter Tile Drag and Drop

● Students say eight words, identify rhymes, and write a four-line rhyming poem with the words.

▲ Students say ten words, identify rhymes, and write a four- or eight-line rhyming poem with the words.

■ Students say twelve words, identify rhymes, and write an eight-line rhyming poem with the words.

LET'S WRITE!

Write in a genre or style.

OBJECTIVES

• Write free-verse poetry.

MATERIALS

• *Let's Write!* Flip Chart Activity 24, paper and pencils

 Grammar Jammer

● Students write a free-verse poem about their first time in a new place, using expressive words.

▲ Students write a free-verse poem about their first time in a new place, using expressive words and imaginative details.

■ Students write a free-verse poem about their experiences in a new situation, using figurative language and imaginative details.

WORDS TO KNOW

Determine word meanings.

OBJECTIVES

• Identify the meanings of compound words.

MATERIALS

• *Words to Know* Flip Chart Activity 24, teacher-made word cards, paper and pencils

 Vocabulary Activities

● Students choose and write five compound words, circle the words that form the compounds, define the words, and write sentences using the words.

▲ Students choose and write seven compound words, circle the words that form the compounds, define the words, and write sentences using the words.

■ Students choose and write ten compound words, circle the words that form the compounds, define the words, and write sentences using the words.

READ FOR MEANING

Use text-based comprehension tools.

OBJECTIVES

• Identify a sequence of events.

MATERIALS

• *Read for Meaning* Flip Chart Activity 24, Leveled Readers, paper and pencils

 Pearson eText
  • Leveled eReaders

 Envision It! Animations

● Students choose a book and write three sentences that tell the story's order of events, using the words *first, next,* and *finally.*

▲ Students choose a book and write four sentences that tell the story's order of events.

■ Students choose a leveled reader and write a paragraph that tells the order of events.

GET FLUENT

Practice fluent reading.

OBJECTIVES

• Read aloud with appropriate expression and attention to punctuation cues.

MATERIALS

• *Get Fluent* Flip Chart Activity 24, Leveled Readers

 Pearson eText
  • Leveled eReaders

● Partners read from a Concept Literacy or Below-Level Reader, practicing correct expression using punctuation cues and providing feedback.

▲ Partners read from an On-Level Reader, practicing correct expression using pronunciation cues and providing feedback.

■ Partners read from an Advanced Reader, practicing correct expression using punctuation cues and providing feedback.

Manage the Stations

Use these management tools to set up and organize your Practice Stations:

Practice Station Flip Charts

Classroom Management Handbook for Differentiated Instruction Practice Stations, p. 42

3 Independent Reading ©

Students should select appropriately complex texts to read and write about independently every day before, during, and after school.

Suggestions for this week's independent reading:
  • Informational text on last week's topic: the difficulty of adapting to a new culture
  • Nonfiction selections about living in a new culture
  • An information-rich Web site about moving to a new culture

BOOK TALK Have partners discuss their independent reading. Tell them to refer to their Reading Logs and paraphrase what each selection was about. Then have students discuss one or more of the following:

Key Ideas and Details
  • Identify the main idea. What key details support it?
  • Think about the details in the text. What conclusions can you draw?

Craft and Structure
  • How is the information in the text organized?
  • Where does the main idea appear in each paragraph?

Integration of Ideas
  • Compare and contrast this text to others you have read.
  • Explain why you think the author has or has not supported his or her ideas well.

 Pearson eText
  • Student Edition
  • Decodable Readers
  • Leveled Readers

 Trade Book Library

 School or Classroom Library

Materials

- Student Edition
- Reader's and Writer's Notebook
- Decodable Reader

© **Bridge to Common Core**

INTEGRATION OF KNOWLEDGE/IDEAS
This week, students will read, write, and talk about foods from different cultures.

Texts This Week
- "Quentin's Complaint"
- "What Does a Baker Do?"
- "Biscuits for Breakfast"
- *Jalapeño Bagels*
- "Foods of Mexico: A Delicious Blend"

Social Studies Knowledge Goals
Students will understand that food
- comes from different cultures
- is shared
- can be a mix from different cultures

Street Rhymes!

All along the city street
There are places you can eat.
[There are tasty treats to eat!]
Try the spicy tacos or the cheese fondue.
Try the baked lasagna or the lobster stew!

- To introduce this week's concept, read aloud the poem several times and ask students to join you.

Content Knowledge Zoom in on ©

Foods from Different Cultures

CONCEPT TALK To further explore the unit concept of Cultures, this week students will read, write, and talk about foods from different cultures. Write the Question of the Week on the board, *How can different cultures contribute to the foods we eat?*

Build Oral Language

TALK ABOUT FOODS FROM DIFFERENT CULTURES Have students turn to pp. 288–289 in their Student Editions. Look at each of the photos. Then use the prompts to guide discussion and create a concept map. Remind students to make pertinent comments and answer questions with appropriate detail.

- What type of food is shown in the small photo on p. 289? (Mexican food) Mexican foods include hot peppers and *spices* that give the food *flavor*. Let's add *Flavors* to our concept map.

- What are the woman and the girl doing? (They are eating turkey and stuffing to celebrate Thanksgiving.) Different cultures celebrate traditions, such as holidays, with special foods. Let's add *Traditions* to the map.

- Why else is it good for us to eat different foods? (They make us healthy.) We get *nutrition* from our food. Let's add *Nutrition* to the map.

- After discussing all the photos, ask: How can different cultures contribute to the foods we eat?

Oral Vocabulary

You've learned
227
Amazing Words ⭐
so far this year!

Let's Talk About

Foods We Eat

- Share ideas about foods that come from different cultures.
- Ask relevant questions about foods unique to specific cultures.
- Pose and answer questions about the foods we eat.

READING STREET ONLINE
CONCEPT TALK VIDEO
www.ReadingStreet.com

288

289

Student Edition, pp. 288–289

CONNECT TO READING Tell students that this week they will be reading about foods from different cultures. Encourage students to add concept-related words to this week's concept map.

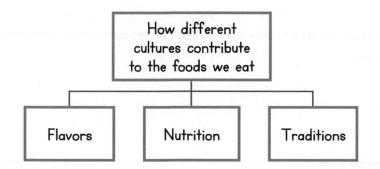

How different cultures contribute to the foods we eat

Flavors | Nutrition | Traditions

eSTREET INTERACTIVE
www.ReadingStreet.com

Pearson eText
- Student Edition

Concept Talk Video

ELL

Preteach Concepts Use the Day 1 instruction on ELL Poster 24 to build background knowledge, develop concepts, and build oral vocabulary.

ELL Support Additional ELL support and modified instruction is provided in the *ELL Handbook* and in the ELL Support Lessons found on the *Teacher Resources DVD-ROM*.

Jalapeño Bagels **288–289**

Common Core State Standards

Language 4. Determine or clarify the meaning of unknown and multiple-meaning word and phrases based on grade 3 reading and content, choosing flexibly from a range of strategies. **Language 6.** Acquire and use accurately grade-appropriate conversational, general academic, and domain-specific words and phrases, including those that signal spatial and temporal relationships (e.g., *After dinner that night we went looking for them*). **Also Speaking/Listening 1.**

Amazing Words

You've learned 2 2 7 words so far.

You'll learn 0 1 0 words this week!

nutrition	grumble
calorie	allergic
flavor	wholesome
spice	grate
nutmeg	agent

Content Knowledge

Build Oral Vocabulary

INTRODUCE AMAZING WORDS "Quentin's Complaint" is about a boy who learns that the foods we eat come from many different countries. Tell students to listen for this week's Amazing Words—*nutrition, calorie,* and *flavor*—as you read the Teacher Read Aloud on p. 289b.

Amazing Words   Robust Vocabulary Routine

1. **Introduce** Write the word *flavor* on the board. Have students say the word aloud with you. In "Quentin's Complaint," Quentin says that foods from other countries have different *flavors*. Does the text include any context clues about the meaning of *flavor*? Supply a student-friendly definition.

2. **Demonstrate** Have students answer questions with appropriate detail to demonstrate understanding. What kind of *flavor* is in chili? Do you like foods with a salty *flavor*?

3. **Apply** Ask students to tell what *flavor* they like the best.

4. **Display the Word** Run your hand under the syllables *fla-vor* as you read the word.

See p. OV•4 to teach *nutrition* and *calorie.*

Routines Flip Chart

AMAZING WORDS AT WORK Reread "Quentin's Complaint" aloud. As students listen, have them notice how the Amazing Words are used in context. build oral vocabulary, lead the class in a discussion about the meanings of th Amazing Words.

Don't Wait Until Friday

MONITOR PROGRESS **Check Oral Vocabulary**

During discussion, listen for students' use of Amazing Words.

If... students are unable to use the Amazing Words in discussion,

then... use the Oral Vocabulary Routine in the Routines Flip Chart to demonstrate words in different contexts.

Teacher Read Aloud

MODEL FLUENCY As you read "Quentin's Complaint," model accuracy with smooth, fluent reading.

Quentin's Complaint

Quentin bounded through the front door and listened for the screen door to slam shut behind him.

"I'm ho-ome!" he called out.

"I'm here in the kitchen," his mother called back. When he came around the corner, there she was, grating onions.

"What's for dinner?" Quentin asked. All of a sudden, he felt hungry. His stomach was grumbling.

"Well, hi to you too!" His mother laughed. "I thought we'd have meat loaf and potatoes. You could help me make a salad," she added.

The expression on Quentin's face changed. "How come we never have anything interesting to eat?" he blurted.

Quentin's mother stopped grating and gave him a puzzled look. "Interesting? Our meals are always delicious," she pointed out.

"I make sure we have good nutrition. And we look at the calorie count."

"I know," Quentin said. "But other kids get to eat things from other countries! Their food has a different flavor from ours. Everything we eat is so *American*."

Quentin's mother got that little smile on her face that always told him she knew something he didn't.

"American?" she answered. "Give me an example."

Quentin thought for a moment. Then he pointed to the three red potatoes resting on the kitchen counter. "Potatoes," he said.

"The first potatoes came from South America," his mother said. "Try again."

Quentin pointed to the red tomato waiting to be sliced into the salad. "Tomatoes," he said.

"Tomatoes also came from South America," his mother said. "Centuries ago, Spanish explorers found them growing there. They took some back to Europe. Later, Europeans brought tomatoes back across the ocean when they emigrated here."

Quentin wrinkled his forehead. He remembered what they had had for dinner the night before. "What about noodles?" he asked.

"Long before United States was a country, people were eating noodles in China and Italy," his mother said.

Quentin was feeling desperate. Finally, he thought of chocolate.

"It came from Mexico and Central America," his mother said.

Quentin could see he had lost the argument, but he didn't really mind. "I never knew those foods came from other parts of the world," he admitted. "I guess they aren't so boring after all."

eSTREET INTERACTIVE
www.ReadingStreet.com

Teacher Resources
• Amazing Word Cards
• ELL Support

ELL Support for Read Aloud Use the modified Read Aloud on p. DI•94 of the ELL Support Lessons on the *Teacher Resources DVD-ROM* to prepare students to listen to "Quentin's Complaint."

Support Listening Comprehension Before listening, have small groups of students discuss traditional foods and meals from their culture. Share with the group. After listening, have students compare their discussions with what they heard in the Read Aloud. For example, have students discuss if their culture's traditional meals have any ingredients from other cultures.

Common Core State Standards
Foundational Skills 3. Know and apply grade-level phonics and word analysis skills in decoding words **Foundational Skills 3.c.** Decode multisyllable words.

Skills Trace

Vowel Patterns *ei, eigh*
Introduce U5W4D1
Practice U5W4D3; U5W4D4
Reteach/Review U5W4D5; U5W5D4
Assess/Test Weekly Test U5W4 Benchmark Test U5
KEY: U=Unit   W=Week   D=Day

Vocabulary Support

You may wish to explain the meaning of these words.

either one or the other
neither not one or the other
sleigh a horse-drawn sled
vein tube-like body part that carries blood

Phonics

Teach/Model

Vowel Patterns *ei, eigh*

CONNECT Write the words *haul* and *paw*. Ask students what they know about the vowel sounds in these words. (*Haul* has /ȯ/ spelled *au*; *paw* has /ȯ/ spelled *aw*.) Today you will learn how to spell and read words with long *a*, long *e*, and long *i* sounds.

USE SOUND-SPELLING CARDS Display Card 64. Point to *ei*. The sound /ē/ can be spelled *ei*. Have students say /ē/ several times as you point to *ei*. Follow the same procedure with Card 65, the sound /ā/ spelled *eigh,* and Card 66, the sound /ī/ spelled *eigh.*

MODEL Write *weigh*. In this word, the letters *e-i-g-h* stand for the sound /ā/. Point to each spelling as you say its sound. Then blend the word: /w/ /ā/, *weigh*. Follow this procedure to model *height* and *receive*.

GROUP PRACTICE Continue the process. This time have students blend with you. Remind students that *ei* can stand for the sounds /ā/ or /ē/ and *eigh* can stand for the sounds /ā/ or /ī/. Tell them that, in certain words, *ei* can stand for the sound /ī/.

sleigh	veiled	weight	either	ceiling
neighbors	reins	neither	vein	height

REVIEW When you see the spelling *ei* in a word, try the sounds /ā/ or /ē/. When you see the spelling *eigh* in a word, try the sounds /ā/ or /ī/.

Guide Practice

MODEL Have students turn to p. 290 in their Student Editions. Each word on this page has the vowel sound /ā/, /ē/, or /ī/. The first word is *either*. I hear /ē/ in the first syllable. In *either*, /ē/ is spelled *ei*. When I say *eight,* I hear /ā/. In *eight,* /ā/ is spelled *eigh*.

GROUP PRACTICE For each word in Words I Can Blend, ask for the sound of each letter or group of letters. Make sure that students identify the correct sounds for the patterns *ei* and *eigh*. Then have them blend the words.

> **Corrective feedback**
> **If...** students have difficulty blending a word,
> **then...** model blending the word and then ask students to blend it with you.

Common Core State Standards
Foundational Skills 3. Know and apply grade-level phonics and word analysis skills in decoding words.

Envision It! | Sounds to Know

ceiling

ei

neighbors

height

eigh

eigh

READING STREET ONLINE
SOUND-SPELLING CARDS
www.ReadingStreet.com

Phonics

Long *a, e, i* Spelled *ei* or *eigh*

Words I Can Blend

e i t h e r

e i g h t

w e i g h

n e i t h e r

h e i g h t

Sentences I Can Read

1. We can either ride or walk the eight blocks to the show.
2. Neither of us wanted to weigh the apples.
3. What is your height?

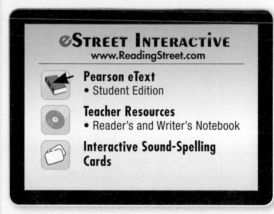

Long ago, a tiny toad princess was given a choice. Either marry a frog king or spend the eight remaining years of her stepfather's reign in a dungeon. She wanted to do neither, but after weighing both choices, she decided to marry the frog.

On the day of the wedding, the princess wore a veil and set out for the frog's marsh in a sleigh. A huge weight lay on her shoulders. There was a difference in height, after all.

On arrival, the toad princess fell in love with the frog and his marsh. She reigned for eighteen joyful years.

You've learned

Long *a, e, i,* Spelled *ei* or *eigh*

290

291

Student Edition, pp. 290–291

Apply

READ WORDS IN ISOLATION After students can successfully segment and blend the words on p. 290 in their Student Editions, point to words in random order and ask students to read them naturally.

READ WORDS IN CONTEXT Have students read each of the sentences on p. 290. Have them identify words in the sentences that have the vowel sounds /ā/, /ē/, and /ī/ spelled *ei* or *eigh.*

Team Talk Pair students and have them take turns reading each of the sentences aloud.

Chorally read the I Can Read! passage on p. 281 with students. Then have them read the passage aloud for themselves.

ON THEIR OWN For additional practice, use *Reader's and Writer's Notebook,* p. 349.

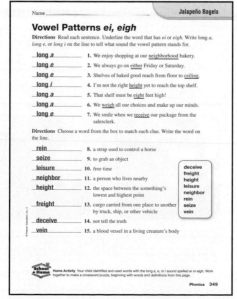

Name _____ Jalapeño Bagels

Vowel Patterns *ei, eigh*

Directions Read each sentence. Underline the word that has *ei* or *eigh.* Write *long a, long e,* or *long i* on the line to tell what sound the vowel pattern stands for.

long *i* 1. We enjoy shopping at our neighborhood bakery.

long *e* 2. We always go on either Friday or Saturday.

long *e* 3. Shelves of baked good reach from floor to ceiling.

long *i* 4. I'm not the right height yet to reach the top shelf.

long *a* 5. That shelf must be eight feet high!

long *a* 6. We weigh all our choices and make up our minds.

long *e* 7. We smile when we receive our package from the salesclerk.

Directions Choose a word from the box to match each clue. Write the word on the line.

rein 8. a strap used to control a horse

seize 9. to grab an object

leisure 10. free time

neighbor 11. a person who lives nearby

height 12. the space between the something's lowest and highest point

freight 13. cargo carried from one place to another by truck, ship, or other vehicle

deceive 14. not tell the truth

vein 15. a blood vessel in a living creature's body

deceive
freight
height
leisure
neighbor
rein
seize
vein

Home Activity Your child identified and used words with the long a, e, or i sound spelled ei or eigh. Work together to make a crossword puzzle, beginning with words and definitions from this page.

Phonics 349

Reader's and Writer's Notebook, p. 349

eSTREET INTERACTIVE
www.ReadingStreet.com

Pearson eText
• Student Edition

Teacher Resources
• Reader's and Writer's Notebook

Interactive Sound-Spelling Cards

ELL

Language Transfer The English sound /ē/ is rare in other languages. English learners may have difficulty distinguishing between /ē/ and /ā/. Provide practice by pronouncing word pairs such as *may/me* and *say/see* and having students echo your pronunciation.

Common Core State Standards

Foundational Skills 3. Know and apply grade-level phonics and word analysis skills in decoding words. **Foundational Skills 3.c.** Decode multisyllable words. **Foundational Skills 3.d.** Read grade-appropriate irregularly spelled words. **Foundational Skills 4.** Read with sufficient accuracy and fluency to support comprehension. **Also Literature 2., 3.**

Decodable Reader 24A

If students need help, then...

Read *Heidi and Her Mom*

READ WORDS IN ISOLATION Have students turn to p. 97 of *Decodable Practice Readers 3.2.* Have students read each word.

Have students read the high-frequency words *was, clothes, said, your, you, there, a, to, pretty, the, of, what, from, would, one,* and *laugh* on the first page.

PREVIEW Have students read the title and preview the story. Tell them that they will read words with the vowel sounds /ā/ and /ē/ spelled *ei,* and the vowel sounds /ā/ and /ī/ spelled *eigh.* Tell students that in certain cases, the vowel sound /ī/ is spelled *ei,* as in *Heidi* and *heist.*

READ WORDS IN CONTEXT Pair students for reading and listen as they read. One student begins. Students read the entire story, switching readers after each page. Partners reread the story. This time the other student begins. Make sure students are monitoring their accuracy when they decode words.

Decodable Practice Reader 24A

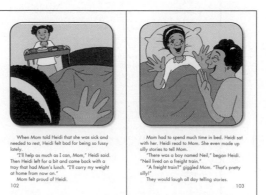

Corrective feedback

If... students have difficulty decoding a word, **then...** refer them to the *Sound-Spelling Cards* to identify the sounds in the word. Then prompt them to blend the word.

- What is the new word?
- Is the new word a word you know?
- Does it make sense in the story?

CHECK DECODING AND COMPREHENSION Have students retell the story to include characters, setting, and events. Then have students find words in the story that have /ā/, /ē/, or /ī/ spelled with the syllabication pattern *ei* or *igh*. Students should supply *Heidi, eight, either, neither, neigh, ceiling, Keith, neighbor, receive, weight, Neil,* and *freight.*

Reread for Fluency

REREAD DECODABLE READER Have students reread *Decodable Practice Reader* 24A to develop automaticity decoding words that have /ā/, /ē/, or /ī/ spelled *ei* or *eigh.*

 Routine | **Oral Rereading**

. **Read** Have students read the entire book orally.

. **Reread** To achieve optimal fluency, students should reread the text three or four times.

Corrective Feedback Listen as students read. Provide corrective feedback regarding their fluency and decoding.

Routines Flip Chart

ELL

Beginning Write several words with the vowel sound /ē/ from the *Decodable Practice Reader* on the board, such as *either, ceiling,* and *receive.* Point to each word as you say it aloud. Then underline the letters that spell the sound /ē/ in each word. Have students repeat the words with you. Repeat the procedure for the sound /ā/, using words such as *weight, eight, neigh,* and *neighbor.*

Intermediate After reading, have students find pairs of rhyming words with the vowel sound /ā/. For example: *weight, eight, freight.*

Advanced After reading the story, have students choose 4 or 5 words with the vowel sounds /ā/ or /ē/ spelled *ei* or *eigh* and write a sentence for each word.

Zoom in on ©

Skills Trace

⚆ **Draw Conclusions**

Introduce U2W3D1; U3W1D1; U5W4D1

Practice U2W3D2; U2W3D3; U2W5D2; U3W1D2; U3W1D3; U3W4D2; U4W5D3; U5W3D2; U5W4D2; U5W4D3; U5W5D2

Reteach/Review U2W3D5; U3W1D5; U5W4D5

Assess/Test Weekly Tests U2W3; U3W1; U5W4

Benchmark Tests U3

KEY: U=Unit   W=Week   D=Day

Comprehension Support

Students may also turn to pp. EI•6 and EI•25 to review the skill and strategy if needed.

Text-Based Comprehension

⚆ **Draw Conclusions**
⚆ **Summarize**

READ Remind students of the weekly concept—Foods from Different Cultures. Have students read "What Does a Baker Do?" on p. 293.

MODEL A CLOSE READ

Think Aloud Have students follow along as you reread the first three paragraphs. The third paragraph explains that bakers need to know what their customers like best. I am going to use the facts given in the selection and common sense to draw conclusions about how bakers know what their customers like best. I think they can ask customers and see what sells the most. Now when I read, I often stop and summarize what has happened to recall important ideas. When I reread the first two paragraphs, I notice that bakers make many things and that they have to get up early. I will draw conclusions and summarize by saying that bakers work very hard.

TEACH Have students read p. 292. Explain that the skill of drawing conclusions and the strategy of summarizing are tools they can use to monitor their understanding as they read. Review the bulleted items and explanations on p. 292. Then have students use a graphic organizer like the one on p. 292 and draw conclusions about why practicing with experienced bakers is a good way for new bakers to learn.

GUIDE PRACTICE Have students reread "What Does a Baker Do?" using the callouts as guides. Then ask volunteers to respond to the questions in the callouts, citing specific examples from the text to support their answers.

Skill The treats are different from bread, cakes, and pies.
Skill They might ask customers what they like.
Strategy A baker bakes bread and other treats. Bakers can work in large stores, neighborhood bakeries, and restaurants. They have to get up early to bake food and sell it the same day. They learn their job by watching other bakers or by going to a special school. Some bakers like to experiment and create their own recipes. Baking food that people like is what makes this career exciting.

APPLY Use *Reader's and Writer's Notebook,* p. 350 for additional practice with drawing conclusions.

Reader's and Writer's Notebook, p. 350

Common Core State Standards
Informational Text 1. Ask and answer questions to demonstrate understanding of a text, referring explicitly to the text as the basis for the answers. **Also Informational Text 2.**

Envision It! | Skill/Strategy

Skill

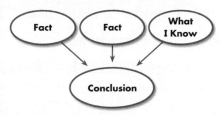

Strategy

READING STREET ONLINE
ENVISION IT! ANIMATIONS
www.ReadingStreet.com

Comprehension Skill

◉ Draw Conclusions

- You draw conclusions when you use facts and details to make decisions about characters or events.

- Think about what you already know to help you draw conclusions.

- Use what you learned about drawing conclusions and a graphic organizer like the one below as you read "What Does a Baker Do?" Then use your conclusion as the topic sentence for a paragraph that tells what a baker does.

```
  Fact     Fact    What
                    I Know

           Conclusion
```

Comprehension Strategy

◉ Summarize

Active readers summarize to help them understand. To summarize, tell the most important ideas or events in logical order, maintaining the meaning of what you read.

What Does a Baker Do?

Have you ever helped an adult bake something? A baker is a person who makes baked goods for a living. A baker makes bread, cakes, pies, and many other treats!

Some bakers work in large stores, some work in small neighborhood bakeries, and some work in restaurants. Baked goods must be fresh, so bakers often get up early in the morning to make goods to be sold that day.

Bakers need to know what kinds of treats people in their neighborhood like. This helps them know what to make and how much.

Many bakers learn their job by working with experienced bakers. They watch, listen, and practice on the job. Some bakers go to special schools to learn how to bake.

Some bakers like to experiment and create their own recipes for their customers' favorite baked goods. Working as a baker can be an exciting career!

Skill What can you conclude about the other treats a baker makes?

Skill How do bakers find out what customers want?

Strategy Summarize the selection. Include why the author concludes that being a baker is an exciting career.

Your Turn!

⏸ **Need a Review?** See the *Envision It! Handbook* for more information about drawing conclusions and summarizing.

▶ **Ready to Try It?** As you read *Jalapeño Bagels*, use what you've learned about drawing conclusions and summarizing to understand the text.

292   293

Student Edition, pp. 292–293

Model Fluent Reading

ACCURACY Have students listen as you read paragraph four of "What Does a Baker Do?" with accuracy. Explain that to read accurately, you read carefully so you don't skip words or say the wrong word.

Routine | Oral Rereading

1. **Read** Have students read paragraph four of "What Does a Baker Do?" orally.

2. **Reread** To achieve optimal fluency, students should reread the text three or four times.

3. **Corrective Feedback** Have students read aloud without you. Provide feedback about their accuracy and encourage them to take their time to read each word correctly.

Routines Flip Chart

⊘STREET INTERACTIVE
www.ReadingStreet.com

Pearson eText
• Student Edition

Envision It! Animations

Teacher Resources
• Reader's and Writer's Notebook

ⒺⓁⓁ

Draw Conclusions Some students may interpret "draw conclusions" literally and assume the skill involves drawing a picture. Clarify for students that when you draw a conclusion, you think about facts and what you already know and make a decision. Provide oral practice by having students draw conclusions about foods.

Common Core State Standards

Writing 7. Conduct short research projects that build knowledge about a topic. **Speaking and Listening 1.** Engage effectively in a range of collaborative discussions (one-on-one, in groups, and teacher-led) with diverse partners on grade 3 topics and texts, building on others' ideas and expressing their own clearly. **Language 4.** Determine or clarify the meaning of unknown and multiple-meaning word and phrases based on grade 3 reading and content, choosing flexibly from a range of strategies. **Language 6.** Acquire and use accurately grade-appropriate conversational, general academic, and domain-specific words and phrases, including those that signal spatial and temporal relationships (e.g., *After dinner that night we went looking for them*).

Selection Vocabulary

Use the following routine to introduce this week's tested selection vocabulary.

bakery a place where bread and cake are made and sold

batch a group of things made at the same time

boils to heat a liquid until it starts to bubble and give off steam

braided three or four strands woven together

dough flour and liquid mixed together to make bread, biscuits, and pastry

ingredients items that something is made from

mixture the combination of things mixed or blended together

SEE IT/SAY IT Write *batch*. Scan across the word with your finger as you say it: *batch*.

HEAR IT Use the word in a sentence. I made a *batch* of cookies for the party.

DEFINE IT Elicit definitions from students. How would you describe to another student what *batch* means? Clarify or give a definition when necessary. Yes, *batch* means a group of things that are made at the same time. Restate the word in student-friendly terms. So if you make a *batch* of cookies, you are making them all at the same time.

Team Talk Is a *batch* of something always a lot of things? What other things can be in a *batch*? Turn and talk to your partner about this. Be prepared to explain your answer. Allow students time to discuss. Ask for examples. Rephrase their examples for usage when necessary or to correct misunderstandings.

MAKE CONNECTIONS Have students discuss the word. Have you ever made a *batch* of cookies or seen a *batch* of something? Turn and talk to your partner about this. Then be prepared to share. Have students share. Rephrase their ideas for usage when necessary or to correct misunderstandings.

RECORD Have students write the word and its meaning.

Continue this routine to introduce the remaining words in this manner.

| Corrective feedback | **If...** students are having difficulty understanding, **then...** review the definitions in small groups. |

Research and Inquiry

Step 1 Identify and Focus Topic

TEACH Discuss the Question of the Week: *How can different cultures contribute to the foods we eat?* Tell students they will research foods from different cultures. They will present their articles to the class on Day 5.

Think Aloud

MODEL I'll start by brainstorming a list of questions about foods from different cultures. I know that special foods are part of celebrating holidays or certain traditions in various cultures. For example, Americans celebrate Thanksgiving with turkey dinners. Some possible questions could be *In what holidays and traditions do foods play an important role? What types of food do people in various cultures cook to celebrate holidays? What are the traditional foods in different cultures?*

GUIDE PRACTICE After students have brainstormed inquiry questions, explain that tomorrow they will conduct research using their questions. Help students identify keywords that will guide their search.

ON THEIR OWN Have students work individually, in pairs, or in small groups to write an inquiry question.

---

eStreet Interactive
www.ReadingStreet.com

Teacher Resources
- Envision It! Pictured Vocabulary Cards
- Tested Vocabulary Cards

21st Century Skills
Internet Guy *Don Leu*

Weekly Inquiry Project

STEP 1	Identify and Focus Topic
STEP 2	Navigate/Search
STEP 3	Analyze Information
STEP 4	Synthesize
STEP 5	Communicate

ELL

Multilingual Vocabulary Students can apply knowledge of their home languages to acquire new English vocabulary by using the Multilingual Vocabulary Lists (*ELL Handbook,* pp. 431–442).

Day 1 SMALL GROUP TIME • Differentiate Vocabulary, p. SG•49

OL On-Level	**SI Strategic Intervention**	**A Advanced**
• **Practice Vocabulary** Amazing Words	• **Reteach Vocabulary** Amazing Words	• **Extend Vocabulary** Amazing Words
• **Read** *Reading Street Sleuth,* pp. 62–63	• **Read** *Reading Street Sleuth,* pp. 62–63	• **Read** *Reading Street Sleuth,* pp. 62–63
		• **Introduce** Inquiry Project

ELL

If... students need more scaffolding and practice with **Vocabulary, then...** use the activities on pp. DI•92–DI•93 in the Teacher Resources section on SuccessNet.

Common Core State Standards

Language 1.g. Form and use comparative and superlative adjectives and adverbs, and choose between them depending on what is to be modified. **Language 2.f.** Use spelling patterns and generalizations (e.g., word families, position-based spellings, syllable patterns, ending rules, meaningful word parts) in writing words.

Spelling Pretest

Vowel Patterns *ei, eigh*

INTRODUCE This week we will spell words with vowel patterns *ei* and *eigh*. As you spell these words, remember to think about letter sounds.

PRETEST Say each word, read the sentence, and repeat the word.

1. ceiling	The party favors hung from the **ceiling.**
2. neighbor	The person who lives next door is my **neighbor.**
3. either	I will go to **either** the mountains or the beach.
4. eighteen	**Eighteen** is one more than seventeen.
5. height	My dad's **height** is 5 feet, 11 inches.
6. neither	**Neither** of those two chairs is the right size.
7. weight	The nurse used the scale to measure our **weight.**
8. leisure	Shooting hoops is a fun **leisure** activity.
9. protein	Milk is an important source of **protein.**
10. freight	There is cargo on the **freight** train.
11. receive	When will we **receive** your invitation?
12. weigh	The packages **weigh** five pounds each.
13. deceive	A lie is meant to **deceive.**
14. sleigh	Eight reindeer pulled the red **sleigh.**
15. conceited	A snobbish person is **conceited.**

Challenge words

16. receipt	The cashier handed us our **receipt.**
17. eightieth	We will celebrate Grandma's **eightieth** birthday.
18. neighborly	Taking cake to neighbors is kind and **neighborly.**
19. deceitful	The **deceitful** person was not to be trusted.
20. featherweight	Smaller wrestlers are in the **featherweight** division.

SELF-CORRECT Have students self-correct their pretests by rewriting misspelled words.

ON THEIR OWN Use *Let's Practice It!* p. 319 on the *Teacher Resources DVD-ROM.*

Let's Practice It! TR DVD•319

Conventions

Comparative and Superlative Adverbs

MAKE CONNECTIONS Write the verb *run* on the board. Point out that the word *fast* can be used to describe *run*. Then ask students which animal runs faster—a dog or a cheetah. Write *faster* next to *run.* Underline the *-er* and explain that this is a comparative adverb. It compares two things. Write *slowly* and ask which runs most slowly—a turtle, a rabbit, or a cat. Underline *most* and explain this compares three or more things.

TEACH Display Grammar Transparency 24, and read aloud the explanation and examples in the box.

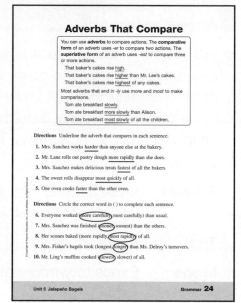

Adverbs That Compare

You can use **adverbs** to compare actions. The **comparative form** of an adverb uses *-er* to compare two actions. The **superlative form** of an adverb uses *-est* to compare three or more actions.

That baker's cakes rise high.
That baker's cakes rise higher than Mr. Lee's cakes.
That baker's cakes rise highest of any cakes.

Most adverbs that end in *-ly* use *more* and *most* to make comparisons.

Tom ate breakfast slowly.
Tom ate breakfast more slowly than Alison.
Tom ate breakfast most slowly of all the children.

Directions Underline the adverb that compares in each sentence.

1. Mrs. Sanchez works harder than anyone else at the bakery.
2. Mr. Lane rolls out pastry dough more rapidly than she does.
3. Mrs. Sanchez makes delicious treats fastest of all the bakers.
4. The sweet rolls disappear most quickly of all.
5. One oven cooks faster than the other oven.

Directions Circle the correct word in ( ) to complete each sentence.

6. Everyone worked (more carefully, most carefully) than usual.
7. Mrs. Sanchez was finished (sooner, soonest) than the others.
8. Her scones baked (more rapidly, most rapidly) of all.
9. Mrs. Fisher's bagels took (longest, longer) than Ms. Delroy's turnovers.
10. Mr. Ling's muffins cooked (slowest, slower) of all.

Unit 5 Jalapeño Bagels   Grammar **24**

Grammar Transparency 24, TR DVD

MODEL Model underlining the adverb that compares in item 1.

GUIDE PRACTICE Guide students to complete items 2–5. Remind them to look for adverbs that end in *-er* or *-est* or adverbs that use *more* and *most* to compare. Record the correct responses on the transparency.

APPLY Have students read sentences 6–10 on the transparency and circle the correct adverb to correctly complete each sentence.

Handwriting

MODEL LETTER FORMATION AND ADJUSTING TO FIT Display capital letters *N, M,* and *U.* Follow the stroke instructions pictured to model letter formation. Explain that writing legibly involves making adjustments to the size of handwriting to make sure it fits the available space. Draw write-on lines on the board and model writing this sentence: *Nick moved from New Mexico to Utah.*

GUIDE PRACTICE Provide write-on lines for students and have them write these sentences: *Manuel is from the Northeast. Nina lives in Uruguay.*

eSTREET INTERACTIVE
www.ReadingStreet.com

Teacher Resources
• Let's Practice It!
• Grammar Transparency
• Daily Fix-It Transparency

Daily Fix-It

1. Marias mom tought her to bake bread. *(Maria's; taught)*
2. Her flower was sifted more sooner than mine. *(flour; sifted sooner)*

Academic Vocabulary

Comparative adverbs compare two people, places, or things. Add *-er* to most adverbs to make them comparative. Use *more* with adverbs that end in *-ly.*

Superlative adverbs compare three or more people, places, or things. Add *-est* to most adverbs to make them superlative. Use *most* with adverbs that end in *-ly.*

ELL

Language Production: Comparative and Superlative Adverbs Write on the board a list of adverbs, such as *quickly, slow, carefully, warm, fun,* and *soon.* Have students read the words and determine whether to use *-er* and *-est* or *more* and *most.* Then use some of the adverbs incorrectly in sentences. For example, say: Cheetahs run the *most* fast of all the animals. Call on students to say the sentence with the correct form.

Jalapeño Bagels   **293d**

Common Core State Standards

Writing 2. Write informative/explanatory texts to examine a topic and convey ideas and information clearly. **Writing 2.a.** Introduce a topic and group related information together; include illustrations when useful to aiding comprehension. **Writing 2.b.** Develop the topic with facts, definitions, and details.

Bridge to Common Core

TEXT TYPES AND PURPOSES

This week students write an invitation requesting someone to come over for dinner.

Expository/Informative/Explanatory Writing

Through reading and discussion, students will gain a deeper understanding of cultures. They will use this knowledge from the texts to write and support their invitations.

Through the week, students will improve their range and content of writing through daily mini-lessons.

5-Day Plan

DAY 1	Read Like a Writer
DAY 2	Organize Your Ideas
DAY 3	Writing Trait: Purpose
DAY 4	Revise: Adding
DAY 5	Proofread for Adverbs

Write Guy *by Jeff Anderson*

Let Me Check My List

Encourage students to keep lists of words they come across that are exciting or interesting to them. This is a great way to improve vocabulary and word choice.

Writing

Invitation

Mini-Lesson   Read Like a Writer

■ **Introduce** An **invitation** is a written request for someone to come to a party or other special event. If you wanted to invite people to a party, would you write an invitation or a short story? This week you will write an invitation.

Prompt	Invite a friend over for dinner, using specific details.
Trait	Focus/Ideas
Mode	Expository/Informative/Explanatory

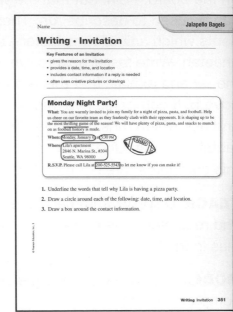

Reader's and Writer's Notebook, p. 351

■ **Examine Model Text** Let's read an example of an invitation. Have students read "Monday Night Party!" on p. 351 of their *Reader's and Writer's Notebook.*

■ **Key Features** A good invitation offers a reason for the special event. It tells readers why they are being invited to the event and what they will be celebrating. Guide students in identifying the reason for Lila's pizza party. Have them underline the words that tell them.

Invitations tell the date, time, and location of the event. Ask students what might happen if an invitation was missing one of these important details.

Invitations provide contact information so readers can ask questions about the event or tell the host whether they will attend. What type of contact information does Lila include in her invitation? (her telephone number) Have students role-play calling Lila to tell her whether they will attend her pizza party.

Invitations are often decorated with pictures or drawings. These get the reader's attention.

Review Key Features

Review the key features of an invitation with students. You might want to post the key features in the classroom for students to reference as they work on their invitations.

Key Features of an Invitation

- gives the reason for the invitation
- provides a date, time, and location
- includes contact information if a reply is needed
- often uses creative pictures or drawings

Routine **Quick Write for Fluency** **Team Talk**

. **Talk** Have pairs take a few minutes to discuss the importance of providing contact information in an invitation.

. **Write** Each student writes three sentences summarizing his or her ideas.

. **Share** Partners read one another's sentences.

Routines Flip Chart

eStreet Interactive
www.ReadingStreet.com

Teacher Resources
- Reader's and Writer's Notebook
- Let's Practice It!

Academic Vocabulary

An **invitation** is a written request for someone to come to a party or other special event.

ELL

Activate Prior Knowledge Read aloud the writing model on p. 313 of the Student Edition and help students understand it. Ask students to tell about a time they sent or received an invitation. Provide sentence frames, such as the following, to help spark discussion:
I was invited to _____.
The party was held at _____.
The day of the party was _____.

Wrap Up Your Day!

✔ **Content Knowledge** Reread Street Rhymes! on p. 288j to students. Ask them what they learned this week about foods from different cultures.

✔ **Oral Vocabulary** Have students use the Amazing Words they learned in context sentences.

✔ **Homework** Send home this week's Family Times newsletter on *Let's Practice It!* pp. 320–321 on the *Teacher Resources DVD-ROM.*

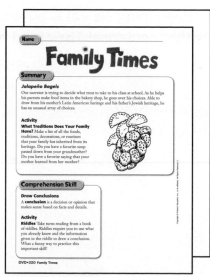

Let's Practice It!
TR DVD•320–321

Preview DAY 2

Tell students that tomorrow they will read about Pablo and his parents' bakery.

Common Core State Standards

Speaking/Listening 1. Engage effectively in a range of collaborative discussions (one-on-one, in groups, and teacher-led) with diverse partners on grade 3 topics and texts, building on others' ideas and expressing their own clearly. **Language 6.** Acquire and use accurately grade-appropriate conversational, general academic, and domain-specific words and phrases, including those that signal spatial and temporal relationships (e.g., *After dinner that night we went looking for them*). **Also Speaking/Listening 1.d.**

Content Knowledge

Foods from Different Cultures

EXPAND THE CONCEPT Remind students of the weekly concept question *How can different cultures contribute to the foods we eat?* Tell students that today they will begin reading *Jalapeño Bagels.* As they read, encourage students to think about how other cultures influence the foods we eat.

Build Oral Language

TALK ABOUT SENTENCES AND WORDS Reread these sentences from the Read Aloud, "Quentin's Complaint."

"I know," Quentin said. "But other kids get to eat things from other countries! Their food has a different flavor from ours. Everything we eat is so American."

• What does *flavor* mean? (the taste of food)
• What is different about the food Quentin's friends eat? (They eat things from other countries. The food they eat tastes different.)
• Why do you think the author has Quentin complain about the food his mom makes? (This allows the author to show, through Quentin's mother, how many of the foods that are part of the American diet in fact come from other countries.)

Team Talk Have students turn to a partner and discuss the following activity. Then ask them to share their results.

• Reorganize the sentences by combining them or changing the order while keeping the meaning of the sentences the same. (Possible response: "Everything we eat is so *American*, but other kids get to eat things from other countries! Their food has a different flavor from ours.")

Build Oral Vocabulary

Amazing Words   Robust Vocabulary Routine

1. Introduce Write the Amazing Word *spice* on the board. Have students say it aloud with you. Relate *spice* to the photographs on pp. 288–289 and "Quentin's Complaint." Why do cooks use *spices* in food? What kinds of *spices* are used in Mexican food? Have students determine the definition of the word. A *spice* is a seasoning from a plant used to flavor food.

2. Demonstrate Have students answer questions to demonstrate understanding. Why might you find different *spices* in foods from different cultures? What flavors do *spices* add to food?

3. Apply Have students apply their understanding. How do your family members use *spices* in their cooking?

4. Display the Word Run your hand under the word as you emphasize the syllables *spi-ces.* Have students say the word.

See p. OV•4 to teach *nutmeg.*

Routines Flip Chart

ADD TO THE CONCEPT MAP Use the photos on pp. 288–289 and the Read Aloud, "Quentin's Complaint," to talk about the Amazing Words: *nutrition, calorie,* and *flavor.* Add these and other concept-related words to the concept map to develop students' knowledge of the topic. Discuss the following questions. Remind students to make pertinent comments and answer questions with appropriate detail during a discussion.

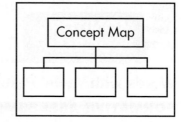

How can foods from different cultures affect our *nutrition?*

Name a food that is high in *calories.* Do you know what culture the food is from?

Why might foods from different cultures have different *flavors?*

Amazing Words

nutrition	grumble
calorie	allergic
flavor	wholesome
spice	grate
nutmeg	agent

Reinforce Vocabulary Use the Day 2 instruction on ELL Poster 24 to teach lesson vocabulary and the lesson concept.

© **Common Core State Standards**

Foundational Skills 3. Know and apply grade-level phonics and word analysis skills in decoding words. **Foundational Skills 3.c.** Decode multisyllable words. **Language 6.** Acquire and use accurately grade-appropriate conversational, general academic, and domain-specific words and phrases, including those that signal spatial and temporal relationships (e.g., *After dinner that night we went looking for them*). **Also Foundational Skills 3.d.**

Phonics

🔄 Vowel Patterns *ei, eigh*

REVIEW Review the /ā/, /ē/, and /ī/ vowel patterns *ei* and *eigh* using *Sound-Spelling Cards* 64, 65, and 66.

READ WORDS IN ISOLATION Have the class read these words. Then point to the words in random order and ask students to read them quickly.

sleigh	reins	veil	weight
neigh	height	freight	neither

Corrective feedback | Model blending decodable words and then ask students to blend them with you.

READ WORDS IN CONTEXT Have the class read these sentences.

Team Talk Have pairs take turns reading the sentences naturally.

The king's evil **reign** lasted for **eight** years.

The robbers appeared to get away with the **heist**.

After the girl **received** her crown, she was full of **conceit**.

Don't Wait Until Friday **MONITOR PROGRESS** Check Word Reading

Words with Vowel Patterns *ei* and *eigh*

FORMATIVE ASSESSMENT Write the following words and have the class read them. Notice which words students miss during the group reading. Call on individuals to read some of the words.

ceiling	leisure	neigh	either
unhappy	usable	hopeless	return
neighed	freighter	unveiled	weightless

Spiral Review
Row 2 reviews words with prefixes and suffixes.

Row 3 contrasts words with prefixes and suffixes and words with vowel patterns *ei, eigh.*

If... students cannot read words with vowel patterns *ei* and *eigh* at this point,

then... use the Day 1 Phonics lesson on p. 290a to reteach vowel patterns *ei* and *eigh.* Use words from the *Decodable Practice Passages* (or Reader). Continue to monitor students' progress using other instructional opportunities during the week. See the Skills Trace on p. 290a.

Literary Terms

Dialogue and Narration

TEACH Tell students that **dialogue** is a conversation in a book, a movie, a play, or a TV show. **Narration** is the recounting of an event or a series of events with accompanying description. A reader experiences the events through the eyes, mind, and voice of the storyteller, called the narrator or speaker.

Think Aloud **MODEL** Let's look at "What Does a Baker Do?" How is narration used in the passage? (It gives information about bakers.) Narration can be used in nonfiction to provide a description. What does the narrator describe in the passage? (what bakers cook and where they work)

GUIDE PRACTICE Have students find examples of narration in *Jalapeño Bagels.* Be sure to point out that dialogue, the conversation between two or more people, is often combined with narration to tell a story.

ON THEIR OWN Have students look for examples of dialogue and narration in other selections of their Student Edition.

eSTREET INTERACTIVE
www.ReadingStreet.com

Pearson eText
• Student Edition

Interactive Sound-Spelling Cards

Academic Vocabulary

dialogue conversation in a book, a movie, a play, or a TV show

narration the recounting by a storyteller of an event or series of events with accompanying description

Common Core State Standards

Language 4. Determine or clarify the meaning of unknown and multiple-meaning words and phrases based on grade 3 reading and content, choosing flexibly from a range of strategies. **Language 4.a.** Use sentence-level context as a clue to the meaning of a word or phrase. **Foundational Skills 4.b.** Read on-level prose and poetry orally with accuracy, appropriate rate, and expression on successive readings. **Also Foundational Skills 4., Language 5.**

Selection Vocabulary

bakery a place where bread and cake are made and sold

batch a group of things made at the same time

boils to heat a liquid until it starts to bubble and give off steam

braided three or four strands woven together

dough flour and liquid mixed together to make bread, biscuits, and pastry

ingredients items that something is made from

mixture the combination of things mixed or blended together

Bridge to Common Core

VOCABULARY ACQUISITION AND USE

Using context clues helps students determine or clarify the meaning of unknown words and enables them to acquire a broad range of academic and domain-specific words. This use of context clues allows students to develop independence in gathering vocabulary knowledge on their own.

Vocabulary Support

Refer students to *Words!* on p. W•7 in the Student Edition for additional practice.

Vocabulary Skill

Unfamiliar Words

READ Have students read "Biscuits for Breakfast" on p. 295. Use the vocabulary skill and strategy as tools to build comprehension.

TEACH CONTEXT CLUES Tell students that they can use context clues to determine the meanings of unfamiliar words. Context clues are the surrounding words that help define the word. When they see an unfamiliar word, they should look for clues that help them determine the meaning.

Think Aloud **MODEL** Write on the board: *I like to shop at the bakery. I buy bread there. Sometimes I buy cakes or rolls.* If I were not sure of the meaning of *bakery,* I would look for context clues. The next sentences tell me that a *bakery* has bread, cakes, and rolls. A *bakery* is also a place where people buy things. I can use those context clues to determine that a *bakery* must be a store that sells baked goods.

GUIDE PRACTICE Write these sentences from "Biscuits for Breakfast" on the board: *Use a fork to add the shortening to the flour, baking powder, and salt. The mixture should look like fine crumbs.* Have students use context clues to determine the meaning of *mixture.* For additional support, use *Envision It! Pictured Vocabulary Cards* or *Tested Vocabulary Cards.*

ON THEIR OWN Have students reread "Biscuits for Breakfast" on p. 295 using context clues to understand the meanings for the selection vocabulary. Encourage them to test the meanings in the sentences. For additional practice, use the *Reader's and Writer's Notebook,* p. 352.

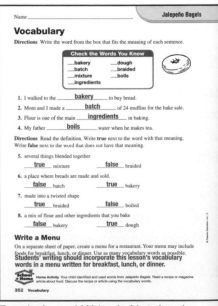

Reader's and Writer's Notebook, p. 352

Common Core State Standards
Language 4.a. Use sentence-level context as a clue to the meaning of a word or phrase. Also Language 4.

Envision It! Words to Know

bakery

batch

dough

boils
braided
ingredients
mixture

READING STREET ONLINE
VOCABULARY ACTIVITIES
www.ReadingStreet.com

Vocabulary Strategy for

Unfamiliar Words

Context Clues Sometimes you come across an unfamiliar word. How can you figure out what the word means? Look at the context, or the words and sentences around the word. You might find clues that can help you figure out the meaning of the word.

1. Read the words and sentences around the word you don't know. Sometimes the author tells you what the word means.

2. If not, use the words and sentences to predict a meaning for the word.

3. Try that meaning in the sentence. Does it make sense?

Read "Biscuits for Breakfast" on page 295. As you read, use context clues to help you understand the meanings of the Words to Know and other unfamiliar words.

Words to Write Reread "Biscuits for Breakfast." Write the directions explaining how to make your favorite breakfast food. Be sure to include the ingredients and the steps. Use words from the Words to Know list.

Biscuits for Breakfast

Would you like something for breakfast that you will not find in a bakery? Make biscuits! You'll need only a few ingredients to make one batch.

⅓ cup shortening

1 ¾ cups flour

2 ½ teaspoons baking powder

¾ teaspoon salt

¾ cup milk

Use a fork to add the shortening to the flour, baking powder, and salt. The mixture should look like fine crumbs. Add enough milk so that the dough rounds into a ball. Put the dough on a floured board. Knead it 10 times and only 10 times.

Roll the dough flat, about ½ inch thick. Cut out round circles using a biscuit cutter or an overturned glass. Place the circles on a baking sheet. Do not let the circles touch one another. Bake at 350° for 10 to 12 minutes or until the biscuits are light brown on top. Serve them with butter and honey.

Forget about braided coffee cakes. When the water boils for your morning tea and you are looking for something to go with it, grab a hot, fresh biscuit.

Your Turn!

⏸ **Need a Review?** For additional help with unfamiliar words, see *Words!*

▶ **Ready to Try It?** Read *Jalapeño Bagels* on pp. 296–309.

294

295

Reread for Fluency

ACCURACY Read aloud paragraph three of "Biscuits for Breakfast" clearly and accurately. Tell students that you are reading the paragraph carefully and without skipping words. Explain the correct terms for reading the fraction, temperature, and numbers in the paragraph.

Routine | Oral Rereading

1. Read Have students read paragraph three of "Biscuits for Breakfast" orally.

2. Reread To achieve optimal fluency, students should reread the text three or four times.

3. Corrective Feedback Have students read aloud without you. Provide feedback about their accuracy. Listen for correct pronunciation and make sure they do not skip any words.

Routines Flip Chart

eSTREET INTERACTIVE
www.ReadingStreet.com

Pearson eText
• Student Edition

Vocabulary Activities

Journal

Teacher Resources
• Envision It! Pictured Vocabulary Cards
• Tested Vocabulary Cards
• Reader's and Writer's Notebook

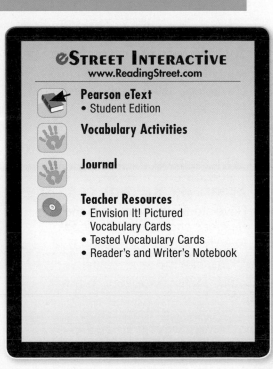

© Common Core State Standards

Literature 7. Explain how specific aspects of a text's illustrations contribute to what is conveyed by the words in a story (e.g., create mood, emphasize aspects of a character or setting). **Literature 10.** By the end of the year, read and comprehend literature, including stories, dramas, and poetry, at the high end of the grades 2–3 text complexity band independently and proficiently.

© Bridge to Common Core

CRAFT AND STRUCTURE

Students analyze the structure of the selection and how its components relate to each other and the whole when they examine its genre. As they preview the illustrations and identify the characters and setting and then prepare to read, they come to see how purpose shapes the content and style of the text.

Academic Vocabulary ©

realistic fiction a made-up story with characters, settings, and events that seem real

Strategy Response Log

Have students use p. 30 in the *Reader's and Writer's Notebook* to review and use the strategy of summarizing.

Text-Based Comprehension

Introduce Main Selection

Student Edition, pp. 296–297

GENRE Remind students that **realistic fiction** tells a made-up story with characters, settings, and events that seem real. Characters' actions and story endings are reasonable and believable. The key features of realistic fiction are realistic characters, realistic settings, and a believable plot.

PREVIEW AND PREDICT Have students read the title and the names of the author and illustrator. Then have them preview the illustrations and identify the characters and setting they see. Have them use the title and the illustrations to predict what the story will be about.

PURPOSE By analyzing *Jalapeño Bagels,* a realistic fiction selection, students will gain knowledge of foods from different cultures.

Access Main Selection

READER AND TASK SUGGESTIONS

Preparing to Read the Text	Leveled Tasks
• Review using context clues to understand unfamiliar words. • Discuss how setting contributes to a story. • Remind students that when they encounter unfamiliar words, they should adjust their reading rate.	• **Structure** If students have difficulty following the chronology of the selection, have them identify the bakery items one-by-one, as Pablo's parents create them. • **Analysis** If students don't understand why Pablo decides to bring jalapeño bagels to school, have them identify the cultural backgrounds of Pablo's parents. Then have them point out which cultural traditions use jalapeño peppers and which prepare bagels.

See Text Complexity Measures for *Jalapeño Bagels* on the tab at the beginning of this week.

READ Tell students that today they will read *Jalapeño Bagels* for the first time. Use the Read for Understanding routine.

Routine   Read for Understanding ©

Deepen understanding by reading the selection multiple times.

1. **First Read**—If students need support, use the **Access Text** note to help them clarify understanding.

2. **Second Read**—Use the **Close Reading** notes to help students draw knowledge from the text.

Day 2   SMALL GROUP TIME • Differentiate Comprehension, p. SG•49

OL On-Level	**SI** Strategic Intervention	**A** Advanced
• **Practice** Selection Vocabulary • **Read** *Jalapeño Bagels*	• **Reteach** Selection Vocabulary • **Read** *Jalapeño Bagels*	• **Extend** Selection Vocabulary • **Read** *Jalapeño Bagels* • **Investigate** Inquiry Project

eStreet Interactive
www.ReadingStreet.com

Pearson eText
• Student Edition

AudioText CD

Teacher Resources
• Reader's and Writer's Notebook

Background Building Audio CD

Access for All

 SI Strategic Intervention

Work with students to set a purpose for reading or, if time permits, have students work with partners to set purposes.

ELL

Build background To build background, review the selection summary in English (*ELL Handbook* p. 169). Use the Retelling Cards to provide visual support for the summary.

 ELL

If... students need more scaffolding and practice with the **Comprehension Skill, then...** use the activities on p. DI•96 in the Teacher Resources section on SuccessNet.

Access Text ⓒ *If students need help, then...*

⊙ DRAW CONCLUSIONS When you draw conclusions, you use what you know and the details you read. Have students draw a conclusion about where Pablo and his parents live in relation to the bakery.

(Think Aloud) MODEL The story doesn't say where Pablo's family lives, but it give clues. In the last paragraph, Pablo's mother awakens Pablo early to go to work. The next sentence says that they walk down the street to the bakery. So, I draw the conclusion that the bakery is just down the street.

Close Reading ⓒ

SYNTHESIS How can you figure out who runs the bakery? (I can draw the conclusion that Pablo's parents run the bakery because they open it and are the only people working there.)

ANALYSIS • TEXT EVIDENCE What do we learn about the story from the use of dialogue and narration on p. 298? (The dialogue sets up the characters and gives us an idea of what they are like. We know what Pablo sounds like and the kinds of questions he asks. The narration adds details. It tells us that a *panaderia* is a bakery and that it is warm and smells good.)

"What should I bring to school on Monday for International Day?" I ask my mother. "My teacher told us to bring something from our culture."

"You can bring a treat from the *panaderia*," she suggests. Panaderia is what Mama calls our bakery. "Help us bake on Sunday—then you can pick out whatever you want."

"It's a deal," I tell her. I like helping at the bakery. It's warm there, and everything smells so good.

Early Sunday morning, when it is still dark, my mother wakes me up.

"Pablo, it's time to go to work," she says.

298

Student Edition, p. 298

ON THEIR OWN Have students reread pp. 298–299 and draw a conclusion about Pablo's relationship with his parents. For additional practice, use *Let's Practice It!* p. 322 on the *Teacher Resources DVD-ROM.*

We walk down the street to the bakery. My father turns on the lights. My mother turns on the ovens. She gets out the pans and ingredients for *pan dulce.* Pan dulce is Mexican sweet bread.

I help my mother mix and knead the dough. She shapes rolls and loaves of bread and slides them into the oven. People tell her she makes the best pan dulce in town.

"Maybe I'll bring pan dulce to school," I tell her.

299

Student Edition, p. 299

ANALYSIS • TEXT EVIDENCE Why does Pablo like helping at the bakery? Use details from the story to support your answer. (On p. 298, he says he likes it because it's warm there and everything smells good.)

© **Common Core State Standards**

Literature 1. Ask and answer questions to demonstrate understanding of a text, referring explicitly to the text as the basis for the answers. **Literature 3.** Describe characters in a story (e.g., their traits, motivations, or feelings) and explain how their actions contribute to the sequence of events.

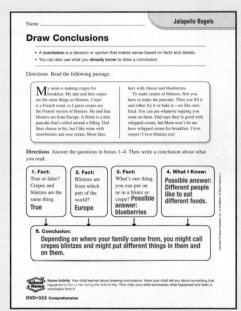

Let's Practice It! TR DVD•322

 **Connect to Social Studies**

Neighborhood Businesses Discuss with students how a neighborhood bakery helps the owners and the residents of the community. For example, by providing food, the bakery helps the residents. The residents, in return, put their money back into the community by helping people, such as the owners, who live there.

Activate Prior Knowledge Create a content web to record students' prior knowledge of bakeries. We are going to read about foods that are made in a bakery. What foods can you find at a bakery? Record students' answers on the web, and add to the web as students read the selection.

1ST READ

Access Text © If students need help, then…

UNFAMILIAR WORDS Have students use context clues to determine the meaning of *empanadas de calabaza* on the top of p. 300.

MODEL The term *empanadas de calabaza* is unfamiliar because it comes from another language. Do you know what language it's from? (Spanish) There are clues that help me figure out the meaning. I see that Pablo explains they are pumpkin turnovers that have a filling and are baked until the dough is brown and flaky.

2ND READ

Close Reading ©

ANALYSIS • TEXT EVIDENCE Use context clues to figure out the meaning of *chango bars* on p. 301. (I see that there are clues in the text that will help me figure out the meaning. Pablo explains that *chango* means "monkey man." So *chango bars* means "monkey man bars." Pablo and his mother have been making sweets and pastries, so *chango bars* is probably a nickname for another type of pastry or dessert.)

Next we make *empanadas de calabaza*—pumpkin turnovers. I'm in charge of spooning the pumpkin filling. Mama folds the dough in half and presses the edges with a fork. She bakes them until they are flaky and golden brown. Some customers come to our bakery just for her turnovers.

300

Student Edition, p. 300

ON THEIR OWN Have students reread p. 300 and use context clues to figure out further information about the meaning of *empanadas de calabaza*. For additional practice with unfamiliar words, use *Reader's and Writer's Notebook,* p. 356.

"Maybe I'll bring empanadas de calabaza instead."
"You'll figure it out," she says. "Ready to make *chango* bars?" Chango means "monkey man."

Student Edition, p. 301

INFERENCE What are Pablo and Mama making? (*empanadas de calabaza* and *chango* bars) Why do you think the author uses the Spanish names for the baked goods? (The author uses the Spanish names for the baked goods to tell the reader that the foods are from Mexican and Spanish-speaking cultures.)

Common Core State Standards

Literature 1. Ask and answer questions to demonstrate understanding of a text, referring explicitly to the text as the basis for the answers. **Language 4.** Determine or clarify the meaning of unknown and multiple-meaning word and phrases based on grade 3 reading and content, choosing flexibly from a range of strategies. **Also Language 4.a.**

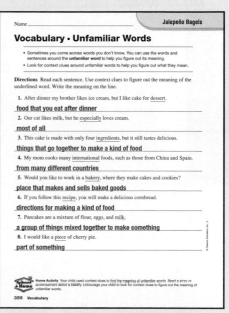

Reader's and Writer's Notebook, p. 356

Connect to Social Studies

Spanish-Speaking Countries Have a volunteer point out the country of Mexico on a world map. Explain that most people in Mexico speak Spanish. Then point out other countries where the Spanish language is spoken, such as Panama, Argentina, Costa Rica, and Spain.

Vocabulary: Expression Focus students' attention on the expression "figure it out" in the second paragraph on p. 301. *Figure out* is an idiom that means "to think out." People might use this idiom when they are trying to make a decision or to understand something. Ask students to share a time when they had to "figure out" something.

Jalapeño Bagels **301a**

Access Text © If students need help, then...

⊙ SUMMARIZE Have students summarize how Pablo helps his mother. (He helps his mother mix and knead the dough, spoons filling into *empanandas de calabaza,* and adds chocolate chips and nuts to the *chango* bars mix.)

(Think Aloud) MODEL When I read, I often stop to summarize what has happened. When I summarize, I try to recall the main events. I remember that first Pablo helped his mother knead dough. I can go back and reread to see what happened next. I want to be sure it makes sense and follows a logical order.

Mama lets me pour in the chocolate chips and nuts. When she's not looking, I pour in more chocolate chips.

"I could bring chango bars. They're my favorite dessert."

"Mine, too," says Mama. "This batch should be especially good. I put in extra chips."

302

Student Edition, p. 302

Close Reading ©

ANALYSIS • TEXT EVIDENCE Why does Pablo help his parents at the bakery? How does he help them? Use details from the story to support your answer. (Pablo needs to choose a food from his culture to bring to International Day. His parents tell him he can bring something from their bakery if he helps them bake on Sunday. Pablo helps his mother bake pastries and sweets from Mexican culture. He helps his father make bagels.)

REREAD CHALLENGING TEXT Have students reread paragraph one on page 303. Students should understand that English is spoken in the United States and that Spanish is spoken in many countries. However, they may not understand that Yiddish is a language spoken by many Jewish people, but it is not the language spoken in a specific country.

ON THEIR OWN Have students reread p. 303 and summarize the events on the page, maintaining meaning and logical order.

If you want to teach this selection in two sessions, stop here.

If you want to continue reading this selection, turn to page 304–305.

My father calls from the back room. "Pablo! Come help me with the bagels!" Papa speaks English and Yiddish. He learned Yiddish from his family in New York City. I know some words too. *Bubbe* means "grandmother." He uses my bubbe's recipe to make the bagels.

First he makes the dough in a big metal bowl. Then he rolls it out into a long rope shape. He cuts off pieces and shows me how to connect the ends in a circle. We put the circles on trays where they sit and rise.

303

Student Edition, p. 303

SYNTHESIS Based on what you have read so far, how do you think the story will develop? (I predict that Pablo will help make more baked goods and will try to decide what to take to school for International Day.)

Common Core State Standards

Literature 1. Ask and answer questions to demonstrate understanding of a text, referring explicitly to the text as the basis for the answers. **Literature 3.** Describe characters in a story (e.g., their traits, motivations, or feelings) and explain how their actions contribute to the sequence of events. **Also Literature 10.**

Access for All

SI Strategic Intervention

Have students work in pairs to discuss the setting shown in the illustrations. Ask them to describe the clues in the illustrations that indicate the setting is a bakery.

A Advanced

Explain that Yiddish is a language that comes from German. It is spoken by some Jewish people. Have students find more information about Yiddish and the people who speak it.

ELL

Vocabulary List the names of the baked goods Pablo and his parents make: *pan dulce, empanadas de calabaza, chango bars, bagels*. Add to the list the names of students' favorite baked goods. Discuss the languages the names come from.

Jalapeño Bagels **303a**

© Common Core State Standards

Writing 7. Conduct short research projects that build knowledge about a topic. **Writing 8.** Recall information from experiences or gather information from print and digital sources; take brief notes on sources and sort evidence into provided categories. **Language 1.g.** Form and use comparative and superlative adjectives and adverbs, and choose between them depending on what is to be modified. **Language 2.f.** Use spelling patterns and generalizations (e.g., word families, position-based spellings, syllable patterns, ending rules, meaningful word parts) in writing words.

© Bridge to Common Core

RESEARCH TO BUILD AND PRESENT KNOWLEDGE

On Day 2 of the weeklong research project, students gather relevant information based on their focused questions from Day 1. They will consult online sources, print sources, and expert sources. They will hone their research skills, evaluate sources for credibility, and learn to bookmark Web sites for quick access. This process enables students to demonstrate an understanding of the subject under investigation. As students access online information, they should always note their sources for a Works Cited page.

Research and Inquiry

Step 2 Navigate/Search

TEACH Have students generate a research plan for gathering relevant information about their topic. Have students review their inquiry questions and decide on the best sources for answers to their questions: online sources, print sources, or expert sources. Remind students to take notes as they gather information. Then encourage students to improve the focus of their research by interviewing a local expert on the topic. Help students to use online directories to locate expert sources to contact.

Think Aloud **MODEL** When looking for information about traditional foods, I found *Challah is a loaf of bread that is traditionally eaten by Jewish people on the Sabbath, holidays, and other ceremonial occasions.* I will use key words from this information, such as *traditional* and *bread,* to find more specific information about traditional breads from other cultures. I will also search for local bakers that I might interview about breads from various cultures.

GUIDE PRACTICE Have students continue their review of Web sites they identified. Show them how to bookmark Web sites. Explain that bookmarks allow students to go on to a Web site immediately, instead of typing in the complete address.

ON THEIR OWN Have students continue to research their topic. Encourage them to interview family or friends as expert sources about different cultures.

Conventions

Comparative and Superlative Adverbs

TEACH Write these sentences: *The turtle is slow. The snail is slower. The sloth is slowest of the three.* Underline *slower* and *slowest.* To compare characteristics, add *-er* to most adjectives. To compare three or more characteristics, add *-est* to most adjectives. Remind students that we can also make comparisons with adverbs. Then write sentences using the phrases *more slowly* and *most slowly.* Explain that we usually use *-er* and *-est* with one-syllable adverbs and *more* and *most* with longer adverbs. Adverbs that end in the suffix *-ly* usually use *more* and *most* to make comparisons.

GUIDE PRACTICE Write the following adverbs of manner: *quickly, softly, soon,* and *early* on the board. Point out that the suffixes *-er* and *-est* are used with *early* because *-ly* is not a suffix in *early.* Guide students in changing each adverb to the appropriate comparative and superlative forms.

Provide students with this sentence about the selection: *Pablo twisted the dough most quickly.* Have students write other sentences about the story using comparative and superlative adverbs and read them aloud.

ON THEIR OWN For additional practice, use *Reader's and Writer's Notebook,* p. 353.

Spelling

Vowel Patterns *ei, eigh*

TEACH Remind students that their spelling words have vowel patterns *ei* and *eigh.* Point out that *ei* often stands for the long e sound, as in *ceiling* or *receive.* Then point out that *eigh* can stand for long a, as in *weight,* or long i, as in *height.*

GUIDE PRACTICE Have students write each spelling word and underline the vowel pattern. Remember to segment the words in your mind and think about letter sounds, word parts, and syllables. Call on students to correctly pronounce each word.

ON THEIR OWN For additional practice, use *Reader's and Writer's Notebook,* p. 354.

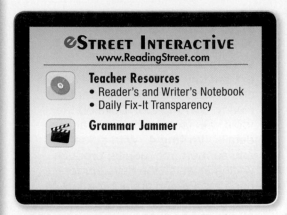

Daily Fix-It

3. Blake and her put wallnuts in the banana bread. *(she; walnuts)*
4. You aught to drink a glass of Milk. *(ought; milk)*

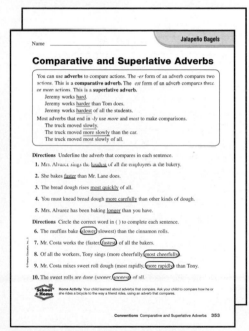

Reader's and Writer's Notebook, pp. 353–354

Conventions To provide students with practice on comparative and superlative adverbs, use the modified grammar lessons in the *ELL Handbook* and Grammar Jammer online at: www.ReadingStreet.com

Common Core State Standards

Writing 2. Write informative/ explanatory texts to examine a topic and convey ideas and information clearly. **Writing 2.b.** Develop the topic with facts, definitions, and details. **Writing 4.** With guidance and support from adults, produce writing in which the development and organization are appropriate to task and purpose. **Writing 5.** With guidance and support from peers and adults, develop and strengthen writing as needed by planning, revising, and editing.

Writing

Invitation

Writing Trait: Organization

INTRODUCE THE PROMPT Remind students that an invitation should offer a reason for the special event and include important details, such as the event's date, location, and time. Have students think about these features as they plan their writing. Then explain that today they will begin the writing process for an invitation. Read aloud the writing prompt.

Writing Prompt

Invite a friend over for dinner, using specific details.

SELECT A TOPIC

Think Aloud The first part of the writing process is selecting a topic. I know I will write an invitation to invite a friend to dinner, but I need to include a reason for the special event. Let's make a web and list reasons why we might invite someone over to dinner. **Display a concept web. Write** *Reasons for a Dinner Party* **in the center oval and model listing ideas.** One reason I might have a dinner party is to welcome someone back from a trip. List the idea and continue brainstorming aloud with students.

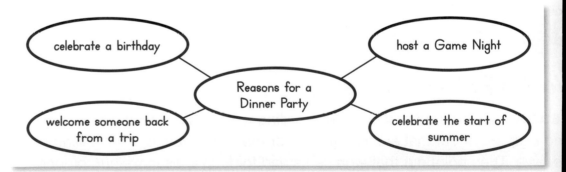

GATHER INFORMATION Have students complete a web of their own. Remind students that at this point they are only brainstorming. They will need to make a final decision about the focus of their invitation a little later.

Corrective feedback As students fill in their webs, move around the room and confer briefly with struggling students. Suggest that these students generate ideas by brainstorming with a partner, drawing pictures, or remembering times they have had friends over for dinner.

Mini-Lesson Organize Your Ideas

eSTREET INTERACTIVE
www.ReadingStreet.com

Teacher Resources
• Reader's and Writer's Notebook

▌ A four-column chart helps you organize ideas. Write heads for each column and fill in details below. Write the first column head: *What*. Fill in details, such as *outdoor barbecue to celebrate the start of summer*.

▌ Next, I will write *When* and *Where* as the heads of the next two columns. Write the heads and fill in party details, such as *Saturday, June 24, 5:00 P.M.,* and *Horner Park*.

▌ I will write RSVP in the last column and include my contact information.

Have students begin a four-column chart for their own invitation using the form on p. 355 of their *Reader's and Writer's Notebook*.

Routine Quick Write for Fluency [Team Talk]

. **Talk** Have pairs discuss how the chart helped them focus their ideas.

. **Write** Each student writes a paragraph summarizing the steps he or she took to plan a draft.

. **Share** Partners read their paragraphs to one another.

Routines Flip Chart

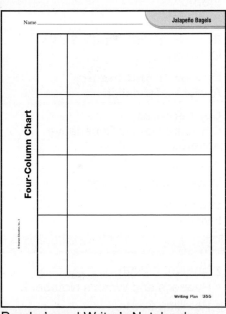

Reader's and Writer's Notebook, p. 355

Wrap Up Your Day!

✔ **Content Knowledge** What did you learn about the different cultures where the foods Pablo's parents made come from?

✔ **Text-Based Comprehension** How were you able to draw conclusions about how Pablo felt about helping in the bakery?

Preview DAY 3

Tell students that tomorrow they will read more about what Pablo decides to bring to International Day.

Materials

- Student Edition
- Reader's and Writer's Notebook
- Retelling Cards
- Decodable Reader

Ⓒ Common Core State Standards

Speaking/Listening 1. Engage effectively in a range of collaborative discussions (one-on-one, in groups, and teacher-led) with diverse partners on grade 3 topics and texts, building on others' ideas and expressing their own clearly. **Language 6.** Acquire and use accurately grade-appropriate conversational, general academic, and domain-specific words and phrases, including those that signal spatial and temporal relationships (e.g., *After dinner that night we went looking for them*).

Content Knowledge

Foods from Different Cultures

EXPAND THE CONCEPT Remind students of the weekly concept question, *How can different cultures contribute to the foods we eat?* Discuss how the question relates to *Jalapeño Bagels.* Encourage students to think about how many of the foods we eat come from different cultures.

Build Oral Language

TALK ABOUT SENTENCES AND WORDS Read sentences from *Jalapeño Bagels,* Student Edition p. 299.

She gets out the pans and ingredients for pan dulce. *Pan dulce is Mexican sweet bread.*

- The phrase *gets out* is an idiom. What does *gets out* mean here? (takes out)
- What other words could be used in place of *gets out? (gathers, collects)*
- Which words in the first sentence are in Spanish? *(pan dulce)*
- What is *pan dulce?* (Mexican sweet bread)
- How do you know what *pan dulce* is? (The second sentence tells what it is.)
- What is the purpose of the second sentence? (Its purpose is to define *pan dulce,* so the reader will know what it is.)

Team Talk Have students combine the sentences and replace the words *gets out.* They can use this sentence frame:

She _____ the pans and ingredients for pan dulce, which is _____.

Build Oral Vocabulary

Robust Vocabulary Routine

Introduce Write the word *grumble* on the board. Have students say it with you. Yesterday we read about pastries and sweets that Pablo baked with his mother. Reading about the foods may have made you feel hungry. Sometimes our stomachs *grumble* when we feel hungry. Have students determine a definition for *grumble*. (When something *grumbles,* it makes a low, heavy sound like thunder.)

Demonstrate Have students answer questions to demonstrate understanding. What is another thing that might *grumble*? (A very heavy truck driving on an uneven street could make a grumbling noise.)

Apply Have students apply their understanding. When has your stomach *grumbled*?

Display the Word Students can decode the sounds in *grumble* and blend them.

See p. OV•4 to teach *allergic*.

Routines Flip Chart

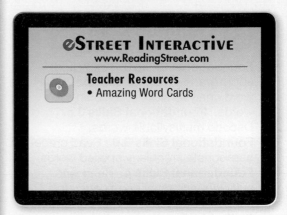

Amazing Words

nutrition	grumble
calorie	allergic
flavor	wholesome
spice	grate
nutmeg	agent

ADD TO THE CONCEPT MAP Discuss the Amazing Words *spice* and *nutmeg.* Add these and other concept-related words to the concept map. Use the following questions to develop students' understanding of the concept. Remind students to make pertinent comments and answer questions with appropriate detail.

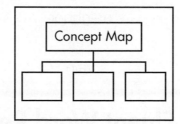

Concept Map

Pablo and his mother add many ingredients to the pastries to give them flavor, such as pumpkin filling and chocolate chips. Think about ingredients we use to flavor food. How are *spices* used to flavor food?

What types of foods might *nutmeg* be used to flavor?

Jalapeño Bagels **304b**

Ⓒ **Common Core State Standards**

Foundational Skills 3. Know and apply grade-level phonics and word analysis skills in decoding words. **Foundational Skills 3.c.** Decode multisyllable words. **Foundational Skills 3.d.** Read grade-appropriate irregularly spelled words. **Foundational Skills 4.** Read with sufficient accuracy and fluency to support comprehension. **Foundational Skills 4.b.** Read on-level prose and poetry orally with accuracy, appropriate rate, and expression on successive readings.

Phonics

🔊 Vowel Patterns *ei, eigh*

MODEL WORD SORTING Write *Long a, Long e,* and *Long i* as heads in a three-column chart. Now we are going to sort words that have the syllabication patterns *ei* and *eigh*. We'll put words with the long *a* vowel sound in the first column. Words with the long *e* vowel sound will go in the second column. Words with the long *i* sound will go in the third column. I will start. Write *weight* and model how to read it, using the Phonics lesson on p. 290a. I hear the vowel sound /ā/ in *weight,* so I will write the word in the first column. I will underline the letters that spell the long *a* sound in *weight: e-i-g-h*. Model reading *either* and *reins* in the same way.

GUIDE PRACTICE Use the practice words from the activity on p. 294c and other words for the word sort. Point to a word. Have students read the word, identify the vowel sound, and tell where it belongs on the chart. Then have them identify the letters that stand for the vowel sound in the word.

> **Corrective feedback** | For corrective feedback, model blending the word to read it.

Long *a*	Long *e*	Long *i*
w<u>eigh</u>t	<u>ei</u>ther	h<u>eigh</u>t
r<u>ei</u>ns	n<u>ei</u>ther	
sl<u>eigh</u>	c<u>ei</u>ling	
n<u>eigh</u>bor		
v<u>ei</u>l		
v<u>ei</u>n		

Fluent Word Reading

MODEL Write *eight*. You know the sounds for *eigh* and *t*. Blend them and read the word: *eight*.

GUIDE PRACTICE Write the words below. Say the sounds in your head for each spelling you see. When I point to the word, we'll read it together. Allow one second per sound previewing time for the first reading.

| neigh | deceive | reindeer | receive | eighty | freight |

ON THEIR OWN Have students read the list above three or four times, until they can read one word per second.

Decodable Passage 24B

...students need help, then...

Read *Sleigh Rides*

READ WORDS IN ISOLATION Have students turn to p. 105 in *Decodable Practice Readers 3.2* and find the first list of words. Each word in this list has long *a*, long *e*, or long *i* spelled *ei* or *eigh*. Be sure that students correctly pronounce the long vowel sound in each word.

Next, have students read the high-frequency words.

PREVIEW Have students read the title and preview the story. Tell them that they will read words that have long *a*, long *e*, or long *i* spelled *ei* or *eigh*.

READ WORDS IN CONTEXT Chorally read the story along with the students. Have students identify words in the story that have long *a*, long *e*, or long *i* spelled *ei* or *eigh*. Make sure that students are monitoring their accuracy when they decode.

Team Talk Pair students and have them take turns reading the story aloud to each other. Monitor students as they read to check for proper pronunciation and appropriate pacing.

eSTREET INTERACTIVE
www.ReadingStreet.com

Pearson eText
• Decodable Reader

Access for All

 Strategic Intervention

If students have difficulty decoding multisyllabic words, have them practice segmenting the sounds, then blending the sounds to pronounce the entire word.

A Advanced

Have students choose three or four words from the story and write a sentence that uses each word.

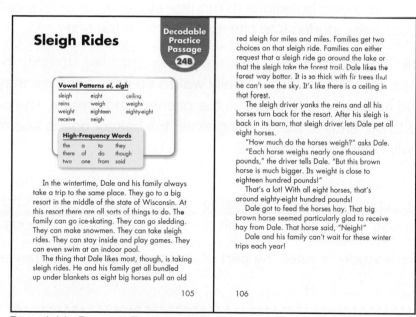

Decodable Practice Passage 24B

Sleigh Rides

Decodable Practice Passage **24B**

Vowel Patterns *ei*, *eigh*

sleigh	eight	ceiling
reins	weigh	weighs
weight	eighteen	eighty-eight
receive	neigh	

High-Frequency Words

the	a	to	they
there	of	do	though
two	one	from	said

In the wintertime, Dale and his family always take a trip to the same place. They go to a big resort in the middle of the state of Wisconsin. At this resort there are all sorts of things to do. The family can go ice-skating. They can go sledding. They can make snowmen. They can take sleigh rides. They can stay inside and play games. They can even swim at an indoor pool.

The thing that Dale likes most, though, is taking sleigh rides. He and his family get all bundled up under blankets as eight big horses pull an old

105

red sleigh for miles and miles. Families get two choices on that sleigh ride. Families can either request that a sleigh ride go around the lake or that the sleigh take the forest trail. Dale likes the forest way better. It is so thick with fir trees that he can't see the sky. It's like there is a ceiling in that forest.

The sleigh driver yanks the reins and all his horses turn back for the resort. After his sleigh is back in its barn, that sleigh driver lets Dale pet all eight horses.

"How much do the horses weigh?" asks Dale.

"Each horse weighs nearly one thousand pounds," the driver tells Dale. "But this brown horse is much bigger. Its weight is close to eighteen hundred pounds!"

That's a lot! With all eight horses, that's around eighty-eight hundred pounds!

Dale got to feed the horses hay. That big brown horse seemed particularly glad to receive hay from Dale. That horse said, "Neigh!"

Dale and his family can't wait for these winter trips each year!

106

 ELL

Pronunciation Have students practice pronouncing words with long *a* spelled *ei* or *eigh* by playing telephone. Have one student whisper the phrase *eight sleighs and eighteen reindeer* to another student. The second student passes the words along to another, and so on.

**Common Core
State Standards**

Literature 1. Ask and answer questions to demonstrate understanding of a text, referring explicitly to the text as the basis for the answers. **Literature 2.** Recount stories, including fables, folktales, and myths from diverse cultures; determine the central message, lesson, or moral and explain how it is conveyed through key details in the text. **Also Speaking/Listening 4.**

Strategy Response Log

Have students revisit the text and use p. 30 in the *Reader's and Writer's Notebook* to summarize the first half of *Jalapeño Bagels*.

Text-Based Comprehension
Check Understanding

Student Edition, pp. 296–297

If... you chose to read *Jalapeño Bagels* in two parts,

then... use the following questions to monitor students' understanding of the selection. Encourage students to cite evidence from the text.

SYNTHESIS Why do Pablo and his parents have to wake up early in the morning when it is still dark? (The family wakes up early because they own a bakery, and it takes time to make all the pastries and breads. The baked goods need to be ready in the morning when the bakery opens and many customers will want to buy them.)

ANALYSIS What clues in the story tell you that Pablo's father is not from a Spanish-speaking culture? (Pablo's father speaks English and Yiddish, not Spanish. He also makes bagels, which are not Spanish baked goods.)

RETELL Have students retell the part of *Jalapeño Bagels* that they read yesterday.

> **Corrective feedback**
> **If...** students leave out important details,
> **then...** have students look back through the illustrations in the selection.

READ Use the **Access Text** and **Close Reading** notes to finish reading *Jalapeño Bagels*.

... you followed the Read for Understanding routine below,
ıen... ask students to retell the selection before you reread *Jalapeño Bagels*.

ETELL Have students retell the part of *Jalapeño Bagels* that they read ɜsterday.

Corrective feedback	**If...** students leave out important details, **then...** have students look back through the illustrations in the selection.

EAD Return to p. 298–299 and use the **2nd Read/Close Reading** notes to read *Jalapeño Bagels*.

Read Main Selection

Routine Read for Understanding

ɜepen understanding by reading the selection multiple times.

- **First Read**—If students need support, use the **Access Text** notes to help them clarify understanding.
- **Second Read**—Use the **Close Reading** notes to help students draw knowledge from the text.

eStreet Interactive
www.ReadingStreet.com

- **Pearson eText**
  - Student Edition
- **AudioText CD**
- **Teacher Resources**
  - Reader's and Writer's Notebook
- **Background Building Audio CD**

ELL

Check Retelling To support retelling, review the multilingual summary for *Jalapeño Bagels* with the appropriate Retelling Cards to scaffold understanding.

Day 3 SMALL GROUP TIME • Differentiate Close Reading, p. SG•49

OL On-Level	SI Strategic Intervention	A Advanced
• **Reread** to Develop Vocabulary • **Read** *Jalapeño Bagels*	• **Reread** to Develop Vocabulary • **Read** *Jalapeño Bagels*	• **Reread** to Extend Vocabulary • **Read** *Jalapeño Bagels* • **Investigate** Inquiry Project

ELL

If... students need more scaffolding and practice with the **Main Selection**, **then...** use the activities on p. DI•97 in the Teacher Resources section on SuccessNet.

Access Text © If students need help, then...

◉ **SUMMARIZE** After students finish reading pp. 304–305, ask them to summarize the story so far. (Pablo helps his mother make pumpkin turnovers and *chango* bars. Then he helps his father make bagels and *challah*.)

Think Aloud **MODEL** When I summarize, I tell the most important ideas in a story. I know that Pablo's parents own a bakery and that he helps them bake. Why is Pablo helping his parents? (to decide what to bring to International Day) What foods do they bake? (*pan dulce,* pumpkin turnovers, *chango* bars, *challah,* bagels)

Close Reading ©

SYNTHESIS • TEXT EVIDENCE

Why are Pablo and his father able to make the *challah* and the bagels at the same time? When do they make the *challah*? What happens next? Use evidence from the text to support your answer. (On p. 303 they were making bagels. On 304, it says "While we are waiting," so they made the *challah* while the bagel dough was rising. When the bagel dough finished rising, Papa boiled the bagels and Pablo sprinkled them with poppy seeds and sesame seeds. Then the bagels went in the oven.)

While we are waiting my father makes *challah,* Jewish braided bread. He lets me practice braiding challah dough at my own counter. It's a lot like braiding hair. The customers say it is almost too beautiful to eat.

"Maybe I'll bring a loaf of challah to school," I tell Papa. He smiles.

When the bagel dough has risen, he boils the bagels in a huge pot of water and fishes them out with a long slotted spoon. I sprinkle on poppy seeds and sesame seeds, and then they go in the oven.

304

Student Edition, p. 304

ON THEIR OWN Have pairs of students review pp. 304–305 of *Jalapeño Bagels* and list important events. Have them share the main events with the class.

"Maybe I could bring sesame-seed bagels with cream cheese."

"No *lox?*" Lox is smoked salmon. My father's favorite bagel is pumpernickel with a smear of cream cheese and lox.

I crinkle my nose. "Lox tastes like fish. Jam is better."

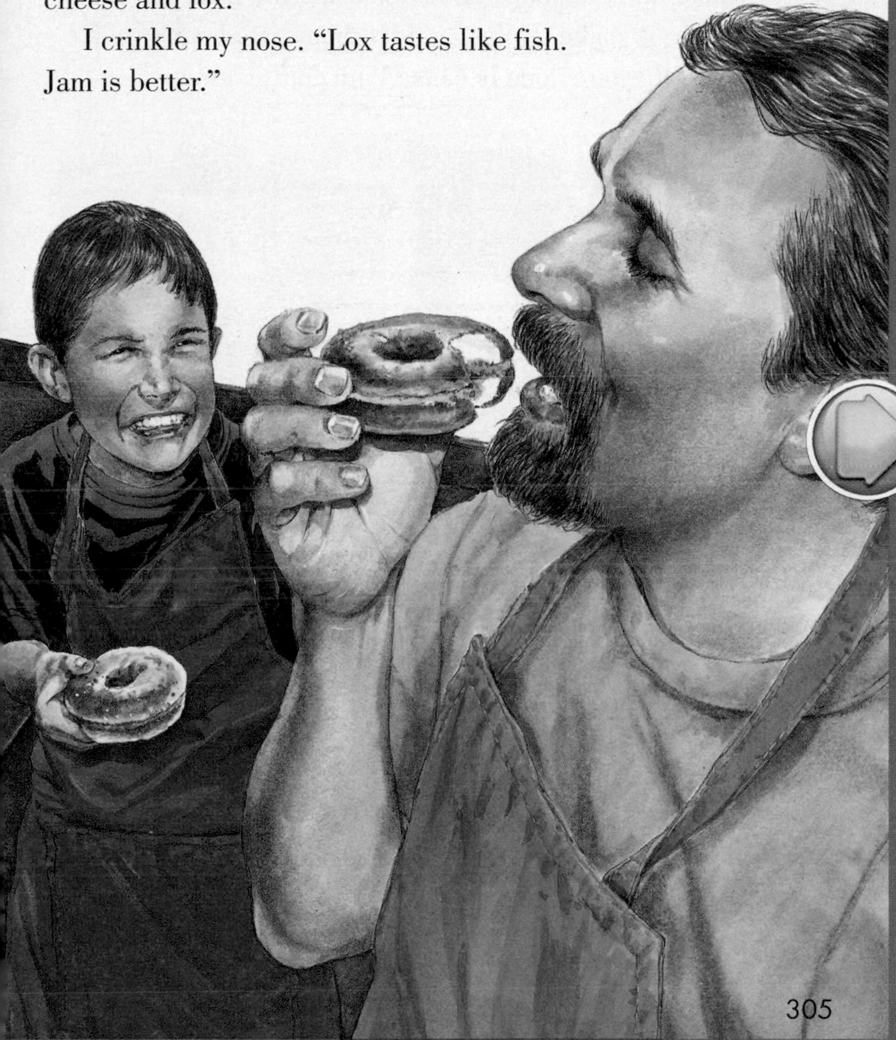

305

Student Edition, p. 305

INFERENCE Why does Papa smile when Pablo says he might bring a loaf of *challah* to school? (Papa is proud that Pablo is considering bringing something from Papa's culture to International Day.)

Common Core State Standards

Literature 1. Ask and answer questions to demonstrate understanding of a text, referring explicitly to the text as the basis for the answers. **Literature 2.** Recount stories, including fables, folktales, and myths from diverse cultures; determine the central message, lesson, or moral and explain how it is conveyed through key details in the text. **Literature 3.** Describe characters in a story (e.g., their traits, motivations, or feelings) and explain how their actions contribute to the sequence of events.

Connect to Social Studies

Jewish Traditions Tell students that *challah* is traditionally eaten by Jewish people on the Sabbath, holidays, and other ceremonial occasions.

ELL

Graphic Organizer Have students create a word log to help them remember food names and keep track of events in the story. Students list the names of the foods Pablo and his parents make, their meanings, and sample sentences. Students should list the names in the order they appear in the story, and use the log to summarize important events in the story.

1ST READ

Access Text © If students need help, then...

⊙ DRAW CONCLUSIONS Ask students to draw a conclusion to answer the question: Does Pablo like lox?

(Think Aloud) **MODEL** A conclusion is a decision you reach that makes sense given the details—including what the illustrations show—in the text you're reading. On page 307, Pablo says everything is good except for the lox. And if I turn back to page 305, I read that Pablo prefers jam to lox. Also, the illustration shows Pablo making a funny face as his father eats lox. The conclusion I draw from this is that Pablo does not like lox.

ON THEIR OWN Have students reread pp. 306–307 and draw a conclusion about how Pablo's parents created the special recipe for jalapeño bagels.

My mother joins us and helps my father make another batch of bagels—*jalapeño* bagels. My parents use their own special recipe. While Papa kneads the dough, Mama chops the jalapeño *chiles*. She tosses them into the dough and adds dried red peppers. We roll, cut, make circles, and let them rise. I can't wait until they are done because I am getting hungry.

306

Student Edition, p. 306

2ND READ

Close Reading ©

ANALYSIS • TEXT EVIDENCE How are the *jalapeño* bagels similar to the other bagels Pablo and his father make? What is different about the *jalapeño* bagels? Use details from the story in your comparison. (The *jalapeño* bagels include the same basic ingredients as the poppy seed and sesame seed bagels. On p. 306 it says Pablo and Papa roll, cut, make circles, and let them rise, so all the bagels are cooked and prepared the same way. However, the *jalapeño* bagels include *jalapeño chiles* and red peppers instead of seeds.)

ANALYSIS Help students generate text-based questions by providing the following question stem: In the selection, why does Pablo _____?

DEVELOP LANGUAGE Have students reread the third sentence on p. 306. What does the word *kneads* mean? What else is something you could *knead* besides dough? Explain.

"Have you decided what you're going to bring to school?" asks Mama.

"It's hard to choose. Everything is so good," I tell her. I look at Papa. "Except for lox."

"You should decide before we open," warns Mama, "or else our customers will buy everything up."

307

Student Edition, p. 307

EVALUATION Do you think that Pablo's parents' bakery is a successful business? Why do you think so? (I can draw the conclusion that the bakery is successful because Pablo's mother says that their customers buy everything up.)

Common Core State Standards

Literature 1. Ask and answer questions to demonstrate understanding of a text, referring explicitly to the text as the basis for the answers. **Literature 3.** Describe characters in a story (e.g., their traits, motivations, or feelings) and explain how their actions contribute to the sequence of events.

Connect to Social Studies

Bagels Explain that Americans began eating bagels in the early 1900s in New York after Eastern European Jews brought the food to the United States. Have students name foods from different cultures that they have tried and liked. Discuss how many foods that we eat regularly originally came from other cultures.

 ELL

Language Transfer: Quotation Marks Students may have difficulty distinguishing dialogue from the rest of a sentence. Tell them that quotation marks are used at the beginning and the end of dialogue. Explain that words such as *said* or *replied* usually are found just before or after dialogue. Make sure students can identify the dialogue on p. 307. Point out that the words *asks, tell,* and *warns* all indicate dialogue.

Jalapeño Bagels **307a**

Access Text © If students need help, then...

Review **SEQUENCE** Have students tell the sequence of the main events that led to Pablo's decision to bring *jalapeño* bagels to school.

Think Aloud **MODEL** Pablo bakes *pan dulce*, pumpkin turnovers, and *chango* bars with Mama. Then he bakes bagels and *challah* with Papa. Finally, they all make *jalapeño* bagels, and because that food is a mixture of both cultures, Pablo decides to bring *jalapeño* bagels.

ON THEIR OWN For additional practice, use *Let's Practice It!* page 323 on the *Teacher Resources DVD-ROM*.

CROSS-TEXT EVALUATION
Use a Strategy to Self-Check How did the Read Aloud, "Quentin's Complaint," help you understand this selection?

I walk past all the sweet breads, chango bars, and bagels.

I think about my mother and my father and all the different things they make in the bakery. And suddenly I know exactly what I'm going to bring.

"Jalapeño bagels," I tell my parents. "And I'll spread them with cream cheese and jam."

"Why jalapeño bagels?" asks Papa.

"Because they are a mixture of both of you. Just like me!"

308

Student Edition, p. 308

Close Reading ©

ANALYSIS • TEXT EVIDENCE Recall the order of steps that Pablo and his father followed to prepare and bake bagels. How is the order of steps in the recipe on p. 309 similar to the sequence they followed? (First, Pablo and his father make the dough. Then they roll it into long rope shapes and connect the ends to make circles. Then they let the dough rise. Next they boil the bagels. Finally, they bake the bagels in the oven. The recipe follows the same sequence of steps.)

SYNTHESIS • TEXT EVIDENCE Using what you learned in this selection, tell what we can learn about food from different cultures. Have students cite examples from the text to support their responses.

CHECK PREDICTIONS Have students return to the predictions they made earlier and confirm whether they were accurate.

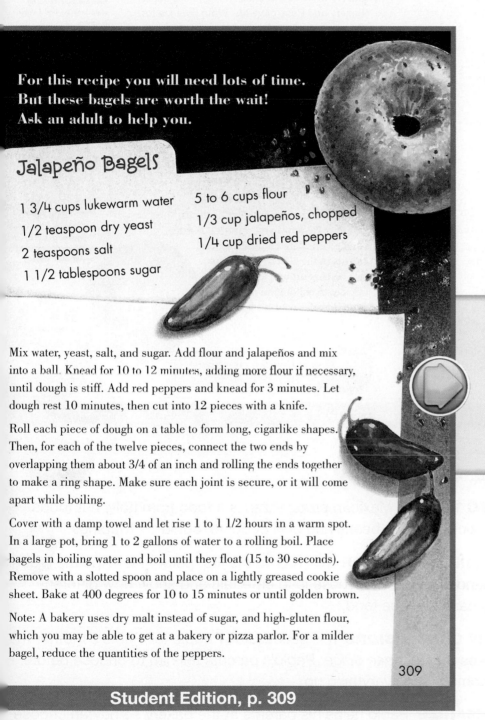

For this recipe you will need lots of time. But these bagels are worth the wait! Ask an adult to help you.

Jalapeño Bagels

1 3/4 cups lukewarm water

1/2 teaspoon dry yeast

2 teaspoons salt

1 1/2 tablespoons sugar

5 to 6 cups flour

1/3 cup jalapeños, chopped

1/4 cup dried red peppers

Mix water, yeast, salt, and sugar. Add flour and jalapeños and mix into a ball. Knead for 10 to 12 minutes, adding more flour if necessary, until dough is stiff. Add red peppers and knead for 3 minutes. Let dough rest 10 minutes, then cut into 12 pieces with a knife.

Roll each piece of dough on a table to form long, cigarlike shapes. Then, for each of the twelve pieces, connect the two ends by overlapping them about 3/4 of an inch and rolling the ends together to make a ring shape. Make sure each joint is secure, or it will come apart while boiling.

Cover with a damp towel and let rise 1 to 1 1/2 hours in a warm spot. In a large pot, bring 1 to 2 gallons of water to a rolling boil. Place bagels in boiling water and boil until they float (15 to 30 seconds). Remove with a slotted spoon and place on a lightly greased cookie sheet. Bake at 400 degrees for 10 to 15 minutes or until golden brown.

Note: A bakery uses dry malt instead of sugar, and high-gluten flour, which you may be able to get at a bakery or pizza parlor. For a milder bagel, reduce the quantities of the peppers.

309

Student Edition, p. 309

ANALYSIS How are the *jalapeño* bagels a mixture of both Mama and Papa? (Bagels come from Papa's Jewish culture. The recipe for *jalapeño* bagels includes *jalapeño chiles* and red peppers from Mama's Mexican culture.)

Common Core State Standards

Literature 1. Ask and answer questions to demonstrate understanding of a text, referring explicitly to the text as the basis for the answers. **Literature 2.** Recount stories, including fables, folktales, and myths from diverse cultures; determine the central message, lesson, or moral and explain how it is conveyed through key details in the text.

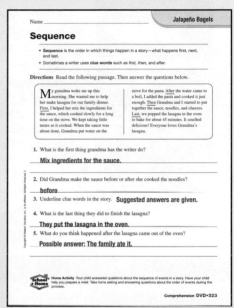

Let's Practice It! TR DVD•323

ELL

Monitor Comprehension Read aloud the first two sentences on p. 308. Model using the reading strategy monitoring comprehension by saying: I wonder what Pablo is thinking as he makes his decision. I know he is thinking about his parents and the foods from the bakery. How does that relate to what food he should bring to school? Read the rest of the page and have students identify why Pablo chooses jalapeño bagels. (Pablo wanted to bring a food that represented both his parents' cultures. Jalapeño bagels are a mixture of both Jewish and Hispanic cultures.)

Common Core State Standards
Literature 1. Ask and answer questions to demonstrate understanding of a text, referring explicitly to the text as the basis for the answers. Also Literature 2., Writing 8.

Envision It! Retell

READING STREET ONLINE
STORY SORT
www.ReadingStreet.com

310

Think Critically

1. In the story, Pablo takes jalapeño bagels to school for International Day because they combine his mother's and his father's cultures. What else can you think of that represents two different cultures? Explain your answer. Text to World

2. Is the narrator of this story first or third person? Why do you think the author chose to write the story from that point of view? What do you think the author's purpose is for writing this story? Think Like an Author

3. Is the family bakery successful? What details from the story support your answer?  Draw Conclusions

4. Summarize the story in two to three sentences. Be sure to use logical order.
   Summarize

5. **Look Back and Write** Look back through the story. Think about the two cultures of Pablo's parents. Now write a paragraph telling why jalapeño bagels are special to Pablo. Be sure to include facts and details from the story in your paragraph.
   Key Ideas and Details • Text Evidence

Meet the Author and the Illustrator

Natasha Wing

Natasha Wing lives in northern California, where she often buys jalapeño bagels at a bakery in town. The bakery, called Los Bagels Bakery and Cafe, gave Ms. Wing the idea for this story. Los Bagels offers many tasty snacks, like Mexican hot chocolate, pumpkin turnovers, and bagels topped with jalapeño jelly.

Ms. Wing is married and has two cats, Toonces and Jemima, and a dog named Sabaka.

Antonio L. Castro

Antonio L. Castro has illustrated many children's books. He is also an artist. He has displayed his art in museums in Texas, Mexico, Spain, and Italy.

Mr. Castro was born in Zacatecas, Mexico. He now lives in Juarez, Mexico, and is considered one of the best artists in the El Paso-Juarez area. He teaches art and local history classes to children in museums and libraries near his home.

Here are more books by Natasha Wing and Antonio L. Castro.

The Night Before Summer Vacation by Natasha Wing

Pájaro Verde/The Green Bird as told by Joe Hayes, illustrated by Antonio L. Castro

Reading Log

Use the *Reader's and Writer's Notebook* to record your independent reading.

311

Common Core State Standards

Literature 1. Ask and answer questions to demonstrate understanding of a text, referring explicitly to the text as the basis for the answers. **Also Literature 2., 10., Writing 2., 10., Speaking/Listening 4., Language 3.**

Bridge to Common Core

RANGE OF READING AND LEVEL OF TEXT COMPLEXITY

To increase students' capacity for reading and comprehending complex texts independently and proficiently, have them read other literary selections by Natasha Wing or about the social studies topic of foods from different cultures. After students read closely for a sustained period of time, they should record their reading in their Reading Logs.

Think Critically

1. **TEXT TO WORLD** Mexican pizza; Pizza is a food from Italy, but foods from Mexico, such as beans and chili peppers, could be toppings.

2. **THINK LIKE AN AUTHOR** The narrator is first person. It helps the reader understand Pablo. The purpose is to entertain and show how different cultures can influence food.

3.  **DRAW CONCLUSIONS** It is successful. People tell Pablo's mother that she makes the best *pan dulce*. Pablo's parents tell him to choose before the customers buy everything up.

4. **SUMMARIZE** Pablo helps his parents at the bakery so he can choose a food. They bake using recipes from his parents' cultures. He takes *jalapeño* bagels because they represent both heritages.

5. **LOOK BACK AND WRITE • TEXT EVIDENCE** To build writing fluency, allow 10–15 minutes.

Scoring Rubric | Look Back and Write

TOP-SCORE RESPONSE A top score response uses details to tell why *jalapeño* bagels are special to Pablo.

A top-score response should include:

• Pablo learns how to make *pan dulce, empanadas de calabaza,* and *chango* bars from his mother's Mexican culture.
• Pablo learns how to make bagels and *challah* from his father's Jewish culture.
• *Jalapeño* bagels use ingredients from both of Pablo's cultures.

Retell

Have students work in pairs to retell the selection, using the retelling strip in the Student Edition or the Story Sort as prompts. Monitor students' retellings.

Scoring Rubric | Narrative Retelling

	4	3	2	1
Connections	Makes connections and generalizes beyond the text	Makes connections to other events, stories, or experiences	Makes a limited connection to another event, story, or experience	Makes no connection to another event, story, or experience
Author's Purpose	Elaborates on author's purpose	Tells author's purpose with some clarity	Makes some connection to author's purpose	Makes no connection to author's purpose
Characters	Describes the main character(s) and any character development	Identifies the main character(s) and gives some information about them	Inaccurately identifies some characters or gives little information about them	Inaccurately identifies the characters or gives no information about them
Setting	Describes the time and location	Identifies the time and location	Omits details of time or location	Is unable to identify time or location
Plot	Describes the problem, goal, events, and ending using rich detail	Tells the problem, goal, events, and ending with some errors that do not affect meaning	Tells parts of the problem, goal, events, and ending with gaps that affect meaning	Retelling has no sense of story

Plan to Assess Retelling

☐ **Week 1** Strategic Intervention
☐ **Week 2** Advanced
☐ **Week 3** Strategic Intervention
☑ **This week assess On-Level students.**
☐ **Week 5** Assess any students you have not yet checked during this unit.

Meet the Author

Have students read about the author Natasha Wing and the illustrator Antonio L. Castro on p. 311. Ask them how the bakery Ms. Wing goes to and the one she writes about are similar. Ask what Mr. Castro teaches.

Read Independently

Have students enter their independent reading information into their Reading Logs.

MONITOR PROGRESS Check Retelling

If... students have difficulty retelling,

then... use the Retelling Cards/Story Sort to scaffold their retellings.

Don't wait until Friday

 **Common Core State Standards**

Foundational Skills 4. Read with sufficient accuracy and fluency to support comprehension.
Foundational Skills 4.b. Read on-level prose and poetry orally with accuracy, appropriate rate, and expression on successive readings. **Writing 8.** Recall information from experiences or gather information from print and digital sources; take brief notes on sources and sort evidence into provided categories.

Fluency

Accuracy

MODEL FLUENT READING Have students turn to p. 304 in *Jalapeño Bagels*. Have students follow along as you read this page. Remind them that when you read accurately, you don't skip words or say the wrong word. Explain that you are going to read carefully and concentrate on saying each word correctly as you read about the special bagels Pablo makes with his parents. Point out that Pablo uses two words from the Spanish language in his description—*jalapeño* and *chiles*. Have students listen as you read slowly and pronounce the words correctly.

GUIDE PRACTICE Have students follow along as you read the page again. Then have them reread the page as a group, without you, until they read accurately without mispronouncing or skipping any words. Ask questions to be sure students comprehend the text. Continue in the same way on p. 305.

Corrective feedback	**If...** students are having difficulty reading with accuracy, **then...** prompt them as follows:
	• Where do you see periods, dashes, and commas?
	• What should you do when you see these marks?
	• Read the sentence again. Pause when you see these marks.

Reread for Fluency

Routine Oral Rereading

1. **Read** Have students read p. 306 of *Jalapeño Bagels*.

2. **Reread** To achieve optimal fluency, students should reread the text three o four times.

3. **Corrective Feedback** Have students read aloud without you. Provide feedback about their accuracy and assist with correct pronunciation as necessary. Encourage them to take their time to read each word correctly.

Routines Flip Chart

Research and Study Skills

Outlining

TEACH Discuss with students that outlining is a way to organize information before writing. Tell students that when they read, they need to take simple notes. Encourage them to look at distinguishing text features to help them find the important information. They can then organize their notes into categories that can become their outline. Using the example below, demonstrate writing a topic outline, which uses phrases to organize information from two or more sources.

Foods from Mexico

Main Dishes

    A. *frijoles* and *tortillas*

    B. *bolillos*

    C. *torta de tamal*

Desserts

    A. *pan dulce*

    B. *empanadas de calabaza*

    C. *chango* bars

Explain to students that an outline helps identify the most important points in research, and how the points are related to each other.

GUIDE PRACTICE Discuss these questions:

How does the outline organize information about foods from Mexico? (The outline organizes the foods into the categories *main dishes* and *desserts*.)

How does outlining help you better understand and remember important points from your research? (An outline helps me organize important points into groups. When I group information into categories, it is easier to remember.)

As students work, make sure they are taking notes and sorting evidence into categories.

ON THEIR OWN Have students review the instructions and complete p. 357 in the *Reader's and Writer's Notebook*.

eSTREET INTERACTIVE
www.ReadingStreet.com

Teacher Resources
• Reader's and Writer's Notebook

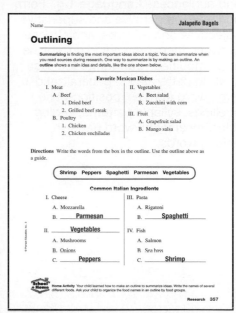

Reader's and Writer's Notebook, p. 357

Build Academic Vocabulary
Supply meanings for the supporting academic vocabulary as needed.
For example:
A **category** is a group of things that are alike in some way.

An **outline** is a list that shows a general plan.

Research and Inquiry

Step 3 Analyze Information

TEACH Tell students that today they will analyze their research findings. Have students sort the information from their notes into an outline. Remind students that an outline is a plan for writing. Then explain that students may have to improve the focus of their research by consulting additional sources, including experts.

Think Aloud **MODEL** Originally I thought that just a few foods were used to celebrate holidays and traditions in various cultures. My online research tells me that many, many different foods are part of traditions in various cultures. In addition, part of my research was to ask a local expert about the topic. I talked with the owner of the bakery near my house, and she gave me information about traditional breads and pastries from different cultures. I will refocus my inquiry question to include information from my expert and from my online research. Now my inquiry question is *What types of breads and pastries do people in various cultures bake to celebrate holidays and traditions?*

GUIDE PRACTICE Have students analyze their findings. They may need to refocus their inquiry question to better fit the information they found. Remind students that if they have difficulty improving their focus they can ask a reference librarian or the local expert for guidance.

Have students continue to take notes and sort the information they gather into the categories within their outline.

ON THEIR OWN Have partners share their outlines and summarize the information they have gathered. Partners should discuss whether they need to collect additional information to answer the inquiry question.

Conventions

Comparative and Superlative Adverbs

REVIEW Remind students that this week they learned about adverbs that compare.

- Comparative adverbs compare two things. Add *-er* to most adverbs to make them comparative. Use *more* with adverbs that end in the suffix *-ly*.

- Superlative adverbs compare three or more things. Add *-est* to most adverbs to make them superlative. Use *most* with adverbs that end in the suffix *-ly*.

CONNECT TO ORAL LANGUAGE
Have the class complete this sentence frame orally.

She sang loudly.

The radio played _____ than she sang.

ON THEIR OWN For additional support, use *Let's Practice It!* p. 324 on the Teacher Resources DVD-ROM.

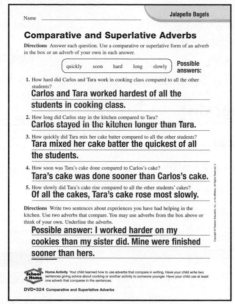

Let's Practice It! TR DVD•324

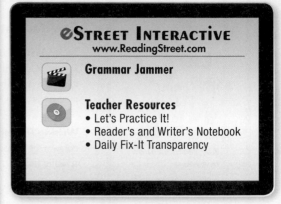

Access for All

SI Strategic Intervention

To practice writing comparative and superlative adverbs, have students work in small groups to write three sentences about cooking. They should write one with *-er* to compare two actions, one with *-est* to compare three or more actions, and one using *more* or *most* with an adverb ending in *-ly*.

Daily Fix-It

5. The students is having blue berry muffins for a snack. *(are; blueberry)*

6. I can finnish mine fastest than you. *(finish; faster)*

Spelling

Vowel Patterns *ei, eigh*

FREQUENTLY MISSPELLED WORDS The words *believe* and *friend* are words that students often misspell. The words *either* and *receive* from your spelling list are also difficult to spell. I'm going to read a sentence. Choose the correct word to complete the sentence and then write it correctly.

1. I will order _____ the taco plate or the fajitas. (either)

2. Liam does not _____ your lie. (believe)

3. Karen is my best _____. (friend)

4. You will _____ the package next Friday. (receive)

ON THEIR OWN For additional practice, use *Reader's and Writer's Notebook*, p. 358.

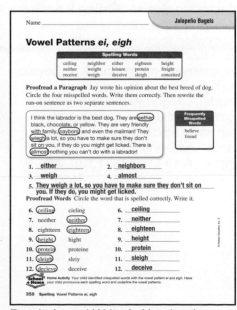

Reader's and Writer's Notebook, p. 358

Jalapeño Bagels **311e**

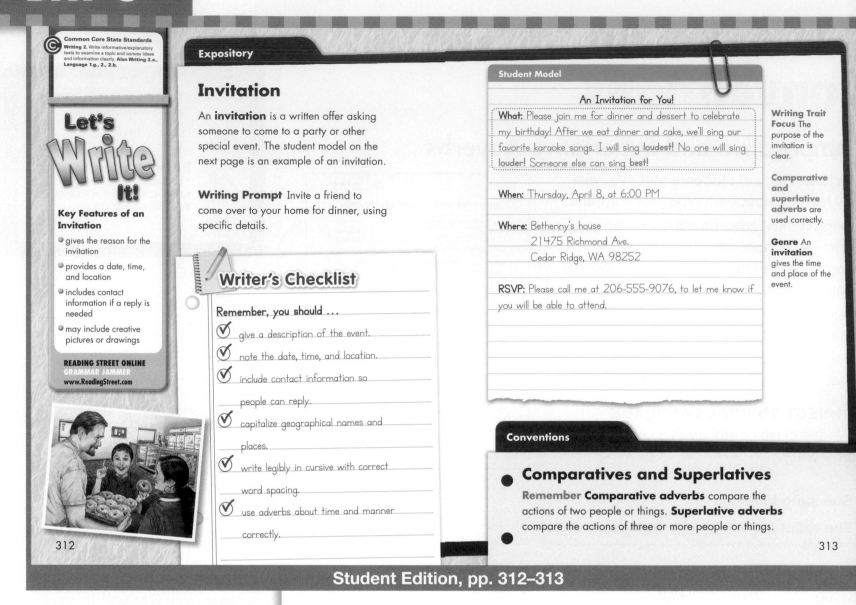

Common Core State Standards
Writing 2. Write informative/explanatory texts to examine a topic and convey ideas and information clearly. Also Writing 2.a., Language 1.g., 2., 2.b.

Let's

It!

Key Features of an Invitation

- gives the reason for the invitation
- provides a date, time, and location
- includes contact information if a reply is needed
- may include creative pictures or drawings

READING STREET ONLINE
GRAMMAR JAMMER
www.ReadingStreet.com

312

Expository

Invitation

An **invitation** is a written offer asking someone to come to a party or other special event. The student model on the next page is an example of an invitation.

Writing Prompt Invite a friend to come over to your home for dinner, using specific details.

Writer's Checklist

Remember, you should . . .

☑ give a description of the event.

☑ note the date, time, and location.

☑ include contact information so people can reply.

☑ capitalize geographical names and places.

☑ write legibly in cursive with correct word spacing.

☑ use adverbs about time and manner correctly.

Student Model

An Invitation for You!

What: Please join me for dinner and dessert to celebrate my birthday! After we eat dinner and cake, we'll sing our favorite karaoke songs. I will sing loudest! No one will sing louder! Someone else can sing best!

When: Thursday, April 8, at 6:00 PM

Where: Bethenny's house
21475 Richmond Ave.
Cedar Ridge, WA 98252

RSVP: Please call me at 206-555-9076, to let me know if you will be able to attend.

Writing Trait Focus The purpose of the invitation is clear.

Comparative and superlative adverbs are used correctly.

Genre An **invitation** gives the time and place of the event.

Conventions

Comparatives and Superlatives

Remember **Comparative adverbs** compare the actions of two people or things. **Superlative adverbs** compare the actions of three or more people or things.

313

Student Edition, pp. 312–313

Common Core State Standards

Writing 2. Write informative/explanatory texts to examine a topic and convey ideas and information clearly. **Writing 2.a.** Introduce a topic and group related information together; include illustrations when useful to aiding comprehension. **Writing 2.b.** Develop the topic with facts, definitions, and details. **Language 2.** Demonstrate command of the conventions of standard English capitalization, punctuation, and spelling when writing. **Also Language 1.g., 2.b., 3.**

Let's Write It!

WRITE AN INVITATION Use pp. 312–313 in the Student Edition. Direct students to read the key features of an invitation that appear on p. 312. Remind students that they can refer to the information in the Writer's Checklist as they write their own invitations.

Read the student model on p. 313. Point out the date, location, and time in the model, as well as Bethenny's contact information.

CONNECT TO CONVENTIONS Remind students that most adverbs that compare three or more actions are formed by adding -*est*. Point out the correct use of the adverb *loudest* in the model.

Writing

Zoom in on ©

Invitation

Writing Trait: Focus/Ideas

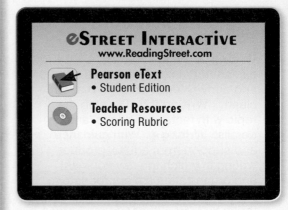

DISPLAY RUBRIC Display Scoring Rubric 24 from the *Teacher Resources DVD-ROM* and review the criteria for each trait under each score. Then, using the model in the Student Edition, choose students to explain why the model should score a 4 for one of the traits. If a student offers that the model should score below 4 for a particular trait, the student should support that response. Remind students that this is the rubric that will be used to evaluate the invitation they write.

Scoring Rubric Invitation

	4	**3**	**2**	**1**
Focus/Ideas	Clear focus and purpose for invitation	Fairly clear focus and purpose for invitation	Unclear focus and purpose for invitation	No attempt made to offer a reason for the event
Organization	Clearly organized details, such as date, time, and location of party	Able to follow details, such as date, time, and location of party	Effort to include details, such as date, time, and location; details for party are unclear	No effort made to include party details, such as date, time, and location
Voice	Writer achieves an animated voice and makes the party sound enticing	Some evidence of animated voice and inviting tone	Attempts an animated voice and inviting tone	No attempt at an animated voice or inviting tone
Word Choice	Strong use of vivid words	Adequate use of vivid words	Weak use of vivid words	No use of vivid words
Sentences	Clear sentences of various lengths and types	Sentences of a few lengths and types	No sentences; little attempt at various lengths and types of sentences	No attempt at sentences; no attempt at various lengths and types of sentences
Conventions	Few, if any, errors; correct use of comparative and superlative adverbs	Several minor errors; mostly correct use of comparative and superlative adverbs	Many errors; inaccurate use of comparative and superlative adverbs	Numerous errors; no use of comparative and superlative adverbs

FOUR-COLUMN CHART Have students refer to the four-column charts they worked on yesterday. If their charts are not complete, allow students a few minutes of class time to add details for their invitation.

WRITE You will use your four-column chart as you write the first draft of your invitation. When you are drafting, don't worry if the invitation does not sound exactly how you want it. You will have a chance to revise it later.

Access for All

A Advanced

Have students brainstorm alternative ways to organize the details in the student model on p. 313. Encourage students to make an outline for each idea. Have partners exchange outlines and check each other's work for inclusion of date, time, location, and contact information. Allow students to use their alternative outlines when drafting their own invitations.

ELL

Invitation Have pairs of students use a four-column chart to organize the date, time, location, and contact information of the student model on p. 313.

DAY 3

Common Core State Standards

Writing 2. Write informative/explanatory texts to examine a topic and convey ideas and information clearly. **Writing 2.b.** Develop the topic with facts, definitions, and details. **Writing 4.** With guidance and support from adults, produce writing in which the development and organization are appropriate to task and purpose. **Writing 10.** Write routinely over extended time frames (time for research, reflection, and revision) and shorter time frames (a single sitting or a day or two) for a range of discipline-specific tasks, purposes, and audiences.

Bridge to Common Core

RANGE OF WRITING

As students progress through the writing project, they routinely write for a range of tasks and purposes. In this lesson, they learn how to establish a purpose for writing an invitation and get ready to draft their invitations.

Writing

Invitation

Mini-Lesson   Writing Trait: Focus/Ideas

■ **Introduce** Discuss the importance of purpose in writing. Explain that there are four common reasons authors write: to persuade, inform, entertain, and express a mood or feeling. Discuss the purpose for writing an invitation. Guide students to understand that the purpose for writing an invitation is to inform readers of a special event. Invitations may also be written to persuade guests to attend the event. Then display Writing Transparency 24A.

Let's Grill!

What: Please join my family in an outdoor barbeque to celebrate the beginning of summer! We will have plenty of hambergers and hot dogs for everyone. After dinner, we will play games. The three-legged race should be the funnest of all! Prizes will be given to the teams that run most fastest.

When: Saturday, June 24th, at 500 PM

Where: Meet us at the picnic tables at horner Park.

R.S.V.P. Please call Mario Ortíz at 309-555-8428 to let me know if you will join us. Hope you can make it!

Unit 5 Jalapeño Bagels   Writing: Model **24A**

Writing Transparency 24A, TR DVD

Drafting Tips

✔ To get started, review your four-column chart.

✔ Make sure to include specific details to inform the reader of your special event.

✔ Focus on getting your ideas down. Don't worry about grammar and mechanics while writing your first draft.

Think Aloud **MODEL** Now I will write my draft. I will use the details from my four-column chart to help organize my ideas. First, I will write a title for my invitation. Because my invitation is for an outside barbecue, will title it *Let's Grill!* Then I will write details about the barbecue to let my reader know when and where it will take place. Because I want to persuade my reader to attend the event, I will also try to make the event sound fun and exciting. I will not worry about grammar and mechanics until I get to the proofreading stage.

Direct students to use the drafting tips to guide them in developing their drafts. Remind them to keep in mind the overall purpose of an invitation to inform and persuade as they write.

eSTREET INTERACTIVE
www.ReadingStreet.com

Teacher Resources
• Writing Transparency

Routine | **Quick Write for Fluency** | **Team Talk**

1. **Talk** Have pairs discuss how they made their special event sound fun and exciting.

2. **Write** Each student writes a sentence about his or her event using a comparative adverb.

3. **Share** Partners read one another's writing and check for correct use of adverbs.

Routines Flip Chart

Access for All

A **Advanced**

Have groups of three or four students discuss and determine the author's purpose for writing *Jalapeño Bagels*. After arriving at a consensus, have each group member find a sentence from the story that supports his or her conclusion.

Wrap Up Your Day!

✔ **Content Knowledge** What did you learn about how Pablo's parents were able to combine their cultures into one food?

✔ **Text-Based Comprehension** *What clues did you use to help you conclude why Pablo chose to bring jalapeño bagels?* Encourage students to cite examples from the text.

Preview DAY 4

Tell students that tomorrow they will read about foods from Mexico.

Materials

- Student Edition
- Reader's and Writer's Notebook
- Decodable Reader

Common Core State Standards

Speaking/Listening 1. Engage effectively in a range of collaborative discussions (one-on-one, in groups, and teacher-led) with diverse partners on grade 3 topics and texts, building on others' ideas and expressing their own clearly. **Language 6.** Acquire and use accurately grade-appropriate conversational, general academic, and domain-specific words and phrases, including those that signal spatial and temporal relationships (e.g., *After dinner that night we went looking for them*).

Content Knowledge

Foods from Different Cultures

EXPAND THE CONCEPT Remind students of the weekly concept question, *How can different cultures contribute to the foods we eat?* Have students discuss how different cultures influenced the things Pablo and his family bakes.

Build Oral Language

Team Talk **TALK ABOUT SENTENCES AND WORDS** Ask students to reread the first sentence of the last paragraph on p. 304.

When the bagel dough has risen, he boils the bagels in a huge pot of water and fishes them out with a long slotted spoon.

- What is a homonym for the word *dough? (doe)*
- What does it mean to "fish" something out? (It means to remove something from whatever it's in.) What are some other examples of when you might "fish" something or someone out? (You might fish leaves out of a swimming pool or fish someone out of a troubling situation.)
- What is a *slotted* spoon? (a spoon with slits or holes) Why does Pablo's father use a slotted spoon to take the bagels out of the boiling water? (If he used a regular spoon, he would remove some of the boiling water with it, but all he wants to remove is the bagel.)

Build Oral Vocabulary

Amazing Words

Robust Vocabulary Routine

1. Introduce Write the word *wholesome* on the board. Have students say it with you. Yesterday we read about bread and bagels that Pablo made with his parents. In appropriate servings, bread is a *wholesome* food. Discuss how whole grains and bread can be part of healthy nutrition. Then have students use context to determine a definition for *wholesome*. (A *wholesome* food is a food that is good for your health.)

2. Demonstrate Have students answer questions to demonstrate understanding. What are examples of other *wholesome* foods? (fruits, vegetables, fish, meat)

3. Apply Have students apply their understanding. What is an antonym for *wholesome*? *(unhealthy)*

4. Display the Word Point out the different sound-spellings in the word as you read it.

See p. OV•4 teach *grate* and *agent*.

Routines Flip Chart

ADD TO THE CONCEPT MAP Discuss the Amazing Words *grumble* and *allergic* and add these and other concept-related words to the concept map. Use the following questions to develop students' understanding of the concept and add words generated in the discussion to the concept map.

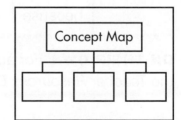

What is your body telling you when it *grumbles*?
What types of food make your stomach *grumble*?
What cultures are they from?
What might happen to someone who is *allergic* to a particular food?

Amazing Words

nutrition	grumble
calorie	allergic
flavor	wholesome
spice	grate
nutmeg	agent

Strategy Response Log

Have students complete p. 30 in the *Reader's and Writer's Notebook*. Then have students work in pairs to summarize "Foods of Mexico: A Delicious Blend."

ELL

Produce Oral Language Use the Day 4 instruction on ELL Poster 24 to extend and enrich language.

Common Core State Standards

Foundational Skills 3. Know and apply grade-level phonics and word analysis skills in decoding words. **Foundational Skills 3.c.** Decode multisyllable words. **Foundational Skills 3.d.** Read grade-appropriate irregularly spelled words.

Phonics

Review Vowel Patterns for /ȯ/

REVIEW SOUND-SPELLINGS To review last week's phonics skill, write *paw, ball, caught, talk,* and *bought.* You studied words like these last week. What do you know about the vowel sound in these words? (Each word has /ȯ/, but the sound has different spelling patterns.) Have students identify the spelling pattern in each word. What letters spell the /ȯ/ sound in *paw?* (*aw*) In *ball?* (*a*) Continue in the same way for /ȯ/ in *caught* (*augh*) and *bought* (*ough*).

Corrective feedback	**If...** students are unable to answer the questions about /ȯ/ spelling patterns, **then...** refer them to *Sound-Spelling Cards* 56, 57, 58, 97, 105, and 106.

GUIDE PRACTICE Draw a six-column chart. When I say a word, think about the letters that spell the vowel sound /ȯ/. Say *walk. Walk* is spelled *w-a-l-k.* The letters *al* stand for /ȯ/. I'll write *walk* in the fourth column. Write each word in the appropriate column. Then have students read the words and ask volunteers to underline the letters that stand for /ȯ/ in each word.

a	au	aw	al	augh	ough
ball	cause	fawn	walk	taught	brought
stall	fault	raw	stalk	daughter	thought
	because	dawn			

ON THEIR OWN For additional practice, use *Let's Practice It!* page 325 on the *Teacher Resources DVD-ROM.*

Name _____ Jalapeño Bagels

Vowel Patterns *a, au, aw, al, augh, ough*
Directions Each word contains a blank space. Replace the blank space with the letter or combination of letters that makes the vowel sound in the word *ball.* Write the word on the line.

1. _al_most __almost__
2. sm_a_ll __small__
3. b_ough_t __bought__
4. cl_aw_ __claw__
5. _aw_ful __awful__
6. st_al_k __stalk__
7. f_au_lt __fault__
8. s_au_ce __sauce__

Directions Each sentence contains two words in ( ). Underline the word that is spelled correctly.

9. Another word for *clumsy* is (akward, <u>awkward</u>).
10. We missed the bus, so we had to (<u>walk</u>, wauk) to school that morning.
11. My brother Theo is the (<u>tallest</u>, taulest) person in the family.
12. I (toot, <u>taught</u>) my little brother how to paint.

Directions Choose three words from the above list and write a sentence for each word.

13. Possible answer: I am almost nine years old.
14. Possible answer: The kitten's claw snagged my sweater.
15. Possible answer: Taylor likes a lot of sauce on his spaghetti.

Home Activity Your child spelled words with the vowel sound in *ball.* These vowel patterns are *a, au, aw, al, augh,* and *ough.* Read and prepare a favorite recipe with your child. Find words with vowel patterns *a, au, aw, al, augh,* and *ough* in the recipe and have your child spell them correctly.

Vowel Patterns *a, au, aw, al, augh, ough* DVD•325

Let's Practice It! TR DVD•325

Fluent Word Reading

Spiral Review

READ WORDS IN ISOLATION Display these words. Tell students that they can already decode some words on this list. Explain that they should know other words because they appear often in reading.

Have students read the list three or four times until they can read at the rate of two to three seconds per word.

Word Reading

annual	rows	very	seen	violets
watched	videos	quiet	their	have
scene	unusual	tail	created	tale
people	giant	many	rose	two

Corrective feedback	**If...** students have difficulty reading whole words, **then...** have them use sound-by-sound blending for decodable words or chunking for words that have word parts, or have them say and spell high-frequency words. **If...** students cannot read fluently at a rate of two to three seconds per word, **then...** have pairs practice the list until they can read the words fluently.

eSTREET INTERACTIVE
www.ReadingStreet.com

 Teacher Resources
• Let's Practice It!

Interactive Sound-Spelling Cards

Access for All

SI Strategic Intervention

To assist students having difficulty with identifying vowel patterns for the sound /ȯ/, focus on two patterns at a time. For example, write words with /ȯ/ spelled *au* and *aw,* such as *cause, fault, haunt, paws, fawn, straw.* Read the words; then have students read the words and identify the letters that spell /ȯ/.

Spiral Review

These activities review:

• previously taught high-frequency words *have, many, people, their, two, very, watched.*

• homophones; syllable pattern CV/VC.

Fluent Word Reading Have students listen to a more fluent reader say the words. Then have them repeat the words.

Graphic Organizer Discuss with students how a graphic organizer such as a 5-column chart can organize information and make it easier to understand and remember. Review the elements of a chart: headings, rows, and columns. Then have students work in pairs to create a 3-column chart that shows their favorite foods for breakfast, lunch, and dinner, including foods from their native cultures.

 **Common Core State Standards**

Foundational Skills 3. Know and apply grade-level phonics and word analysis skills in decoding words. **Foundational Skills 3.c.** Decode multisyllable words. **Foundational Skills 3.d.** Read grade-appropriate irregularly spelled words. **Foundational Skills 4.** Read with sufficient accuracy and fluency to support comprehension. **Foundational Skills 4.c.** Use context to confirm or self-correct word recognition and understanding, rereading as necessary.

Fluent Word Reading

READ WORDS IN CONTEXT Display these sentences. Call on individuals to read a sentence. Then randomly point to review words and have students read them. To help you monitor word reading, high-frequency words are underlined and decodable words are italicized.

MONITOR PROGRESS Sentence Reading

Dad read a tale about a <u>very</u> *quiet giant*.
Her garden has *rows* of *violets* and <u>two</u> *rose* bushes.
<u>Have</u> you ever *seen* a horse with such an *unusual tail*?
<u>Their</u> yard was the *scene* of our *annual* picnic.
<u>Many</u> <u>people</u> <u>watched</u> the *videos* we *created*.

If... students are unable to read an underlined high-frequency word,

then... read the word for them and spell it, having them echo you.

If... students have difficulty reading an italicized decodable word,

then... guide them in using sound-by-sound blending or chunking.

Reread for Fluency

Have students reread the sentences to develop automaticity decoding words.

Routine Oral Rereading

1. **Read** Have students read all the sentences orally.

2. **Reread** To achieve optimal fluency, students should reread the sentences three or four times.

3. **Corrective Feedback** Listen as students read. Provide corrective feedback regarding their fluency and decoding.

Routines Flip Chart

Decodable Passage 24C

students need help, then...

Read *Miranda Turns Eight*

READ WORDS IN ISOLATION Have students turn to p. 107 in *Decodable Practice Readers 3.2* and find the first list of words. Each word in this list has long *a*, long *e*, or long *i* spelled *ei* or *eigh*. Let's blend and read these words. Be sure that students identify the correct vowel sound in each word.

Next, have students read the high-frequency words.

PREVIEW Have students read the title and preview the story. Tell them that they will read words with long *a*, long *e*, and long *i* spelled *ei* and *eigh*.

READ WORDS IN CONTEXT Chorally read the story along with the students. Have students identify words in the story that have long *a*, long *e*, and long *i* spelled *ei* or *eigh*. Make sure that students are monitoring their accuracy when they decode.

Team Talk Pair students and have them take turns reading the story aloud to each other. Monitor students as they read to check for proper pronunciation and appropriate pacing.

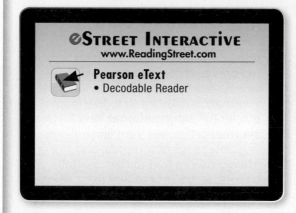

eSTREET INTERACTIVE
www.ReadingStreet.com

Pearson eText
• Decodable Reader

Access for All

A Advanced

Have students write their own sentences using some of the decodable words found in the sentences on p. 314e.

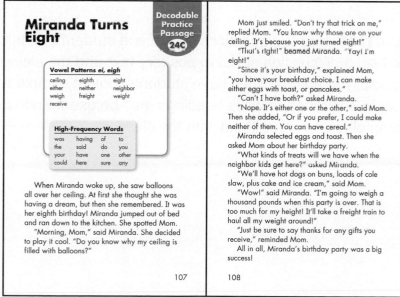

Decodable Practice Passage 24C

Common Core State Standards

Informational Text 5. Use text features and search tools (e.g., key words, sidebars, hyperlinks) to locate information relevant to a given topic efficiently. **Informational Text 7.** Use information gained from illustrations (e.g., maps, photographs), and the words in a text to demonstrate understanding of the text (e.g., where, when, why, and how key events occur).

 **Bridge to Common Core**

KEY IDEAS AND DETAILS

Examining the structure and features of expository texts enables students to determine the organizational flow of the information presented and how to quickly access certain information within the text. By reading the text closely and paying attention to text features, students can determine the main idea and summarize the key details.

Social Studies in Reading

Expository Text

INTRODUCE Explain to students that what we read is structured differently depending on the author's reasons for writing and what kind of information he/she wishes to convey. Different types of texts are called genres. Tell them that expository text is one type of genre.

DISCUSS THE GENRE Remind students that they have read many types of expository text this year, including a photo essay and a magazine article. Review the elements and characteristics of expository text to activate students' prior knowledge. Ask the following questions:

- What is the purpose of expository text? (Possible response: The purpose of expository text is to give information about something or to explain the nature of an object, idea, or theme.)
- What are some text features that you might find in expository text? (Possible responses: Expository text can include photos or graphics and text features such as diagrams, maps, a table of contents, headings, or an index.)
- How can headings help you understand the information in expository text? (Possible responses: Headings organize and categorize the information in expository text. Headings give a general preview of the information included in a section.)

GROUP PRACTICE Use the questions above and students' detailed responses to lead a discussion about expository text and the elements it includes, especially headings. Then have students look at sample texts in the class or library to see different ways headings may be used. Encourage them to list their examples and share them with the class.

READ Tell students that they will now read an expository text that tells about the cultures and foods that have blended to form Mexican cuisine. Have the class think about how the headings organize the information in the text.

Day 4 **SMALL GROUP TIME • Differentiate Vocabulary, p. SG•49**

OL On-Level	**SI** Strategic Intervention	**A** Advanced
Develop Language Using Amazing Words	• **Review/Discuss** Amazing Words	• **Extend** Amazing Words and Selection Vocabulary
Read "Foods of Mexico: A Delicious Blend"	• **Read** "Foods of Mexico: A Delicious Blend"	• **Read** "Foods of Mexico: A Delicious Blend"
		• **Organize** Inquiry Project

 ELL

If... students need more scaffolding and practice with the **Amazing Words,**
then... use the Routine on pp. xxxvi–xxxvii in the *ELL Handbook.*

Common Core State Standards
Informational Text 5. Use text features and search tools (e.g., key words, sidebars, hyperlinks) to locate information relevant to a given topic efficiently.
Also Informational Text 7.

Social Studies in Reading

Genre
Expository Text

• Expository text explains or describes the main idea about a topic, using facts and details.

• Graphic sources show the information visually.

• Text features, such as headings, italicized words, and captions help readers to predict, locate, and verify the information.

• As you read "Foods of Mexico," use the text features to predict, locate, and verify information about the topic.

314

Foods of Mexico
a Delicious Blend

From *Viva Mexico! The Foods*
by George Ancona

Panza llena, corazón contento is an old Mexican proverb that means "a full belly makes for a happy heart." The foods of Mexico are a treat to see, smell, taste, and eat.

Native Foods

The early people of Mexico developed maize (corn) from a small wild plant. They grew many varieties of maize: white, red, yellow, black, and other color combinations.

Between rows of corn they planted tomatoes, beans, chiles, pumpkins, sweet potatoes, and squash. They also raised avocados and amaranth, a nutritious grain that was ground into flour for tortillas and bread. Fields and forests supplied fruits, peanuts, cacao (cocoa) beans, honey, and mushrooms.

Chiles · Tuna · Nopal · Cacao beans · Beans · Jiotilla · Avocado · Amaranth · Peanuts · Guayaba · Chayote · Tomatoes · Sweet potatoes · Honey · Squash

315

Let's Think About...
According to the title, what is the topic going to be? How does the proverb help introduce the main idea about the topic?
Expository Text

1

Let's Think About...
What facts and details that support the main idea can you learn from the photos and captions?
Expository Text

2

Student Edition, pp. 314–315

Common Core State Standards

Informational Text 5. Use text features and search tools (e.g., key words, sidebars, hyperlinks) to locate information relevant to a given topic efficiently. **Informational Text 7.** Use information gained from illustrations (e.g., maps, photographs) and the words in a text to demonstrate understanding of the text (e.g., where, when, why, and how key events occur).

Access Text ©

TEACH Genre: Expository Text Have students preview "Foods of Mexico: A Delicious Blend" (from *Viva Mexico! The Foods*) on pp. 314–317. Tell them that the selection is expository text. Expository text is writing that explains the nature of an object, an idea, or a theme. **Then ask:** What do you think this expository text will be about? How do you know?

Corrective feedback | **If...** students are unable to predict what the text will be about, **then...** use the model to guide students in skimming and scanning.

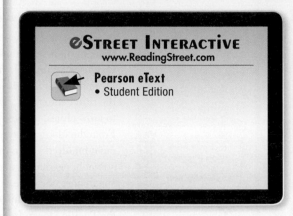
 Think Aloud

MODEL In expository text, there are often headings that tell what different parts of the text are about. I can read the headings to determine what it will be about.

ON THEIR OWN Have students work in pairs to read the headings and preview the text in "Foods of Mexico: A Delicious Blend." Have them write what they think the text will be about.

Close Reading ©

ANALYSIS • TEXT EVIDENCE Why did the author include the labeled photograph on p. 315? (It helps readers understand the text. They might recognize some of the foods and not have known their names.)

EVALUATION Do you think that the early people of Mexico were skilled farmers? Why do you think so? (The early people of Mexico were skilled farmers because they knew how to grow many types of plants. They also developed many varieties of maize.)

Genre

LET'S THINK ABOUT... As you read "Foods of Mexico: A Delicious Blend," use Let's Think About in the Student Edition to help students focus on the features of an expository text.

The title tells me that the topic is going to be the delicious foods of Mexico. The proverb is a good introduction to the topic because it is also from Mexican culture and let's the reader know that the text will be about food.

The photos show me what each food looks like and the captions tell me the name of each food.

Access for All

SI Strategic Intervention

Discuss the photograph on p. 315. Have students list the foods in a T-chart and tell what they know about the foods (e.g., uses, taste, texture).

A Advanced

Have students use a cookbook or online sources to find a recipe that contains at least one of the native Mexican foods discussed on p. 315.

Access Content Have students preview the text by reading the title and looking at the photographs and other graphic aids. Ask them what the main topic of the text is. (food) Next, have students read the photograph labels aloud. If students recognize a word, have them share what they know about it.

The Spanish Flavor

The Spanish who came to the New World brought their traditions with them. Over the centuries Spain had had many influences. From the Greeks, who colonized Spain in the fifth century B.C., the Spanish learned to grow olives, grapes, and chickpeas. From the Moors, who ruled their country for eight hundred years, they learned to plant spinach, eggplants, artichokes, watermelons, sugarcane, and lime, lemon, and orange trees.

Spanish ships called galleons sailed across the Pacific Ocean from Spanish colonies in Asia. They brought many foods and spices with them. Rice from Asia together with Mexico's native beans *(frijoles)* and tortillas became the staple food of Mexico. African slaves who were brought to New Spain also added their ways of cooking.

Beans *(frijoles)*

Rice

Tortillas or Bolillos?

The Spanish planted wheat because they preferred wheat bread to the native corn tortillas. They baked little rolls called *bolillos*. Serving *bolillos* was a status symbol among Europeans. But Mexicans never gave up their tortillas. Eventually the settlers began to eat them too.

Today it isn't necessary to choose between a *tamal* or a *bolillo*. Street-corner food vendors sell a breakfast snack that blends two cultures: a sliced *bolillo* with a hot tamale inside. This is called a *torta de tamal*, a tamale sandwich.

Tamales

Like seeds blown by the wind, people came to Mexico from distant lands, and they settled and flowered. The foods they brought with them blended with native cooking. The result is a Mexican cuisine that has traces of distant lands.

Bolillos

Let's Think About...

How do the headings in this selection organize the text?

Expository Text

❸

Let's Think About...

What do italicized words indicate? How do you know?

Expository Text

❹

Let's Think About...

Reading Across Texts In this article, people from distant lands blended their foods with the foods of the Mexican people. How did Pablo's family in *Jalapeño Bagels* also do this?

Writing Across Texts Use the recipe at the end of *Jalapeño Bagels* to help you create a step-by-step recipe for a food you can make that combines two cultures.

316

317

Student Edition, pp. 316–317

Common Core State Standards

Informational Text 5. Use text features and search tools (e.g., key words, sidebars, hyperlinks) to locate information relevant to a given topic efficiently. **Informational Text 7.** Use information gained from illustrations (e.g., maps, photographs) and the words in a text to demonstrate understanding of the text (e.g., where, when, why, and how key events occur).

Access Text ©

TEACH Genre: Expository Text Remind students that expository text can include photos or graphics and text features such as diagrams, maps, a table of contents, headings, or an index. Have them discuss how text features help them understand information in expository text. Then ask: What do headings tell you about the information that will be presented in the text?

Corrective feedback

If... students are unable to explain how headings help preview the text,

then... use the model to guide students to use headings to preview text.

Think Aloud **MODEL** I know that expository text can include graphics and text features such as headings. Headings organize the information presented and also give a quick preview of ideas or topics in the text. The headings in this text tell me that foods native to Mexico and Spanish foods will be discussed in the text.

ON THEIR OWN Have students work in pairs to write three headings that might appear in an expository text about their favorite type of food.

Close Reading ©

ANALYSIS How was the development of Spanish and Mexican cuisines similar? (Spanish and Mexican cuisines are both blends of foods from different cultures. Spanish cuisine includes foods from the Greeks and the Moors. Mexican cuisine includes native foods and foods from Spain, including those the Spanish adopted from other countries.)

EVALUATION Why is the heading on p. 317 "Tortillas or Bolillos?" (The heading tells the reader that people choose between *tortillas* and *bolillos*. It leads the reader to expect to learn what is different about these foods.)

Genre

LET'S THINK ABOUT... features of an expository text.

The headings in the text organize the information into sections about native foods of Mexico, the Spanish influence on Mexican cuisine, and how the two cultures blend.

The italicized words are the Spanish words for different kinds of food. I know this because the words are defined in the text.

Reading and Writing Across Texts

Have students create a T-chart to record information about how Pablo's family blended foods together and how Mexican cuisine blends foods together. Then have students list steps to include when writing a recipe, based on the recipe on p. 309, such as "list ingredients and measurements" and "give directions." Have them follow the steps to write their own recipe.

 Connect to Social Studies

Pasta Even though people think of tomato sauce and pasta being native to Italian cuisine, the tomato was imported back to Europe after explorers arrived in the Americas. Also, the pasta noodle made—from flour, water, and sometimes egg—has been found in ancient cuisines from China to Syria.

Professional Development: Make Personal and Cultural Connections
"We should constantly search for ways to link academic content with what students already know or what is familiar to them from their family or cultural experiences. This not only validates children's sense of identity, but it also makes the learning more meaningful." —Dr. Jim Cummins

Cultural Connections Have students work in small groups to discuss foods from their cultures and whether they recognize any of the foods native to their cultures in American cuisine.

Common Core State Standards
Language 4.a. Use sentence-level context as a clue to the meaning of a word or phrase. Also Foundational Skills 4., Speaking/Listening 4., Language 4.

Let's **Learn It!**

READING STREET ONLINE
ONLINE STUDENT EDITION
www.ReadingStreet.com

Vocabulary

Unfamiliar Words

Context Clues Use context clues to find the meanings of unfamiliar words while you are reading. The words or sentences around an unfamiliar word may provide clues to its meaning.

Practice It! Select three Words to Know words. Reread *Jalapeño Bagels*. Use context clues to determine the meaning of each word. Write the meaning of each word as it is used in the story. Record the words or phrases you used as context clues.

Fluency

Accuracy

When you read aloud it is important to pronounce words correctly. This will help everyone understand the meaning of the story you are reading.

Practice It! Read aloud pages 298–299 of *Jalapeño Bagels* with a partner. Take turns listening to each other to make sure you are both reading the words correctly.

318

Media Literacy

Get Ready For Middle School

Make contributions and work productively with others.

Advertisement

Ads inform people about and persuade them to buy a product or service or go to a place. An ad can be on the radio, on TV, in a newspaper, or on the Internet.

Practice It! Prepare a two-minute radio ad that persuades people to buy jalapeño bagels, and perform it for the class. Use sounds to influence them to buy the bagels. How would your ad change if you were creating a Web site for the bagels instead?

Tips

Listening ...
• Sit quietly, facing the speaker.
• Listen to identify persuasive techniques.

Speaking ...
• Use expression and persuasive techniques.

Teamwork ...
• Ask and answer questions about how communication changes when moving from the radio to the Internet.

319

Student Edition, pp. 318–319

Common Core State Standards

Foundational Skills 4. Read with sufficient accuracy and fluency to support comprehension. **Speaking/Listening 4.** Report on a topic or text, tell a story, or recount an experience with appropriate facts and relevant, descriptive details, speaking clearly at an understandable pace. **Language 4.** Determine or clarify the meaning of unknown and multiple-meaning word and phrases based on grade 3 reading and content, choosing flexibly from a range of strategies. **Language 4.a.** Use sentence-level context as a clue to the meaning of a word or phrase. **Also Foundational Skills 4.b., Speaking/Listening 1.b., Language 3.**

Fluency

Accuracy

GUIDE PRACTICE Use the Student Edition activity as an assessment tool. Make sure the reading passage is at least 200 words in length. As students read aloud with partners, walk around to make sure they read with accuracy.

Don't Wait Until Friday

MONITOR PROGRESS Check Fluency

FORMATIVE ASSESSMENT As students reread, monitor their progress toward their individual fluency goals.
Current Goal: 102–112 words correct per minute
End-of-Year Goal: 120 words correct per minute

If... students cannot read fluently at a rate of 102–112 words correct per minute,

then... have students practice with text at their independent levels.

Vocabulary

⊙ Unfamiliar Words

TEACH UNFAMILIAR WORDS • CONTEXT CLUES Tell students that sometimes when they read they will come across words they don't know. Remind them to use context clues to determine the meaning of unfamiliar words. They should look at the context, or the words and sentences around the word, for clues to the meaning of the unfamiliar word.

GUIDE PRACTICE Write *boils* on the board. Have a volunteer read aloud the first paragraph on p. 304 of *Jalapeño Bagels*. Then say this sentence aloud and write it on the board: *As soon as the water boils, you can put the pasta in.* Guide students to use the context clues in the paragraph and sentence to determine the meaning of *boils*.

ON THEIR OWN Walk around the room as students work in small groups to determine the meaning of three unfamiliar words in *Jalapeño Bagels*. Check that students record the words and phrases they are using as clues to figure out the meaning of each word.

Media Literacy

Radio Advertisement

TEACH Discuss advertising with students. Ask them to describe **advertisements** that they have seen or heard on the radio, in newspapers and magazines, on television, and on Web sites. Discuss the techniques used to communicate the message. (Print uses text and images, radio uses spoken words and sounds, and Web sites and television use spoken words and images.) Point out that radio commercials use engaging, conversational language and repeat information to reinforce the message. They also include sounds that attract listeners' attention and entice them to want the product.

GUIDE PRACTICE Give students time to prepare their radio advertisements. Be sure that students communicate the main message more than once. Remind them to use expression and convey excitement.

ON THEIR OWN Have students perform their commercials for the class. Remind them to speak coherently at an appropriate rate and volume and employ eye contact.

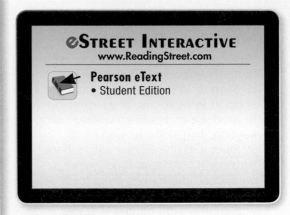

Advertisement
Explain that a good advertisement presents a persuasive argument to buy a product. Tell students that a persuasive presentation states a clear position and provides relevant support. Students can use relevant facts, details, examples, quotations, statistics, stories, and anecdotes to support their arguments. They can also use persuasive language to influence others.

Academic Vocabulary ©
advertisement a written display or oral announcement meant to sell a product or service

© Bridge to Common Core

PRESENTATION OF KNOWLEDGE AND IDEAS
As students plan their advertisements, they recognize the elements of an advertisement and the techniques of persuasion, including engaging language, repetition, and sound effects. Students can make strategic use of digital media to record their advertisements or add images, music, and sound effects.

ELL

Vocabulary: Context Clues
Provide students with additional contextualized definitions for unfamiliar words. Demonstrate any words that can be acted out, and use illustrations and other visuals to clarify the relevant meanings of words. Have students illustrate the meaning of the word to confirm understanding.

Jalapeño Bagels **319a**

Common Core State Standards

Writing 2.b. Develop the topic with facts, definitions, and details. **Writing 6.** With guidance and support from adults, use technology to produce and publish writing (using keyboarding skills) as well as to interact and collaborate with others. **Writing 10.** Write routinely over extended time frames (time for research, reflection, and revision) and shorter time frames (a single sitting or a day or two) for a range of discipline-specific tasks, purposes, and audiences. **Language 1.g.** Form and use comparative and superlative adjectives and adverbs, and choose between them depending on what is to be modified. **Language 2.f.** Use spelling patterns and generalizations (e.g., word families, position-based spellings, syllable patterns, ending rules, meaningful word parts) in writing words.

Research and Inquiry

Step 4 Synthesize

TEACH Have students synthesize their research findings and results. Remind them that when they synthesize, they integrate important information and relevant ideas from various sources to create an answer to their inquiry question. Remind students that they can sort the information they gather into categories in an outline. Explain that their outline will help them synthesize and organize the information for their article and presentation.

GUIDE PRACTICE Have students use a word processing program to prepare an outline for their articles and presentations on Day 5. Check to see that students' outlines organize the most important points from their research and include details to support each main point.

ON THEIR OWN Have students write their articles, making sure to include details to support their main ideas. Then have them practice their presentations.

Conventions

omparative and Superlative Adverbs

EST PRACTICE Remind students that
rammar skills, such as using comparative
nd superlative adverbs to discuss time and
anner, are often assessed on important
sts. Remind students to add -er to most
dverbs to make them comparative. Add
st to make most adverbs superlative. Use
ore and most with adverbs that end in the
uffix -ly.

N THEIR OWN For additional practice,
se *Reader's and Writer's Notebook,* p. 359.

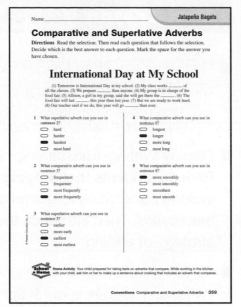

Reader's and Writer's Notebook,
p. 359

Spelling

Vowel Patterns *ei, eigh*

PRACTICE SPELLING STRATEGY Write
e words from the spelling list on the board.
ave students read and spell each word
orally. Have students work with a partner
 use each word in a sentence. Ask several
irs to share their sentences. Remind stu-
nts to segment words by letter sounds,
llables, and word parts, when applicable.

N THEIR OWN For additional prac-
e, use *Let's Practice It!* page 326 on the
acher Resources DVD-ROM.

Let's Practice It! TR DVD•326

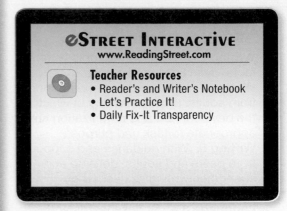

Daily Fix-It

7. Charles had went to school more
   earlier than Ms. Lawrence. *(Charles
   went or had gone; school earlier)*

8. He braught a big bassket of bagels.
   (brought; basket)

© Bridge to Common Core

**CONVENTIONS OF STANDARD
ENGLISH**

As students form and use
comparative and superlative
adverbs and correctly spell words
with the vowel patterns *ei* and
eigh, they are demonstrating
command of the conventions of
standard English. Your guidance
will help them use correct
grammar, usage, and spelling to
convey meaning when they speak
and write.

Write Guy *by Jeff Anderson*

Focus Your Revising

In the revising process, students can easily get bogged down by everything that needs to be fixed. Revising one aspect at a time helps students focus their efforts and concentrate on one task, while making it easier for you as a teacher to fully explain and reteach the concept, moving students toward correctness. Sometimes less really is more.

Writing Zoom in on ©

Invitation

Mini-Lesson Revise: Adding

- Yesterday we wrote an invitation inviting a friend over to dinner. Today we will revise our drafts. The goal is to make our writing clearer, more interesting, and more informative.

- Display Writing Transparency 24B. Remind students that revising does not include corrections to grammar and mechanics. Then introduce the revising strategy of adding.

- As you revise, ask yourself whether your invitation includes enough specific details to inform your reader about the event. For example, our outdoor barbecue invitation tells readers to meet us at the picnic tables at a park. We can add the detail *the southwest corner of Horner Park* to help readers find the exact location of the party. Have students read their invitations and look for places to add specific details about their event.

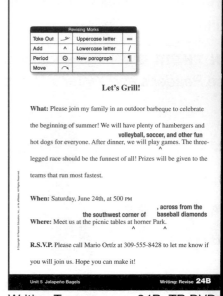

Writing Transparency 24B, TR DVD

Tell students that in addition to adding informative details, they should also look for places to replace non-descriptive language with more vivid words.

Revising Tips
✔ Check that details are well-organized and specific enough to inform your readers.
✔ Review writing for varied sentence types and lengths.
✔ Make sure that your tone is friendly and engaging.

PEER CONFERENCING • PEER REVISION Have pairs of students exchange papers for peer revision. After partners have read each other's invitations, have the reader summarize the details of the invitation to see whether they are what the writer intended. Have partners tell where they would add information to improve the invitations. Remind students to begin their critique with a compliment or strength of the invitation.

Have students revise their invitations using the key features of an invitation as well as the suggestions offered by their partner during Peer Revision. Be sure students are using the revising strategy of adding.

Corrective feedback | Circulate around the room to monitor students and confer with them as they revise. Remind students correcting errors that they will have time to edit tomorrow. They should be working on content and organization today.

Routine Quick Write for Fluency Team Talk

- **Talk** Have pairs discuss what a dinner party with Pablo and his family from *Jalapeño Bagels* might be like.

- **Write** Each student writes a paragraph describing the event.

- **Share** Partners read each other's paragraphs and check for specific details about the event.

Routines Flip Chart

eStreet Interactive
www.ReadingStreet.com
Teacher Resources
• Writing Transparency

ELL

Peer Revision Provide students with sentence starters to use during peer conferencing, such as: *I liked the way you _____*, and *Can you add details to explain _____?*

Wrap Up Your Day!

✔ **Content Knowledge** Have students discuss what they learned about Mexican food.

✔ **Oral Vocabulary** Monitor students' use of oral vocabulary as they respond to this question: *Do you think the spices in the foods from Mexico make them wholesome and full of nutrition?*

✔ **Story Structure** Discuss how dialogue between the characters helps students understand text.

Preview DAY 5

Remind students to think about how foods can come from more than one culture.

DAY 5
at a Glance

Materials

- Student Edition
- Weekly Test
- Reader's and Writer's Notebook

ⓒ **Bridge to Common Core**

INTEGRATION OF KNOWLEDGE/IDEAS
This week, students have integrated content presented in diverse media and analyzed how different texts address similar topics. They have developed knowledge about foods from different cultures to expand the unit topic of Cultures.

Social Studies Knowledge Goals
Students have learned that food
- comes from different cultures
- is shared
- can be a mix from different cultures

Content Knowledge

Foods from Different Cultures

REVIEW THE CONCEPT Have students look back at the reading selections to find examples that best demonstrate how different cultures contribute to the foods we eat.

Build Oral Language

REVIEW AMAZING WORDS Display and review this week's concept map. Remind students that this week they have learned ten Amazing Words related to foods from different cultures. Have students use the Amazing Words and the concept map to answer the Question of the Week, *How can different cultures contribute to the foods we eat?*

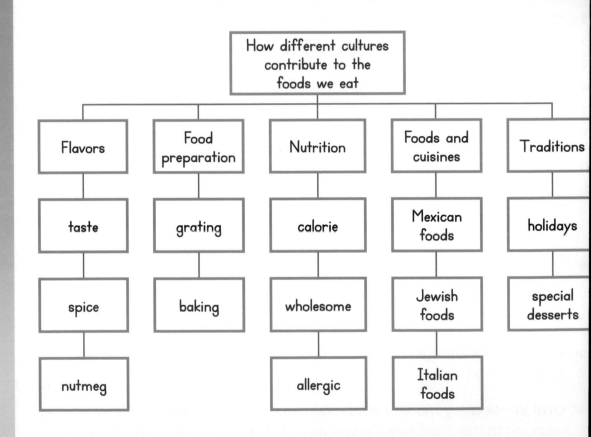

Build Oral Vocabulary

Team Talk **CONNECT TO AMAZING IDEAS** Have pairs of students discuss how the Question of the Week connects to the question for this unit of study: *What happens when two ways of life come together?* Tell students to use the concept map and what they have learned from this week's discussions and reading selections to form an Amazing Idea—a realization or "big idea" about Cultures. Remind partners to answer questions with appropriate detail and to give suggestions that build on each other's ideas. Then ask pairs to share their Amazing Ideas with the class.

Amazing Ideas might include these key concepts:

People can blend foods from different cultures to create new dishes and cuisines.

Foods from different cultures may contribute new flavors to the foods we eat.

Different cultures may contribute new methods for preparing and cooking food.

Foods from different cultures contribute to the nutritional value of the foods we eat.

WRITE ABOUT IT Have students write a few sentences about their Amazing Idea, beginning with "This week I learned . . ."

eSTREET INTERACTIVE
www.ReadingStreet.com

Concept Talk Video

Teacher Resources
• Amazing Word Cards

Story Sort

Amazing Words

nutrition	grumble
calorie	allergic
flavor	wholesome
spice	grate
nutmeg	agent

MONITOR PROGRESS **Check Oral Vocabulary**

FORMATIVE ASSESSMENT Have individuals use this week's Amazing Words to describe foods from different cultures. Monitor students' abilities to use the Amazing Words and note which words you need to reteach.

If... students have difficulty using the Amazing Words,

then... reteach using the Oral Vocabulary Routine on pp. 289a, 294b, 304b, 314b, OV•4.

Check Concepts and Language
Use the Day 5 instruction on ELL Poster 24 to monitor students' understanding of the lesson concept.
Concept Map Work with students to add new words to the concept map.

Jalapeño Bagels **319g**

Zoom in on ©

© Common Core State Standards

Literature 1. Ask and answer questions to demonstrate understanding of a text, referring explicitly to the text as the basis for the answers. **Foundational Skills 3.** Know and apply grade-level phonics and word analysis skills in decoding words. **Language 4.a.** Use sentence-level context as a clue to the meaning of a word or phrase. **Also Literature 3.**

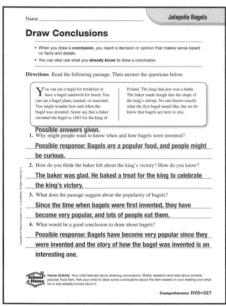

Let's Practice It! TR DVD•327

Selection Vocabulary

bakery a place where bread and cake are made and sold

batch a group of things made at the same time

boils to heat a liquid until it starts to bubble and give off steam

braided three or four strands woven together

dough flour and liquid mixed together to make bread, biscuits, and pastry

ingredients items that something is made from

mixture the combination of things mixed or blended together

Text-Based Comprehension

Review ⊙ Draw Conclusions

TEACH Review the definition of draw conclusions. Remind students that you draw conclusions when you use facts and details to make decisions. For additional support, have students review p. EI•6 on draw conclusions.

GUIDE PRACTICE Have student pairs give an example of a conclusion they can draw about information in the story *Jalapeño Bagels*.

ON THEIR OWN For additional practice, use *Let's Practice It!* p. 327 on the *Teacher Resources DVD-ROM*.

Vocabulary Skill

Review ⊙ Unfamiliar Words

TEACH Remind students that sometimes they can use context clues to determine the meanings of unfamiliar words.

GUIDE PRACTICE Review with students how to use context clues to determine the meaning of *braided* on p. 304.

ON THEIR OWN Have students practice using context clues to figure out the meanings of the words *ingredients* and *mixture* on p. 295.

Phonics

Review Vowel Patterns *ei, eigh*

TEACH Write the following sentences on the board. Have students read each one, first quietly to themselves and then aloud as you track the print.

1. Neither of our neighbors received today's newspaper.
2. The school nurse measured our height and weight.
3. My father painted the ceiling in his leisure time.
4. The freight was sent either by truck or train.
5. My eighteen-year-old brother is conceited.

Team Talk Have students discuss with a partner which words have the vowel sounds /ā/, /ē/, and /ī/ spelled *ei* or *eigh*. Ask them to identify the letters that spell the vowel sound in each word. Then call on individuals to share with the class.

Literary Terms

Review Dialogue and Narration

TEACH Have students reread pp. 302–306 of *Jalapeño Bagels*. Remind students that narration is the telling of a story or recounting of events in fiction or nonfiction. When people in the story speak, they use dialogue.

GUIDE PRACTICE Discuss how narration is used to tell the story in *Jalapeño Bagels*. Ask students to say why the author tells the story through the eyes, mind, and voice of Pablo, the narrator. Have students point out examples of narration and dialogue from the section and discuss.

ON THEIR OWN Have students make a T-chart with the headings *narration* and *dialogue*. Remind them that dialogue, the conversation between two or more people, is often combined with narration to tell a story. Have students list the events and information they learn from the narration under *narration* and what they learn from the dialogue under *dialogue*.

eStreet Interactive
www.ReadingStreet.com

Pearson eText
• Student Edition

Teacher Resources
• Let's Practice It!

ELL

Articulation Tip If students have trouble pronouncing words with long vowel spelling patterns *ei* or *eigh*, demonstrate how to pronounce them by slowly repeating words. Have students practice saying the words until they develop confidence.

Jalapeño Bagels **319i**

Common Core State Standards

Informational Text 10. By the end of the year, read and comprehend informational texts, including history/social studies, science, and technical texts, at the high end of the grades 2–3 text complexity band independently and proficiently. **Foundational Skills 4.** Read with sufficient accuracy and fluency to support comprehension.

Plan to Assess Fluency

☐ **Week 1** Advanced

☐ **Week 2** Strategic Intervention

☐ **Week 3** On-Level

☑ **This week assess Strategic Intervention students.**

☐ **Week 5** Assess any students you have not yet checked during this unit.

Set individual goals for students to enable them to reach the year-end goal.

• Current Goal: 102–112 WCPM

• Year-End Goal: 120 WCPM

Assessment

Monitor Progress

FLUENCY Make two copies of the fluency passage on p. 319k. As the student reads the text aloud, mark mistakes on your copy. Also mark where the student is at the end of one minute. To check the student's comprehension of the passage, have him or her retell what was read. To figure words correct per minute (WCPM), subtract the number of mistakes from the total number of words read in one minute.

RATE

Corrective feedback	**If...** students cannot read fluently at a rate of 102–112 WCPM, **then...** make sure they practice with text at their independent reading level. Provide additional fluency practice by pairing nonfluent readers with fluent readers.
	If... students already read at 120 WCPM, **then...** have them read a book of their choice independently.

ELL

If... students need more scaffolding and practice with **Conventions and Writing,** **then...** use the activities on pp. DI•99–DI•100 in the Teacher Resources section on SuccessNet.

Day 5 **SMALL GROUP TIME • Differentiate Reteaching, p. SG•49**

OL On-Level	**SI Strategic Intervention**	**A Advanced**
• **Practice** Comparative and Superlative Adverbs	• **Review** Comparative and Superlative Adverbs	• **Extend** Comparative and Superlative Adverbs
• **Reread** *Reading Street Sleuth,* pp. 62–63	• **Reread** *Reading Street Sleuth,* pp. 62–63	• **Reread** *Reading Street Sleuth,* pp. 62–63
		• **Communicate** Inquiry Project

Name _____

Making Challah

Making challah bread for the Sabbath is a tradition in many   11

Jewish families. The Sabbath is a day of rest. Many families share a   24

special dinner and spend time playing with family members. Challah   34

may be bought at a bakery. But many sons and daughters learn to   47

make it from an old family recipe. Some families have used the same   60

one for many generations.   64

First, the best bread ingredients are sought: flour, yeast, sugar,   74

salt, and eggs. The ingredients are mixed together. They are kneaded,   85

squeezing the dough between flour-covered hands until it is smooth.   95

The dough is left to rise in a warm place. After the first rising, the   110

mixture is punched down and left to rest for a few minutes. Then the   124

dough is separated into three pieces and braided into one long loaf.   136

The bread is set out to rise a second time.   146

Some people put poppy seeds or sesame seeds on top of the loaf.   159

Most people brush the uncooked dough with raw egg to give the crust   172

a glossy brown color when it is done baking.   181

Family recipes for challah may be different, but most families   191

agree that it is important to make bread for your family with loving   204

thoughts.   205

MONITOR PROGRESS   • **Check Fluency**

@ **Common Core
State Standards**

Literature 1. Ask and answer
questions to demonstrate
understanding of a text, referring
explicitly to the text as the basis
for the answers. **Literature 10.** By the
end of the year, read and comprehend
literature, including stories, dramas,
and poetry, at the high end of the
grades 2–3 text complexity band
independently and proficiently.

Assessment

Monitor Progress

For a written assessment of Vowel Patterns *ei, eigh,* Drawing Conclusions,
and Selection Vocabulary, use Weekly Test 27, pp. 139–144.

⊙ DRAW CONCLUSIONS Use "Arnie's Idea" on p. 319m to check students'
understanding of drawing conclusions.

1. What was Arnie's idea? Arnie's idea was to bake pizzas with foods from
   many different cultures.

2. Why do you think people at the fair wanted to try more than one kind of
   pizza? I can draw the conclusion that people enjoyed the pizzas and were
   curious to try the different ingredients.

3. Why did Tess say that Arnie's idea was a great idea? Tess thought Arnie's
   idea was a great idea because the third graders handed out all of the pizzas
   and their booth was very popular at the fair.

**Corrective
feedback** | **If...** students are unable to answer the comprehension
questions,
then... use the Reteach lesson in *First Stop*.

Name _____

Arnie's Idea

The neighborhood public school was planning an International Fair. Kids and adults would display crafts, jewelry, and costumes from all over the world.

Mrs. Lanning's third graders wanted to do something really special to demonstrate that Americans eat foods from many different countries.

"How about making pizza?" suggested Arnie.

"That isn't such a good idea because pizza is just an Italian-American food," said Tess. "What about other countries?"

"Well, I meant we should bake pizzas in a special way," explained Arnie.

Then Arnie described his idea to the class.

On the evening of the fair, the third grade class had a large, colorful booth. Across the top, a sign said "Pizzas of the World." The class made little pizzas using ideas from all around the world. The Mexican pizza had taco sauce, cheese, and ground beef on it. The Chinese pizza had vegetables and little shrimp. The kids also made Jamaican pizza, German pizza, Indian pizza, Vietnamese pizza, and more.

Mrs. Lanning baked little pizza after pizza in an oven. The third graders served little pizzas to a long line of kids, parents, and teachers. Most people wanted to try more than one kind.

Tess, Arnie, and all the third graders were busy the whole evening of the fair. When it was finally over, the third grade class had no pizza left!

As the class cleaned up, Tess looked at Arnie and said, "Hey, Arnie, I told you this wasn't such a good idea."

Then she added, "It was a great idea!"

MONITOR PROGRESS   • Draw Conclusions

Common Core State Standards

Speaking/Listening 1.b. Follow agreed-upon rules for discussions (e.g., gaining the floor in respectful ways, listening to others with care, speaking one at a time about the topics and texts under discussion). **Speaking/Listening 4.** Report on a topic or text, tell a story, or recount an experience with appropriate facts and relevant, descriptive details, speaking clearly at an understandable pace. **Language 1.g.** Form and use comparative and superlative adjectives and adverbs, and choose between them depending on what is to be modified. **Language 2.f.** Use spelling patterns and generalizations (e.g., word families, position-based spellings, syllable patterns, ending rules, meaningful word parts) in writing words.

Research and Inquiry

Step 5 Communicate

PRESENT IDEAS Have students share their inquiry results by presenting their articles and giving a brief talk on their research. Have students use the outline that they created on Day 3 to guide their talk.

SPEAKING Remind students how to be good speakers and how to communicate effectively with their audience.

• Respond to relevant questions with appropriate details.

• Speak clearly and loudly.

• Keep eye contact with audience members.

• Speak at an appropriate rate so that audience members can easily understand the ideas communicated.

LISTENING Remind students of these tips for being a good listener.

• Wait until the speaker has finished before raising your hand to ask a relevant question.

• Be polite, even if you disagree.

LISTEN TO IDEAS Have students listen attentively to the various presentations. Have them make pertinent comments, closely related to the topic.

Spelling Test

Vowel Patterns *ei, eigh*

To administer the spelling test, refer to the directions, words, and sentences on p. 293c.

Conventions

Comparative and Superlative Adverbs

MORE PRACTICE Remind students that comparative adverbs compare two things and often end in *-er*. Superlative adverbs compare three or more or things and often end in *-est*. Comparative and superlative adverbs that end in the suffix *-ly* use *more* and *most*.

GUIDE PRACTICE Have students think of animals to complete the sentences.

_____ **runs fast.**

_____ **runs faster than** _____ .

_____ **runs fastest of all.**

ON THEIR OWN Write these sentences on the board. Have students read aloud each sentence and replace the underlined phrase with the correct form of the adverb. Students should complete *Let's Practice It!* page 328 on the *Teacher Resources DVD-ROM.*

1. **The rolls bake <u>more quicker</u> than the bread.** (more quickly)
2. **The cheetah runs <u>most fastest</u> of any animal.** (fastest)
3. **Today the bus traveled <u>slowly</u> than yesterday.** (more slowly)
4. **My phone rings <u>most quietly</u> than Sara's.** (more quietly)

Daily Fix-It

9. Matt creeated a knew recipe for muffins. *(created; new)*
10. The muffins has strawberrys inside. *(have; strawberries)*

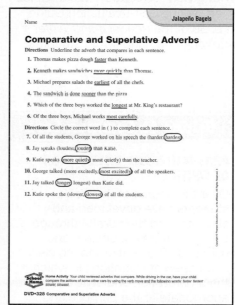

Let's Practice It! TR DVD•328

Common Core State Standards

Writing 5. With guidance and support from peers and adults, develop and strengthen writing as needed by planning, revising, and editing. **Language 1.** Demonstrate command of the conventions of standard English grammar and usage when writing or speaking. **Language 1.g.** Form and use comparative and superlative adjectives and adverbs, and choose between them depending on what is to be modified. **Language 2.** Demonstrate command of the conventions of standard English capitalization, punctuation, and spelling when writing. **Also Writing 6, 10.**

Teacher Note

Writing Self-Evaluation Make copies of the Writing Self-Evaluation Guide on p. 39 of the *Reader's and Writer's Notebook* and hand out to students.

Bridge to Common Core

PRODUCTION AND DISTRIBUTION OF WRITING

Over the course of the week, students have developed and strengthened their drafts through planning, revising, editing, and rewriting. The final drafts are clear and coherent invitations in which the organization and style are appropriate to the purpose and audience.

Writing

Invitation

REVIEW REVISING Remind students that yesterday they revised their invitations. Today they will proofread them.

Mini-Lesson | Proofread

Proofread for Adverbs

- **Teach** When we proofread, we look closely at our work, searching for errors in mechanics. Today we will focus on making sure we have used comparative and superlative adverbs correctly.

- **Model** Display Writing Transparency 24C. Let's look at a sentence from the invitation we started yesterday. I see a problem in the fifth sentence with the phrase *most fastest*. To form most superlative adverbs, you add *-est*. For adverbs that end in the suffix *-ly,* you use the word *most*. But you do not use *most* with adverbs that use the *-est* form. Because *fastest* ends with *-est,* I will take out the word *most*. Have

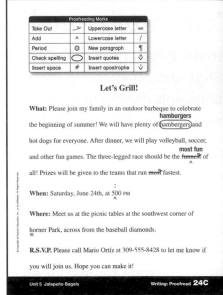

Writing Transparency 24C, TR DVD

students reread their invitations and check for correct use of comparative and superlative adverbs. Then explain to students that they should reread their invitations several times, each time looking for different types of errors spelling, punctuation, capitalization, and grammar. Have students pay particular attention to the time of their event, checking for proper use of the colon.

PROOFREAD Display the Proofreading Tips. Ask students to proofread their compositions, using the Proofreading Tips and paying particular attention to comparative and superlative adverbs. Circulate around the room answering students' questions. Then have pairs proofread one another's invitations.

Proofreading Tips

- ✔ Be sure that all adverbs are used correctly.
- ✔ Check for correct use of the colon when writing times (e.g., 5:00).
- ✔ Remember to capitalize geographical names and places.

eStreet Interactive
www.ReadingStreet.com

Teacher Resources
• Writing Transparency
• Reader's and Writer's Notebook

PRESENT Have students incorporate revisions and proofreading edits into their invitations to create a final draft. Remind students that invitations often include illustrations. Have students copy their invitations on a folded sheet of cardstock and illustrate the final draft, or they can use an invitation template from a desktop publishing program or the Internet. Have students type their final draft into the template and add photographs or clip art.

Routine   Quick Write for Fluency   Team Talk

1. **Talk** Have pairs discuss what they learned about invitations this week.

2. **Write** Each student writes a paragraph comparing the features of an invitation and the features of a friendly letter.

3. **Share** Partners read their paragraphs to each other.

Routines Flip Chart

Wrap Up Your Week!

Foods from Different Cultures

How can different cultures contribute to the foods we eat?

Think Aloud In *Jalapeño Bagels* and "Foods of Mexico: A Delicious Blend," we learned about foods from different countries and cultures.

Team Talk Have students recall their Amazing Ideas about cultures and use these ideas to help them demonstrate their understanding of the Question of the Week.

Next Week's Concept
City Life and Country Life

How does city life compare to life in the country?

Poster Preview Prepare students for next week by using Week 5 ELL Poster 25. Read the Talk-Through to introduce the concept and vocabulary. Ask students to identify and describe actions in the art.

Selection Summary Send home the summary of next week's selection, *Me and Uncle Romie,* in English and in students' home languages, if available in the *ELL Handbook*. They can read the summary with family members.

How does city life compare to life in the country? Tell students that next week they will read about a boy who travels from North Carolina to spend the summer in New York City.

Preview Next Week

Assessment Checkpoints for the Week

Weekly Assessment

Use pp. 139–144 of *Weekly Tests* to check:

✔ **Phonics/Word Analysis** Vowel Patterns *ei, eigh*

✔ **Comprehension** Draw Conclusions

✔ **Review** **Comprehension** Sequence of Events

✔ **Selection Vocabulary**

bakery	braided	ingredients
batch	dough	mixture
boils		

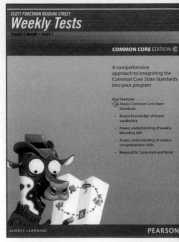

Weekly Tests

Differentiated Assessment

Advanced

Use pp. 139–144 of *Fresh Reads for Fluency and Comprehension* to check:

✔ **Comprehension** Draw Conclusions

✔ **Review** **Comprehension** Sequence

✔ **Fluency** Words Correct Per Minute

SI
Strategic Intervention

OL
On-Level

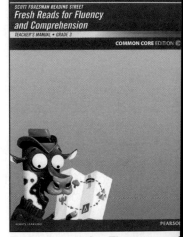

Fresh Reads for Fluency and Comprehension

Managing Assessment

Use *Assessment Handbook* for:

✔ **Weekly Assessment Blackline Masters for Monitoring Progress**

✔ **Observation Checklists**

✔ **Record-Keeping Forms**

✔ **Portfolio Assessment**

Assessment Handbook

TEACHER NOTES

DAY 1   Differentiate Vocabulary

- **Word Knowledge** Amazing Words
- **Read** "Pizza, Pizza Everywhere"
- **Inquiry** Identify Questions

"Pizza, Pizza Everywhere,"
pp. 62–63

DAY 2   Differentiate Comprehension

- **Word Knowledge** Selection Vocabulary
- **Access Text** Read *Jalapeño Bagels*
- **Inquiry** Investigate

DAY 3   Differentiate Close Reading

- **Word Knowledge** Develop Vocabulary
- **Close Reading** Read *Jalapeño Bagels*
- **Inquiry** Investigate

DAY 4   Differentiate Vocabulary

- **Word Knowledge** Amazing Words
- **Read** "Foods of Mexico: A Delicious Blend"
- **Inquiry** Organize

DAY 5   Differentiate Reteaching

- **Conventions** Comparative and Superlative Adverbs
- **Reread** "Pizza, Pizza Everywhere" or Leveled Readers
- **Inquiry** Communicate

Teacher Guides and Student pages can be found in the Leveled Reader Database.

 Place English Language Learners in the groups that correspond to their reading abilities.
If... students need scaffolding and practice,
then... use the ELL Notes on the instructional pages.

Independent Practice

Independent Practice Stations

See pp. 288h and 288i for Independent Stations.

Pearson Trade Book Library

See the Leveled Reader Database for lesson plans and student pages.

Reading Street Digital Path

Independent Practice Activities are available in the Digital Path.

Independent Reading

See p. 288i for independent reading suggestions.

Common Core State Standards

Literature 1. Ask and answer questions to demonstrate understanding of a text, referring explicitly to the text as the basis for the answers. **Informational Text 2.** Determine the main idea of a text; recount the key details and explain how they support the main idea. **Foundational Skills 4.** Read with sufficient accuracy and fluency to support comprehension. **Language 4.** Determine or clarify the meaning of unknown and multiple-meaning words and phrases based on grade 3 reading and content, choosing flexibly from a range of strategies. **Language 6.** Acquire and use accurately grade-appropriate conversational, general academic, and domain-specific words and phrases, including those that signal spatial and temporal relationships (e.g., *After dinner that night we went looking for them*).

Independent Reading Options

Trade Book Library

eSTREET INTERACTIVE
www.ReadingStreet.com

Teacher Guides are available on the Leveled Reader Database.

If... students need more scaffolding and practice with **Vocabulary, then...** use the activities on pp. DI•92–DI•93 in the Teacher Resources section on SuccessNet.

On-Level

① Build Word Knowledge
Practice Amazing Words

DEFINE IT Elicit the definition for the word *flavor* from students. Ask: How would you explain *flavor* to another student? (Possible response: *Flavor* is the taste of food or drink.) Clarify or give a definition when necessary. Continue with the words *calorie* and *nutrition*.

Team Talk **TALK ABOUT IT** Have students internalize meanings. Ask: How can you group the Amazing Words together in a sentence? (Possible response: When I choose foods, I think about *flavor, nutrition,* and *calorie* counts.) Allow time for students to play with the words. Review the concept map with students. Discuss other words they can add to the concept map.

② Text-Based Comprehension
Read

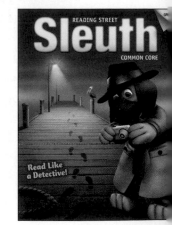

READ ALOUD "Pizza, Pizza Everywhere" Have partners read "Pizza, Pizza Everywhere" from *Reading Street Sleuth* on pp. 62–63.

ACCESS TEXT Discuss the Sleuth Work section with students before they work on it. Remind students that they can use these steps with other texts they read.

Gather Evidence Have partners work together to note details from the text that tell how pizzas look and taste differently around the world. Invite students to note on their list what country those details relate to.

Ask Questions Have partners share their questions with each other. Talk together about how students might approach a chef with these questions.

Make Your Case Have students discuss their opinions, sharing convincing evidence from the text to explain their opinions.

 On-Level

Build Word Knowledge
Practice Selection Vocabulary

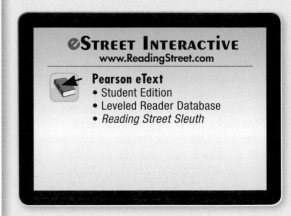
eSTREET INTERACTIVE
www.ReadingStreet.com

Pearson eText
• Student Edition
• Leveled Reader Database
• *Reading Street Sleuth*

bakery	batch	boils	braided
dough	ingredients	mixture	

DEFINE IT Discuss the definition for the word *bakery* with students. Ask: How would you describe a *bakery* to another student? (Possible response: A *bakery* is a place where people make and sell bread.) Continue with the remaining words.

Team Talk **TALK ABOUT IT** Have pairs use the selection vocabulary in sentences to internalize meaning. Ask: How can you group the selection vocabulary words together in a sentence? (Possible response: Your *dough mixture* contained many *ingredients*.) Allow time for students to play with the words and then share their sentences.

Read
Jalapeño Bagels

If you read *Jalapeño Bagels* during whole group time, then use the following instruction.

ACCESS TEXT Reread the dialogue on p. 298. Ask: Why does Pablo's mother wake him up early? (so he can go work at the bakery with his parents) Why does Pablo go to the bakery? (to help his parents and choose something to bring for International Day) How does Pablo feel about the bakery? (He likes it because it is warm and smells good.)

Have students identify sections from today's reading that they did not completely understand. Reread them aloud and clarify misunderstandings.

If you are reading *Jalapeño Bagels* during small group time, then return to p. 298–303a to guide the reading.

More Reading for Group Time

ON-LEVEL

Reviews
• Draw Conclusions
• Summarize
• Selection Vocabulary

Use this suggested Leveled Reader or other text at student's instructional level.

eSTREET INTERACTIVE
www.ReadingStreet.com

Use the Leveled Reader Database for lesson plans and student pages for *Kapuapua's Magic Shell*.

SMALL GROUP TIME

Ⓒ Common Core State Standards

Literature 1. Ask and answer questions to demonstrate understanding of a text, referring explicitly to the text as the basis for the answers. **Informational Text 7.** Use information gained from illustrations (e.g., maps, photographs), and the words in a text to demonstrate understanding of the text (e.g., where, when, why, and how key events occur). **Language 4.** Determine or clarify the meaning of unknown and multiple-meaning words and phrases based on grade 3 reading and content, choosing flexibly from a range of strategies. **Language 6.** Acquire and use accurately grade-appropriate conversational, general academic, and domain-specific words and phrases, including those that signal spatial and temporal relationships (e.g., *After dinner that night we went looking for them*). **Also Writing 2.a.**

OL On-Level

❶ Build Word Knowledge
Develop Vocabulary

REREAD FOR VOCABULARY Reread the first paragraph on p. 304. Introduce: Let's read this paragraph and think about what *customers* means. To help students understand the word *customers,* remind students that a *bakery* is a kind of business. Ask: Who buys the breads and other goods at the bakery? Have students use online sources to find out more information about customers.

❷ Read

Jalapeño Bagels

If you read *Jalapeño Bagels* during whole group time, then use the following instruction.

CLOSE READING Read pp. 304–305. Have students search the text and make a list of all the food words in the order that they appear. (*challah, bread, loaf, bagel, dough, poppy seeds, sesame seeds, cream cheese, lox, salmon, pumpernickel, fish, jam*)

Ask: In what categories would you put the foods from your list? (Some foods are baked—*challah,* bread, bagel; some of the foods go on top of baked foods—cream cheese, jam, lox, or salmon.) How do these words help you understand what Pablo's parents do? (I can see all the things that his parents make, the ingredients in the foods, and what people put on the baked goods.)

If you are reading *Jalapeño Bagels* during small group time, then return to pp. 304–309a to guide the reading.

If... students need more scaffolding and practice with the **Main Selection, then...** use the activities on p. DI•97 in the Teacher Resources section on SuccessNet.

On-Level

Build Word Knowledge

Practice Amazing Words

| nutrition | calorie | flavor | spice | nutmeg |
| grumble | allergic | wholesome | grate | agent |

Team Talk **LANGUAGE DEVELOPMENT** Have students practice building more complex sentences. Display a sentence starter and have students add al phrases or clauses using the Amazing Words. For example: The _____ eal _____. (The *wholesome* meal / had great *flavor* / and provided us / with enty of *nutrition*.) Guide students to add at least three phrases or clauses er sentence.

Read

"Foods of Mexico: A Delicious Blend"

BEFORE READING Read loud the genre information bout expository text on p. 14. Remind students that the urpose of expository text is to xplain a topic. Have students eview "Foods of Mexico: A Delicious Blend" and set a purpose for reading.

How do photos help explain the topic? (The labels identify the food.)

Why are some words in italic (slanted) type? (They are foreign.)

DURING READING Have students read with you. Ask:

What is covered in the section titled "Native Foods"? (foods of the early people of Mexico)

What is covered in the section titled "The Spanish Flavor"? (foods and spices brought to Mexico from Spain)

What is covered in the last section? (the difference between Spanish rolls made from wheat, called *bolillos,* and Mexican corn tortillas)

AFTER READING Have students share their reactions to "Foods of Mexico: A Delicious Blend." Then have them write a paragraph describing their favorite od and what culture or cultures they think it comes from.

eStreet Interactive
www.ReadingStreet.com

Pearson eText
• Student Edition
• Leveled Reader Database

SMALL GROUP TIME

Independent Reading Options

Trade Book Library

eStreet Interactive
www.ReadingStreet.com

Teacher Guides are available on the Leveled Reader Database.

Jalapeño Bagels **SG•53**

OL On-Level

Ⓒ Common Core State Standards

Informational Text 1. Ask and answer questions to demonstrate understanding of a text, referring explicitly to the text as the basis for the answers. **Informational Text 2.** Determine the main idea of a text; recount the key details and explain how they support the main idea. **Foundational Skills 4.** Read with sufficient accuracy and fluency to support comprehension. **Writing 4.** With guidance and support from adults, produce writing in which the development and organization are appropriate to task and purpose. **Writing 10.** Write routinely over extended time frames (time for research, reflection, and revision) and shorter time frames (a single sitting or a day or two) for a range of discipline-specific tasks, purposes, and audiences. **Language 1.g.** Form and use comparative and superlative adjectives and adverbs, and choose between them depending on what is to be modified. **Also Language 6.**

More Reading for Group Time

ON-LEVEL

Reviews
• Draw Conclusions
• Summarize
• Selection Vocabulary

Use this suggested Leveled Reader or other text at students' instructional level.

eSTREET INTERACTIVE
www.ReadingStreet.com

Use the Leveled Reader Database for lesson plans and student pages for *Kapuapua's Magic Shell.*

① Build Word Knowledge
Practice Comparative and Superlative Adverbs

IDENTIFY Ask a volunteer to read aloud the instruction about comparative and superlative forms of adverbs on p. 313 and discuss their form and function. Have students work in teams to reread the invitation to find examples of how the author used comparative and superlative adverbs. Allow time for students to discuss their examples and correct any misunderstandings.

② Text-Based Comprehension
Read

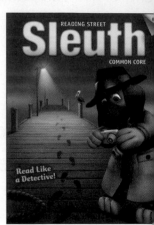

REREAD "Pizza, Pizza Everywhere" Have partners reread "Pizza, Pizza Everywhere."

EXTEND UNDERSTANDING Talk together about the wide variety of ingredients found on pizzas. Have students share the oddest ingredient they have ever had on pizza.

PERFORMANCE TASK • Prove It! Have students write a recipe for their own pizza using interesting and unique pizza toppings. Review with students the format of a recipe before they begin to write.

COMMUNICATE Have pairs share their recipes with each other. Encourage discussion about the kinds of toppings students used.

SI Strategic Intervention

1 Reteach Amazing Words

Repeat the definition of the word. We learned that *flavor* refers to the way food or drinks taste. Then use the word in a sentence. My favorite *flavor* of ice cream is chocolate.

Team Talk TALK ABOUT IT Have students take turns using the word *flavor* in a sentence. Continue this routine to practice the Amazing Words *nutrition* and *calorie*. Review the concept map with students. Discuss other words they can add to the concept map.

> **Corrective feedback**
>
> **If...** students need more practice with the Amazing Words, **then...** use visuals from the Student Edition or online sources to clarify meaning.

2 Text-Based Comprehension

Read

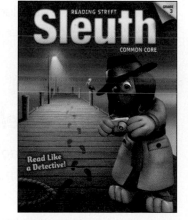

READ "Pizza, Pizza Everywhere" Have students track the print as you read "Pizza, Pizza Everywhere" from *Reading Street Sleuth* on pp. 62–63.

ACCESS TEXT Discuss the Sleuth Work section with students and provide support as needed as they work on it. Remind students that they can use these steps with other texts they read.

Gather Evidence Talk together about details from the text that tell how pizzas look and taste differently around the world. With students, make a list of these details, noting which country each detail relates to.

Ask Questions Talk together about questions students might ask a chef. Have pairs role-play asking questions and answering as "chef." As students role-play, encourage them to ask both factual and opinion questions.

Make Your Case Have students select a position on the issue. Then have them partner with someone who took the same position to make a list of evidence from the text to help justify their opinions.

---

eStreet Interactive
www.ReadingStreet.com

Pearson eText
- Student Edition
- Leveled Reader Database
- *Reading Street Sleuth*

More Reading for Group Time

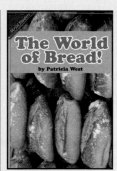

CONCEPT LITERACY
Practice
Concept Words

BELOW-LEVEL
Reviews
- Draw Conclusions
- Summarize
- Selection Vocabulary

Use these suggested Leveled Readers or other text at student's instructional level.

eStreet Interactive
www.ReadingStreet.com

Use the Leveled Reader Database for lesson plans and student pages for *Bread!* and *The World of Bread!*

SMALL GROUP TIME

Common Core State Standards

Literature 1. Ask and answer questions to demonstrate understanding of a text, referring explicitly to the text as the basis for the answers. **Language 4.** Determine or clarify the meaning of unknown and multiple-meaning words and phrases based on grade 3 reading and content, choosing flexibly from a range of strategies. **Language 4.a.** Use sentence-level context as a clue to the meaning of a word or phrase. **Language 5.** Demonstrate understanding of word relationships and nuances in word meanings.

① Build Word Knowledge
Reteach Selection Vocabulary

DEFINE IT Describe *braided* to a friend. Give a definition when necessary. Restate the word in student-friendly terms and clarify meaning with a visual. *Braided* means woven in a pattern. Hair may be *braided*. Page 304 shows *braided* bread.

bakery	batch	boils	braided
dough	ingredients	mixture	

Team Talk **TALK ABOUT IT** Have you ever seen *braided* hair? Turn and talk to your partner about this. Allow time for students to discuss. Ask for examples. Rephrase students' examples for usage when necessary or to correct misunderstandings. Continue with the remaining words.

Corrective feedback | **If...** students need more practice with selection vocabulary, **then...** use the *Envision It! Pictured Vocabulary Cards.*

② Read
Jalapeño Bagels

If you read *Jalapeño Bagels* during whole group time, then use the instruction below.

ACCESS TEXT Reread the dialogue on p. 298. Ask questions to check understanding. Who is Pablo? (a boy whose parents own a bakery) What is Pablo's problem? (He doesn't know what to bring to school for International Day.) Why does he get up early on Sunday? (He is going to help his parents at the bakery and pick out something for school.) Why does Pablo enjoy helping at the bakery? (He likes that the bakery is warm and smells good.)

Have students identify sections they did not understand. Reread them aloud. Clarify the meaning of each section to build understanding.

If you are reading *Jalapeño Bagels* during small group time, then return to pp. 298–303a to guide the reading.

Independent Reading Options

Trade Book Library

eSTREET INTERACTIVE
www.ReadingStreet.com

Teacher Guides are available on the Leveled Reader Database.

Strategic Intervention

❶ Build Word Knowledge

Develop Vocabulary

REREAD FOR VOCABULARY Reread the first paragraph on p. 304.
Introduce: Let's read this paragraph and think about what *customers* means.
To help students understand the word *customers,* remind students that a bakery is a business. Then ask questions related to the context, such as: Who is talking about the challah? What do they say about it? Who buys things from businesses?

Corrective feedback | **If...** students have trouble understanding the word *customers,* **then...** guide students to consult a thesaurus for other words with similar meanings.

❷ Read

Jalapeño Bagels

If you read *Jalapeño Bagels* during whole group time, then use the instruction below.

CLOSE READING Read p. 304–305. Have students search through the text to find time-order words. As a class, make a list of these words in the order they occur and retell what happened in the story. *(While, When, then)*

Now use the time-order words you listed to retell what happened in this part of the story. (While they waited, Pablo and his father make challah. When the bagel dough rises, Pablo's father boils the bagels. Then they go into the oven.)

If you are reading *Jalapeño Bagels* during small group time, then return to p. 304–309a to guide the reading.

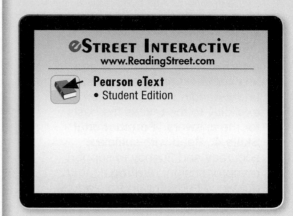

eStreet Interactive
www.ReadingStreet.com

Pearson eText
• Student Edition

SMALL GROUP TIME

ELL

If... students need more scaffolding and practice with the **Main Selection, then...** use the activities on p. DI•97 in the Teacher Resources section on SuccessNet.

Strategic Intervention

© Common Core State Standards

Informational Text 1. Ask and answer questions to demonstrate understanding of a text, referring explicitly to the text as the basis for the answers. **Foundational Skills 4.** Read with sufficient accuracy and fluency to support comprehension. **Writing 4.** With guidance and support from adults, produce writing in which the development and organization are appropriate to task and purpose. **Language 1.g.** Form and use comparative and superlative adjectives and adverbs, and choose between them depending on what is to be modified. **Language 6.** Acquire and use accurately grade-appropriate conversational, general academic, and domain-specific words and phrases, including those that signal spatial and temporal relationships (e.g., *After dinner that night we went looking for them*). **Also Writing 10.**

1 Build Word Knowledge
Review Amazing Words

nutrition	calorie	flavor	spice	nutmeg
grumble	allergic	wholesome	grate	agent

Team Talk **LANGUAGE DEVELOPMENT** Have students practice building more complex sentences. Display a sentence starter and have students add oral phrases or clauses using the Amazing Words. For example: The _____ meal _____. (The *wholesome* meal got its *flavor* / from a *spice* called *nutmeg*.) Guide students to add at least two phrases or clauses per sentence.

Corrective feedback | **If...** students have difficulty using the Amazing Words orally, **then...** review the meaning of each of the words.

2 Read
"Foods of Mexico: A Delicious Blend"

BEFORE READING Read aloud the genre information about expository text on p. 314. Remind students that the purpose of expository text is to explain a topic. Recall the Leveled Reader *The World of Bread! The World of Bread!* is also expository text. How does it give information about bread? (It gives a photograph and a paragraph or two about each kind of bread.) Then have students scan the pages for headings, photographs, and captions.

DURING READING Have students perform a choral reading of the selection Stop to discuss Spanish words, unfamiliar words, and proper nouns.

AFTER READING Have students share their reactions to the paired selection. Then guide them through the Reading Across Texts and Writing Across Texts activities. When did the Spanish learn about rice? (when they established colonies in Asia) What did you learn about Mexican food from reading this book? (Mexican food is the result of blending Spanish influences with foods eaten by early people of Mexico.)

If... students need more scaffolding and practice with **Amazing Words, then...** use the Routine on pp. xxxvi–xxxvii in the *ELL Handbook*.

SI Strategic Intervention

eStreet Interactive
www.ReadingStreet.com

Pearson eText
- Student Edition
- Leveled Reader Database
- *Reading Street Sleuth*

Build Word Knowledge

Review Comparative and Superlative Adverbs

IDENTIFY Ask a volunteer to read aloud the instruction about comparative and superlative forms of adverbs on p. 313. Have students work in teams to reread the invitation to find examples of how the author used comparative and superlative adverbs. Allow time for students to discuss their examples and correct any misunderstandings.

Text-Based Comprehension

Read

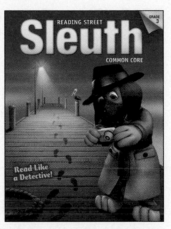

REREAD "Pizza, Pizza Everywhere" Have partners reread "Pizza, Pizza Everywhere," with partners alternating paragraphs.

EXTEND UNDERSTANDING Take a poll of students' favorite and least favorite toppings in the United States. Then ask students to vote on which toppings they'd most like to try from another country's pizza.

PERFORMANCE TASK • Prove It! Have students write a recipe for their own pizza using interesting and unique pizza toppings. Talk together about a recipe format, highlighting the need to list ingredients, the amount of ingredients, and steps to bake the pizza.

COMMUNICATE Have students share their recipes with another student. Invite discussion about the baking techniques used in the recipes. Were they similar or different? Have students explain their answers.

More Reading for Group Time

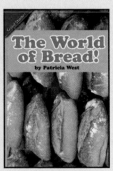

CONCEPT LITERACY
Practice
Concept Words

BELOW-LEVEL
Reviews
- Draw Conclusions
- Summarize
- Selection Vocabulary

Use these suggested Leveled Readers or other text at student's instructional level.

eStreet Interactive
www.ReadingStreet.com

Use the Leveled Reader Database for lesson plans and student pages for *Bread!* and *The World of Bread!*

A Advanced

© **Common Core State Standards**

Literature 1. Ask and answer questions to demonstrate understanding of a text, referring explicitly to the text as the basis for the answers. **Informational Text 2.** Determine the main idea of a text; recount the key details and explain how they support the main idea. **Foundational Skills 4.** Read with sufficient accuracy and fluency to support comprehension. **Writing 7.** Conduct short research projects that build knowledge about a topic. **Language 4.** Determine or clarify the meaning of unknown and multiple-meaning words and phrases based on grade 3 reading and content, choosing flexibly from a range of strategies. **Also Writing 8., Language 6.**

1 Build Word Knowledge

Extend Amazing Words

Team Talk Have students define *flavor*. Discuss synonyms for *flavor*. Continue with *nutrition* and *calorie*. Have students use all three words in a sentence.

2 Text-Based Comprehension

Read

READ "Pizza, Pizza Everywhere" Have students read "Pizza, Pizza Everywhere" from *Reading Street Sleuth* on pp. 62–63.

ACCESS TEXT Discuss the Sleuth Work section with students before they work on it. Remind students that they can use these steps with other texts they read.

Gather Evidence Have students note details from the text that tell how pizzas look and taste different around the world. Invite students to note on their list what country those details relate to.

Ask Questions Have partners share their questions with each other. If time permits, have students research local pizza places, writing a letter to one of the chefs in town.

Make Your Case Have students discuss their opinions, sharing convincing evidence from the text and their own personal experiences to explain their opinions.

3 Inquiry: Extend Concepts

IDENTIFY QUESTIONS Have students think about questions they have about their favorite foods and use these questions to create an annotated menu that tells the country of origin of the foods, their ingredients, and their characteristics (spicy, cheesy, crunchy, and so on). Throughout the week, the[y] will gather information. On Day 5, they will present what they have learned.

If... students need more scaffolding and practice with **Vocabulary, then...** use the activities on pp. DI•92–DI•93 in the Teacher Resources section on SuccessNet.

A Advanced

Build Word Knowledge

Extend Selection Vocabulary

Team Talk Have partners use the selection vocabulary in sentences to interalize their meanings. Have students use as many of the words as they can while making sure the sentence is grammatically correct. (Possible response: The *bakery* had all the *ingredients* I needed for making *dough*.) Continue with additional selection vocabulary words.

bakery	batch	boils	braided
dough	ingredients	mixture	

Read

Jalapeño Bagels

If you read *Jalapeño Bagels* during whole group time, then use the instruction below.

ACCESS TEXT Have students reread the dialogue on p. 298. Discuss what readers learn about the narrator from the opening dialogue. (He is a young person named Pablo. His parents run a bakery. He needs to bring something from his culture to school for International Day. He is going to help at the bakery so he can decide what to bring.)

Ask: Why did the writer begin the story with the characters speaking? (It is a good way to introduce the characters and let them tell the story.)

If you are reading *Jalapeño Bagels* during small group time, then return to pp. 298–303a to guide the reading.

Inquiry: Extend Concepts

INVESTIGATE Encourage students to use materials at their independent reading levels or student-friendly search engines to identify relevant and credible sites to gather information about the origins and ingredients of their favorite foods. Have students consider how they will present their information.

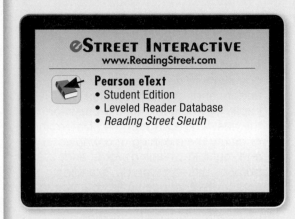

eSTREET INTERACTiVE
www.ReadingStreet.com
Pearson eText
• Student Edition
• Leveled Reader Database
• *Reading Street Sleuth*

More Reading for Group Time

Mixing, Kneading, and Baking: The Baker's Art

by Francelia Sevin

ADVANCED

Reviews
• Drawing Conclusions
• Summarizing

Use this suggested Leveled Reader or other text at student's instructional level.

eSTREET INTERACTiVE
www.ReadingStreet.com

Use the Leveled Reader Database for lesson plans and student pages for *Mixing, Kneading, and Baking: The Baker's Art.*

SMALL GROUP TIME

A Advanced

① Build Word Knowledge
Develop Vocabulary

REREAD FOR VOCABULARY Reread the first paragraph on p. 304. Let's read this paragraph to find out what *customers* means. Discuss meaning and context with students.

② Read
Jalapeño Bagels

If you read *Jalapeño Bagels* during whole group time, then use the instruction below.

CLOSE READING Read pp. 304–305. Have students create a T-chart with headings *Baked Foods* and *Toppings.* Then have

students search the text for food words. After identifying the words, students should think of ways to classify them and sort the words to fill in the chart.

Baked Foods	Toppings
challah	sesame seeds and poppy seeds
bread	cream cheese
bagels	lox
	jam

Ask: How do these words help you understand what Pablo and his father are doing? (They tell what they are making and the ingredients that go on them.) What do these words tell you about the characters? (Lox, *challah*, and bagels are Jewish foods, so they show that the father is Jewish. Pablo doesn't like lox.

If you are reading *Jalapeño Bagels* during small group time, then return to pp. 304–309a to guide the reading.

③ Inquiry: Extend Concepts

INVESTIGATE Provide time for students to investigate their topics in books or online. If necessary, help them locate information that is focused on their topic.

Independent Reading Options

Trade Book Library

eStreet Interactive
www.ReadingStreet.com

Teacher Guides are available on the Leveled Reader Database.

A Advanced

Build Word Knowledge

Extend Amazing Words and Selection Vocabulary

nutrition	calorie	flavor	agent
spice	nutmeg	grumble	
allergic	wholesome	grate	

bakery	batch	boils
braided	dough	ingredients
mixture		

Team Talk Have students practice building more complex sentences. Display a sentence starter and have students add oral phrases or clauses using the Amazing Words and the selection vocabulary.

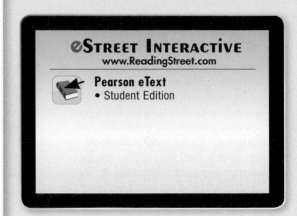

eSTREET INTERACTIVE
www.ReadingStreet.com

Pearson eText
• Student Edition

Read

"Foods of Mexico: A Delicious Blend"

BEFORE READING Review the panel information on expository text on p. 314. Then have students use the text features to set a purpose for reading.

DURING READING Encourage students to think critically and creatively. For example, ask: What main idea do you think the author wants you to understand? (Mexican cuisine is a blend of European cultures and the foods of early people of Mexico.) How do details in the section titled "Tortillas or Bolillos?" support this main idea? (Mexicans blend native and European traditions in the torta de tamal, or tamale sandwich.) Which of the foods would you most like to try? Why? (Students should identify a food from the selection.)

AFTER READING Guide students through the Reading Across Texts and Writing Across Texts activities.

Inquiry: Extend Concepts

ORGANIZE INFORMATION Provide time for students to organize their information into a format that will effectively communicate their findings to their audience. Provide any necessary materials or computer time.

SMALL GROUP TIME

Independent Reading Options

Trade Book Library

eSTREET INTERACTIVE
www.ReadingStreet.com

Teacher Guides are available on the Leveled Reader Database.

Jalapeño Bagels **SG•63**

© Common Core State Standards

Informational Text 1. Ask and answer questions to demonstrate understanding of a text, referring explicitly to the text as the basis for the answers. **Foundational Skills 4.** Read with sufficient accuracy and fluency to support comprehension. **Writing 4.** With guidance and support from adults, produce writing in which the development and organization are appropriate to task and purpose. **Speaking/Listening 4.** Report on a topic or text, tell a story, or recount an experience with appropriate facts and relevant, descriptive details, speaking clearly at an understandable pace. **Language 1.g.** Form and use comparative and superlative adjectives and adverbs, and choose between them depending on what is to be modified. **Also Speaking/Listening 1.a., 1.b.**

More Reading for Group Time

Mixing, Kneading, and Baking: The Baker's Art

by
Francelia Sevin

ADVANCED

Reviews
• Drawing Conclusions
• Summarize

Use this suggested Leveled Reader or other text at students' instructional level.

eStreet Interactive
www.ReadingStreet.com

Use the Leveled Reader Database for lesson plans and student pages for *Mixing, Kneading, and Baking: The Baker's Art.*

A Advanced

① Build Word Knowledge
Extend Comparative and Superlative Adverbs

IDENTIFY AND EXTEND Ask a volunteer to read aloud the instruction abou comparative and superlative forms of adverbs on p. 313. Have students work in teams to reread the invitation to find examples of how the author used com parative and superlative adverbs. Then encourage students to write their own invitations using the appropriate adverbs. Allow time for students to discuss their work and correct any misunderstandings.

② Text-Based Comprehension
Read

REREAD "Pizza, Pizza Everywhere" Have partners reread the selection. Encourage them to discuss which country's pizza they would most like to try.

EXTEND UNDERSTANDING Talk together about why pizza ingredients vary so much around the world. How do the ingredients reflect a country's culture?

PERFORMANCE TASK • Prove It! Have students write a recipe for their own pizza using interesting and unique pizza toppings. Encourage students to be detailed in their recipes so others can easily follow it.

COMMUNICATE Have students share their recipes with a small group. Encourage discussion about the ease or difficulty of making this recipe.

③ Inquiry: Extend Concepts

COMMUNICATE Have students share their inquiry projects on the origins and ingredients of their favorite foods with the rest of the class. Provide the following tips for presenting.
• Explain unfamiliar words.
• Make eye contact with the audience and point to visuals as you speak.
• Ask questions to make sure your audience understands the information.

Indiana Common Core Edition

This Week's Target Skills and Strategies

Target Skills and Strategies	Ⓒ Common Core State Standards for English Language Arts	Indiana Academic Standards for English Language Arts
Phonics and Spelling 🔊 Skill: Suffixes -y, -ish, -hood, -ment	**CCSS Foundational Skills 3.** Know and apply grade-level phonics and word analysis skills in decoding words. **(Also CCSS Foundational Skills 3.b., CCSS Language 2.e.)**	**IN 3.1.8** Use knowledge of prefixes and suffixes to determine the meaning of words.
Text-Based Comprehension 🔊 Skill: Author's Purpose	**CCSS Informational Text 6.** Distinguish their own point of view from that of the author of a text.	**IN 3.2** Students read and understand grade-level-appropriate material.
🔊 **Strategy:** Background Knowledge	**CCSS Informational Text 1.** Ask and answer questions to demonstrate understanding of a text, referring explicitly to the text as the basis for the answers.	**IN 3.2.2** Ask questions and support answers by connecting prior knowledge with literal information from the text. **(Also IN 3.2.3)**
Vocabulary 🔊 Skill: Homonyms **Strategy:** Context Clues	**CCSS Language 4.** Determine or clarify the meaning of unknown and multiple-meaning words and phrases based on *grade 3 reading and content,* choosing flexibly from a range of strategies. **(Also CCSS Language 4.a.)**	**IN 3.1.6** Use sentence and word context to find the meaning of unknown words.
Fluency **Skill:** Appropriate Phrasing	**CCSS Foundational Skills 4.** Read with sufficient accuracy and fluency to support comprehension. **(Also CCSS Foundational Skills 4.b.)**	**IN 3.1.3** Read aloud grade-level-appropriate literary and informational texts fluently and accurately and with appropriate timing, change in voice, and expression.
Listening and Speaking Retelling	**CCSS Speaking/Listening 4.** Report on a topic or text, tell a story, or recount an experience with appropriate facts and relevant, descriptive details, speaking clearly at an understandable pace.	The Indiana Academic Standards for Listening and Speaking are not currently assessed on ISTEP+ assessments. Educators and students should implement the Common Core Standards for Speaking and Listening as soon as possible.
Six-Trait Writing **Trait of the Week:** Conventions	**CCSS Language 2.** Demonstrate command of the conventions of standard English capitalization, punctuation, and spelling when writing. **(Also CCSS Language 1.h., CCSS Language 1.i.)**	**IN 3.6** Students write using Standard English conventions appropriate to this grade level.
Writing Book Review	**CCSS Writing 1.a.** Introduce the topic or book they are writing about, state an opinion, and create an organizational structure that lists reasons.	**IN 3.6.7** Write responses to literature.
Conventions **Skill:** Conjunctions	**CCSS Language 1.h.** Use coordinating and subordinating conjunctions.	**IN 3.6** Students write using Standard English conventions appropriate to this grade level.

This Week's Cross-Curricular Standards and Resources

Cross-Curricular Indiana Academic Standards for Social Studies

Social Studies
IN 3.3.11 Identify and describe the relationship between human systems and physical systems and the impact they have on each other.
IN 3.3.9 Identify factors that make the region unique, including cultural diversity, industry, the arts and architecture.

Reading Street Sleuth

The Harlem Renaissance on Canvas; pp. 64–65

Follow the path to close reading using the Super Sleuth tips:

- Gather Evidence
- Ask Questions
- Make Your Case
- Prove it!

More Reading in Science and Social Studies

Concept Literacy

Below Level

On Level

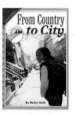
Advanced

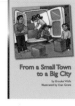
ELL

ELD

ISBN-13: 978-0-328-73391-0   ISBN-10: 0-328-73391-1

Your 90-Minute Reading Block

	Whole Group	Formative Assessment	Small Group OL On Level SI Strategic Intervention A Advanced	Daily Independent Options
		How do I make my small groups flexible?	What are my other students reading and learning every day in Small Groups?	What do my other students do when I lead Small Groups?

DAY 1

Whole Group
Content Knowledge
  Build Oral Language/Vocabulary
Phonics/Word Analysis
Read Decodable Reader
Text-Based Comprehension
Selection Vocabulary
Research and Inquiry
  Step 1–Identify and Focus Topic
Spelling Pretest
  Connect to Phonics/Word Analysis

Formative Assessment
Monitor Progress
Check Oral Vocabulary

Small Group
Differentiate Vocabulary
Build Word Knowledge
OL Practice Amazing Words
SI Reteach Amazing Words
A Extend Amazing Words
OL SI A Text-Based Comprehension
Read *Reading Street Sleuth*, pp. 64–65 or Leveled Readers
A Inquiry Project
ELL Access Vocabulary

Daily Independent Options

★ **Independent Reading** ©
Suggestions for this week's independent reading:
• Informational texts on last week's social studies topic: how different cultures contribute to the foods we eat
• A high-quality newspaper article about food in our culture
• A nonfiction book by a favorite author

DAY 2

Content Knowledge
  Build Oral Language/Vocabulary
Phonics/Word Analysis
Vocabulary Skill
Text-Based Comprehension
  Read Main Selection, using Access Text Notes
Research and Inquiry
  Step 2–Navigate/Search
Spelling
  Connect to Phonics/Word Analysis

Monitor Progress
Formative Assessment:
Check Word Reading

Differentiate Comprehension
Build Word Knowledge
OL Practice Selection Vocabulary
SI Reteach Selection Vocabulary
A Extend Selection Vocabulary
OL SI A Access Text
Read *Me and Uncle Romie*
A Inquiry Project
ELL Access Comprehension Skill

Book Talk
Foster critical reading and discussion skills through independent and close reading.

Students should focus on discussing one or more of the following:
• Key Ideas and Details
• Craft and Structure
• Integration of Ideas

DAY 3

Content Knowledge
  Build Oral Language/Vocabulary
Phonics/Word Analysis
Read Decodable Passage
Text-Based Comprehension
  Read Main Selection, using Close Reading Notes
Fluency
Research and Inquiry
  Step 3–Analyze Information
Spelling
  Connect to Phonics/Word Analysis

Monitor Progress
Check Retelling

Differentiate Close Reading
OL SI **Reread to Develop Vocabulary**
A **Reread to Extend Vocabulary**
OL SI A **Close Reading**
Read *Me and Uncle Romie*
A Inquiry Project
ELL Access Main Selection

Pearson eText
• Student Edition
• Decodable Readers
• Leveled Readers

Trade Book Library

DAY 4

Content Knowledge
  Build Oral Language/Vocabulary
Phonics/Word Analysis
Read Decodable Passage
Read Content Area Paired Selection with Genre Focus
Let's Learn It!
  Vocabulary/Fluency/Listening and Speaking
Research and Inquiry
  Step 4–Synthesize
Spelling
  Connect to Phonics/Word Analysis

Monitor Progress
Check Fluency

Differentiate Vocabulary
Build Word Knowledge
OL Develop Language Using Amazing Words
SI Review/Discuss Amazing Words
A Extend Amazing Words and Selection Vocabulary
OL SI A Text-Based Comprehension
Read "Country to City"
A Inquiry Project
ELL Access Amazing Words

Materials from School or Classroom Library

Independent Stations
Practice Last Week's Skills
★ Focus on these activities when time is limited.
Word Wise
Word Work
★ **Read for Meaning**
Let's Write!
Words to Know
★ **Get Fluent**

DAY 5

Content Knowledge
  Build Oral Language/Vocabulary
Text-Based Comprehension
Vocabulary Skill
Phonics/Word Analysis
Assessment
  Fluency, Comprehension
Research and Inquiry
  Step 5–Communicate
Spelling Test
  Connect to Phonics/Word Analysis

Monitor Progress
Formative Assessment:
Check Oral Vocabulary

Monitor Progress
Fluency; Comprehension

Differentiate Reteaching
OL **Practice Conjunctions**
SI **Review Conjunctions**
A **Extend Conjunctions**
OL SI A **Text-Based Comprehension**
Reread *Reading Street Sleuth*, pp. 64–65 or Leveled Readers
A Inquiry Project
ELL Access Conventions and Writing

Assessment Resources

Common Core
Weekly Tests, pp. 145–150

Common Core Fresh Reads for Fluency and Comprehension, pp. 145–150

Common Core
Unit 5 Benchmark Test

Common Core Success Tracker, ExamView, and Online Lesson Planner

Teaching the Common Core State Standards This Week

The Common Core State Standards for English Language Arts are divided into strands for **Reading** (including **Foundational Skills**), **Writing**, **Speaking and Listening**, and **Language**. The chart below shows some of the content you will teach this week, strand by strand. Turn to this week's 5-Day Planner on pages 320d–320e to see how this content is taught each day.

Reading Strand

- **Phonics/Word Analysis:** Suffixes *-y*, *-ish*, *-hood*, *-ment*
- **Text-Based Comprehension:** Author's Purpose; Background Knowledge
- **Fluency:** Appropriate Phrasing

- **Literary Terms:** Onomatopoeia
- **Genre:** Main Selection: Historical Fiction; Paired Selection: Online Reference Sources

Common Core State Standards for English Language Arts

Writing Strand

- **Writing Mini-Lesson:** Book Review
- **Trait:** Conventions
- **Look Back and Write:** Text Evidence

Speaking and Listening Strand

- **Content Knowledge:** Build Oral Language
- **Listening and Speaking:** Retelling
- **Research and Inquiry**

Language Strand

- **Oral Vocabulary: Amazing Words** *skyscraper, taxicab, scamper, scurry, vendor, hurl, meager, gutter, bitter, ramble*
- **Vocabulary:** Homonyms; Context Clues
- **Selection Vocabulary:** *flights, stoops, ruined, fierce, treasure, feast, cardboard, pitcher*

- **Academic Vocabulary:** *conjunction, critique, historical fiction, free verse, alliteration, assonance, narrative poem, organization*
- **Conventions:** Conjunctions
- **Spelling:** Suffixes *-y*, *-ish*, *-hood*, *-ment*

Text-Based Comprehension

Text Complexity Measures

Use the rubric to familiarize yourself with the text complexity of *Me and Uncle Romie*.

Bridge to Complex Knowledge

Quantitative Measures	Lexile	620L
	Average Sentence Length	9.42
	Word Frequency	3.63

Qualitative Measures	Levels of Meaning	understand historical fiction and the symbolism in the collages
	Structure	conventional structure
	Language Conventionality and Clarity	close alignment of images and text; natural, conversational language
	Theme and Knowledge Demands	references to other cultural experiences; singular perspective; figurative language; perspective that may be similar to that of many readers

Reader and Task Suggestions	**FORMATIVE ASSESSMENT** Based on assessment results, use the **Reader and Task Suggestions** in Access Main Selection to scaffold the selection or support independence for students as they read *Me and Uncle Romie*.

READER AND TASK SUGGESTIONS	
Preparing to Read the Text	**Leveled Tasks**
• Review strategies for understanding homonyms. • Discuss how authors use factual information in historical fiction. • Remind students to adjust their reading rate when they encounter unfamiliar vocabulary and concepts.	• **Levels of Meaning • Analysis** Students may not understand how to recognize historical fiction. Have them identify events in the story that show it is set in the past. • **Theme and Knowledge Demands** The many sightseeing destinations James visits in New York City may confuse some students. Have them make a note of places in the story with which they are unfamiliar.

Recommended Placement Both the qualitative and quantitative measures suggest this text should be placed in the Grade 2–3 text complexity band, which is where both the Common Core State Standards and *Scott Foresman Reading Street* have placed it.

Focus on Common Core State Standards ©

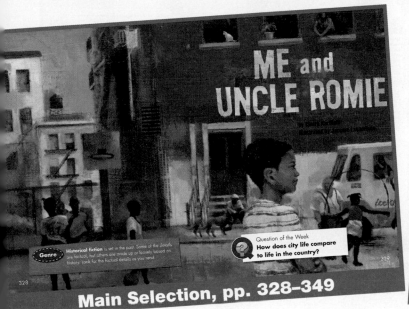

Main Selection, pp. 328–349

Paired Selection, pp. 354–357

Text-Based Comprehension

◉ **Author's Purpose**
CCSS Informational Text 6.

◉ **Background Knowledge**
CCSS Informational Text 1.

Fluency

Appropriate Phrasing
CCSS Foundational Skills 4.,
CCSS Foundational Skills 4.b.

Writing and Conventions

Trait: Conventions
CCSS Language 1.h.,
CCSS Language 1.i.,
CCSS Language 2.

Writing Mini-Lesson: Book Review
CCSS Writing 1.a.

Conventions: Conjunctions
CCSS Language 1.h.

Oral Vocabulary

Amazing Words

skyscraper	hurl
taxicab	meager
scamper	gutter
scurry	bitter
vendor	ramble

CCSS Language 6.

Selection Vocabulary

◉ **Homonyms**
CCSS Language 4.

Context Clues
CCSS Language 4.,
CCSS Language 4.a.

cardboard	flights	stoops
feast	pitcher	treasure
fierce	ruined	

Spelling

Suffixes -y, -ish, -hood, -ment
CCSS Foundational Skills 3.b.,
CCSS Language 2.e.

rocky	childish
foolish	parenthood
rainy	crunchy
childhood	bumpy
selfish	payment
treatment	sleepy
movement	shipment
neighborhood	

Challenge Words

assignment	environment
livelihood	guilty
stylish	

Listening and Speaking

Retelling
CCSS Speaking/Listening 4.

Preview Your Week

How does city life compare to life in the country?

Main Selection, pp. 328–349

Paired Selection, pp. 354–357

Genre: Historical Fiction

◉ **Vocabulary:** Homonyms

◉ **Text-Based Comprehension:** Author's Purpose

21st Century Skills

Online Reference Sources

Build Content Knowledge (Zoom in on ©)

Time for SOCIAL STUDIES

KNOWLEDGE GOALS
Students will understand that

- city life is busy
- cities have tall buildings
- the country has farms

THIS WEEK'S CONCEPT MAP
Develop a concept-related graphic organizer like the one below over the course of this week.

How city life and country life compare

| Animals | Buildings | Transportation |

BUILD ORAL VOCABULARY
This week, students will acquire the following academic vocabulary/domain-specific words.

Amazing Words

skyscraper	vendor	gutter
taxicab	hurl	bitter
scamper	meager	ramble
scurry		

OPTIONAL CONCEPT-BASED READING Use the Digital Path to access readers offering different levels of text complexity.

Concept Literacy   Below-Level   On-Level   Advanced   ELL   ELD

This Week's Digital Resources

eStreet Interactive
www.ReadingStreet.com

Get Ready to Read

 Concept Talk Video   Use this video on the Digital Path to engage interest and introduce the weekly concept of cultures.

 Pearson eText   Read the eText of the Student Edition pages on Pearson SuccessNet for comprehension and fluency support.

 Envision It! Animations   Use this vivid animation on the Digital Path to explain the target comprehension skill, Author's Purpose.

Read and Comprehend

 Journal   Use the Word Bank on the Digital Path to have students write sentences using this week's selection vocabulary words.

 Background Building Audio CD   This audio CD provides important background information about cultures to help students read and comprehend the weekly texts.

 Pearson eText   Read the eText of the main selection, *Me and Uncle Romie,* and the paired selection, "Country to City," with audio support on Pearson SuccessNet.

 Vocabulary Activities   A variety of interactive vocabulary activities on the Digital Path help students practice selection vocabulary and concept-related words.

 Story Sort   Use the Story Sort Activity on the Digital Path after reading *Me and Uncle Romie* to involve students in summarizing.

Language Arts

 Grammar Jammer   Select a colorful animation on the Digital Path to provide an engaging grammar lesson that will draw students' attention.

 Pearson eText   Find the Student Edition eText of the Let's Write It! and Let's Learn It! pages with audio support on Pearson SuccessNet.

Additional Resources

 Teacher Resources DVD-ROM Use the following resources on the TR DVD or on Pearson SuccessNet throughout the week:

- Amazing Word Cards
- Reader's and Writer's Notebook
- Writing Transparencies
- Daily Fix-It Transparencies
- Scoring Rubrics
- Grammar Transparencies
- ELL Support
- Let's Practice It!
- Graphic Organizers
- Vocabulary Cards

This Week's Skills

Phonics/Word Analysis
Suffixes -y, -ish, -hood, -ment

Comprehension
👁 **Skill:** Author's Purpose
👁 **Strategy:** Background Knowledge

Language
👁 **Vocabulary:** Homonyms
Conventions: Conjunctions

Fluency
Appropriate Phasing

Writing
Book Review

5-Day Planner

DAY 1

Get Ready to Read

Content Knowledge 321a
Oral Vocabulary: *skyscraper, taxicab, scamper, scurry*

> **Monitor Progress**
> Check Oral Vocabulary

Phonics/Word Analysis 322a
👁 Suffixes -y, -ish, -hood, -ment
READ Decodable Reader 25A
Reread for Fluency

Read and Comprehend

Text-Based Comprehension 324a
👁 Author's Purpose
👁 Background Knowledge

Fluency 324–325
Appropriate Phrasing

Selection Vocabulary 325a
cardboard, feast, fierce, flights, pitcher, ruined, stoops, treasure

Language Arts

Research and Inquiry 325b
Identify and Focus Topic

Spelling 325c
Suffixes -y, -ish, -hood, -ment, Pretest

Conventions 325d
Conjunctions

Handwriting 325d
Cursive Letters *V, W, Y*

Writing 325e
Book Review

DAY 2

Get Ready to Read

Content Knowledge 326a
Oral Vocabulary: *vendor, hurl*

Phonics/Word Analysis 326c
Suffixes -y, -ish, -hood, -ment

> **Monitor Progress**
> Check Word Reading

Literary Terms 326d
Onomatopoeia

Read and Comprehend

Vocabulary Skill 326e
👁 Homonyms

Fluency 326–327
Appropriate Phrasing

Text-Based Comprehension 328–329
READ *Me and Uncle Romie* —1st Read

Language Arts

Research and Inquiry 339b
Navigate/Search

Conventions 339c
Conjunctions

Spelling 339c
Suffixes -y, -ish, -hood, -ment

Writing 339d
Book Review

DAY 3

Get Ready to Read

Content Knowledge 340a
Oral Vocabulary: *meager, gutter*

Word Analysis 340c
Fluent Word Reading
DECODE AND READ
Decodable Practice Passage 25B

Read and Comprehend

Text-Based Comprehension 340e
Check Understanding
READ *Me and Uncle Romie*
—2nd Read
Monitor Progress Check Retelling

Fluency 351b
Appropriate Phrasing

Language Arts

Research and Study Skills 351c
Electronic Text

Research and Inquiry 351d
Analyze Information

Conventions 351e
Conjunctions

Spelling 351e
Suffixes *-y, -ish, -hood, -ment*

Writing 352–353
Book Review

DAY 4

Get Ready to Read

Content Knowledge 354a
Oral Vocabulary: *bitter, ramble*

Phonics/Word Analysis 354c
Review Vowel Patterns *ei, eigh*
Fluent Word Reading
DECODE AND READ
Decodable Practice Passage 25C

Read and Comprehend

21st Century Skills 354g
Online Reference Sources
READ "Country to City"
—Paired Selection

Fluency 358–359
Appropriate Phrasing
Monitor Progress Check Fluency

Vocabulary Skill 359a
Homonyms

Listening and Speaking 359a
Retelling

Language Arts

Research and Inquiry 359b
Synthesize

Conventions 359c
Conjunctions

Spelling 359c
Suffixes *-y, -ish, -hood, -ment*

Writing 359d
Book Review

DAY 5

Get Ready to Read

Content Knowledge 359f
Review Oral Vocabulary
Monitor Progress
Check Oral Vocabulary

Read and Comprehend

Text-Based Comprehension 359h
Review Author's Purpose

Vocabulary Skill 359h
Review Homonyms

Phonics/Word Analysis 359i
Review Suffixes *-y, -ish, -hood, -ment*

Literary Terms 359i
Review Onomatopoeia

Assessment 359j, 359l
Monitor Progress
Fluency; Author's Purpose

Language Arts

Research and Inquiry 359n
Communicate

Spelling 359o
Suffixes *-y, -ish, -hood, -ment*, Test

Conventions 359o
Conjunctions

Writing 359p
Book Review

Wrap Up Your Week! 359q

Me and Uncle Romie **320e**

Access for All

What do I do in group time?
It's as easy as 1-2-3!

1 TEACHER-LED SMALL GROUPS ➔ **2** INDEPENDENT PRACTICE STATIONS ➔ **3** INDEPENDENT READING

Small Group Time

Ⓒ Bridge to Common Core

SKILL DEVELOPMENT
- Author's Purpose
- Background Knowledge
- Homonyms

DEEP UNDERSTANDING
This Week's Knowledge Goals
Students will understand that
- city life is busy
- cities have tall buildings
- the country has farms

1 Small Group Lesson Plan

	DAY 1 Differentiate Vocabulary	**DAY 2** Differentiate Comprehension
OL On-Level pp. SG•66–SG•70	**Build Word Knowledge** Practice Amazing Words **Text-Based Comprehension** Read *Reading Street Sleuth*, pp. 64–65 or Leveled Readers	**Build Word Knowledge** Practice Selection Vocabulary **Access Text** Read *Me and Uncle Romie*
SI Strategic Intervention pp. SG•71–SG•75	**Build Word Knowledge** Reteach Amazing Words **Text-Based Comprehension** Read *Reading Street Sleuth*, pp. 64–65 or Leveled Readers	**Build Word Knowledge** Reteach Selection Vocabulary **Access Text** Read *Me and Uncle Romie*
A Advanced pp. SG•76–SG•80	**Build Word Knowledge** Extend Amazing Words **Text-Based Comprehension** Read *Reading Street Sleuth*, pp. 64–65 or Leveled Readers	**Build Word Knowledge** Extend Selection Vocabulary **Access Text** Read *Me and Uncle Romie*
Independent Inquiry Project	Identify Questions	Investigate
ELL If... students need more scaffolding and practice with...	**Vocabulary,** then... use the activities on pp. DI•117–DI•118 in the Teacher Resources section on SuccessNet.	**Comprehension Skill,** then... use the activities on p. DI•121 in the Teacher Resources section on SuccessNet.

Build Text-Based Comprehension

Me and Uncle Romie

Reading Street Sleuth

- Provides access to grade-level text for all students
- Focuses on finding clues in text through close reading
- Builds capacity for complex text

Optional Leveled Readers

| Concept Literacy | Below-Level | On-Level | Advanced | ELL | ELD |

DAY 3

Differentiate Close Reading

Reread to Develop Vocabulary
Close Reading
Read *Me and Uncle Romie*

Reread to Develop Vocabulary
Close Reading
Read *Me and Uncle Romie*

Reread to Extend Vocabulary
Close Reading
Read *Me and Uncle Romie*

Investigate

Main Selection,
then... use the activities on p. DI•122 in the Teacher Resources section on SuccessNet.

DAY 4

Differentiate Vocabulary

Build Word Knowledge
Develop Language Using Amazing Words
Text-Based Comprehension
Read "Country to City"

Build Word Knowledge
Review/Discuss Amazing Words
Text-Based Comprehension
Read "Country to City"

Build Word Knowledge
Extend Amazing Words and Selection Vocabulary
Text-Based Comprehension
Read "Country to City"

Organize

Amazing Words,
then... use the Routine on pp. xxxvi–xxxvii in the *ELL Handbook*.

DAY 5

Differentiate Reteaching

Practice Conjunctions
Text-Based Comprehension
Reread *Reading Street Sleuth*, pp. 64–65 or Leveled Readers

Review Conjunctions
Text-Based Comprehension
Reread *Reading Street Sleuth*, pp. 64–65 or Leveled Readers

Extend Conjunctions
Text-Based Comprehension
Reread *Reading Street Sleuth*, pp. 64–65 or Leveled Readers

Communicate

Conventions and Writing,
then... use the Grammar Transition Lessons on pp. 312–386 in the *ELL Handbook*.

② Independent Stations

Practice Last Week's Skills

⭐ Focus on these activities when time is limited.

WORD WISE

Spell and use words in sentences.

OBJECTIVES

• Spell words with vowel patterns *ei, eigh.*

MATERIALS

• *Word Wise* Flip Chart Activity 25, teacher-made word cards, paper and pencils

 Letter Tile Drag and Drop

● Students write five words with vowel patterns *ei, eigh,* write sentences using the words, and think of other words with the same vowel pattern.

▲ Students write seven words with vowel patterns *ei, eigh*, write sentences using the words, and think of other words with the same vowel pattern.

■ Students write nine words with vowel patterns *ei, eigh,* write sentences using the words, and think of other words with the same vowel pattern.

WORD WORK

Identify and pronounce words.

OBJECTIVES

• Identify and pronounce words with vowel patterns *ei, eigh.*

MATERIALS

• *Word Work* Flip Chart Activity 25, teacher-made word cards, paper and pencils

 Letter Tile Drag and Drop

● Students say eight words and sort them in a T-chart with columns labeled *ei* and *eigh.*

▲ Students say ten words and sort them in a T-chart with columns labeled *ei* and *eigh.*

■ Students say twelve words and sort them in a T-chart with columns labeled *ei* and *eigh.* Then they add rhyming words to the chart.

LET'S WRITE!

Write a personal letter.

OBJECTIVES

• Write an invitation.

MATERIALS

• *Let's Write* Flip Chart Activity 25, paper and pencils

 Grammar Jammer

● Students write an invitation to a friend for an imaginary play date and use colons in the start and end times.

▲ Students write an invitation to a friend for an imaginary birthday party and use colons in the start and end times.

■ Students write an invitation to a friend for an imaginary event of their choosing and use colons in the start and end times.

WORDS TO KNOW

Determine word meanings.

OBJECTIVES

• Identify the meanings of unfamiliar words.

MATERIALS

• *Word Wise* Flip Chart Activity 25, magazines, dictionary, paper and pencils

 Vocabulary Activities

● Students find three unfamiliar words in a magazine, look up their meanings, and write sentences using the words.

▲ Students find four unfamiliar words in a magazine, look up their meanings, and write sentences using the word and context clues.

■ Students find six unfamiliar words in a magazine and use context clues and a dictionary to determine their meanings.

READ FOR MEANING

Use text-based comprehension skills.

OBJECTIVES

• Draw conclusions.

MATERIALS

• *Read for Meaning* Flip Chart Activity 25, Leveled Readers, paper and pencils

 Pearson eText
• Leveled eReaders

 Envision It! Animations

● Students read a book and write one sentence in which they draw a conclusion about one of the characters.

▲ Students read a book, write one sentence in which they draw a conclusion about a character or event and a sentence that identifies support for the conclusion.

■ Students read a book and write a short paragraph in which they draw a conclusion and identify support for the conclusion.

GET FLUENT

Practice fluent reading with a partner.

OBJECTIVES

• Read aloud with accuracy.

MATERIALS

• *Get Fluent* Flip Chart Activity 25, Leveled Readers

 Pearson eText
• Leveled eReaders

● Partners take turns reading aloud with accuracy from a Concept Literacy Reader or a Below-Level Reader and providing feedback.

▲ Partners take turns reading aloud with accuracy from an On-Level Reader and providing feedback.

■ Partners take turns reading aloud with accuracy from an Advanced Reader and providing feedback.

Manage the Stations

Use these management tools to set up and organize your Practice Stations:

Practice Station Flip Charts

Classroom Management Handbook for Differentiated Instruction Practice Stations, p. 43

3 Independent Reading ©

Students should select appropriate complex texts to read and write about independently every day before, during, and after school.

Suggestions for this week's independent reading:
• Informational texts on last week's social studies topic: how different cultures contribute to the foods we eat
• A high-quality newspaper article about food in our culture
• A nonfiction book by a favorite author

BOOK TALK Have partners discuss their independent reading for the week. Tell them to refer to their Reading Logs and paraphrase what each selection was about. Then have students focus on discussing one or more of the following:

Key Ideas and Details
• What is the main idea of the text? List details that support it.
• What inferences can you draw from what the author says in the text?

Craft and Structure
• What is the author's purpose and point of view?
• List details that help you identify the author's point of view.

Integration of Ideas
• What argument does the author make in the text?
• How well does the author support his or her claims?

 Pearson eText
• Student Edition
• Decodable Readers
• Leveled Readers

 Trade Book Library

 School or Classroom Library

Materials

- Student Edition
- Reader's and Writer's Notebook
- Decodable Reader

Ⓒ **Bridge to Common Core**

INTEGRATION OF KNOWLEDGE/IDEAS
This week, students will read, write, and talk about city life and country life.

Texts This Week
- "Nature in the City"
- "New York City"
- "A Different Treasure Hunt"
- *Me and Uncle Romie*
- "Country to City"

Social Studies Knowledge Goals
Students will understand that
- city life is busy
- cities have tall buildings
- the country has farms

Street Rhymes!

City: The vendors are selling pretzels to eat.
Commuters are traveling on busy streets.
Country: The hillsides are planted with crops far and wide.
And people ramble through the countryside.

- To introduce this week's concept, read aloud the poem several times and ask students to join you.

Content Knowledge

City Life and Country Life

CONCEPT TALK To further explore the unit concept of Cultures, this week students will read, write, and talk about how living in the city compares to living in the country. Write the Question of the Week on the board, *How does city life compare to life in the country?*

Build Oral Language

TALK ABOUT CITY LIFE AND COUNTRY LIFE Have students turn to pp. 320–321 in their Student Editions. Look at each of the photos. Then use the prompts to guide discussion and create a concept map.

- What kinds of animals might *scamper* or *scurry*? (rabbits, deer) Are those city or country animals? (country) Are there animals in both the country and the city? (yes) What kinds? (horses, dogs, cats, cows) Let's add *Animals* to our concept list.

- Do you see *skyscrapers* in the city or the country? (city) What kinds of buildings are in the country? (houses, barns) Both places have buildings. Let's add *Buildings* to our concept list.

- How is it different to get around in the city and the country? (In the city, there is public transportation. In both places, people walk.) Let's add *Transportation* to the concept map.

- After discussing the photos, ask: How does city life compare to life in the countr

Oral Vocabulary

Let's Talk About

City and Country Life

- Ask relevant questions about urban and rural life.
- Express opinions about life in the city versus life in the country.
- Describe life in the city or the country.

READING STREET ONLINE
CONCEPT TALK VIDEO
www.ReadingStreet.com

Student Edition, pp. 320–321

CONNECT TO READING Tell students that this week they will be reading about a boy who lives in the country and visits a city. Throughout the week, encourage students to add concept-related words to this week's concept map.

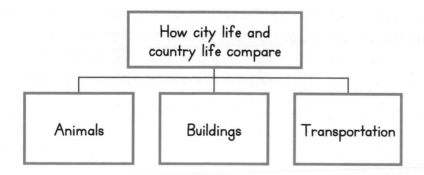

How city life and country life compare
- Animals
- Buildings
- Transportation

eSTREET INTERACTIVE
www.ReadingStreet.com

Pearson eText
- Student Edition

Concept Talk Video

ELL

Preteach Concepts Use the Day 1 instruction on ELL Poster 25 to build knowledge, develop concepts, and build oral vocabulary.

ELL Support Additional ELL support and modified instruction is provided in the *ELL Handbook* and in the ELL Support lessons on the *Teacher Resources DVD-ROM*.

Me and Uncle Romie **320–321**

Amazing Words

You've learned **2 3 7** words so far.

You'll learn **0 1 0** words this week!

skyscraper	hurl
taxicab	meager
scamper	gutter
scurry	bitter
vendor	ramble

Content Knowledge

Build Oral Vocabulary

INTRODUCE AMAZING WORDS "Nature in the City" on p. 321b is about nature preserves in big cities. Tell students to listen for this week's Amazing Words—*skyscraper, taxicab, scamper,* and *scurry*—as you read the Teacher Read Aloud on p. 321b.

Amazing Words   Robust Vocabulary Routine

1. **Introduce** Write the word *skyscraper* on the board. Have students say it aloud with you. In "Nature in the City," *skyscrapers* line busy streets. How does the context help you understand the meaning of *skyscraper*? Supply a student-friendly definition.

2. **Demonstrate** Have students answer questions to demonstrate understanding. How do you get to the top floors of a *skyscraper*? How can you tell a *skyscraper* from other buildings on a street?

3. **Apply** Have students who have seen a *skyscraper* describe it. Have them tell how they feel when they look at *skyscrapers* from the ground.

4. **Display the Word** Run your hand under the two parts of the compound word *sky-scraper* as you read the word. Have students say the word again.

See p. OV•5 to teach *taxicab, scamper,* and *scurry.*

Routines Flip Chart

AMAZING WORDS AT WORK Reread "Nature in the City" aloud. As students listen, have them notice how the Amazing Words are used in context. To build oral vocabulary, lead the class in a discussion about the Amazing Words meanings. Remind students to answer questions with appropriate detail.

Don't Wait Until Friday **MONITOR PROGRESS** **Check Oral Vocabulary**

During discussion, listen for students' use of Amazing Words.

If... students are unable to use the Amazing Words in discussion,

then... use the Oral Vocabulary Routine in the Routines Flip Chart to demonstrate words in different contexts.

Teacher Read Aloud

MODEL FLUENCY As you read "Nature in the City," model appropriate phrasing by grouping words in a meaningful way and paying attention to punctuation cues.

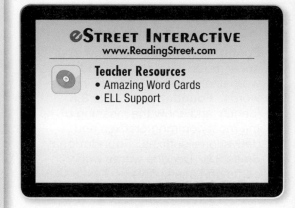

eSTREET INTERACTIVE
www.ReadingStreet.com

Teacher Resources
• Amazing Word Cards
• ELL Support

Nature in the City

What kinds of sounds do you hear in the city? You hear a car and a taxicab honking their horns at each other. You hear people talking and big machines roaring. Cities around the world are getting louder every day.

Not all the sounds in big cities are loud. Some of the biggest cities in Texas also have different, softer kinds of sounds. Sounds like birds singing in bushes and wind rushing through trees. Sounds like hear cool water flowing gently over rocks. Sounds that rabbits make when they scamper through woods and that squirrels make when they scurry through fields.

The area around Austin is called the Edwards Plateau. A long time ago, it belonged to the animals. Some very special animals still make their homes in Austin. Bats live under the bridges, and foxes live in the canyons. Salamanders swim in the springs, and birds nest in the trees. However as the city has gotten bigger, it is harder for animals to live here and for plants to survive.

Studies have been done to learn what makes people who live in cities happy. We've learned that many people feel happy when they spend time in city parks or nature preserves. Nature preserves are places people can visit to see plants and animals living in their natural habitats, or homes.

The people of Austin understand the importance of such places. They work

hard to keep their city green. Green cities have clean air and clear streams with clean water.

In 2007, Austin became a Community Wildlife Habitat. This means that city-planners work to keep the animals safe. They build nature preserves so there is plenty of food and shelter for the animals. People are taught to care for the animals and understand their needs.

Today Austin has over 200 parks and 12 nature preserves scattered around town. There are over 50 miles of trails for hiking. One of these trails winds up a hill. From there, you can see a skyscraper or two lining a busy city street.

Another city in Texas, Fort Worth, has done a spectacular job of preserving the beauty of nature. At the Fort Worth Botanical Gardens, you can see a variety of gardens and garden types, including a Japanese garden and a fragrance garden. If you take a walk on the Texas Native Forest Boardwalk, you can learn about native trees and efforts that are being made to conserve them.

As our cities grow larger, we need to protect these special places where plants can grow as they were meant to grow. We need to save land for the animals without changing the way they live. Then we can hear nature not far from our doorsteps. We can feel good about helping animals by giving them the space they need to live and grow.

Support Listening Comprehension
To increase understanding of the academic vocabulary heard in the Read Aloud, use visuals to support understanding of words students may not know, such as *taxi, skyscraper, nature preserve,* and *canyons.* You may also consider bringing in images of Austin or Fort Worth.

ELL Support for Read Aloud Use the modified Read Aloud on p. DI•119 of the ELL Support lessons on the *Teacher Resources DVD-ROM.*

Common Core State Standards

Foundational Skills 3. Know and apply grade-level phonics and word analysis skills in decoding words. **Foundational Skills 3.a.** Identify and know the meaning of the most common prefixes and derivational suffixes. **Foundational Skills 3.b.** Decode words with common Latin suffixes.

Skills Trace

⊚ **Suffixes -y, -ish, -hood, -ment**
Introduce U5W5D1
Practice U5W5D2, U5W5D3
Reteach/Review U5W5D5, U6W1D4
Assess/Test Weekly Test U5W5
Benchmark Test U5
KEY: U=Unit W=Week D=Day

Vocabulary Support

You may wish to explain the meanings of these words.

falsehood a lie or an untruth

entertainment the act of entertaining; something done to interest or amuse others

Word Analysis

Teach/Model

🔊 **Suffixes -y, -ish, -hood, -ment**

CONNECT Write *leader* and *conductor*. Point out that students have already studied words with suffixes. Ask them to read each word and identify the suffix. Today you will learn how to spell and read words with other suffixes.

MODEL Write *squeaky*. When I see a word with a suffix, I break it into parts. I read the base word first. Cover the *-y* and read the base word. Uncover the *-y*. Next, I read the suffix. Then I put the parts together to read the word. Have students read the word with you. *Squeaky* is a two-syllable word formed from the base word *squeak* and the suffix *-y*. Adding *-y* changes the noun *squeak* to an adjective, *squeaky*.

GROUP PRACTICE Write the words below. Have the group read the words with you. Then have them identify each base word and the suffix that has been added. Discuss the meaning of each suffix.

yellowish	healthy	entertainment	thirsty	adulthood
payment	falsehood	stormy	frosty	brownish

REVIEW What do you know about reading words with suffixes? When you see a word with a suffix, break it into parts. Read the base word first. Then read the suffix. Put the parts together to read the whole word.

Guide Practice

MODEL Have students turn to p. 322 in their Student Editions. Each word on this page has a suffix. The first word, *bumpy*, has the suffix *-y*. The word *boyish* has the suffix *-ish*. *Childhood* has the suffix *-hood*. *Enjoyment* has the suffix *-ment*, and *funny* has the suffix *-y*.

GROUP PRACTICE For each word in Words I Can Blend, ask students to segment the word by identifying the base word and the suffix. Then have them put the parts together to read the words.

Corrective feedback	**If...** students have difficulty reading a word, **then...** model reading the parts and then the whole word, and then ask students to read it with you.

Phonics

🔊 Suffixes -y, -ish, -hood, -ment

Envision It! Sounds to Know

neighborhood

suffix -hood

greenish

suffix -ish

equipment

suffix -ment

sandy

suffix -y

READING STREET ONLINE
SOUND-SPELLING CARDS
www.ReadingStreet.com

Words I Can Blend

bumpy

boyish

childhood

enjoyment

funny

Sentences I Can Read

1. It is difficult to ride on the bumpy street.
2. Nate has had a boyish grin since childhood.
3. I get a lot of enjoyment from funny stories.

322

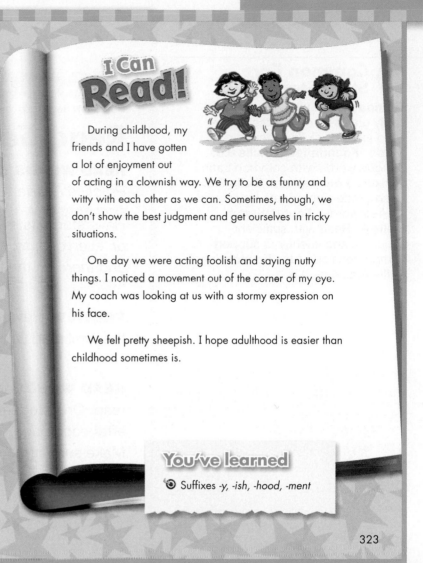

I Can Read!

During childhood, my friends and I have gotten a lot of enjoyment out of acting in a clownish way. We try to be as funny and witty with each other as we can. Sometimes, though, we don't show the best judgment and get ourselves in tricky situations.

One day we were acting foolish and saying nutty things. I noticed a movement out of the corner of my eye. My coach was looking at us with a stormy expression on his face.

We felt pretty sheepish. I hope adulthood is easier than childhood sometimes is.

You've learned
🔊 Suffixes -y, -ish, -hood, -ment

323

Student Edition, pp. 322–323

Apply

READ WORDS IN ISOLATION After students can successfully combine the word parts to read the words on p. 322 in their Student Editions, point to words in random order and ask students to read them naturally.

READ WORDS IN CONTEXT Have students read each of the sentences on p. 322. Have them identify words in the sentences that have the suffixes -y, -ish, -hood, and -ment.

Team Talk Pair students and have them take turns reading each of the sentences aloud.

Chorally read the I Can Read! passage on p. 323 with students. Then have them read the passage aloud to themselves.

ON THEIR OWN For additional practice, use Reader's and Writer's Notebook, p. 360.

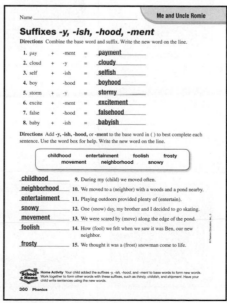

Name _____ **Me and Uncle Romie**

Suffixes -y, -ish, -hood, -ment
Directions Combine the base word and suffix. Write the new word on the line.

1. pay	+	-ment	=	payment
2. cloud	+	-y	=	cloudy
3. self	+	-ish	=	selfish
4. boy	+	-hood	=	boyhood
5. storm	+	-y	=	stormy
6. excite	+	-ment	=	excitement
7. false	+	-hood	=	falsehood
8. baby	+	-ish	=	babyish

Directions Add -y, -ish, -hood, or -ment to the base word in ( ) to best complete each sentence. Use the word box for help. Write the new word on the line.

childhood	entertainment	foolish	frosty
movement	neighborhood	snowy	

childhood   9. During my (child) we moved often.
neighborhood 10. We moved to a (neighbor) with a woods and a pond nearby.
entertainment 11. Playing outdoors provided plenty of (entertain).
snowy   12. One (snow) day, my brother and I decided to go skating.
movement   13. We were scared by (move) along the edge of the pond.
foolish   14. How (fool) we felt when we saw it was Ben, our new neighbor.
frosty   15. We thought it was a (frost) snowman come to life.

School + Home **Home Activity** Your child added the suffixes -y, -ish, -hood, and -ment to base words to form new words. Work together to form other words with these suffixes, such as thirsty, childish, and shipment. Have your child write sentences using the new words.

360 Phonics

Reader's and Writer's Notebook, p. 360

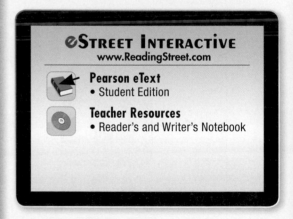

eStreet Interactive
www.ReadingStreet.com

Pearson eText
• Student Edition

Teacher Resources
• Reader's and Writer's Notebook

ELL

Language Transfer Point out to Spanish speakers that the suffix -ment does not have the same meaning as the suffix -mente in Spanish. In English, the suffix is often used to change a verb into a noun (enjoy/enjoyment). In Spanish, -mente is used to change an adjective into an adverb (rápido, rápidamente).

Me and Uncle Romie **322–323**

Common Core State Standards

Foundational Skills 3. Know and apply grade-level phonics and word analysis skills in decoding words. **Foundational Skills 3.b.** Decode words with common Latin suffixes. **Foundational Skills 3.d.** Read grade-appropriate irregularly spelled words. **Foundational Skills 4.** Read with sufficient accuracy and fluency to support comprehension. **Also Foundational Skills 3.a., 4.a., 4.b.**

Decodable Reader 25A

If students need help, then...

Read *Selfish Shelly*

READ WORDS IN ISOLATION Have students turn to p. 109 of *Decodable Practice Readers* 3.2. Have students read each word.

Have students read the high-frequency words *was, a, what, wanted, very, the, of, everyone, to, they, could, any, said, warm, sure, friends, one, been, having,* and *there* on the first page.

PREVIEW Have students read the title and preview the story. Tell them that they will read words with the suffixes *-y, -ish, -hood,* and *-ment.*

READ WORDS IN CONTEXT Pair students for reading and listen as they read. One student begins. Students read the entire story, switching readers after each page. Partners reread the story. This time the other student begins. Make sure students are monitoring their accuracy when they decode words.

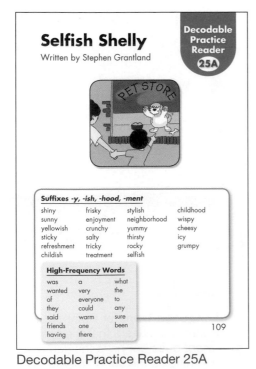

Decodable Practice Reader 25A

eSTREET INTERACTIVE
www.ReadingStreet.com

Pearson eText
• Decodable Reader

Interactive Sound-Spelling Cards

Corrective feedback	**If...** students have difficulty decoding a word, **then...** refer them to the *Sound-Spelling Cards* to identify the word parts. Have them read the word parts individually and then together to say the word.

- What is the new word?
- Is the new word a word you know?
- Does it make sense in the story?

CHECK DECODING AND COMPREHENSION Have students retell the story to include characters, setting, and events. Then have students find words in the story that have the suffixes *-y, -ish, -hood,* and *-ment.* Students should supply *shiny, childhood, neighborhood, crunchy, sticky, icy, rocky, treatment, risky, sunny, wispy, yummy, refreshment, grumpy, selfish, stylish, enjoyment, yellowish, cheesy, thirsty, tricky,* and *childish.*

Reread for Fluency

REREAD DECODABLE READER Have students reread *Decodable Practice Reader 25A* to develop automaticity decoding words with suffixes.

Routine Oral Reading

- **Read** Have students read the entire book orally.

- **Reread** To achieve optimal fluency, students should reread the text three or four times.

- **Corrective Feedback** Listen as students read. Provide corrective feedback regarding their fluency and decoding.

Routines Flip Chart

Suffixes

Beginning Write words with the suffix *-ish* from the *Decodable Practice Reader,* such as *selfish, stylish,* and *childish.* Cover the suffix in each word and read the base word aloud. Then uncover the suffix and read that syllable. Have students put the word parts together to read the word with you. Repeat the procedure for the suffixes *-y, -hood,* and *-ment.*

Intermediate After reading, have students each choose a word with the suffix *-y, -ish, -hood,* or *-ment.* Have them write sentences that use the words. Then have them each identify the base word and write a second sentence that uses that word.

Advanced After reading the story, have students choose four or five words with the suffixes *-y, -ish, -hood,* and *-ment* and write a sentence for each word.

Common Core State Standards

Informational Text 6. Distinguish their own point of view from that of the author of a text. **Foundational Skills 4.b.** Read on-level prose and poetry orally with accuracy, appropriate rate, and expression on successive readings. **Also Informational Text 1., Foundational Skills 4.**

Skills Trace

Author's Purpose

Introduce U1W5D1; U2W4D1; U5W5D1

Practice U1W5D2; U1W5D3; U2W4D2; U2W4D3; U3W1D2; U3W3D2; U5W5D2; U5W5D3; U6W1D2

Reteach/Review U1W5D5; U2W4D5; U5W5D5

Assess/Test Weekly Tests U1W5; U2W4; U5W5
Benchmark Test U3

KEY: U=Unit W=Week D=Day

Comprehension Support

Students may also turn to pp. EI•2 and EI•18 to review the skill and strategy if necessary.

Text-Based Comprehension

Author's Purpose
Background Knowledge

READ Remind students of the weekly concept—City Life and Country Life. Have students read "New York City" on p. 325.

MODEL A CLOSE READ

Think Aloud Have students follow along as you reread paragraph 2 of "New York City." This paragraph gives information about a famous building in New York. Is the author's purpose to inform, persuade, entertain, or express feelings? **(The author's purpose is to persuade the reader to visit New York City because it has amazing buildings.)**

I have never been to New York City, but I have seen it in movies and TV shows. I saw pictures of it in a book. I remember seeing skyscrapers. This helps me understand how tall the Empire State Building is.

TEACH Have students read p. 324. Explain to students that the skill of author's purpose and the strategy of background knowledge are tools they can use to help them better understand what they read. Then have students look back at "New York City" and use a graphic organizer like the one on p. 324 to figure out the author's purpose for writing the passage.

GUIDE PRACTICE Have students reread "New York City" using the callouts as guides. Then ask volunteers to respond to the questions in the callouts, citing specific examples from the text to support their answers.

Skill The author wants to persuade me to visit New York City.

Strategy I know that New York City has a large population and a lot of buildings.

Strategy I know that the Statue of Liberty is very tall.

APPLY Use *Reader's and Writer's Notebook*, p. 361 for additional practice with author's purpose.

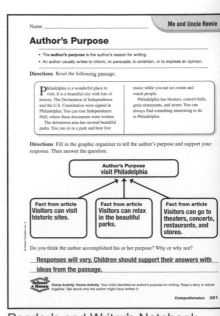

Reader's and Writer's Notebook, p. 361

Envision It! Skill Strategy

Skill

Author's Purpose

Strategy

Background Knowledge

READING STREET ONLINE
ENVISION IT! ANIMATIONS
www.ReadingStreet.com

Comprehension Skill

Author's Purpose

- Sometimes authors tell you their purposes for writing. They write to inform, entertain, persuade, or express an opinion.

- An author can write to try to persuade you to think or do something by using "loaded words," or strong words.

- Use what you learned about author's purpose and a graphic organizer like the one below as you read "New York City." Then write a paragraph explaining the author's purpose.

Author's Purpose

Fact from article | Fact from article | Fact from article

Comprehension Strategy

Background Knowledge

Good readers use what they already know to help them understand their reading. As you read, make connections to your own life. Have you ever seen or experienced what you are reading about? This will help you understand what you read.

NEW YORK CITY

I'm going to talk you into coming to New York City. It's a terrific place to visit. There are many things to see and do. New York City is the largest city in the United States.

In New York City you can visit the Empire State Building. This grand building opened in 1931. It is 102 stories tall! For many years, it was the tallest building in the world.

The Statue of Liberty is a breathtaking place! This statue stands on Bedloe's Island in New York Harbor. The Statue of Liberty rises to more than 300 feet. People come from all over the world to see this famous statue.

If you enjoy great plays and musical events, Broadway, a street in the center of New York City, has it all. It is the most famous theater district in the country. You will enjoy your visit and have a wonderful time when you come to New York!

Skill What is the author's stated purpose for writing?

Strategy What do you already know about New York City?

Strategy What do you already know about the Statue of Liberty?

Your Turn!

⏸ **Need a Review?** See the *Envision It! Handbook* for help with author's purpose and background knowledge.

▶ **Ready to Try It?** As you read *Me and Uncle Romie*, use what you've learned about author's purpose and background knowledge to understand the text.

324   325

Model Fluent Reading

APPROPRIATE PHRASING Have students listen as you read paragraph 2 of "New York City" with appropriate phrasing. Explain that you use the punctuation to guide the way you phrase the sentences.

Routine   Paired Reading

- **Select a Passage** For "New York City," use the whole passage.

- **Reading 1** Students read the entire passage, switching readers at the end of each paragraph.

- **Reading 2** Partners reread the passage. This time the other student begins.

- **Reread** For optimal fluency, have partners continue to read three or four times.

- **Corrective Feedback** Listen as students read. Listen to make sure they pause when appropriate and provide feedback as needed.

Routines Flip Chart

eStreet Interactive
www.ReadingStreet.com

📖 **Pearson eText**
• Student Edition

🎬 **Envision It! Animations**

💿 **Teacher Resources**
• Reader's and Writer's Notebook

Author's Purpose Have a student find sentences with dates in them. Have a volunteer find a sentence that tells how tall something is. Explain that these sentences tell facts and facts are used to inform.

Me and Uncle Romie **324–325**

Common Core State Standards

Writing 7. Conduct short research projects that build knowledge about a topic. **Language 4.** Determine or clarify the meaning of unknown and multiple-meaning words and phrases based on grade 3 reading and content, choosing flexibly from a range of strategies. **Also Language 4.a.**

Selection Vocabulary

Use the following routine to introduce this week's tested selection vocabulary.

cardboard thick, stiff paper

feast a meal with a lot of food

fierce frightening, scary

flights sets of stairs

pitcher a person who throws a baseball to a batter

ruined destroyed or damaged

stoops small porches with steps, usually at the front of a house

treasure valuables; prizes

SEE IT/SAY IT Write *pitcher*. Scan across the word with your finger as you say it: *pitch-er.*

HEAR IT Use the word in a sentence. Sally is the *pitcher* for our softball team.

DEFINE IT Elicit definitions from students. What does the word *pitcher* mean in this sentence? Clarify or give a definition when necessary. Yes, it means "the person who throws the ball to the batter." Restate the word in student-friendly terms. The *pitcher* throws the ball to the batters during a soft-ball or baseball game.

Team Talk Is the *pitcher* the most important player on a team? Turn and talk to your partner about this. Be prepared to explain your answer. Allow students time to discuss. Ask for examples. Rephrase their examples for usage when necessary or to correct misunderstandings.

MAKE CONNECTIONS Have students discuss the word. Have you ever seen a *pitcher* or been the *pitcher* on a team? Turn and talk to your partner about this. Then be prepared to share. Have students share. Rephrase their ideas for usage when necessary or to correct misunderstandings.

RECORD Have students write the word and its meaning.

Continue this routine to introduce the remaining words in this manner.

Corrective feedback | **If...** students are having difficulty understanding, **then...** review the definitions in small groups.

Research and Inquiry

Step 1 | Identify and Focus Topic

TEACH Discuss the Question of the Week: *How does city life compare to life in the country?* Tell students they will research how family life in cities and the country are alike and different. They will write articles to present to the class on Day 5.

Think Aloud

MODEL I'll start by brainstorming a list of questions about city life and country life. I know that people have families in both places. First, I wonder how families are changed by the kind of place they live in. I am interested in sports. We play a lot of soccer where I live in the country, but I wonder if kids can play soccer in the city. Some possible questions could be *Are the sports you can play in the city the same as in the country? What kinds of sports leagues are there in different places?* and *What kinds of sports do families play together?*

GUIDE PRACTICE After students have brainstormed open-ended inquiry questions, explain that tomorrow they will conduct online research using their questions. Help students identify keywords that will guide their search.

ON THEIR OWN Have students work individually, in pairs, or in small groups to write an inquiry question.

eSTREET INTERACTIVE
www.ReadingStreet.com

Teacher Resources
• Envision It! Pictured Vocabulary Cards
• Tested Vocabulary Cards

21st Century Skills
Internet Guy *Don Leu*

Weekly Inquiry Project

STEP 1	Identify and Focus Topic
STEP 2	Navigate/Search
STEP 3	Analyze Information
STEP 4	Synthesize
STEP 5	Communicate

Multilingual Vocabulary Students can apply knowledge of their home languages to acquire new English vocabulary by using the Multilingual Vocabulary Lists (*ELL Handbook*, pp. 443–444).

If... students need more scaffolding and practice with **Vocabulary, then...** use the activities on pp. DI•117–DI•118 in the Teacher Resources section on SuccessNet.

Day 1 | SMALL GROUP TIME • Differentiate Vocabulary, p. SG•65

OL On-Level	**SI Strategic Intervention**	**A Advanced**
• **Practice Vocabulary** Amazing Words	• **Reteach Vocabulary** Amazing Words	• **Extend Vocabulary** Amazing Words
• **Read** *Reading Street Sleuth,* pp. 64–65	• **Read** *Reading Street Sleuth,* pp. 64–65	• **Read** *Reading Street Sleuth,* pp. 64–65
		• **Introduce** Inquiry Project

Ⓒ Common Core State Standards

Foundational Skills 3.a. Identify and know the meaning of the most common prefixes and derivational suffixes. **Foundational Skills 3.b.** Decode words with common Latin suffixes. **Language 1.h.** Use coordinating and subordinating conjunctions. **Language 2.e.** Use conventional spelling for high-frequency and other studied words and for adding suffixes to base words (e.g., *sitting, smiled, cries, happiness*).

Spelling Pretest

Suffixes -y, -ish, -hood, -ment

INTRODUCE Tell students to think of words that end with the suffixes *-y (sleepy), -ish (sheepish), -hood (brotherhood),* and *-ment (department).* Remember to divide the words with suffixes into base word and suffix to spell them.

PRETEST Say each word, read the sentence, and repeat the word.

1.	**rocky**	This is a **rocky** beach.
2.	**foolish**	Anthony regretted his **foolish** behavior.
3.	**rainy**	**Rainy** days make me feel sad.
4.	**childhood**	**Childhood** should be a time of learning.
5.	**selfish**	Sometimes it is **selfish** not to share.
6.	**treatment**	I went to the doctor for **treatment.**
7.	**movement**	Cops tracked the robber's **movement.**
8.	**neighborhood**	My **neighborhood** is friendly.
9.	**childish**	They think his pouting is **childish.**
10.	**parenthood**	**Parenthood** can be stressful.
11.	**crunchy**	This **crunchy** cereal is delicious.
12.	**bumpy**	The bus bounced on the **bumpy** road.
13.	**payment**	I received **payment** after I did the job.
14.	**sleepy**	At the end of the day, Sarah was **sleepy.**
15.	**shipment**	Henry mailed the **shipment.**

Challenge words

16.	**assignment**	I need to finish my math **assignment.**
17.	**livelihood**	Writing stories for money is her **livelihood.**
18.	**stylish**	That purple sweater is very **stylish** right now.
19.	**environment**	Saving the **environment** is an important topic.
20.	**guilty**	The child felt **guilty** for spilling the juice on the rug.

SELF-CORRECT Have students self-correct their pretests by rewriting misspelled words.

ON THEIR OWN Use *Let's Practice It!* page 329 on the *Teacher Resources DVD-ROM.*

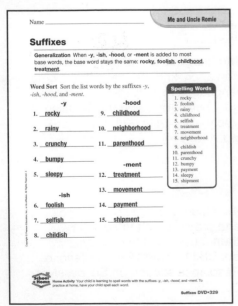

Let's Practice It! TR DVD•329

Conventions

Conjunctions

MAKE CONNECTIONS Ask students to name things that are a set or represent a choice, such as *peanut butter and jelly, cats or dogs.* Write the words on the board. Then underline the conjunctions. Explain that conjunctions connect words or ideas.

TEACH Display Grammar Transparency 25, and read aloud the explanation and examples in the box. Point out the ways to use *and, but, or,* and *because.*

MODEL Model writing the correct conjunction from the sentences in items 1 and 2. Apply the rules for conjunctions to show how you determined the conjunction in each.

GUIDE PRACTICE Guide students to complete items 3–5. Remind them to think about whether the sentences adding information or showing a choice, difference, or reason. Record the correct responses on the transparency.

APPLY Have students read sentences 6–10 on the transparency and circle the correct word in the parentheses to complete each sentence.

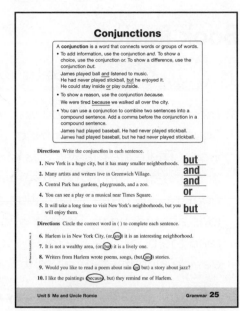

Conjunctions

A **conjunction** is a word that connects words or groups of words.

- To add information, use the conjunction *and.* To show a choice, use the conjunction *or.* To show a difference, use the conjunction *but.*
  James played ball <u>and</u> listened to music.
  He had never played stickball, <u>but</u> he enjoyed it.
  He could stay inside <u>or</u> play outside.
- To show a reason, use the conjunction *because.*
  We were tired <u>because</u> we walked all over the city.
- You can use a conjunction to combine two sentences into a compound sentence. Add a comma before the conjunction in a compound sentence.
  James had played baseball. He had never played stickball.
  James had played baseball, but he had never played stickball.

Directions Write the conjunction in each sentence.

1. New York is a huge city, but it has many smaller neighborhoods. **but**
2. Many artists and writers live in Greenwich Village. **and**
3. Central Park has gardens, playgrounds, and a zoo. **and**
4. You can see a play or a musical near Times Square. **or**
5. It will take a long time to visit New York's neighborhoods, but you will enjoy them. **but**

Directions Circle the correct word in ( ) to complete each sentence.

6. Harlem is in New York City, (or,(and) it is an interesting neighborhood.
7. It is not a wealthy area, (or,(but) it is a lively one.
8. Writers from Harlem wrote poems, songs, (but,(and) stories.
9. Would you like to read a poem about rain (or) but) a story about jazz?
10. I like the paintings (because), but) they remind me of Harlem.

Unit 5 Me and Uncle Romie   Grammar **25**

Grammar Transparency 25, TR DVD

Handwriting

MODEL LETTER FORMATION AND SPACING Display the uppercase cursive letters *V, W,* and *Y.* Follow the stroke instruction pictured to model letter formation. Explain that writing legibly means that the space between letters is not too large or too small. Model writing this sentence with proper letter spacing: *Vicky asked Wayne if he knows Yvonne.* Make sure the letters aren't too light, dark, or jagged.

GUIDE PRACTICE Have students write these sentences. *What is the capital of West Virginia? Young's Yo-Yo Shop sells games.* Circulate around the room, guiding students.

Daily Fix-It

1. Jeffs uncle lives in a city neighborhod. *(Jeff's; neighborhood)*
2. His sister and him visits Uncle Jim every summer. *(he; visit)*

Academic Vocabulary

A **conjunction** is a word that connects words or groups of words.

Conjunctions Write two sentences that use two of the conjunctions. Provide support for students based on their proficiency levels:

Beginning Read the sentences aloud and have students echo. Then have them say the conjunction used in each sentence.

Intermediate Have students write the sentences and circle the conjunctions. Have them tell the purpose of each conjunction.

Advanced Remove the conjunctions from the sentences, and have students rewrite them with the missing information.

 Common Core State Standards

Writing 1. Write opinion pieces on topics or texts, supporting a point of view with reasons. **Writing 1.a.** Introduce the topic or text they are writing about, state an opinion, and create an organizational structure that lists reasons.

Bridge to Common Core

TEXT TYPES AND PURPOSES

This week students will write a book review.

Opinion Writing

Students will demonstrate understanding of the texts they are studying by offering opinions through writing. They will use essential components, such as valid reasoning and relevant evidence, to write a book review.

Through the week, students will improve the range and content of their writing through daily mini-lessons.

5-Day Plan

DAY 1	Read Like a Writer
DAY 2	Preparing to Review
DAY 3	Organizing Your Draft
DAY 4	Revise: Adding
DAY 5	Proofread for Conjunctions

Write Guy *by Jeff Anderson*

Trait-by-Trait Organization

Organization is a trait of good writing, but let's not be so concerned with form that we forget about meaning. A student may develop a good way to communicate ideas that does not precisely follow the format we expect.

Writing

Book Review

Mini-Lesson   **Read Like a Writer**

■ **Introduce** This week you will write a critique. A critique is a review of someone's work. There are many kinds of critiques, and one of them is a **book review.** A book review gives information and opinions about a book. People who have not read the book use the review to help them decide whether they want to read it.

Prompt	Think about a story or book you have read recently. Write a book review of it, explaining to readers whether they should read it.
Trait	Conventions
Mode	Opinion/Persuasive

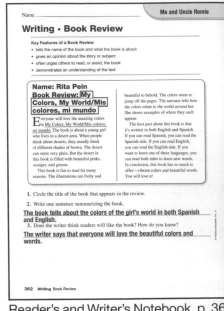

Reader's and Writer's Notebook, p. 362

■ **Examine Model Text** Let's read an example of a book review for a book called *My Colors, My World/Mis colores, mi mundo.* Have students read the book review on p. 362 of their *Reader's and Writer's Notebook.*

■ **Key Features** Book reviews should include the title of the book being reviewed. The title of the book should be underlined in a review. Have students circle the title of the book in the model.

A book review also tells what the book is about. Have students write a sentence summarizing the book.

Book reviews either urge readers to read or to avoid the book. What is the writer of this book review trying to persuade the reader to do? Have students list reasons the writer thinks others should read the book.

A good book review demonstrates that the writer has a good understanding of what the book is about. Discuss whether the writer demonstrates a good understanding of the text.

Review Key Features

Review the key features of a book review with students. You may want to post the key features in the classroom for students to refer to as they work on their book reviews.

Key Features of a Book Review

- tells the name of the book and what the book is about
- gives an opinion about the story or subject
- often urges others to read, or avoid, the book
- demonstrates an understanding of the text

Routine | Quick Write for Fluency | Team Talk

Talk Pairs discuss the key features of a book review.

Write Each student writes two sentences about where a book review might appear.

Share Partners read aloud their writing to one another.

Routines Flip Chart

eSTREET INTERACTIVE
www.ReadingStreet.com

Teacher Resources
- Reader's and Writer's Notebook
- Let's Practice It!

Academic Vocabulary ©

A **critique** is a review of a piece of writing, drama, music, or other work of art.

 ELL

Book Review Read the writing model aloud and help students understand it. Remind students that book reviews tell about the book and then encourage their audience to read it or to avoid it. Ask students what qualities make a good book.

Wrap Up Your Day!

✔ **Content Knowledge** Reread "Street Rhymes!" on p. 320j to students. Ask them what they learned today about country life and city life.

✔ **Oral Vocabulary** Have students use the Amazing Words they learned in context sentences.

✔ **Homework** Send home this week's Family Times newsletter on *Let's Practice It!* pp. 330–331 on the *Teacher Resources DVD-ROM.*

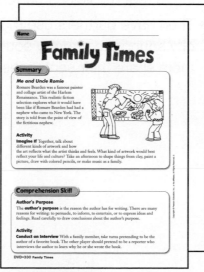

Let's Practice It!
TR DVD•330–331

Preview DAY 2

Tell students that tomorrow they will read about a boy who visits the city.

Materials

- Student Edition
- Reader's and Writer's Notebook

© Common Core State Standards

Speaking/Listening 1. Engage effectively in a range of collaborative discussions (one-on-one, in groups, and teacher-led) with diverse partners on grade 3 topics and texts, building on others' ideas and expressing their own clearly. **Language 6.** Acquire and use accurately grade-appropriate conversational, general academic, and domain-specific words and phrases, including those that signal spatial and temporal relationships (e.g., *After dinner that night we went looking for them*). **Also Language 1.h., 5.b.**

Content Knowledge

City Life and Country Life

EXPAND THE CONCEPT Remind students of the weekly concept question, *How does city life compare to life in the country?* Tell students that today they will begin reading *Me and Uncle Romie.* As they read, encourage students to think about how life in the city compares to life in the country.

Build Oral Language

TALK ABOUT SENTENCES AND WORDS Reread a sentence from the Read Aloud, "Nature in the City."

Some of the biggest cities in Texas also have different, softer kinds of sounds. . . . Sounds that rabbits make when they scamper through woods and that squirrels make when they scurry through fields.

- What does *scamper* mean? Use context clues to help you determine the meaning. (to run quickly)

- How can you retell this sentence in a simpler way? (Bigger cities also have the quieter sounds that animals make running through the woods and fields)

- Why might the author include these descriptions? (to show that not all sounds in the city are loud; cities have quiet sounds too)

Team Talk Have students turn to a partner and discuss the following question. Then ask them to share their responses.

- What types of sounds have you heard in a city? In the country? (cars honking, street musicians performing; crickets chirping, tractors plowing)

- Then have partners use their responses to create a sentence that compares city sounds to country sounds. Remind them to use conjunctions. Have them share their sentences.

Build Oral Vocabulary

Amazing Words

Robust Vocabulary Routine

Introduce Write the Amazing Word *vendor* on the board. Have students say it aloud with you. Relate *vendor* to "New York City." *What kinds of vendors might you see on the streets in New York?* (You might see vendors selling food, hats, or books.) Have students use context clues to determine the definition of the word. *A vendor is someone who sells things, usually outdoors.*

Demonstrate Have students answer questions to demonstrate understanding. *What kinds of vendors have you seen at a fair? What might a vendor say to get your attention?*

Apply Have students apply their understanding. *Would you buy a house from a vendor? What is something you might buy from a vendor?*

Display the Word Run your hand under the word parts *vend-or* as you read the word. Have students say the word.

See p. OV•5 to teach *hurl*.

Routines Flip Chart

ADD TO THE CONCEPT MAP Use the photos on pp. 320–321 and the Read Aloud, "Nature in the City," to discuss differences between country life and city life and to talk about the Amazing Words *taxicab, scamper, scurry,* and *skyscraper.* Add these and other concept-related words to the concept map to develop students' knowledge of the topic. Discuss the following questions. Encourage students to build on others' ideas when they answer.

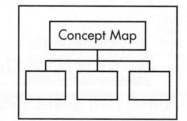

What would you see *scurry* down a country lane? Down a city street?

How do *skyscrapers* and *taxicabs* go together?

What animals *scamper* in both the city and the country?

eSTREET INTERACTIVE
www.ReadingStreet.com

Teacher Resources
• Amazing Word Cards
• Graphic Organizers

Amazing Words

skyscraper	hurl
taxicab	meager
scamper	gutter
scurry	bitter
vendor	ramble

Reinforce Vocabulary Use the Day 2 instruction on ELL Poster 25 to teach selection vocabulary and discuss the weekly concept.

Me and Uncle Romie **326b**

© **Common Core State Standards**

Literature 4. Determine the meaning of words and phrases as they are used in a text, distinguishing literal from nonliteral language. **Foundational Skills 3.a.** Identify and know the meaning of the most common prefixes and derivational suffixes. **Foundational Skills 3.b.** Decode words with common Latin suffixes. **Language 6.** Acquire and use accurately grade-appropriate conversational, general academic, and domain-specific words and phrases, including those that signal spatial and temporal relationships (e.g., *After dinner that night we went looking for them*). **Also Foundational Skills 3.**

Word Analysis

❂ Suffixes -y, -ish, -hood, -ment

REVIEW Review the suffixes *-y, -ish, -hood,* and *-ment,* pointing out that suffixes are added at the end of base words. Display these words. Have the class decode the words. Then point to the words in random order and ask students to read them quickly.

READ WORDS IN ISOLATION Have the class read these words. Then point to the words in random order and ask students to read them quickly.

knighthood	wooly	Scottish	girlhood
treatment	boyish	honesty	grayish

> **Corrective feedback** | Model reading the base word and then the suffix, and then ask students to read the word with you.

READ WORDS IN CONTEXT Have the class read these sentences.

Team Talk Have pairs take turns reading the sentences naturally.

My **English** grandmother likes to tell stories about her **neighborhood.**
Bravery was important in the olden days.
The **measurement** of the wall was off by two inches.

Don't Wait Until Friday **MONITOR PROGRESS** Check Word Reading

FORMATIVE ASSESSMENT Write the following words and have the class read them. Notice which words students miss during the group reading. Call on individuals to read some of the words.

tasty	reddish	brotherhood	enjoyment
planner	pianist	hostess	editor
unlikely	unselfish	reworked	discontented

Spiral Review
Row 2 reviews words with suffixes *-er, -ist, -ess, -or.*

Row 3 contrasts words with prefixes and suffixes.

If... students cannot read words with suffixes at this point,

then... use the Day 1 Word Analysis lesson on p. 322a to reteach suffixes. Use words from the *Decodable Practice Passages* (or Reader). Continue to monitor students' progress using other instructional opportunities during the week. See the Skills Trace on p. 322a.

Literary Terms

Onomatopoeia

TEACH Tell students that words that sound like their meanings are called onomatopoeia. These sound words, such as *buzz* and *clang,* help reinforce meanings, dramatize events, and appeal to the senses.

Think Aloud **MODEL** Let's look at "New York City." When I think of the sounds of cities, I think of onomatopoeia. There's the *honk-honk* of car horns and the *screech* of cars hitting their brakes. Can you think of other words to describe city sounds? (Students should identify onomatopoeic words.)

GUIDE PRACTICE Point out an example of onomatopoeia on p. 332 of *Me and Uncle Romie*. Have students read the words *chug-a-chug-a-chug-a-chug* aloud and notice how they sound like the sound of a train.

ON THEIR OWN Have students find other examples of onomatopoeia in other selections of their Student Edition.

Common Core State Standards

Language 4. Determine or clarify the meaning of unknown and multiple-meaning words and phrases based on grade 3 reading and content, choosing flexibly from a range of strategies. **Language 4.a.** Use sentence-level context as a clue to the meaning of a word or phrase. **Also Foundational Skills 4., 4.b., Language 4.d., 5.**

Selection Vocabulary

cardboard thick, stiff paper

feast a meal with a lot of food

fierce frightening, scary

flights sets of stairs

pitcher a person who throws a baseball to a batter

ruined destroyed or damaged

stoops small porches with steps, usually at the front of a house

treasure valuables; prizes

 Bridge to Common Core

VOCABULARY ACQUISITION AND USE

Using context clues helps students determine or clarify the meaning of unknown words and enables them to acquire a broad range of academic and domain-specific words. By consulting a dictionary to find alternate word choices, they demonstrate the ability to gather vocabulary knowledge on their own.

Vocabulary Support

Refer students to *Words!* on p. W•11 in the Student Edition for additional practice.

Vocabulary Skill

Homonyms

READ Have students read "A Different Treasure Hunt" on p. 327. Use the vocabulary skill and strategy as tools to build comprehension.

TEACH CONTEXT CLUES Students can use context clues to determine the meanings of words that may be homonyms. Discuss the first paragraph on p. 326. Explain how context clues can help determine the different meanings of the homonym *saw*. Continue with other homonyms.

Think Aloud **MODEL** Write on the board: *I see pots of flowers on all the front stoops of the houses. The boy stoops down to pick up a coin off the sidewalk. Stoops* is a homonym. I can figure out the meaning of each homonym by reading the words around it. In the first sentence, the stoops are on the front of apartments. This homonym means "small porches at the front of the house." In the second sentence, the boy stoops down to the sidewalk. This word is a verb. What does this homonym mean? **(bend over)**

GUIDE PRACTICE Write these sentences on the board: *I ran up three flights of stairs to get to the third floor. The family left their carry-on luggage behind after their flight.* Have students determine the meaning of *flight* using context clues. Let students use a dictionary to confirm their answers. For additional support, use *Envision It! Pictured Vocabulary Cards* or *Tested Vocabulary Cards.*

ON THEIR OWN Have students reread "A Different Treasure Hunt" on p. 327. Have students identify the context clues that help them define each selection vocabulary word before they write their responses. For additional practice, use *Reader's and Writer's Notebook,* p. 363.

Name _____ **Me and Uncle Romie**

Vocabulary

Directions Underline the word that completes each sentence. Write the word on the line.

Check the Words You Know			
__flights	__fierce	__stoops	__treasure
__pitcher	__feast	__ruined	__cardboard

1. Our team's ___**pitcher**___ struck everyone out.
   pitcher   treasure
2. My neighbors' ___**stoops**___ needed repairs to the broken stairs.
   fierce   stoops
3. After my aunt discovered the chest in the attic, she found a ___**treasure**___
   feast   treasure
4. My grandmother made us a special ___**feast**___ for the holiday.
   flights   feast
5. I walked up three ___**flights**___ of stairs.
   treasure   flights

Directions Write the word from the box that completes each sentence.

6. The lion looked very ___**fierce**___ when it growled.
7. We packed the books in a ___**cardboard**___ box.
8. I ate so much at the ___**feast**___ that I'm not hungry now.
9. The cake was ___**ruined**___ when she dropped it on the floor.
10. The ring from my grandfather is something to keep as a ___**treasure**___

Write a Thank-You Note

On a separate sheet of paper, write a thank-you note that James might write to Uncle Romie after his visit. Use as many vocabulary words as possible. **Students should use vocabulary in a thank-you note from Me and Uncle Romie to his Uncle Romie.**

Home Activity Your child has identified and used the vocabulary words from Me and Uncle Romie. Read a story about a family together. Have a conversation with your child about your family, using some of the vocabulary words in this lesson.

Vocabulary 36

Reader's and Writer's Notebook, p. 363

Common Core State Standards
Language 4.a. Use sentence-level context as a clue to the meaning of a word or phrase. Also Language 4., 5.

Envision It! Words to Know

cardboard

feast

treasure

fierce
flights
pitcher
ruined
stoops

**READING STREET ONLINE
VOCABULARY ACTIVITIES**
www.ReadingStreet.com

Vocabulary Strategy for

⊙ Homonyms

Context Clues You may read a familiar word that doesn't make sense in the sentence. The word could be a homonym. Homonyms are words that are pronounced and spelled the same, but have different meanings. For example, *saw* means "looked at" and "a tool for cutting." Use the context—the words and sentences around the word—to figure out the correct meaning.

1. Reread the words and sentences around the word that doesn't make sense.

2. Draw a conclusion about another meaning for the word using context clues.

3. Try the meaning in the sentence. Does it make sense?

Read "A Different Treasure Hunt" on page 327. Use context clues to help you find the meanings of homonyms.

Words to Write Reread "A Different Treasure Hunt." Write your answer to the question at the end of the selection. Give reasons for your answer. Use homonyms and words from the Words to Know list in your answer.

A DIFFERENT TREASURE HUNT

The summer I turned eight, my family moved from New York City to North Carolina. In the city, we climbed four flights of stairs to our apartment. The building was ten stories high! People sat on their front stoops and listened to the noise. I was a pitcher on the neighborhood baseball team.

In North Carolina, we live in a house. All the houses have front porches and yards. At night it is very dark and quiet. At first, I thought my life was ruined.

My mother saw my fierce face. She suggested I have a treasure hunt, but instead of looking for gold, I should look for baseball players. She promised to help by preparing a feast with all my favorite food. I made signs on cardboard and posted them at the grocery store, the library, and the post office. The signs said:

I'm looking for baseball players.
Come to 124 Willow Street
June 28 at 2:00 P.M.
FREE FOOD!

Do you think anyone showed up?

Your Turn!

⏸ **Need a Review?** For additional help with homonyms, see *Words!*

▶ **Ready to Try It?** Read *Me and Uncle Romie* on pp. 328–349.

326

327

Student Edition, pp. 326–327

Reread for Fluency

APPROPRIATE PHRASING Read paragraph 2 of "A Different Treasure Hunt," pausing for commas and periods to emphasize appropriate phrasing. Tell students to notice the punctuation as they follow along.

Routine   Paired Reading

Select a Passage For "A Different Treasure Hunt," use the whole passage.

Reading 1 Students read the entire passage, switching readers at the end of each paragraph.

Reading 2 Partners reread the passage. This time the other student begins.

Reread For optimal fluency, have partners continue to read three or four times.

Corrective Feedback Listen as students read. Provide feedback about whether they should pause and where it makes sense to stop.

Routines Flip Chart

eSTREET INTERACTIVE
www.ReadingStreet.com

Pearson eText
• Student Edition

Vocabulary Activities

Journal

Teacher Resources
• Envision It! Pictured Vocabulary Cards
• Tested Vocabulary Cards
• Reader's and Writer's Notebook

© Common Core State Standards

Literature 10. By the end of the year, read and comprehend literature, including stories, dramas, and poetry, at the high end of the grades 2–3 text complexity band independently and proficiently. **Also Literature 7.**

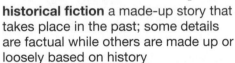

© Bridge to Common Core

CRAFT AND STRUCTURE

Students analyze how portions of the text relate to the selection as a whole when they preview. As they prepare to read, they come to see how its genre impacts the content and style of the text.

Academic Vocabulary ©

historical fiction a made-up story that takes place in the past; some details are factual while others are made up or loosely based on history

Strategy Response Log

Have students use p. 31 in the *Reader's and Writer's Notebook* to identify the characteristics of historical fiction.

Text-Based Comprehension

Introduce Main Selection

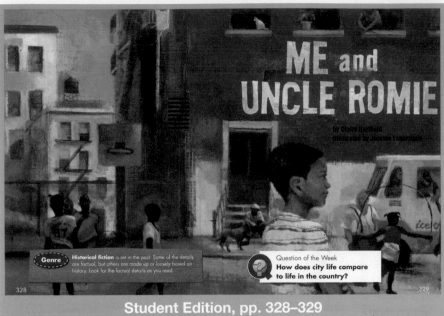

Student Edition, pp. 328–329

GENRE Remind students that **historical fiction** tells a made-up story that takes place in the past. Some details in historical fiction are factual, but other details are made up or loosely based on history. The setting of historical fiction is important as it demonstrates how the characters lived at the time the story takes place.

PREVIEW AND PREDICT Have students read the title, the author, and the illustrator for *Me and Uncle Romie*. Have them use the title and illustrations to predict what they will find out as they read.

PURPOSE By analyzing *Me and Uncle Romie,* an example of historical fiction, students will gain knowledge about city life and country life.

Access Main Selection

READER AND TASK SUGGESTIONS	
Preparing to Read the Text	**Leveled Tasks**
• Review strategies for understanding homonyms. • Discuss how authors use factual information in historical fiction. • Remind students to adjust their reading rate when they encounter unfamiliar vocabulary and concepts.	• **Levels of Meaning • Analysis** Students may not understand how to recognize historical fiction. Have them identify events in the story that show it is set in the past. • **Theme and Knowledge Demands** The many sightseeing destinations James visits in New York City may confuse some students. Have them make a note of places in the story they are unfamiliar with.

See Text Complexity Measures for *Me and Uncle Romie* on the tab at the beginning of this week.

READ Tell students that today they will read *Me and Uncle Romie* for the first time. Use the Read for Understanding routine.

Routine Read for Understanding ©

Deepen understanding by reading the selection multiple times.

1. **First Read**—If students need support, then use the **Access Text** notes to help them clarify understanding.

2. **Second Read**—Use the **Close Reading** notes to help students draw knowledge from the text.

Day 2 SMALL GROUP TIME • Differentiate Comprehension, p. SG•65

OL On-Level	**SI** Strategic Intervention	**A** Advanced
• **Practice** Selection Vocabulary • **Read** *Me and Uncle Romie*	• **Reteach** Selection Vocabulary • **Read** *Me and Uncle Romie*	• **Extend** Selection Vocabulary • **Read** *Me and Uncle Romie* • **Investigate** Inquiry Project

eSTREET INTERACTIVE
www.ReadingStreet.com

Pearson eText
• Student Edition

AudioText CD

Teacher Resources
• Reader's and Writer's Notebook

Background Building Audio CD

Access for All

 SI Strategic Intervention
Work with students to set a purpose for reading, or if time permits, have students work with partners to set purposes.

A Advanced
Have students trace on a United States map the route James most likely took from North Carolina to New York City.

ELL

Build Background To build background, review the selection summary in English (*ELL Handbook*, p. 175). Use the Retelling Cards to provide visual support for the summary.

If... students need more scaffolding and practice with the **Comprehension Skill, then...** use the activities on p. DI•121 in the Teacher Resources section on SuccessNet.

Access Text ⓒ *If students need help, then...*

ⓐ AUTHOR'S PURPOSE Why does the author describe Uncle Romie before the boy meets him? (She wants the reader to understand how the boy pictures Uncle Romie so the reader can understand why the boy is nervous.)

Think Aloud MODEL To figure out why the author describes Uncle Romie, I first think about how she describes him. She says he is "a bald-headed, fierce-eyed giant," and makes it clear that the boy finds him scary. I think the author wants the reader to understand why the boy is nervous.

Close Reading ⓒ

ANALYSIS • TEXT EVIDENCE How does the author help you understand that the boy is nervous about the trip? Cite evidence from the text to support your answer. (In the last paragraph on p. 331, the boy says he is lucky to get to ride on the train, but then he thinks "maybe." The author wrote this to show that the boy is unsure about the trip.)

t was the summer Mama had the twins that I first met my uncle Romie. The doctor had told Mama she had to stay off her feet till the babies got born. Daddy thought it was a good time for me to visit Uncle Romie and his wife, Aunt Nanette, up north in New York City. But I wasn't so sure. Mama had told me that Uncle Romie was some kind of artist, and he didn't have any kids. I'd seen his picture too. He looked scary—a bald-headed, fierce-eyed giant. No, I wasn't sure about this visit at all.

330

Student Edition, p. 330

ON THEIR OWN Have students reread pp. 330–331 to find other reasons the writer wrote what she did. For additional practice with author's purpose, see *Let's Practice It!* page 332 on the *Teacher Resources DVD-ROM.*

The day before I left home was a regular North Carolina summer day. "A good train-watching day," my friend B. J. said.

We waited quietly in the grass beside the tracks. B. J. heard it first. "It's a'coming," he said. Then I heard it too—a low rumbling, building to a roar. *WHOOO—OOO!*

"The *Piedmont!*" we shouted as the train blasted past.

"I'm the greatest train-watcher ever," B. J. boasted.

"Yeah," I answered, "but tomorrow I'll be *riding* a train. I'm the lucky one."

Lucky, I thought as we headed home. *Maybe.*

331

Student Edition, p. 331

INFERENCE • TEXT EVIDENCE What conclusion can you draw about the relationship between the boy and B.J.? What evidence can you use to draw this conclusion? (They seem to be very good friends, probably because they share an interest in trains. On p. 331, when the boy spends a "regular North Carolina summer day," he spends it with B.J. watching trains. The two boys boast playfully to each other about being great at identifying trains and getting to ride on an actual train.)

Common Core
State Standards

Literature 1. Ask and answer questions to demonstrate understanding of a text, referring explicitly to the text as the basis for the answers. **Literature 10.** By the end of the year, read and comprehend literature, including stories, dramas, and poetry, at the high end of the grades 2–3 text complexity band independently and proficiently. **Also Literature 3.**

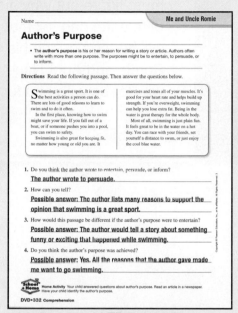

Let's Practice It! TR DVD•332

Connect to
Social Studies

The Importance of Trains Trains were very important to the expansion of the United States. Long before there were airplanes, people and freight traveled throughout the United States by train. Up until World War II, most Americans traveled long distances by train, and train service was available from coast to coast.

ELL

Activate Content Knowledge Create a web to record students' prior knowledge of trains. We're going to read about a boy who likes to watch trains and takes a trip on a train. What do you know about trains? Where have you seen them? How do trains move? On what do they travel?

Me and Uncle Romie **331a**

Access Text © If students need help, then...

Review DRAW CONCLUSIONS Why does James tell his mother he will miss the way she makes his birthday special? (James will be celebrating his birthday in New York instead of at home with his mother.)

Think Aloud **MODEL** To understand why James will miss the way his mother makes his birthday special, I must figure out why his birthday will be different. I can tell that James's birthday will happen during his visit with Uncle Romie and Aunt Nanette, so his mother will not be with him for it.

Close Reading ©

ANALYSIS How does Daddy probably think James's birthday will be? (Daddy says Romie is a good man and notes that Nanette will be there too, so he probably feels Romie and Nanette will help James celebrate and have a nice birthday.)

That evening I packed my suitcase. Voices drifted up from the porch below.

"Romie's got that big art show coming up," Mama said quietly. "I hope he's not too busy for James, especially on his birthday."

"Romie's a good man," Daddy replied. "And Nanette'll be there too."

The light faded. Mama called me into her bedroom. "Where's my good-night kiss?" she said.

I curled up next to her. "I'll miss the way you make my birthday special, Mama. Your lemon cake and the baseball game."

"Well," Mama sighed, "it won't be those things. But Uncle Romie and Aunt Nanette are family, and they love you too. It'll still be a good birthday, honey."

Mama pulled me close. Her voice sang soft and low. Later, in my own bed, I listened as crickets began their song and continued into the night.

The next morning I hugged Mama good-bye, and Daddy and I headed for the train. He got me seated, then stood waving at me from the outside. I held tight to the jar of pepper jelly Mama had given me for Uncle Romie.

"ALL A-BOARD!" The conductor's voice crackled over the loudspeaker.

The train pulled away. *Chug-a-chug-a-chug-a-chug.* I watched my town move past my window—bright-colored houses, chickens strutting across the yards, flowers everywhere.

332

Student Edition, p. 332

EVALUATION • TEXT EVIDENCE How do you think James feels about the trip? Cite evidence from the text to support your answer. (He is still nervous. He stays up late listening to crickets instead of getting a good night's sleep, and once on the train he holds tight to the jar of pepper jelly for Uncle Romie, which shows he is nervous about losing it.)

ON THEIR OWN Have students use the information on p. 332 to draw other conclusions about James's trip. For additional practice with drawing conclusions, see *Let's Practice It!* page 333 on the *Teacher Resources DVD-ROM.*

333

Student Edition, p. 333

ANALYSIS Help students generate text-based questions by providing the following question stem: In the selection, what does Mama say when _____?

© **Common Core State Standards**

Literature 1. Ask and answer questions to demonstrate understanding of a text, referring explicitly to the text as the basis for the answers. **Literature 3.** Describe characters in a story (e.g., their traits, motivations, or feelings) and explain how their actions contribute to the sequence of events. **Literature 10.** By the end of the year, read and comprehend literature, including stories, dramas, and poetry, at the high end of the grades 2–3 text complexity band independently and proficiently.

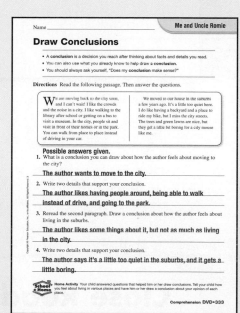

Let's Practice It! TR DVD•333

ELL

Extend Language Point out the contractions *Nanette'll* and *It'll* on p. 332. Explain that this particular type of contraction or blending of subject and verb (*Nanette will* and *It will*) occurs only in informal dialogue and is not considered standard English.

Me and Uncle Romie **333a**

Access Text  If students need help, then...

HOMONYMS Point out the word *kind* on p. 334. Tell students that it is a homonym. Have them identify the word's meaning as it is used in the sentence in the story.

Think Aloud **MODEL** What do we call words that have the same pronunciation and the same spelling but different meanings? (homonyms) I found two entries for *kind* in the dictionary. Which meaning of *kind* is the author using? (When used before *of,* the word *kind* means "nearly; almost; somewhat.")

After a while I felt hungry. Daddy had packed me a lunch and a dinner to eat one at a time. I ate almost everything at once. Then my belly felt tight and I was kind of sleepy. I closed my eyes and dreamed about Mama and Daddy getting ready for those babies. Would they even miss me?

Later, when I woke up, I ate the last bit of my dinner and thought about my birthday. Would they make my lemon cake and take me to a baseball game in New York?

The sky turned from dark blue to black. I was getting sleepy all over again.

"We're almost there, son," the man next to me said.

Then I saw it . . . New York City. Buildings stretching up to the sky. So close together. Not like North Carolina at all.

334

Student Edition, p. 334

Close Reading

INFERENCE • TEXT EVIDENCE

How long do you think it takes James to get from North Carolina to New York City? Cite evidence from the text to support your answer. (The text says that James leaves in the morning and that his father packs him a lunch and a dinner to eat on the train. Also, the text says that they sky turns from blue to black, which means that by the time James gets to New York City, it is night. I think it would have taken at least nine hours to reach New York City.)

ON THEIR OWN Have students use context clues to figure out the meaning of *last* as it is used in the second paragraph on p. 334. ("the only part left") For additional practice with homonyms, see *Reader's and Writer's Notebook,* p. 367.

"Penn Station! Watch your step," the conductor said, helping me down to the platform. I did like Daddy said and found a spot for myself close to the train. Swarms of people rushed by. Soon I heard a silvery voice call my name. This had to be Aunt Nanette. I turned and saw her big smile reaching out to welcome me.

She took my hand and guided me through the rushing crowds onto an underground train called the subway. "This will take us right home," she explained.

335

Student Edition, p. 335

ANALYSIS • TEXT EVIDENCE What does James notice and think when he first sees New York City? What does that tell you about North Carolina? Cite the page and provide details from the selection. (On p. 334, James immediately notices the buildings "stretching up to the sky. So close together." He thinks it looks nothing like North Carolina. It makes me think there is more space in North Carolina.)

Common Core State Standards

Literature 1. Ask and answer questions to demonstrate understanding of a text, referring explicitly to the text as the basis for the answers. **Literature 3.** Describe characters in a story (e.g., their traits, motivations, or feelings) and explain how their actions contribute to the sequence of events. **Language 4.a.** Use sentence-level context as a clue to the meaning of a word or phrase. **Also Literature 10., Language 4.d.**

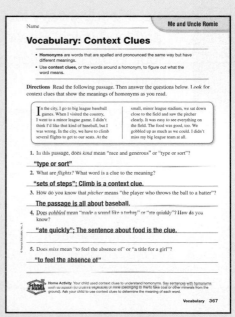

Reader's and Writer's Notebook, p. 367

ELL

Verbs Review the irregular verbs used on pp. 334–335. Show how each verb changes and help students practice the verbs to memorize them.

feel	felt	felt
eat	ate	eaten
say	said	said
see	saw	seen
hear	heard	heard

Me and Uncle Romie **335a**

1ST READ

Access Text © If students need help, then...

◉ BACKGROUND KNOWLEDGE

Ask students if they think James's initial descriptions or ideas of Uncle Romie are accurate now that he's seen Uncle Romie. (When I look at the illustration of Uncle Romie on p. 337, he doesn't seem fierce-looking. James's ideas might not be accurate.)

Think Aloud MODEL On p. 330, how does James describe Uncle Romie's picture? (bald-headed, fierce-looking giant) On p. 337, how is Uncle Romie described? (heavy footsteps, giant, deep and loud voice) How does Uncle Romie look in the illustration on p. 337? (friendly and nice)

2ND READ

Close Reading ©

EVALUATION • TEXT EVIDENCE

What kind of artist is Uncle Romie? How does James react when he learns this? Read the part of the story that tells you the kind of artist Uncle Romie is. (On p. 337, Aunt Nanette says that Uncle Romie is a collage artist. James thinks that sounds easy.)

Home was like nothing I'd ever seen before. No regular houses anywhere. Just big buildings and stores of all kinds—in the windows I saw paints, fabrics, radios, and TVs.

We turned into the corner building and climbed the stairs to the apartment—five whole flights up. *Whew!* I tried to catch my breath while Aunt Nanette flicked on the lights.

"Uncle Romie's out talking to some people about his big art show that's coming up. He'll be home soon," Aunt Nanette said. She set some milk and a plate of cookies for me on the table. "Your uncle's working very hard, so we won't see much of him for a while. His workroom—we call it his studio—is in the front of our apartment. That's where he keeps all the things he needs to make his art."

336

Student Edition, p. 336

ON THEIR OWN Have students tell why using background knowledge can help them understand and enjoy a story.

 Common Core State Standards

Literature 1. Ask and answer questions to demonstrate understanding of a text, referring explicitly to the text as the basis for the answers. **Literature 7.** Explain how specific aspects of a text's illustrations contribute to what is conveyed by the words in a story (e.g., create mood, emphasize aspects of a character or setting). **Literature 10.** By the end of the year, read and comprehend literature, including stories, dramas, and poetry, at the high end of the grades 2–3 text complexity band independently and proficiently.

"Doesn't he just paint?" I asked.

"Uncle Romie is a collage artist," Aunt Nanette explained. "He uses paints, yes. But also photographs, newspapers, cloth. He cuts and pastes them onto a board to make his paintings."

"That sounds kinda easy," I said.

Aunt Nanette laughed.

"Well, there's a little more to it than that, James. When you see the paintings, you'll understand. Come, let's get you to bed."

Lying in the dark, I heard heavy footsteps in the hall. A giant stared at me from the doorway. "Hello there, James." Uncle Romie's voice was deep and loud, like thunder. "Thanks for the pepper jelly," he boomed. "You have a good sleep, now." Then he disappeared down the hall.

Access for All

SI Strategic Intervention

Have students work in pairs to reread pp. 336–337, identifying passages they don't understand and using rereading, reading ahead, or the illustrations to clarify.

337

Student Edition, p. 337

ANALYSIS • TEXT EVIDENCE Where would you find a description of James's regular home to contrast it with the description of his new home? (I would look back at p. 332 at the description of what he saw looking out the moving train and compare and contrast that information with the description on p. 336.)

Background Knowledge Discuss students' prior knowledge of types of housing. In this story, James goes to an apartment. How would you describe an apartment? What other kinds of houses are there? How are they like apartments? How are they different?

Me and Uncle Romie **337a**

Access Text © If students need help, then...

➤ **AUTHOR'S PURPOSE** Ask students why they think the author describes the things James does on his first day in New York. (She wants to show that he is having a good time.)

(Think Aloud) MODEL What did James do on his first day in New York? (He went to a market, played stickball, and ate ice cream and barbecue.) How would you describe a day filled with these activities? (fun) What is the author saying about James's first day? (He had fun.)

ON THEIR OWN Have students reread p. 338 to find other reasons why the author wrote what she did.

Close Reading ©

ANALYSIS Why did the author use ellipsis between each of the activities in the fourth paragraph on p. 338? (She is showing that James and Aunt Nanette did not do all of the activities in one day and that this is just a sampling of some of the activities they did.)

The next morning the door to Uncle Romie's studio was closed. But Aunt Nanette had plans for both of us. "Today we're going to a neighborhood called Harlem," she said. "It's where Uncle Romie lived as a boy."

Harlem was full of people walking, working, shopping, eating. Some were watching the goings-on from fire escapes. Others were sitting out on stoops greeting folks who passed by—just like the people back home calling out hellos from their front porches. Most everybody seemed to know Aunt Nanette. A lot of them asked after Uncle Romie too.

We bought peaches at the market, then stopped to visit awhile. I watched some kids playing stickball. "Go on, get in that game," Aunt Nanette said, gently pushing me over to join them. When I was all hot and sweaty, we cooled off with double chocolate scoops from the ice cream man. Later we shared some barbecue on a rooftop way up high. I felt like I was on top of the world.

As the days went by, Aunt Nanette took me all over the city—we rode a ferry boat to the Statue of Liberty . . . zoomed 102 floors up at the Empire State Building . . . window-shopped the fancy stores on Fifth Avenue . . . gobbled hot dogs in Central Park.

But it was Harlem that I liked best. I played stickball with the kids again . . . and on a really hot day a whole bunch of us ran through the icy cold water that sprayed out hard from the fire hydrant. In the evenings Aunt Nanette and I sat outside listening to the street musicians playing their saxophone songs.

338

Student Edition, p. 338

CHECK PREDICTIONS Have students look back at the predictions they made earlier and discuss whether they were accurate. Then have students preview the rest of the selection and either adjust their predictions accordingly or make new predictions.

339

Student Edition, p. 339

If you want to teach this selection in two sessions, stop here.

If you want to continue reading this selection, turn to page 340–341.

INFERENCE James and Aunt Nanette ate barbecue on a rooftop. What did James mean when he felt like he was "on top of the world"? (James felt as if he were even higher than the rooftop. He also felt happy—the idiom "on top of the world" means "everything is going well.")

Common Core State Standards

Literature 1. Ask and answer questions to demonstrate understanding of a text, referring explicitly to the text as the basis for the answers. **Literature 4.** Determine the meaning of words and phrases as they are used in a text, distinguishing literal from nonliteral language. **Literature 10.** By the end of the year, read and comprehend literature, including stories, dramas, and poetry, at the high end of the grades 2–3 text complexity band independently and proficiently.

Access for All

SI Strategic Intervention

Working in small groups, have students make a collage that portrays what James and Aunt Nanette did while in New York. Let each group display and describe the collage.

A Advanced

Discuss why James might like Harlem best, comparing the things he does there with the things he does in other places around New York and noting the connection with Uncle Romie's childhood.

ELL

Graphic Organizer Help students make a web to record and organize details about all the different things that James does with Aunt Nanette in New York.

Me and Uncle Romie **339a**

Bridge to Common Core

RESEARCH TO BUILD AND PRESENT KNOWLEDGE

On Day 2 of the weeklong research project, students gather relevant information based on their focused questions from Day 1. They consult informational texts as well as digital sources, use text features to find information, and assess the credibility of each one. This process enables students to demonstrate an understanding of the subject under investigation. As students access online information, they should always note their sources for a Works Cited page.

Research and Inquiry

Step 2 Navigate/Search

TEACH Have students generate a research plan for gathering relevant information. Discuss with students how they might search the Internet using their inquiry questions and keywords. Tell them to skim and scan each site for information that helps them answer their inquiry question or leads them to specific information that will be useful. Bold or italicized words may be clues to what kind of information the Web site will provide. Have students look for other features, such as headings, illustrations, captions, or highlighting. Remind them to take notes as they gather information from multiple sources.

 MODEL When I started looking for soccer teams, I found professional ones and some in other parts of the country. When I added my local area to my keywords, I got more helpful information. When I went to the site, I looked for the boldfaced heads and read captions on pictures to help me get more information.

GUIDE PRACTICE Have students continue their review of Web sites they identified. Remind students that some Web sites are more reliable than others. Explain that Web addresses ending in *.gov, .org,* or *.edu* are more likely to have reliable information than some sites ending in *.com.*

ON THEIR OWN Have students identify valid and reliable sources and discuss the importance of citing valid and reliable sources.

Conventions

Conjunctions

TEACH Write this sentence: *Uncle Romie and Aunt Nanette are family, and they love you too.* Ask students to identify the coordinating conjunction in this sentence. (*and*) Remind students that a *conjunction* is a word that connects words or groups of words.

GUIDE PRACTICE Write the following sentences on the board: *I wish I could go to the movies. I don't have any allowance left.* Ask students which coordinating conjunction could be used to join the sentences together. (*but*) Help students join the two sentences into one compound sentence.

ON THEIR OWN For more practice, use *Reader's and Writer's Notebook,* p. 364.

Spelling

Suffixes -y, -ish, -hood, -ment

TEACH Remind students that their spelling words for this week include the suffixes *-y, -ish, -hood,* and *-ment.* Model again how to spell words with these suffixes. The parts in *foolish* are *fool* and *ish.* First, I spell the base word. Write *fool.* Then I write the suffix. Write *ish.* Then I spell *foolish:* f-o-o-l-i-s-h.

GUIDE PRACTICE Write the remaining spelling words on the board. Have students write them and underline each base word.

ON THEIR OWN For more practice, use *Reader's and Writer's Notebook,* p. 365.

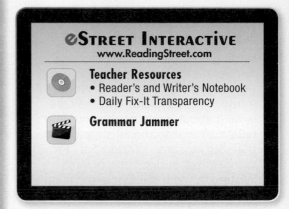

eStreet Interactive
www.ReadingStreet.com

Teacher Resources
• Reader's and Writer's Notebook
• Daily Fix-It Transparency

Grammar Jammer

Daily Fix-It

3. It was a rainey day, and we played baseball anyway. *(rainy; but)*
4. I played in the outfield, and catched a fly ball. *(outfield and; caught)*

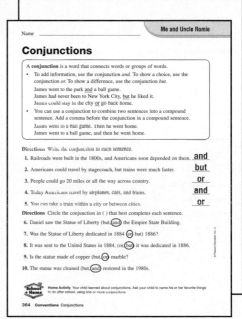

Reader's and Writer's Notebook, pp. 364–365

Conventions To provide students with practice on conjunctions, use the modified grammar lessons in the *ELL Handbook* and the Grammar Jammer online at:
www.ReadingStreet.com

Conjunctions To help students differentiate between *and, but,* and *or,* ask students questions while using physical cues, such as *Would you like to use a crayon or a marker?* (Hold out one and then the other.) or *Would you like to use a pencil and an eraser?* (Hold out both.)

© Common Core State Standards

Writing 1. Write opinion pieces on familiar topics or texts, supporting a point of view with reasons. **Writing 1.a.** Introduce the topic or text they are writing about, state an opinion, and create an organizational structure that lists reasons. **Writing 1.b.** Provide reasons that support the opinion. **Writing 4.** With guidance and support from adults, produce writing in which the development and organization are appropriate to task and purpose.

Writing

Book Review

Writing Trait: Organization

INTRODUCE THE PROMPT Review the key features of a book review and remind students to think about these features as they plan their writing. Explain that today they will begin the writing process for a book review that either encourages their audience to read the book or discourages them from reading the book. They are, in effect, writing responses to texts. Read aloud the writing prompt.

Writing Prompt

Think about a story or book you have read recently. Write a book review of it, explaining to readers whether they should read it.

SELECT A TOPIC

Think Aloud A book review is a piece of writing that discusses the good and bad qualities of a book. A negative review doesn't necessarily mean that the writer dislikes the book. Critiques can be positive too. I want to write a book review about a book I really liked. Let's make a list of books we really enjoy and reasons we like them. Display a T-chart. Ask students to name titles to add to the list. Remind students that they will choose a book to generate a first draft of their book review.

Books We Like	Reasons We Like These Books
How a Plant Grows	Interesting subject and pictures
Charlotte's Web	Interesting plot and creative characters
Amelia Earhart: Free in the Skies	Humorous and unlikely situations
How to Eat Fried Worms	Funny and gross story

Corrective feedback Circulate around the room as students choose a book to write about. If students are having trouble choosing a book, provide a list of titles of popular books from the classroom or school library. Ask struggling students to tell you which book they like best out of the last three books they have read.

e STREET INTERACTIVE
www.ReadingStreet.com

Teacher Resources
• Reader's and Writer's Notebook
• Graphic Organizer

Mini-Lesson | Preparing to Review

Display the book review graphic organizer. I want to write a book review about the book <u>How a Plant Grows</u>. I will write this title on the first line of the graphic organizer. This book does not have an illustrator listed, so I won't write anything on that line.

This book is about plants and how they grow. I will write this information on the *Plot or Nonfiction Topic* line. I really liked the subject and pictures so I will write this on the *My Opinion* line. In the box I will write additional information. Write *I learned a lot about how seeds travel*.

Have students begin their own book reviews using the form on p. 366 of their *Reader's and Writer's Notebook*.

Routine | Quick Write for Fluency | Team Talk

1. **Talk** Have pairs discuss the books they want to review.

2. **Write** Each student writes a few sentences about the book.

3. **Share** Partners read one another's writing and ask questions.

Routines Flip Chart

Reader's and Writer's Notebook,
p. 366

Wrap Up Your Day!

✔ **Content Knowledge** What did you learn about life in North Carolina?

✔ **Text-Based Comprehension** What do you think the author's purpose was in telling this story?

Preview DAY 3

Tell students that tomorrow they will read more about James and Uncle Romie.

Content Knowledge
Oral Vocabulary

Phonics/Word Analysis
Ⓢ Suffixes -y, -ish, -hood, -ment

Text-Based Comprehension
Ⓢ Author's Purpose
Ⓢ Background Knowledge

Fluency
Appropriate Phrasing

Research and Study Skills
Electronic Text

Research and Inquiry
Analyze Information

Conventions
Conjunctions

Spelling
Suffixes -y, -ish, -hood, -ment

Writing
Book Review

Materials

- Student Edition
- Reader's and Writer's Notebook
- Retelling Cards
- Decodable Reader

Ⓒ Common Core State Standards

Speaking/Listening 1. Engage effectively in a range of collaborative discussions (one-on-one, in groups, and teacher-led) with diverse partners on grade 3 topics and texts, building on others' ideas and expressing their own clearly. **Speaking/Listening 1.c.** Ask questions to check understanding of information presented, stay on topic, and link their comments to the remarks of others. **Speaking/Listening 1.d.** Explain their own ideas and understanding in light of the discussion. **Language 6.** Acquire and use accurately grade-appropriate conversational, general academic, and domain-specific words and phrases, including those that signal spatial and temporal relationships (e.g., *After dinner that night we went looking for them*).

Content Knowledge

City Life and Country Life

EXPAND THE CONCEPT Remind students of the weekly concept question, *How does city life compare to life in the country?* Tell students that today they will continue reading *Me and Uncle Romie.* Encourage students to think about how living in the city compares to living in the country.

Build Oral Language

TALK ABOUT SENTENCES AND WORDS Reread this sentence from Student Edition p. 332.

I watched my town move past my window—bright-colored houses, chickens strutting across the yards, flowers everywhere.

- James is on the train when he watches his "town move past my window." The town isn't really moving—the train is moving. Why do you think the author didn't just write "I moved past my town"? (The author wanted to show that James doesn't really want to leave his town.)
- What does *strutting* mean? (walking about with a proud attitude)
- What are some synonyms for the word *strutting?* (prancing, parading, marching)
- What is another way the author could have described the houses instead of using the adjective *bright-colored?* (colorful, showy, vivid)
- Why do you think the author chose the words *strutting* and *bright-colored?* (Answers will vary.)

Team Talk Have students work in pairs to replace words in the sentence without changing meaning.

I watched my town move past my window—_____ houses, chickens _____ across the yards, flowers everywhere.

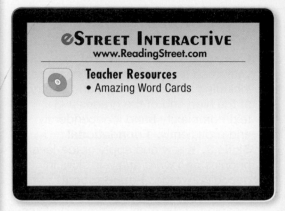

Build Oral Vocabulary

Amazing Words

Robust Vocabulary Routine

1. **Introduce** Write the word *meager* on the board. Have students say it with you. Yesterday, you read that James and Aunt Nanette shared barbecue. They each only ate a *meager* amount because they weren't very hungry. Have students determine a definition of *meager*. (*Meager* means "a small or little amount.")

2. **Demonstrate** Have students answer questions to demonstrate understanding. Was the double chocolate scoop ice cream James ate a *meager* amount? Explain. (No, because a double scoop is a lot of ice cream.)

3. **Apply** Have students apply their understanding. What is the opposite of a *meager* meal? (a feast)

4. **Display the Word** Students can decode the sounds in *meager* and blend them.

See p. OV•5 to teach *gutter*.

Routines Flip Chart

ADD TO THE CONCEPT MAP Discuss the Amazing Words *vendor* and *hurl*. Add these and other concept-related words to the concept map. Use the following questions to develop students' understanding of the concept.

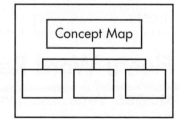

Concept Map

A pitcher *hurls* a baseball to the batter. Think about what the verb *hurl* means. Pantomime *hurling* a ball.

What *vendors* did James see in the city? How are they like *vendors* in the country?

Amazing Words

skyscraper	hurl
taxicab	meager
scamper	gutter
scurry	bitter
vendor	ramble

Expand Vocabulary Use the Day 3 instruction on ELL Poster 25 to help students expand vocabulary.

Common Core State Standards

Literature 10. By the end of the year, read and comprehend literature, including stories, dramas, and poetry, at the high end of the grades 2–3 text complexity band independently and proficiently. **Foundational Skills 3.** Know and apply grade-level phonics and word analysis skills in decoding words. **Foundational Skills 3.a.** Identify and know the meaning of the most common prefixes and derivational suffixes. **Foundational Skills 3.b.** Decode words with common Latin suffixes. **Foundational Skills 3.d.** Read grade-appropriate irregularly spelled words.

Word Analysis

Suffixes -y, -ish, -hood, -ment

MODEL WORD SORTING Write -y, -ish, -hood, and -ment as headings in a four-column chart. Now we are going to sort words. We'll put words with the suffix -y in the first column. Words with the suffix -ish will go in the second column. Words with the suffix -hood will go in the third column. Words with the suffix -ment will go in the fourth column. I will start. Write *statement* and model how to read it, using the lesson on p. 322a. *Statement* is made up of the base word *state* and the suffix -ment, so I will write it in the last column. Model reading *shaky* and *excitement* in the same way.

GUIDE PRACTICE Use the practice words from the activities on p. 322a for the word sort. Point to a word. Have students read the word, identify its parts, and tell where it should be written on the chart.

> **Corrective feedback** For corrective feedback, model reading the base word and the suffix, and then putting the word parts together to read the whole word.

-y	-ish	-hood	-ment
shaky	yellowish	adulthood	statement
healthy	brownish	falsehood	excitement
stormy			payment
thirsty			entertainment
frosty			

Fluent Word Reading

MODEL Write *basement*. I see the base word *base* and the suffix -ment. When I put the parts together I can read the word *basement*. How does the suffix change the meaning of the base word? (The suffix changes the word to a place. A *basement* is the lowest part of a building.)

GUIDE PRACTICE Write the words below. Look for word parts you know. When I point to a word, we'll read it together. Allow one second per word par previewing time for the first reading.

development	contentment	environment	stylish
guilty	livelihood	assignment	knighthood

ON THEIR OWN Have students read the list above three or four times, until they can read one word per second.

Decodable Passage 25B

If students need help, then...

Read *A Stormy Day*

READ WORDS IN ISOLATION Have students turn to p. 117 in *Decodable Practice Readers 3.2* and find the first list of words. Each word in this list has a suffix. Be sure that students correctly pronounce the suffix in each word.

Next, have students read the high-frequency words.

PREVIEW Have students read the title and preview the story. Tell them that they will read words that include the suffixes -*y*, -*ish*, -*hood*, and -*ment*.

READ WORDS IN CONTEXT Chorally read the story along with students. Have students identify words in the story that include the suffixes -*y*, -*ish*, -*hood*, and -*ment*. Make sure that students are monitoring their accuracy when they decode words.

Team Talk Pair students and have them take turns reading the story aloud to each other. Monitor students as they read to check for proper pronunciation and appropriate pacing.

Access for All

Ⓐ **Advanced**

Have students come up with lists of other words that have the suffixes -*y*, -*ish*, -*hood,* and -*ment*. Have them choose two or three words and write sentences that use the words.

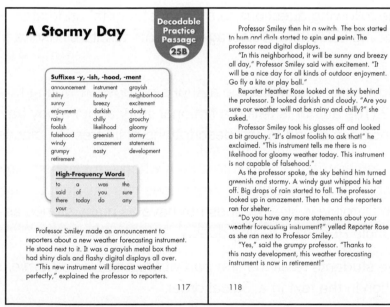

Decodable Practice Passage 25B

© Common Core State Standards

Literature 1. Ask and answer questions to demonstrate understanding of a text, referring explicitly to the text as the basis for the answers. **Literature 2.** Recount stories, including fables, folktales, and myths from diverse cultures; determine the central message, lesson, or moral and explain how it is conveyed through key details in the text. **Literature 3.** Describe characters in a story (e.g., their traits, motivations, or feelings) and explain how their actions contribute to the sequence of events.

Strategy Response Log

Have students revisit p. 31 in the *Reader's and Writer's Notebook* to add additional information about historical fiction.

Text-Based Comprehension

Check Understanding

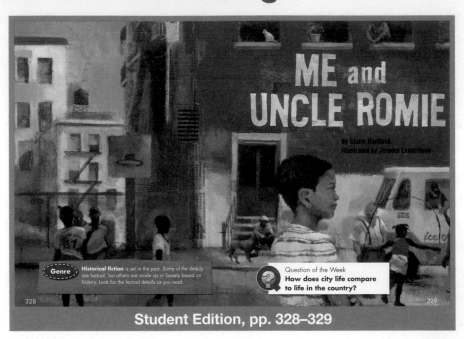

Student Edition, pp. 328–329

If... you chose to read *Me and Uncle Romie* in two parts,
then... use the following questions to monitor students' understanding of pp. 328–339 of the selection. Encourage students to cite evidence from the text.

ANALYSIS How can you tell that the author's purpose in writing this story is to entertain? (The author is telling a fictional story about a boy having an adventure. It includes dialogue and descriptions of interesting places.)

INFERENCE James tries to catch his breath when Aunt Nanette takes him u five flights of stairs to her apartment. What does this say about what James's house in North Carolina is like? (It does not have as many stories as Aunt Nanette and Uncle Romie's building does.)

RETELL Have students retell the first part of *Me and Uncle Romie,* summarizing information in the text in a logical order.

> **Corrective feedback**
> **If...** students leave out important details,
> **then...** have students look back through the illustrations in the selection.

READ Use the **Access Text** and **Close Reading** notes to finish reading *Me and Uncle Romie.*

eStreet Interactive
www.ReadingStreet.com

Pearson eText
- Student Edition

AudioText CD

Teacher Resources
- Reader's and Writer's Notebook

f... you followed the Read for Understanding routine below,
hen... ask students to retell the selection before you reread *Me and Uncle Romie.*

RETELL Have students retell *Me and Uncle Romie,* summarizing information n the text in a logical order.

Corrective feedback	**If...** the students leave out important details, **then...** have students look back through the illustrations in the selection.

EAD Return to p. 330–331 and use the **2nd Read/Close Reading** notes to eread *Me and Uncle Romie.*

Read Main Selection

Routine Read for Understanding

eepen understanding by reading the selection multiple times.
- **First Read**—If students need support, then use the **Access Text** notes to help them clarify understanding.
- **Second Read**—Use the **Close Reading** notes to help students draw knowledge from the text.

ELL

Check Retelling To support retelling, review the multilingual summary for *Me and Uncle Romie* with the appropriate Retelling Cards to scaffold understanding.

Day 3 SMALL GROUP TIME • Differentiate Close Reading, p. SG•65

OL On-Level	SI Strategic Intervention	A Advanced
Reread to Develop Vocabulary **Read** *Me and Uncle Romie*	• **Reread** to Develop Vocabulary • **Read** *Me and Uncle Romie*	• **Reread** to Extend Vocabulary • **Read** *Me and Uncle Romie* • **Investigate** Inquiry Project

ELL

If... students need more scaffolding and practice with the **Main Selection,**
then... use the activities on p. DI•122 in the Teacher Resources section on SuccessNet.

Access Text © If students need help, then...

⟲ BACKGROUND KNOWLEDGE

Why do you think James feels his birthday will be ruined? (He is probably worried that spending his birthday with his uncle won't be special.)

Think Aloud **MODEL** I think about how I feel about birthdays and how I would feel if I were James. James probably thinks that his uncle won't celebrate his birthday in the same way that his mother does, which will be different and, because of this, not as special. He probably thinks there won't be a lemon cake or a baseball game.

On rainy days I wrote postcards and helped out around the apartment. I told Aunt Nanette about the things I liked to do back home—about baseball games, train-watching, m birthday. She told me about the special Caribbean lemon an mango cake she was going to make.

My uncle Romie stayed hidden away in his studio. But I wasn't worried anymore. Aunt Nanette would make my birthday special.

4 . . . 3 . . . 2 . . . 1 . . . My birthday was almost here! And then Aunt Nanette got a phone call.

"An old aunt has died, James. I have to go away for her funeral. But don't you worry. Uncle Romie will spend your birthday with you. It'll be just fine."

Close Reading ©

EVALUATION • TEXT EVIDENCE

What new event in the story makes James think his birthday is ruined? Cite evidence from the text. (On p. 340, we learn that Aunt Nanette has to leave because her aunt died. James thought Aunt Nanette would make his birthday special. But now he has to spend it with Uncle Romie. James thinks Uncle Romie doesn't know about cakes or birthdays, which will ruin his birthday.)

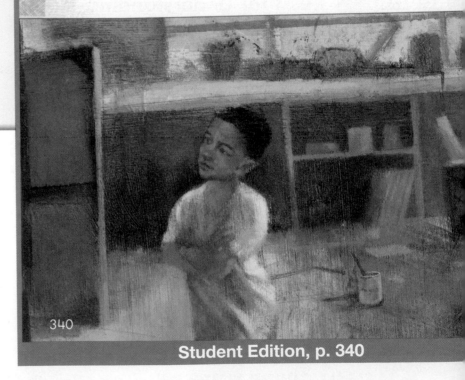

340

Student Edition, p. 340

ON THEIR OWN Have students reread the section to find other ways they can relate to James's experiences.

That night Aunt Nanette kissed me good-bye. I knew it would not be fine at all. Uncle Romie didn't know about cakes or baseball games or anything except his dumb old paintings. My birthday was ruined.

When the sky turned black, I tucked myself into bed. I missed Mama and Daddy so much. I listened to the birds on the rooftop—their songs continued into the night.

The next morning everything was quiet. I crept out of bed and into the hall. For the first time the door to Uncle Romie's studio stood wide open. What a glorious mess! There were paints and scraps all over the floor, and around the edges were huge paintings with all sorts of pieces pasted together.

341

Student Edition, p. 341

INFERENCE Why does Uncle Romie most likely stay inside his studio with the door closed while James is visiting? (Uncle Romie is busy working in his studio. He might not want to be distracted.)

 Common Core State Standards

Literature 1. Ask and answer questions to demonstrate understanding of a text, referring explicitly to the text as the basis for the answers. **Literature 3.** Describe characters in a story (e.g., their traits, motivations, or feelings) and explain how their actions contribute to the sequence of events. **Literature 10.** By the end of the year, read and comprehend literature, including stories, dramas, and poetry, at the high end of the grades 2–3 text complexity band independently and proficiently.

 Connect to Social Studies

Birthday Traditions Children around the world celebrate their birthdays in different ways. Chinese children pay their respects to their parents and receive money as a gift. Children from England find money mixed in with the birthday cake. Children from India wear colorful clothes and pass out candy to their classmates.

Access for All

SI Strategic Intervention
Point out "4 ... 3 ... 2 ...1 ..." in the text and help students understand it indicates four days passing. Have students tell other ways the author could have conveyed this information to the reader.

Background Knowledge Before students read p. 341, help them complete a concept map about art supplies. Remind them that Uncle Romie is an artist but that James has never seen Uncle Romie's art studio. Let students add to the map as they read the page and look at the illustration.

Access Text  If students need help, then...

AUTHOR'S PURPOSE Have students reread the first paragraph on p. 342. What is the author trying to say about Harlem? (She is trying to say that Harlem is alive with activity.)

(Think Aloud) MODEL I try to picture what James sees in Uncle Romie's paintings. The images communicate all of the activity on the streets of Harlem. I think the author is trying to help us appreciate the excitement of Harlem.

I saw saxophones, birds, fire escapes, and brown faces. *It's Harlem,* I thought. *The people, the music, the rooftops, and the stoops.* Looking at Uncle Romie's paintings, I could *feel* Harlem—its beat and bounce.

Then there was one that was different. Smaller houses, flowers, and trains. "That's home!" I shouted.

"Yep," Uncle Romie said, smiling, from the doorway. "That's the Carolina I remember."

342

Student Edition, p. 342

Close Reading

ANALYSIS • TEXT EVIDENCE How is James discovering he is like his uncle? Use evidence from the text to support your answer. (When James and his uncle talk about North Carolina, they find they both have similar memories and a love of pepper jelly.)

Common Core State Standards

Literature 1. Ask and answer questions to demonstrate understanding of a text, referring explicitly to the text as the basis for the answers. **Literature 3.** Describe characters in a story (e.g., their traits, motivations, or feelings) and explain how their actions contribute to the sequence of events. **Literature 6.** Distinguish their own point of view from that of the narrator or those of the characters. **Literature 10.** By the end of the year, read and comprehend literature, including stories, dramas, and poetry, at the high end of the grades 2–3 text complexity band independently and proficiently.

ON THEIR OWN Have students explain why the author has Uncle Romie say *Mmm* on p. 343.

"Mama says you visited your grandparents there most every summer when you were a kid," I said.

"I sure did, James. *Mmm.* Now that's the place for pepper jelly. Smeared thick on biscuits. And when Grandma wasn't looking . . . I'd sneak some on a spoon."

"Daddy and I do that too!" I told him.

We laughed together, then walked to the kitchen for a breakfast feast—eggs, bacon, grits, and biscuits.

"James, you've got me remembering the pepper jelly lady. People used to line up down the block to buy her preserves."

"Could you put someone like that in one of your paintings?" I asked.

343

Student Edition, p. 343

Access for All

SI Strategic Intervention

Review with students how to use context clues around unfamiliar words, such as *feast* and *smeared,* to figure out the meanings. Have students use the definition in place of the word in the sentence to see if it makes sense.

REREAD CHALLENGING TEXT Have students reread p. 343 to clarify the people who James and Uncle Romie are talking about. The text mentions grandparents, a kid, Grandma, Daddy, and the pepper jelly lady. Discuss with students who these people are.

Author's Purpose Have partners read James and Uncle Romie's dialogue aloud with accuracy. Have them explain why informal dialogue shows that the author's purpose is to entertain.

Me and Uncle Romie **343a**

Access Text © If students need help, then...

Review **DRAW CONCLUSIONS** Why did James tear into the birthday packages from home?

(Think Aloud) **MODEL** I think about birthdays and other occasions when people receive gifts. If someone is excited to see what's inside a package, he or she will usually quickly rip off the paper. What does it mean that James "tore into the packages"? (He ripped off the packaging with excitement so that he could immediately see the gifts he got.)

Close Reading ©

SYNTHESIS What do James and Uncle Romie have in common? How does having something in common with someone affect how you feel about that person? (Uncle Romie lived in North Carolina and used to sneak pepper jelly and watch the trains like James does. He also knows about baseball. People who have something in common can understand each other, usually are friends, and can talk about their common experiences. Uncle Romie understands James and can make his birthday special.)

"I guess I could." Uncle Romie nodded. "Yes, that's a memory just right for sharing. What a good idea, James. Now let's get this birthday going!"

He brought out two presents from home. I tore into the packages while he got down the pepper jelly and two huge spoons. Mama and Daddy had picked out just what I wanted—a special case for my baseball cards, and a model train for me to build.

"Pretty cool," said Uncle Romie. "I used to watch the trains down in North Carolina, you know."

How funny to picture big Uncle Romie lying on his belly!

"B. J. and me, we have contests to see who can hear the trains first."

"Hey, I did that too. You know, it's a funny thing, James. People live in all sorts of different places and families. But the things we care about are pretty much the same. Like favorite foods, special songs, games, stories . . . and like birthdays." Uncle Romie held up two tickets to a baseball game!

It turns out Uncle Romie knows all about baseball— he was even a star pitcher in college. We got our mitts and set off for the game.

Way up in the bleachers, we shared a bag of peanuts, cracking the shells with our teeth and keeping our mitts ready in case a home run ball came our way. That didn't happen—but we sure had fun.

344

Student Edition, p. 344

DEVELOP VOCABULARY Have students reread the seventh paragraph on p. 344. What does *pitcher* mean? What does it mean that Uncle Romie was a "star pitcher"?

Student Edition, p. 345

INFERENCE • TEXT EVIDENCE Why did Uncle Romie get out two spoons with the jelly? (Uncle Romie and James will eat the jelly with spoons like they talked about on p. 343.)

Common Core State Standards

Literature 1. Ask and answer questions to demonstrate understanding of a text, referring explicitly to the text as the basis for the answers. **Literature 3.** Describe characters in a story (e.g., their traits, motivations, or feelings) and explain how their actions contribute to the sequence of events. **Literature 10.** By the end of the year, read and comprehend literature, including stories, dramas, and poetry, at the high end of the grades 2–3 text complexity band independently and proficiently.

Access for All

A Advanced

As students read the story, have them complete a Venn diagram that compares and contrasts James and Uncle Romie. Let them use their diagrams to discuss how the two became friends.

Sequence Have pairs of students draw a comic strip that depicts the story events on pp. 341–345. Help students differentiate between the characters' memories and the events in the story.

Me and Uncle Romie **345a**

1ST READ

Access Text © If students need help, then...

🎯 AUTHOR'S PURPOSE Have students explain why the author uses conversations to tell about Uncle Romie's paintings. (It is a way to explain what they look like without showing pictures of them and without lengthy descriptions of them.)

(Think Aloud) **MODEL** What does the text tell you about Uncle Romie's paintings? ("Remember our first train ride from Chicago to New York" tells that the painting is of a train. "That guitar-playing man reminds me of my Uncle Joe" tells that the painting is of a man playing a guitar.)

2ND READ

Close Reading ©

ANALYSIS How can context clues help you figure out the meaning of the word *conversations* at the bottom of page 346? (The text at the top of p. 347 tells what people are saying and paragraph 3 says "strangers talking." This helps me understand that *conversations* means "instances when people are talking to each other.")

Aunt Nanette came home that night. She lit the candles, and we all shared my Caribbean birthday cake.

After that, Uncle Romie had to work a lot again. But at the end of each day he let me sit with him in his studio and talk. Daddy was right. Uncle Romie is a good man.

The day of the big art show finally came. I watched the people laughing and talking, walking slowly around the room from painting to painting. I walked around myself, listening to their conversations.

346

Student Edition, p. 346

ON THEIR OWN Have students explain why the author mentions that Uncle Romie's paintings remind people of special things in their lives.

"Remember our first train ride from Chicago to New York?" one lady asked her husband.

"That guitar-playing man reminds me of my Uncle Joe," said another.

All these strangers talking to each other about their families and friends and special times, and all because of how my uncle Romie's paintings reminded them of these things.

Later that night Daddy called. I had a brand-new brother and sister. Daddy said they were both bald and made a lot of noise. But he sounded happy and said how they all missed me.

This time Aunt Nanette and Uncle Romie took me to the train station.

347

INFERENCE • TEXT EVIDENCE Do you think Uncle Romie's art show was successful? Use facts from the text to support your answer. (I think it was successful because the text says people were laughing and talking as they slowly looked at the paintings. The comments people made about the paintings were all positive.)

Common Core State Standards

Literature 1. Ask and answer questions to demonstrate understanding of a text, referring explicitly to the text as the basis for the answers. **Literature 4.** Determine the meaning of words and phrases as they are used in a text, distinguishing literal from nonliteral language. **Literature 10.** By the end of the year, read and comprehend literature, including stories, dramas, and poetry, at the high end of the grades 2–3 text complexity band independently and proficiently. **Language 4.a.** Use sentence-level context as a clue to the meaning of a word or phrase.

Access for All

 Strategic Intervention

Have students use a graphic organizer to list events, in order, as they occur in the story. Let them use organizers to retell the story in their own words.

Background Knowledge Have students tell if they have ever seen art in a museum or art show. Encourage them to share what their experiences were like. Have them describe their favorite art piece that was on display.

Me and Uncle Romie **347a**

1ST READ

Access Text © If students need help, then...

◎ HOMONYMS Have students use context clues to determine the meaning of *streak* as it is used in the last sentence on p. 348.

(Think Aloud) MODEL A *streak* can be "a long, thin mark," or "a short period" such as a *streak* of bad luck. *Streak* can also mean "to move very fast." When I substitute these definitions in the sentence, "to move very fast" seems to be what the author intended.

ON THEIR OWN Have students write a sentence for each meaning of *streak.*

CROSS-TEXT EVALUATION
Use a Strategy to Self-Check How did "New York City" on page 325 help you understand this selection?

"Here's a late birthday present for you, James," Uncle Romie said, holding out a package. "Open it on the train, wh don't you. It'll help pass the time on the long ride home."

I waved out the window to Uncle Romie and Aunt Nanette until I couldn't see them anymore. Then I ripped off the wrappings!

And there was my summer in New York. Bright sky in one corner, city lights at night in another. Tall buildings. Baseball ticket stubs. The label from the pepper-jelly jar. And trains. One going toward the skyscrapers. Another going away.

Back home, I lay in the soft North Carolina grass. It was the first of September, almost Uncle Romie's birthday. I watched the birds streak across the sky.

348

Student Edition, p. 348

2ND READ

Close Reading ©

ANALYSIS Use context clues to tell the meaning of the homonym *like* in paragraph 1 on page 349. (I know that James is back from his summer in New York, and he is thinking that the birds are also back. This tells how James and the birds are similar. The meaning of *like* is "the same or similar.")

SYNTHESIS What is the theme, or big idea, of this story? (The theme of the story is that even though people come from different places and backgrounds, they care about the same things like favorite foods, family, birthdays, and special times.)

SYNTHESIS • TEXT EVIDENCE Using what you learned in this selection, tell how city life is different from country life. Have students cite examples from the text to support their responses.

CHECK PREDICTIONS Have students return to the predictions they made earlier and confirm whether they were accurate.

Rooftop birds, I thought. *Back home from their summer in New York, just like me.* Watching them, I could still feel the city's beat inside my head.

A feather drifted down from the sky. In the garden tiger lilies bent in the wind. *Uncle Romie's favorite flowers.* I yanked off a few blossoms. And then I was off on a treasure hunt, collecting things that reminded me of Uncle Romie.

I painted and pasted them together on a big piece of cardboard. Right in the middle I put the train schedule. And at the top I wrote:

349

Student Edition, p. 349

Common Core State Standards

Literature 1. Ask and answer questions to demonstrate understanding of a text, referring explicitly to the text as the basis for the answers. **Literature 2.** Recount stories, including fables, folktales, and myths from diverse cultures; determine the central message, lesson, or moral and explain how it is conveyed through key details in the text. **Literature 10.** By the end of the year, read and comprehend literature, including stories, dramas, and poetry, at the high end of the grades 2–3 text complexity band independently and proficiently. **Language 4.a.** Use sentence-level context as a clue to the meaning of a word or phrase. **Also Language 5.c., 6.**

Access for All

 Strategic Intervention

Have students find examples of italicized text throughout the story. Have them identify what the italics show. Have them copy the passages that show thought and punctuate them with quotation marks.

 Advanced

Have students write an additional page to the story that shows what happens after Uncle Romie's birthday or how Uncle Romie reacts to James's present.

Idioms Point out paragraph 1 on p. 348 and explain to students that "pass the time" means "to do something to keep busy when waiting." If I look at a magazine in a doctor's waiting room, am I doing it to pass the time? What might you do to pass the time while waiting at a bus stop?

Me and Uncle Romie **349a**

Common Core State Standards
Literature 1. Ask and answer questions to demonstrate understanding of a text, referring explicitly to the text as the basis for the answers. Also Literature 2., Writing 8.

Envision It! Retell

READING STREET ONLINE
STORY SORT
www.ReadingStreet.com

350

Think Critically

1. Compare and contrast North Carolina and New York City back in the 1920s. How are these places alike and different from where you live now? **Text to World**

2. Is this story written in first or third person? Why do you think the author wrote from this point of view?
Think Like an Author

3. Read "Meet the Author" on page 351. Why did the author write this story? Why do you think the author chose to write this selection as historical fiction and not as a biography like *Rocks in His Head*? Explain your answer with evidence from the text.
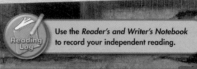 **Author's Purpose**

4. What did you know about New York City or Harlem before you read the story? How did your knowledge help you as you read? 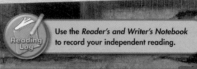 **Background Knowledge**

5. **Look Back and Write** Look back at the adventures James had in New York City. Now write about why you would or would not like to visit Uncle Romie in Harlem. Provide evidence to support your answer.
Key Ideas and Details • Text Evidence

Meet the Author and the Illustrator

Claire Hartfield and Jerome Lagarrigue

Claire Hartfield began taking dance lessons when she was five. Dance is her way of telling stories. In *Me and Uncle Romie*, she wanted to show how an artist can use art to tell stories. Although *Me and Uncle Romie* is fiction, it is based on the life of collage artist Romare Bearden.

Today, Ms. Hartfield is a lawyer in Chicago.

Jerome Lagarrigue grew up in Paris, France, in a family of artists. His art has appeared in magazines, and he has illustrated several picture books. Mr. Lagarrigue teaches drawing and painting in New York City. For *Me and Uncle Romie*, he used some elements of collage in his paintings—like Romare Bearden.

Read some books about great art projects.

Loo-Loo, Boo, and Art You Can Do by Denis Roche

Recycled Crafts Box by Laura C. Martin

 Use the *Reader's and Writer's Notebook* to record your independent reading.

351

Student Edition, pp. 350–351

Common Core State Standards

Literature 1. Ask and answer questions to demonstrate understanding of a text, referring explicitly to the text as the basis for the answers. **Also Literature 2., Writing 1., Speaking/Listening 2.**

Bridge to Common Core

RANGE OF READING AND LEVEL OF TEXT COMPLEXITY

To increase students' capacity for reading and comprehending complex texts independently and proficiently, have them read other historical fiction selections about different cultures. After students read closely for a sustained period of time, they should record their reading in their Reading Logs.

Think Critically

1. **TEXT TO WORLD** In the 1920s, North Carolina was mostly rural and Ne York City was a big city with skyscrapers. Answers will vary for the secon part of the question.

2. **THINK LIKE AN AUTHOR** The story is written in the first person. The author wanted the reader to see the story from James's viewpoint.

3. 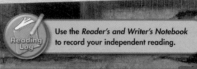**AUTHOR'S PURPOSE** She wrote the story to show how an artist car use art to tell stories. The genre allowed the author to include facts and made-up descriptions to show what life in New York was like back then a seen through a young boy's eyes.

4. 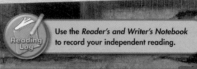**BACKGROUND KNOWLEDGE** I knew that New York City is a big cit This helped me because I expected James to find it very different from North Carolina.

5. **LOOK BACK AND WRITE • TEXT EVIDENCE** To build writing fluency assign a 10–15 minute time limit.

Scoring Rubric Look Back and Write

TOP-SCORE RESPONSE A top score response uses details to tell why students would or would not like to visit Uncle Romie.

A top-score response should include:

• positive or negative descriptions about New York City and the things people can do there

• positive or negative descriptions about art and art exhibits

• positive or negative aspects of leaving home

• solid reasons that support students' opinions

Retell

Have students work in pairs to retell the selection, using the retelling strip in the Student Edition or the Story Sort as prompts. Monitor students' retellings.

Scoring Rubric Narrative Retelling

	4	3	2	1
Connections	Makes connections and generalizes beyond the text	Makes connections to other events, stories, or experiences	Makes a limited connection to another event, story, or experience	Makes no connection to another event, story, or experience
Author's Purpose	Elaborates on author's purpose	Tells author's purpose with some clarity	Makes some connection to author's purpose	Makes no connection to author's purpose
Characters	Describes the main character(s) and any character development	Identifies the main character(s) and gives some information about them	Inaccurately identifies some characters or gives little information about them	Inaccurately identifies the characters or gives no information about them
Setting	Describes the time and location	Identifies the time and location	Omits details of time or location	Is unable to identify time or location
Plot	Describes the problem, goal, events, and ending using rich detail	Tells the problem, goal, events, and ending with some errors that do not affect meaning	Tells parts of the problem, goal, events, and ending with gaps that affect meaning	Retelling has no sense of story

MONITOR PROGRESS Check Retelling

If... students have difficulty retelling,

then... use the Retelling Cards/Story Sort to scaffold their retellings.

Plan to Assess Retelling

☐ **Week 1** Strategic Intervention
☐ **Week 2** Advanced
☐ **Week 3** Strategic Intervention
☐ **Week 4** On-Level
☑ **This week assess any students you have not yet checked during this unit.**

Meet the Author and the Illustrator

Have students read about the author Claire Hartfield and illustrator Jerome Lagarrigue on p. 351. Ask them why they think Ms. Hartfield chose to base the story on Romare Bearden's life and why Mr. Lagarrigue used collage in some of his paintings.

Read Independently

Have students enter their independent reading into their Reading Logs.

 **Common Core State Standards**

Informational Text 5. Use text features and search tools (e.g., key words, sidebars, hyperlinks) to locate information relevant to a given topic efficiently. **Foundational Skills 4.** Read with sufficient accuracy and fluency to support comprehension. **Foundational Skills 4.b.** Read on-level prose and poetry orally with accuracy, appropriate rate, and expression on successive readings. **Also Writing 8.**

Fluency

Appropriate Phrasing

MODEL FLUENT READING Have students turn to p. 336 of *Me and Uncle Romie*. Have students follow along as you read the page. Point out how dashes and other punctuation marks guide the way you phrase the sentences.

GUIDE PRACTICE Have students follow along as you read the page again. Then have them reread the pages with partners until they can read them with appropriate phrasing and no mistakes. Continue in this way with p. 337.

| Corrective feedback | **If...** students are having difficulty reading with appropriate phrasing, **then...** prompt them as follows:
- Where can we break up this sentence? Which words are related?
- Read the sentence again. Pause after each group of words.
- Tell me the sentence. Now read it with pauses after each group of words. |

Reread for Fluency

Routine Paired Reading

1. **Select a Passage** For *Me and Uncle Romie*, use p. 343.

2. **Reading 1** Students read the entire page, switching readers at the end of each paragraph.

3. **Reading 2** Partners reread the page. This time the other student begins.

4. **Reread** For optimal fluency, have partners continue to read three or four times.

5. **Corrective Feedback** Listen as students read. Provide feedback and encourage students to pause briefly at the ends of phrases.

Routine Flip Chart

Research and Study Skills

Electronic Text

TEACH Ask students if they have ever used the Internet to find the answer to a question. If possible, display a search engine page on your classroom computer. Review these terms and concepts:

Search engines can help you locate information on the Internet.

A search engine links you to Web sites that may be related to your topic.

At the top of the search engine is a box to type in keywords. Search engines locate these keywords on various Web sites and display those sites on the screen.

Have groups of students discuss keywords they might use to research a given topic.

GUIDE PRACTICE Discuss these questions:

Why should you try different search engines? (Each search engine is linked to different Web sites, so different search engines give different results.)

How can you narrow your search? (Possible response: I could add more keywords.)

Have groups use different search engines to answer the same question. Have them compare the keywords they chose and see their different results.

ON THEIR OWN Have students review and complete p. 368 of the *Reader's and Writer's Notebook*.

eStreet Interactive
www.ReadingStreet.com

Teacher Resources
• Reader's and Writer's Notebook

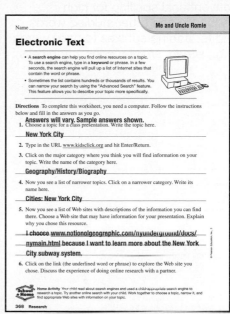

Reader's and Writer's Notebook, p. 368

Professional Development: What ELL Experts Say About Paired Reading "When students participate in shared reading and echo the spoken text or read the words aloud chorally, anxiety about pronunciation or decoding errors is reduced."
—Dr. Georgia Earnest García

© Common Core State Standards

Writing 8. Recall information from experiences or gather information from print and digital sources; take brief notes on sources and sort evidence into provided categories. **Foundational Skills 3.a.** Identify and know the meaning of the most common prefixes and derivational suffixes. **Foundational Skills 3.b.** Decode words with common Latin suffixes. **Language 1.h.** Use coordinating and subordinating conjunctions. **Language 2.e.** Use conventional spelling for high-frequency and other studied words and for adding suffixes to base words (e.g., *sitting, smiled, cries, happiness*).

Research and Inquiry

Step 3 Analyze Information

TEACH Tell students that today they will analyze their research findings. Hav students sort the information from their notes into an outline. This outline should include categories such as main ideas and supporting details. Remind students that an outline is a plan for writing. Then explain that students may have to improve the focus of their research by interviewing experts.

Think Aloud **MODEL** While scanning a Web site, I noticed that there are many sports and games played in both the city and the country. I talked to youth soccer league coach, and she said that even though soccer is popular in cities, there are some sports that are more popular there. I decided to focus on if any sports are more popular in one place or the other. Now my inquiry question is *Which sports and games are most popular in the city and which are most popular in the country?*

GUIDE PRACTICE Have students analyze their findings. They may need to refocus their inquiry question to better fit the information they found. Remind students that if they have difficulty improving their focus, they can ask a reference librarian or the local expert for guidance.

ON THEIR OWN Have partners share their outlines and summarize the infor mation they have gathered. Partners should discuss whether they need to co lect additional information to answer the inquiry question.

Conventions

Conjunctions

REVIEW Remind students that this week they learned about conjunctions. Introduce the conjunction *therefore* and review *and, or, but,* and *because*.

Conjunctions are words that connect words or groups of words.

To show a result of something, use *therefore*.

To add information, use *and*.

To show a choice, use *or*.

To show a difference, use *but*.

To show a reason, use *because*.

Because and *therefore* can also be used as transitions.

CONNECT TO ORAL LANGUAGE Have the class complete these sentence frames orally.

> After school, I _____ and _____.
>
> My mother said _____, therefore I will _____.

ON THEIR OWN For additional support, use *Let's Practice It!* page 334 on the *Teacher Resources DVD-ROM.*

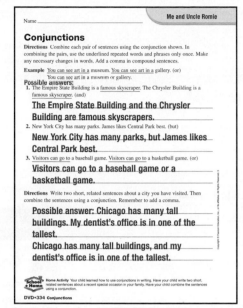

Let's Practice It! TR DVD•334

Spelling

Suffixes -y, -ish, -hood, -ment

FREQUENTLY MISSPELLED WORDS The words *different* and *very* are words that students often misspell. Think carefully before you write these words. Have students practice writing the words by writing sentences using each word.

1. I want to watch a _____ television show. (different)

2. This television show is _____ boring. (very)

3. I like birds _____ much. (very)

ON THEIR OWN For additional support, use *Reader's and Writer's Notebook,* p. 369.

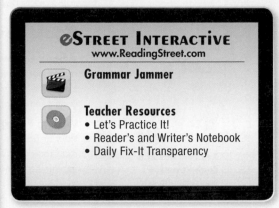

Access for All

SI Strategic Intervention

Create flashcards for *therefore, because, and, but,* and *or.* Write *result, reason, information, choice,* and *difference* on the back of the cards. Have partners practice identifying the purposes of the conjunctions by using the flashcards.

Daily Fix-It

5. My mom spent her child hood in New York city. *(childhood; City)*

6. She say it is busiest there than in North Carolina. *(says; busier)*

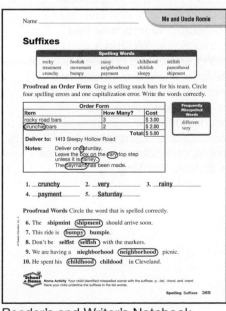

Reader's and Writer's Notebook, p. 369

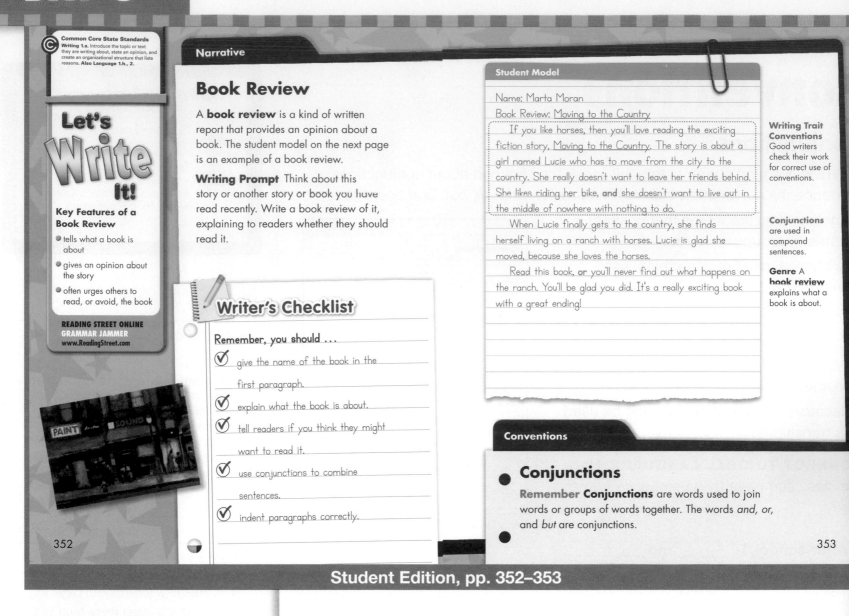

Let's Write It!

Key Features of a Book Review

- tells what a book is about
- gives an opinion about the story
- often urges others to read, or avoid, the book

READING STREET ONLINE
GRAMMAR JAMMER
www.ReadingStreet.com

352

Narrative

Book Review

A **book review** is a kind of written report that provides an opinion about a book. The student model on the next page is an example of a book review.

Writing Prompt Think about this story or another story or book you have read recently. Write a book review of it, explaining to readers whether they should read it.

Writer's Checklist

Remember, you should . . .

☑ give the name of the book in the first paragraph.

☑ explain what the book is about.

☑ tell readers if you think they might want to read it.

☑ use conjunctions to combine sentences.

☑ indent paragraphs correctly.

Student Model

Name: Marta Moran

Book Review: Moving to the Country

    If you like horses, then you'll love reading the exciting fiction story, Moving to the Country. The story is about a girl named Lucie who has to move from the city to the country. She really doesn't want to leave her friends behind. She likes riding her bike, **and** she doesn't want to live out in the middle of nowhere with nothing to do.

    When Lucie finally gets to the country, she finds herself living on a ranch with horses. Lucie is glad she moved, because she loves the horses.

    Read this book, **or** you'll never find out what happens on the ranch. You'll be glad you did. It's a really exciting book with a great ending!

Writing Trait
Conventions Good writers check their work for correct use of conventions.

Conjunctions are used in compound sentences.

Genre A **book review** explains what a book is about.

Conventions

Conjunctions

Remember Conjunctions are words used to join words or groups of words together. The words *and, or,* and *but* are conjunctions.

353

Student Edition, pp. 352–353

Common Core State Standards

Writing 1.a. Introduce the topic or text they are writing about, state an opinion, and create an organizational structure that lists reasons. **Writing 1.c.** Use linking words and phrases (e.g., *because, therefore, since, for example*) to connect opinion and reasons. **Language 1.h.** Use coordinating and subordinating conjunctions. **Language 1.i.** Produce simple, compound, and complex sentences. **Writing 1., 1.b.**

Let's Write It!

WRITE A BOOK REVIEW Use pp. 352–353 in the Student Edition. Direct students to read the key features of a book review, which appear on p. 352. Remind students that they can refer to the information in the Writer's Checklist as they write their own book reviews.

Read the student model on p. 353. Point out the underlined title in the model and the paragraphs that explain what the book is about.

CONNECT TO CONVENTIONS Remind students that a conjunction is a word that connects words or groups of words. Point out the correct use of conjunctions in compound sentences in the model.

Writing

 Zoom in on

Book Review

Writing Trait: Conventions

DISPLAY RUBRIC Display Scoring Rubric 25 from the *Teacher Resources DVD-ROM* and go over the criteria for each trait under each score. Then, using the model in the Student Edition, choose students to explain why the model should score a 4 for one of the traits. If a student offers that the model should score below 4 for a particular trait, the student should offer support for that response. Remind students that this is the rubric that will be used to evaluate the book reviews they write.

Scoring Rubric Book Review

	4	3	2	1
Focus/Ideas	Clear, focused review with many supporting details	Most ideas in review clear and supported	Some ideas in review unclear or off-topic	Review with no clarity or development
Organization	Organized logically, no gaps; clearly presented book topic	Organized logically, few gaps; book topic presented	Organizational pattern attempted but not clear; book topic unclear	No organizational pattern evident; book topic not presented clearly
Voice	Engaging; shows writer's feelings/opinion about subject	Evident voice connecting with reader; shows writer's feelings	Weak voice; weak display of writer's feelings/opinion about subject	Flat writing with no voice; writer doesn't state his/her opinion
Word Choice	Vivid, precise word choice	Accurate word choice	Limited or repetitive word choice	Incorrect or very limited word choice
Sentences	Clear sentences of various lengths and types; correct punctuation	Sentences of a few lengths and types; mostly correct punctuation	Sentences of similar length and type; weak use of punctuation	No attempt at sentences of various lengths or types; incorrect or no punctuation
Conventions	Few, if any, errors; correct use of conjunctions	Several minor errors; mostly correct use of conjunctions	Many errors; weak use of conjunctions	Numerous errors; incorrect or no use of conjunctions

BOOK REVIEW Have students take out the review forms they worked on yesterday. If their forms are not complete, allow additional time to complete them.

WRITE You will be using your review forms to help you write the paragraphs as you develop the first draft of your book review. When you are drafting, don't worry if your review doesn't sound exactly as you want it. You will have a chance to revise it tomorrow.

Access for All

 Advanced

Challenge students to create a book review that compares two different books. Have them describe both books and tell how they are alike and different. Then have them write an opinion about which book they think is better.

Plot or Topic Help students with organizing the plot or topic of the book they have chosen to review.

Beginning Have students orally describe the plot or topic of the book. Help them make notes to use while drafting.

Intermediate Help students create a beginning-middle-end chart for the plot or a main idea and details chart for the topic of the book they will review.

Advanced Have students create a main idea and details chart or a beginning-middle-end chart for the plot or topic of the book they plan to review.

Me and Uncle Romie **353a**

Common Core State Standards

Writing 1.a. Introduce the topic or text they are writing about, state an opinion, and create an organizational structure that lists reasons. **Writing 1.b.** Provide reasons that support the opinion. **Language 2.** Demonstrate command of the conventions of standard English capitalization, punctuation, and spelling when writing. **Language 2.a.** Capitalize appropriate words in titles. **Also Writing 1.**

Bridge to Common Core

RANGE OF WRITING

As students progress through the writing project, they routinely write for a range of tasks, purposes, and audiences. In this lesson, they learn how to organize a draft, making sure all elements of a book review are included.

Writing

Book Review

Mini-Lesson Organizing Your Draft

■ **Introduce** Explain to students that organizing a review means making sure to include all of the elements of a book review and demonstrating understanding of the book. Display the Drafting Tips for students. Remind them that the focus of drafting is to record their ideas using organized paragraphs. Then display Writing Transparency 25A and explain the process of drafting.

Name: Rita Pein
Book Review: How Plants Grow

I think readers will really enjoy How Plants Grow by Bobbie Kalman. The book tells about the amazing process that happens when plants grow from seeds. Readers learn that each part of a plant has a special job. For example, the leaves are responsible for making food. The stems carry water and minerals to the plant.

The subject, illustrations, and photos are very interesting. I enjoyed learning about plants. There are neat illustrations. The book also includes many photographs.

How Plants Grow showed me that Plants are carried in many different ways Some seeds are carried through water, such as rivers but lakes. Other seeds fly thrugh the wind. Sometimes animals can carry seeds, too.

I think everyone should read this book therefore plants are such an important parts of human life.

Unit 5 Me and Uncle Romie   Writing: Model **25A**

Writing Transparency 25A, TR DVD

Drafting Tips

✔ To get started, study your review form.

✔ Read aloud parts of your review. Ask yourself: *Is my information in the review organized so that the writing makes sense?*

✔ Don't worry about grammar or mechanics while drafting. You'll concentrate on them during the revising stage.

Think Aloud **MODEL** I'm going to write the first draft of a book review about How Plants Grow. When I draft, I develop my ideas. I don't worry about revising or proofreading because those tasks will come later will refer to my book review graphic organizer to make sure that I include a the elements I need to generate a complete review.

Have students use the drafting tips as a guide as they draft their book reviews. Remind them to check their work carefully for presentation of ideas, organize their ideas into coherent paragraphs, and make sure to underline the book title.

Writing Trait: Conventions

Review the importance of conventions in writing. Good writers follow the rules for writing. Remind students that the important words in book titles begin with capital letters and that they should check the book to be sure to use appropriate capital letters when they write the title. Also remind them to underline the title to identify it as a title. Point out the book review title <u>How Plants Grow</u> and note that the three words in the title begin with capital letters.

Routine   Quick Write for Fluency   Team Talk

. **Talk** Pairs talk about two details they want to include in their book reviews.

. **Write** Each student writes two sentences about these details.

. **Share** Partners read and check each other's writing for the correct use of conjunctions.

Routines Flip Chart

eStreet Interactive
www.ReadingStreet.com

Teacher Resources
• Writing Transparency

Access for All

SI Strategic Intervention

Have groups of two or three students work together to confirm organization in their drafts. Each student in the group should ask the question: *Is the information in the review organized so that the writing makes sense?*

Wrap Up Your Day!

✔ **Content Knowledge** Have students discuss the differences between city and country life.

✔ **Text-Based Comprehension** How can understanding the author's purpose help you understand the story?

Preview DAY 4

Tell students that tomorrow they will read about using online reference sources.

Materials

- Student Edition
- Reader's and Writer's Notebook
- Decodable Reader

Ⓒ Common Core State Standards

Speaking/Listening 1. Engage effectively in a range of collaborative discussions (one-on-one, in groups, and teacher-led) with diverse partners on grade 3 topics and texts, building on others' ideas and expressing their own clearly. **Language 4.a.** Use sentence-level context as a clue to the meaning of a word or phrase. **Language 6.** Acquire and use accurately grade-appropriate conversational, general academic, and domain-specific words and phrases, including those that signal spatial and temporal relationships (e.g., *After dinner that night we went looking for them*).

Content Knowledge

City Life and Country Life

EXPAND THE CONCEPT Remind students of the weekly concept question, *How does city life compare to life in the country?* Have students discuss what they have learned about the differences between city life and country life.

Build Oral Language

TALK ABOUT SENTENCES AND WORDS Ask students to reread these sentences from the second paragraph of Student Edition, p. 349.

A feather drifted down from the sky. In the garden tiger lilies bent in the wind.

- What does the word *drifted* mean? (to be carried along by currents of air) What are some synonyms and antonyms for the word *drifted*? Have students turn to a partner to share. (synonyms: *floated, wandered;* antonyms: *fell quickly, fell heavily*)

- What does the word *bent* mean? (became crooked or curved) What are some synonyms and antonyms for the word *bent*? Have students turn to a partner to share. (synonyms: *curved, stooped, bowed;* antonyms: *straightened, stood*)

- Using your understanding of the words *drifted* and *bent,* how can you restate the sentences in your own words? Have student pairs share their ideas. (Possible response: *A feather floated down slowly from the sky. In the garden tiger lilies stooped in the wind.*)

- Do the two sentences make you think of a stormy day or a breezy day? Why?

Build Oral Vocabulary

Amazing Words

Robust Vocabulary Routine

1. Introduce Write the Amazing Word *bitter* on the board. Have students say it aloud with you. *James felt* bitter *when Aunt Nanette left and he found out he was going to have to spend his birthday with Uncle Romie.* Supply a student-friendly definition: *Bitter* describes something that causes sharp pain or grief.

2. Demonstrate Have students answer questions to demonstrate understanding. *How do you know James felt* bitter? (He says that his birthday is ruined.) *How do* bitter *winds feel?* (They cause sharp pain.) *Are you happy when you feel* bitter? (no)

3. Apply Have students apply their understanding. Have them name synonyms for *bitter*. (biting, sharp, unpleasant)

4. Display the Word Have students divide the word *bitter* into two chunks, and then read the word: *bit-ter.*

See p. OV•5 to teach *ramble.*

Routines Flip Chart

Amazing Words

skyscraper	hurl
taxicab	meager
scamper	gutter
scurry	bitter
vendor	ramble

Strategy Response Log

Have students rewrite the characteristics of historical fiction in their Strategy Response logs on p. 31 of the *Reader's and Writer's Notebook.* Then have them compare *Me and Uncle Romie* to another example of historical fiction they have read or know about.

ADD TO THE CONCEPT MAP Discuss the Amazing Words *gutter* and *meager.* Add these and other concept-related words to the concept map. Use the following questions to develop students' understanding of the concept.

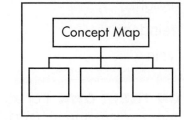

Concept Map

Gutters catch and carry off rainwater. Where have you seen *gutters*?

When do you eat *meager* amounts of food? Could this happen in the city or in the country?

ELL

Produce Oral Language Use the Day 4 instruction on ELL Poster 25 to extend and enrich language.

© Common Core State Standards

Foundational Skills 3. Know and apply grade-level phonics and word analysis skills in decoding words. **Foundational Skills 3.d.** Read grade-appropriate irregularly spelled words. **Language 6.** Acquire and use accurately grade-appropriate conversational, general academic, and domain-specific words and phrases, including those that signal spatial and temporal relationships (e.g., *After dinner that night we went looking for them*).

Name _____   **Me and Uncle Romie**

Vowel Patterns *ei, eigh*

Directions Read each word. Write the vowel sound for the underlined letters.

1. neighbor **long a**	5. ceiling **long e**
2. reindeer **long a**	6. sleigh **long a**
3. height **long i**	7. receive **long e**
4. weigh **long a**	8. weird **long e**

Directions Choose a word from the box that completes each sentence. Write it on the line.

either   neighs   deceive   receipt   weight   reins   seize

9. The guard yelled, "_____ **Seize** _____ her!"
10. Save the _____ **receipt** _____ in case you want to return the shirt.
11. Amazingly, the horse _____ **neighs** _____ to count objects.
12. The veterinarian checked the dog's _____ **weight** _____ on the scale.
13. We will meet _____ **either** _____ Kara or her mother at the school.
14. The rider held tightly to the horse's _____ **reins** _____ .
15. The child tried to _____ **deceive** _____ her parents.

Home Activity Your child identified and wrote words with the vowel patterns *ei* and *eigh*. Tell your child about a family event. Have your child identify and spell words with the vowel patterns *ei* and *eigh*.

Vowel Patterns *ei, eigh* DVD•335

Let's Practice It! TR DVD•335

Phonics

Review Vowel Patterns *ei, eigh*

REVIEW SOUND-SPELLINGS To review last week's phonics skill, write *veil* and *eight.* You studied words like these last week. What do you know about the vowel sounds in these words? (Both words have the long *a* sound.) What letters stand for the sound /ā/ in *veil*? (*ei*) In *eight*? (*eigh*) Continue in the same way for /ē/ in *ceiling* and *receive* and /ī/ in *height*.

> **Corrective feedback** | If students are unable to answer the questions about the vowel patterns, refer them to *Sound-Spelling Cards* 64, 65, and 66.

GUIDE PRACTICE Display a three-column chart. When I say a word, listen for the long vowel sound. Shake your head if the word has /ā/. Point to your knee if the word has /ē/. Point to your eye if the word has /ī/. Say the words in the following chart in random order. After students identify the vowel sound of *ei* or *eigh,* write the word in the appropriate column. Then have students read the words and ask volunteers to underline the letters that spell the long vowel sound in each word.

/ā/	/ē/	/ī/
neighbor	seize	height
weigh	deceive	eiderdown
neigh	receipt	sleight
freight	ceiling	
reindeer		
vein		

ON THEIR OWN For additional practice, use *Let's Practice It!* p. 335 on the *Teacher Resources DVD-ROM.*

Fluent Word Reading

Spiral Review

READ WORDS IN ISOLATION Display these words. Tell students that they can already decode some words on this list. Explain that they should know other words because they appear often in reading.

Have students read the list three or four times until they can read at the rate of two to three seconds per word.

Word Reading

all	watch	aunt	saw	meat
saucer	would	taught	fawns	stalking
raw	deer	paused	thought	your
ant	should	meet	two	dear

Corrective feedback

If... students have difficulty reading whole words,
then... have them use sound-by-sound blending for decodable words or chunking for words that have word parts, or have them say and spell high-frequency words.

If... students cannot read fluently at a rate of two to three seconds per word,
then... have pairs practice the list until they can read it fluently.

eSTREET INTERACTIVE
www.ReadingStreet.com

Teacher Resources
• Let's Practice It!

Interactive Sound-Spelling Cards

Access for All

SI Strategic Intervention

To assist students having difficulty with the vowel patterns *ei* and *eigh*, focus on only one vowel sound at a time. Write words with /ā/ spelled *ei* and *eigh* on separate cards. Have students sort the words by long *a* spelling and then read all the words.

Spiral Review

These activities review

• previously taught high-frequency words *watch*, *would*, *should*, *two*, *your*.
• vowel patterns for /ȯ/ spelled *a*, *au*, *aw*, *augh*, *ough*; homophones.

Fluent Word Reading Have students listen to a more fluent reader say the words. Then have listening students repeat the words.

© **Common Core State Standards**

Foundational Skills 3. Know and apply grade-level phonics and word analysis skills in decoding words. **Foundational Skills 3.b.** Decode words with common Latin suffixes. **Foundational Skills 3.d.** Read grade-appropriate irregularly spelled words. **Foundational Skills 4.** Read with sufficient accuracy and fluency to support comprehension.

Access for All

 Advanced

Have students write their own sentences using some of the decodable words found in the Monitor Progress sentences.

Fluent Word Reading

READ WORDS IN CONTEXT Display these sentences. Call on individuals to read a sentence. Then randomly point to review words and have students read them. To help you monitor word reading, high-frequency words are underlined and decodable words are italicized.

MONITOR PROGRESS Sentence Reading

We *paused* to <u>watch</u> the <u>two</u> *fawns*.
You <u>should</u> not eat *raw meat*.
Paul <u>would</u> like me to *meet* his *dear* friends.
Dad *taught* me *all* about *stalking deer*.
I *thought* I saw an *ant* on <u>your</u> *saucer*.

If... students are unable to read an underlined high-frequency word,

then... read the word for them and spell it, having them echo you.

If... students have difficulty reading an italicized decodable word,

then... guide them in using sound-by-sound blending or chunking.

Reread for Fluency

Have students reread the sentences to develop automaticity decoding words.

Routine Oral Rereading

1. **Read** Have students read all the sentences orally.

2. **Reread** To achieve optimal fluency, students should reread the sentences three or four times.

3. **Corrective Feedback** Listen as students read. Provide corrective feedback regarding their fluency and decoding.

Routines Flip Chart

Decodable Passage 25C

If students need help, then...

Read *Messy Jim*

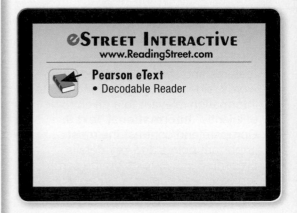

eSTREET INTERACTIVE
www.ReadingStreet.com

Pearson eText
• Decodable Reader

READ WORDS IN ISOLATION Have students turn to p. 119 in *Decodable Practice Readers* 3.2 and find the first list of words. Each word in this list has a suffix added to the base word. Be sure that students correctly pronounce the suffix in each word.

Next, have students read the high-frequency words.

PREVIEW Have students read the title and preview the story. Tell them that they will read words with the suffixes *-y*, *-ish*, *-hood,* and *-ment*.

READ WORDS IN CONTEXT Chorally read the story along with the students. Have students identify words in the story that include the suffixes *-y*, *-ish*, *-hood,* and *-ment*. Make sure that students are monitoring their accuracy when they decode words.

Team Talk Pair students and have them take turns reading the story aloud to each other. Monitor students as they read to check for proper pronunciation and appropriate pacing.

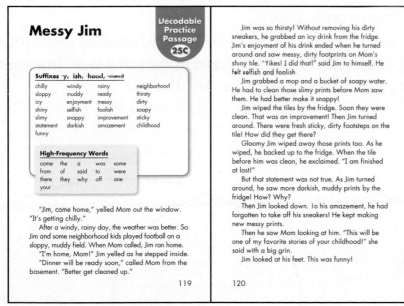

Decodable Practice Passage 25C

Suffixes

Beginning After reading, have students find pairs of words that end with the same suffix.

Intermediate Have students work in pairs to chorally reread paragraphs from the Decodable Practice Passage.

Advanced After reading the story, have students choose two or three words with the suffixes *-y*, *-ish*, *-hood,* or *-ment* and write a sentence for each word.

Me and Uncle Romie **354f**

DAY 4

 Common Core State Standards

Informational Text 5. Use text features and search tools (e.g., key words, sidebars, hyperlinks) to locate information relevant to a given topic efficiently. **Informational Text 9.** Compare and contrast the most important points and key details presented in two texts on the same topic.

Bridge to Common Core

KEY IDEAS AND DETAILS

Recognizing how online reference sources and traditional reference sources differ will lead students to research more effectively and choose the sources that best suit their needs. Understanding the Internet will lead students to Web sites and links that provide information explicitly.

21st Century Skills

Online Reference Sources

INTRODUCE Explain to students that technology is all around us. Tell them that online reference sources are one type of technology we use today. Ask students to share what they already know about online reference sources, such as what they are and when to use them.

DISCUSS REFERENCE SOURCES Discuss with students some of the reference sources they have used. What reference materials have you used to write informational articles? (encyclopedias, almanacs, and atlases) Explain: In the past, people had to go to libraries to find reference materials. They looked through the books and took notes. They could not take the reference materials home. Now you can search on the Internet and easily find reference materials.

GROUP PRACTICE Display a Venn diagram like the one below. Label the sides *Books* and *Online*. Ask the following questions:

- How are reference books and online reference materials different? (Possible responses: Reference books are on different shelves of the library, and online references are found on a computer. Some Web sites even give you different reference sources in one place. Online reference materials may be updated often, but only the newest books are up-to-date. Online materials have easy links to other sites.)

- How are reference books and online reference materials alike? (Possible responses: The information is organized in the same way. The sources look alike. They usually contain the same information.)

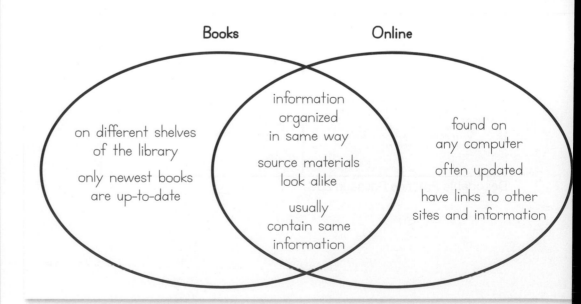

Team Talk Have students work in pairs to list the benefits of using online reference sources. Let them share their lists with the class.

READ Tell students they will now read about a student who uses online reference sources to get information. Have the class think about times when using online reference sources for this purpose might be helpful and what conventions might be necessary.

Cognates The French word *technologie*, the Italian word *tecnologia,* and the Spanish word *tecnología* may be familiar to speakers of those languages as cognates for *technology*.

Day 4 SMALL GROUP TIME • Differentiate Vocabulary, p. SG•65

OL On-Level	**SI** Strategic Intervention	**A** Advanced
Develop Language Using Amazing Words	• **Review/Discuss** Amazing Words	• **Extend** Amazing Words and Selection Vocabulary
Read "Country to City"	• **Read** "Country to City"	• **Read** "Country to City"
		• **Organize** Inquiry Project

If... students need more scaffolding and practice with the **Amazing Words,**
then... use the Routine on pp. xxxvi–xxxvii in the *ELL Handbook.*

Student Edition, pp. 354–355

Common Core State Standards

Informational Text 5. Use text features and search tools (e.g., key words, sidebars, hyperlinks) to locate information relevant to a given topic efficiently. **Informational Text 9.** Compare and contrast the most important points and key details presented in two texts on the same topic. **Informational Text 10.** By the end of the year, read and comprehend informational texts, including history/social studies, science, and technical texts, at the high end of the grades 2–3 text complexity band independently and proficiently.

Access Text ©

TEACH 21st Century Skills: Online Reference Sources Have students preview "Country to City" on pp. 354–357. Have students look at the information on p. 355 and ask: What text features helped Denise learn about Romare Bearden?

Corrective feedback | **If...** students are unable to identify text features on a Web site, **then...** use the model to guide students through the page.

Think Aloud

MODEL I know that information in online reference sources is organized in a way that is similar to how information is organized in print reference sources. I see the heading *Encyclopedia* that tells me the kind of reference used and the name of the Web site. I see the heading *Romare Bearden* and a bulleted list of facts. Sometimes information will include links to other sources of information related to the topic.

ON THEIR OWN Have students work in pairs to search other online reference sources for information on Romare Bearden. Discuss with them how the information is organized and how the same information could be presented in other formats.

Close Reading ©

ANALYSIS • TEXT EVIDENCE Reread p. 355. What do you learn about Romare Bearden in "Country to City" that connects to events in *Me and Uncle Romie?* What can you conclude from this? (Romare Bearden lived in North Carolina and in Harlem like Uncle Romie and James. Romare Bearden was a collage artist like Uncle Romie. I conclude that *Me and Uncle Romie* is a story based on the life of a real person.)

ANALYSIS Based on the types of online sources here, what kinds of information can you find about Romare Bearden? (I can find out where and when he was born, what his childhood was like, the types of collages he created.)

Access for All

SI Strategic Intervention

Have pairs of students make a two-column chart labeled *Romare Bearden* and *Uncle Romie*. In the first column, have them list where Romare Bearden was born, where he lived, and what he is best known for. Then have them find the same facts about Uncle Romie and add to the chart. Help students conclude that Uncle Romie and Romare Bearden are the same person.

A Advanced

Have students brainstorm other search topics they could use when researching information on Romare Bearden's life, such as *collage artists* and *Harlem Renaissance*.

Access Content Have students preview the text by locating the words *North Carolina* and *New York* in the encyclopedia entry on Romare Bearden and then finding the atlas and almanac entry for each state on the following pages.

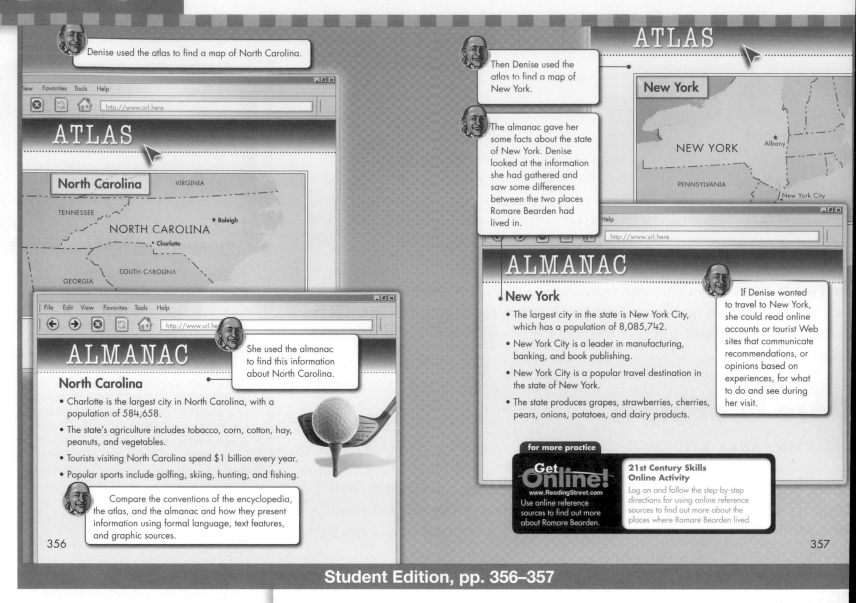

Student Edition, pp. 356–357

356

357

Common Core State Standards

Informational Text 5. Use text features and search tools (e.g., key words, sidebars, hyperlinks) to locate information relevant to a given topic efficiently. **Informational Text 9.** Compare and contrast the most important points and key details presented in two texts on the same topic. **Informational Text 10.** By the end of the year, read and comprehend informational texts, including history/social studies, science, and technical texts, at the high end of the grades 2–3 text complexity band independently and proficiently.

Access Text ©

TEACH 21st Century Skills: Online Reference Sources Have students identify the two reference sources on pp. 356–357. Then ask: How is the infor mation in an atlas different from that provided by an almanac?

Corrective feedback | **If...** students are unable to contrast the two reference sources, **then...** use the model to guide students in how they are different.

Think Aloud **MODEL** I see maps for each state in the atlases. I see a list of facts about each state in the almanacs. Atlases provide maps and almanacs provide facts.

ON THEIR OWN Have students search an online encyclopedia, atlas, and almanac for information about their state. Then have them compare and contrast the key details about their state in the online encyclopedia, atlas, and almanac.

Close Reading

ANALYSIS • TEXT EVIDENCE What types of graphic sources do the online materials on pp. 356–357 include? Would you expect to find this kind of information in a story such as *Me and Uncle Romie*? (The graphic sources are a map of each state and lists of what each state is known for. This kind of information is more common in reference material than in a story.)

ANALYSIS How do you know that the author's purpose in writing "Country to City" is to inform? (The passage includes facts about Denise's online search that inform the reader about online reference sources and about Romare Bearden.)

Get Online!

Online Reference Sources

FOR MORE PRACTICE Show students how to locate Web sites by clicking on the appropriate links. Be sure that they follow the step-by-step directions for finding articles about Harlem. Discuss with students how the information in an encyclopedia is different from that found in a dictionary.

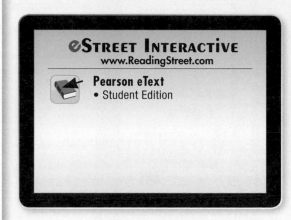

eStreet Interactive
www.ReadingStreet.com

Pearson eText
• Student Edition

Connect to Social Studies

History of Almanacs Almanacs have been written for hundreds of years. Published annually and according to the calendar, they often show times of ocean tides, solar eclipses, and lunar eclipses. The name *almanac* comes from a medieval Arabic word, but early almanacs have been traced back to the ancient Greeks. They used almanacs to list weather changes that they traced to astronomical computations.

Graphic Organizers Provide support to students as they create a T-chart to show the differences between an atlas and an almanac. Help them add details in each column.

Let's

Learn

It!

READING STREET ONLINE
ONLINE STUDENT EDITION
www.ReadingStreet.com

Vocabulary

Homonyms

Context Clues Remember that homonyms are words that have the same pronunciations and spellings, but different meanings. You can use nearby words and phrases to tell which meaning is being used in a sentence.

Practice It! Write two definitions for the homonym *pupil*. Then read the following sentence: *The pupil sat in the middle of the classroom.* Now circle the definition that is used in this sentence. Write down the other words or phrases in the sentence that tell you which definition is being used.

Fluency

Appropriate Phrasing

When you group together words and phrases according to the punctuation and meaning of a sentence, the story flows more smoothly.

Practice It! Read aloud page 340 of *Me and Uncle Romie* with a partner. Do you and your partner group certain words and phrases differently? Which way helps you better understand the story?

358

Listening and Speaking

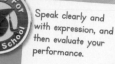

Speak clearly and with expression, and then evaluate your performance.

Retelling

Retelling a story means to tell what happened in the story in your own words. Retellings include the most important events.

Practice It! Work in groups of three to retell *Me and Uncle Romie*. Listen for cues to know when your part begins. Each group member should talk the same amount of time.

Tips

Listening . . .
- Listen attentively.
- Respond to the literature, taking turns to ask questions and make comments.

Speaking . . .
- Determine your purpose for speaking.
- Speak clearly, with expression.
- Use transition words correctly.

Teamwork . . .
- Answer questions with detail.

359

Student Edition, pp. 358–359

Fluency

Appropriate Phrasing

GUIDE PRACTICE Use the Fluency activity as an assessment tool. Be sure the reading passage is at least 200 words long. As students read, make sure their phrasing is correct and that they group words together correctly.

Don't Wait Until Friday **MONITOR PROGRESS** **Check Fluency**

FORMATIVE ASSESSMENT As students reread, monitor progress toward their individual fluency goals. Current Goal: 102–112 words correct per minute. End-of-Year Goal: 120 words correct per minute.

If... students cannot read fluently at a rate of 102–112 words correct per minute,

then... have students practice with text at their independent levels.

Vocabulary Skill

◉ Homonyms

TEACH HOMONYMS • CONTEXT CLUES Remind students that homonyms are words that have the same pronunciation but different meanings. Write the sentence *Uncle Romie's apartment* was *several stories tall.* Have students tell definitions for the word *stories.* Underline the context clues in the sentence that tell which meaning is used.

GUIDE PRACTICE Have students write two sentences that illustrate different meanings for each of the following homonyms: *second, match, bowl.* Have them underline the context clues in each sentence.

ON THEIR OWN As students work independently, make sure they also know the meaning of *pupil* as a part of the eye. Check to make sure they can identify the context clues in the sentence.

Listening and Speaking

Retelling

TEACH Explain to students that when they retell a story, it is important to be a good listener and a good speaker. Remind speakers to determine their purpose for speaking: to inform, to persuade, or to entertain. When they retell the story, they should use good pronunciation, look at their audience, and use a good rate and volume. Remind the audience to listen attentively and to raise their hands before asking any relevant questions or making pertinent comments.

GUIDE PRACTICE Help students break the story into three parts that are equal in length. Have students practice their parts using a timer to keep them the same length. Ask students to think about the words they would choose for an audience of kindergarten children or one of parents and teachers.

ON THEIR OWN Have groups take turns retelling *Me and Uncle Romie.* Allow time for a question and answer session for each group. Encourage students to ask and answer questions with appropriate detail and provide suggestions that build on the ideas of others.

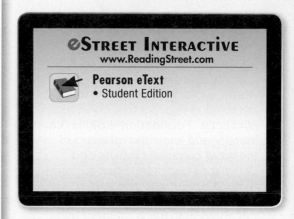

eStreet Interactive
www.ReadingStreet.com

Pearson eText
• Student Edition

Retelling

Remind students that the rate and pace at which they speak will help them effectively communicate the ideas and emotions in the story. Suggest that they vary the rate and pace for effect, emphasize key words, and use emotion in their voices when communicating a character's feelings.

© Bridge to Common Core

PRESENTATION OF KNOWLEDGE AND IDEAS

As students retell stories, they should use appropriate phrasing and present their retellings in an organized fashion. Students should understand their target audience and choose a style and language appropriate to that audience.

Common Core State Standards

Informational Text 5. Use text features and search tools (e.g., key words, sidebars, hyperlinks) to locate information relevant to a given topic efficiently. **Foundational Skills 3.a.** Identify and know the meaning of the most common prefixes and derivational suffixes. **Foundational Skills 3.b.** Decode words with common Latin suffixes. **Writing 2.** Write informative/explanatory texts to examine a topic and convey ideas and information clearly. **Writing 2.b.** Develop the topic with facts, definitions, and details. **Language 1.h.** Use coordinating and subordinating conjunctions. **Language 2.e.** Use conventional spelling for high-frequency and other studied words and for adding suffixes to base words (e.g., *sitting, smiled, cries, happiness*).

Research and Inquiry

Step 4 Synthesize

TEACH Have students synthesize their research findings and results. Remind them that when they synthesize, they integrate important information and relevant details from various sources to create an answer to their inquiry questions. Explain that their outline will help them synthesize and organize the information for their article and presentation.

GUIDE PRACTICE Meet with students and review their material. Have them use a word processing program for their articles. If students have not collected enough information to answer their inquiry questions, then guide them in revisiting online resources and doing further research, including interviewing experts.

ON THEIR OWN Have students finish writing their informational articles and then write a brief explanation of their research findings. Then have them organize and combine information and plan their presentations.

Conventions

Conjunctions

TEST PRACTICE Remind students that grammar skills, such as coordinating conjunctions, are often assessed on important tests. Remind students that conjunctions are words that connect words or groups of words. Review the conjunction *because*. To show a reason, use the conjunction *because*. I fell asleep early *because* I was tired. Then review *and, or, but,* and *therefore*.

ON THEIR OWN For additional practice, use *Reader's and Writer's Notebook,* p. 370.

Reader's and Writer's Notebook, p. 370

Spelling

Suffixes -y, -ish, -hood, -ment

PRACTICE SPELLING STRATEGY Supply pairs of students with index cards on which the spelling words have been written. Have one student read a word while the other writes it. Then have students switch roles. Have them use the cards to check their spelling and correct any misspelled words.

ON THEIR OWN For additional practice, use *Let's Practice It!* page 336 on the *Teacher Resources DVD-ROM*.

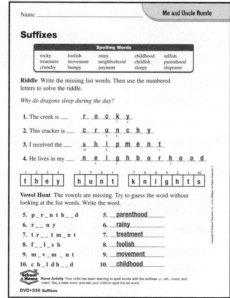

Let's Practice It! TR DVD•336

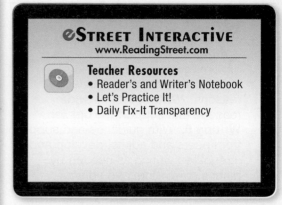

eSTREET INTERACTIVE
www.ReadingStreet.com

Teacher Resources
• Reader's and Writer's Notebook
• Let's Practice It!
• Daily Fix-It Transparency

Daily Fix-It

7. Her and me lived with our familys in New York City. *(She and I; families)*

8. On Sundays, childrn feed the ducks and gooses in Central Park. *(children; geese)*

 Bridge to Common Core

CONVENTIONS OF STANDARD ENGLISH

As students identify and use conjunctions and spell words with suffixes *-y, -ish, -hood,* and *-ment* they are demonstrating command of the conventions of standard English. Your guidance will help them use correct grammar, usage, and spelling to convey meaning when they speak and write.

ELL

Suffixes Write the spelling words on note cards with the suffixes separated from their base words. Provide support for students based on their proficiency levels:

Beginning Have students match the cards by referring to their spelling lists.

Intermediate Have students match the cards and then write the complete words.

Advanced Remove the suffixes. Have students write the complete spelling words by looking at the base words.

Me and Uncle Romie **359c**

Common Core State Standards

Writing 1. Write opinion pieces on familiar topics or texts, supporting a point of view with reasons. **Writing 1.b.** Provide reasons that support the opinion. **Writing 5.** With guidance and support from peers and adults, develop and strengthen writing as needed by planning, revising, and editing.

Write Guy by *Jeff Anderson*

Show Off—in a Good Way

Post students' successful sentences or short paragraphs. Celebrate students as writers. Select a sentence of the week, and write it large! Students learn from each other's successes.

Writing Zoom in on ©

Book Review

Mini-Lesson | Revise: Adding

■ Yesterday we wrote book reviews about books that we've read. Today we will revise our drafts. The goal is to make your writing clearer, more interesting, and more informative.

■ Display Writing Transparency 25B. Remind students that revising does not include corrections of grammar and mechanics. Tell them that this will be done during the lesson as they proofread their work. Then introduce the revising strategy of adding.

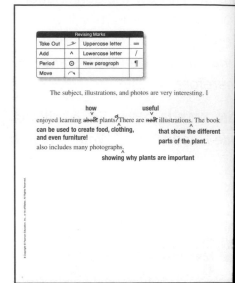

Writing Transparency 25B, TR DVD

■ When you revise, ask yourself *How can I make my writing more informative and interesting?* The revising strategy adding is when you add more details to your sentences to better explain or describe what you are writing about. The second paragraph of my book review is very plain. I'll revise the first sentence by adding the text *how plants can be used to create food, clothing, and even furniture!* Then I'll revise the second sentence by replacing the word *neat* with *useful* and adding the words *that show the different parts of the plant* after the word *illustrations*. Finally, I'll add the text *showing why plants are important* to the end of the third sentence. Reread your review for places where you might want to add informative and interesting details.

Tell students that as they revise, not only should they look for places where they might add information to help make their reviews clearer, better organized, and more interesting, but they should also make sure they have organized their ideas into coherent paragraphs.

Revising Tips

✔ Check your work to make sure the writing is well organized.

✔ Add specific information or details to make your writing more interesting and support your opinion.

PEER CONFERENCING • PEER REVISION Have pairs of students exchange papers for peer revision. Students should write three questions about their partner's writing. Tell students that their questions should focus on where the partner could revise by adding information to make the writing clearer.

Have students revise their book reviews using the key features of a book review and questions or suggestions from their partners. Be sure students are using the revising strategy of adding.

| **Corrective feedback** | Circulate around the room to monitor and confer with students as they revise. Remind students correcting errors that they will have time to edit tomorrow. They should be working on content and organization today. |

Routine   Quick Write for Fluency   `Team Talk`

- **Talk** Pairs discuss the selection, *Me and Uncle Romie.*

- **Write** Each student writes a one-paragraph review of the story.

- **Share** Students read their own writing to their partner and then check the partner's writing for one or more of the key features of a book review.

Routines Flip Chart

ELL

Showing Opinions Provide additional phrases for students to use to show their opinions, such as *the book does not; I enjoyed; I do not understand why; the illustrations are; the book could use more,* etc.

Wrap Up Your Day!

✔ **Content Knowledge** What did you learn about life in North Carolina and New York?

✔ **Oral Vocabulary** Monitor students' use of oral vocabulary as they respond: *Do you think you will see animals scurry and scamper in sky-scrapers in the city?*

✔ **Text Features** Discuss how understanding the climax helps students understand text.

Preview DAY 5

Remind students to think about how city life compares to country life.

ⓒ Bridge to Common Core

INTEGRATION OF KNOWLEDGE/IDEAS
This week, students have integrated content presented in diverse media and analyzed how different texts address similar topics. They have developed knowledge about life in the city compared to life in the country to expand the unit topic of Cultures.

Social Studies Knowledge Goals
Students have learned that
• city life is busy
• cities have tall buildings
• the country has farms

Content Knowledge
City Life and Country Life

REVIEW THE CONCEPT Have students look back at the reading selections to find examples that best demonstrate comparing city life to country life.

Build Oral Language

REVIEW AMAZING WORDS Display and review this week's concept map. Remind students that this week they have learned ten Amazing Words related to comparing city life and country life. Have students use the Amazing Words and the concept map to answer the Question of the Week, *How does city life compare to life in the country?*

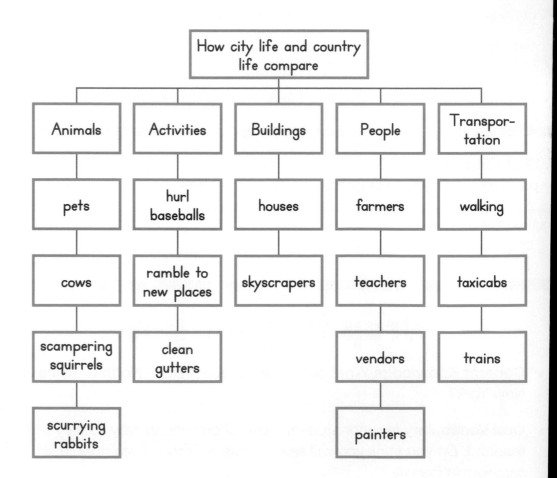

eSTREET INTERACTIVE
www.ReadingStreet.com

Concept Talk Video

Teacher Resources
• Amazing Word Cards

Story Sort

Build Oral Vocabulary

Team Talk **CONNECT TO AMAZING IDEAS** Have pairs of students discuss how the Question of the Week connects to the question for this unit of study: *What happens when two ways of life come together?* Tell students to use the concept map and what they have learned from this week's discussions and reading selections to form an Amazing Idea—a realization or "big idea" about Cultures. Remind partners to pose and answer questions with appropriate detail and to give suggestions that build on each other's ideas. Then ask pairs to share their Amazing Ideas with the class.

Amazing Ideas might include these key concepts:

City life and country life are two different ways of life.

People who live in the city often have the same interests as people who live in the country.

Although people come from different ways of life, they can find common interests and form friendships.

WRITE ABOUT IT Have students write a few sentences about their Amazing Idea, beginning with "This week I learned . . ."

Amazing Words

skyscraper	hurl
taxicab	meager
scamper	gutter
scurry	bitter
vendor	ramble

MONITOR PROGRESS **Check Oral Vocabulary**

FORMATIVE ASSESSMENT Have individuals use this week's Amazing Words to describe city life and country life. Monitor students' abilities to use the Amazing Words and note which words you need to reteach.

If... students have difficulty using the Amazing Words,

then... reteach using the Oral Vocabuary Routine on pp. 321a, 326b, 340b, 54b, and OV•5.

ELL

Check Concepts and Language Use the Day 5 instruction on ELL Poster 25 to monitor students' understanding of the lesson concept.

Me and Uncle Romie **359g**

© Common Core State Standards

Literature 4. Determine the meaning of words and phrases as they are used in a text, distinguishing literal from nonliteral language. **Informational Text 6.** Distinguish their own point of view from that of the author of a text. **Foundational Skills 3.b.** Decode words with common Latin suffixes. **Language 4.a.** Use sentence-level context as a clue to the meaning of a word or phrase. **Language 4.b.** Determine the meaning of the new word formed when a known affix is added to a known word (e.g., *agreeable/disagreeable, comfortable/uncomfortable, care/careless, heat/preheat*).

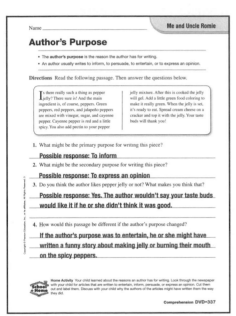

Let's Practice It! TR DVD•337

Selection Vocabulary

cardboard thick, stiff paper

feast a meal with a lot of food

fierce frightening, scary

flights sets of stairs

pitcher a person who throws a baseball to a batter

ruined destroyed or damaged

stoops small porches with steps, usually at the front of a house

treasure valuables; prizes

Text-Based Comprehension

Review ⊙ Author's Purpose

TEACH Review the definition of author's purpose on p. 324. Remind students that the author's purpose is the reason or reasons the author has for writing. Writers may write to inform, persuade, entertain, or express an opinion. For additional support, have students review p. EI•2 on author's purpose.

GUIDE PRACTICE Have students find an example that illustrates the author's purpose in *Me and Uncle Romie*. Remind them that using background knowledge can help them determine the author's purpose. Then have pairs tell what the author's purpose is.

ON THEIR OWN For additional practice, use *Let's Practice It!* page 337 on the *Teacher Resources DVD-ROM*.

Vocabulary Skill

Review ⊙ Homonyms

TEACH Remind students to use context clues to help them understand the meanings of homonyms.

GUIDE PRACTICE Write on the board: *I got tired after I walked down four flights of stairs*. Review with students how context clues can help them determine the meaning of the homonym *flights* in the sentence.

ON THEIR OWN Have students write sentences to illustrate two meanings for the homonyms *flights* and *stoops*. Let them exchange papers with a partner and use context clues to identify the correct meaning of each homonym.

Word Analysis

Review Suffixes -y, -ish, -hood, -ment

TEACH Write the following sentences on the board. Have students read each one, first quietly to themselves and then aloud as you track the print.

1. My neighborhood was filled with excitement about the festival.
2. This juicy orange is a very healthy snack.
3. Our homework assignment is lengthy.
4. She says it's childish to get dirty playing in the mud.
5. What is Ted's punishment for his dishonesty?

Team Talk Have students discuss with a partner which words have the suffixes -y, -ish, -hood, or -ment. Ask them to identify the base word and the suffix in each word. Then call on individuals to share with the class.

Literary Terms

Review Onomatopoeia

TEACH Have students reread p. 336 of *Me and Uncle Romie.* Remind them that onomatopoeia describes words that sound like their meaning.

GUIDE PRACTICE Find an example of onomatopoeia on p. 336. Discuss why the author used *Whew!* Have students find another example of onomatopoeia on p. 332.

ON THEIR OWN Have students reread p. 348. Have them identify onomatopoeic words the author could have used on James's train ride home.

eStreet Interactive
www.ReadingStreet.com

Pearson eText
• Student Edition

Teacher Resources
• Let's Practice It!

ELL

Using Words with Suffixes Have students provide base words to orally complete sentences with words that use a base word plus a suffix. For example: *Someone who is **dirty** is covered with* (dirt). *A **foolish** man acts like a* (fool).

Me and Uncle Romie **359i**

**Ⓒ Common Core
State Standards**

Foundational Skills 4. Read with sufficient accuracy and fluency to support omprehension. **Foundational Skills 4.b.** Read on-level prose and poetry orally with accuracy, appropriate rate, and expression on successive readings.

Plan to Assess Fluency

☐ **Week 1** Advanced

☐ **Week 2** Strategic Intervention

☐ **Week 3** On-Level

☐ **Week 4** Strategic Intervention

☑ **This week assess any students you have not yet checked during this unit.**

Set individual goals for students to enable them to reach the year-end goal.

• Current Goal: 102–112 WCPM

• Year-End Goal: 120 WCPM

Assessment

Monitor Progress

FLUENCY Make two copies of the fluency passage on p. 359k. As the student reads the text aloud, mark mistakes on your copy. Also mark where the student is at the end of one minute. To check the student's comprehension of the passages have him or her retell what was read. To figure words correct per minute (WCPM), subtract the number of mistakes from the total number of words read in one minute.

RATE

Corrective feedback	**If...** students cannot read fluently at a rate of 102–112 WCPM, **then...** make sure they practice with text at their independent reading level. Provide additional fluency practice by pairing nonfluent readers with fluent readers.
	If... students already read at 120 WCPM, **then...** have them read a book of their choice independently.

ⒺⓁⓁ

If... students need more scaffolding and practice with **Conventions and Writing,**
then... use the Grammar Transition Lessons on pp. 312–386 in the *ELL Handbook*.

Day 5 SMALL GROUP TIME • Differentiate Reteaching, p. SG•65

OL On-Level	**SI Strategic Intervention**	**A Advanced**
• **Practice** Conjunctions • **Reread** *Reading Street Sleuth*, pp. 64–65	• **Review** Conjunctions • **Reread** *Reading Street Sleuth*, pp. 64–65	• **Extend** Conjunctions • **Reread** *Reading Street Sleuth*, pp. 64–65 • **Communicate** Inquiry Project

Hunting Treasure

"What fine feast have you prepared for the crew's enjoyment?" 10

the captain asked as he opened the hatch and went down the short 23

flight of steps to the kitchen. He had to bend down to enter the low 38

doorway. 39

"The usual, Sir," I said as cheerfully as possible. *Ruined soup,* 50

moldy apples, and lumpy oatmeal is what I thought. I poured the 62

captain a cup of goat's milk from my pitcher. 71

I had left my childhood home in London to make my livelihood as 84

a cook at sea. I would have been better off living in a garbage dump. 99

I was sleepy and cold the entire voyage. But now it was spring, and 113

our voyage was almost over. 118

"Land ho!" a voice called from aloft. 125

At last! I went up on deck. There was a fair green strip of land 140

before us. The next morning, I set out with my shipmates to explore it. 154

The captain came seeking furs and spices. I had more practical things 166

in mind. 168

I searched the creek sides for green sprouts that are good to 180

eat. I filled my cap full of walnuts from the ground. Then, in an open 195

meadow, I found what I had been dreaming of for months. Fresh 207

strawberries, treasure enough for this ship's cook. 214

MONITOR PROGRESS   • Check Fluency

 **Common Core State Standards**

Literature 1. Ask and answer questions to demonstrate understanding of a text, referring explicitly to the text as the basis for the answers. **Literature 3.** Describe characters in a story (e.g., their traits, motivations, or feelings) and explain how their actions contribute to the sequence of events.

Assessment

Monitor Progress

For a written assessment of Suffixes, Author's Purpose, and Selection Vocabulary, use Weekly Test 25, pages 145–150.

✆ AUTHOR'S PURPOSE Use "The Last Night" on p. 359m to check students' understanding of author's purpose.

1. What is Warren worried about? (Warren is moving from a farm to a city, and he wonders if he will be happy in a city.)

2. What is the author's purpose in writing paragraph 1? (The author is writing to give a description of Warren's farm.)

3. Why does the author describe the city in paragraph 2? (This shows all the good things Warren is looking forward to.)

> **Corrective feedback** | **If...** students are unable to answer the comprehension questions,
> **then...** use the Reteach lesson in *First Stop*.

The Last Night

Warren gazed out the upstairs bedroom window into the night. The moon shone brightly and lit up the farmyard. Warren studied the old wooden barn, the towering silo, and the animal pens. He took a deep breath. Through the window screen he could smell the farm. He could smell animals and fields of hay. He loved the summertime smells of this farmland. Then Warren heard a distant train whistling as it rumbled through a rail crossing on its way to the city.

Warren took another deep breath and wondered what his new life would be like. Tomorrow his family would move into that huge city. Warren was looking forward to it. The city was full of excitement. There were busy people rushing around. There were zoos and museums. There were baseball parks and football stadiums. There were interesting things to do and interesting people to meet. City living would be a great adventure.

Yet Warren felt sad tonight. He knew he would miss this old farm. He would miss the sounds of roosters in the morning, of cows waiting to be milked, of pigs snorting as they gobbled down their food.

Warren wondered if he would ever again ride on a tractor or climb in a hayloft. He wondered if his mom and dad would be happy working in the city. City work would have to be easier than farming!

Warren leaned closer to the window and to the farm outside it. Would he be happy in the city?

MONITOR PROGRESS • Author's Purpose

Common Core State Standards

Speaking/Listening 4. Report on a topic or text, tell a story, or recount an experience with appropriate facts and relevant, descriptive details, speaking clearly at an understandable pace. **Language 1.h.** Use coordinating and subordinating conjunctions. **Language 2.e.** Use conventional spelling for high-frequency and other studied words and for adding suffixes to base words (e.g., *sitting, smiled, cries, happiness*).

Research and Inquiry

Step 5 Communicate

PRESENT IDEAS Have students share their inquiry results by presenting their information and giving a brief talk about their research.

SPEAKING Remind students how to be good speakers and how to communicate effectively with their audience.

• Respond to relevant questions with appropriate details.

• Speak clearly and loudly.

• Keep eye contact with audience members.

LISTENING Review with students these tips for being a good listener.

• Wait until the speaker has finished before raising your hand to ask a relevant question or make a comment.

• Be polite, even if you disagree.

• Sit up straight and listen attentively.

LISTEN TO IDEAS Have students listen attentively to the various informational articles. Have them make pertinent comments, closely related to the topic.

Spelling Test

Suffixes -y, -ish, -hood, -ment

To administer the spelling test, refer to the directions, words, and sentences on p. 325c.

Conventions

Conjunctions

MORE PRACTICE Remind students that conjunctions are words that connect words or groups of words.

To add information, use the conjunction *and*.

To show a choice, use the conjunction *or*.

To show a difference, use the conjunction *but*.

To show a result, use the conjunction *therefore*.

To show a reason, use *because*.

GUIDE PRACTICE Have students work with a partner to list the conjunction that goes with each action.

show a difference (but)	show a reason (because)

ON THEIR OWN Write these sentences. Have students use the correct conjunctions to complete the sentences. Students should complete *Let's Practice It!* page 338 on the *Teacher Resources DVD-ROM*.

1. I like strawberries, _____ I like bananas better. (but)

2. The sunset is pink _____ orange. (and)

3. It is raining, _____ I will need an umbrella. (therefore)

4. I am unprepared _____ I forgot my gym bag. (because)

5. Do you want sausage _____ bacon for breakfast? (or)

eSTREET INTERACTIVE
www.ReadingStreet.com

Teacher Resources
• Let's Practice It!
• Daily Fix-It Transparency

Daily Fix-It

9. There is much trafic in the city, there is not much in the country. *(traffic; city, but)*

10. Arent the city sights interesting to James and she? *(Aren't; her)*

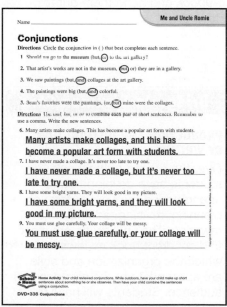

Let's Practice It! TR DVD•338

Common Core State Standards

Writing 10. Write routinely over extended time frames (time for research, reflection, and revision) and shorter time frames (a single sitting or a day or two) for a range of discipline specific tasks, purposes, and audiences. **Language 1.** Demonstrate command of the conventions of standard English grammar and usage when writing or speaking. **Language 1.h.** Use coordinating and subordinating conjunctions. **Language 2.** Demonstrate command of the conventions of standard English capitalization, punctuation, and spelling when writing. **Also Writing 5.**

Teacher Note

Writing Self-Evaluation Make copies of the Writing Self-Evaluation Guide on p. 39 of the *Reader's and Writer's Notebook* and hand them out to students.

Bridge to Common Core

PRODUCTION AND DISTRIBUTION OF WRITING

Over the course of the week, students have developed and strengthened their drafts through planning, revising, editing, and rewriting. The final drafts are clear and coherent book reviews in which the organization and style are appropriate to the purpose and audience. Students will have used valid reasoning to support their opinions.

Writing Zoom in on

Book Review

REVIEW REVISING Remind students that yesterday they revised their book reviews, paying particular attention to adding details that would make their writing more interesting and informative. Today they will proofread their book reviews.

Mini-Lesson Proofread

Proofread for Conjunctions

■ **Teach** When we proofread, we look closely at our work, searching for errors in mechanics such as spelling, capitalization, punctuation, and grammar. Today we will focus on making sure conjunctions are used correctly.

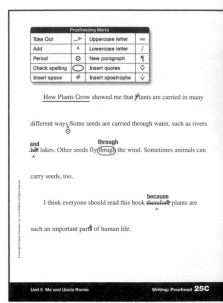

Writing Transparency 25C, TR DVD

■ **Model** Let's look at the last few paragraphs of my book review from yesterday. Display Writing Transparency 25C. Explain that you will look for errors in the use of conjunctions. In the second sentence, I used *but* instead of *and*. In the last sentence, I used *therefore* instead of *because*. Point out the title in the first line. I also need to underline <u>How Plants Grow</u> because it is the title of the book. Now I will reread the review several more times looking for errors. Explain to students that they should reread their reviews a number of times, each time looking for different types of errors: spelling, punctuation, capitalization, grammar, and any specific requirements of the writing product, such as underlining the book title.

PROOFREAD Display the Proofreading Tips. Ask students to proofread their reviews using the Proofreading Tips and paying particular attention to conjunctions. Circulate around the room answering students' questions. When students have finished editing their own work, have pairs proofread each other's book reviews.

Proofreading Tips

✔ Be sure that conjunctions are being used correctly.

✔ Do not rely solely on a word processing spell-checker; use a dictionary to find and double-check spelling.

eSTREET INTERACTIVE
www.ReadingStreet.com

Teacher Resources
- Writing Transparency
- Reader's and Writer's Notebook

PRESENT Have students incorporate revisions and proofreading edits into their book reviews to create a final draft. Then have small groups create book review magazines, including a table of contents, from their writing. Have them find or create art for the cover of their book reviews. Then have each student complete the Writing Self-Evaluation Guide.

Routine   Quick Write for Fluency   Team Talk

1. **Talk** Pairs discuss what they learned about reviewing books this week.

2. **Write** Each person writes a few sentences about why someone might want to read book reviews.

3. **Share** Partners read their writing to their partner.

Routines Flip Chart

Wrap Up Your Week!

City Life and Country Life

How does city life compare to life in the country?

 **MODEL** In *Me and Uncle Romie* and "Country to City," we learned about what it's like to live in the country and what it's like to live in the city.

Team Talk Have students recall their Amazing Ideas about cultures and use these ideas to help them demonstrate their understanding of the Question of the Week.

Concept for Unit 6 Week 1
Symbols of Freedom

Why do we have symbols that represent freedom?

Poster Preview Prepare students for Unit 6 Week 1 by using Unit 6 Week 1 ELL Poster 26. Read the Talk-Through to introduce the concept and vocabulary. Ask students to identify and describe actions in the art.

Selection Summary Send home the summary of the Unit 6 Week 1 selection, *The Story of the Statue of Liberty,* in English and in students' home languages, if available in the *ELL Handbook.* They can read the summary with family members.

Why do we have symbols that represent freedom? Tell students that in Unit 6, Week 1 they will read narrative nonfiction about one of the symbols of freedom in the United States.

Preview Unit 6, Week 1

Common Core State Standards
Literature 10. By the end of the year,
read and comprehend literature, including
stories, dramas, and poetry, at the high
end of the grades 2–3 text complexity
band independently and proficiently.
Also Literature 5.,
Foundational Skills 4.b.

Poetry

- **Narrative poems** tell a story. Their stories can be simple, dramatic, humorous, or even a little sad.

- A narrative poem can be told in **free verse.** This means that it doesn't have **rhyme** patterns or a regular **rhythm,** or **cadence.** The words may appear in unusual ways, sometimes even without punctuation.

- A free verse poem may use the words and rhythms of everyday speech.

- A poet may use **alliteration,** or the repeated sounds of consonants, or **assonance,** the repeated sounds of vowels, to create more vivid images.

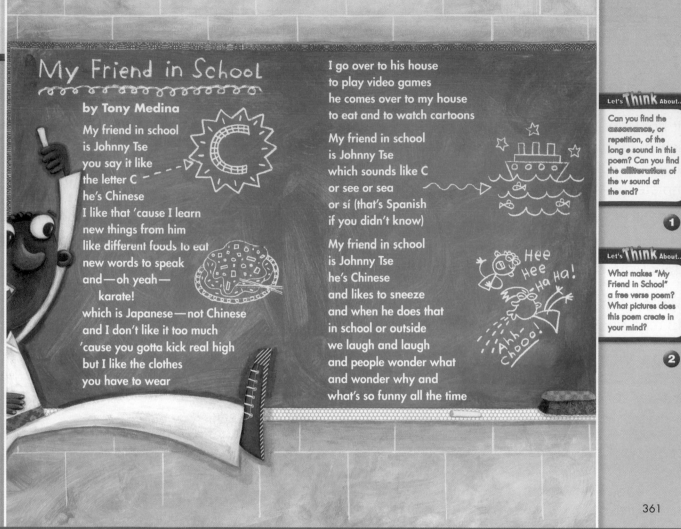

My Friend in School

by Tony Medina

My friend in school
is Johnny Tse
you say it like
the letter C
he's Chinese
I like that 'cause I learn
new things from him
like different foods to eat
new words to speak
and—oh yeah—
    karate!
which is Japanese—not Chinese
and I don't like it too much
'cause you gotta kick real high
but I like the clothes
you have to wear

I go over to his house
to play video games
he comes over to my house
to eat and to watch cartoons

My friend in school
is Johnny Tse
which sounds like C
or see or sea
or sí (that's Spanish
if you didn't know)

My friend in school
is Johnny Tse
he's Chinese
and likes to sneeze
and when he does that
in school or outside
we laugh and laugh
and people wonder what
and wonder why and
what's so funny all the time

Hee Hee Ha Ha!

Ahh-Choooo!

Let's Think About...

Can you find the assonance, or repetition, of the long e sound in this poem? Can you find the alliteration of the w sound at the end?

1

Let's Think About...

What makes "My Friend in School" a free verse poem? What pictures does this poem create in your mind?

2

360   361

Student Edition, pp. 360–361

Common Core State Standards

Literature 10. By the end of the year, read and comprehend literature, including stories, dramas, and poetry, at the high end of the grades 2–3 text complexity band independently and proficiently. **Also Literature 5., Foundational Skills 4.b.**

Academic Vocabulary ©

free verse poems that do not have rhymes or regular rhythm

Poetry

Free Verse

TEACH Review the definition of free verse on p. 360. Remind students that poems written in free verse do not have rhymes or regular rhythm but are clearly not prose.

GUIDE PRACTICE Have students discuss "My Friend in School." Point out that most lines begin with lowercase letters and there is little punctuation. Ask them to think about all the information the poet gives the reader or listener.

ON THEIR OWN Have students read the poem aloud. Have them first read it as if it were prose. Then have them read it carefully, thinking about the best way to group the words. Encourage them to try different ways to read the poem and discuss which they like best.

eSTREET INTERACTIVE
www.ReadingStreet.com

Pearson eText
• Student Edition

Alliteration and Assonance

TEACH Review the definitions of alliteration and assonance on p. 360. Explain that poets often use alliteration or assonance to create a musical effect. They also use these techniques to draw attention to important words in a poem.

GUIDE PRACTICE Have students compare ways in which the narrator talks and ways in which they might really say the same thing. Have them notice the run-on quality to the speech.

ON THEIR OWN Have students read the poem with expression. Remind them to pause slightly after reading each line so the listener can focus on the repetition of sounds.

Let's Think About...

I can find the assonance using the long *e* sound. It is in *Tse* many times and in the verse with *C*, *see*, *sea,* and *sí*. There is alliteration at the end of the poem in the phrases *wonder what* and *wonder why*.

"My Friend in School" is free verse because there is no rhyme, regular rhythm, or cadence. Many of the words and rhythms are like regular speech. The poem creates a picture of two boys, one Chinese and one not, who are having fun together and laughing a lot about silly things.

Academic Vocabulary

alliteration the repeated sounds of consonants

assonance the repeated sounds of vowels

Access for All

 Strategic Intervention

Have students make up alliterative phrases using their names. Have them illustrate the name (e.g., Silly Sam, Muddy Max).

A **Advanced**

Have students work together to write a short poem that emphasizes the long *a* sound.

Assonance Explain to students that poets often use assonance to create musical effects. However, the spellings of the same sounds can be very different. Make a chart with students of all the words with different spellings of the long *e* sound in the poem, such as *Tse, C, see, sea,* and *sí*. Have them add other words they know either in English or their own languages.

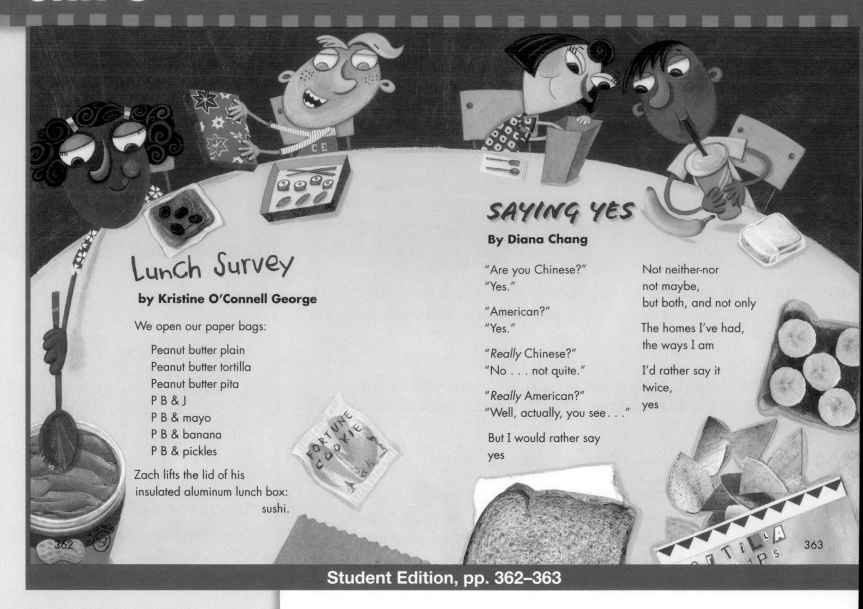

Student Edition, pp. 362–363

Lunch Survey

by Kristine O'Connell George

We open our paper bags:

Peanut butter plain
Peanut butter tortilla
Peanut butter pita
P B & J
P B & mayo
P B & banana
P B & pickles

Zach lifts the lid of his
insulated aluminum lunch box:
sushi.

362

SAYING YES

By Diana Chang

"Are you Chinese?"
"Yes."

"American?"
"Yes."

"*Really* Chinese?"
"No . . . not quite."

"*Really* American?"
"Well, actually, you see. . ."

But I would rather say
yes

Not neither-nor
not maybe,
but both, and not only

The homes I've had,
the ways I am

I'd rather say it
twice,
yes

363

Common Core State Standards

Literature 10. By the end of the year, read and comprehend literature, including stories, dramas, and poetry, at the high end of the grades 2–3 text complexity band independently and proficiently. **Writing 3.** Write narratives to develop real or imagined experiences or events using effective technique, descriptive details, and clear event sequences. **Also Literature 5., Foundational Skills 4.b.**

Acedemic Vocabulary ©

narrative poem a poem that tells a story

Poetry

Narrative Poems

TEACH Review the definition of narrative poems on p. 360. Remind students that narrative poems can be funny, sad, quiet, or dramatic. The important thing is that they tell a story.

GUIDE PRACTICE Have students discuss the story in "Lunch Survey" and identify why "Lunch Survey" is a narrative poem. (It tells a story.) Point out the similarity and difference between "We open our paper bags" and "Zach lifts the lid of his insulated aluminum lunch box." (Everyone is taking out lunch, but only Zach has a lunch box instead of a paper bag.)

ON THEIR OWN Have students read the poem aloud, pausing before the last line to make it stand out.

Close Reading ©

EVALUATION Why do you think the author chose to write "Lunch Survey" as free verse? (The story works well when it lists all the lunches. The sameness might be lost in a rhyme.)

ANALYSIS What would be different if you told the story in "Saying Yes" in prose? (I would probably identify the speakers. I would also add punctuation and probably some more words to make the text more clear.)

ANALYSIS In the second half of "Saying Yes," what idea is the speaker trying to express? (She is a whole rather than a half. She is more rather than less. She is the sum of all of her experiences.)

Practice Fluent Reading

APPROPRIATE PHRASING Have partners read "Saying Yes" aloud, one student reading only lines 1, 3, 5, and 7, and the other reading all the other lines. (Students can then switch parts.) Encourage the student reading the main speaker's lines to use a clipped, conversational tone for the dialogue, and a slower, more reflective tone for the second half of the poem.

Writing Poetry

Have students write a poem about a kind of food, sports, or clothing that has become a part of American culture but originated elsewhere. (To get students started, you might write *egg roll*, *soccer*, and *poncho* on the board.) Invite students to read their works aloud, grouping poems by culture, if possible.

Access for All

SI **Strategic Intervention**
Work with students to list the information given in "Lunch Survey" so they can "see" the narrative.

A **Advanced**
Have students work in pairs to write free verse poems about what they see people eating during lunch.

Discuss with students the different foods they bring for lunch. Have them take turns naming their favorite lunch foods.

Assessment Checkpoints for the Week

Weekly Assessment

Use pp. 145–150 of *Weekly Tests* to check:

✔ **Phonics** Suffixes *-y, -ish, -hood, -ment*

✔ **Comprehension** Author's Purpose

✔ **Review** **Comprehension** Draw Conclusions

✔ **Selection Vocabulary**

cardboard	pitcher
feast	ruined
fierce	stoops
flights	treasure

Weekly Tests

Differentiated Assessment

A
Advanced

OL
On-Level

SI
Strategic
Intervention

Use pp. 145–150 of *Fresh Reads for Fluency and Comprehension* to check:

✔ **Comprehension** Author's Purpose

✔ **Review** **Comprehension** Draw Conclusions

✔ **Fluency** Words Correct Per Minute

Fresh Reads for Fluency and Comprehension

Managing Assessment

Use *Assessment Handbook* for:

✔ **Weekly Assessment Blackline Masters for Monitoring Progress**

✔ **Observation Checklists**

✔ **Record-Keeping Forms**

✔ **Portfolio Assessment**

Assessment Handbook

TEACHER NOTES

DAY 1 Differentiate Vocabulary

- **Word Knowledge** Amazing Words
- **Read** "The Harlem Renaissance on Canvas"
- **Inquiry** Identify Questions

"The Harlem Renaissance on Canvas," pp. 64–65

DAY 2 Differentiate Comprehension

- **Word Knowledge** Selection Vocabulary
- **Access Text** Read *Me and Uncle Romie*
- **Inquiry** Investigate

DAY 3 Differentiate Close Reading

- **Word Knowledge** Develop Vocabulary
- **Close Reading** Read *Me and Uncle Romie*
- **Inquiry** Investigate

DAY 4 Differentiate Vocabulary

- **Word Knowledge** Amazing Words
- **Read** "Country to City"
- **Inquiry** Organize

DAY 5 Differentiate Reteaching

- **Conventions** Conjunctions
- **Reread** "The Harlem Renaissance on Canvas" or Leveled Readers
- **Inquiry** Communicate

Teacher Guides and Student pages can be found in the Leveled Reader Database.

 Place English Language Learners in the groups that correspond to their reading abilities.
If... students need scaffolding and practice,
then... use the ELL Notes on the instructional pages.

Independent Practice

Independent Practice Stations

See pp. 320h and 320i for Independent Stations.

Pearson Trade Book Library

See the Leveled Reader Database for lesson plans and student pages.

Reading Street Digital Path

Independent Practice Activities are available in the Digital Path.

Independent Reading

See p. 320i for independent reading suggestions.

On-Level

© Common Core State Standards

Literature 1. Ask and answer questions to demonstrate understanding of a text, referring explicitly to the text as the basis for the answers. **Informational Text 3.** Describe the relationship between a series of historical events, scientific ideas or concepts, or steps in technical procedures in a text, using language that pertains to time, sequence, and cause/effect. **Foundational Skills 4.** Read with sufficient accuracy and fluency to support comprehension. **Speaking/Listening 1.** Engage effectively in a range of collaborative discussions (one-on-one, in groups, and teacher-led) with diverse partners on grade 3 topics and texts, building on others' ideas and expressing their own clearly. **Language 4.** Determine or clarify the meaning of unknown and multiple-meaning words and phrases based on grade 3 reading and content, choosing flexibly from a range of strategies. **Language 4.a.** Use sentence-level context as a clue to the meaning of a word or phrase.

Independent Reading Options

Trade Book Library

eStreet Interactive
www.ReadingStreet.com

Teacher Guides are available on the Leveled Reader Database.

If... students need more scaffolding and practice with **Vocabulary, then...** use the activities on pp. DI•117–DI•118 in the Teacher Resources section on SuccessNet.

① Build Word Knowledge
Practice Amazing Words

DEFINE IT Elicit the definition for the word *skyscraper* from students. Ask: How would you describe a *skyscraper* to another student? (Possible response: A *skyscraper* is a very tall city building.) Clarify or give a definition when necessary. Continue with the words *taxicab* and *scurry.*

Team Talk **TALK ABOUT IT** Have students internalize meanings. Ask: How can you group the Amazing Words together in a sentence? (Possible response: In the big city, busy people *scurry* from *taxicabs* to the doors of *skyscrapers.*) Allow time for students to play with the words. Review the concept map with students. Discuss other words they can add to the concept map.

② Text-Based Comprehension
Read

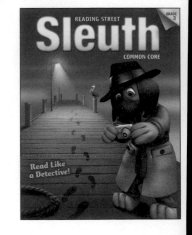

READ ALOUD "The Harlem Renaissance on Canvas" Have partners read "The Harlem Renaissance on Canvas" from *Reading Street Sleuth* on pp. 64–65.

ACCESS TEXT Discuss the Sleuth Work section with students before they work on it. Remind students that they can use these steps with other texts they read.

Gather Evidence Have partners work together to list details from the text. Invite students to share an interesting detail.

Ask Questions Have students share the painter they chose and the questions they would like to find answers for. Talk together about the sources students may use to find answers to their questions. If time permits, have partners research the answer to one of their questions.

Make Your Case Encourage students to revisit the text to identify evidence that supports their opinions. Have students share their opinion and the evidence that supports it.

On-Level

1 Build Word Knowledge
Practice Selection Vocabulary

cardboard	feast	fierce	flights
pitcher	ruined	stoops	treasure

DEFINE IT Discuss the definition for the word *treasure* with students. Ask: How would you describe a *treasure* to another student? (Possible response: A *treasure* is something valuable and often secret.) Continue with the remaining words.

Team Talk **TALK ABOUT IT** Have pairs use the selection vocabulary in sentences to internalize meaning. Ask: How can you pair the selection vocabulary words together in a sentence? (Possible response: I keep my *treasure* in a *cardboard* box under the *flight* of stairs.) Allow time for students to play with the words and then share their sentences.

2 Read
Me and Uncle Romie

If you read *Me and Uncle Romie* during whole group time, then use the following instruction.

ACCESS TEXT Reread the first two paragraphs on p. 336. Ask students to check understanding. How does James react to walking along the city streets? (He is amazed by how different the city is from his home.) What surprises him about the city? (There are no regular houses, just buildings and stores.) How do you know that James is not used to climbing lots of stairs? (James counts the flights and says "Whew!" when he reaches the top.)

Have students identify sections from today's reading that they did not completely understand. Reread them aloud and clarify misunderstandings.

If you are reading *Me and Uncle Romie* during small group time, then return to pp. 330–339a to guide the reading.

eSTREET INTERACTIVE
www.ReadingStreet.com

Pearson eText
• Student Edition
• Leveled Reader Database
• *Reading Street Sleuth*

SMALL GROUP TIME

More Reading for Group Time

ON-LEVEL

Reviews
• Author's Purpose
• Background Knowledge
• Selection Vocabulary

Use this suggested Leveled Reader or other text at students' instructional level.

eSTREET INTERACTIVE
www.ReadingStreet.com

Use the Leveled Reader Database for lesson plans and student pages for *Bobby's New Apartment*.

On-Level

Common Core State Standards

Literature 1. Ask and answer questions to demonstrate understanding of a text, referring explicitly to the text as the basis for the answers. **Foundational Skills 4.** Read with sufficient accuracy and fluency to support comprehension. **Language 4.** Determine or clarify the meaning of unknown and multiple-meaning words and phrases based on grade 3 reading and content, choosing flexibly from a range of strategies. **Language 4.a.** Use sentence-level context as a clue to the meaning of a word or phrase.

① Build Word Knowledge
Develop Vocabulary

REREAD FOR VOCABULARY Reread the last two paragraphs on p. 344. Introduce: Let's read these paragraphs to find out what *bleachers* means. To help students understand the word *bleachers,* ask questions related to context, such as: Where are James and Uncle Romie? Where do people sit when they go to a baseball game? Have students use online sources to find out more information about bleachers.

② Read
Me and Uncle Romie

If you read *Me and Uncle Romie* during whole group time, then use the following instruction.

CLOSE READING Read pp. 341–342. Have students search the text to find words and phrases that describe Uncle Romie's studio. As a class, make a list on the board. (*glorious mess, paints and scraps all over, huge painting, pieces pasted together, saxophones, birds, fire escapes, brown faces, beat and bounce, smaller houses, flowers, trains*)

Ask: What does James learn about Uncle Romie from his studio? (He learns that Uncle Romie is talented. James can see and feel Harlem. He also learns that Uncle Romie remembers growing up in North Carolina.) How are the images of Harlem and North Carolina different? (Harlem: musical instruments, fire escapes, buildings, and brown people. North Carolina: houses, flowers, and trains.)

If you are reading *Me and Uncle Romie* during small group time, then return to pp. 340–349a to guide the reading.

If... students need more scaffolding and practice with the **Main Selection,** **then...** use the activities on p. DI•122 in the Teacher Resources section on SuccessNet.

 **On-Level**

1 Build Word Knowledge
Practice Amazing Words

skyscraper	taxicab	scamper	scurry	vendor
hurl	meager	gutter	bitter	ramble

Team Talk **LANGUAGE DEVELOPMENT** Have students practice building more complex sentences. Display a sentence starter and have students add oral phrases or clauses using the Amazing Words. For example: The man _____. (The man jumped out of the *taxicab,* / grabbed a hot dog / from the *vendor,* / and *scurried* / into the *skyscraper.*) Guide students to add at least three phrases or clauses per sentence.

2 Read
"Country to City"

BEFORE READING Read aloud the genre information about online reference sources on p. 354. Explain that these sources can help students find information for research papers. Have students preview "Country to City" and set a purpose for reading. What is the purpose of the text boxes in the selection? (They tell what Denise did as she explored the online sources.)

DURING READING Have students read with you.

- Why is this selection called "Country to City"? (Romare Bearden was born in the country and later moved to the city.)

- In what format do the article on Romare Bearden and the almanac entry present information? (bulleted lists)

- In what way is a bulleted list a helpful way to present information? (It is easy to review a page quickly and find exactly what you are seeking.)

- On the maps, what does the star symbol mean? (It indicates the state capital.)

AFTER READING Have students share their reaction to "Country to City." Then have them research a state of their choice online and make a list of facts like those shown.

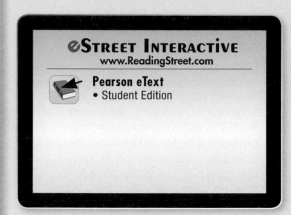

eSTREET INTERACTIVE
www.ReadingStreet.com

Pearson eText
• Student Edition

SMALL GROUP TIME

Independent Reading Options

Trade Book Library

eSTREET INTERACTIVE
www.ReadingStreet.com

Teacher Guides are available on the Leveled Reader Database.

OL On-Level

Common Core State Standards

Literature 1. Ask and answer questions to demonstrate understanding of a text, referring explicitly to the text as the basis for the answers. **Informational Text 3.** Describe the relationship between a series of historical events, scientific ideas or concepts, or steps in technical procedures in a text, using language that pertains to time, sequence, and cause/ effect. **Foundational Skills 4.** Read with sufficient accuracy and fluency to support comprehension. **Writing 7.** Conduct short research projects that build knowledge about a topic. **Speaking/Listening 1.** Engage effectively in a range of collaborative discussions (one-on-one, in groups, and teacher-led) with diverse partners on grade 3 topics and texts, building on others' ideas and expressing their own clearly **Language 4.** Determine or clarify the meaning of unknown and multiple-meaning words and phrases based on grade 3 reading and content, choosing flexibly from a range of strategies. **Also Language 1.h., 4.a.**

More Reading for Group Time

ON-LEVEL

Reviews
• Author's Purpose
• Background Knowledge
• Selection Vocabulary

Use this suggested Leveled Reader or other text at students' instructional level.

eSTREET INTERACTIVE
www.ReadingStreet.com

Use the Leveled Reader Database for lesson plans and student pages for *Bobby's New Apartment*.

① Build Word Knowledge
Practice Conjunctions

IDENTIFY Choral read the Conventions note at the bottom of p. 353 and discuss conjunctions. Write a list of the conjunctions on the board. Have partners reread the model book review and make a list of all the conjunctions the author used. Allow time for students to discuss their examples and correct any misunderstandings.

② Text-Based Comprehension
Read

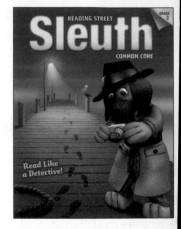

REREAD "The Harlem Renaissance on Canvas" Have partners reread "The Harlem Renaissance on Canvas."

EXTEND UNDERSTANDING Talk together about the importance of the move of African Americans from southern rural towns to northern cities.

PERFORMANCE TASK • Prove It! Help students find a painting from the Harlem Renaissance online. Have each student study the painting and write a paragraph describing what the painting shows about African American life. Encourage students to note something they learned about African American life from studying this painting.

COMMUNICATE Have students share their paragraphs with a partner. Invite students to discuss similarities and differences between the paintings they researched.

SI Strategic Intervention

1 Build Word Knowledge
Reteach Amazing Words

Repeat the definition of the word *skyscraper*. We learned that a *skyscraper* is a very tall building in the city. Then use the word in a sentence. I like to go to the top of *skyscrapers* and see the view.

Team Talk **TALK ABOUT IT** Have students take turns using the word *skyscraper* in a sentence. Continue this routine to practice the Amazing Words *taxicab* and *scurry*. Review the concept map with students. Discuss other words they can add to the concept map.

> **Corrective feedback** | **If...** students need more practice with the Amazing Words, **then...** use visuals from the Student Edition or online sources to clarify meaning.

2 Text-Based Comprehension
Read

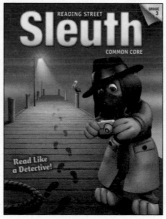

READ "The Harlem Renaissance on Canvas" Have students track the print as you read "The Harlem Renaissance on Canvas" from *Reading Street Sleuth* on pp. 64–65.

ACCESS TEXT Discuss the Sleuth Work section with students and provide support as needed as they work on it. Remind students that they can use these steps with other texts they read.

Gather Evidence Talk together and list evidence from the text about the importance of the Harlem Renaissance. Invite students to state what they feel is the most convincing piece of evidence.

Ask Questions Have students work with a partner to choose a painter and list questions they would like to research. Talk together about the sources students may use to find answers to their questions. If time permits, have partners research the answer to one of their questions.

Make Your Case Have students find another student who chose the same profession. Have them work together to make a list of reasons to support their choice. Remind students to revisit the text for evidence that may support their reasoning.

More Reading for Group Time

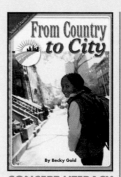

CONCEPT LITERACY
Practice
Concept Words

BELOW-LEVEL
Reviews
• Author's Purpose
• Background Knowledge
• Selection Vocabulary

Use these suggested Leveled Readers or other text at students' instructional level.

Use the Leveled Reader Database for lesson plans and student pages for *From Country to City* and *A Walk Around the City*.

SMALL GROUP TIME

Strategic Intervention

1 Build Word Knowledge
Reteach Selection Vocabulary

DEFINE IT Describe a *pitcher* to a friend. Give a definition when necessary. Restate the word in student-friendly terms and clarify meaning with a visual. A *pitcher* is the person who throws the ball to the batters. Page 345 shows a baseball game.

cardboard	feast	fierce	flights
pitcher	ruined	stoops	treasure

Team Talk **TALK ABOUT IT** Have you ever seen a pitcher at a baseball game? Turn and talk to your partner about this. Allow time for students to discuss. Ask for examples. Rephrase students' examples for usage when necessary or to correct misunderstandings. Continue with the remaining words.

Corrective feedback | **If...** students need more practice with selection vocabulary, **then...** use the *Envision It! Pictured Vocabulary Cards.*

2 Read
Me and Uncle Romie

If you read *Me and Uncle Romie* during whole group time, then use the instruction below.

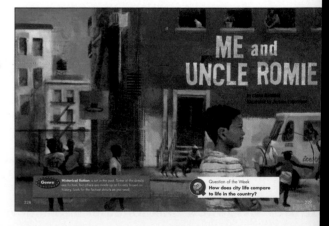

ACCESS TEXT Reread the first two paragraphs on p. 336. Ask students to check understanding. What does James see as he walks down the street? (big buildings, stores of all kinds) What doesn't he see? (regular houses) How does he react to what he sees and doesn't see? (He is amazed by how different the city is from his home.) How do you know that James is not used to climbing lots of stairs? (James counts the flights and says "Whew!" when he reaches the top.)

Have students identify sections they did not understand. Reread them aloud. Clarify the meaning of each section to build understanding.

If you are reading *Me and Uncle Romie* during small group time, then return to pp. 330–339a to guide the reading.

SI Strategic Intervention

1 Build Word Knowledge
Develop Vocabulary

REREAD FOR VOCABULARY Reread the last two paragraphs on p. 344. Let's read these paragraphs to find out what *bleachers* means. To help students understand the word *bleachers,* ask questions related to context, such as: Where do people usually sit when the go to watch sports events? Where are James and Uncle Romie sitting? How does the picture on p. 345 help you understand the word? What is another word for *bleachers?*

Corrective feedback | **If...** students have difficulty understanding the word *bleachers,* **then...** guide students to a dictionary or thesaurus to find more information about the word.

2 Read
Me and Uncle Romie

If you read *Me and Uncle Romie* during whole group time, then use the instruction below.

CLOSE READING Read pp. 341–342. Have students search the text to find time references that help show the sequence of the events in the story. Make a list of these time-order words in the order they occur and then retell what happened in the story. (*That night, When the sky turned, The next morning, For the first time, Then there was*)

Now use the time-order words you listed to retell what happened in this part of the story. (*That night Aunt Nanette said goodbye to James. When the sky turned black, James went to bed. The next morning, James snuck into Uncle Romie's studio. For the first time, he saw Uncle Romie's pictures. Then he saw a picture of North Carolina.*)

If you are reading *Me and Uncle Romie* during small group time, then return to pp. 340–349a to guide the reading.

SMALL GROUP TIME

ELL

If... students need more scaffolding and practice with the **Main Selection, then...** use the activities on p. DI•122 in the Teacher Resources section on SuccessNet.

Me and Uncle Romie **SG•73**

Strategic Intervention

Common Core State Standards

Literature 1. Ask and answer questions to demonstrate understanding of a text, referring explicitly to the text as the basis for the answers. **Foundational Skills 4.** Read with sufficient accuracy and fluency to support comprehension. **Writing 7.** Conduct short research projects that build knowledge about a topic. **Speaking/Listening 1.** Engage effectively in a range of collaborative discussions (one-on-one, in groups, and teacher-led) with diverse partners on grade 3 topics and texts, building on others' ideas and expressing their own clearly. **Language 1.h.** Use coordinating and subordinating conjunctions. **Language 4.** Determine or clarify the meaning of unknown and multiple-meaning words and phrases based on grade 3 reading and content, choosing flexibly from a range of strategies. **Language 4.a.** Use sentence-level context as a clue to the meaning of a word or phrase.

1 Build Word Knowledge
Review Amazing Words

skyscraper	taxicab	scamper	scurry	vendor
hurl	meager	gutter	bitter	ramble

Team Talk **LANGUAGE DEVELOPMENT** Have students practice building more complex sentences. Display a sentence starter and have students add oral phrases or clauses using the Amazing Words. For example: The skyscraper _____. (The *skyscraper* was so tall / that the *taxicabs* / looked like *scurrying* ants.) Guide students to add at least two phrases or clauses.

> **Corrective feedback** | **If...** students have difficulty using Amazing Words orally, **then...** review the meaning of each of the words.

2 Read
"Country to City"

BEFORE READING Read aloud the genre information about online reference sources on pp. 354–357. *Me and Uncle Romie* is based on a real-life artist, Romare Bearden. This selection shows how to use  online references to show how you can learn more about him. Then have students note the different online sources reprinted in the article.

DURING READING Lead students in a choral reading of the selection. Stop to discuss concepts and terms such as *Harlem Renaissance.* How could you learn more about the Harlem Renaissance if you were sitting at a computer? (You could search in an online encyclopedia.)

AFTER READING Have students share their reactions to the selection. Then guide students through the Get Online! activity.

- What did you learn from the online almanac about North Carolina and New York? (statistics, such as their populations, and facts, such as sources of income)
- What did you learn from *Me and Uncle Romie* about North Carolina and New York? (an idea of what it is like to be in those places)

 ELL

If... students need more scaffolding and practice with Amazing Words, **then...** use the Routine on pp. xxxvi–xxxvii in the *ELL Handbook.*

SI Strategic Intervention

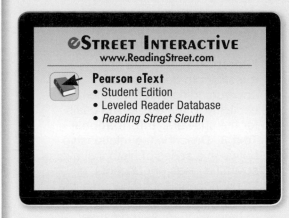

eStreet Interactive
www.ReadingStreet.com

Pearson eText
• Student Edition
• Leveled Reader Database
• *Reading Street Sleuth*

1 Build Word Knowledge
Review Conjunctions

IDENTIFY Choral read the Conventions note at the bottom of p. 353 to review conjunctions. Write a list of the conjunctions on the board. Have partners reread the model book review and make a list of all the conjunctions the author used. Allow time for students to discuss their examples and correct any misunderstandings.

2 Text-Based Comprehension
Read

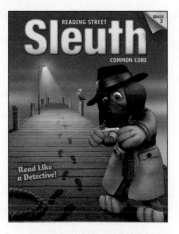

REREAD "The Harlem Renaissance on Canvas" Have partners reread "The Harlem Renaissance on Canvas," with partners alternating paragraphs.

EXTEND UNDERSTANDING Talk together about the kind of people Laura Wheeler Waring painted. Have students share why they believe she painted famous people.

PERFORMANCE TASK • Prove It! Help students find a painting from the Harlem Renaissance online. Have each student study the painting and write a paragraph describing what the painting shows about African American life. Encourage students to use descriptive words and phrases to describe the paintings.

COMMUNICATE Have students share their paragraphs with a partner. Invite students to discuss what they learned about African American life while researching Harlem Renaissance paintings.

More Reading for Group Time

CONCEPT LITERACY
Practice
Concept Words

BELOW-LEVEL
Reviews
• Author's Purpose
• Background Knowledge
• Selection Vocabulary

Use these suggested Leveled Readers or other text at students' instructional level.

eStreet Interactive
www.ReadingStreet.com

Use the Leveled Reader Database for lesson plans and student pages for *From Country to City* and *A Walk Around the City.*

SMALL GROUP TIME

A Advanced

Common Core State Standards

Literature 1. Ask and answer questions to demonstrate understanding of a text, referring explicitly to the text as the basis for the answers. **Informational Text 3.** Describe the relationship between a series of historical events, scientific ideas or concepts, or steps in technical procedures in a text, using language that pertains to time, sequence, and cause/effect. **Foundational Skills 4.** Read with sufficient accuracy and fluency to support comprehension. **Speaking/Listening 1.** Engage effectively in a range of collaborative discussions (one-on-one, in groups, and teacher-led) with diverse partners on grade 3 topics and texts, building on others' ideas and expressing their own clearly. **Language 4.** Determine or clarify the meaning of unknown and multiple-meaning words and phrases based on grade 3 reading and content, choosing flexibly from a range of strategies. **Language 4.a.** Use sentence-level context as a clue to the meaning of a word or phrase. **Also Writing 7.**

1 Build Word Knowledge

Extend Amazing Words

Team Talk Have students define *skyscraper*. Discuss other names for or ways to describe a skyscraper. Continue with *taxicab* and *scurry*.

2 Text-Based Comprehension

Read

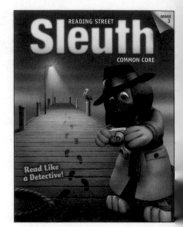

READ "The Harlem Renaissance on Canvas" Have students read "The Harlem Renaissance on Canvas" from *Reading Street Sleuth* on pp. 64–65.

ACCESS TEXT Discuss the Sleuth Work section with students before they work on it. Remind students that they can use these steps with other texts they read.

Gather Evidence Have students list details from the text. Invite them to share a compelling reason as to why the Harlem Renaissance was important to American culture.

Ask Questions Talk together about the painters students chose to research. Have students discuss sources they may use to find answers to their questions. If time permits, have partners research the answer to one of their questions.

Make Your Case Encourage students to make a list of reasons, listing them from the most important to least important. Talk together about the profession they chose and why.

3 Inquiry: Extend Concepts

IDENTIFY QUESTIONS Have students think about questions they have about the art of Romare Bearden and use these questions to explore his art, find an example that interests them, and learn how and from what materials he created it. On Day 5, they will present what they have learned.

If... students need more scaffolding and practice with **Vocabulary, then...** use the activities on pp. DI•117–DI•118 in the Teacher Resources section on SuccessNet.

A Advanced

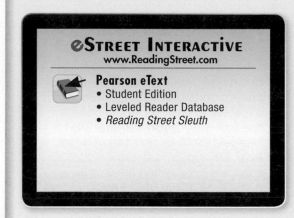

eStreet Interactive
www.ReadingStreet.com

Pearson eText
• Student Edition
• Leveled Reader Database
• *Reading Street Sleuth*

1 Build Word Knowledge

Extend Selection Vocabulary

Team Talk Have partners use the selection vocabulary in sentences to internalize their meanings. Have students use as many of the words as they can while making sure the sentence is grammatically correct. (Possible response: The *fierce* flood *ruined* the *cardboard* box that the *pitcher* kept his baseball *treasures* in.) Continue with additional selection vocabulary words.

cardboard	feast	fierce	flights
pitcher	ruined	stoops	treasure

2 Read

Me and Uncle Romie

If you read *Me and Uncle Romie* during whole group time, then use the instruction below.

ACCESS TEXT Reread the first two paragraphs on p. 336. Discuss the differences between James's home and the city where he visits Uncle Romie. (Differences include the fact that there are no regular houses on the city streets, only big buildings and stores. People live in apartments, not houses.)

Ask: How does the author show you the differences between the city and the country? (She reveals the differences through James's eyes and his actions, such as counting the number of flights.)

If you are reading *Me and Uncle Romie* during small group time, then return to pp. 330–339a to guide the reading.

3 Inquiry: Extend Concepts

INVESTIGATE Encourage students to use materials at their independent reading levels or student-friendly search engines to identify relevant and credible sites to gather information about Romare Bearden's art. Have students consider how they will present their information.

More Reading for Group Time

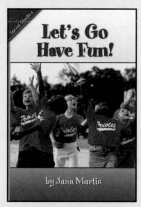

Let's Go Have Fun!

by Jana Martin

ADVANCED

Reviews
• Author's Purpose
• Background Knowledge

Use this suggested Leveled Reader or other text at students' instructional level.

eStreet Interactive
www.ReadingStreet.com

Use the Leveled Reader Database for lesson plans and student pages for *Let's Go Have Fun!*

SMALL GROUP TIME

© Common Core State Standards

Literature 1. Ask and answer questions to demonstrate understanding of a text, referring explicitly to the text as the basis for the answers. **Informational Text 5.** Use text features and search tools (e.g., key words, sidebars, hyperlinks) to locate information relevant to a given topic efficiently. **Foundational Skills 4.** Read with sufficient accuracy and fluency to support comprehension. **Language 4.** Determine or clarify the meaning of unknown and multiple-meaning words and phrases based on grade 3 reading and content, choosing flexibly from a range of strategies. **Language 4.a.** Use sentence-level context as a clue to the meaning of a word or phrase. **Also Writing 7.**

Independent Reading Options

Trade Book Library

eSTREET INTERACTIVE
www.ReadingStreet.com

Teacher Guides are available on the Leveled Reader Database.

ELL

If... students need more scaffolding and practice with the **Main Selection, then...** use the activities on p. DI•122 in the Teacher Resources section on SuccessNet.

SG•78 Cultures • Unit 5 • Week 5

A Advanced

① Build Word Knowledge
Develop Vocabulary

REREAD FOR VOCABULARY Reread the fourth and fifth paragraphs on p. 343. Let's read this paragraph to find out what *preserves* are. Discuss meaning and context with students.

② Read
Me and Uncle Romie

If you read *Me and Uncle Romie* during whole group time, then use the instruction below.

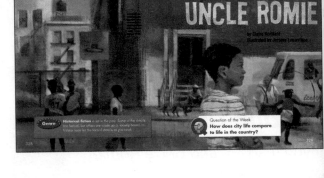

CLOSE READING Read pp. 341–342. Have students create a T-chart with the heads **Night** and **Day.** Have students search through text for words or details about how James feels the night before his birthday and words or details that tell how he feels on the morning of his birthday.

Night	Day
not fine at all	glorious mess
ruined	beat and bounce
sky turned black	That's home!

Ask: How does James feel the night before his birthday? (He's disappointed, lonely, and upset.) How does he feel the next morning when he sees Uncle Romie's art? (He's amazed and excited.)

If you are reading *Me and Uncle Romie* during small group time, then return to pp. 340–349a to guide the reading.

③ Inquiry: Extend Concepts

INVESTIGATE Provide time for students to investigate their topics in books or online. If necessary, help them locate information that is focused on their topics.

A Advanced

1 Build Word Knowledge

Extend Amazing Words and Selection Vocabulary

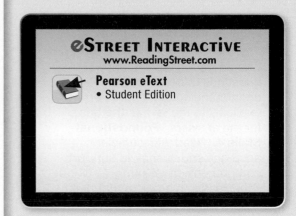

eStreet Interactive
www.ReadingStreet.com

Pearson eText
• Student Edition

skyscraper	taxicab	scamper	scurry
vendor	hurl	meager	gutter
bitter	ramble		

cardboard	feast	fierce
flights	pitcher	ruined
stoops	treasure	

Team Talk Have students practice building more complex sentences. Display a sentence starter and have students add oral phrases or clauses using the Amazing Words and the selection vocabulary. For example: The skyscraper _____. (The *skyscraper* was so tall / that people *scampered* / up many *flights* of stairs / to reach the top, / where they could enjoy a view / that they would always *treasure*.)

2 Read

"Country to City"

BEFORE READING Read the panel information on online sources on p. 354. Have students use the text features to set a purpose for reading and then read "Country to City" on their own.

DURING READING Ask students to consider how this selection differs from most other readings in the book.

How is the information in these Web pages presented differently from information in a story? (It is organized in bulleted lists and graphics rather than paragraphs.)

How does the format of the encyclopedia and almanac entries make the text easier to read? (It is easy to find the specific facts or details you need.)

AFTER READING Have students complete the Get Online! activity.

3 Inquiry: Extend Concepts

ORGANIZE INFORMATION Provide time for students to organize their information into a format that will effectively communicate their findings to their audience. Provide any necessary materials, such as poster board and markers and other supplies, or computer time.

Independent Reading Options

Trade Book Library

eStreet Interactive
www.ReadingStreet.com

Teacher Guides are available on the Leveled Reader Database.

Common Core State Standards

Literature 1. Ask and answer questions to demonstrate understanding of a text, referring explicitly to the text as the basis for the answers. **Foundational Skills 4.** Read with sufficient accuracy and fluency to support comprehension. **Writing 7.** Conduct short research projects that build knowledge about a topic. **Speaking/ Listening 1.** Engage effectively in a range of collaborative discussions (one-on-one, in groups, and teacher-led) with diverse partners on grade 3 topics and texts, building on others' ideas and expressing their own clearly. **Speaking/Listening 4.** Report on a topic or text, tell a story, or recount an experience with appropriate facts and relevant, descriptive details, speaking clearly at an understandable pace. **Language 1.h.** Use coordinating and subordinating conjunctions.

More Reading for Group Time

Let's Go Have Fun!

by Jana Martin

ADVANCED

Reviews
• Author's Purpose
• Background Knowledge

Use this suggested Leveled Reader or other text at students' instructional level.

eSTREET INTERACTIVE
www.ReadingStreet.com

Use the Leveled Reader Database for lesson plans and student pages for *Let's Go Have Fun!*

A Advanced

1 Build Word Knowledge
Extend Conjunctions

IDENTIFY AND EXTEND Choral read the bottom of p. 353 and have students discuss conjunctions. Encourage students to name the conjunctions they know. Have partners reread the model book review and make a list of all the conjunctions the author used. Then encourage students to write a single-paragraph book review of their favorite story using a mix of conjunctions. Allow time for students to discuss their work and correct any misunderstandings.

2 Text-Based Comprehension
Read

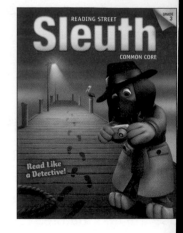

REREAD "The Harlem Renaissance on Canvas" Have partners reread "The Harlem Renaissance on Canvas." Have partners discuss how the new opportunities African Americans had as they moved to the cities affected their lives.

EXTEND UNDERSTANDING Discuss the idea of artists capturing what life is like during important periods in history. Discuss how artists did that during the Harlem Renaissance as well as other important times in American history.

PERFORMANCE TASK • Prove It! Help students find paintings from the Harlem Renaissance online. Have each student study a painting and write a paragraph describing what the painting shows about African American life. Encourage students to talk about the painters and the kinds of work they painted as well.

COMMUNICATE Have students share their paragraphs with a small group. Invite students to share new questions about the Harlem Renaissance these paintings raised for them.

3 Inquiry: Extend Concepts

COMMUNICATE Have students share their inquiry projects on Romare Bearden's art with the rest of the class. Provide the following tips for presenting.
• Match your tone of voice and your pitch to your content.
• Make eye contact with the audience and point to visuals as you speak.
• Speak at an appropriate rate.

UNIT 5

Cultures

What happens when two ways of life come together?

During this week, you may wish to:

☑ Choose content to **review** based on progress monitoring

☑ Focus on **target skills** or use the **flexible plan** to adjust instruction

☑ Provide opportunities for interacting with texts by using **model text** in the *Reader's* and *Writer's Notebook*

☑ Develop students' understanding of genre and text structure using the **Strategy Response Log** in the *Reader's* and *Writer's Notebook*

DAY 1	DAY 2	DAY 3	DAY 4	DAY 5
REVIEW WEEK 1	REVIEW WEEK 2	REVIEW WEEK 3	REVIEW WEEK 4	REVIEW WEEK 5
Suki's Kimono	*I Love Saturdays y domingos*	*Good-Bye, 382 Shin Dang Dong*	*Jalapeño Bagels*	*Me and Uncle Romie*
How does culture influence the clothes we wear?	How are cultures alike and different?	Why is it hard to adapt to a new culture?	How can different cultures contribute to the foods we eat?	How does city life compare to life in the country?
• **Amazing Words** *traditional, fret, scarves, fabric, acceptable, inspire, robe, drape, elegant, stylish*	• **Amazing Words** *clan, dwelling, shield, headdress, concentrate, barbeque, belief, chant, procession, settler*	• **Amazing Words** *native, homeland, aspect, advantage, sponsor, habit, impolite, manner, conscious, insult*	• **Amazing Words** *nutrition, calorie, flavor, spice, nutmeg, grumble, allergic, wholesome, grate, agent*	• **Amazing Words** *skyscraper, taxicab, scamper, scurry, vendor, hurl, meager, gutter, bitter, ramble*
Text-Based Comprehension Compare and Contrast; Visualize	**Text-Based Comprehension** Main Idea and Details; Inferring	**Text-Based Comprehension** Sequence; Monitor and Clarify	**Text-Based Comprehension** Draw Conclusions; Summarize	**Text-Based Comprehension** Author's Purpose; Background Knowledge
Phonics Syllable Pattern CV/VC	**Phonics** Homophones	**Phonics** Vowel Patterns *a, au, aw, al, augh, ough*	**Phonics** Vowel Patterns *ei, eigh*	**Phonics** Suffixes *-y, -ish, -hood, -ment*
Vocabulary Synonyms; Context Clues	**Vocabulary** Homophones; Context Clues	**Vocabulary** Compound Words; Word Structure	**Vocabulary** Unfamiliar Words; Context Clues	**Vocabulary** Homonyms; Context Clues
• **Fluency** Rate	• **Fluency** Accuracy	• **Fluency** Expression and Punctuation Cues	• **Fluency** Accuracy	• **Fluency** Appropriate Phrasing
• **Conventions** Adjectives and Articles	• **Conventions** Comparative and Superlative Adjectives	• **Conventions** Adverbs	• **Conventions** Comparative and Superlative Adverbs	• **Conventions** Conjunctions
• **Spelling** Syllable Pattern CV/VC	• **Spelling** Homophones	• **Spelling** Vowel Patterns *a, au, aw, al, augh, ough*	• **Spelling** Vowel Patterns *ei, eigh*	• **Spelling** Suffixes *-y, -ish, -hood, -ment*

Preview Your Week

What happens when two ways of life come together?

DAY 1

Student Edition, pp. 198–199

Genre: Realistic Fiction
Phonics: Syllable Pattern CV/VC
Text-Based Comprehension: Compare and Contrast

DAY 2

Student Edition, pp. 230–231

Genre: Realistic Fiction
Phonics: Homophones
Text-Based Comprehension: Main Idea and Details

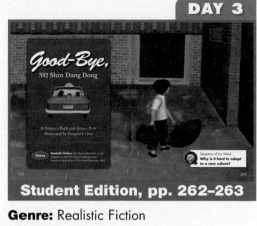

DAY 3

Student Edition, pp. 262–263

Genre: Realistic Fiction
Phonics: Vowel Patterns for /ȯ/
Text-Based Comprehension: Sequence

DAY 4

Student Edition, pp. 296–297

Genre: Realistic Fiction
Phonics: Vowel Patterns *ei, eigh*
Text-Based Comprehension: Draw Conclusions

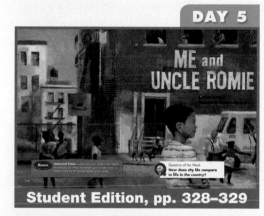

DAY 5

Student Edition, pp. 328–329

Genre: Historical Fiction
Phonics: Suffixes *-y, -ish, -hood, -ment*
Text-Based Comprehension: Author's Purpose

Reinforce Content Knowledge

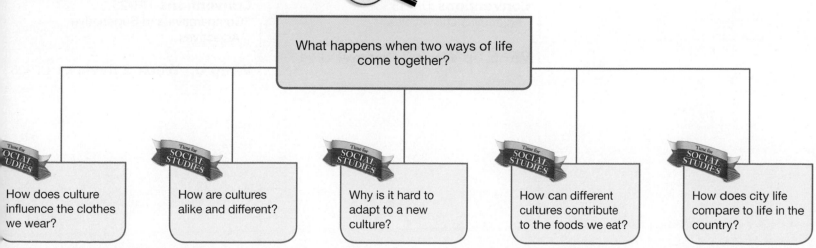

What happens when two ways of life come together?

| How does culture influence the clothes we wear? | How are cultures alike and different? | Why is it hard to adapt to a new culture? | How can different cultures contribute to the foods we eat? | How does city life compare to life in the country? |

5-Day Planner

DAY 1 Review Week 1

Get Ready to Read

Content Knowledge UR•6
Oral Vocabulary: *traditional, fret, scarves, fabric, acceptable, inspire, robe, drape, elegant, stylish*

Read and Comprehend

Text-Based Comprehension
UR•8–13
🔘 Compare and Contrast

Vocabulary Skill UR•10–13
🔘 Synonyms

Fluency UR•13
Appropriate Rate

Language Arts

Word Analysis UR•14
🔘 Syllable Pattern CV/VC

Spelling UR•14
Syllable Pattern CV/VC

Conventions UR•15
Adjectives and Articles

Wrap Up Week 1 Review! UR•15

DAY 2 Review Week 2

Get Ready to Read

Content Knowledge UR•16
Oral Vocabulary: *clan, dwelling, shield, headdress, concentrate, barbecue, belief, chant, procession, settler*

Read and Comprehend

Text-Based Comprehension
UR•18–23
🔘 Main Idea and Details

Vocabulary Skill UR•20–23
🔘 Homophones

Fluency UR•23
Accuracy

Language Arts

Word Analysis UR•24
🔘 Homophones

Spelling UR•24
Homophones

Conventions UR•25
Comparative and Superlative
Adjectives

Wrap Up Week 2 Review! UR•25

DAY 3 Review Week 3

Get Ready to Read

Content Knowledge UR•26
Oral Vocabulary: *native, homeland, aspect, advantage, sponsor, habit, impolite, manner, conscious, insult*

Read and Comprehend

Text-Based Comprehension
UR•28–33
◉ Sequence

Vocabulary Skill UR•30–33
◉ Compound Words

Fluency UR•33
Expression

Language Arts

Phonics UR•34
◉ Vowel Patterns for /ȯ/

Spelling UR•34
Vowel Patterns *au, aw, augh, ou, ough*

Conventions UR•35
Adverbs

Wrap Up Week 3 Review! UR•35

DAY 4 Review Week 4

Get Ready to Read

Content Knowledge UR•36
Oral Vocabulary: *nutrition, calorie, flavor, spice, nutmeg, grumble, allergic, wholesome, grate, agent*

Read and Comprehend

Text-Based Comprehension
UR•38–43
◉ Draw Conclusions

Vocabulary Skill UR•40–43
◉ Unfamiliar Words

Fluency UR•43
Accuracy

Language Arts

Phonics UR•44
◉ Vowel Patterns *ei, eigh*

Spelling UR•44
Vowel Patterns *ei, eigh*

Conventions UR•45
Comparative and Superlative Adverbs

Wrap Up Week 4 Review! UR•45

DAY 5 Review Week 5

Get Ready to Read

Content Knowledge UR•46
Oral Vocabulary: *skyscraper, taxicab, scamper, scurry, vendor, hurl, meager, gutter, bitter, ramble*

Read and Comprehend

Text-Based Comprehension
UR•48–53
◉ Author's Purpose

Vocabulary Skill UR•50–53
◉ Homonyms

Fluency UR•53
Appropriate Phrasing

Language Arts

Word Analysis UR•54
◉ Suffixes *-y, -ish, -hood, -ment*

Spelling UR•54
Suffixes *-y, -ish, -hood, -ment*

Conventions UR•55
Conjunctions

Wrap Up Week 5 Review! UR•55

Access for All
Small Group Lesson Plan
★ Focus on these activities when time is limited.

	DAY 1 Review Week 1 pages UR•6–UR•15	DAY 2 Review Week 2 pages UR•16–UR•25
OL On-Level	**Review** ★• Compare and Contrast • Synonyms • Read with Appropriate Rate ★• Quick Write for Fluency	**Review** ★• Main Idea and Details ★• Homophones • Read with Accuracy ★• Quick Write for Fluency
SI Strategic Intervention	**Reteach and Review** • Content Knowledge • Oral Vocabulary ★• Syllable Pattern CV/VC ★• Compare and Contrast • Synonyms • Read with Appropriate Rate • Spelling ★• Adjectives and Articles ★• Quick Write for Fluency	**Reteach and Review** • Content Knowledge • Oral Vocabulary ★• Homophones ★• Main Idea and Details • Homophones • Read with Accuracy • Spelling ★• Comparative and Superlative Adjectives ★• Quick Write for Fluency
A Advanced	**Extend** ★• Compare and Contrast • Synonyms ★• Quick Write for Fluency	**Extend** ★• Main Idea and Details • Homophones ★• Quick Write for Fluency
ELL	**Reteach and Review** • Content Knowledge • Oral Vocabulary • ELL Poster ★• Syllable Pattern CV/VC ★• Compare and Contrast • Synonyms • Read with Appropriate Rate • Spelling ★• Adjectives and Articles ★• Quick Write for Fluency	**Reteach and Review** • Content Knowledge • Oral Vocabulary • ELL Poster ★• Homophones ★• Main Idea and Details • Homophones • Read with Accuracy • Spelling ★• Comparative and Superlative Adjectives ★• Quick Write for Fluency

Build Oral Vocabulary

REVIEW AMAZING WORDS Display the Amazing Words for *Suki's Kimono*. Remind students that the words are related to the week's concept.

Amazing Words

Robust Vocabulary Routine

1. **Review** Ask students for definitions of the words, starting at the top of the list. Listen for accurate definitions. Prompt students to connect the words to the unit concept of Cultures whenever possible.

2. **Demonstrate** Have students use two or more Amazing Words in the same sentence. Guide the discussion by providing an example that shows the meaning of each word. *Clothing that is stylish in one culture may not be acceptable in another.* Follow this pattern to the end of the list, covering as many of the ten words as possible.

3. **Apply** Assign the words in random order and have students come up with more new sentences for them. *To show that you are becoming more comfortable using these Amazing Words, think up more new sentences for them.*

Routines Flip Chart

AMAZING WORDS AT WORK Have students use the Retelling Cards/Story Sort for *Suki's Kimono* to talk about the Amazing Words.

CONNECT TO READING Tell students that today they will be rereading passages from *Suki's Kimono* and reading "Aaron's First Day." As they read, ask students to think about how culture influences the clothes we wear.

eSTREET INTERACTIVE
www.ReadingStreet.com

Big Question Video

Concept Talk Video

Teacher Resources
• Amazing Word Cards

Story Sort

Amazing Words

traditional	inspire
fret	robe
scarves	drape
fabric	elegant
acceptable	stylish

Build Background Use ELL Poster 21 to review the Week 1 lesson concept and to practice oral language. Point out and read the question: *How does culture influence the clothes we wear?*

Once in a while, Suki would lift her arms and let the butterfly sleeves flutter in the breeze. It made her feel like she'd grown her own set of wings.

Let's **Think** About...

How do you feel when others tease you? How might Suki feel?
Background Knowledge

When they reached the school, Mari and Yumi hurried across the yard to a group of their friends. Suki stopped and looked around. Some of the children turned and stared at her, and others giggled and pointed at her kimono.

But Suki ignored them.

204 **5**

She took a seat on a swing to wait for the bell. A girl dressed in overalls just like a pair Suki had at home sat on the swing beside her.

"Hi, Suki," said the girl.

"Hi, Penny," said Suki.

"How come you're dressed so funny?" Penny asked. "Where did you get those shoes?"

Suki lifted her feet off the sand and wiggled her toes. "I'm not dressed funny," she said. "My grandma gave me these shoes."

Suki started pumping her legs. After a moment, Penny did the same, and soon they were both swinging as fast and as high as they could. *Swoosh, swoosh,* up and up.

Let's **Think** About...

What do you think might happen next for Suki and Penny?
Predict

6

205

Student Edition, pp. 204–205

Common Core State Standards

Literature 1. Ask and answer questions to demonstrate understanding of a text, referring explicitly to the text as the basis for the answers. **Literature 3.** Describe characters in a story (e.g., their traits, motivations, or feelings) and explain how their actions contribute to the sequence of events.

Access Text ©

REVIEW ⊙ COMPARE AND CONTRAST Review the definitions of compare and contrast on p. 194. Remind students that when they compare and contrast two or more things, they tell how the things are alike and different. Tell students that clue words sometimes signal that things are being compared or contrasted.

GUIDE PRACTICE Point out the clue words *same* and *both* in the last paragraph on p. 205. Have students explain how Suki and Penny are alike in this paragraph. Have them look at the illustrations to explain how the two girls are different.

ON THEIR OWN Have students look at the illustrations again and reread the text on p. 205 to find something else that is being compared and contrasted.

Close Reading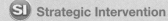

ANALYSIS Reread the bottom of p. 204. Compare and contrast how Suki and her sisters interact with the other students at school. Suki's sisters immediately join a group of their friends. Suki stays by herself.

INFERENCE When the other children laugh and point at Suki's kimono, Suki ignores them and sits on a swing by herself. Why do you think she does this? She thinks the other students are judging her because she's wearing unusual clothing.

INFERENCE Penny recognizes that Suki is dressed differently, but she swings with her anyway. How does Penny's loyalty help Suki get through her first day of school? Suki probably feels more comfortable knowing that her friend Penny accepts her for who she is.

eStreet Interactive
www.ReadingStreet.com

Pearson eText
• Student Edition

Access for All

SI Strategic Intervention

Have students make a T-Chart with "Compare" in the left column and "Contrast" in the right column. Tell students to list similarities and differences between characters as they read.

A Advanced

Have students write a few sentences about the role Penny plays in the story. Ask volunteers to read their compositions aloud.

On the first day of school, Suki wanted to wear her kimono. Her sisters did not approve.

"You can't wear that," said Mari. "People will think you're weird."

"You can't wear that," said Yumi. "Everyone will laugh, and no one will play with you."

"You need something new, Suki."

"You need something cool."

But Suki shook her head. She didn't care for new. She didn't care for cool. She wanted to wear her favorite thing. And her favorite thing was her kimono.

Let's Think About...
How does the art help you form a picture in your mind of Suki in her kimono?
Visualize

1

Suki's obāchan had given her the kimono. The first time Suki wore it, her obāchan took her to a street festival where they slurped bowls of slippery, cold sōmen noodles and shared a cone of crunchy, shaved ice topped with a sweet red bean sauce.

Under strings of paper lanterns, Suki joined her obāchan in a circle dance. She followed her and copied her movements, trying to be as light and as graceful. She watched the other women and children who danced, especially those who were dressed in cotton kimonos like her.

Let's Think About...
The words in this description are meant to help you visualize. What can you do if you don't understand them?
Monitor and Clarify

2

200

201

Student Edition, pp. 200–201

Common Core State Standards

Literature 1. Ask and answer questions to demonstrate understanding of a text, referring explicitly to the text as the basis for the answers. **Literature 3.** Describe characters in a story (e.g., their traits, motivations, or feelings) and explain how their actions contribute to the sequence of events. **Language 4.a.** Use sentence-level context as a clue to the meaning of a word or phrase.

Access Text ©

REVIEW ⊙ SYNONYMS Review the definition of synonyms on p. 196. Remind students that a synonym is a word that has the same or almost the same meaning as another word. Explain that an author can use a synonym of a word as a clue to the meaning of the word, as well as the context in which the word appears.

GUIDE PRACTICE Point out the word *graceful* on p. 201. Have students look for a synonym for *graceful* in the same sentence. *(light)* Ask a volunteer to demonstrate light movements and explain that when movements are graceful, they are also light.

ON THEIR OWN Use *Let's Practice It!* p. 342 on the *Teacher Resources DVD-ROM* for additional practice with synonyms.

Let's Practice It! TR DVD•342

Close Reading ©

DEVELOP LANGUAGE What synonym does the author use to help you figure out the meaning of the word *followed* on p. 201? **The synonym used for *followed* is *copied*.**

ANALYSIS Compare and contrast Suki's personality with her sisters' personalities. **Suki is an independent thinker who is not afraid to be herself. Her sisters follow the crowd; they seek approval from others.**

INFERENCE Suki's sisters are willing to dress as others want them to in order to feel accepted. How do you think this makes them feel? **Suki's sisters probably feel sad and hurt that they can't express themselves freely.**

ANALYSIS Suki and her grandmother enjoy a traditional Japanese street festival. What does Suki do and how does she feel at the festival? How does the experience of the festival affect her feelings about the kimono? **Suki has a fun time wearing her kimono, dancing with her grandmother, and eating new foods. Her memories of the festival help make the kimono her favorite thing.**

eSTREET INTERACTIVE
www.ReadingStreet.com

Pearson eText
• Student Edition

Teacher Resources
• Let's Practice It!

Access for All

SI Strategic Intervention
Have students work in pairs to write one sentence using the synonyms *followed* and *copied* and one sentence using the synonyms *light* and *graceful*.

A Advanced
Have students work in pairs to write sentences using a synonym as a context clue for a more difficult word. Then have students share their sentences with the class.

Read the story. **Answer** the questions.

Aaron's First Day

"I don't get it, Mom," Aaron said. Since we moved, I can't wear what I want anymore. Why do I have to look like everyone else?"

"Now, Aaron," said Mom, "that's hardly what a school uniform means. Rules are rules, and uniforms are the rule in your new school. I don't hear your sister complaining."

"She *wants* to look like everyone else," Aaron replied.

"Uniforms aren't all bad," Mom continued. "With a uniform, you don't even have to think about dressing for school. You can just get out a pair of pants and a shirt, and you're ready to go."

Aaron thought about when his favorite baseball team, the Arrows, would be in town. He always wore one of their orange and purple jerseys to school. Now, he'd have to wear his school uniform instead.

The next morning, Aaron came into the kitchen in his brand new uniform.

"Your uniform looks sharp," said Dad. Then he looked at Aaron's shoes. "Wait a minute. Are those orange and purple shoelaces part of the school uniform?"

"The rules don't mention shoelaces," Aaron pointed out.

His parents decided to let Aaron wear the orange and purple laces, but he brought along some plain white ones, just in case.

When he got to school, Aaron walked into his classroom and found a seat. No one seemed to notice his shoelaces. They didn't seem to notice him at all, as a matter of fact. The other kids were talking and laughing as if they'd known each other their whole lives.

Comprehension DVD•343

When recess time came, Aaron noticed a girl looking at him. *Oh no, she is coming over to talk,* Aaron thought, nervously.

"Are you an Arrows fan like I am?" she asked shyly.

"How'd you know?" Aaron asked, surprised.

"Your shoelaces!" she said, giggling and pointing.

Aaron looked down. He'd forgotten all about the shoelaces.

"Yeah, my favorite team is the Arrows," Aaron told her. "I used to live close enough to the ballpark that I could go to some of their games."

The girl said, "My name is Ashley. My brother just started pitching for the Arrows this summer! We're going to see him pitch in the playoffs this weekend. Maybe you'd like to go with us."

"You bet I would," said Aaron, excitedly. "I'll even wear my shoelaces!"

---

1. How is Aaron's new school different from his old one?

   <u>**He has to wear a uniform at his new school.**</u>

2. How are Aaron and his sister different?

   <u>**Possible response: His sister wants to look like everyone else in**</u>
   <u>**her class; he does not.**</u>

3. What is the same about Aaron and the girl at school who talks to him?

   <u>**They both like a baseball team named the Arrows.**</u>

School + Home **Home Activity** Your child compared and contrasted characters and places in a story. Have your child choose two people in your family or neighborhood and tell how they are alike and how they are different.

DVD•344 Comprehension

Let's Practice It! TR DVD•343–34

Common Core State Standards

Literature 1. Ask and answer questions to demonstrate understanding of a text, referring explicitly to the text as the basis for the answers. **Literature 3.** Describe characters in a story (e.g., their traits, motivations, or feelings) and explain how their actions contribute to the sequence of events. **Literature 10.** By the end of the year, read and comprehend literature, including stories, dramas, and poetry, at the high end of the grades 2–3 text complexity band independently and proficiently. **Foundational Skills 3.** Know and apply grade-level phonics and word analysis skills in decoding words. **Language 4.a.** Use sentence-level context as a clue to the meaning of a word or phrase. **Also Foundational Skills 4.b.**

Access Text ©

Have students read "Aaron's First Day" and respond to the questions.

REVIEW COMPARE AND CONTRAST What is the same about Aaron and the girl at school who talks to him? They both like a baseball team named the Arrows.

Review with students that a clue word often signals when things are being compared or contrasted. In the sentence *Are you an Arrows fan like I am?*, the word *like* shows sameness. It signals that the two students have something in common.

REVIEW VISUALIZE What words help you visualize what Aaron experiences when he walks into his classroom? The other kids were talking and laughing as if they'd known each other their whole lives.

REVIEW ⊙ SYNONYMS What is a synonym for the word *jersey* in paragraph 5? *shirt* How do you know this? Aaron remembers when he could choose which shirt he wanted to wear at his old school. If his favorite baseball team was in town, he always wore one of their jerseys.

Review with students that they can determine the meaning of an unfamiliar word by looking at nearby words and sentences for a synonym of the word. Ask students to use context clues to find a meaning for *uniform* in paragraph 2.

REVIEW ⊙ COMPARE AND CONTRAST How are Aaron and his sister different? His sister wants to look like everyone else in her class; he does not.

Sometimes there are no clue words signaling a comparison or contrast. The reader may need to read several paragraphs to determine whether a person, place, or thing is being compared to or contrasted with another. Ask students to find another example of compare and contrast in the story.

Reread for Fluency

MODEL FLUENT READING Read aloud the first four paragraphs of "Aaron's First Day" on p. 343, keeping your rate comfortable. Explain to students that you are reading the passage neither too slowly nor too quickly because you want your readers to understand what you are saying. Explain that you are pausing when you see a comma or period.

Routine   Oral Reading

1. **Select a Passage** Read the first four paragraphs of "Aaron's First Day."

2. **Model** Have students listen as you read at an appropriate rate.

3. **On their own** Have students read orally.

4. **Reread** For optimal fluency, students should reread three or four times at an appropriate rate.

5. **Corrective Feedback** Listen as students read. Provide corrective feedback regarding their oral reading, paying special attention to rate.

Routines Flip Chart

Common Core State Standards

Foundational Skills 3. Know and apply grade-level phonics and word analysis skills in decoding words. **Writing 10.** Write routinely over extended time frames (time for research, reflection, and revision) and shorter time frames (a single sitting or a day or two) for a range of discipline-specific tasks, purposes, and audiences. **Language 1.a.** Explain the function of nouns, pronouns, verbs, adjectives, and adverbs in general and their functions in particular sentences. **Also Language 2.f.**

Let's Practice It! TR DVD•341

Reader's and Writer's Notebook, pp. 371–372

Word Analysis

REVIEW ⊙ SYLLABLE PATTERN CV/VC Review the syllable pattern CV/VC using *Sound-Spelling Card* 116.

Use *Let's Practice It!* p. 341 on the *Teacher Resources DVD-ROM*.

READ WORDS IN ISOLATION Point out that students know how to read these words. Have students read the words together. Allow several seconds previewing time for the first reading.

READ WORDS IN CONTEXT Point out that there are many words in the sentences that students already know. Have students read the sentences together.

> **Corrective feedback**
>
> **If...** students have difficulty reading the syllable pattern CV/VC,
>
> **then...** guide them in using the word parts strategy. Have students read all the words repeatedly until they can read the words fluently. Then have students read each sentence repeatedly until they can read the sentences fluently.

Spelling

REVIEW SYLLABLE PATTERN CV/VC Write *create, medium,* and *pioneer*. Point out that these words have the CV/VC syllable pattern. Remind students that they have learned how to spell words with the CV/VC syllable pattern.

SPELLING STRATEGY Review words with the syllable pattern CV/VC by having students follow the spelling strategy for spelling these words.

> **We spell some words incorrectly because we say them wrong.**
>
> **Step 1: Say the word correctly. Listen to the sound of each letter.**
>
> **Step 2: Say the word again as you write it.**

ON THEIR OWN Use p. 371 of the *Reader's and Writer's Notebook* for additional practice with spelling words with the syllable pattern CV/VC.

Conventions

REVIEW ADJECTIVES AND ARTICLES Review **adjective** and **article** with students.

GUIDE PRACTICE Read the following sentences. Have students identify the adjectives and articles in each sentence.

1. I have a blue jacket.
2. The book is funny.
3. An elephant has a gray trunk.

ON THEIR OWN For additional practice, use the *Reader's and Writer's Notebook,* p. 372.

Routine   Quick Write for Fluency   Team Talk

1. **Talk** Have pairs discuss how clothing from different cultures has influenced modern American fashion.

2. **Write** Each student writes a paragraph describing clothing from different cultures, using adjectives and articles.

3. **Share** Partners read their paragraphs to one another.

Routines Flip Chart

---

eSTREET INTERACTIVE
www.ReadingStreet.com

Teacher Resources
• Reader's and Writer's Notebook
• Let's Practice It!

Interactive Sound-Spelling Cards

Writing Workshop
Use the writing process lesson on pages WP•1–WP•10 for this week's writing instruction.

Wrap Up Week 1 Review!

✔ **Content Knowledge** What cultures influence our clothes?

✔ **Compare and Contrast** Compare the cultures and clothing discussed in this week's selections.

✔ **Synonyms** How can learning synonyms help you learn new words?

✔ **Homework** Send home this week's Family Times newsletter on *Let's Practice It!* pp. 339–340 on the *Teacher Resources DVD-ROM.*

Let's Practice It!
TR DVD•339–340

Preview DAY 2

Tell students that tomorrow they will review *I Love Saturdays y domingos.*

Content Knowledge
Review Oral Vocabulary

Text-Based Comprehension
Review 🔎 Main Idea and Details

Selection Vocabulary
Review 🔎 Homophones

Fluency
Accuracy

Phonics/Word Analysis
Review 🔎 Homophones

Spelling
Review Homophones

Conventions
Review Comparative and Superlative Adjectives

Writing
Quick Write for Fluency

Materials

• Student Edition
• Retelling Cards
• Sound-Spelling Cards
• Reader's and Writer's Notebook

Ⓒ Common Core State Standards

Speaking/Listening 1. Engage effectively in a range of collaborative discussions (one-on-one, in groups, and teacher-led) with diverse partners on grade 3 topics and texts, building on others' ideas and expressing their own clearly. **Language 6.** Acquire and use accurately grade-appropriate conversational, general academic, and domain-specific words and phrases, including those that signal spatial and temporal relationships (e.g., *After dinner that night we went looking for them*).

Content Knowledge

Comparing Cultures

REVISIT THE CONCEPT Today students will explore how the question for this unit of study connects to *I Love Saturdays y domingos.* Remind students of the Question of the Week, *How are cultures alike and different?*

Build Oral Language

DISCUSS CULTURES Remind students of the question for this unit of study, *What happens when two ways of life come together?* Use the prompts and the concept map from Week 2 to discuss similarities and differences when two cultures come together.

• How can we appreciate more than one culture?
• How can the beliefs of one culture be similar to beliefs of another culture?
• What can we learn from people from different cultures?

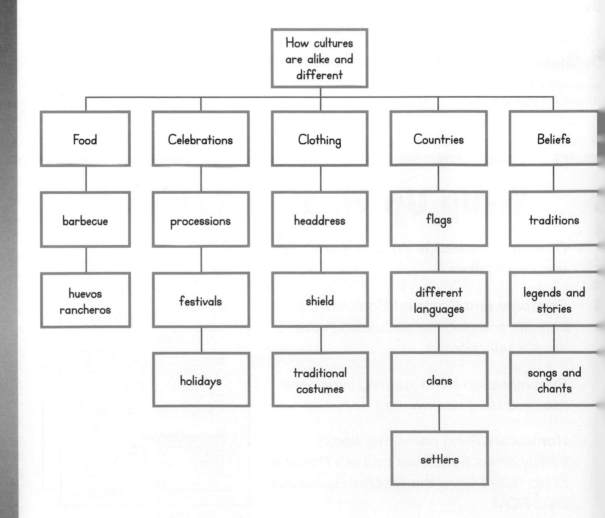

Build Oral Vocabulary

REVIEW AMAZING WORDS Display the Amazing Words for *I Love Saturdays y domingos.* Remind students that the words are related to the week's concept.

Amazing Words

Robust Vocabulary Routine

1. **Review** Ask students for definitions of the words, starting at the top of the list. Listen for accurate definitions. Prompt students to connect the words to the unit concept of Cultures whenever possible.

2. **Demonstrate** Have students use two or more Amazing Words in the same sentence. Guide the discussion by providing an example that shows the meaning of each word. *The Bear clan of the Hopi tribe stood in front of the dwelling.* Follow this pattern to the end of the list, covering as many of the ten words as possible.

3. **Apply** Assign the words in random order and have students come up with more new sentences for them. To show that you are becoming more comfortable using these Amazing Words, think up more new sentences for them.

Routines Flip Chart

AMAZING WORDS AT WORK Have students use the Retelling Cards/Story Sort for *I Love Saturdays y domingos* to talk about the Amazing Words.

CONNECT TO READING Tell students that today they will be rereading passages from *I Love Saturdays y domingos* and reading "Nana and Poppi." As they read, ask students to think about similarities and differences when two cultures come together.

eSTREET INTERACTIVE
www.ReadingStreet.com

Big Question Video

Concept Talk Video

Teacher Resources
• Amazing Word Cards

Story Sort

Amazing Words

clan	barbecue
dwelling	belief
shield	chant
headdress	procession
concentrate	settler

ELL

Build Background Use ELL Poster 22 to review the Week 2 lesson concept and to practice oral language. Point out and read the question: *How are cultures alike and different?*

On Saturdays, Grandma serves me breakfast: milk, scrambled eggs, and pancakes. The pancakes are spongy. I like to put a lot of honey on my pancakes.

Grandma asks me, "Do you like them sweetheart?" And I answer, "Oh, yes, Grandma, I love them!"

Los domingos, Abuelita serves me a large glass of papaya juice and a plate of eggs called *huevos rancheros.* The *huevos rancheros* are wonderful. No one makes them better than *Abuelita.*

Abuelita asks me if I like them: —*¿Te gustan, hijita?* First I need to swallow, and then I answer: —*Sí, Abuelita, ¡me encantan!*

234

Grandma has a tabby cat. Her name is Taffy. I roll on the carpet and call, "Come, Taffy, let´s play."

Abuelita has a dog. His name is *Canelo.* When I go out to the garden, *Canelo* follows me. I call out to him: —*Ven, Canelo. ¡Vamos a jugar!*

235

Student Edition, pp. 234–235

Common Core State Standards

Literature 1. Ask and answer questions to demonstrate understanding of a text, referring explicitly to the text as the basis for the answers. **Literature 2.** Recount stories, including fables, folktales, and myths from diverse cultures; determine the central message, lesson, or moral and explain how it is conveyed through key details in the text.

Access Text ©

REVIEW ⦾ MAIN IDEA AND DETAILS Review the definitions of main idea and details on p. 226. Remind students that the main idea is the most important idea about the topic. Details tell more about the main idea.

GUIDE PRACTICE Have students read p. 234 and discuss what the first four paragraphs have in common with the last three. Help them to see that the main idea is that the girl's grandmothers make her breakfast.

ON THEIR OWN Have students work in pairs to list details from p. 234 that support the main idea.

Close Reading ©

SYNTHESIS • TEXT EVIDENCE How is the main idea in the first paragraph on p. 235 like the main idea in the second paragraph? What are some details that are alike? The main idea in each paragraph is that the grandmother has a pet. Details that are alike include that each animal has a name and that the girl likes to play with each pet.

ANALYSIS Contrast the pets that the grandmothers have. Is their choice of pet something influenced by culture? Grandma has a cat, and *Abuelita* has a dog. Culture hasn't affected their choice of pet because people from different cultures have cats and dogs for pets.

ANALYSIS The girl's grandmothers make her special breakfasts. How are the breakfasts both different and alike? They are different because Grandma serves milk, scrambled eggs, and pancakes with honey, while *Abuelita* serves papaya juice and *huevos rancheros.* They are alike because the girl loves them both.

Access for All

SI Strategic Intervention

Write the following three sentences on the board: *Dogs are fun to play with. Dogs are loving animals. Dogs are easy to take care of.* Ask students to identify the main idea for those sentences.

A Advanced

Have students write two sentences that can be details to support the main idea *My grandmothers make breakfast for me.*

Grandpa has a beautiful aquarium. He keeps it very clean. "Look at that big fish!" Grandpa says, and points to a big yellow fish. "I like the little ones," I answer. It's fun to watch the big and little fish. I watch, my nose pressed against the glass, for a long time.

Abuelito takes me to the seashore. He loves to walk by the ocean. We sit on the pier and look down at the water.

—*Mira el pez grande*— Abuelito says. He points to a big fish.

—*Me gustan los chiquitos*— I answer, and show him some little silver fish that are nibbling by a rock.

We stay at the pier *un buen rato,* for a long time.

238

Grandpa knows I love surprises. One Saturday, when I arrive, he has blown up a bunch of balloons for me. The balloons look like a big bouquet of flowers: yellow, red, orange, blue, and green.

"What fun, Grandpa" I say, and run with my balloons up and down the yard.

Un domingo, Abuelito also has a special surprise for me. He has made me a kite. The kite is made of colored paper and looks like a giant butterfly: *amarillo, rojo, anaranjado, azul, y verde.*

—*¡Qué divertido, Abuelito!*— I say. And I hold on to the string of my kite as it soars high in the air.

239

Student Edition, pp. 238–239

Common Core State Standards

Literature 1. Ask and answer questions to demonstrate understanding of a text, referring explicitly to the text as the basis for the answers. **Literature 3.** Describe characters in a story (e.g., their traits, motivations, or feelings) and explain how their actions contribute to the sequence of events. **Foundational Skills 4.c.** Use context to confirm or self-correct word recognition and understanding, rereading as necessary. **Language 4.a.** Use sentence-level context as a clue to the meaning of a word or phrase.

Access Text ©

REVIEW ◎ HOMOPHONES Review the definition of homophones on p. 228. Remind students that they can often use context clues to figure out the meanings of homophones.

GUIDE PRACTICE Point out the word *nose* on p. 238. Have students find a homophone for *nose* on p. 239. *(knows)* Ask students to explain the two meanings of the words. Have them use context clues to know which word is correct on each page. Have them use each word in a sentence that shows understanding of the meaning.

ON THEIR OWN Use *Let's Practice It!* p. 346 on the *Teacher Resources DVD-ROM* for additional practice with homophones.

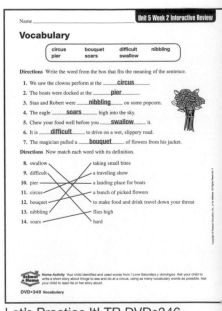

Let's Practice It! TR DVD•346

Close Reading ©

DEVELOP LANGUAGE On p. 239, the text says the kite "soars high in the air." How can you tell which homophone (*soars* or *sores*) is correct? **I know that when something *soars*, it flies high in the air. *Sores* are things that hurt. A kite would *soar*, not *sore*.**

EVALUATION • TEXT EVIDENCE Look at p. 239. How are the details about each grandfather similar? **Both grandfathers bring the girl a present. Both presents are colorful.**

ANALYSIS Dialogue is important in stories because it allows the reader to hear the different characters' voices. On p. 238, we hear Grandpa and *Abuelito's* voices and know that *Abuelito* speaks Spanish. Think of another selection where dialogue is important. How did the dialogue help you understand the story? **The dialogue in *Tops & Bottoms* told me what kind of characters Hare and Bear are.**

INFERENCE Describe how the girl probably feels when she spends time with her grandfathers. Explain why you think so. **The girl probably feels happy and loved because she has fun and sees interesting things, and both Grandpa and *Abuelito* give her surprises.**

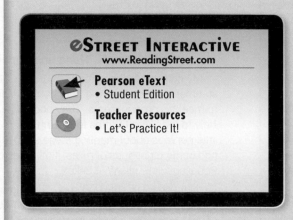

Access for All

SI **Strategic Intervention**
Write the following words on the board: *two, know, son,* and *hear.* Have students write a homophone for each word.

A **Advanced**
Have students think of a pair of homophones and use both words in one sentence. Have them write the sentence with blanks for the homophones. Have partners fill in the blanks.

Name_____

Read the story. **Answer** the questions.

Nana and Poppi

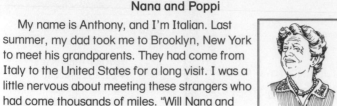

My name is Anthony, and I'm Italian. Last summer, my dad took me to Brooklyn, New York to meet his grandparents. They had come from Italy to the United States for a long visit. I was a little nervous about meeting these strangers who had come thousands of miles. "Will Nana and Poppi speak English?" I asked.

"Not very well," my dad said. "They know a few words, but they speak mostly Italian. The important thing is that they want to meet you. I've told them so much about you."

We went through the door of a big apartment building. "Nana and Poppi are staying with my cousin on the sixth floor," explained Dad, "so we have to take the elevator."

We got off on the sixth floor and rang the buzzer of apartment 612. An older man answered. "Poppi!" Dad cried as he hugged him. "Anthony, this is your great-grandfather Alfredo, but you may call him Poppi." I shook hands politely with Poppi and said, "Hello." He said, "Buongiorno," and motioned for me to come inside. Then he walked slowly to a couch and sat down.

Inside the apartment, Dad walked over to kiss and hug an older woman sitting in an armchair. *She was wearing a long, black dress. She must be my great-grandmother,* I thought. When I said hello, she smiled and said something in Italian to my dad. They both laughed, and then I didn't know what to do.

Name_____

"Come with me, Anthony," Dad whispered.

"Where are we going?" I whispered back.

"Come see what Nana made today." Dad pointed to a kitchen counter and said, "Nana said she made these just for you. I told her how much you love cannolis. This is her own secret cannoli recipe. See what you think." As I bit into one of the light, gooey pastries, I could taste the love that Nana had baked right into it.

"These are the best cannolis I've ever tasted!" I said, my mouth full. "Nana makes the best cannolis ever!"

---

1. What is this story mostly about?

   A boy named Anthony meets his great-grandparents from Italy.

2. What are some details that tell you about Poppi? Underline them. **Suggested answers are given.**

3. What are two details that tell you about Nana?

   Possible responses: She wears a long, black dress, she is a good baker, and she doesn't speak much English.

4. Underline the sentence below that tells the main idea of this story.

   Cannolis are a kind of Italian dessert.

   Family members can show love in many ways.

   Families can live in apartments or houses.

Let's Practice It! TR DVD•347–348

Ⓒ Common Core State Standards

Literature 1. Ask and answer questions to demonstrate understanding of a text, referring explicitly to the text as the basis for the answers. **Literature 2.** Recount stories, including fables, folktales, and myths from diverse cultures; determine the central message, lesson, or moral and explain how it is conveyed through key details in the text. **Foundational Skills 4.b.** Read on-level prose and poetry orally with accuracy, appropriate rate, and expression on successive readings. **Foundational Skills 4.c.** Use context to confirm or self-correct word recognition and understanding, rereading as necessary. **Also Language 4.a.**

Access Text Ⓒ

Have students read "Nana and Poppi" and respond to the questions.

REVIEW ◉ MAIN IDEA AND DETAILS What is this story mostly about? A boy named Anthony meets his great-grandparents from Italy.

Tell students that when they are trying to determine the main idea, they should ask themselves *What is the story all about?* Remind them to look for details to support the main idea.

REVIEW ◉ INFERRING In the fourth paragraph on p. 347, the great-grandfather says *"Buongiorno"* to Anthony. Reread the first paragraph. What can you infer that the great-grandfather said? Since the great-grandfather is from Italy, I know he is speaking Italian. Since Anthony had said "Hello" and the great-grandfather responded with *"Buongiorno,"* I can infer that *buongiorno* is a greeting in Italian.

REVIEW ⊙ HOMOPHONES What is a homophone for the word *made* on p. 348? *maid* What is the meaning of each word? Use each in a sentence. *Made* is the past tense of *make. Maid* means "a person whose job is to do housework." *Nana made delicious cannolis. The maid cleaned up the kitchen.*

Review with students that homophones are words that are pronounced the same but have different meanings and spellings. They can use context clues as they read to figure out which word and meaning is correct. Have students use the homophones *blue* and *blew* in a sentence. *The boy blew his blue horn.*

REVIEW ⊙ MAIN IDEA AND DETAILS What are some details that tell about Poppi? (older man, walked slowly)

Remind students that details are information that tell more about the main idea. Ask students to find details that tell about Nana. (She wears a long, black dress. She is a good baker. She doesn't speak much English.)

Reread for Fluency

MODEL FLUENT READING Remind students that it is important to read with accuracy in order to understand what we are reading. Model reading the first paragraph of "Nana and Poppi" on p. 347 with accuracy and have students track the print as you read.

Routine | Paired Reading

. **Select a Passage** Pair students and have them read "Nana and Poppi."

. **Reading 1** Students read the story, switching readers at the end of each page.

. **Reading 2** Partners reread the story. This time the other partner begins.

. **Reread** For optimal fluency, have partners continue to read three or four times.

. **Corrective Feedback** Listen to students read and provide corrective feedback regarding their accuracy.

Routines Flip Chart

© Common Core State Standards

Foundational Skills 4.c. Use context to confirm or self-correct word recognition and understanding, rereading as necessary. **Language 1.g.** Form and use comparative and superlative adjectives and adverbs, and choose between them depending on what is to be modified. **Language 2.e.** Use conventional spelling for high-frequency and other studied words and for adding suffixes to base words (e.g., *sitting, smiled, cries, happiness*). **Also Writing 10.**

Let's Practice It! TR DVD•345

Reader's and Writer's Notebook, p. 373

Word Analysis

REVIEW ⊙ HOMOPHONES Review homophones using *Sound-Spelling Card 137.*

Use *Let's Practice It!* p. 345 on the *Teacher Resources DVD-ROM.*

READ WORDS IN ISOLATION Point out that students know how to read these words. Have students read the sentences together. Allow several seconds previewing time for the first reading.

READ WORDS IN CONTEXT Point out that there are many words that students already know. Have students determine together which homophone fits the definition.

Corrective feedback	**If...** students have difficulty reading homophones, **then...** guide them in using the word parts strategy. Have students read all the words in each sentence repeatedly until they can read the words fluently. Then have students read each word repeatedly until they can read the homophones fluently.

Spelling

REVIEW HOMOPHONES Write *to, too,* and *two.* Point out that these words are homophones. Remind students that they have learned how to spell homophones.

SPELLING STRATEGY Review homophones by having students follow the spelling strategy for spelling these words.

> **Step 1: Ask yourself: Which part of the word gives me a problem?**
>
> **Step 2: Underline your problem part.**
>
> **Step 3: Picture the word. Focus on the problem part.**

ON THEIR OWN Use p. 373 of the *Reader's and Writer's Notebook* for additional practice with spelling homophones.

Conventions

REVIEW COMPARATIVE AND SUPERLATIVE ADJECTIVES Adjectives describe things. Review **comparative** and **superlative adjectives** with students.

GUIDE PRACTICE Read the following sentences. Have students identify the comparative and superlative adjectives.

1. A grown dog is **bigger** than a puppy.
2. This is the **longest** book I've ever read.
3. Justine is **faster** than Toni, but Kima is our **fastest** runner.

ON THEIR OWN For additional practice, use the *Reader's and Writer's Notebook,* p. 374.

Routine | **Quick Write for Fluency** | **Team Talk**

1. **Talk** Have pairs discuss the traditions and celebrations they have learned about.

2. **Write** Students each write a few sentences about traditions or celebrations, using adjectives to compare and contrast them.

3. **Share** Students read each other's writing and check for comparative and superlative adjectives.

Routines Flip Chart

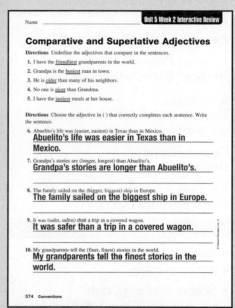

eStreet Interactive
www.ReadingStreet.com

Teacher Resources
• Reader's and Writer's Notebook
• Let's Practice It!

Interactive Sound-Spelling Cards

Reader's and Writer's Notebook, p. 374

Writing Workshop
Use pages WP•1–WP•10 for this week's writing instruction.

Wrap Up Week 2 Review!

✓ **Content Knowledge** How are cultures alike and different?

✓ **Main Idea and Details** What are the main ideas and details in this week's selections?

✓ **Homophones** How can learning homophones help you learn new words?

Preview DAY 3

Tell students that tomorrow they will review *Good-Bye, 382 Shin Dang Dong.*

Content Knowledge
Review Oral Vocabulary

Text-Based Comprehension
Review ⊚ Sequence

Selection Vocabulary
Review ⊚ Compound Words

Fluency
Expression and Punctuation Cues

Phonics/Word Analysis
Review ⊚ Vowel Patterns for /ȯ/

Spelling
Review Vowel Patterns *au, augh, ou, ough*

Conventions
Review Adverbs

Writing
Quick Write for Fluency

Materials

- Student Edition
- Retelling Cards
- Sound-Spelling Cards
- Reader's and Writer's Notebook

Ⓒ Common Core State Standards

Speaking/Listening 1. Engage effectively in a range of collaborative discussions (one-on-one, in groups, and teacher-led) with diverse partners on grade 3 topics and texts, building on others' ideas and expressing their own clearly. **Language 6.** Acquire and use accurately grade-appropriate conversational, general academic, and domain-specific words and phrases, including those that signal spatial and temporal relationships (e.g., *After dinner that night we went looking for them*).

Content Knowledge

Adapting to a New Culture

REVISIT THE CONCEPT Today students will explore how the question for this unit of study connects to *Good-Bye, 382 Shin Dang Dong.* Remind students of the Question of the Week, *Why is it hard to adapt to a new culture?*

Build Oral Language

DISCUSS CULTURES Remind students of the question for this unit of study, *What happens when two ways of life come together?* Use the prompts and the concept map from Week 3 to discuss how adapting to one culture from another can be difficult.

- What things might people bring from their homeland to a new country?
- Why is it an advantage to have a sponsor in a new country?
- Why might people have to change their habits when they move to a new place?

Build Oral Vocabulary

REVIEW AMAZING WORDS Display the Amazing Words for *Good-Bye, 382 Shin Dang Dong*. Remind students that the words are related to the week's concept.

Amazing Words   Robust Vocabulary Routine

1. **Review** Ask students for definitions of the words, starting at the top of the list. Listen for accurate definitions. Prompt students to connect the words to the unit concept of Cultures whenever possible.

2. **Demonstrate** Have students use two or more Amazing Words in the same sentence. Guide discussion by providing an example that shows the meaning of each word. *Learning a new language is one* aspect *of leaving your* homeland *and moving to a new country.* Follow this pattern to the end of the list, covering as many of the words as possible.

3. **Apply** Assign the words in random order and have students come up with more new sentences for them. *To show that you are becoming more comfortable using these Amazing Words, think up more new sentences for them.*

Routines Flip Chart

AMAZING WORDS AT WORK Have students use the Retelling Cards/Story Sort for *Good-Bye, 382 Shin Dang Dong* to talk about the Amazing Words.

CONNECT TO READING Tell students that today they will be rereading passages from *Good-Bye, 382 Shin Dang Dong* and reading "The Big Move." As they read, ask students to think about the difficulties of adapting to one culture from another.

eStreet Interactive
www.ReadingStreet.com

Big Question Video

Concept Talk Video

Teacher Resources
• Amazing Word Cards

Story Sort

Amazing Words

native	habit
homeland	impolite
aspect	manner
advantage	conscious
sponsor	insult

ELL

Build Background Use ELL Poster 23 to review the Week 3 lesson concept and to practice oral language. Point out and read the question: *Why is it hard to adapt to a new culture?*

Soon after we returned, family and friends began to arrive, carrying pots and plates of food. One by one they took off their shoes, then entered the house. Grandmother was dressed in her most special occasion *hanbok.* She set up the long *bap sang* and before I could even blink, on it were a big pot of dumpling soup and the prettiest pastel rice cakes I had ever seen. Kisuni and I peeled and sliced our chummy and carefully arranged the pieces on a plate.

Then everybody ate and sang traditional Korean songs and celebrated in a sad way. Love and laughter and tears rippled through our house. How I wanted to pack these moments into a big brown box and bring them with me to America.

Kisuni and I sneaked outside and sat beneath the willow tree. We watched the rain with glum faces.

"Kisuni, I wish we never had to move from this spot," I said.

"Me, too," she sighed. "Jangmi, how far away is America?"

"My mom says that it's halfway around the world. And my dad told me that when the moon is shining here, the sun is shining there. That's how far apart we'll be," I moaned.

"That's really far," Kisuni moaned back.

We watched the rain and grew more glum than ever. Then Kisuni perked up.

"So when you're awake, I'll be asleep. And when I'm awake, you'll be asleep," she declared. "At least we'll always know what the other one is doing."

268

269

Student Edition, pp. 268–269

Common Core State Standards

Literature 1. Ask and answer questions to demonstrate understanding of a text, referring explicitly to the text as the basis for the answers. **Literature 7.** Explain how specific aspects of a text's illustrations contribute to what is conveyed by the words in a story (e.g., create mood, emphasize aspects of a character or setting).

Access Text ©

REVIEW ◎ SEQUENCE Review the definition of sequence on p. 258. Remind students that the sequence is the order in which events happen in a story. Tell students that they can look for transition words that signal sequence, such as *first, next,* and *then.*

GUIDE PRACTICE Ask students to look for transition words as they read p. 269. Have them identify the sequence.

ON THEIR OWN Have partners use transition words to summarize the sequence on p. 269.

Close Reading ©

ANALYSIS What transition words and phrases does the author use on p. 269? *Soon after, Then* Identify another place on this page where the author could use a transition word or phrase to signal the sequence. The author could add the word *Next* at the beginning of the third paragraph.

INFERENCE What does Jangmi mean when she says that everybody "celebrated in a sad way"? Even though they were doing things they normally do to celebrate an occasion—singing and eating special foods—they were sad because the occasion was that Jangmi's family was moving away.

SYNTHESIS • TEXT EVIDENCE Using both the illustration and the text, explain what a *bap sang* is. The text says that Grandmother set up a *bap sang* and soon a pot of soup and rice cakes were on it. The picture shows a long colorful table with a pot, rice cakes, and other dishes on it. So a *bap sang* must be a meal table.

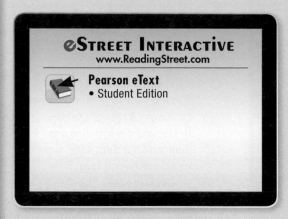

Access for All

SI Strategic Intervention

List transition words and phrases on the board. Model using them to summarize the sequence of events in the first paragraph on p. 269. Then ask students to use these words and phrases in their summaries of the entire page.

A Advanced

Have students summarize the sequence of events in a favorite fiction selection.

That moment our faces brightened. But a moment later we had to say good-bye.

Kisuni held back her tears. "Promise you'll write to me, Jangmi."

"I promise, Kisuni."

It was time to go to the airport.

"Kimpo Airport," Dad instructed the taxi driver.

The taxi slowly pulled away. I looked at our beautiful home one last time. Like rain on the window, tears streaked down my face.

"Good-bye, 382 Shin Dang Dong!" I cried.

270

On the long ride to the airport, Dad asked me, "Do you want to know what your new home looks like?"

"Okay," I shrugged.

"Let's see," Dad began, "it's a row house."

"A house that's attached to other houses," Mom explained.

"And inside the house are wooden floors," Dad added.

"No *ondal* floors?" I asked him. "How will we keep warm in the winter without ondal floors?"

"There are radiators in every room!" Mom said with an enthusiastic clap. "And a fireplace in the living room! Imagine!"

No, I could not imagine that. In our home we had a fire in the cellar called the *ondal*. It stayed lit all the time. The heat from the ondal traveled through underground pipes and kept our wax-covered floors warm and cozy. A fireplace in the living room sounded peculiar to me.

"And the rooms are separated by wooden doors," Mom added.

"No rice-paper doors?" I wondered.

My parents shook their heads. "No, Jangmi."

My eyes closed with disappointment. I had a hard time picturing this house. Would it ever feel like home?

271

Student Edition, pp. 270–271

Common Core State Standards

Literature 1. Ask and answer questions to demonstrate understanding of a text, referring explicitly to the text as the basis for the answers. **Literature 3.** Describe characters in a story (e.g., their traits, motivations, or feelings) and explain how their actions contribute to the sequence of events. **Foundational Skills 3.** Know and apply grade-level phonics and word analysis skills in decoding words. **Language 4.** Determine or clarify the meaning of unknown and multiple-meaning words and phrases based on grade 3 reading and content, choosing flexibly from a range of strategies.

Access Text ©

REVIEW ⊙ COMPOUND WORDS Review how to identify a compound word on p. 260. Remind students that they can look for two small words in a long word. They may be able to use the meaning of the two small words to determine the meaning of the compound word.

GUIDE PRACTICE Point out the word *airport* on p. 270. Have students identify the two small words in the compound word. Ask them to use the meaning of these words to determine the meaning of the compound word.

ON THEIR OWN Use *Let's Practice It!* p. 350 on the *Teacher Resources DVD-ROM* for additional practice with compound words.

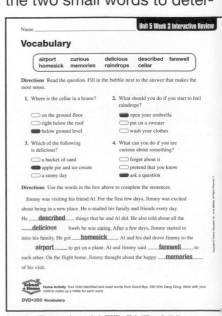

Let's Practice It! TR DVD•350

Close Reading ©

DEVELOP LANGUAGE What are the two small words in the compound word *fireplace* on p. 271? *fire, place* Use the meaning of these words to determine the meaning of this compound word. A fire is a collection of wood that is burning. A place is a location. A fireplace is a location inside a home where a fire burns.

INFERENCE Summarize the sequence on p. 270. Jangmi says good-bye to Kisuni, gets in a taxi, and says good-bye to her home. Why do you think Jangmi says good-bye to her home as well as her friend? Jangmi says good-bye to her home because, like her friend, it is something she loves, and she will miss it once she is gone.

ANALYSIS In what ways is Jangmi's American home unlike her Korean home? It is a row house, attached to other houses, and it has wooden floors, wooden doors, and a fireplace. Her Korean home had an ondal to heat the home through the floors and rice-paper doors.

Access for All

SI **Strategic Intervention**
Write *airport* and *fireplace* on the board. Draw a line to divide each compound word into two small words. Have students repeat this process with the word *underground*. Have partners use word structure to define each word.

A **Advanced**
Have students identify compound words in another selection and use word structure to determine each word's meaning.

DAY 3
Week 3

Name _____

Read the story. **Answer** the questions.

The Big Move

Moving from Colorado to Florida is like moving to another country, Will thought. He looked around his new neighborhood and tried to figure out what was so different. There were palm trees instead of pine trees. The air felt wet and sticky against his skin, instead of fresh and dry. He was sure there was something else, though. Suddenly, he knew. The mountains were missing! Almost everywhere he looked in Colorado, he could see the Rocky Mountains, often with snow on them. Florida was as flat as a pancake. There would be no more sled rides and no more snowball fights. Will felt sad and bored.

With nothing better to do, he reviewed what had brought them to Florida. <u>First,</u> there was the day his mom came home crying. She had lost her job as a chef in Denver. <u>Then,</u> for weeks, his mom tried to find a new job in Colorado. Nothing seemed as interesting as her old job, and nothing paid very well, either. <u>Finally,</u> his mom broke the news to him.

"Will, I can't find a job here in Colorado, so we'll have to move. We can't afford to live here without work for me."

Once Will's mom decided they should move, she learned about a few jobs she thought she would enjoy. The best one was in Miami, Florida. It sounded like a long way from Colorado, and it was. They packed all their belongings in a rental van. They said goodbye to all their friends, and then they were on the road.

Comprehension DVD•351

Name _____

Will enjoyed seeing new places on the trip to Florida. The first night away from home, they spent at Will's cousin's house. Will and his cousin stayed up late playing games and talking. The second night, his mom treated them to a stay in a motel with a swimming pool. The next morning, they crossed the state line. They were finally in Florida!

That far south, Will started to notice that the nights don't cool off as they do in Colorado. It is hot and humid all day in Florida and can be hot and humid all night, too. The heat made Will and his mom grumpy. So far, the move didn't feel very good to Will. Then they stopped for lunch in a beach town. Will had never seen the ocean or tasted its salty water. After an afternoon of playing in the waves, he decided that maybe Florida wasn't so bad after all!

1. Reread paragraph 2. Underline the time-order words that give clues about the order of events *before* the move.
Suggested answers are given.

2. What did Will and his mom do with all their belongings?

   They packed them in a van.

3. What happened first, next, and last during the trip to Florida?

   1. They stopped at Will's cousin's house. 2. They stayed in a

   motel. 3. They crossed the state line.

4. What did Will do after lunch in the beach town?

   He played in the waves.

School + Home Home Activity Your child identified the sequence of events in a realistic story. Do an activity with your child. Then help him or her recall the sequence of events that you followed together.

DVD•352 Comprehension

Let's Practice It! TR DVD•351–35

Access Text ©

Have students read "The Big Move" and respond to the questions.

REVIEW SEQUENCE Reread paragraph 2. Identify the time-order words that give clues about the order of events *before* the move. *First, Then, Finally*

Tell students that the sequence is the order in which events in a story happen. They can look for words and phrases that show what happens first, next, and last.

REVIEW MONITOR AND CLARIFY What could you do if you read the first two paragraphs and you did not understand why Will and his mother are moving to Florida? reread the text; read on to find more information

eStreet Interactive
www.ReadingStreet.com

Teacher Resources
• Let's Practice It!

REVIEW ⊙ COMPOUND WORDS What are the two small words in the compound word *snowball* on p. 351? *snow, ball* Use the word structure strategy to determine the meaning of the word *snowball.* I break the word into its two parts. I know that *snow* is frozen water. I know that a *ball* is a round object you throw. I put the two word parts together and understand that a *snowball* is a round object you throw that is made of snow.

Review with students that a compound word is made up of two small words. They can use the meanings of the small words to help them figure out the meaning of the compound word. Have students find other examples of compound words in the story and use the word structure strategy to determine their meaning.

REVIEW ⊙ SEQUENCE What happened first, next, and last during the trip to Florida? 1. They stopped at Will's cousin's house. 2. They stayed in a motel. 3. They crossed the state line.

Have students use time-order words to summarize these events with a partner.

Reread for Fluency

MODEL FLUENT READING Read p. 351 of "The Big Move" aloud using appropriate expression. Explain to students that you adjust your voice level to show excitement or sadness, and use punctuation cues to decide how to read and where to pause or stop.

Routine   Paired Reading

- **Select a passage** Use the entire text of "The Big Move." Divide students into pairs.

- **Reading 1** Students read the entire story, switching readers at the end of each paragraph.

- **Reading 2** Partners reread the story. This time the other student begins.

- **Reread** For optimal fluency, have partners continue to read three or four times.

- **Corrective Feedback** Listen as students read. Provide feedback about their expression. Encourage them to adjust their voice levels to stress important words and phrases.

Routines Flip Chart

© **Common Core State Standards**

Foundational Skills 3. Know and apply grade-level phonics and word analysis skills in decoding words. **Language 1.a.** Explain the function of nouns, pronouns, verbs, adjectives, and adverbs in general and their functions in particular sentences. **Language 2.f.** Use spelling patterns and generalizations (e.g., word families, position-based spellings, syllable patterns, ending rules, meaningful word parts) in writing words. **Also Writing 10.**

Let's Practice It! TR DVD•349

Reader's and Writer's Notebook, p. 375

Phonics

REVIEW ⊙ VOWEL PATTERNS FOR /ȯ/ Review vowel patterns *a, au, aw, al, augh,* and *ough* using *Sound-Spelling Cards* 56, 57, 58, 97, 105, and 106.

Use *Let's Practice It!* p. 349 on the *Teacher Resources DVD-ROM.*

READ WORDS IN ISOLATION Point out that students know how to blend these words. Have students read the words in each row together. Allow several seconds previewing time for the first reading.

READ WORDS IN CONTEXT Point out that there are many words in the sentences that students already know. Have students read the sentences together.

Corrective feedback	**If...** students have difficulty reading the vowel patterns *a, au, aw, al, augh,* and *ough,* **then...** guide them in using sound-by-sound blending. Have students read all the words in each row repeatedly until they can read the words fluently. Then have students read each sentence repeatedly until they can read the sentences fluently.

Spelling

REVIEW VOWEL PATTERNS *au, augh, ou, ough* The vowel sound in *ball* can be spelled *au, augh,* and *ough:* bec**au**se, t**augh**t, b**ough**t. The vowel pattern *ou* can spell short *u,* as in **touch,** and the vowel sound in **could.**

SPELLING STRATEGY Review words with vowel patterns *au, augh, ou,* or *ough* by having students follow the spelling strategy for spelling these words.

Step 1: Ask yourself: Which part of the word gives me a problem?

Step 2: Underline your problem part.

Step 3: Picture the word. Focus on the problem part.

ON THEIR OWN Use p. 375 of the *Reader's and Writer's Notebook* for additional practice with spelling words with the vowel patterns *au, augh, ou,* and *ough.*

Conventions

REVIEW ADVERBS An **adverb** describes an action. Adverbs can tell how, when, or where something happens. Adverbs often end in -*ly*.

GUIDE PRACTICE Read the following sentences. Have students identify the adverb in each sentence.

1. Chin Sen **recently** came to the United States.
2. My uncle lives **nearby.**
3. Daniel set the vase down **carefully.**
4. That store is **always** closed on Sundays.

ON THEIR OWN For additional practice, use the *Reader's and Writer's Notebook,* p. 376.

Routine   Quick Write for Fluency   Team Talk

1. **Talk** Have pairs discuss ways of life in different cultures.
2. **Write** Each student writes a paragraph about life in different cultures, using adverbs to describe actions.
3. **Share** Partners read each other's writing and check for adverbs.

Routines Flip Chart

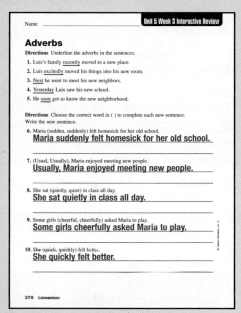

eSTREET INTERACTIVE
www.ReadingStreet.com

Teacher Resources
• Reader's and Writer's Notebook
• Let's Practice It!

Interactive Sound-Spelling Cards

Name _____   Unit 5 Week 3 Interactive Review

Adverbs

Directions Underline the adverbs in the sentences.

1. Luis's family <u>recently</u> moved to a new place.
2. Luis <u>excitedly</u> moved his things into his new room.
3. <u>Next</u> he went to meet his new neighbors.
4. <u>Yesterday</u> Luis saw his new school.
5. He <u>soon</u> got to know the new neighborhood.

Directions Choose the correct word in ( ) to complete each new sentence. Write the new sentence.

6. Maria (sudden, suddenly) felt homesick for her old school.
   Maria suddenly felt homesick for her old school.

7. (Usual, Usually), Maria enjoyed meeting new people.
   Usually, Maria enjoyed meeting new people.

8. She sat (quietly, quiet) in class all day.
   She sat quietly in class all day.

9. Some girls (cheerful, cheerfully) asked Maria to play.
   Some girls cheerfully asked Maria to play.

10. She (quick, quickly) felt better.
    She quickly felt better.

376 Convention

Reader's and Writer's Notebook, p. 376

Writing Workshop

Use pages WP•1–WP•10 for this week's writing instruction.

Wrap Up Week 3 Review!

✔ **Content Knowledge** How do you think you would adapt to a new culture or way of life?

✔ **Sequence** What is the sequence of events in the selection?

✔ **Compound Words** How can learning compound words help you learn new words?

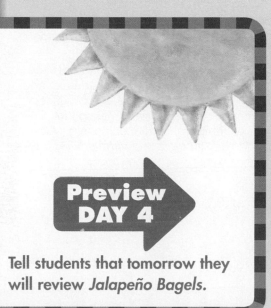

Preview DAY 4

Tell students that tomorrow they will review *Jalapeño Bagels.*

Content Knowledge
Review Oral Vocabulary

Text-Based Comprehension
Review Draw Conclusions

Selection Vocabulary
Review Unfamiliar Words

Fluency
Accuracy

Phonics/Word Analysis
Review Vowel Patterns *ei, eigh*

Spelling
Review Vowel Patterns *ei, eigh*

Conventions
Review Comparative and Superlative Adverbs

Writing
Quick Write for Fluency

Materials

- Student Edition
- Retelling Cards
- Sound-Spelling Cards
- Reader's Writer's Notebook

Common Core State Standards

Speaking/Listening 1. Engage effectively in a range of collaborative discussions (one-on-one, in groups, and teacher-led) with diverse partners on grade 3 topics and texts, building on others' ideas and expressing their own clearly. **Language 6.** Acquire and use accurately grade-appropriate conversational, general academic, and domain-specific words and phrases, including those that signal spatial and temporal relationships (e.g., *After dinner that night we went looking for them*).

Content Knowledge

Foods from Different Cultures

REVISIT THE CONCEPT Today students will explore how the question for this unit of study connects to *Jalapeño Bagels*. Remind students of the Question of the Week, *How can different cultures contribute to the foods we eat?*

Build Oral Language

DISCUSS CULTURES Remind students of the question for this unit of study, *What happens when two ways of life come together?* Use the prompts and the concept map from Week 4 to discuss how different cultures can influence the foods we eat.

- What are some ingredients that come from other cultures?
- What are examples of flavors that usually go with a certain culture?
- What foods do you like that come from a culture other than your own?

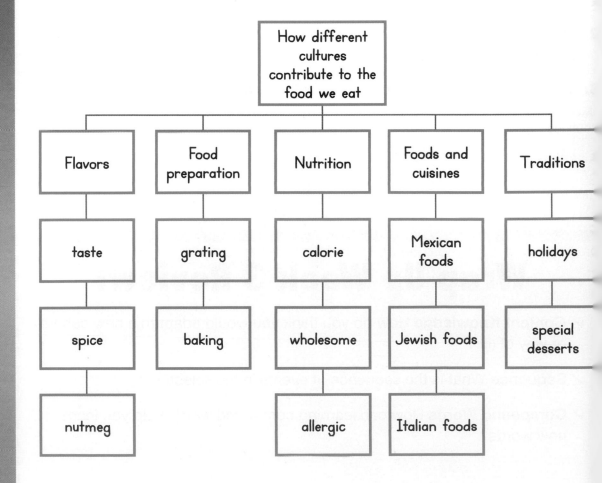

Build Oral Vocabulary

REVIEW AMAZING WORDS Display the Amazing Words for *Jalapeño Bagels*. Remind students that the words are related to the week's concept.

Amazing Words
Robust Vocabulary Routine

1. **Review** Ask students for definitions of the words, starting at the top of the list. Listen for accurate definitions. Prompt students to connect the words to the unit concept of Cultures whenever possible.

2. **Demonstrate** Have students use two or more Amazing Words in the same sentence. Guide the discussion by providing an example that shows the meaning of each word. *Nutmeg* is a *spice* used to *flavor* desserts. Follow this pattern to the end of the list, covering as many of the ten words as possible.

3. **Apply** Assign the words in random order and have students come up with more new sentences for them. To show that you are becoming more comfortable using these Amazing Words, think up more new sentences for them.

Routines Flip Chart

AMAZING WORDS AT WORK Have students use the Retelling Cards/Story Sort for *Jalapeño Bagels* to talk about the Amazing Words.

CONNECT TO READING Tell students that today they will be rereading passages from *Jalapeño Bagels* and reading "A Very Bad Day." As they read, ask students to think about how different cultures can influence the foods we eat.

Amazing Words

nutrition	grumble
calorie	allergic
flavor	wholesome
spice	grate
nutmeg	agent

ELL

Build Background Use ELL Poster 24 to review the Week 4 lesson concept and to practice oral language. Point out and read the question: *How can different cultures contribute to the foods we eat?*

Mama lets me pour in the chocolate chips and nuts. When she's not looking, I pour in more chocolate chips.

"I could bring chango bars. They're my favorite dessert."

"Mine, too," says Mama. "This batch should be especially good. I put in extra chips."

302

My father calls from the back room. "Pablo! Come help me with the bagels!" Papa speaks English and Yiddish. He learned Yiddish from his family in New York City. I know some words too. *Bubbe* means "grandmother." He uses my bubbe's recipe to make the bagels.

First he makes the dough in a big metal bowl. Then he rolls it out into a long rope shape. He cuts off pieces and shows me how to connect the ends in a circle. We put the circles on trays where they sit and rise.

303

Student Edition, pp. 302–303

Common Core State Standards

Literature 1. Ask and answer questions to demonstrate understanding of a text, referring explicitly to the text as the basis for the answers. **Literature 3.** Describe characters in a story (e.g., their traits, motivations, or feelings) and explain how their actions contribute to the sequence of events.

Access Text ©

REVIEW © DRAW CONCLUSIONS Review the explanation of drawing conclusions on p. 292. Remind students that you draw conclusions when you use facts and details in the text and what you already know to make decisions about characters and events.

GUIDE PRACTICE Have students reread p. 302 of *Jalapeño Bagels* and use facts and details in the text to draw conclusions about how Pablo and his mother feel about chocolate chips. Provide prompts such as: Does Pablo like chocolate chips? How do you know? How can you tell how Pablo's mother feels about chocolate chips?

ON THEIR OWN Have students reread p. 302 of *Jalapeño Bagels* and draw conclusions about whether Pablo told his mother he added extra chocolate chips to the *chango* bars.

Close Reading ©

SYNTHESIS Reread the first paragraph on p. 303 of *Jalapeño Bagels*. Why do you think that Pablo's father uses the family recipe to make bagels? Pablo's father probably uses the family recipe because he knows it well and he knows his customers enjoy the bagels.

INFERENCE Pablo and his mother both add extra chips to the batch of *chango* bars. Do you think the author meant this to be funny? Why or why not? Yes, it is funny because Pablo thinks he is sneaking in more chips, but his mother had already done so. Now there will be lots and lots of extra chips in the bars.

ANALYSIS Pablo's family's bakery is successful. Based on what you have read, why is it successful? Pablo's mother and father make the food by hand and with love. They work together and care about the foods they bake.

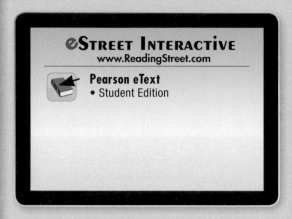

eSTREET INTERACTIVE
www.ReadingStreet.com

Pearson eText
• Student Edition

Access for All

SI Strategic Intervention

Review pp. 302–303 of *Jalapeño Bagels* with students and guide them to use facts from the story and what they know to draw conclusions about Pablo's relationship with his parents.

A Advanced

Have students use facts from the text and background knowledge to discuss whether this batch of *chango* bars will be really good or not.

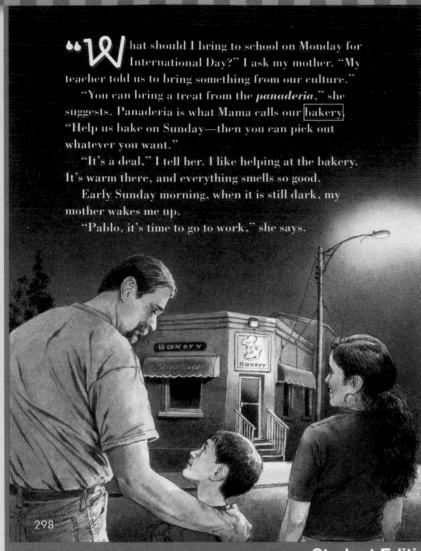

"What should I bring to school on Monday for International Day?" I ask my mother. "My teacher told us to bring something from our culture."

"You can bring a treat from the *panaderia*," she suggests. Panaderia is what Mama calls our bakery. "Help us bake on Sunday—then you can pick out whatever you want."

"It's a deal," I tell her. I like helping at the bakery. It's warm there, and everything smells so good.

Early Sunday morning, when it is still dark, my mother wakes me up.

"Pablo, it's time to go to work," she says.

We walk down the street to the bakery. My father turns on the lights. My mother turns on the ovens. She gets out the pans and ingredients for *pan dulce*. Pan dulce is Mexican sweet bread.

I help my mother mix and knead the dough. She shapes rolls and loaves of bread and slides them into the oven. People tell her she makes the best pan dulce in town.

"Maybe I'll bring pan dulce to school," I tell her.

298

299

Student Edition, pp. 298–299

Common Core State Standards

Literature 1. Ask and answer questions to demonstrate understanding of a text, referring explicitly to the text as the basis for the answers. **Language 4.** Determine or clarify the meaning of unknown and multiple-meaning words and phrases based on grade 3 reading and content, choosing flexibly from a range of strategies. **Language 4.a.** Use sentence-level context as a clue to the meaning of a word or phrase.

Access Text ©

REVIEW ⊙ UNFAMILIAR WORDS Review the definitions of unfamiliar words and context clues on p. 294. Remind students that you read the words and sentences around an unfamiliar word to look for context clues that can help you determine its meaning.

GUIDE PRACTICE Point out that *panaderia* on p. 298 may be unfamiliar because it is from another language. Ask students if they know what language the word is from. Have students use context clues to determine its meaning. Ask volunteers to share their meanings and the context clues they found.

ON THEIR OWN Use *Let's Practice It!* p. 354 on the *Teacher Resources DVD-ROM* for additional practice with unfamiliar words.

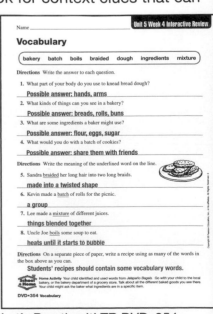

Name _____

Unit 5 Week 4 Interactive Review

Vocabulary

| bakery | batch | boils | braided | dough | ingredients | mixture |

Directions Write the answer to each question.

1. What part of your body do you use to knead bread dough?
   Possible answer: hands, arms
2. What kinds of things can you see in a bakery?
   Possible answer: breads, rolls, buns
3. What are some ingredients a baker might use?
   Possible answer: flour, eggs, sugar
4. What would you do with a batch of cookies?
   Possible answer: share them with friends

Directions Write the meaning of the underlined word on the line.

5. Sandra braided her long hair into two long braids.
   made into a twisted shape
6. Kevin made a batch of rolls for the picnic.
   a group
7. Lee made a mixture of different juices.
   things blended together
8. Uncle Joe boils some soup to eat.
   heats until it starts to bubble

Directions On a separate piece of paper, write a recipe using as many of the words in the box above as you can.
   Students' recipes should contain some vocabulary words.

Home Activity Your child identified and used words from *Jalapeño Bagels*. Go with your child to the local bakery, or the bakery department of a grocery store. Talk about all the different baked goods you see there. Your child might ask the baker what ingredients are in a specific item.

DVD•354 Vocabulary

Let's Practice It! TR DVD•354

Close Reading ©

DEVELOP LANGUAGE What context clues could you use to figure out the meaning of *ingredients* on p. 299? **The text says Pablo's mother turns on the oven and gets out pans and ingredients for *pan dulce*. It also says *pan dulce* is a sweet bread. I know she is going to bake something. I know when you bake something, you need flour and sugar and other things to mix together before you put them in a pan. I think *ingredients* must be the things she needs to make *pan dulce*.**

EVALUATION What do you think Pablo's mother's *pan dulce* tastes like? Why do you think so? **I think that Pablo's mother's *pan dulce* tastes sweet and delicious. I think it's sweet because its name means "sweet bread." I think her *pan dulce* is probably delicious because people say it is the best *pan dulce* in town.**

INFERENCE • TEXT EVIDENCE Do you think that Pablo's mother enjoys working in the bakery? Why or why not? Give examples from the text to support your answer. **I think that she must like it because she is very good at baking and people like her food. They say her *pan dulce* is the best.**

EVALUATION Are the foods from Pablo's family's bakery a good thing to bring to International Day at Pablo's school? Why? **Yes, the foods that Pablo's parents make are good to bring to International Day because they come from several different cultures. They show how different cultures contribute to the foods we eat.**

eStreet Interactive
www.ReadingStreet.com

Pearson eText
• Student Edition

Teacher Resources
• Let's Practice It!

Access for All

SI **Strategic Intervention**
Guide students to identify the context clues that surround the words. Discuss how each clue helps them figure out the meaning of the word.

A **Advanced**
Have students pick one word from the selection and look it up in a dictionary or glossary. Then have them write one or two sentences using the word with context clues. Have other students read the sentences, find the context clues, and tell the meaning of the word.

Name_____

Read the story. Then follow the directions and answer the questions.

A Very Bad Day

Kiran walked home glumly. It had been a very bad day and he was not in a good mood. He pushed open the front door and started up the stairs.

"Kiran, is that you?" his mom called from the kitchen.

Kiran didn't answer her. He went into his room and shut the door. He decided he might as well start on his homework. He didn't have anything better to do. Normally, he would go over to Pedro's house to play, but not today. Today he wasn't going anywhere near Pedro.

Kiran got out his math homework and stared at it. His bad day had all started with math. He had gotten a math test back. Now he pulled the test out of his folder and looked at it.

"Kiran, I'm disappointed in you," Mr. Murch had said as he handed Kiran back the test. "I know you can do better."

Kiran knew he could do better, too. That's why he was so mad at himself. Plus, everything had just gone downhill from there. It happened like that sometimes. One bad thing would just lead to another, until the whole day was ruined.

Kiran crumpled up the math test and threw it into the wastebasket. That was one test that wasn't going on the fridge. He lay back on his bed and put his arms under his head, staring at the ceiling.

Then he heard his mom calling. "Kiran, why don't you come down for a snack?" she yelled.

Kiran was feeling hungry. He got off his bed and trudged down the stairs. His mom had put samosas out on the table. Samosas were Kiran's favorite snack. He loved the crispy dough pieces filled with spicy potatoes and peas.

"Wow, thanks Mom," he said as he bit into one. Somehow, she could always make him feel better.

_____

1. Why caused Kiran's bad day?

   He got a bad grade on his math test.

2. Underline two sentences in the story that help you draw that conclusion. **Possible answers are given.**

3. Why do you think Kiran's mom made him his favorite snack?

   Possible answer: She figured out that Kiran had a bad day in school and she wanted to help him feel better.

School + Home **Home Activity** Your child drew conclusions by connecting prior knowledge or experiences with information he or she read in the story. Have your child tell why Kiran said he wasn't going anywhere near Pedro today and explain his or her reasoning.

Comprehension DVD•355

DVD•356 Comprehension

Let's Practice It! TR DVD•355–35

Literature 1. Ask and answer questions to demonstrate understanding of a text, referring explicitly to the text as the basis for the answers. **Literature 3.** Describe characters in a story (e.g., their traits, motivations, or feelings) and explain how their actions contribute to the sequence of events. **Foundational Skills 4.b.** Read on-level prose and poetry orally with accuracy, appropriate rate, and expression on successive readings. **Language 4.** Determine or clarify the meaning of unknown and multiple-meaning words and phrases based on grade 3 reading and content, choosing flexibly from a range of strategies. **Language 4.a.** Use sentence-level context as a clue to the meaning of a word or phrase.

Access Text ©

Have students read "A Very Bad Day" and respond to the questions.

REVIEW ◉ DRAW CONCLUSIONS What caused Kiran's bad day? He got a bad grade on his math test.

Remind students that they can draw conclusions about characters and story events based on facts and details in a story. Point out that the story includes many details that help you draw a conclusion about what caused Kiran's bad day: He got a math test back that morning; his teacher was disappointed in him; he was mad at himself; he threw the test in the wastebasket.

REVIEW ◉ SUMMARIZE Summarize the main events that happen when Kiran gets home from a bad day at school. When Kiran gets home, he goes to his room to do homework. In his room, he thinks about the events of his bad day. He recalls getting a bad grade on his math test and thinks about the other bad events that followed from there. His mother calls him downstairs for a snack. Finally, he feels better.

REVIEW ⊙ UNFAMILIAR WORDS What context clues help you figure out the meaning of the unfamiliar word *samosa*? What is the meaning of the word? The words and sentences around the unfamiliar word *samosa* tell me that it is a snack with crispy dough, spicy potatoes, and peas. A *samosa* is a pastry stuffed with spicy potatoes and peas.

Remind students that they can use the words and sentences around an unfamiliar word to predict a meaning for the word. Then they can try their meaning in the sentence to see if it makes sense.

REVIEW ⊙ DRAW CONCLUSIONS Why do you think Kiran's mom made him his favorite snack? She figured out that Kiran had a bad day in school, and she wanted to make him feel better.

Remind students that they can use what they already know to help them draw conclusions about characters and story events. Have students discuss how family members cheer them up when they are sad or have had a bad day. Discuss how their prior experience helps them draw a conclusion about why Kiran's mom made him his favorite snack.

Reread for Fluency

MODEL FLUENT READING Read aloud the first three paragraphs of "A Very Bad Day" on p. 355 to model reading carefully and without skipping words. Remind students that to read accurately, you read carefully so you don't skip words or say the wrong word.

Routine | Oral Rereading

1. **Read** Have students read "A Very Bad Day" orally.

2. **Reread** To achieve optimal fluency, students should reread the text three or four times.

3. **Corrective Feedback** Have students read aloud without you. Provide feedback about their accuracy and encourage them to take their time to read each word correctly.

Routines Flip Chart

Common Core State Standards

Foundational Skills 3. Know and apply grade-level phonics and word analysis skills in decoding words. **Language 1.g.** Form and use comparative and superlative adjectives and adverbs, and choose between them depending on what is to be modified. **Language 2.f.** Use spelling patterns and generalizations (e.g., word families, position-based spellings, syllable patterns, ending rules, meaningful word parts) in writing words. **Also Writing 10.**

Let's Practice It! TR DVD•353

Reader's and Writer's Notebook, p. 377

Phonics

REVIEW ◉ VOWEL PATTERNS *ei, eigh* Review vowel patterns *ei* and *eigh* using *Sound-Spelling Cards* 64, 65, and 66.

Use *Let's Practice It!* p. 353 on the *Teacher Resources DVD-ROM*.

READ WORDS IN ISOLATION Point out that students know how to blend these words. Have students read the words in the row together. Allow several seconds previewing time for the first reading.

READ WORDS IN CONTEXT Point out that there are many words in the sentences that students already know. Have students read the sentences together.

| Corrective feedback | **If...** students have difficulty reading the vowel sounds *ei* and *eigh*, **then...** guide them in using sound-by-sound blending. Have students read all the words in the row repeatedly until they can read the words fluently. Then have students read each sentence repeatedly until they can read the sentences fluently. |

Spelling

REVIEW VOWEL PATTERNS *ei, eigh* The vowel pattern *ei* often spells long *e*: **ceiling**. The vowel pattern *eigh* can spell long *a* or long *i*: **neighbor, weight, height.**

SPELLING STRATEGY Review words with the vowel pattern *ei* and *eigh* by having students follow the spelling strategy for spelling these words.

Step 1: Ask yourself: Which part of the word gives me a problem?

Step 2: Underline your problem part.

Step 3: Picture the word. Focus on the problem part.

ON THEIR OWN Use p. 377 of the *Reader's and Writer's Notebook* for additional practice with spelling words with the vowel patterns *ei* and *eigh*.

Conventions

REVIEW COMPARATIVE AND SUPERLATIVE ADVERBS Review **comparative adverb** and **superlative adverb** with students.

GUIDE PRACTICE Read the following sentences. Have students identify the comparative and superlative adverbs in each sentence.

1. Helen finished her homework **sooner** than Kelley.
2. After the play, we clapped **loudest** in the whole audience.
3. My cake tasted **better** than Mike's, but Ken's cake tasted **best.**

ON THEIR OWN For additional practice, use the *Reader's and Writer's Notebook,* p. 378.

Routine · Quick Write for Fluency · Team Talk

1. **Talk** Have pairs discuss combining foods from different cultures.

2. **Write** Each student writes a few sentences about a favorite food from a different culture using comparative adverbs.

3. **Share** Partners read their own writing to each other and check for correct usage of comparative adverbs.

Routines Flip Chart

eSTREET INTERACTIVE
www.ReadingStreet.com

Teacher Resources
• Reader's and Writer's Notebook
• Let's Practice It!

Interactive Sound-Spelling Cards

Name _____

Unit 5 Week 4 Interactive Review

Comparative and Superlative Adverbs

Directions Underline the adverb that compares in each sentence.
1. Bread bakes longer than biscuits do.
2. The big oven heats more quickly than the other ovens.
3. Of all the breads, the banana bread will be done soonest.
4. Mrs. Stone kneads dough harder than Kelly does.
5. Of all the neighbors, Mrs. Lopez works most slowly.

Directions Choose the correct word in ( ) to complete each sentence. Write the new sentence.
6. Of all the girls, Jo learned (more quickly, most quickly) how to bake breads.
Of all the girls, Jo learned most quickly how to bake breads.
7. She worked (hard, hardest) of all on her tomato bread.
She worked hardest of all on her tomato bread.
8. Everyone eats her pumpkin bread (faster, fastest) than any other bread.
Everyone eats her pumpkin bread faster than any other bread.
9. Uncle Dan compliments Jo (more frequently, most frequently) than I do.
Uncle Dan compliments Jo more frequently than I do.
10. Jo stays in the kitchen (longer, longest) than Mom.
Jo stays in the kitchen longer than Mom.

378 Conventions

Reader's and Writer's Notebook, p. 378

Writing Workshop
Use pages WP•1–WP•10 for this week's writing instruction.

Wrap Up Week 4 Review!

✔ **Content Knowledge** What cultures contribute to the foods we eat?

✔ **Draw Conclusions** What conclusions can you draw from the selection?

✔ **Unfamiliar Words** How can you use context clues to help you find the meanings of unfamiliar words?

Preview DAY 5

Tell students that tomorrow they will review *Me and Uncle Romie.*

Review
Week 5

Materials

- Student Edition
- Retelling Cards
- Sound-Spelling Cards
- Reader's and Writer's Notebook

Ⓒ Common Core State Standards

Speaking/Listening 1. Engage effectively in a range of collaborative discussions (one-on-one, in groups, and teacher-led) with diverse partners on grade 3 topics and texts, building on others' ideas and expressing their own clearly. **Language 6.** Acquire and use accurately grade-appropriate conversational, general academic, and domain-specific words and phrases, including those that signal spatial and temporal relationships (e.g., *After dinner that night we went looking for them*).

Content Knowledge

City Life and Country Life

REVISIT THE CONCEPT Today students will explore how the question for this unit of study connects to *Me and Uncle Romie*. Remind students of the Question of the Week, *How does city life compare to life in the country?*

Build Oral Language

DISCUSS CULTURES Remind students of the question for this unit of study, *What happens when two ways of life come together?* Use the prompts and the concept map from Week 5 to discuss what might happen when city life and country life come together.

- What might happen if a vendor from the country moved her business to a city?
- How would country life change if a skyscraper were built on a farm?
- What might a taxicab driver do for work in the country?

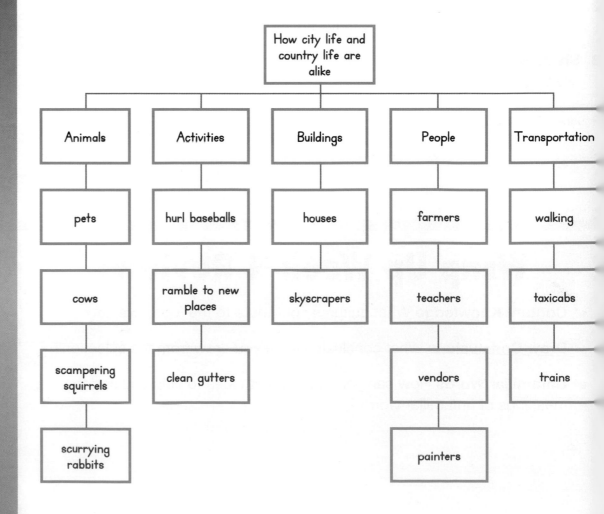

Build Oral Vocabulary

REVIEW AMAZING WORDS Display the Amazing Words for *Me and Uncle Romie.* Remind students that the words are related to the week's concept.

Amazing Words

Robust Vocabulary Routine

1. **Review** Ask students for definitions of the words, starting at the top of the list. Listen for accurate definitions. Prompt students to connect the words to the unit concept of Cultures whenever possible.

2. **Demonstrate** Have students use two or more Amazing Words in the same sentence. Guide the discussion by providing an example that shows the meaning of each word. *I was late and had to scurry across the street to catch a taxicab to get a ride to my office in the skyscraper.* Follow this pattern to the end of the list, covering as many of the ten words as possible.

3. **Apply** Assign the words in random order and have students come up with more new sentences for them. *To show that you are becoming more comfortable using these Amazing Words, think up more new sentences for them.*

Routines Flip Chart

AMAZING WORDS AT WORK Have students use the Retelling Cards/Story Sort for *Me and Uncle Romie* to talk about the Amazing Words.

CONNECT TO READING Tell students that today they will be rereading passages from *Me and Uncle Romie* and reading "Meet Me in St. Louis." As they read, ask students to think about what might happen when city life and country life come together.

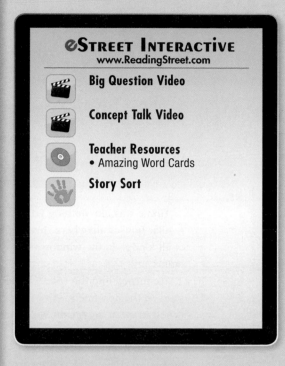

eSTREET INTERACTIVE
www.ReadingStreet.com

Big Question Video

Concept Talk Video

Teacher Resources
• Amazing Word Cards

Story Sort

Amazing Words

skyscraper	hurl
taxicab	meager
scamper	gutter
scurry	bitter
vendor	ramble

Build Background Use ELL Poster 25 to review the Week 5 lesson concept and to practice oral language. Point out and read the question: *How does city life compare to life in the country?*

Home was like nothing I'd ever seen before. No regular houses anywhere. Just big buildings and stores of all kinds—in the windows I saw paints, fabrics, radios, and TVs.

We turned into the corner building and climbed the stairs to the apartment—five whole flights up. *Whew!* I tried to catch my breath while Aunt Nanette flicked on the lights.

"Uncle Romie's out talking to some people about his big art show that's coming up. He'll be home soon," Aunt Nanette said. She set some milk and a plate of cookies for me on the table. "Your uncle's working very hard, so we won't see much of him for a while. His workroom—we call it his studio—is in the front of our apartment. That's where he keeps all the things he needs to make his art."

336

"Doesn't he just paint?" I asked.

"Uncle Romie is a collage artist," Aunt Nanette explained. "He uses paints, yes. But also photographs, newspapers, cloth. He cuts and pastes them onto a board to make his paintings."

"That sounds kinda easy," I said.

Aunt Nanette laughed.

"Well, there's a little more to it than that, James. When you see the paintings, you'll understand. Come, let's get you to bed."

Lying in the dark, I heard heavy footsteps in the hall. A giant stared at me from the doorway. "Hello there, James." Uncle Romie's voice was deep and loud, like thunder. "Thanks for the pepper jelly," he boomed. "You have a good sleep, now." Then he disappeared down the hall.

337

Student Edition, pp. 336–337

© Common Core State Standards

Literature 1. Ask and answer questions to demonstrate understanding of a text, referring explicitly to the text as the basis for the answers. **Literature 3.** Describe characters in a story (e.g., their traits, motivations, or feelings) and explain how their actions contribute to the sequence of events. **Language 3.a.** Choose words and phrases for effect.*

Access Text ©

REVIEW ⊙ AUTHOR'S PURPOSE Review the definition of author's purpose on p. 324. Remind students that authors write to inform, entertain, persuade, or express an opinion.

GUIDE PRACTICE Have students read the first two paragraphs on p. 336. Have students identify the author's purpose in writing this passage. Have them identify facts that show the author's purpose is to inform the reader what the city looks like to James.

ON THEIR OWN Have students read p. 337. In pairs, have students discuss and identify the author's purpose in writing this passage.

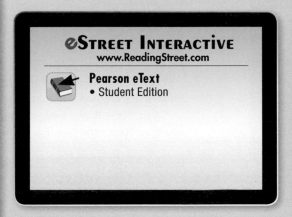

Close Reading ©

ANALYSIS On p. 336, the author had James think *"Whew!"* Does an author use words like this to inform, entertain, persuade, or express an opinion? Entertain. Words like *whew* are expressions that give the reader a feeling about someone or something. They are usually meant to entertain.

ANALYSIS • TEXT EVIDENCE James says that Aunt Nanette's home is like nothing he has ever seen before. How is it different from what James is used to? How do you know? How does James feel as he looks around? Give examples from the text to support your answer. On p. 336, it says that the kinds of houses are different. Instead of "regular houses," there are big buildings and "stores of all kinds." James feels surprised at how different everything is.

INFERENCE • TEXT EVIDENCE Reread the last paragraph on page 337. How do you think James feels about his uncle after their first meeting? He probably feels a little scared of his uncle. James describes Uncle Romie as having heavy footsteps and a deep and loud voice that booms. He also says that Uncle Romie was a giant in the doorway.

Access for All

SI Strategic Intervention

Have students make a web graphic organizer with facts from the story in the outer circles. Have them use the facts to determine the author's purpose and write that in the center.

A Advanced

Have students make a T-chart labeled *Same* and *Different* to compare their homes to Aunt Nanette's as described on pp. 336–337.

I saw saxophones, birds, fire escapes, and brown faces. *It's Harlem,* I thought. *The people, the music, the rooftops, and the stoops.* Looking at Uncle Romie's paintings, I could *feel* Harlem—its beat and bounce.

Then there was one that was different. Smaller houses, flowers, and trains. "That's home!" I shouted.

"Yep," Uncle Romie said, smiling, from the doorway. "That's the Carolina I remember."

"Mama says you visited your grandparents there most every summer when you were a kid," I said.

"I sure did, James. *Mmm.* Now that's the place for pepper jelly. Smeared thick on biscuits. And when Grandma wasn't looking . . . I'd sneak some on a spoon."

"Daddy and I do that too!" I told him.

We laughed together, then walked to the kitchen for a breakfast feast—eggs, bacon, grits, and biscuits.

"James, you've got me remembering the pepper jelly lady. People used to line up down the block to buy her preserves."

"Could you put someone like that in one of your paintings?" I asked.

342

343

Student Edition, pp. 342–343

Common Core State Standards

Literature 1. Ask and answer questions to demonstrate understanding of a text, referring explicitly to the text as the basis for the answers. **Language 4.** Determine or clarify the meaning of unknown and multiple-meaning words and phrases based on grade 3 reading and content, choosing flexibly from a range of strategies. **Language 4.a.** Use sentence-level context as a clue to the meaning of a word or phrase.

Access Text ©

REVIEW ⊙ HOMONYMS Review the definition of homonyms on p. 326. Remind students that they should use context clues to figure out the meaning of a homonym.

GUIDE PRACTICE Point out the word *trains* on p. 342. Have students discuss possible meanings of *train* ("a line of railroad cars hooked together and pulled"; "to make or become fit by exercise or diet"). Point out that context clues show *trains* is a noun, so the first meaning makes sense.

ON THEIR OWN Use *Let's Practice It!* p. 358 on the *Teacher Resources DVD-ROM* for additional practice with homonyms.

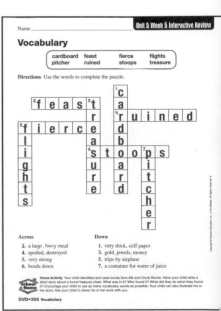

Let's Practice It! TR DVD•358

Close Reading ©

DEVELOP LANGUAGE Look at the word *beat* on p. 342. What part of speech is it? How can context clues help you determine its meaning? *Beat* is a noun. I can look at the words around *beat* to figure out its meaning. Since the sentence talks about "beat and bounce," it must mean something like "rhythm."

ANALYSIS • TEXT EVIDENCE Read the first paragraph on p. 342. What is the author trying to persuade the reader about Harlem? The author is trying to persuade the reader that Harlem is lively. It has "beat and bounce."

INFERENCE How would you describe Uncle Romie's feelings for North Carolina? He seems to have fond memories of North Carolina, which he visited every summer as a child.

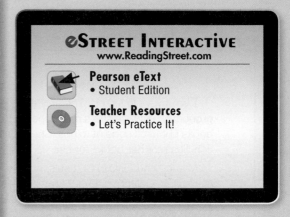

Access for All

SI Strategic Intervention

Have students look up the homonyms *train* and *beat* in a dictionary to find how many different meanings each word has.

A Advanced

Have students determine the meaning for the homonym *block* in paragraph 5 on p. 343. Have them write sentences that illustrate the different meanings for *block*.

Name_____

Read the story. Then follow the directions and answer the questions.

Meet Me in St. Louis

I've always loved art. The only thing I love more than art is my grandma, because she's really special. She's a writer who writes books about all sorts of things. She says that when I get older, I can illustrate her books for her.

My dad and I live in St. Louis, but my grandma lives far away from us, in California. Every winter, she comes here to St. Louis to visit me and during the summer, I go to California and stay with her.

I love staying at Grandma's house because her sheets smell like sunshine and there's always something baking in her kitchen. Best of all, she doesn't worry about what I'm doing. I can draw all day if I want to. It's not like here at home, where my dad is always telling me to stop drawing and go out to play.

I never get to see Grandma on her birthday because her birthday is in the spring and she doesn't visit then. But I always make her a nice card. This year I worked especially hard on it. The card took me a whole week to make. It was a picture of Grandma and me swimming near her house in California.

School + Home **Home Activity** Your child read a story and identified the author's purpose and point of view. Ask your child to retell the story from the point of view of Janelle's dad or grandma.

Comprehension DVD•359

When I finished the card, I put it in the mail for her. Then, the morning of her birthday, I called her from my room as soon as I woke up. I called her on her cell phone and she answered after the first ring. "Happy Birthday, Grandma!" I shouted into the phone. "Did you get my card?"

"No, Janelle" she replied. "I didn't get it, but I will soon, I'm sure."

"What do you mean?" I asked, confused.

Grandma started to laugh. "I didn't get it because I'm not home. I flew into St. Louis late last night when you were already asleep. I'm downstairs in your kitchen. Surprise!"

1. Reread the beginning of the story. Why do you think the author explained how far away Grandma lived?

   to make Grandma's visit even more of a surprise for Janelle

2. Some stories tell facts about a topic. Others try to get you to agree with something. Many stories are written to entertain a reader. Which kind of story is this? How do you know?

   This story is written to entertain a reader. It has characters, setting, and a plot.

3. What do you think is the author's purpose for writing this story?

   to tell an interesting story about a Grandma and a girl who are very close

DVD•360 Comprehension

Let's Practice It! TR DVD•359–360

Common Core State Standards

Literature 1. Ask and answer questions to demonstrate understanding of a text, referring explicitly to the text as the basis for the answers. **Foundational Skills 4.** Read with sufficient accuracy and fluency to support comprehension. **Language 4.** Determine or clarify the meaning of unknown and multiple-meaning words and phrases based on grade 3 reading and content, choosing flexibly from a range of strategies. **Language 4.a.** Use sentence-level context as a clue to the meaning of a word or phrase.

Access Text ©

Have students read "Meet Me in St. Louis" and respond to the questions.

REVIEW AUTHOR'S PURPOSE Some stories tell facts about a topic. Others try to get you to agree with something. Many stories are written to entertain a reader. Which kind of story is this? How do you know? **This story is written to entertain a reader. It has characters, setting, and a plot.**

REVIEW BACKGROUND KNOWLEDGE Think about birthday celebrations you have seen. How do you think Janelle feels about celebrating her grandmother's birthday with her? **I think Janelle is happy to celebrate her grandmother's birthday with her because birthday celebrations are happy occasions.**

eStreet Interactive
www.ReadingStreet.com

Teacher Resources
• Let's Practice It!

REVIEW ◉ HOMONYMS Use context clues to tell the meaning of the homonym *sheets* in paragraph 3 on p. 359. I know there can be sheets of paper, sheets of glass, sheets of ice, and sheets that you sleep on. It says Grandma's "sheets smell like sunshine." I know that sometimes the sheets on my bed smell really good. They could smell like sunshine. The other kinds of sheets wouldn't smell like that. *Sheets* must mean "cloth on a bed to sleep on or under."

REVIEW ◉ AUTHOR'S PURPOSE What do you think is the author's purpose for writing this story? The purpose is to tell an entertaining, interesting story about a grandma and a girl who are very close.

Reread for Fluency

MODEL FLUENT READING Remind students that it is important to read with appropriate phrasing. This will help them understand what they are reading. Model reading the first paragraph of "Meet Me in St. Louis" on p. 359 with the appropriate phrasing. Have students track the print as you read.

Routine Paired Reading

1. **Select a Passage** For "Meet Me in St. Louis," use the whole passage.

2. **Reading 1** Students read the entire story, switching readers at the end of each page.

3. **Reading 2** Partners reread the story. This time the other student begins.

4. **Reread** For optimal fluency, have partners continue to read three or four times.

5. **Corrective Feedback** Listen to students read and provide corrective feedback regarding their phrasing.

Routines Flip Chart

Word Analysis

REVIEW ⊙ SUFFIXES -y, -ish, -hood, -ment Review the suffixes *-y, -ish, -hood,* and *-ment* using *Sound-Spelling Cards* 168, 170, 174, and 177.

Use *Let's Practice It!* p. 357 on the *Teacher Resources DVD-ROM.*

READ WORDS IN ISOLATION Point out that students know how to read these words. Have students combine the base word with the suffix and read the new word together. Allow several seconds previewing time for the first reading. Then have students match the words with the definitions.

Corrective feedback	**If...** students have difficulty reading the suffixes *-y, -ish, -hood,* and *-ment,* **then...** guide them in using the word parts strategy. Have students read all the words repeatedly until they can read the words fluently.

Let's Practice It! TR DVD•357

Reader's and Writer's Notebook, p. 379

Spelling

REVIEW SUFFIXES -y, -ish, -hood, -ment Write *rocky, foolish, childhood,* and *movement.* Point out that these words have the suffixes *-y, -ish, -hood,* and *-ment.* Remind students that they have learned how to spell words with these suffixes.

SPELLING STRATEGY Review words with the suffixes *-y, -ish, -hood,* and *-ment* by having students follow the spelling strategy for spelling these words.

Step 1: Identify the base word.

Step 2: Draw a line between the base word and the suffix.

Step 3: Study each word part to remember the spelling.

ON THEIR OWN Use p. 379 of the *Reader's and Writer's Notebook* for additional practice with spelling words with the suffixes *-y, -ish, -hood,* and *-ment.*

Conventions

REVIEW CONJUNCTIONS A **conjunction** connects words or groups of words. Review conjunctions with students.

GUIDE PRACTICE Have students identify the conjunctions in these sentences.

1. Yesterday I ate an apple **and** a pear.
2. Will Carl **and** Angie be at the game, **or** will they miss it?
3. You can come with me **and** Jan, **but** we might meet Pete **or** Lou.

ON THEIR OWN For additional practice, use the *Reader's and Writer's Notebook,* p. 380.

Routine — Quick Write for Fluency — Team Talk

1. **Talk** Have pairs talk about how life in the country and life in the city are different.

2. **Write** Each student writes a paragraph about the differences between country and city life, using conjunctions.

3. **Share** Students read their own writing to their partners, who then check for proper use of conjunctions.

Routines Flip Chart

---

eStreet Interactive
www.ReadingStreet.com

Teacher Resources
• Reader's and Writer's Notebook
• Let's Practice It!

Interactive Sound-Spelling Cards

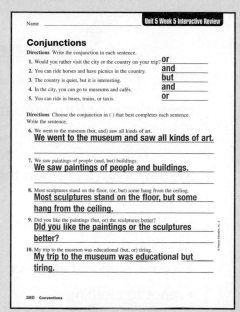

Reader's and Writer's Notebook, p. 380

Writing Workshop
Use pp. WP•1–WP•10 for this week's writing instruction.

Wrap Up Week 5 Review!

✔ **Content Knowledge** Where would you like to live—in the city or in the country?

✔ **Author's Purpose** What different purposes may an author have for writing?

✔ **Homonyms** How can you use context clues to help you understand homonyms?

Preview Unit 6

Use p. 359q to preview Unit 6 Week 1 with students.

Wrap Up Your Unit!

Zoom in on ©

Discuss Content Knowledge Gained Through Reading

What happens when two ways of life come together?

WEEK 1

How does culture influence the clothes we wear?

Students have learned that people

- wear special clothes for holidays
- wear traditional clothing
- react to clothing

WEEK 2

How are cultures alike and different?

Students have learned that cultures

- have similarities and differences
- usually value family
- can be tied to countries

WEEK 3

Why is it hard to adapt to a new culture?

Students have learned that a new culture means

- a new home and neighborhood
- a new language
- new traditions

How do people feel about cultures that are different from their own?

- They like to try other cultures' foods and admire their traditions.
- Sometimes they are excited to learn about new cultures.
- Sometimes they are unsure what to think about other cultures because they are so different.

Discuss with students the selections they have explored surrounding the idea of cultures. Throughout discussions, students should support their comments and ideas with evidence from the texts.

How do two ways of life come together in each of the selections you read?

- *Suki's Kimono:* Suki wears her Japanese kimono to her American school and teaches others about it.
- *I Love Saturdays y domingos:* The girl has different experiences with her grandparents from two cultures
- *Good-Bye, 382 Shin Dang Dong:* Jangmi moves from Korea to America.
- *Jalapeño Bagels:* Pablo experiences foods from each of his parents' cultures.
- *Me and Uncle Romie:* James experiences life in the country at home and life in the city when he goes to visit his uncle.

WEEK 4

How can different cultures contribute to the foods we eat?

Students have learned that food

- comes from different cultures
- is shared
- can be a mix from different cultures

WEEK 5

How does city life compare to life in the country?

Students have learned that

- city life is busy
- cities have tall buildings
- the country has farms

Talk about cultures.

Think of a time you experienced something from another culture. Describe what it was like. (Responses will vary.)

Team Talk Have students work in pairs to talk about the Amazing Ideas related to cultures that they discussed each week. Then have students use these ideas to help demonstrate their understanding of the question, *What happens when two ways of life come together?*

Amazing Words

You've learned **247** words this year!

You've learned **050** words this unit to use as you talk about cultures.

Assessment Checkpoints for the Week

Unit Assessment

Use Unit 5 *Benchmark Tests* to check:

✔ **Passage Comprehension**

✔ **Phonics**

✔ **Vocabulary Skills**

✔ **Writing Conventions**

✔ **Writing**

✔ **Fluency**

Benchmark Tests

Managing Assessment

Use *Assessment Handbook* for:

✔ **Weekly Assessment Blackline Masters for Monitoring Progress**

✔ **Observation Checklists**

✔ **Record-Keeping Forms**

✔ **Portfolio Assessment**

Assessment Handbook

Writing Trait Skills Trace

All of the writing traits taught in Scott Foresman Reading Street are dimensions of good writing. The chart below shows you the writing traits taught each week of the unit. In the column on the right, the criteria to achieve the Indiana Writing Applications Rubric top score are identified. For an overview of the Indiana Writing Applications Rubric and the Language Conventions Rubric, see the back of this page.

	Writing Trait of the Week/ Weekly Selection	Indiana Writing Applications/Language Conventions Rubric Top Score Point Criteria
		A Score Point 6 paper is rare. It fully accomplishes the task and has a distinctive quality that sets it apart as an outstanding performance.
Week 1	Organization *Suki's Kimono* **Writing Prompt** Write a letter to the editor about an issue occurring in your community or school.	**Does the writing have clear order?** **Does it** • follow a clear sequence with a beginning, a middle, and an end? • have a logical progression of main ideas and support?
Week 2	Conventions *I Love Saturdays y domingos* **Writing Prompt** *I Love Saturdays y domingos* is a personal narrative about the cultures in a girl's family. Think about the things that are important to you, such as happy memories. Now write a personal narrative about one of your happy memories.	There are no errors that impair the flow of communication. Errors that appear will generally be of the first-draft variety; they have a minor impact on the overall communication.
Week 3	Word Choice *Good-bye 382 Shin Dang Dong* **Writing Prompt** Think about a time you were new to something or someplace. Write a free verse poem about the experience.	**Does the writing sample exhibit exceptional word usage? Does it** • include dynamic words and provide rich details, strong verbs, and/or vivid descriptions? • demonstrate control of a challenging vocabulary?
Week 4	Focus/Ideas *Jalapeño Bagels* **Writing Prompt** Invite a friend to come over to your home for dinner, using specific details.	**Does the writing stay fully focused? Does it** • stay on the topic? • avoid rambling and/or repeating information? **Does the writing sample include thorough and complete ideas? Does it** • include in-depth information and supporting details? • fully explore many facets of the topic?
Week 5	Conventions *Me and Uncle Romie* **Writing Prompt** Think about this story or another story or book you have read recently. Write a book review of it, explaining to readers whether they should read it.	There are no errors that impair the flow of communication. Errors that appear will generally be of the first-draft variety; they have a minor impact on the overall communication.

For tips on **Publishing/Presenting** a Persuasive Essay, see Step 5 on the Unit 5 Writing Process tab.

Indiana Writing Resources

Use these resources to build writing skills during and after the teaching of Unit 5.

Reader's and Writer's Notebook

Writing Rubrics and Anchor Papers

Digital Resources
• Online Journal
• Online Writing Transparencies
• Grammar Jammer

Teacher Resources DVD-ROM
• Reader's and Writer's Notebook
• Let's Practice It!
• Graphic Organizers
• Writing Transparencies

ISBN-13: 978-0-328-73391-0   ISBN-10: 0-328-73391-1

Indiana Writing Rubrics

Indiana Writing Applications Rubric Overview

The released Indiana Writing Applications Rubric Overview can be used to score the Unit 5 Writing Process Persuasive Essay on pp. WP•1–WP•10 and other writing assignments.

Writing Prompt Write to persuade your parents to let you travel to another country, dress in a special way, or eat a particular food.

Purpose Convince parents to accept an idea

Audience Parents

Score Level	Ideas and Content	Organization	Style
	Does the writing sample	Does the writing sample	Does the writing sample
6	• stay fully focused? • include thorough and complete ideas?	• have clear order?	• exhibit exceptional word usage? • exhibit writing that is fluent and easy to read? • display a strong sense of audience?
5	• stay focused? • include many relevant ideas?	• have clear order?	• exhibit more than adequate word usage? • exhibit writing that is fluent and easy to read? • display a sense of audience?
4	• stay mostly focused? • include some relevant ideas?	• have order?	• exhibit adequate word usage? • exhibit writing that is readable? • display some sense of audience?
3	• exhibit less than minimal focus? • include few relevant ideas?	• have some order?	• exhibit minimal word usage? • exhibit writing that is mostly readable? • display little sense of audience?
2	• exhibit less than minimal focus? • include few relevant ideas?	• have little order?	• exhibit less than minimal word usage? • exhibit writing that is hard to read? • display little sense of audience?
1	• have little or no focus? • include almost no relevant ideas?	• have little or no order?	• exhibit less than minimal word usage? • exhibit writing that is hard to read? • display little or no sense of audience?

NOTE: This chart is only a brief summary of the score points. It is not appropriate to use this summary as the sole tool in scoring student papers.

Indiana Language Conventions Rubric Overview

Score Level	Command of Language Skills
4	In a Score Point 4 paper, there are no errors that impair the flow of communication. Errors that appear will generally be of the first-draft variety; they have a minor impact on the overall communication.
3	In a Score Point 3 paper, errors are occasional but do not impede the flow of communication; the writer's meaning is not seriously obscured by language errors.
2	In a Score Point 2 paper, errors are generally frequent and may cause the reader to stop and reread part of the writing. While some aspects of the writing may be more consistently correct than others, the existing errors do impair communication. With a little extra effort on the reader's part, it is still possible to discern most, if not all, of what the writer is trying to communicate.
1	In a Score Point 1 paper, errors are serious and numerous; they cause the reader to struggle to discern the writer's meaning. Errors are frequently of a wide variety. There may be sections where it is impossible to ascertain what the writer is attempting to communicate.

Writing on Reading Street

DAILY WRITING FOCUS

Quick Writes for Fluency

- Use the Quick Write routine for **writing on demand**.
- The Quick Write **prompt and routine** extend skills and strategies from daily writing lessons.
- Daily 10-minute **mini-lessons** focus instruction on the **traits** and **craft** of good writing.
- **Writing Traits** are focus/ideas, organization, voice, word choice, sentences, and conventions.
- **Craft** includes drafting strategies, revising strategies, and editing strategies.

WEEKLY WRITING FOCUS

Writing Forms and Patterns

- Instruction focuses on a different **product** each week.
- Mini-lessons and models help students learn key features and **organizational patterns**.
- Use **mentor text** every week as a model to exemplify the traits of good writing.
- **Grade 3 Products** include fables, friendly letters, news articles, autobiographies, summaries, realistic fiction, and more.
- **Grade 3 Organizational Patterns** include poetic forms, compare and contrast, main idea and details, narratives, letters, and more.

UNIT WRITING FOCUS

Writing Process

- Six **writing process** lessons provide structure to move students through the steps of the writing process.
- One-week and two-week pacing (see the back of this Tab) allows lessons to be used in **Writing Workshops**.
- The **steps of the writing process** are Plan and Prewrite, Draft, Revise, Edit, and Publish and Present.
- **Grade 3 Writing Process Products** include personal narratives, how-to reports, cause-and-effect essays, problem-solution essays, persuasive essays, and research reports.

Persuasive Essay

PROCESS WRITING STEPS	© COMMON CORE STATE STANDARDS FOR ENGLISH LANGUAGE ARTS	TIPS FOR UNIT 5 PROCESS WRITING
① Plan and Prewrite	Writing 1.a., Writing 5.	As students prepare to **prewrite**, suggest that they examine a model of the type of text they will be writing.
② Draft	Writing 1.a., Writing 5.	As students **draft** their writing, show them how to use a graphic organizer to categorize and organize their ideas.
③ Revise	Writing 1.a., Writing 5., Language 1.g.	Before students **revise** their drafts, refer them to the *Revising Checklist*.
④ Edit	Writing 5., Writing 6.	As students **edit** their writing, remind them to use proofreading marks.
⑤ Publish and Present	Writing 6.	When students are ready to **publish** their writing, have them use the Scoring Rubric to evaluate their own writing.

Alternate Pacing Plans for Unit Writing Projects

Sometimes you want to spend more time on writing – perhaps you do a **Writing Workshop.** Below you will find one- or two-week plans for the unit-level writing projects.

1-WEEK PLAN	Day 1	Day 2	Day 3	Day 4	Day 5
1 Plan and Prewrite	■	■			
2 Draft			■		
3 Revise				■	
4 Edit					■
5 Publish and Present					■

2-WEEK PLAN	Day 1	Day 2	Day 3	Day 4	Day 5	Day 6	Day 7	Day 8	Day 9	Day 10
1 Plan and Prewrite	■	■	■	■						
2 Draft					■	■	■			
3 Revise								■		
4 Edit									■	
5 Publish and Present										■

Grade 3 Unit Writing Projects

UNIT WRITING PROCESS PROJECTS	
UNIT 1	Personal Narrative
UNIT 2	How-to Report
UNIT 3	Cause-and-Effect Essay
UNIT 4	Problem-Solution Essay
UNIT 5	Persuasive Essay
UNIT 6	Research Report

UNIT 21ST CENTURY WRITING PROJECTS	
UNIT 1	E-Pen Pals
UNIT 2	Story Exchange
UNIT 3	Photo Writing
UNIT 4	Classroom Profile
UNIT 5	E-Newsletter
UNIT 6	Discussion Forum

You can find all of the Unit 21st Century Writing Projects in the Teacher Resources section on SuccessNet.

Persuasive Essay

Academic Vocabulary ⒸⒺ

In a **persuasive essay,** a writer establishes a position and uses details to support that position and to convince readers to agree with it.

Writing Prompt

Write to persuade your parents to let you travel to another country, dress in a special way, or eat a particular food.

Purpose Convince parents to accept an idea.

Audience parents

INTRODUCE GENRE AND PROMPT In this writing process lesson, you will study a persuasive essay and use this genre to write a response to the prompt. In a persuasive essay, a writer tries to convince a reader to act or believe in a certain way.

INTRODUCE KEY FEATURES

Key Features of a Persuasive Essay

- establishes a clear position on an issue or question
- supports the position with details, reasons, facts, and examples as evidence
- tries to convince readers to think or act in a certain way
- uses persuasive words to make reasons more convincing
- often organizes ideas and facts in order of importance

Introduce Genre Write *persuasive* on the board. Explain to students that this word describes anything that tries to convince people to think or act in a certain way. Write *essay* on the board. Explain that this word names a short piece of writing. Therefore, a *persuasive essay* is a short piece of writing that tries to convince people to think or act in a certain way. Discuss with students the key features of a persuasive essay that appear on this page.

Writing 1. Write opinion pieces on familiar topics or texts, supporting a point of view with reasons. **Writing 1.a.** Introduce the topic or text they are writing about, state an opinion, and create an organizational structure that lists reasons. **Writing 1.b.** Provide reasons that support the opinion. **Writing 5.** With guidance and support from peers and adults, develop and strengthen writing as needed by planning, revising, and editing.

Plan and Prewrite

Mini-Lesson Reading Like a Writer

■ **Examine Model Text** Let's look at an example of a persuasive essay in which a student tries to convince a parent to let him make a particular food. Display and read aloud to students "Pizza Proposal" on Writing Transparency WP29. Ask them to identify key features of a persuasive essay in the student model.

■ **Evaluate Model Text** Display and read aloud "Traits of a Good Persuasive Essay" on Writing Transparency WP30. Discuss each trait as it is shown in the model. For Focus/Ideas, ask students to explain what the writer's position is. Point out that the writing is focused because it discusses that position and only that position. For Organization, tell students that the writer gives several reasons to support his position. Ask students to name the reasons. Proceed in the same way for the remaining traits, defining them when necessary and helping students identify examples of the traits in the model.

Pizza Proposal

Danny and Josh are coming over tonight, and the three of us would like to make a pizza. Our teacher, Mr. Lorenzo, gave us a recipe. After making dough and rolling it out very flat, you put sauce and different toppings on the dough. I would like to put cheese, sausage, mushrooms, peppers, and olives on our pizza. Doesn't that sound delicious? But we can't make this pizza without your permission and your help.

First, you won't have to do any work. I will help you shop for all of the ingredients, and we will clean up the kitchen when we are done. Second, it will be fun and educational to make our own pizza. It will also be safe because I know you will help us with the oven. Third, you can eat as much of the pizza as you want! Most importantly, pizza is one of the best foods we could eat because it is full of nourishing things such as cheese and vegetables.

This will be a great project for all of us. Please say yes to fun, learning, and good nutrition.

Unit 5 Persuasive Essay • PLAN and PREWRITE   Writing Process **29**

Writing Transparency WP29, TR DVD

Traits of a Good Persuasive Essay

Focus/Ideas	Essay stays focused on topic.
Organization	Writer organizes reasons in order of importance.
Voice	Writer shows personality and persuasiveness.
Word Choice	Writer uses persuasive words (*fun, educational, safe, most importantly, best*).
Sentences	Sentences are of varied lengths and kinds, including a question and an exclamation.
Conventions	Writer has good control of spelling, grammar, capitalization, and punctuation.

Unit 5 Persuasive Essay • PLAN and PREWRITE   Writing Process **30**

Writing Transparency WP30, TR DVD

GENERATE IDEAS FOR WRITING The writing prompt tells you the general topic of your writing assignment: persuading your parents to let you travel to another country, dress in a special way, or eat a particular food. Now you need to think of a specific topic: the particular country, type of dress, or food you will present and support in your essay. First, generate a list of as many possible topics as you can.

USE RANGE OF STRATEGIES Encourage students to try a range of strategies for generating ideas, including these:

✔ Review foods, clothing, and places described in the selections in the unit. Write lists and add additional items to each list.

✔ Write a brief journal entry about a trip they would like to take.

✔ In small groups, brainstorm reasons that have proven effective in persuading parents or others to take a particular action.

NARROW TOPIC Once you have generated a list of topics, you need to narrow your choices to one topic. Have students look more closely at each of their topics and think about why it is or is not the most suitable topic for the assignment. They might ask: *Would I have to persuade my parents to let me do this? Can I think of good reasons that would convince my parents?*

Topics	Evaluate
wear my Indian sari to school	I can do this on International Day.
eat food from Thailand	I wouldn't have to persuade my parents to let me do this.
visit France on the school trip in fifth grade ★	I would really like to do this; it would take some persuading.

Corrective feedback

If... students have trouble thinking of possible reasons in support of their position,

then... suggest that they imagine a similar situation in which they tried to persuade their parents to allow them to do something and write brief notes on the kinds of reasons they used.

Write Guy *by Jeff Anderson*

Use Mentor Texts

Although it is not a persuasive essay, a main selection in this unit has persuasive elements. *Good-Bye, 382 Shin Dang Dong,* gives reasons why Jangmi will like living in America. Invite students to examine the text to find these reasons. Tell them they will need to include reasons to support their position in the persuasive essay they will write.

Access for All

SI Strategic Intervention

For an alternative writing prompt, use the following: Think about going to a friend's house after school. Write a paragraph about why you want to visit your friend. Use persuasive words that will help convince your parent to let you go.

A Advanced

For an alternative writing prompt, use the following: Write a persuasive essay about studying in a different country. Find facts about the country that will help you persuade a parent to let you go there. Use the facts as well as examples and other supporting details as reasons in your essay.

Common Core State Standards

Writing 1.a. Introduce the topic or text they are writing about, state an opinion, and create an organizational structure that lists reasons. **Writing 1.b.** Provide reasons that support the opinion.

1 Plan and Prewrite

Mini-Lesson Planning a First Draft

■ **Use a Persuasion Chart** Display Writing Transparency WP31 and read it aloud to students.

Think Aloud **MODEL** This student wants to persuade her parents to allow her to go on the fifth-grade class trip to France. The writer has categorized her ideas by writing them in the Introduction, Reasons, and Conclusion boxes on this graphic organizer. Now that she has organized her ideas, she can start writing beginning, middle, and ending paragraphs for the first draft of her essay.

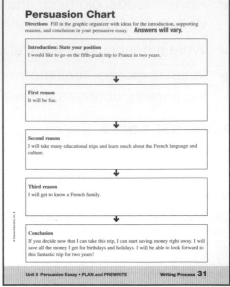

Persuasion Chart

Directions Fill in the graphic organizer with ideas for the introduction, supporting reasons, and conclusion in your persuasive essay. **Answers will vary.**

Introduction: State your position
I would like to go on the fifth-grade trip to France in two years.

↓

First reason
It will be fun.

↓

Second reason
I will take many educational trips and learn much about the French language and culture.

↓

Third reason
I will get to know a French family.

↓

Conclusion
If you decide now that I can take this trip, I can start saving money right away. I will save all the money I get for birthdays and holidays. I will be able to look forward to this fantastic trip for two years!

Unit 5 Persuasive Essay • PLAN and PREWRITE   Writing Process **31**

Writing Transparency WP31, TR DVD

■ Have students use *Reader's and Writer's Notebook,* p. 381 to help them plan their first draft. Before you begin writing, use this graphic organizer to categorize and organize your ideas about your position, opinions, reasons, and conclusion and to plan the paragraphs for your essay.

Name _____   Writing Process Unit 5

Persuasion Chart

Directions Fill in the graphic organizer with ideas for the introduction, supporting reasons, and conclusion in your persuasive essay. **Answers will vary.**

Introduction: State your position.

↓

First reason

↓

Second reason

↓

Third reason (most important)

↓

Conclusion

Unit 5 Writing Process **381**

Reader's and Writer's Notebook, p. 381

 Draft

DISPLAY RUBRIC Display Scoring Rubric WP5 from the *Teacher Resources DVD-ROM.* Review with students the criteria for each trait under each score. Explain that they need to keep these criteria in mind as they develop drafts of their persuasive essays. Remind them that this is the rubric that will be used to evaluate their persuasive essays when they are finished.

Scoring Rubric — Persuasive Essay

	4	3	2	1
Focus/Ideas	Well-focused essay; clear position	Generally focused essay; clear position	Essay lacking focus; unclear position	Essay without focus; no clear position
Organization	Supporting details given in order of importance	Supporting details given in fairly clear order	Supporting details given in confused order	No order; no supporting details
Voice	Sincere, persuasive voice	Voice somewhat sincere, persuasive	No clear, persuasive voice	Uninvolved or indifferent
Word Choice	Uses strong persuasive words to make reasons and opinions convincing	Uses some persuasive words	Uses few persuasive words	No attempt to use persuasive words
Sentences	Variety of strong, clear sentences	Mostly clear sentences; some variety	Little or no variety; some unclear sentences	Incoherent sentences or short, choppy sentences
Conventions	Few, if any, errors	Some minor errors	Many errors	Numerous serious errors

PREPARE TO DRAFT Have students review the persuasion charts they worked on earlier. Ask them to make sure that their persuasion charts are complete. If they are not, have students finish them now. You will be using your persuasion chart as you write the draft of your persuasive essay. Don't worry if your draft doesn't sound exactly the way you want your essay to sound. You will have a chance to revise your draft later.

> **Corrective feedback**
>
> **If...** students do not grasp the connection between the Scoring Rubric and their persuasive essays,
> **then...** have them help you use the Scoring Rubric to evaluate and score one or more traits of the model persuasive essay on Writing Transparency WP29.

Access for All

SI Strategic Intervention
Ask students to share their persuasion charts with you or more able writers. Discuss with them how to organize and/or add to their reasons or supporting details.

ELL

Prepare to Draft Have students name the supporting details they want to use for their position. Help them restate their position and supporting details as complete sentences. Record the sentences on the board. Have students copy the sentences.

Common Core State Standards

Writing 1.a. Introduce the topic or text they are writing about, state an opinion, and create an organizational structure that lists reasons. **Writing 1.b.** Provide reasons that support the opinion. **Writing 5.** With guidance and support from peers and adults, develop and strengthen writing as needed by planning, revising, and editing. **Language 1.g.** Form and use comparative and superlative adjectives and adverbs, and choose between them depending on what is to be modified.

Name_____   **Writing Process Unit 5**

Use Persuasive Words

Persuasive words convince readers to take an action or agree with the writer's position. Here are some different kinds of persuasive words:
  Words that state that an action is necessary: *should, must, important*
  Words that compare: *best, most delicious, most important*
  Words that describe positive traits: *educational, healthful, safe, effective*

Directions Write sentences for your persuasive essay. Use the kind of persuasive word shown. Underline your persuasive words.

1. Word that states that an action is necessary
_____
_____

2. Word that compares
_____
_____

3. Word that describes positive traits
_____
_____

4. Any kind of persuasive word
__**Answers should be based on the provided**__
__**hints and should be complete sentences**__
with appropriate capitalization and
punctuation.

382 Unit 5 Writing Process

Reader's and Writer's Notebook, p. 382

---

② Draw

Draft

■ **Use Persuasive Words** Display and read aloud Writing Transparency WP32. Discuss the different kinds of persuasive words. Ask students to identify the persuasive words in each sentence and tell into which category the persuasive words fit.

 MODEL Suppose I want to convince you to see a movie I've seen. I might say, "You should see this movie. It's the best movie I've ever seen." I used the persuasive words *should* and *best.* When I write a persuasive essay, I do the same thing: I use words that try to convince readers to take an action. I use words that make the action sound appealing.

Use Persuasive Words
Persuasive words convince readers to take an action or agree with the writer's position. Here are some different kinds of persuasive words:
  Words that state that an action is necessary: *should, must, important, ought*
  Words that compare: *best, most delicious, most important*
  Words that describe positive traits: *educational, healthful, safe, effective*

Directions Underline the persuasive words in each sentence.

1. Salads are the tastiest and most nourishing meals you can eat.

2. Everyone should have the educational experience of traveling to a different country.

3. Africa is the perfect place for a trip because it has the most unusual plants and animals.

4. You must try lobster because it is more delicious than any other seafood.

Unit 5 Persuasive Essay • DRAFT   Writing Process **32**

Writing Transparency WP32, TR DVD

■ Have students use *Reader's and Writer's Notebook,* p. 382 to practice writing sentences with persuasive words.

Tips for Including Strong Adjectives

✔ Use adjectives that suggest traits the readers value.

✔ Choose sensory words to help readers see, hear, touch, taste, and smell what is described.

✔ Use the comparative forms of adjectives to be more persuasive.

DEVELOP DRAFT Remind students that the focus of drafting is to get their ideas down in an organized way. Display the Tips for Including Strong Adjectives for students. Direct them to use what they learned about persuasive words and strong adjectives as they write their drafts.

③ Revise

Mini-Lesson | Writer's Craft: Add Adverbs

■ One way to revise writing is to use adverbs that give specific details. Adding adverbs will help make writing clearer and more coherent. This in turn will make writing easier for the audience to understand and appreciate. **Discuss this example with students.**

| **General** | A trip to Paris will help me learn to speak French. |
| **More Specific** | A trip to Paris will help me learn to speak French <u>easily</u> and <u>naturally</u>. |

Have students practice using adverbs to add specific details on *Reader's and Writer's Notebook,* p. 383.

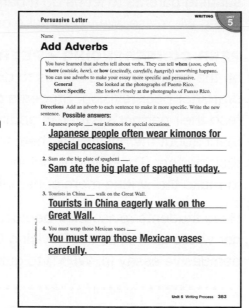

Reader's and Writer's Notebook, p. 383

REVISE MODEL Display Writing Transparency WP33 and use it to model revising. Point out the revising marks, which students should use when they revise their work. This is part of a persuasive essay about a future trip to France. In the fourth sentence, the writer added the adverb *maturely* to add a specific detail about the students' behavior. The writer also added the persuasive words *educational* and *the perfect* to make her reasons more persuasive.

Ask students to point out and explain other revisions the writer made. (The writer made the phrase *a good learning experience* even more persuasive by changing it to *the best learning experience in the world.*)

Writing Transparency WP33, TR DVD

Access for All

 Advanced

As they revise their work, have students consider ways to improve it.

• Use one strong adjective or adverb with each reason.

• Try to include a question and an exclamation.

• Make sure the supporting details specifically appeal to the audience.

ⒺⓁⓁ

Support Writing Use the following strategies to help students complete Writing Transparency WP32:

• Discuss words that communicate that action should be taken, such as *should, must,* and *ought,* and model them in sentences.

• Explain that some words describe traits most people admire, such as *educational, healthful,* and *safe,* so they are especially persuasive. Have students use these words in sentences.

Persuasive Essay **WP•7**

© Common Core State Standards

Writing 1.b. Provide reasons that support the opinion. **Writing 5.** With guidance and support from peers and adults, develop and strengthen writing as needed by planning, revising, and editing. **Writing 6.** With guidance and support from adults, use technology to produce and publish writing (using keyboarding skills) as well as to interact and collaborate with others. **Language 3.a.** Choose words and phrases for effect.*

3 Revise

REVISE DRAFT Earlier we wrote drafts of persuasive essays about persuading parents to let us do a particular action. Now we will revise our drafts. When we revise, we try to make our writing clearer and more interesting.

PEER CONFERENCING • PEER REVISION Write the Revising Checklist on the board or make copies to distribute. Have pairs of students exchange drafts for peer revision. Students can use the checklist to help them as they read their partner's paper. In addition to listing at least one genuine compliment about the essay, ask them to write at least three revision suggestions for their partner. These might include where to add persuasive words and adverbs to make the writing more coherent and convincing for the audience.

Have students revise their persuasive essays using the suggestions their partner wrote as well as the Revising Checklist and the list of key features of a persuasive essay (p. WP•1) to guide them.

Corrective feedback	**If...** students are making spelling, mechanics, and grammar corrections, **then...** remind them that they will make those kinds of corrections later when they edit. When they revise, they should be working on the content and organization of their draft.

Revising Checklist

Focus/Ideas

✔ Is the persuasive essay focused on a position to convince a parent?

✔ Are there supporting details to strengthen the position?

Organization

✔ Are the reasons explained in order from the least important to the most important?

Voice

✔ Is the writer's voice persuasive and sincere?

✔ Does the writer's voice speak to the audience?

Word Choice

✔ Are persuasive words used to convince readers to take an action or agree with the position?

Sentences

✔ Have adverbs been used to add specific details that make the writing clearer and more coherent?

✔ Are sentences different lengths and kinds?

 **Edit**

Mini-Lesson   Editing Strategy: Sentence by Sentence

■ Suggest that students use this editing strategy as they check their work: Read sentence by sentence. As you read each sentence, check for correct spelling, grammar, punctuation, and capitalization.

■ Display Writing Transparency WP34 and use it to model the sentence-by-sentence editing strategy. Point out the proofreading marks, which students should use when they edit their work. As I check sentence by sentence, I see that *France,* a proper noun, should be capitalized. In the next sentence, instead of the word *week,* its homophone *weak* has been used.

Writing Transparency WP34, TR DVD

■ Ask students to point out and explain the other edits the writer made. (In the last sentence, the possessive pronoun *your* should be used, not the contraction *you're.* Also, the adverb *soonest* should be changed to *sooner* since two things are being compared: now and two years from now.)

Have students edit the paragraph on *Reader's and Writer's Notebook,* p. 384 using proofreading marks.

You can create your own rubric using items from the rubric on p. WP•5 and your own additions and changes, and have students use it to edit their own drafts for spelling, grammar, punctuation, and capitalization. Tell them to use proofreading marks to indicate needed corrections.

Technology Tips

Students who write their persuasive essays on computers should keep these tips in mind as they edit:

✔ Determine margins, line lengths, borders, shading, paragraph indents, and other features using the Format menu.

✔ See whether their word processor has templates, such as those for different writing formats. Sometimes these will be in a menu item called Templates or Project Gallery.

Write Guy *by Jeff Anderson*
What Do You Notice?

When students are editing one another's writing, ask, "What do you notice?" Giving students the responsibility of commenting on what they find effective in peer writing helps them build self-confidence, and they often begin to notice features of the writing they might not have otherwise.

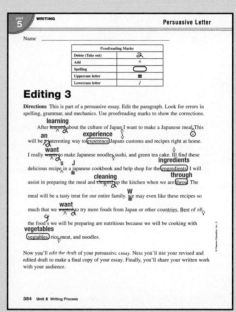

Reader's and Writer's Notebook, p. 384

Support Editing When reviewing a student's draft, emphasize ideas rather than errors. Observe whether there are consistent grammatical errors. If so, they may reflect the writing conventions of the home language. Choose one or two skills, and use the appropriate lessons in the *ELL Handbook* to explicitly teach the English conventions.

Publish and Present

OPTIONS FOR PRESENTING Point out that, as students read on *Reader's and Writer's Notebook,* p. 384, publishing their writing is the last step in the writing process. Have them incorporate peer suggestions and their own revisions and proofreading edits into their persuasive essay to write or use a computer to create a final draft. Offer them two options for presenting their work:

Give their persuasive essays to the parent or parents they wrote to.	Make a class book containing their persuasive essays.

Mini-Lesson Evaluating Writing

■ Display and read aloud Writing Transparency WP35. Model how to evaluate a persuasive essay using the Scoring Rubric on p. WP•5.

 MODEL I would give this persuasive essay a 4. It is focused on one topic: persuading parents to let the writer travel to another country. The reasons are developed and in order from least important to most important. The writer is sincere and convincing. She uses persuasive words and phrases effectively. Short and long sentences as well as questions and exclamations are included. Grammar, mechanics, and spelling are excellent.

> **A Trip to Remember**
>
> As you know, each year some of the fifth graders at our school take a trip to France. They stay with French families for a week. I will be able to go on this trip in two years. I want to ask your permission for the trip sooner.
>
> First of all, the trip is so much fun. Can you imagine traveling to Europe with your good friends? Many adults, both teachers and parents, go on the trip. They say that past groups have behaved maturely. Second, we will go on many educational outings. I will learn so much about French history and art! This trip will be the perfect introduction for studying French in high school and college. Third, we will stay in the home of a French family. Getting to know people with a different language and culture from our own is the best learning experience in the world.
>
> I think you should give me permission for this trip so I can start saving money now. Then I can look forward to fun, educational outings, and meeting a French family for two years!
>
> Unit 5 Persuasive Essay • PUBLISH and PRESENT   Writing Process **35**

Writing Transparency WP35, TR DVD

■ Have students use the Scoring Rubric to evaluate their persuasive essays. Encourage them to use the evaluation process to help them identify areas for improvement in their future writing. Remind students to use transition words and phrases to show the connection between their opinions and the reasons for them.

Looking for Teacher Resources and other important information?

Go online to **Pearson SuccessNet**

eSTREET INTERACTIVE
www.ReadingStreet.com

In the *First Stop* on Reading Street, you will find the following information.

- Research into Practice on Reading Street
- Guide to Reading Street
- Assessment on Reading Street
- Customize Writing on Reading Street
- Small Group Instruction on Reading Street

- ELL on Reading Street
- Customize Literacy on Reading Street
- 21st Century Skills on Reading Street
- Teacher Resources for Grade 3
- Index

Oral Vocabulary for **Suki's Kimono**

LET'S LEARN
Amazing Words

Oral Vocabulary Routine

DAY 1

fret

1. **Introduce** To *fret* means "to worry about something."
2. **Demonstrate** Mom *fretted* because we were a half hour late.
3. **Apply** Have students show how someone might act if they were *fretting*.
4. **Display the Word** Identify the letters and sounds for initial fr/*fr*/.

scarves

1. **Introduce** *Scarves* are long pieces of cloth people wrap loosely around their necks.
2. **Demonstrate** I put on *scarves* to warm my neck during a cold winter day.
3. **Apply** Have students tell where else they might wear a scarf.
4. **Display the Word** Identify the letters and sounds for the irregular plural *-ves*. Students can read the word after you.

fabric

1. **Introduce** *Fabric* is another word for cloth.
2. **Demonstrate** Janelle's dress was made of a beautiful, shiny *fabric*. The *fabric* had gold threads woven into it.
3. **Apply** Have students describe the *fabric* of some of the clothing they're wearing.
4. **Display the Word** Identify the short vowel sound in each syllable of *fab-ric*.

DAY 2

inspire

1. **Introduce** If something *inspires* you, it makes you want to create something, such as a poem, music, or art.
2. **Demonstrate** Vincent was *inspired* to paint when he saw the ocean. The clothing designer was *inspired* by the beautiful fabrics of India.
3. **Apply** Have students tell about a time something *inspired* them. What did they do?
4. **Display the Word** Identify the long *i* vowel sound in the word part *-spire*.

DAY 3

drape

1. **Introduce** If you *drape* a piece of cloth, you arrange it gracefully.
2. **Demonstrate** Josie *draped* the cloth over her shoulders and pretended it was a cape. We *draped* the table with a cheerful tablecloth.
3. **Apply** Have students explain how they would *drape* a large piece of fabric.
4. **Display the Word** Identify the letters and sounds for initial /dr/*dr* and the long *a* vowel sound. Students can decode this word.

DAY 4

stylish

1. **Introduce** *Stylish* means to be in fashion or in the latest style.
2. **Demonstrate** Jess was unhappy because she thought her dress was old and no longer *stylish*. *Stylish* people are always in fashion.
3. **Apply** Help students understand that *stylish* has to do with fads and trends. Have them list other examples of being *stylish*.
4. **Display the Word** Run your hand under the word parts *sty-lish* as you read the word.

Oral Vocabulary for **I Love Saturdays y domingos**

LET'S LEARN
Amazing Words

Oral Vocabulary Routine

DAY 1

dwelling
1. **Introduce** A *dwelling* is the place where someone or something lives.
2. **Demonstrate** The Hupa *dwellings* were made of cedar wood.
3. **Apply** Have students describe their own *dwelling* or the kind of dwelling they would like to have.
4. **Display the Word** Identify the short *e* vowel sound in *dwelling*.

shield
1. **Introduce** A *shield* is a piece of metal, leather, or plastic carried on the arm to protect the body. A *shield* can also be anything used to protect.
2. **Demonstrate** The knight's *shield* protected him from the arrows whizzing around him.
3. **Apply** Have students think of things that can act as *shields*.
4. **Display the Word** Identify the letters and sounds for initial /sh/*sh*. Students can decode this word.

headdress
1. **Introduce** A *headdress* is a decoration worn on the head for a special occasion.
2. **Demonstrate** The Sioux chief wore a *headdress* of feathers and beads.
3. **Apply** Have students describe additional examples of ornamental *headdresses*.
4. **Display the Word** Point out the two words *head* and *dress* that make up the compound word *headdress*.

DAY 2

barbecue
1. **Introduce** A *barbecue* is an outdoor meal where meat is cooked over an open fire or on a grill.
2. **Demonstrate** We had a *barbecue* at the state park last Saturday.
3. **Apply** Have students tell what they most like to eat at a *barbecue*.
4. **Display the Word** Run your hand under the word parts *bar-be-cue* as you read the word.

DAY 3

chant
1. **Introduce** *Chant* means "to say words or phrases over and over in rhythm."
2. **Demonstrate** Malia knows many jump-rope *chants*. The class often sings a times-table *chant*.
3. **Apply** Have students recite other *chants* they know, such as jump-rope rhymes and cheers at sporting events.
4. **Display the Word** Students can decode the word *chant*. Have them name other words that begin with /ch/.

DAY 4

settler
1. **Introduce** A *settler* is someone who goes to live in a place that is new to him or her.
2. **Demonstrate** Native Americans were the first *settlers* in California. Later, *settlers* came to California from Spain.
3. **Apply** Have students tell some problems they think the first *settlers* in a place might have.
4. **Display the Word** Point out the base word *settle* in *settler*. Identify the suffix *-er*.

Oral Vocabulary for **Good-Bye, 382 Shin Dang Dong**

LET'S LEARN
Amazing Words

Oral Vocabulary Routine

DAY 1

native
1. **Introduce** A *native* is a person who was born in a particular place.
2. **Demonstrate** I am a *native* of Texas, but my parents are *natives* of New York.
3. **Apply** Have students complete this sentence: I am a *native* of _____.
4. **Display the Word** Point out that the word *native* has a single consonant between two vowels and that the first vowel sound is a long *a* (V/CV pattern). Students can decode the word.

homeland
1. **Introduce** *Homeland* is the place that is someone's home or native land.
2. **Demonstrate** Jen spoke with the tourists who said their *homeland* is Bolivia.
3. **Apply** Have students discuss their own or their ancestors' *homelands.*
4. **Display the Word** Run your hand under the syllables *home-land* as you read the word. Point out that this is a compound word made up of the words *home* and *land.*

aspect
1. **Introduce** An *aspect* is a particular feature or characteristic of something.
2. **Demonstrate** The mayor's committee looked at every *aspect* of the proposal for a new mall.
3. **Apply** Have students suggest *aspects* they would consider if they were a committee choosing new playground equipment.
4. **Display the Word** Identify the short *e* vowel sound in the second syllable.

DAY 2

habit
1. **Introduce** A *habit* is an action someone does so often that it is done without thinking about it.
2. **Demonstrate** Biting your fingernails is a bad *habit.* Drinking water is a good *habit.*
3. **Apply** Explain that *habits* can be healthy, unhealthy, or neutral. Have students give examples of some good *habits.*
4. **Display the Word** Identify the short *i* vowel sound in the syllable *it.*

DAY 3

manner
1. **Introduce** *Manner* is a way of acting or behaving.
2. **Demonstrate** It is considered good *manners* to say "please" and "thank you."
3. **Apply** Have students give examples of good *manners.* If you have students from another culture in your class, ask them to give an example of good *manners* from their native culture.
4. **Display the Word** Run your hand under the syllables *man-ner* as you read the word.

DAY 4

insult
1. **Introduce** To *insult* someone means "to do something rude or disrespectful that hurts a person's feelings or their pride."
2. **Demonstrate** John was *insulted* when I said that he was too young to play the game. In some countries, it is an *insult* to refuse food.
3. **Apply** Have students give an example of something that would *insult* them.
4. **Display the Word** Run your hand under the syllables *in-sult* as you read the word.

Oral Vocabulary for **Jalapeño Bagels**

Oral Vocabulary Routine

DAY 1

nutrition
1. **Introduce** *Nutrition* means "food or nourishment."
2. **Demonstrate** We need to eat a variety of foods to get the right *nutrition.* There are many foods that give you good *nutrition.*
3. **Apply** Have students name some foods that they think are high in *nutrition.*
4. **Display the Word** Run your hand under the word parts *nu-tri-tion* as you read the word.

calorie
1. **Introduce** A *calorie* is a unit that measures the amount of energy a food contains.
2. **Demonstrate** Some foods are very high in *calories.* If we eat more *calories* than we use up, we will gain weight.
3. **Apply** Have students name foods they think may be high in *calories.*
4. **Display the Word** Run your hand under the syllables *cal-or-ie* as you read the word.

DAY 2

nutmeg
1. **Introduce** *Nutmeg* is a spice used in cooking. It is the hard seed of a tree. It is dried and then grated or ground.
2. **Demonstrate** We grated the *nutmeg.* We put *nutmeg* and cinnamon in the cookies.
3. **Apply** Work with students to list recipes that might have *nutmeg* in them.
4. **Display the Word** Identify the short vowel in each syllable.

DAY 3

allergic
1. **Introduce** To be *allergic* to something means you have an unpleasant reaction to it.
2. **Demonstrate** Some people are *allergic* to peanuts. Susan is *allergic* to cats.
3. **Apply** Have students name other things that they know of that people are *allergic* to.
4. **Display the Word** Run your hand under the syllables *al-ler-gic* as you read the word. Clap the syllables with students.

DAY 4

grate
1. **Introduce** To *grate* something means "to break it into small pieces by rubbing it against a rough surface."
2. **Demonstrate** Mom showed us how to *grate* the lemon peel. We *grated* cheese for the tacos.
3. **Apply** Pantomime the act of *grating* something, such as cheese. Have students suggest things they may have seen their parents *grate* when cooking.
4. **Display the Word** Identify long *a* spelled *a_e* in *grate.* Students can decode the word.

agent
1. **Introduce** An *agent* is something that produces an effect by its action.
2. **Demonstrate** Yeast is the *agent* that causes bread to rise. Insects such as bees are *agents* of fertilization.
3. **Apply** Have students tell what the *agent* might be for the following effects: clothes getting clean in the washer, ice melting.
4. **Display the Word** Identify the /j/ sound spelled *g.* Students can decode this word.

Oral Vocabulary for Me and Uncle Romie

LET'S LEARN
Amazing Words

Oral Vocabulary Routine

DAY 1

scamper

1 **Introduce** To *scamper* means "to run or move quickly."

2 **Demonstrate** We watched the rabbit *scamper* across the yard. The squirrel *scampered* up the tree.

3 **Apply** Have students show how someone might *scamper*. Then have them use *scamper* in a sentence to describe someone or something moving.

4 **Display the Word** Identify the short *a* vowel sound in the first syllable.

scurry

1 **Introduce** To *scurry* means "to go or move in a hurry."

2 **Demonstrate** Let's *scurry* to our seats because the movie is about to start. The children *scurried* after their parents.

3 **Apply** Have students name another Amazing Word that is a synonym for *scurry*.

4 **Display the Word** Identify the long *e* sound spelled *y* in *scurry*.

taxicab

1 **Introduce** A *taxicab* is an automobile that can be hired to take people where they want to go. A *taxicab* is also called a *taxi* or a *cab*.

2 **Demonstrate** Mom and Dad called a *taxicab* to take them to the airport.

3 **Apply** Have students who have ridden in a *taxicab* describe the ride. Have students tell when they might take a *taxicab* to go somewhere.

4 **Display the Word** Run your hand under the word parts *tax-i-cab* as you read the word.

DAY 2

hurl

1 **Introduce** To *hurl* means "to throw something hard and fast."

2 **Demonstrate** Bob can really *hurl* the ball. We watched the pitcher as he *hurled* a strike.

3 **Apply** Have students name a synonym for *hurl*.

4 **Display the Word** Students can decode this word.

DAY 3

gutter

1 **Introduce** The *gutter* is a channel or ditch along the side of a street or road that carries off wastewater.

2 **Demonstrate** The *gutters* in the streets were filled with water after the storm. The car wheels splashed water from the *gutter* onto the people standing on the corner.

3 **Apply** Have students tell why many streets have *gutters*.

4 **Display the Word** Identify the short *u* vowel sound. Students can decode this word.

DAY 4

ramble

1 **Introduce** To *ramble* means "to wander about, or to walk without any particular place to go."

2 **Demonstrate** I love to *ramble* through the woods. We *rambled* around the old farm.

3 **Apply** Have students name a synonym for *ramble*.

4 **Display the Word** Identify the syllable pattern C + *le* in *ramble*.

ACKNOWLEDGMENTS

Teacher's Edition

Text

KWL Strategy: The KWL Interactive Reading Strategy was developed and is used by permission of Donna Ogle, National-Louis University, Skokie, Illinois, co-author of *Reading Today and Tomorrow,* Holt, Rinehart & Winston Publishers, 1988. (See also the *Reading Teacher,* February 1986, pp. 564–570.)

Photographs

Cover (B) ©Mark Kostich/Getty Images, (Bkgd) ©Chlaus Lotscher/ Getty Images

Every effort has been made to secure permission and provide appropriate credit for photographic material. The publisher deeply regrets any omission and pledges to correct errors called to its attention in subsequent editions.

Unless otherwise acknowledged, all photographs are the property of Pearson Education, Inc.

Student Edition

Student Edition, p. 552

Student Edition, p. 553

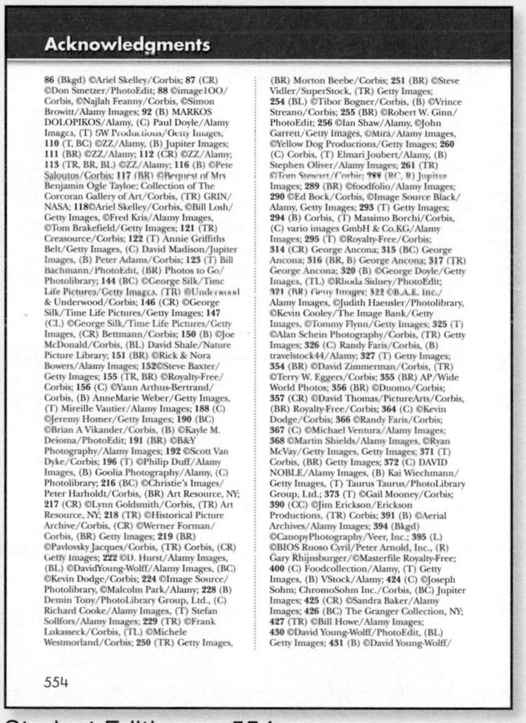

Student Edition, p. 554

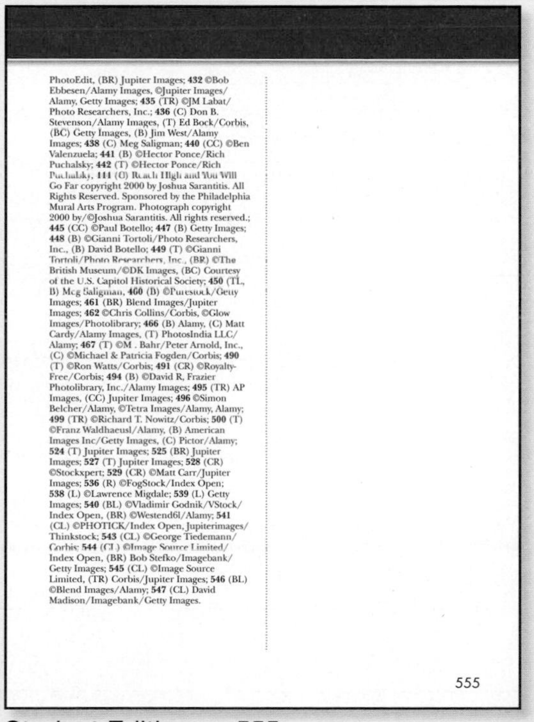

Student Edition, p. 555

TEACHER NOTES

Looking for Teacher Resources and other important information?

Go online to Pearson SuccessNet

In the *First Stop* on Reading Street, you will find the following information.

- Research into Practice on Reading Street
- Guide to Reading Street
- Assessment on Reading Street
- Customize Writing on Reading Street
- Small Group Instruction on Reading Street

- ELL on Reading Street
- Customize Literacy on Reading Street
- 21st Century Skills on Reading Street
- Teacher Resources for Grade 3
- Index

Looking for Teacher Resources and other important information?

Go online to Pearson SuccessNet

eStreet Interactive
www.ReadingStreet.com

In the *First Stop* on Reading Street, you will find the following information.

- Research into Practice on Reading Street
- Guide to Reading Street
- Assessment on Reading Street
- Customize Writing on Reading Street
- Small Group Instruction on Reading Street

- ELL on Reading Street
- Customize Literacy on Reading Street
- 21st Century Skills on Reading Street
- Teacher Resources for Grade 3
- Index